BORROMINI
and the Roman Oratory

The Architectural History Foundation/MIT Press Series

I.   *On Domestic Architecture,* Sebastiano Serlio's Sixth Book.
Introductions by James S. Ackerman, Adolf K. Placzek, and
Myra Nan Rosenfeld. 1978.

II.   *Space Into Light, The Churches of Balthasar Neumann,*
by Christian F. Otto. 1979.

III.   *Borromini and the Roman Oratory, Style and Society,*
by Joseph Connors. 1980.

Joseph Connors is Associate Professor, Department of Art History and
Archaeology, Columbia University, New York.

Special thanks go to the National Endowment for the Humanities, whose
generous grant helped make possible the publication of this book.

The Foundation gratefully acknowledges the support of the Ford, Hearst
and Kaufmann Foundations, The International Telephone and Telegraph
Corporation, Skidmore, Owings & Merrill, Samuel I. Newhouse, Jr., and
Mrs. Barnett Newman.

BORROMINI
and the Roman Oratory

Style and Society

Joseph Connors

The Architectural History Foundation
New York

The MIT Press
Cambridge, Massachusetts, and London, England

Designed by Glenn Ruby

Library of Congress Cataloging in Publication Data.
 Connors, Joseph.
  Borromini and the Roman oratory.
  (The Architectural History Foundation/MIT Press
series; 3)
  Includes bibliography and index.
  1. Oratorio dei Filippini, Rome. 2. Borromini,
Francesco, 1599–1667. 3. Architecture, Baroque—Italy—
Rome (City) 4. Oratorians. I. Title.
NA5620.07C66   726'.4   80-16111
ISBN 0-262-03071-3

Photographic Sources

To Françoise Connors

Contents

Acknowledgments   ix
List of Abbreviations   xi

Introduction   1

1 Filippo Neri and the
   Early History of the Vallicella   5

2 The Projects of Paolo Maruscelli   13

3 Borromini's Oratory and Facade   23

4 The Construction of the Casa   41

5 Finance, Function, Imagery   59

6 The Urban Context of the Casa   81

7 Conclusion   95

Appendix I: Outline of Dates   101
Appendix II: Paolo Maruscelli   107
Notes   113

Documents   141

Catalogue of Drawings   165

The Plates   295

List of Works Cited   361
Index   369

Acknowledgments

The greatest debt I incurred in Rome was to the late Marchese Giovanni Incisa della Rocchetta, who introduced me to the many problems surrounding the Casa dei Filippini, listened patiently to every idea, and gave me access to his transcriptions from the *Libri dei decreti* of the Congregation, which in published form will become the basic source material for future research on art and architecture at the Vallicella. Padre Patrick Dalos, then Preposito of the Congregation of the Oratory, and Padre Guido Martinelli, expert archivist, extended every courtesy; to them and to those Oratorians who helped me in my work go my warmest thanks. My visits to the building and its many rooms were received with great courtesy by the staffs of the public agencies to whom it is entrusted: the Decima Ripartizione del Comune di Roma, the Biblioteca Vallicelliana, the Biblioteca Comunale, the Archivio Storico Capitolino, and the Istituto Storico per il Medio Evo. I am grateful to Dr. Walter Koschatzky for allowing me to inspect the Borromini drawings in the Albertina in 1973. For their resources and the assistance of their staffs I am grateful to the Biblioteca Vaticana, the Archivio di Stato di Roma, the Harvard Libraries, and the other libraries mentioned in the text, but in particular to the Bibliotheca Hertziana and the University of Chicago Library, where most of this book was researched or written. Karin Einaudi, Hellmut Lorenz, and Thomas Gordon Smith helped with photographs. To those who shared their ideas I am deeply indebted, among many others to Anthony Blunt, Rolf Ermeller, Klaus Güthlein, William Maguire, Ronald Malmstrom, Tod Marder, John Mitchell, Jennifer Montagu, Lionello Neppi, John Pinto, and Rosalia Varoli.

Perhaps this is the appropriate place to mention the importance to my graduate education of the teaching of Ernst Kitzinger and Sydney Freedberg, as well as the good fortune I had in beginning the study of Borromini under Richard Krautheimer and Henry Millon in 1971; all continued to give generously of their time when their teaching duties were long past, often when the work most needed it and they could least afford to give it. Three scholars left their mark on every page, in a literal sense, by reading the manuscript with great care, but also in an intellectual sense, by writing the books on which the present study is all too obviously based: James Ackerman, Christoph Frommel, and Howard Hibbard. Every one of these people made this a better book; none is responsible for errors that remain. As the dedication indicates, Françoise Connors helped me more than I can express.

To Harvard University I am grateful for the old-fashioned generosity that allowed me to begin graduate studies and travel to Rome, and to the National Gallery in Washington for a Chester Dale Fellowship in 1973–74, when most of the present research was carried out. A grant from the University of Chicago Humanities Division helped with photographic expenses, and final revisions of the text were completed thanks to a grant from the American Council of Learned Societies. I am indebted to all of these great institutions for supporting my research, and to the Architectural History Foundation for publishing the book that resulted.

Abbreviations

Alb.	Vienna, Albertina, Ital. Architektur-Zeichnung.
ASR	Archivio di Stato di Roma.
AV	Archivio della Congregazione dell'Oratorio a S. Maria in Vallicella.
BV	Biblioteca Vaticana.
Brauer-Wittkower	Heinrich Brauer and Rudolf Wittkower, *Die Zeichnungen des Gianlorenzo Bernini* (Römische Forschungen der Bibliotheca Hertziana, IX), 2 vols., Berlin, 1931.
C	Corpus of Borromini drawings, also abbreviated as Thelen.
CRM	ASR, Corporazioni religiose maschili.
de Bernardi Ferrero	Daria de Bernardi Ferrero, *L'opera di Francesco Borromini nella letteratura artistica e nelle incisioni dell'età barocca,* Turin, 1967.
Decr.	*Libri dei decreti della Congregazione dell'Oratorio,* AV, C.I.6 to C.I.10. The numbering system used here refers to the transcripts from the *decreti* prepared by G. Incisa della Rocchetta for the *Archivio della Società Romana di Storia Patria,* CII, 1981.
Dialogo	Virgilio Spada, *Descrittione della nostra fabrica . . . ,* AV, C.II.7, n.d. [ca. 1648–49]. Published in G. Incisa della Rocchetta, "Un dialogo del p. Virgilio Spada sulla fabbrica dei Filippini," *Archivio della Società Romana di Storia Patria,* XC, 1967, 165–211.
Ehrle, "Spada"	Francesco Ehrle, "Dalle carte e dai disegni di Virgilio Spada (d. 1662) (Codd. Vaticani lat. 11257 e 11258)," *Atti della Pontificia Accademia Romana di Archeologia,* Ser. III, Memorie, II, 1928, 1–98.
Ferrerio-Falda	P. Ferrerio and G. B. Falda, *Palazzi di Roma,* ed. G. G. de Rossi, Rome, I, n.d. [1655 ff.]; II, n.d. [1670–77].

Frommel	Christoph Frommel, *Der Römische Palastbau der Hoch-renaissance* (Römische Forschungen der Bibliotheca Hertziana, XXI), 3 vols., Tübingen, 1973.
Gasbarri	Carlo Gasbarri, *L'Oratorio romano dal cinquecento al novecento,* Rome, 1962.
GR	*Guide rionali di Roma,* prepared by Carlo Pietrangeli and others, 1968 ff.
Hempel	Eberhard Hempel, *Francesco Borromini* (Römische Forschungen des Kunsthistorischen Institutes Graz), Vienna, 1924.
Hess, "Chiesa Nuova"	Jacob Hess, "Contributi alla storia della Chiesa Nuova (S. Maria in Vallicella)," *Scritti di storia dell' arte in onore di Mario Salmi,* III, Rome, 1963, 215–38 and 431–33; reprinted in J. Hess, *Kunstgeschichtliche Studien zu Renaissance und Barock,* Rome, 1967, 353–67. Citations are from the reprint.
Hibbard, *Maderno*	Howard Hibbard, *Carlo Maderno and Roman Architecture 1580–1630,* London, 1971.
Hibbard, *Licenze*	Howard Hibbard, "Di alcune licenze rilasciate dai Mastri di Strade per opere di edificatione a Roma (1586–'89, 1602–'34)," *Bolletino d'arte,* LII, 1967 [published 1970], 99–117.
Huelsen, *Chiese*	Christian Huelsen, *Le chiese di Roma nel medio evo,* Florence, 1927.
JSAH	*Journal of the Society of Architectural Historians.*
Martinelli, *Roma ricercata*	Fioravante Martinelli, *Roma ricercata nel suo sito, et nella scuola di tutti gli antiquarij,* Rome, 1st ed. 1644, 2nd ed. 1650, 3rd ed. with plates by D. Barrière 1658.
Martinelli-D'Onofrio	Fioravante Martinelli, *Roma ornata dall'architettura, pittura e scoltura,* Bibl. Casanatense, MS 4984, n.d. [1660–62]. Published by C. D'Onofrio as *Roma nel seicento,* Florence, 1969.
Nolli	G. B. Nolli, *La nuova topografia di Roma,* Rome, 1748.
Opera I	Francesco Borromini, *Opera . . . cioè La Chiesa, e Fabrica della Sapienza di Roma,* ed. Sebastiano Giannini, Rome, 1720.
Opera II	Francesco Borromini, *Opera . . . cioè L'Oratorio, e Fabrica per l'Abitazione De PP. dell'Oratorio di S. Filippo Neri di Roma,* ed. Sebastiano Giannini, Rome, 1725. Also entitled *Opus Architectonicum.*
Opera III	Francesco Borromini, Monograph on S. Carlo alle Quattro Fontane, ed. Sebastiano Giannini, Rome, n.d.

Opus MS	Francesco Borromini and Virgilio Spada, Description or *Piena relatione* of the Casa dei Filippini, AV. C.II.6, n.d. [1646–47]. Published in 1725 by S. Giannini as *Opera* II or *Opus Architectonicum.*
Opus	Each citation gives both chapter in Roman numerals (which applies both to the MS and the 1725 edition), and the page number in Arabic numerals (which applies only to the MS).
p.	palmo romano (= 0.223 m.).
Passeri-Hess	Jacob Hess, *Die Künstlerbiographien von Giovanni Battista Passeri* (Römische Forschungen der Bibliotheca Hertziana, XI), Leipzig and Vienna, 1934.
Pollak	Oskar Pollak, *Die Kunsttätigkeit unter Urban VIII.,* I, Vienna-Augsburg-Cologne, 1928.
Ponnelle and Bordet	L. Ponnelle and L. Bordet, *Saint Philippe Néri et la société romaine de son temps (1515–1595),* Paris, 1929. References are to the English translation of R. F. Kerr, *St. Philip Neri and the Roman Society of his Times,* London, 1932.
Portoghesi, *Cultura*	Paolo Portoghesi, *Borromini nella cultura europea,* Rome, 1964.
Portoghesi, *Disegni*	Paolo Portoghesi, *Disegni di Francesco Borromini* (exhibition catalogue), Rome, 1967.
Portoghesi, *Linguaggio*	Paolo Portoghesi, *Borromini, architettura come linguaggio,* Rome and Milan, 1967.
Ragguagli	Marcello del Piazzo, ed., *Ragguagli borrominiani,* Rome, 1968.
Röm. Ved.	Hermann Egger, *Römische Veduten. Handzeichnungen aus dem XV.–XVIII. Jahrhundert,* 2 vols., Vienna and Leipzig, I, 1911; II, 1931.
Russo, "Piazza della Chiesa Nuova"	Maria T. Russo, "Il contributo della Congregazione dell'Oratorio alla topografia romana: Piazza della Chiesa Nuova," *Studi Romani,* XIII, 1965, 21–43.
Smither, *Oratorio*	Howard E. Smither, *A History of the Oratorio. Volume I: The Oratorio in the Baroque Era: Italy, Vienna, Paris,* Chapel Hill, 1977.
Studio	D. de Rossi, *Studio d'architettura civile . . . ,* Rome, I, 1702; II, 1711; III, 1721.
Thelen	Heinrich Thelen, *Francesco Borromini. Die Handzeichnungen,* I. Abteilung: Zeitraum von 1620/32, text and plate volumes, Graz, 1967. Contains C 1 to C 82.
Thelen, *Disegni*	Heinrich Thelen, *Francesco Borromini. Mostra di disegni e documenti vaticani,* Vatican City, 1967.

Thelen, *70 disegni*	Heinrich Thelen, *70 disegni di Francesco Borromini dalle collezioni dell'Albertina di Vienna,* Rome, 1958.
▽	*Scudo,* the Roman unit of currency divided into 100 *baiocchi.*
Via Giulia	L. Salerno, L. Spezzaferro, and M. Tafuri, *Via Giulia,* Rome, 1973.
Wittkower	Rudolf Wittkower, *Art and Architecture in Italy 1600–1750* (The Pelican History of Art), Harmondsworth, 1st ed. 1958, 2nd ed. 1965, 3rd ed. 1973. References are to the third paperback edition.

BORROMINI
and the Roman Oratory

Introduction

The church of S. Maria in Vallicella and the Casa dei Filippini next to it together form one of the largest masses of construction in the Renaissance quarter of Rome. Seen on a map or from the air, the two buildings constitute a sturdy block, roughly pentagonal in shape, around which the smaller structures and winding streets of the area seem to eddy (Figs. 1, 2, 4). On the ground the complex is announced by the peculiar feature of "twin" facades (Fig. 8). It is an uneven pair of images; the church facade on the right gives the definite impression of being the senior partner, the larger and more formal of the two. Finished by 1606 and fronting a church built between 1575 and 1593, it was the creation of the first Oratorians, the "old lions"[1] who had known Filippo Neri (1515–95) personally and who had joined with him in founding the original Congregation of the Oratory in 1575. The other facade seems by comparison a warmer and more exotic image, unorthodox in ornament, curved in plan, more fluid in its boundaries (Fig. 12). Begun in 1637 on the designs of Francesco Borromini, it was, along with the oratory and residence behind it, the creation of the second generation of Oratorians, priests who in many cases had never known the saint and who had looser ties with the world of the Counter Reformation. The transition between these two generations, the shift in ideals and the way in which the corporate personality of these men slowly assumed an architectural form are the themes of this book.

The Casa dei Filippini was a complex residential building that harbored many rooms and functions (Figs. 5, 6). The most important space was the oratory itself, which stood in the southwest corner of the building, covered in part by the left half of the oratory facade; it was an eccentric location, and the visitor who passed through the door at the center of the facade soon found that he was entering the oratory not in the middle but along one of its narrow ends. The room was a delicately skeletal structure which opened out at several levels into loggie reserved for singers and important spectators (Figs. 29–37). Its presence gave a ceremonial and semipublic character to the whole south wing of the building. Behind the other half of the facade stood the *portaria,* a porter's lodge with a door to the oratory and a few reception rooms (Figs. 44, 45); at the extreme right side of the facade, a stately portal offered access to the first courtyard (Fig. 43) and, when the appropriate doors were opened, a view down a generous loggia into the heart of the building. If the visitor turned left he would pass along the first courtyard (Fig. 47) and come to the main ceremonial staircase of the casa (Figs. 55–59). Climbing it, he would find on the *piano nobile* the *forestaria,* a set of waiting rooms reserved for visiting dignitaries and their entourages (Figs. 61–64); on the floor above he would find the grand *salone* of the Vallicella library (Fig. 65), which in its original state was smaller than it now appears and had a number of annexes that no longer exist, such as a gallery for maps, a museum for coins and medals, and the archives of the Congregation. On the other hand, if the visitor stayed at ground level and walked straight ahead he would soon find himself in the orbit of the church, close to rooms that were more sacral in character and thus more sumptuously decorated. Entering a dark corridor (Fig. 69), he would find on his left the entrance to the sacristy, a bulky, problematic room that was already standing when Borromini took over the commission (Fig. 72). The entrance to the church stood on the right; once again, if doors were opened a vista was created across the Vallicella transept, through the point where the visitor was standing, and into the sacristy, where it terminated in Algardi's statue of S. Filippo (Fig. 71). Nearby was a spiral staircase leading to a small cluster of preciously decorated rooms that guarded relics of the saint and stood as close as possible to the chapel in the church where his body lay (Figs. 73–80). A few steps more and the dark corridor opened up into a broad and sunlit loggia along the garden courtyard; originally this courtyard was much larger than it is now, planted with vines and potted trees, watered by fountains, and surrounded on the north and west by suites of generous residential rooms (Fig. 83; Cat. 85g, 89c). To the west of the garden, lodged behind the shadow of the Vallicella apse, stood a small third courtyard, triangular in shape, used for receiving supplies (Fig. 95). The wing between these two courtyards contained the rooms used for dining and the ceremonies of communal life: the oval refectory (Fig. 88); the *lavamani* in front of it, with its fountains in the shape of giant tulips (Figs. 85–87); and, on the floor above, the oval recreation room with its colossal marble fireplace (Fig. 90). The northwest corner of the building, which seems like the back to us but was then the front in terms of the original traffic patterns of the area, was given an unusual facade in the form of a cluster of giant brick pilasters with a clocktower looming over it; one dial of the clock faced out, another in, and at the top a belvedere provided a high platform from which the whole structure could be surveyed (Fig. 23).

Complex as the casa is, it does belong to a larger generic class, the type of institutional residence that was developed for the new religious groups that sprang up in Rome in the wake of the Counter Reformation. These residences were for the most part austere and unappealing buildings which found no place in contemporary architectural theory and tend to baffle modern attempts at analysis.[2] Paradoxically, they seem to stand simultaneously for poverty and for wealth. On the one hand, the founding fathers of these institutions embraced monastic ideals and rejected the usual insignia of status and power; on the other hand, it was seldom long before the institution attached itself to some great cardinal or prelate and thereby gained access to immense wealth, sometimes achieving overnight what would have taken generations of acquisitiveness in a normal family. The man who took it under his wing would add the institution's house to an older and more traditional spectrum of commissions, such as the family palace and villa, or the chapel and church facade, which were designed to glorify a magnate (Fig. 104). This pattern of patronage enabled the new institutions to build on a vast scale, but it also led to frequent conflicts over the expression of wealth in the new buildings. For example, when Pope Gregory XIII saw the modest rubble walls of the Collegio Romano going up in 1582, he immediately ordered them demolished and rebuilt in a more "magnificent" manner; similarly, in 1599 Cardinal Odoardo Farnese announced to the Jesuits that the facade of their house, the Casa Professa, "would be built in his way, that is to say, splendidly, and not humbly, as the fathers were inclined."[3] As a result of such encounters these buildings came to project a hesitant and inconsistent public image: severe, restrained in decoration, "more martial than apollonian,"[4] but at the same time announcing the power of the patron to expropriate great tracts of land in the most densely populated parts of the city. The buildings proclaimed a dual allegiance, both to the austere ideals of the founders, whose primitive rooms were often encased like a relic inside the new fabric, and to the glory of a dynasty, whose arms they were obliged to display on the facade.[5]

Encounters like these also took place during the construction of the Casa dei Filippini, but there the conflict was not with any princely patron, but rather between the Oratorians and Borromini. No group in Roman society was more vocal in their distrust of ornament, no architect more creative in producing it. The result was an uneasy partnership, full of strain and discord, which both sides describe with the metaphor of the refractory horse, Borromini lamenting the "bridle" placed upon him, and the Congregation wanting to "hold the reins."[6] At the end Borromini summed up his experience by saying, "I had to serve a Congregation of souls so meek that in the matter of ornament they held my hand, and in places I had to obey their will rather than art."[7] Although the matter is usually dismissed as a simple conflict between artistic exuberance and a strong Puritan strain, deeper values may lie beneath the surface when the problem of ornament is raised. The attempt to investigate this problem has influenced the methodology of the chapters that follow in several specific ways. I have tried to see the design in terms of concrete images when that seemed appropriate, to detect the kinds of borrowed associations that an image might bring with it, and to be particularly attentive whenever the documents attach some nuance of meaning to materials or motifs. Since the relations between architect and patron were often turbulent, I have tried to reconstruct the mechanisms of decision-making in some detail, and to define the amount of constraint and improvisation in the final result. Whenever the classic varieties of formal analysis seemed to lead to a static picture, I have turned instead to a more genetic analysis and have attempted to follow the growth of various images over time, whether their movement was rapid, as in the case of the oratory facade, or imperceptibly slow, as in the case of the urban spaces around the building. Finally, however rudimentary the results might be, I have tried to grasp something of the seventeenth-century spectator's psychology of perception and the ways in which it might be manipulated by the use of ornament, by patterns of movement through the building, and by prints. The ultimate goal is to explain what Borromini did at the Casa dei Filippini. But in building the casa the architect was serving the institution, and the institution in turn was interpreting values that had been formed before Borromini's birth, so to understand his achievement it is necessary to begin long before the cornerstone of the oratory was laid in 1637, namely, with Filippo Neri and his impact on the society of Late-Renaissance Rome.

1

Filippo Neri and the
Early History of the Vallicella

The Roman Oratory was the creation of a unique and powerful personality, Filippo Neri. When Filippo first arrived in Rome in 1533 or 1534, aged about eighteen, he was intent on pursuing some sort of devout life but still had no clear direction, no plans for ordination, and no thought of founding a religious order. The life he led was partly gregarious and urban, partly isolated and eremitical. He frequented the Florentine community in the *banchi* area of the city, where he drew attention by his fervor and whimsical good humor as well as by his selfless devotion to the poor in the hospitals; it soon became clear that he possessed strong powers of personal attraction and deep affections drew men to him "as the magnet draws iron." However, he also sought out the solitude of the catacombs and the remote basilicas beyond the fringes of the populous areas, where he prayed alone and eventually experienced moments of ecstasy. In 1544 he seems to have undergone a profound mystical experience that left physical traces on him in the form of tremors, detached ribs, and an enlarged heart. (Later the flaming heart amid stars and lilies became the saint's heraldry [Figs. 38, 89; Cat. 41]). The dichotomy between these two kinds of existence was finally resolved when Filippo chose the urban side of life and decided to make Rome his field of operations rather than the Indies or some distant desert. In 1548 he joined with his confessor, Padre Persiano Rosa, in organizing the Trinità de' Pellegrini, a confraternity of laymen dedicated to the care of poor pilgrims, particularly those arriving for the Jubilee of 1550. Filippo was finally ordained in 1551, at the age of thirty-six, and at that time he changed his residence, becoming a chaplain in the church of S. Girolamo della Carità on the Via Monserrato. It was here that the Oratory was born and first flourished.[1]

Filippo conceived of himself primarily as a confessor, and all of his time was organized around his penitents and their needs. He heard their confessions on weekday mornings, and in the long, idle afternoons he invited them back to his rooms for edifying conversations or commentaries on a text. Toward evening he would walk with them to one of the major basilicas; later an inner circle of penitents would return to S. Girolamo for a final session of prayer and penance. Filippo soon became a confessor of great repute, and many people came to hear the afternoon discourses and the inspired, informal *ragionamento sopra il libro.* By 1554 his rooms had become inadequate and the afternoon session had to be held in an attic or granary over the nearby church. It was at this time that the word "oratory" was first used for the room in which the new type of devotion was held; later "Oratory" came to signify the devotion itself.[2] By 1565 the exercise had become highly popular and was given a more structured form. While the listeners assembled, a book would be read aloud. Then one of Filippo's chosen disciples would preach an informal sermon and engage in dialogue with a second disciple, who commented on what the first had said. Then would follow an *elaborato sermone* on the lives of the saints, death, the afterlife, and so forth. The next part was an annalistic narrative of church history, while the final sermon paraphrased the life of a saint. The exercise lasted about three hours in all and closed with the singing of motets by professional musicians. Its popularity rested on its informal tone: the subject matter was concrete and unscholastic; the sermons were unprepared and delivered from a seat rather than a pulpit; men came and left as they pleased. The participants were laymen drawn from a broad spectrum of society; they continued to pursue secular careers and to wear the dress befitting their rank and station. The normal Oratory was held on weekday afternoons, but on Sundays and feast days there was also a more "gala" and recreational Oratory, one organized around walks in the campagna and activities like vernacular singing, sermons by children, and the distribution of delicacies in the hospitals. During Carnival the Sunday Oratory was organized to compete with more secular entertainment: there was a pilgrimage to the seven basilicas, including music and a meal in a suburban *vigna,* and women could attend as well as men.[3]

As the Oratory grew, an inner circle of disciples gradually emerged, laymen with a special attachment to Filippo who spoke and preached during the devotion and who habitually returned to his rooms for evening prayer. At first there were no plans to organize these men into any sort of congregation or religious order. In 1563–64, however, when Filippo was asked by the Florentines to become rector of S. Giovanni dei Fiorentini, he sent some of his closest followers, who took orders as priests and went to live at S. Giovanni. This small group of chaplains formed the nucleus of the future Congregation of the Oratory. They performed sacerdotal duties in the church, established simple rules of communal living, and continued to walk to S. Girolamo for the afternoon Oratory, which eventually was moved to the neighborhood of S. Giovanni in 1574, where it was held in the small church of S. Orsola della Pietà.[4] The community at S. Giovanni grew steadily in number, from three in 1564 to thirteen in 1568, with more joining in 1571 and 1575. Eventually they began to feel the need for greater independence. In 1569–71 there was some thought of moving the Oratory to Milan; after tensions with the Florentine Nation in 1574–75 vague plans were aired for merger with the Barnabites or Jesuits. Clearly it was time for the Filippini to strike out on their own. Filippo thought of requesting one of a number of churches, such as S. Cecilia a Monte Giordano or S. Maria in Monticelli alla Regola, or of moving to a site on the Tiber

island. The matter was finally settled in an unexpected way on July 15, 1575 when
Gregory XIII officially recognized the Congregation of the Oratory and assigned
it to the small and dilapidated church of S. Maria in Vallicella.[5]

Filippo had not planned to found a congregation, but when one came into being
in the course of events he helped shape it into a unique body quite different from
a typical religious order. In contrast to the monarchical organization of the Jesuits,
Filippo insisted on government by consensus; in the words of Baronius, "Our saint
did not wish the government to belong to a single person, but that it should be
a kind of well-ordered republic."[6] Each member had to be consulted when the first
draft of the Constitutions was prepared in 1583. There was to be perfect equality
among all fathers. Furthermore, the Filippini were to be a secular congregation of
priests bound together by charity but not by vows. In this respect they stood apart
not only from the Jesuits and Theatines, but also from other groups of secular
priests, such as the Oblates of Milan, whose Rule of 1581 imposed vows of
obedience and stability and encouraged a vow of poverty. Although the Filippini
were not allowed to accept benefices or keep servants or a coach, they still were
not bound to poverty; anyone who had a patrimony was entitled to keep it and was
expected to contribute to the expenses of the house. The rejection of vows was
fundamental in defining the character of the Roman Oratory. It set the Filippini
off from the Oratory in Naples, where, after 1584, sterner ideals prevailed and
there was common property, uniform dress, and a strict novitiate on the model of
a religious order. Vows were excluded expressly by the Roman Oratory in a decree
of 1589, more emphatically in the so-called Last Testament of 1595, and defini-
tively in 1612, when the Constitutions were given papal approval. The Filippini
intended to remain a body of free men.[7]

When Ignatius of Loyola arrived in Rome in 1537, he had already planned the
Society of Jesus and needed only three years to secure papal approval. His Company was organized on the model of an army in the field, capable of moving at a
moment's notice and undertaking any task in any part of the world.[8] In contrast,
the Congregation of the Oratory was not recognized until forty-two years after
Filippo's arrival in Rome. It had coalesced without much forethought; it shunned
centralized authority; it was equipped to take up only one task in one city. Both
the Congregation and the Oratory were rooted in local conditions. What was true
of the institution also came to be true of their architecture: the new church and
eventually the new residence did not follow a rigidly preconceived plan, but took
shape in a series of improvised responses to the environment and to the changing
needs of the Congregation.

S. Maria in Vallicella

The Vallicella area formed part of a larger region called the Tarentum in antiquity
and was linked, because of hot springs and traces of volcanic activity, with a cult
of the underworld.[9] On the northwest the ground level rose toward what seems

to be an artificial mound, Monte Giordano, whereas on the south it declined toward an open drainage canal known as the Euripus; the name Vallicella, or "little valley," comes from a mild depression which formerly marked the terrain around the modern Piazza della Chiesa Nuova. In antiquity the buildings in the area apparently followed alignments almost parallel to those of the Pantheon and the Stadium of Domitian.[10] By the Middle Ages, however, the ancient streets had been obliterated, and in their place there evolved a new system of ramifying arteries that connected the Vatican with a market area broadly scattered between the Campo de' Fiori and the Piazza Navona. This network began at the Ponte S. Angelo and soon split into two different routes, "Parione and Pellegrino, the most famous and crowded streets of Rome"[11] (Figs. 1–4). On the south the Via del Pellegrino (also called the Via dei Banchi Vecchi, Via degli Orefici, Via Mercatoria, and Via Florea) pursued a sinuous course to the Campo de' Fiori, forking once at the Via Monserrato and once again at the Via dei Cappellari. It was the street of bankers, notaries, auditors, of both the old and the new Cancelleria, and of the papal post; in its more distant reaches it became the street of haberdashers, hatters, and smiths of precious metals. It was paved in brick as far as the Chiavica di S. Lucia, but it was not punctuated by any major open space between the Piazza di Ponte and the Piazza della Cancelleria. On the north the Via di Parione (also called the Via Papale, Via dei Banchi Nuovi, or Via del Governo) rose on higher ground to skirt the edge of Monte Giordano and then to continue down to the Piazza di Pasquino, the Gesù, and the Palazzo Venezia. It was the main ceremonial route of the city, used for processions such as the *possesso,* in which the pope traveled from the Vatican to the Lateran to assume temporal power. At the high point of its ascent it opened into the Piazza di Monte Giordano, an important intersection and a center of economic activity in the form of inns, horsetraders, and *rigattieri* or dealers in used objects. Under Paul III the piazza had been enlarged and freed from medieval encumbrances; in 1544–46 the Via di Panico was opened to bring traffic to the area directly from the Ponte S. Angelo.[12] Nearby stood S. Cecilia a Monte Giordano, the major church of the area, which had been rebuilt with a new facade by 1604 (Fig. 3; Cat. 8).[13]

Compared to the strategic position of S. Cecilia, the old church of S. Maria in Vallicella stood in a backwater that was badly drained, poorly served by roads, and equally far removed from the major arteries to the north and south (Cat. 15). In the mid-Cinquecento it was an area of prostitutes and general ill fame: "Whenever one wanted to exaggerate some infamy, one said that it would never have been committed even at the Pozzo Bianco,"[14] a term that referred to the marble well head then standing in front of the old facade. The church itself was a simple basilica which had been in existence since 1145–53; by 1575 it was a dark, half-buried ruin. Filippo had originally planned just to restore the church, but he soon decided on a total reconstruction. The old basilica was demolished and the land cleared. The lines of a new plan were being laid out on the site when Filippo suddenly ordered a major expansion in the building's size. "Allargate più" was the command he twice repeated, and the line of the future left wall was twice moved farther out. Finally, when the foundation trenches were dug, a massive Roman wall, 12 palmi thick, was discovered and used as the foundation for the entire left side of the church and for part of the facade.[15]

The architect at this stage of operations was an obscure builder called Matteo da Castello. In response to Filippo's enlargement he produced a new design closely resembling the Gesù in plan: eight side chapels flanked an aisleless nave, while the crossing was flanked by shallow transepts and covered with a cupola.[16] The plan was particularly appropriate at this time, since S. Maria in Vallicella was still a dependency of S. Lorenzo in Damaso and hence under the jurisdiction of Cardinal Farnese, the patron of the Gesù and the man whom Filippo hoped to attract as Protector of the Congregation.[17] Work began in 1575, and after two years the nave was complete; the decoration of the chapels was undertaken by private patrons between 1577 and 1582. The nave was covered with a wooden ceiling and decorated with cornice stuccoes by Domenico Fontana "after the usage of the Early Church."[18] Lack of funds prevented major construction from continuing after 1577, and so for eleven years the nave stood as a large unfinished box, sealed from the weather by a rustic facade on one end and a temporary wall of leather-covered planks on the other.

Even in this fragmentary state it soon became clear that the rebuilt church would be an entirely new foundation, and that it should no longer be subject to the same jurisdiction as the medieval basilica. In 1578 there was a move to change its name to S. Gregorio Nuovo, and Cardinal Farnese was instructed to release it from his control, an act which he performed with reluctance in 1580. A new and promising patron appeared in 1580–81 in the person of Cardinal Pierdonato Cesi, then papal legate to Bologna. Cesi was anxious to compete with Farnese and was delighted to find a church that could rival the Gesù. He felt that he could assert his own rights and those of his family with greater ease over a congregation of secular priests than over a normal religious order. In return for the "heroic sums" that he resolved to expend, he exacted important privileges. The senior prelate in the family was to be Protector and Visitor over the Congregation's affairs, with the right of intervention; other Cesi ecclesiastics would be accorded the right to vote; finally, both the church and the casa would bear the Cesi arms. Cesi pledged ∇30,000 for the church and spoke of further expenditures for the house; in all he gave the somewhat smaller sum of ∇21,000, including a bequest of ∇8,000 which came after his death in 1586.[19]

Plans changed with patronage. In 1586–88 major innovations were introduced into the design which tended to make the church look less like the Gesù and more like S. Giovanni dei Fiorentini, the Congregation's former home. The ideas probably came from Filippo himself; Giacomo della Porta, the architect of S. Giovanni, offered advice and drawings; Martino Longhi the Elder was the architect who actually put the changes into effect. The existing nave was enlarged by a drastic rebuilding of all the side chapels: tunnel-like side aisles were cut through the lateral walls of the chapels, while the rear walls were demolished and replaced by large protruding apses (Fig. 6). As a result it could be said that "the balustrades [of the chapels] now stand where the altars had formerly stood."[20] In addition the remaining parts of the church were finally constructed: the transept in 1588, the choir and drumless cupola in 1590–91. In 1592–93 the nave ceiling was removed and replaced by a massive barrel vault, built in two stages to spread out the expense.

When the body of the church was complete, the Congregation could finally turn its attention to the facade. Funds were pledged by Monsignor Angelo Cesi, Bishop of Todi and brother of the deceased cardinal. The design of Fausto Rughesi was chosen over those of three competitors in 1593–94, and work was begun in 1594. It soon stopped because of difficulties with the foundations, complicated by flooding and other problems, and it was not resumed for a decade. The right edge of the facade was set in place in 1604; the main cornice was reached in 1605; the upper story apparently was finished around or shortly after 1606, the year of Monsignor Cesi's death.[21]

Early Projects for the Casa dei Filippini

The transfer to the Vallicella immediately posed the problem of a residence for the growing Congregation. Temporary accommodations were provided in older houses located behind the new nave: it was here that the Filippini moved in April 1577, and here that the Oratory was installed in a converted stable (Cat. 15, no. 23). These buildings were cramped and uncomfortable, and furthermore they stood on land that would eventually be occupied by the transept and choir; thus from the outset it was realized that to complete the church it would be necessary to provide a new casa. To this end Cardinal Cesi began to acquire property to the north and east. The convent of S. Elisabetta was purchased and presented to the Congregation in 1581–82 (Cat. 15, no. 7); the neighboring Casa degli Arditi in 1582–83 (Cat. 15, nos. 11–12); and other houses in 1585 and 1586, until two entire blocks, one large and one small, were under the control of the Congregation (Cat. 15, nos. 4–12, 13–16).[22] This land was earmarked for the new residence.

The first projects for the Casa dei Filippini occur on drawings of 1586–87 by Martino Longhi for completing the church (Cat. 1a, 1b).[23] They envisage a house of moderate size with a spacious central courtyard. They show an oratory concealed behind a plain domestic exterior. There are also a sacristy, refectory, service rooms, guest quarters, circular domestic staircase, and straight ceremonial staircase, as well as the residential rooms on the upper floors. The shops that line the northern and eastern wings are a reminder that the building itself—like most members of the Congregation—was expected to be self-supporting.[24] The drawings also reveal a subtle but persistent motivation behind the construction, that of territorial expansion. All but one of the projects call for the expropriation of a block of houses lying to the east of the Congregation's property and the extension of the building as far as the main cross-street of the area, the Vicolo del Governo (Fig. 4; Cat. 1a, 1b).

For the moment, however, nothing came of these projects, and the Filippini continued to live in the *casa vecchia,* an agglomeration of older buildings haphazardly adapted to their needs. For all of its inconveniences, and in spite of the harsh verdict of younger men who saw it as "a motley assortment of houses and shacks, full of a thousand degrading annoyances,"[25] it was the *casa vecchia* that contributed more than any other building to the shaping of the program for the new casa. Its layout is known from a plan of 1618–21 (Cat. 8) and from a few documentary references.[26] The doorkeeper's lodge was originally installed on the Via di Parione but was moved to the south side of the building in 1586 (Cat. 15, nos. 11, 5–6); thus it set the pattern of a formal entrance on the more secluded side and a wagon gate for supplies on the busier and more commercial street to the north (Cat. 15, no. 2).[27] On the interior there was a cloister or loggia as well as the usual service areas: kitchen, refectory, larder, pharmacy, wardrobe, tailor's workshop, staircases, and several cisterns. There was a library large enough to be described as "commoda"; its shelving was later transferred to the new casa, where it can still be seen (Fig. 68).[28] The Filippini lived in *cellette,* sometimes more than one to a room. Filippo himself lived in the *casa vecchia* for twelve years and died there in 1595; his apartment consisted of two rooms on the top floor, outfitted with a rooftop loggia to indulge his love of solitary prayer in places of great height.[29]

The most important room in the *casa vecchia* was the oratory, a large hall built as a sacristy in 1593 but converted to use as an oratory in 1595.[30] It stood behind the right transept of the church and was entered from the Via di Parione (Cat. 8). The exterior of the oratory was entirely undistinguished, in spite of projects intended to give it a more monumental entrance portico (Cat. 4a).[31] The interior was dark and damp. Apparently this was the room used for the performances of Cavalieri's *Rappresentatione di anima et di corpo* in February 1600, when many of the Sacred College attended.[32] There were no balconies to elevate musicians above the audience, although a document of 1638 does mention internal windows from which the Oratory could be heard in seclusion.[33] The room was no longer used as an oratory after 1640, but it survived intact until 1673–75, when a new street was cleared along the right flank of the church and most of the *casa vecchia* destroyed.[34]

For a long time it appeared certain that the Congregation would always live to the east of S. Maria in Vallicella, whether in the old casa or in a new one. The land to the west of the church seemed permanently out of reach; the Congregation's property stopped at the Via di Pizzomerlo, and for decades this important cross-street served as an effective boundary to expansion. In 1611, however, a new presence appeared in the area. The Barnabites of Milan attempted to buy up the large isola which lay between the Piazza Sforza on the south and the Piazza di Monte Giordano on the north. On this site they planned a basilica dedicated to S. Carlo Borromeo, identical in size and plan to the Vallicella but oriented in the opposite direction, with its facade facing northward (Figs. 98, 99).[35] Under the spur of competition the Filippini suddenly turned their sights westward. They brought suit against the Barnabites on the grounds that it was unedifying and uncanonical to have two major churches in such close proximity. They produced affidavits testifying that they had intended to buy property in the Monte Giordano area as early as 1605, and that they had designed a convent there many years before. They bought houses in and around the threatened isola.[36] Eventually the Barnabites withdrew, turning their attention instead to the construction of S. Carlo ai Catinari. The Filippini continued to acquire property in the area, and in 1614 a brief of Paul V allowed them to purchase all houses in "the greater and the lesser isola."[37] The "lesser isola" bordering on the Piazza di Monte Giordano came under their control in 1614, the land later occupied by their sacristy in 1616–18, and the houses along the Via di Pizzomerlo in 1619–21.[38] Permission was finally given to close the street on October 11, 1621, only a month after the last house had been bought; and at the same time the parish of S. Cecilia was dissolved and the church turned over to the Congregation.[39] These expropriations represented the point of no return. The Congregation was now legally bound to construct its residence to the west of the Vallicella, and it was simply a matter of establishing an adequate plan.

The projects drawn up in these years reflect a mood of expansion (Cat. 6a, 6b, 7a, 7b).[40] They show a building almost twice the size of the previous projects, furnished with twenty-four or twenty-five shops instead of a mere nine or fourteen, and designed with more residential space than the Filippini would have known how to use. On one drawing the casa boldly occupies the Via di Pizzomerlo; on another the street is left open and the two separate halves of the casa are joined by an elevated bridge. In spite of ingenious touches, however, the amateur draftsmanship of the projects is symptomatic of deeper flaws: none of the designs is thoughtful in its use of space or responsive to the topography of the Monte Giordano area, and none escapes the defects of unpremeditated and explosive growth. Had the casa been built at this stage, it would have been a grim and forbidding structure.

The heritage which the first generation of Oratorians left to their successors was a complex and problematic one. There was obviously the church itself, which cast its massive shadow over all future planning. As splendid as the Vallicella may have been, from a topographical point of view it followed the wrong alignments and faced in the wrong direction; the Barnabite project of 1611 (Fig. 99) epitomized all of the Congregation's lost opportunities. There was also the habit, established during the construction of the church, of erecting a building piecemeal and changing the design while work was in progress. Finally, there was the idiosyncratic corporate structure that had evolved after the Congregation moved to the Vallicella, one that shunned established models and chose to steer a middle course between the austerities of monasticism and the worldliness of the papal court. None of the early projects for a Casa dei Filippini quite managed to express the unique *qualità* of the new institution. That advance was to come only in the 1620s, when its corporate character came into sharper focus, and a new generation of architects created an imagery to express its place in the social order of seventeenth-century Rome.

2

The Projects of Paolo Maruscelli

The dates 1621–36 mark a period of slow gestation in the planning of the casa. In terms of actual construction it was an unproductive time. The sacristy and a small cluster of rooms around Filippo's chapel were the total results of fifteen years of work: not only was the accomplishment meager in itself, but it was also soon eclipsed in the frenetic phase of building activity ushered in by Borromini in 1637. If the period has any importance it must be sought beneath the stagnant surface, in the steady ferment that was gradually transforming the Oratorians into sophisticated patrons of architecture. It was a time when the institution grew and matured: Filippo was canonized in 1622 and the ensuing years saw an influx of new men, like Virgilio Spada, who later left an indelible stamp on the building. In these years the basic program for the casa was written, the underlying models selected, the mechanisms of patronage established, and the plan cast in a form which seemed to be definitive. Every subsequent architect had to come to grips with the project forged in this period, and none more than Borromini. Owing in part to his efforts, the project and its author, Maruscelli, were later forgotten, but it can be reconstructed from surviving documents and drawings and used to shed light on the form and meaning of the final building.

Mario Arconio (1621–23)

The architect for the first phase of building operations was an obscure personality named Mario Arconio (1575–1635?).[1] Arconio was a painter turned architect who eventually decided to forsake the arts and become a courtier and cupbearer in the service of Cardinal Camillo Borghese, later Pope Paul V. Unluckily, however, he deserted the cardinal just before his election as pope in 1605. Seeing his hopes of preferment dashed, Arconio applied for a provincial governorship and spent most of the pontificate in the town of Cori. He returned to Rome shortly before Paul V's death and was at work for the Congregation as a property assessor in September 1620.[2] It was the right time to be on hand. The Congregation received permission to close the Vicolo di Pizzomerlo in 1621, and for legal reasons it was important to begin work on the new casa with the greatest dispatch. At this juncture the Oratorians turned to Arconio for a plan.

A pair of drawings that can be dated to this period on internal evidence appears to represent Arconio's project (Cat. 8, 9).[3] The first drawing is a survey of the neighboring property, drawn in conjunction with his work as an assessor of houses. The second is a plan for a new casa with three courtyards, a number of shops and service rooms, and an oratory at the northwest corner of the building, close to the site of the parish church of S. Cecilia. In some respects it is a prophetic project. It is the first to endow the oratory with an ecclesiastical facade, and the first to acknowledge the importance of the Piazza di Monte Giordano; both ideas were to recur in Borromini's building. A keen sensitivity to the topography of the area was the great merit of Arconio's plan but at the same time its great drawback. The south wing of the project is shown meeting the side of the church at an oblique angle, a device encouraged by the example of the Collegio Romano and by the desire to avoid unnecessary demolition. Arconio allowed this obliqueness to be communicated to every internal wall in the building, so that even the sacristy and the north wing of the casa meet the axis of the Vallicella at an angle slightly greater than 90 degrees. The logic of oblique alignments became less compelling with time, and eventually contributed to Arconio's undoing. The sacristy foundations were begun according to his plan in 1621–23, but by 1624 there were complaints about "errore nelle misurare," a phrase that in this case seems to refer to misalignments.[4] A new architect was needed to remedy the situation and prepare fresh drawings, and one was found in the person of Paolo Maruscelli (1596–1649), a young and inexperienced assessor who had been in the Congregation's employ since 1622.[5]

Maruscelli's Casa Projects (1624–29)

Maruscelli represented a change of generation in the planning of the new casa. Aged twenty-eight, he stood at the beginning of an active and successful career.[6] In contrast to the courtier-architect who preceded him, Maruscelli was an erudite professional, a book collector who eventually assembled one of the best architectural libraries of early Seicento Rome. To judge from his many preserved drawings he had a better hand than Arconio, a finer sense of design, and a more acute grasp of the problems that stalked the commission. He injected a new orthogonal discipline into the design, and abandoned much of his predecessor's concern with the topography of the area. His early sketches (Cat. 12a, 12d) constitute what might be called the embryology of the casa: they show the plan in formation and the oratory on an internal migration toward the southern part of the building. These preliminary efforts eventually resulted in a complete project preserved in the form of several drawings. The first shows the project superimposed over a plan of the houses existing on the site (Cat. 14); the others formed part of a set of presentation drawings that rendered the entire casa in minute detail and identified the function of every room with a caption number (Cat. 20b, 21).

This caption project of 1627 is one of the key documents in the building's history.[7] In it Maruscelli included most of the rooms and services later found in the finished building: the oratory, porter's lodge, audience rooms, sacristy with three service rooms attached to one side, main stairway, refectory, kitchen, library, recreation rooms, storage space, and extensive living quarters for the members of the Congregation. The oratory was already placed off-center in the southwest corner of the building, in the location it occupies today. The rest of the casa was organized around a series of three courtyards: an entrance courtyard on the south, a large garden courtyard on the north, and a small irregular service court in the northeast corner. Except for the short bend along the Via di Parione, the plan never departs from the orthogonal: all of the principal wings run parallel to the axis of the Vallicella or meet it at strict right angles. The main entrance corridor, which is not placed in the center of the casa but is allowed to skirt the sides of the two larger courtyards, is designed more in the spirit of a Bolognese than a Roman palace.[8] The most ingenious feature of the project is the way it is organized around a series of enfilades: doors planned at three key points would have afforded the passerby in the street uninterrupted vistas stretching several hundred feet into the heart of the building.[9]

Although the caption project did indeed exhibit many of the architect's personal aesthetic preferences, like any institutional design it was a joint endeavor, formed in close collaboration with the patrons, subject to their criticisms, and expressive of their ideas. It was drawn up at a time when the architectural thought of the Oratorians was rapidly maturing. In 1622 Virgilio Spada (1596–1662) entered the Congregation. This younger son of a noble family from the Romagna brought with him a residue of ambition, a broad range of worldly experience, and a fascination with architecture that survived his conversion to the Oratorian way of life.[10] It seems that Spada took an active interest in the casa and its finances from a very early date, although he was not officially appointed to the building committee until 1627. In a few pages of notes surviving from that year he encapsulates the kind of competitive eclecticism that had gone into the caption project.[11] He compares the new sacristy to that of the Gesù, the entrance loggia to the similar loggia in the Casa Professa, the oratory itself to the church of S. Spirito dei Napoletani, the refectory to the one at S. Salvatore in Lauro, and the garden to the Dominican garden at the Minerva. He subjects institutional buildings like the Collegio Romano and the Minerva convent to close scrutiny, and in the process of criticism he manages to hit upon a number of useful ideas, such as sunken corridors and *loggie scoperte,* or open terraces, which were turned to good account in Maruscelli's drawings.[12] With the pride of an intelligent amateur Spada later maintained that the entire building was his own design;[13] the claim is obviously overstated, but nonetheless there was certainly a period of fruitful interchange, possibly even a sense of partnership, between Spada and Maruscelli in the years around 1627.

When the break came between the two men ten years later, recriminations were all the more bitter because their early working relationship had been so close.[14]

Even after presentation drawings had been submitted the design was still not complete. The drawings were then subject to review in what was called a *consulta*, a time-honored practice by which outside architects were called in for criticism and advice. *Consulte* are encountered in the earlier history of the Vallicella and in the construction of many large institutional buildings, particularly those of the Jesuits.[15] The procedure worked in the following fashion. The consultant was shown a design and asked for his comments. He was free to respond in a number of ways, either by offering a verbal opinion (a *parere*) or by submitting a drawing of his own. These counterdesigns were apparently a form of nonverbal criticism, not competitive bids for the commission; they remained the property of the Congregation and accumulated in a growing file. If the patron accepted any of the criticisms or innovations that came out of a *consulta*, the house architect was obliged to accept it and incorporate it into his design. The practice obviously limited an architect's personal freedom but did not necessarily threaten his position. At its best the *consulta* was a source of fresh ideas; at its worst it could degenerate into design-by-committee; in all cases it meant that the final design was a collaborative effort to which conventional notions of intellectual property no longer entirely applied.

In the case of Maruscelli's caption project, the *consulta* of 1627 is documented in unusually precise detail. The original drawings still exist, as well as records noting the criticisms they evoked; a final set of revised drawings shows exactly how the criticisms affected the design. The consultants were Gaspare de Vecchi, G. B. Soria, and apparently Girolamo Rainaldi; in Spada's notes of 1627, their advice is distilled into a series of specific recommendations. First, they advised that the casa be kept lower and airier and that the mezzanine story be eliminated. Second, the loggia along the south side of the garden courtyard should be removed, since it would block light from the sacristy. Third, the first short flight of the staircase should be widened and reduced from ten steps to six. Fourth, it was thought that the larger rooms above the oratory vault would profit more from a northern than a southern exposure. In addition, there were some minor criticisms. Access to some rooms was judged difficult, particularly to the *guardarobba* and the rooms along the north wing of the service courtyard. The connection between the main staircase and the corridor servicing the top floor was rightly questioned. Finally, some difficulty was anticipated in lighting the rooms that stood in the shadow of the Vallicella apse, and there was a proposal to increase the number of windows in the refectory.[16]

Maruscelli accepted most of these criticisms and incorporated them into a set of three large and elegant drawings that constitute his final, definitive project (Cat. 23a, 23b, 23c). In keeping with the instructions to reduce the height of the casa, the mezzanine story was eliminated, the oratory vault lowered 10 palmi, and the *piano nobile* loggia reduced from 34 to 30 palmi in height. A low, narrow walkway replaced the loggia next to the sacristy service rooms. The garden courtyard was expanded from seven to eight bays in length; since the street door in the west facade was no longer symmetrical around a central bay, it was closed and one of the three axes of vision into the casa suppressed. The first flight of the main staircase was widened and shortened according to instructions, although access to the upper stories of the building remained problematical.[17]

Final approval of these revisions was delayed for two more years. Between 1627 and 1629 Maruscelli's attentions were diverted to work on the piazza then being cleared in front of the Vallicella.[18] Finally in 1629 the padri were reminded that the drawings for the new building had been approved by "the leading architects of Rome," shown to Urban VIII, and deposited with the Mastri di Strade. They decided to demolish the church of S. Cecilia and to assert their legal claim to the site by beginning the foundation walls of the north wing "according to Maruscelli's latest drawing."[19] Eight years of demolition, legal maneuvers, and cautious planning had elapsed since the first stone had been laid for the sacristy, but at last the Congregation possessed the ultimate, definitive design. Work could and did begin in earnest.

Construction (1629–34)

The first part of the project to be undertaken was the sacristy. Arconio's foundations of 1621 were only partial and were slightly misaligned; they were straightened and extended in 1630, and the walls and vault of the room were completed by the end of that year.[20] The three small service rooms that line the north flank of the sacristy were approved in 1632 and built in the summer of 1633.[21] The corridor that runs between the sacristy and the Vallicella transept was temporarily covered in 1631 and completed, to a height of two stories, in late 1633 (Fig. 69).[22] Pietro da Cortona's fresco in the center of the sacristy vault dates from the latter half of 1633,[23] and the elegant *credenzoni,* the walnut chests that line the room, from 1634.[24] On September 8, 1634, the feast of the Nativity of the Virgin, the sacristy was inaugurated even before its outfitting and decoration were complete.[25] Work then shifted to the nearby complex of rooms located behind the Chapel of S. Filippo (Figs. 73–80). Originally this space had been allotted to a number of pedestrian functions, but in 1634 it was redesigned around an architectural relic, the saint's private chapel, which was transported stone by stone from the old casa. This complex was built in 1635 and its interior decoration completed by April 1636.[26] In late 1636 work was under way on the high altar of the sacristy, which was Maruscelli's last contribution to the casa.[27]

Sacristy, service rooms, corridor, and complex around the saint's chapel: these comprised Maruscelli's achievement after thirteen years of work. It amounted to only a handful of rooms at the core of a larger project, too limited in scope to exclude subsequent change, but too central to be sidestepped by future architects. These rooms still exist embedded within the present building, and naturally enough they still bear the clear imprint of Maruscelli's style. The sacristy is a near twin of his earlier sacristy at S. Andrea della Valle: both rooms are large vaulted halls with two stories of windows and altar recesses flanked by pairs of doors (Fig. 112).[28] The impressive twin doorframes that face each other across the entrance corridors of both sacristies form one of his most characteristic patterns of design (Figs. 69, 113, 114). The corridor at the Casa dei Filippini has an unorthodox pilaster membering which Borromini later criticized and contrasted with his own more conventional forms (Fig. 70).[29] Two of Maruscelli's enfilades are still visible in the present casa: one running north to south through this corridor, the other running east to west through the Vallicella transept and terminating in the high altar of the sacristy (Fig. 71). Finally, Maruscelli's style is evident in a number of marble doorframes scattered throughout this part of the casa: the twin portals mentioned above (Fig. 69); the door inside the church transept, later transformed by the addition of Borrominian volutes (Fig. 71); the entrance to the Anticamera del Santo (Fig. 79); and three other portals in the area around Filippo's chapel (Fig. 73, nos. 6, 7; Fig. 75).

Sources and Imagery

In the design of doorframes and enfilades Maruscelli was free to leave his mark on the building, but in weightier matters of corporate symbolism he was expected to become a transparent personality, totally devoted to the expression of his patrons' ideas. His great achievement was to forge a new residential imagery for the Congregation, a goal which he accomplished by quoting a number of distinct residential types in his drawings, in particular, a Venetian convent, a Milanese archepiscopal palace, and a Roman *famiglia* palace. Each of these buildings was capable of engaging some aspect of the Oratorians' sympathy and of reflecting some facet of their self-conception; fused together in a single design, they created a relatively faithful mirror for the Congregation's image and aspirations as they stood in the 1620s.

First, Maruscelli drew on Palladio's Convent of the Carità in Venice, or rather on the woodcut of the building in the *Quattro libri,* as the model for his basic organization of space;[30] his north-south section of the casa is taken directly from the print (Fig. 115; Cat. 23a). Both projects show a large vaulted hall standing between two courtyards that are connected by continuous corridors on all levels; both show a narrow walkway designed to connect the two halves of the building; and both have garden courtyards that extend for a greater distance on the upper stories than on the ground floor. The Carità offered a paradigm of textbook classicism and of elegant design in inexpensive materials. Although built in the spirit of the Roman Renaissance for patrons with Roman roots, it nevertheless stood outside the mainstream of Roman institutional building. For a Congregation anxious not to look like Jesuits or Theatines, the Carità was an uncontaminated model.

Second, Maruscelli derived the ornament of his courtyards from the *canonica,* or courtyard, of the archepiscopal palace in Milan (Fig. 117; Cat. 23a).[31] Pellegrino Tibaldi's ornament there is the source of Maruscelli's heavy triple keystones in the lower story, keystones with animal heads in the upper story, Ionic capitals with grotesque masks, and a type of idiosyncratic bracket which extends from the Ionic capitals up into the eaves of the roof. For a Congregation deeply concerned with the role of ornament, Milan was the logical choice. The *canonica* had been designed in 1564 and built in 1571–1604 to satisfy Carlo Borromeo's demands for an "edifying" architecture, one devoid of frivolities, imbued with the spirit of reform, and at the same time impressive enough to symbolize the representative functions of the archdiocese. In addition, the project recalled long-standing personal links between the Congregation and Milan.[32] Borromeo had been Filippo's correspondent and protector. He was a visitor at the Vallicella and an early contributor to its expenses. He repeatedly urged Filippo to establish the Oratory in Milan; in 1571 he offered the Filippini the Brera as a home;[33] later he founded his secular Oblates to take the Congregation's place. In 1663 a chapel was dedicated to him in the Vallicella, opposite Filippo's, to express the spiritual kinship that had existed between these two lights of the Counter Reformation;[34] Maruscelli's project would have expressed the same idea at a much earlier date.

Finally, Maruscelli betrays his most important source in the drawing of the west facade: it imitates the front of the Palazzo della Famiglia Borghese, built in 1624–27 opposite the better known Palazzo Borghese to house the horses and part of the retinue of a papal nephew, Scipione Borghese (Fig. 118; Cat. 23c).[35] The comparison is based on visual evidence and confirmed in documents and drawings. Both facades are composed of a pair of projections, three bays wide, which enframe a long central section. Both deceive the eye in the same way: the left projection of each facade is the front of a normal sequence of rooms and shops, while the right projection, at first sight identical to the one on the left, is really a mask for the narrow end of a long, vaulted hall. In one case the hall served as the Borghese stables, in the other as the oratory of the Filippini. In Spada's notes of 1627 a particular suite of rooms in the Palazzo della Famiglia Borghese is mentioned as the model for the apartments of the senior Oratorian fathers.[36] One of the architects of the Palazzo della Famiglia Borghese, G. B. Soria, appropriately served as an outside consultant for Maruscelli's project in 1627.[37] Finally, the exact medium of transmission has been preserved: two plans of the Palazzo della Famiglia Borghese, possibly by Soria himself, still exist in the Vallicella archives (Figs. 119, 120).[38] They show other similarities in distribution and planning between the two designs, and unmistakably document the Congregation's interest in this novel building type.

One might wonder why the Oratorians singled out the palace of a *famiglia.* The answer lies in their steady search for an imagery adapted to their special status in Roman society. On the one hand, the residence of a *famiglia* was clearly on a lower level than the palace of a cardinal or a secular prince. It was a dignified and efficient type of design that allowed a moderate amount of display and provided high standards of comfort and privacy for a large number of men. On the other hand, while it avoided sumptuous effects, this kind of architecture was clearly not barren or monastic. In defining its corporate status the Congregation had emphatically rejected the monastic model. It had inherited Filippo's pragmatic attitude towards material goods, expressed in the phrase, "Habeat, retineat, sed videat ne qua sit lis" ("Let him have and keep it, only being careful that there is no litigation").[39] Repelled equally by monastic poverty and nepotistic wealth, the Filippini attempted to find a middle ground in architecture as well as in life.[40] They plundered the convents and institutions of the religious orders for functional ideas, but judged them inappropriate as sources of expressive imagery. Those vast severe buildings, which housed men vowed to poverty, had paradoxically become monuments to immense wealth. It was felt that the Collegio Romano, the Casa Professa, the Theatine house at S. Andrea della Valle, the Benedictine monastery in Trastevere "were built by princes, who are expected to support grand enterprises." In contrast, "the Filippini, who were building their own residence, accorded the highest priority to modesty."[41] It was the right balance between modesty and dignity that the *famiglia* model provided, the *via media* between excessive display and excessive austerity.

It was also an image that expressed the proximity between the Oratorians and the world of the papal court. In Gregory XIII's eyes the Congregation had been instituted for the purpose of spreading reform among the members of the courtier class.[42] The Oratory was organized around the courtiers' leisured afternoons; it was courtiers who flocked to hear the music, and courtiers who supplied many of the new recruits. In time the Congregation became a breeding ground that sent its men back out as the heads of many important *famiglie:* it provided the majordomo for the household of Carlo Borromeo in 1566, for that of Cardinal Alessandrino in 1567 and again in 1570, and for that of the Archbishop of Piacenza in 1568; it supplied Clement VIII with the *maestro di camera* for the Vatican palace in 1592.[43] These men left with the blessing of the Congregation, but there were others who left because the pull of the court was simply too strong. When the documents of the 1620s mention the visits of cardinals and dignitaries to the old casa, they express a fear that the court would draw off the Congregation's best blood, that "the finest members would become courtiers, with the danger of forsaking the community for ecclesiastical honors."[44] The coming and going between these two worlds eventually had its effect on the planning of the new casa. Conversion to the Oratory meant a profound change of heart, the crossing of an inward chasm, but nevertheless a man was not forced to burn all of his bridges behind him, and in terms of architecture there was hardly any distance to travel at all. It was the palace of a worldly *famiglia* which he left, and the palace of a spiritual *famiglia* to which he came.

In later years, when he had to explain how he had come by the commission, Borromini tried to assert that his predecessor had never bothered to produce a unified project for the casa, or had not done so until it was too late.[45] As he knew, the charge was false. By 1627 Maruscelli had designed a project that was complete to the most minute detail, that had been criticized, revised, and legally deposited, and that was ready to be built in stages as funds became available. At this stage the project was already a hybrid in the sense that it drew from a number of different prototypes for functional ideas and for the keynotes of its imagery. The fusion of architectural types runs deeper, however, than one designer's personal eclecticism. It was a trend engrained in the commission, inevitable as long as the corporate personality of the Congregation was in flux, and destined to continue, even to accelerate, after Maruscelli had been replaced by a far greater architect.

3

Borromini's Oratory and Facade

The Change of Architects

In the early days of 1637, when the Congregation decided to begin work on the oratory, the commission was still in Maruscelli's hands. By all rights it should have stayed there. The plan, imagery, and most of the basic functional ideas were his, and there was no recorded dissatisfaction with the way he had conducted the work for thirteen years. Nevertheless, in the first half of 1637 a series of unforeseen events led to Maruscelli's resignation and replacement by Borromini, who continued work on the building for an additional thirteen years and brought it close to completion. Borromini's sudden ascendancy at the casa remains one of the puzzling features of its history. Up to 1636 "no one knew him at all."[1] The first mention of his name comes in a document of December 1636, which links him to the high altar then being installed in the sacristy (Cat. 28); at this point he seems to have been working under Maruscelli, and was one of a number of outsiders called in to help outfit the room.[2] In the course of the next five months he managed to insinuate himself into the Congregation's favor. On May 2, 1637 he was paid for "misure e disegni"; one week later, on May 10, his design for the oratory was singled out by the Deputies of the Congregation as "più a proposito" and he was forced upon Maruscelli as an associate architect. The collaboration between the two men was brief and unfruitful. Maruscelli drew his last payment on June 20, 1637 and amid bitter remarks left Borromini in sole charge of the commission.[3]

The underlying reasons for this change deserve elucidation, not only to explain why Borromini became the architect, but also to understand the kind of constraints under which he later had to work. There are two types of evidence on which to draw: first, some texts composed more than a decade after the events in question; and second, a group of plans drawn up by various architects in 1637. The texts are written entirely from Borromini's point of view and contain many distortions, and the drawings are opaque and at first glance unhelpful, yet when all the sources are examined together a coherent picture begins to emerge.

The earliest account of how the commission changed hands occurs in a manuscript, later called the *Opus Architectonicum,* that Borromini and Spada composed together in about 1647:

In those days the Congregation employed Arconio and subsequently Maruscelli to design the sacristy in its present form and fix it on its present site . . ., without, as far as I know, establishing the design of the rest of the building at the same time, which caused discord in the window alignments and the levels of the floors. . . .

To return to the origin of my introduction into the Congregation's service: once the sacristy was completed . . ., the padri turned their attention to the oratory. Since they had already selected the site, they had various drawings made both by their own and by other architects, but none proved satisfactory. There seemed to be no way of spacing the windows to maintain the proper symmetry and to obey a loggia on the interior, nor of putting the door in the proper place. After much research, many drawings, and meetings of the Congregation, a drawing by Paolo Maruscelli was found to be the best, or the least flawed, even though there were obvious defects in the placement of the door, in the oblique window jambs, and in fenestration without the slightest rule or order. These mistakes were accepted as inevitable [and are shown in] the following drawing of Maruscelli's.

At this juncture I was proposed to the Preposito, who was then P. Angelo Saluzzi. . . . He explained his feelings to me and requested that I try to come up with new solutions. I encountered the same problem of enforced obedience to an internal loggia and to a series of unequal arches. Since the corner pier of the courtyard was thicker than any of the other piers, it insured that the distance between the center of the last courtyard arch and the center of the adjacent loggia [to the left] would be greater than the distance between the center of this same arch and the center of the adjacent arch [to the right]. As a result, when viewed from inside the oratory, the windows which align with these arches would seem to be irrationally spaced. Nevertheless, after I had worked on it for a time and done many drawings which were constantly criticized by Padre Virgilio Spada, an amateur of architecture whom the Preposito consulted, I finally did a drawing to everyone's satisfaction, which solved all the difficulties by inserting two loggie or porticoes at either end of the oratory, which keep the windows in order. . . .

In the middle of the oratory on one side there is a niche with the seat from which sermons are delivered, on the opposite side a niche with the image of S. Filippo. This niche corresponds to the thick corner pier of the loggia, and is precisely the device which puts order in the fenestration. . . .[4]

The second account of these events is contained in the *Dialogo* of about 1649, a work composed by Spada as a more popular and less technical version of the *Opus:*

Spada: The floor level of the sacristy and consequently of the rest of the casa was 4 palmi higher than that of the church. However, it was considered improper for the oratory door to be on a higher level than the doors of the adjacent church. Furthermore, a loggia was supposed to run along the [north] flank of the oratory, and the oratory windows had to align with the arches of this loggia and with the [flights of] the nearby staircase. The distances [between the windows] were not all the same, and the discrepancy was going to be reflected on the piazza side. Paolo Maruscelli, then the Congregation's architect, drew up many plans, but all were riddled with mistakes and architectural solecisms. He could not find any way to avoid them, but only to minimize their frequency. Before I became Preposito myself I was summoned by Padre Saluzzi for my opinion, but I withheld my approval when I saw that errors were engrained in the very plan of the building. Saluzzi became totally involved in the affair, and dealt with one architect after another, but without result. Finally Francesco Borromini was proposed to him as a young man of judgment and imagination from Milan. No one knew him at all. His first plan had some imperfections and did not meet with my approval. His second struck home. When I saw it I said, "He has got it. No need to look further. If an angel descended from heaven, he could not do a drawing with fewer errors. There is no error in this design, no license, no offense against good architecture." And so Saluzzi took him on as second architect.

Interlocutor: So you were not the one who introduced Borromini into the Congregation's service. And yet Rome believes that it was you who launched his career.

Spada: It was Padre Angelo Saluzzi, who was Preposito at the time. I did not know Borromini then, and when I became Preposito, he was already in the service of the Congregation. . . .[5]

This is the story that these accounts tell. When it came time to build the oratory the site was already chosen, but an impasse arose over certain technical problems such as the proper level of the oratory floor and the proper fenestration to answer the so-called problem of the thicker corner pier, which seemed to defy solution. Within the Congregation one man became obsessed with these difficulties, namely, Angelo Saluzzi, Preposito between 1632 and 1638.[6] Saluzzi called in Spada, not to propose a solution or to recommend a new architect, but to point out flaws in any designs that might come their way: Spada was to act as Saluzzi's critical eye. Together they scrutinized the solutions offered by several outside architects. Finally, Borromini was asked for drawings, and on his second try he managed to solve the problem of fenestration. He was entirely unknown, but because he had succeeded where everyone else had failed, he was taken on as a second architect.

That Borromini should have been able to impress a patron with the brilliance of his drawings goes without saying. Nevertheless, what is annoying about these accounts are the small inaccuracies and exaggerations that make it look as if a story were being fabricated. Maruscelli cannot be accused of designing the sacristy in isolation from a larger scheme. Details like the problem of the thicker corner pier should not have been so important; in fact, if a hostile critic had raised this point a few years earlier at the cloister of S. Carlo alle Quattro Fontane, it would have been Borromini's turn to acknowledge a mistake and forfeit a commission. Furthermore one gets the sense that the texts are playing on old fears that had lingered on among the Filippini ever since the construction of the Vallicella, fears in particular of having to demolish something already built because of inadequate planning.

The surviving drawings, in contrast to the texts, tell a more subtle and revealing story. Five plans seem to be related to the design of the oratory in early 1637: one that is anonymous, two that appear to be by Girolamo Rainaldi, and one each by Borromini and Giovanni Battista Mola.[7] Fortunately they can be arranged in sequence to form a continuous series. The guiding principle for sorting them out is that the drawings closer to Maruscelli's old design are earlier, while those closer to the oratory as it was actually built are later. The main surprise is that the drawing by Borromini (Cat. 29) stands at the very start of the series. Although it is more scrupulously drawn than anything by Maruscelli, nevertheless it takes over the basic logic of Maruscelli's fenestration, in which the end projection of the oratory sets the basic pattern and the windows are designed from the outside in. It makes no attempt to grapple with the problem of the thicker corner pier, but it does, on the other hand, show two important innovations: an entrance corridor placed on axis with the courtyard, and a facade which is indented, articulated by pilasters, and ready to be transformed into a mild curve. The drawing is followed by two uninventive plans, one anonymous (Cat. 30) and one by Mola (Cat. 31); both accept the innovations of Borromini's drawing but offer few significant improvements of their own. The real advances come in the next set of plans by Girolamo Rainaldi, a senior member of the profession who had served the Congregation as a consultant in the previous decade (Cat. 30, 33). It was Rainaldi who first formulated the problem of the thicker corner pier and who simultaneously devised its solution. His stark, unadorned drawings treat the plan as an exercise in architectural scansion: they make the fenestration conform to a strict rhythm in the way a line of verse might conform to a given meter. The windows on the north side of the oratory are aligned with the staircase and the adjacent loggia, features that might be called the internal skeleton of the building. A basic rhythm is thus established which is transmitted across the room by symmetry and which ultimately emerges on the outer wall. Thus the south facade becomes one of the most interesting and prophetic features of Rainaldi's drawings. It takes its alignment not from the oratory but from the courtyard behind it; the facade becomes a faithful reflection of the internal skeleton of the building. Once formulated, the logic of this idea was to persist throughout the subsequent history of the design and to emerge, amid considerable embellishment, in the facade as it was eventually built (Cat. 41). The last significant drawing in the series would have been another plan by Borromini. The sheet itself is missing, but it would have shown an oratory similar to the one in Cat. 39, in which all of Rainaldi's suggestions are taken up and combined with new ideas of Borromini's own. It was this lost drawing that "struck home" and swept Borromini into the position of associate architect.

At first sight it might seem that these are competition drawings. In fact, later in his career, shortly after Maruscelli's death in 1649, Borromini attempted to circulate the story of a nationwide competition for the design of the casa. This version of events appears for the first time in a document of 1650–52, a *Relatione* composed by the prior of S. Carlo alle Quattro Fontane but based on information supplied by Borromini himself:

> When the Oratorians of S. Filippo Neri decided to build their oratory and residence, every architect of Rome, ambitious for renown and honor, tried to obtain the commission, usually with the backing of influential cardinals or noblemen. These highly placed recommendations caused confusion and dissension among the fathers, and so to spare offence they adopted the following course of action. Notices were posted on the streetcorners of Rome and in the major cities of Italy, which announced that the architects who wanted to compete for the building should appear on an assigned date. Specifications would be given out, and the one who produced the best drawings would be selected by secret ballot. A great number of architects responded to the invitation, among them Borromini, unsponsored and unknown. When all the drawings had been considered, the superiority of Borromini's design was obvious to everyone, and he was duly selected as architect of the Congregation.[8]

The story is designed to evoke the great competitions of the early baroque age: the competition for the moving of the obelisk in 1585, that for the completion of St. Peter's in 1606, or that for the design of S. Maria della Salute in Venice in 1630.[9] And yet the whole account is at variance with the Congregation's established habits of patronage. Aside from a small competition of 1593, when Rughesi was chosen to build the Vallicella facade,[10] the Oratorians preferred outside consultations as a means of arriving at the best possible design. Unlike a competition, a *consulta* was a gradual and cumulative affair. Competitors worked in isolation, but a consultant was always informed of the ideas accumulated by his predecessors, of "tutti li fatti fin hora," by being shown the latest drawing on hand.[11] Competitors fought to win a commission, and in their plans originality was a virtue; consultants could only hope to influence a design that someone else would execute, and with them total originality could be a vice. Consultants were at their best when they offered small, incremental improvements to an established design; they were problem-solvers and are described as such in an important passage of the *Opus* that mentions "another major difficulty, over which many architects sweated when they were consulted by order of the Preposito."[12] When a group of drawings can be arranged in a clear sequence that shows steady, cumulative refinement in a design, then the evidence points to a consultation and not to a competition. And this is the case with the drawings for the oratory.

There still remains the problem of Borromini's sudden rise. Once a *consulta* had run its course, the normal procedure would have been to turn the file of drawings and *pareri,* or critical opinions, over to the house architect, in this case still Maruscelli, and let him execute the building. Instead, the Congregation turned again to Borromini, for reasons that will probably never be entirely clear. Borromini had shown that he could make brilliant use of other consultants' ideas. The *esatezza* of his graphite drawings, what one might call their sharp-edged accuracy, exerted a strong appeal; and it was probably through his drawing style, possibly through his work in the sacristy under the brother Taddeo Landi (Cat. 28), that he first came to Spada's notice.[13] In the 1630s Spada was on the lookout for young talent, and Borromini was not the only *giovane,* or discontented young man, who had walked out of Bernini's shop, "dissatisfied that his glory should augment someone else's fortune," whom Spada tried to patronize.[14] Furthermore, Borromini was not chosen by the Congregation at large but by a small steering group within it, the Four Deputies along with the Preposito.[15] In the governing structure of the Oratorians the General Congregation of all voting fathers decided on matters of general importance such as finance, but the "ordinary difficulties" of the building were left to the Deputies, who ran the consultations and chose the architect. Under this arrangement the plan could be divorced from the designer. Maruscelli's plan had long since been approved by the General Congregation and remained in effect, but in 1637 the Four Deputies chose Borromini to execute it; in effect, he was picked not as an innovator but as the conservator of a long-established design. It was a strange situation to be in. On the one hand, the young architect was bursting with ideas and anxious to surpass everything that Maruscelli or anyone else could teach him; on the other hand, the Congregation at large was profoundly suspicious of anything that could be called "caprice" or "singularity," and in case of doubt it was prone to fall back on the rule "not to innovate in anything at all."[16] Borromini of course seized his chance, but from that day forward he found himself in a situation that severely limited his freedom. Each departure from the familiar plan, each revision in the shape or location of a room, each change in material or ornament had to be presented to the General Congregation and justified in terms that they could understand. Borromini's famous outburst, "I would certainly never have entered this profession only to become a copyist,"[17] is an index of his frustration in this role. If the relations between the architect and his patrons were stormy, and if at the end Borromini felt that his hands had been tied and his talents bridled, the reasons were evident at the outset and were built into the very mechanisms of patronage.

Construction and Design of the Oratory

Materials had already begun to accumulate during the consultations, and once the design was settled, construction proceeded rapidly. The foundations were laid between May and July 1637. The pedestal, or *zoccolo,* and the fine brickwork required for the new facade were authorized in July 1637. The walls rose in great haste, and by May 1638 the room was ready to be vaulted. A contract for stuccoing the interior was concluded between October and November 1638, with a term of eight months allowed for completion of the work. Fittings for the exterior, such as the wooden window frames and the main entrance portal, were in preparation in November and December 1638. The vault fresco was commissioned from

Romanelli in April 1639 and completed by June 1640. The oratory was finally inaugurated on August 15, 1640, the Feast of the Assumption. At that time, and for over a year thereafter, it stood as an isolated building (Cat. 38), surrounded by houses in various stages of demolition or decay, cut off from the church by the vestiges of a public street, and fronted by the half-finished curve of the strange facade.[18]

The oratory was one of Borromini's most constrained commissions, and what he accomplished there is all the more impressive when one realizes the limitations imposed on him from the outset. The Filippini were committed to a more or less standardized Counter-Reformational oratory.[19] It had to be a rectangular room with at least two doors—one public and one private—and with a clear sense of direction from the rear to the altar at the front. Furthermore, it had to embody all the innovations accumulated during the consultation process, in particular five important features that are expressed most clearly in Rainaldi's drawings (Cat. 33, 39): the altar loggia, the spiral staircase, the small closet in the southwest corner, the two niches in the long sides of the room, and of course the fenestration that followed the logic of the thicker corner pier. Borromini's task was to take ideas that were not his own and fuse them into a convincing, unified whole. He achieved this goal by tackling problems of structure and by concentrating on two key features of the design: the twin porticoes at the narrow ends of the room and the great vault above it.

The porticoes were thin masonry screens which had little effect on the real shape or layout of the room but did expand its apparent size by transforming two of its boundaries into transparent screens (Figs. 31, 34). Although both porticoes were supposed to look identical from the center of the oratory, the spaces that lay beyond them were quite different: one was a narrow altar loggia, while the other was a generous entrance space nearly twice as wide, greater in height, covered by a beautiful billowing vault (Fig. 39), and lit at either end by a dramatic display of hidden lighting (Figs. 40, 41). But the porticoes are there for more than visual effect; in fact, they work a profound transformation in the structure of the oratory, making it simultaneously more stable and more skeletal. Maruscelli's oratory would have violated a seventeenth-century rule of statics, namely, that "an isolated angle will give way," meaning that any very large vault placed at the corner of a building and left unbuttressed on two adjacent sides would be prone to collapse at the angle where these two sides meet.[20] His mistake was corrected in the consultation drawings and in the final building by interposing the altar loggia between the vault and the outer wall. The wall now functioned as a buttress rather than as a direct support, providing what would have been called *contrasto* against the *forza della volta,* rather than *appoggio.* [21] Other steps were taken to augment this basic measure: the imperiled angle was thickened; the small hexagonal closets in this corner of the room, which were considered useful in keeping dangerous thrusts at a distance, were tied with chains; and a large chain was immured in the musicians' choir. At the other end of the room the portico was less isolated and consequently less troublesome. Flat architraves were used to carry thrusts over the cardinals' loggia to a *muro maestro,* a solid bearing wall which now forms a partition between the *portaria-forestaria* area and the oratory proper.[22]

Once these steps had been taken to ensure the stability of the vault, the porticoes themselves could be reduced to the barest skeletal minimum, and in fact they remain unsurpassed in the architect's work for their slenderness and height. There are loose analogies to their design in the point-support systems of Gothic architecture, but a more pertinent model can be found in then recent architecture closer to Rome, namely, the porticoes of S. Teresa in Caprarola, designed by Girolamo Rainaldi in 1621 (Fig. 121).[23] Thus the man who contributed many of the basic elements in the oratory plan also contributed the key feature of its elevation. Borromini went even further and drew on Rainaldi's repertoire of decorative ornament: the Ionic capitals of the oratory and the small stepped window frames of its entrance loggia have close precedents in S. Teresa. Nevertheless, it is precisely ornament that marks the parting of the ways between the two architects. Rainaldi used it to embellish the traditional foci of a design, the doorframes, windows, and altarpieces; Borromini used it to reveal the basic lines of force within a structure. He believed that "the beauty of piers . . . consists in allowing their edges to rise uninterrupted and unimpeded,"[24] and so he did everything in his power to accentuate the effect of vertical rise. His window frames reinforce the slender piers without making them seem any thicker; his arches are made to appear thinner, flatter, and more fragile than they really are; his horizontal elements are dissolved into a series of perforated screens (Fig. 34). Borromini left behind a vivid if eccentric metaphor of his intentions in the balustrades of the two loggie. The alternating balusters were meant to remind the spectator, or at least the reader of the *Opus,* that nature produced not only tree trunks, which are thick at the roots and diminish as they rise, but also the human body, which is broader at the level of the torso than at the level of the feet.[25] The image is something of an anti-Palladian taunt, but it clearly conveys Borromini's intention, in the face of a tradition that prized stability above all else, to impart a sense of agility and spring to masonry construction.

The huge webbed vault is the crowning feature of the oratory (Fig. 29). Its broad surface is decorated by a system of flat bands which are described in one of the workmen's contracts as "ribs in the manner of a cupola."[26] In fact these so-called ribs perform no structural function, but instead are there to take the idea of a skeletal architecture beyond what the actual statics of the room would allow into the realm of metaphor. They convey the impression that the oratory is not merely vaulted, but covered by a "lofty cupola,"[27] or more precisely by a Lombard tiburio, a species of cupola in which the drum is suppressed and the windows are pierced directly into the ascending curve of the dome. The central panel is designed to evoke a real oculus, and its original fresco, Romanelli's *Coronation of the Virgin,* was intended as a sequel to the *Assumption* over the main altar, as though successive mysteries of the Virgin could be seen unfolding beyond the confines of a skeletal cage.[28]

Borromini later claimed that this interest in skeletal structure came not from Gothic architecture but from one of the last places one would now look, namely, from the concrete vaulting of Roman thermal halls:

> I wanted to follow ([added:] in some measure) the practice of the ancients, who would not dare to rest a vault directly on a wall, but who instead rested its entire weight on columns or piers [*pilastri*] which they planted in the corners of the room, so that the adjacent walls served only to buttress these piers, as one can observe in Hadrian's Villa, in S. Maria degli Angeli in the Baths of Diocletian, and elsewhere, and as I observed in a recent excavation for the Marchese del Bufalo near the Lateran hospital, where corner piers were found supporting the vault of an underground temple.[29]

This skeletal vision of Roman structural systems has hardly any parallel before the days of nineteenth-century rationalism,[30] but in a sense it goes too far and ties the oratory more closely to Roman precedent than it really deserves. Only the narrow ends of the oratory are skeletal; the sides remain heavy mural masses (Fig. 37). In the corners there are neither columns nor piers but canted corner pilasters that have no precedent in any ruin; in fact, the oratory is farther from the vaults of Roman baths than many buildings by architects like the Tibaldi family or Maderno.[31] Borromini seemed to want to justify his design by citing a precedent that was always somewhere in his consciousness but that surfaced only in obscure parts of the building (Fig. 30) or in unexecuted designs (Cat. 66r).

The importance of Borromini's innovations lies more in the realm of psychology, since their cumulative effect was to bring about a subtle shift in the way the room was perceived. The twin porticoes, the canted corner pilasters, the vault-turned-cupola, and the ribs converging on the central oval, all acted on the visitor's eye to convert an orthodox longitudinal plan into something approximating a centralized space. Part of the effect depended on the kind of conditioning a spectator experienced as he moved through the building: walking under one of the displays of hidden lighting and perforated structure at the entrances to the oratory would have made him more susceptible to the impossible image of an open oculus at the center of the vault (Figs. 29, 40, 41). All the ornamental detail inside the oratory joined in this assault on cold reason, stretching and squeezing an uncongenial space to make it approximate a more central and skeletal ideal, one expressed with fewer inhibitions in the grand project for a Pamphilj chapel that Borromini later sketched to the east of the Vallicella (Fig. 128). From the point of view of function the new shape was better than the old, since the altar was never used and the Oratory as a devotion centered on the pulpit; but from the point of view of tradition an oval oratory was unheard of, and as soon as Borromini was gone the old image of a room with a head and a foot began to reassert itself. In 1652 the high altar was rebuilt and the west portico buried under a lavish array of alabaster columns and marble revetment (Fig. 31).[32] The delicate perceptual base on which Borromini's achievement rested was immediately shattered, and the colorful new ornament reestablished the clear sense of direction that had characterized all the projects drafted before his arrival.

The Oratory Facade

The *Opus Architectonicum* introduces the oratory facade with an arresting image:

> Since the institution was called the Congregation of the Oratory, it was judged necessary to build a facade as a visible symbol of the oratory and of the pious exercises held inside. Having a facade of its own would make it clear that this was the precious gem in the ring of the Congregation.[33]

The metaphor of the gem in the ring is vivid but inaccurate, since there are two facades—church and oratory; a comparison with any normal building of this type, or even with Maruscelli's original project (Fig. 13), forces the historian to pose three essential questions. First, why was the oratory given a special facade at all? Second, what might it have meant in seventeenth-century terms to build a facade in brick, as opposed to the travertine of its grander neighbor? And third, were there earlier stages through which the design might have passed, corresponding to changing ideas as to how it should be perceived?

The response to the first question is ambiguous: there was no clear-cut imperative either for a facade or against it, but only a series of contradictory precedents that could be marshaled on either side of the issue. The early usage of the Congregation spoke against the idea of an ecclesiastical facade. As a devotional exercise the Oratory did not include the mass or any formal liturgy, and so it could be held in any room with adequate space, from the saint's own chambers to a former stable.[34] None of the projects drawn up during Filippo's lifetime gave the oratory a prominent facade (Cat. 1a, 1b). On the contrary, they tend to follow the traditional model of the Oratorio di S. Giovanni Decollato, which was placed at right angles to the adjacent church and given an exterior of plain rubble. This arrangement not only eliminated visual competition between the church and oratory, but also spared the architects the awkward task of fitting a traditional facade to the long side of a rectangular room.

Positive arguments in favor of a facade began to gather momentum only in the decades after Filippo's death in 1595. The example of small independent oratories with facades, like S. Marcello, the Gonfalone, and the Caravita, gradually grew more compelling.[35] An Oratorian musical publication of 1599, the *Tempio armonico,* lent currency to the image of a facade as a symbol for a spiritual edifice of sacred music.[36] In Arconio's project of 1621–23 the oratory was put on the Via di Monte Giordano, more or less on the site of the church of S. Cecilia, and given a facade commensurate with its urban importance (Cat. 9). In Maruscelli's projects of 1627 the Congregation decided to take a step backward and eliminate the facade, and so the oratory was subsumed on the outside under the larger image of a *famiglia* palace (Fig. 13; Cat. 23c). One senses an opposition party gaining ground. According to baroque decorum, church facades were considered the preserve of great prelates and the upper aristocracy, whose coats of arms and, often, coronets appear in their pediments.[37] For a Congregation of free men building a home without princely patronage a facade was not the right image, and one still catches echoes of the opposition in some of the metaphors of the *Opus,* particularly when the oratory is called the offspring of the church.[38] The arguments of the other side, in favor of a facade, can be heard in the equally charged metaphor of the gem in the ring, but how this side gained the upper hand so quickly in 1637 is not clear; perhaps it was Spada's doing. In the years just before Borromini reintroduced the idea of an ecclesiastical facade for the oratory, from 1634 to 1636, Spada was in charge of the design and construction of the facade of S. Paolo in Bologna, which was built to commemorate his nephew's impending marriage into the nobility of that city, and which takes its place alongside a number of classic Roman facades as a partial model for Borromini's design (Fig. 124).[39]

Born amid opposition and compromise, the oratory facade was expected by everyone to maintain a certain deference toward its older and more solemn neighbor, and to express its lower rank, like any inequality in a courtier society, through nuances of attire: "It was judged proper that the oratory facade should be smaller, less ornate, and of inferior material."[40] It was not only smaller, but the fictive podium on which it stood was kept as low as the podium under the church, even at the cost of a general lowering of door thresholds and floor levels throughout the casa. Although it may not seem so at first sight, it was kept rather less ornate than the Vallicella facade, and when compared to the robust and heavy ornament on some facades in the Maderno tradition, particularly S. Susanna, Borromini's details seem extraordinarily lean and spare. The capitals of the lower story were transformed into skeletal abstractions of a proper order *(ossatura di buon ordine),* leaving the so-called bell that stands at the core of an orthodox capital but omitting all freehand carving except for the volutes.[41] Finally, the facade was built in brick, a harsh and stringent requirement that Borromini ingeniously turned to his own advantage. It allowed him first to create a polychrome image, in which the yellow of the fine brickwork, the rusty brown of the rougher brick, the wood of the window frames, and the grayish white of the travertine ornament harmonize in an extraordinarily warm and mellow way. It further allowed him to turn the niches of the lowest story, which derive from Vignola's basic idea that a niche could double as a window, into fantastic allusions to the so-called pumpkin vaults of Hadrianic antiquity.[42] And, finally, it permitted him to express rather fine and nuanced ideas about the status of his patrons, ideas that can best be understood by examining the various contexts in which brick is used in the Roman ambient.

In the sixteenth and seventeenth centuries the Roman building trades were capable of furnishing two common types of wall: rubble or brick, *muro rustico* or *cortina.* Rubble was obviously cheaper and less ostentatious, and coated with stucco that turned brownish gray with time, it was the ubiquitous material of vernacular construction. Brick was more expensive and was available in a greater range of quality, from relatively simple work called *cortina rustica* through a spectrum of imperceptible gradations to walls of impeccable craftsmanship, which are referred to as *cortina arrotata, cortina di mattoni tagliati,* or *pianelle tagliate.* [43] Walls built in extremely fine brickwork with relieving arches and other features that imitate ancient models began to appear with some frequency in palaces of the early sixteenth century from the circle of Raphael and Sangallo, such as the palaces of the Baldassini and the Salviati, or of the Vescovo di Cervia (Fig. 127);[44] this earlier revival, sponsored by an aristocracy anxious to combine fine craftsmanship with antique allusion, would have lent something of a borrowed aura to the brickwork of the oratory. In some complex buildings a combination of techniques was used, such as the Palazzo Farnese with its rubble masonry on the ground floor and its fine brickwork on the upper stories. However, no building exhibits quite as much of the spectrum of possibilities as the Casa dei Filippini, where the domestic wings are built of rubble masonry and *cortina rustica,* the flanking wings of the facade of a finer type of *cortina,* and the curved facade itself of a *cortina* of extreme refinement.[45]

To judge from the *decreti,* the type of brickwork was a highly sensitive issue for the Filippini, but what exact meanings they read into the material must remain a matter for conjecture. The Jesuits were becoming known for fine brickwork, and some Oratorians may not have wanted to be left behind.[46] The possibilities of borrowed grandeur from the fine brickwork of the Renaissance must have been evident to more worldly patrons, and *cortina* of the highest quality was beginning to make an appearance in buildings like the Palazzo Barberini. There was the appeal of allusion to antiquity, not only to the unknown *torrione,* or ruin, that Borromini mentions in the *Opus* but also to a vast number of imposing ruins, of which the tomb of Annia Regilla may be the best surviving example.[47] But finally it may have been the stoic overtones of ancient brickwork, the note of republican austerity, that finally won the Filippini over. While a modern archaeologist would date fine brickwork of the Annia Regilla type to the concrete revolution that, broadly speaking, began under Nero and characterized progressive architecture throughout late antiquity, Borromini's chronology was different. For instance, in the excavations that he conducted under the Lateran in 1656, the brickwork of the structures he unearthed was taken as proof of a pre-Neronian date, before marble had been introduced into residential design and "Asiatic luxury dealt the Republic its final blow."[48] The *Opus* is misleading when it speaks of brickwork only in terms of modesty; in the seventeenth century it was apparently a multivalent symbol, expressive of a wide range of social values, from Renaissance elegance to the sturdy virtues of republican days.

It is tempting to view the oratory facade in static terms, as a grand idea that came instantaneously into being and only awaits a formal analysis subtle enough to reveal the harmonics of its perfection. However, a more fruitful approach may be to stress instead the sources of the design and the element of improvisation in it. When Borromini came to the oratory the stage for the facade was already set: the podium underneath it and the main cornice would have to match the podium and cornice of the Vallicella facade, while the lateral boundaries were set by the church on the right and Maruscelli's projection on the left. Borromini took a negative space and gave it positive value. When it first appears on his early consultation drawing (Cat. 29) the facade is indented in plan but not quite curved; it is five bays wide and, to judge from the pilaster widths, two stories high surmounted by an attic. It is not yet entirely ecclesiastical in character. Some idea of its appearance can be obtained from the side facade of S. Carlo alle Quattro Fontane, which was designed slightly later on the same principles.[49] Because it is set into what had been a featureless gap, the facade no longer fully covers the space that it symbolizes and announces; instead it creates an illusion, like the false bindings on a library shelf:

> I decided to deceive the sight [*ingannare la vista*] of the passerby, and to construct the facade as though . . . the altar were on line with the central door, so that one half of the facade covers part of the oratory, while the other half covers the guest room area.[50]

This basic idea, which was picked up in the later consultation drawings (Cat. 33) and carried over into the final building, represented a radical break with tradition, but it allowed the architect to create a growing image, unanchored to the spaces behind it, which would go through two further phases of expansion before reaching its definitive form.

The second stage of the facade—the one actually put into execution when the oratory was begun in 1637—is shown in plan in Catalogue 39 and reconstructed in Figure 14, stage 2.[51] Except for some of the ornament, the lower story was physically equivalent to what we see in the present building, but it was conceived in a different way, that is, as a five-bay facade built in fine brickwork and flanked by two bays of rougher brick that were visualized as a kind of backdrop rather than as part of the facade proper. The reconstruction of the upper story remains hypothetical, but it was probably narrower than the lower story—three bays wide—and connected to the lower story by the common convention of volutes. Practically every element in the design had some precedent in the Roman facade tradition. The idea of a facade in fine materials flanked by backdrops of rougher brick bordered by brick *bugnati,* or quoins, comes from S. Giacomo degli Incurabili, built by Volterra and Maderno in 1600–08 (Fig. 122).[52] As in Maderno's facade of St. Peter's, a giant order of pilasters was used to encompass rows of windows that had a distinctly domestic look.[53] Like many facades in the tradition of S. Susanna (Fig. 125), the oratory facade followed a clear logic of layering, so that as one approaches the center it seems to be made up of three superimposed strata. But unlike Maderno's facades, there is no crescendo of ornament or of columns toward the middle. Instead, the repetition of four identical niches brings the oratory facade closer to some of the severe facades of the age of Sixtus V, such as Martino Longhi the Elder's unexecuted project for the Vallicella or his executed facade at S. Girolamo degli Schiavoni (Fig. 123).[54]

At the oratory the logical, layered system of the Cinquecento facade is not abolished but inflected, bent inward like a malleable clay mass recoiling, so to speak, from the impact of the eye. The pilaster clusters at either end of the oratory facade can best be understood by thinking of a facade like that of S. Girolamo degli Schiavoni, or of S. Paolo in Bologna (where the facade turns a corner, and the system of pilasters continues around the side), bent inward by some sort of frontal impact: the side pilasters hold firm, the front pilasters bend, and the angle in between is stretched into the extraordinary form that Borromini used (Figs. 12, 123, 124). The columnar centerpiece found in many conventional facades is replaced by a convex bulge, a part of the facade that the *Opus* compares to the human breast;[55] the pilasters on either side of this bulge, each of which curves in two directions, are thus to be understood as part pilaster and part column-substitute. Since the bays flanking the bulge are rather flat,[56] the effect of a concave curve is conveyed mostly by the cornice of the outer bays, which protrudes far more dramatically than anything below it, not so much like arms embracing the visitor as like abstract wings hovering over his head.

Although there did exist a few curved facades in the Renaissance and the early seventeenth century, there seems to be no allusion to them here either in the general form or in any of the specific details.[57] On the other hand, there is an explicit allusion in the *Opus* to the fact that the design was originally modeled in a soft material like wax or clay: "If the building could somehow be made all of a single piece of terra cotta without any joints, it would certainly be a splendid thing."[58] Furthermore, the indented space into which the facade was set encouraged the idea of layers pushed inward. Finally, there may also be some allusion to seventeenth-century theories of optical distortion, particularly in the choice of the word "ingannare" to describe what is going on. Buried in the rather dry geometry of a book of 1625, Pietro Accolti's *Lo inganno de gl' occhi,* is a theorem about the way sight acts like a radius emanating from a fixed center and describing the arc of a circle.[59] According to this logic, flat surfaces should be perceived with more distortion than curved surfaces, since the larger they get the farther they depart from the natural curve of the visual field. In his arcane way Accolti formulated the geometry of the impact of the eye; Borromini dramatized the theorem and superseded it with a powerful work of art. For once, the stiff formality of the Cinquecento facade tradition was relaxed, and the distant frontal view demanded by these old-fashioned architectural pictures was replaced by a new regard for the spectator's glance, which the oratory facade always manages to catch no matter how close the viewer stands or how obliquely he approaches.

If the curve of the facade conveys the feeling of movement in plan, movement within its surface is expressed by the ornamental detail. Countersunk panels in the brickwork dematerialize the mass and create the impression that hidden doors may open at any time. The main entablature was fixed at a height insufficient for the kind of tall, slender windows that Borromini wanted in his oratory, and so the windows drift up into a zone where they are hardly ever found and their frames cut into the architrave like arrowheads, severing horizontal links and creating a sense of sheer vertical rise. Finally, many of the forces that are expressed abstractly in the ornament of the facade are personified in the cherub who looks out over the central window (Fig. 19). He gives the impression of being intensely alive. His smile is vivacious and his hair unkempt; his very naturalistic wings reinforce the feeling of protective hovering conveyed by the main entablature; unlike his cousins on innumerable Roman facades, who appear in pediments permanently reserved for them, he has to carve out his own place, which he does so suddenly and unexpectedly that the hood above him swells and the consoles on either side no longer seem to be supports acting against weight but rather anchors acting against uplift.[60] Like Borromini's whole facade, his right to exist is based solely on energy and daring.

In August 1638 this five-bay facade, which had been built as high as the main cornice, was rendered obsolete by the Congregation's decision to move the library from its original position behind the Vallicella to a new location behind the upper story of the oratory facade, which "being of a different order could be elevated as much as necessary."[61] An increase in height called for a proportionate increase in width and put Borromini in the dilemma of having to enlarge a lower story that already existed. A hasty and radical enlargement is recorded on one of his plans (Cat. 41), but his final solution was much simpler. The two flanking bays of rough brickwork, which had formerly served as a mere backdrop to the design, were now incorporated into the total image; volutes tie them to the upper story, and the *bugnato* on either side came to mark the boundaries of the new seven-bay design (Fig. 14, stage 3; Cat. 41). It was a perceptual rather than a physical enlargement, and characteristically it was reinforced by changes in the ornament. Twin portals were planned for the new outer bays, although in the end only one of them was carried out. Inside the two *bugnati,* curved window frames impart a generous and expansive feeling to the space, while outside them the window frame gives the feeling of being pinched and cramped (Fig. 20). The ornament around the door on the central balcony was made to repeat on a small scale some of the larger themes of the new facade, particularly in the way a laurel swag chains two small volutes to the motif in the center. Finally, the extraordinary pediment, which has precedents only on a much smaller scale in the ornament of Maderno and Cortona,[62] announces emphatically that the curved can be combined with the straight, which is very much the theme of the expanded facade.

It is thus as a flexible, growing image that the oratory facade must be understood, one that began on a modest scale and was subsequently allowed to spread over a broad field as the program and ambitions behind it expanded. In this process the role played by ornament was of immense importance. Ornament was the artist's brushstroke, the means by which an unlikely image was blocked out on the surface of the building and given the semblance of reality. Some of the details used to cement the illusion were ordinary Roman conventions, like volutes, twin portals, and *bugnati;* others, like the central niche and its illusion of depth, go back to the extraordinary way in which Borromini manipulated the conventions of architectural draftsmanship.[63] Fused together into an illusion of great persuasive power, they prepared the spectator to accept an image that in the strictest sense had no right to be there. Nevertheless, it was not an image entirely without difficulties, and in the two decades following its completion Borromini returned to it twice to tackle problems he felt it still posed.

First was the problem of imbalance, since in spite of its expansion the oratory facade was still smaller and less ornate than the Vallicella facade. During the first few months of Innocent X's papacy in 1644 there was hope of a new commission at the Vallicella which would have allowed Borromini to integrate the oratory facade into a larger and more satisfying context. He was asked to design a monumental Pamphilj Chapel along the right flank of the church, and although an obvious precedent was suggested, namely, the Chapel of Sixtus V at S. Maria Maggiore, he turned instead to antiquity and proposed a mausoleum drawn from Montano's engravings (Figs. 128, 129).[64] The whole complex was conceived as a pendant to the casa, and it was given a facade that would have reflected the oratory facade in mirror symmetry. Everything that had come to characterize the original, including the curved plan and the fenestration reflecting the logic of the thicker corner pier, found its way into the duplicate. If built it would have been part of a triple rather than a mere double facade, the ultimate baroque expression of the idea of controlled context that had had its modest beginnings in the brick walls flanking the facades of S. Giacomo degli Incurabili and S. Susanna.

The other problem was one of contradictory clues. Some elements in the facade pointed to a five-bay design, others to a design seven bays wide, and in either case the whole mirage depended on a breed of spectator attuned to faint overtones and subtle suggestions. Did such spectators exist? Apparently in the early years they did not, and the first draftsmen who depict the facade, even with Spada standing over their shoulders, tend to treat it in literalistic terms. Either they include too much, by showing the entire south front of the building (Cat. 85f), or too little, by showing only the five curved bays (Cat. 86f). It was evidently an ambiguous image, and after a time Borromini felt it necessary to step in and clarify how he wanted it read. In a drawing and a pair of prints that are connected with his publication enterprise of 1658–60 (Fig. 16; Cat. 89b, 90), he showed the facade in an idealized state, seven bays wide, freestanding on both sides, bounded by canted pilasters in the spirit of the Propaganda Fide, and redesigned along a deep and dramatic curve. It is as though all of the chains of Oratorian patronage had been snapped, and the original idea, after twenty years of incubation, had detached itself from the casa and begun to lead a viable existence on its own. These prints provided a gestalt that soon dominated the way in which the image was viewed, and it is the idealized, enlarged facade that pervades the *veduta* tradition of the late baroque era, from Falda to Piranesi, and exerts a lingering influence on early modern photographs (Fig. 12, Cat. 98a).[65]

According to the *Opus,* redesigning the oratory led to redesigning the entire casa: "Since the alterations I had to make in the oratory had repercussions elsewhere, I was forced to put my hand to the entire design with the hope of improving many of its parts."[66] Thus it is in the role of the reluctant innovator that Borromini introduces his work in the rest of the casa. To understand the full significance of what he did it is necessary to turn from the oratory to the residential and more purely functional wings of the building, or, in the metaphorical language of the period, from the precious gem to the ring in which it was set.

4

The Construction of the Casa

In 1638, the year the oratory was vaulted, it would have been difficult for the casual observer to sense any guiding plan in the structures rising around the Vallicella. The parts already built were entirely disconnected. The oratory was still a free-standing block; the sacristy was surrounded on three sides by partly demolished houses; at the northern edge of the site a wall built in 1629[1] on the ruins of S. Cecilia remained without linkage to the rest of the building. Even after 1638, when construction got under way in earnest, the growth of the casa would still have seemed haphazard, with wings radiating outward like crooked spokes from a central hub.

Beneath the appearance of haphazard growth, however, there was a careful logic at work, one based not on aesthetic preference but on legal and functional consider-ations. The first priority was to advance without delay to the outermost limits of the proposed plan. The wall of 1629 on the north and the oratory of 1637 on the south staked out the Congregation's claim on the site, and helped to satisfy the clause in the Gregorian expropriation law stipulating that a house could be slated for demolition only if it was surrounded on two sides by an expanding building.[2] The second priority was to complete the sacral parts of the program, specifically the sacristy and oratory, before the domestic.[3] The third priority was to build functional rooms like the kitchen and the refectory at a relatively early stage so that they could be linked to the old casa and put into use even before the main residential wings had been begun. Underlying all these considerations was a careful respect for the topography of the site: the preexisting street pattern, now obliterated and invisible, then provided a series of compelling boundaries that marked the limits of each building campaign (Cat. 14).

After the oratory was finished the rest of the casa was built in three separate phases over a period of thirty-five years (Fig. 7). Each campaign was of a different nature and duration. The first was both long and intense; it was the time when the major functional and ceremonial rooms were built. Between 1638 and 1641 work was concentrated on the refectory wing and the service rooms that surrounded it; between 1641 and 1643 work shifted to the first courtyard and to the completion of the porter's lodge, guest quarters, library, and the remainder of the oratory facade. The second campaign of 1647–50 was brief; it focused on the north wing of the casa ending in the Monte Giordano facade. It marked the end of Borromini's term as architect; when he left in 1652 the casa still stood open on its eastern and western flanks. The third and final campaign of 1659–75 was more dilatory: it saw the completion of the west wing by Camillo Arcucci in 1659–62, and of the Spada chapel and the wing on the east side of the service courtyard by Carlo Rainaldi in 1668–75. During these three campaigns the design was in a state of continual evolution, and by 1675 the completed casa looked quite different from the plans that had been approved in 1637. To understand what happened it will be helpful to examine the work of each campaign in turn.

First Campaign: The Refectory and the Service Courtyard (1638–41)

The service rooms behind the Vallicella apse were the functional heart of the building. Maruscelli had designed them as an interlocking unit that could be of service to the residents of the old casa even before the new building was complete. Furthermore, his library (Cat. 20b, no. 22) was designed to serve temporarily as an elevated bridge to the old building while the new one was in construction, partly as a measure of convenience but also to minimize the feeling of internal schism that the building program was threatening to create within the Congregation.[4]

From the outset Borromini felt compelled to modify these arrangements. Possibly in his eyes the courtyard was cramped, the library dimly lit, and the refectory too close to the public street for complete privacy. In his first plan (Cat. 39) he merely switched the location of various services, but in his second (Cat. 40) he took the more drastic step of eliminating the wing behind the apse. The kitchen was relocated in the "elbow" wing, the *sala di ricreazione* was now placed above the refectory, and the library was banished from the courtyard altogether. In addition, there were far-reaching alterations in the shape of some of the rooms. The refectory in particular went through a series of metamorphoses from Maruscelli's conventional rectangular plan: to a rectangle with canted corners (Cat. 39), then to a narrow dodecagon (Cat. 40), and finally to an oval (Cat. 59), which appears to have been adopted just as foundations were begun in January 1639.[5]

The extent of building during this first campaign was fixed by topographical factors. The wings under construction were carried as far as the edges of the *vicoli,* or narrow lanes that still traversed the site, and there they stopped, whether these points corresponded to any natural cesurae in the design or not. The refectory wing was begun at the wall of the saint's room complex, which had been standing since 1633, and continued to the north as far as the Via di Parione, or more accurately, as far as the wall that had been built on the site of S. Cecilia in 1629.[6] Construction then turned to the west, occupying the site of S. Cecilia and stopping at the line of its demolished facade. To the east, the "elbow" wing followed the bend in the Via di Parione and stopped at the second cross-street, the narrow Vicolo del Corallo. Thus the whole complex under construction came to form roughly the shape of the letter T. For the time being the ends of the cross-bar of the T were left with the rough and amputated look that characterizes much unfinished Roman building; this condition was eventually remedied on the west but is still partly visible at the eastern end (Fig. 96).

From the information given in the *Opus* it is possible to form a precise idea of what the rooms in these wings were used for and what they looked like in their original state. Some deserve detailed consideration, particularly the refectory, the recreation room immediately above it, the *dispensa* or larder, the square staircase, the so-called *piazza d'arme* or distribution room, the kitchen and adjacent rooms, and finally the living quarters on the upper floors.

The principal room of this area, the refectory,[7] was one of Borromini's more carefully studied interiors (Fig. 84, no. 1; Figs. 88, 89). Its floor level was sunk 4 palmi below the level of the adjacent garden courtyard, a device used to increase the clear height under the vault (34 palmi) and to improve the proportions of the space. The plan was changed from a simple rectangle to an oval circumscribed within a rectangle, something like the plan of S. Carlo alle Quattro Fontane reduced to rudimentary form. This shape had numerous advantages. It improved the apparent proportions of the room, provided four storage closets in the "triangles" left over along the perimeter of the oval, and reinforced the structure of the vault, which no longer had to rest on any unbuttressed walls. It also had acoustical advantages and improved face-to-face visibility for the fifty-six to fifty-eight men who could be seated at the thirteen tables that followed the oval curvature of the refectory walls.[8]

Above the refectory, the *sala di ricreazione,* known simply as the sala, was built along an identical oval plan (Fig. 90). Triangular spaces were left along its periphery similar to the spaces below. Instead of sinking the floor to achieve satisfying proportions, the vault was raised to a clear height of 44 palmi. As the construction of the sala began in January 1640, Spada submitted a report "endorsed by the architect" which demonstrated why the room could not be built on a simple rectangular plan; presumably he stressed the danger of placing a vault on unbuttressed and isolated walls.[9] Aesthetic factors may also have been involved, since at this time the architect was showing a consistent preference for patterns of interlocking curves; the design of the chimneypiece installed in the sala in August 1641, with its oval hearth and convex mantel set into a concave wall, closely reflects the design of the library balcony then under construction at the center of the oratory facade (Fig. 91).

In traditional convent design the room in front of the refectory was called the *lavamani* (Fig. 84, no. 8; Figs. 85, 86, 87). It was usually rectangular in shape and equipped with two wall fountains, used for handwashing, which flanked the entrance to the refectory. Maruscelli had followed this conventional plan but Borromini chose to depart from it and to project a series of experimental vestibules that combined the function of *lavamani* and transit corridor (Cat. 39a, 40a). In its final form his *lavamani* was unusually small and dark. He compensated for its size by placing the fountains in the center of the space and carving large niches out of the walls which facilitated circulation and expedited the washing ritual. And he compensated for the darkness by installing windows on three sides which allowed at least borrowed light, "lume di lume,"[10] to filter dimly into the room. The fountains themselves were among the masterpieces of Borromini's decorative sculpture: they drew heavily on a type of fountain then current in monastic design (Fig. 107), where multiple basins, heraldic ornament, and spigots in the form of "animalletti" were common; but they also bore the personal stamp of their creator, particularly in the way they combined geometry with a sense of exotic vegetal growth.[11]

To the north of the *lavamani* stood a long series of rooms that lined the Via di Parione and came to form the cross-bar of the T.[12] The spaces on the ground floor were entirely devoted to the storage and preparation of food. The *dispensa* stood at the extreme west end of the wing on the site of the demolished church of S. Cecilia (Fig. 84, no. 13). It was equipped with cellar and mezzanine for the storage of foods in unusually moist or dry conditions. A narrow corridor connected the *dispensa* with a room to the east known humorously as the *piazza d'arme* (Fig. 84, no. 10), where food and wine were marshaled before being served; a double basin was set into its north wall for washing and cooling foods, and wooden pantries along its walls served for temporary storage. To the east of the *piazza d'arme* room a small triangular room served as a transition to the bent "elbow" wing; as the name *lavapiatti* implies, it was used for dishwashing but also for cleaning meat, and marble sinks were installed along the outer wall for this purpose (Fig. 84, no. 14). Next in line was the kitchen (Fig. 84, no. 15), which was the largest room in the wing, measuring 24 by 40 palmi with a clear height of 34 palmi under the vault. Under normal working conditions it must have been dark and smoky. A huge hearth dominated the room, containing several ovens, a water-boiler, and stone trays for roasts; the street windows were all sealed to prevent smoke and heat from escaping and entering the residential rooms above, and aside from the large chimney the only ventilation came from windows on the service courtyard. Adjoining the kitchen were two vaulted workrooms with mezzanines. The first (Fig. 84, no. 16) was used for working pasta; its mezzanine had a window that overlooked the kitchen and allowed a lay brother to spy on the activities of the employees. The second room (Fig. 84, no. 17) had three small booths which were used to store dirty wash, meat freshly arrived from the butcher, and leftovers; its mezzanine was reserved for the hired cook; the adjacent mezzanine installed over a staircase was used by the cook's assistant. The irregular space at the east end of the wing, where construction had left off, was used for a small spiral staircase to reach the mezzanines, a privy for the kitchen personnel, and a ramp used for bringing pack animals and supplies into the cellar (Fig. 84, nos. 18, 19).

At the center of the wing Borromini built the square staircase (Fig. 84, no. 11) that was to provide the main vertical route through the casa: "I confess that nothing in that building gave me more satisfaction than this staircase."[13] Although this pride seems inordinate, the steps did combine all of the virtues that often eluded contemporary staircase design: ease of ascent, adequate step width, low and constant riser height, and adequate clearance between each flight. An ingenious system of iron balustrades and slanting sills provided abundant light for each landing without disturbing the fenestration on the exterior (Figs. 92, 93). Following common practice, a privy was built at the top of the staircase and the closed well or "anima" used as a shaft for the disposal of waste.[14]

After the ground floor rooms were complete the Congregation turned their attention to the residential quarters, which were to occupy the upper floors along the Via di Parione. Although only a small number of rooms were involved—space for twelve fathers—their design was of great importance, since the floor levels and corridor dimensions carried out in this wing would have to be maintained throughout the entire building. In June 1640 the Congregation voted on the matter.[15] They endorsed the system of sunken corridors long since proposed by Maruscelli, but they added another story to his project, bringing the total back up to four. They approved the standard type of suite that appears on most of the early drawings (Cat. 20b, 39), consisting of a single large *camera* and a single small *camerino* for each padre. This arrangement was later abandoned in favor of larger apartments, but at least one specimen of the one-and-one-half-room suite was built (Cat. 80, 81, 115b).

The construction during this campaign naturally had an effect on the two courtyards flanking the T-shaped wing, the small service courtyard on the east and the large garden courtyard on the west. For all practical purposes the service courtyard[16] was nearly completed at this time (Fig. 95). It consisted of a small trapezoidal space, ungraciously named the "riffiuto della fabrica," which was used for the reception of supplies and for the storage of water. The space was closed on the north by a narrow loggia; above it were corridors that serviced the three upper floors of residential rooms; the brick piers of this loggia come closer than anything else in the building to the functional plainness typical of *famiglia* palace design.[17] On the west stood the massive refectory block, with a small makeshift loggia, or *portichetto,* at its foot. The courtyard was still unfinished on the east, where there was a narrow temporary gate and a stretch of the Vicolo del Corallo still connecting the Via di Parione with the back door of S. Maria in Vallicella. The huge apse of the church loomed over the courtyard on the south; attached to it was an elevated wooden walkway that connected the old casa with the new, following a route through the saint's rooms and terminating near the sacristy.[18]

During this campaign Borromini left the definitive impress of his design on the garden courtyard (Figs. 25, 83).[19] The success of courtyards of this sort depended on two factors: the overall massing and the details of the architectural order. The massing had to be designed so that the open space of the court was not overwhelmed by the height of the surrounding wings; "aria colata,"[20] the stale darkness of light-well courtyards, was a danger to be avoided at any cost. Maruscelli's solution was to have the building descend in steps from the outer wings to the inner courtyard (Cat. 23a). Sun terraces, or *loggie scoperte,* increased the area exposed to light and air, and the roof of the outer wings was pitched to be invisible from any point in the courtyard. This design was satisfactory as long as the outer wings did not rise to excessive heights; it was ruined by a decision of the patron in 1640 to add an extra story to the building.[21] Borromini realized from the outset that the massing was not under his control and so he concentrated his attention on the architectural order. For Maruscelli's Tuscan and Ionic pilasters he substituted colossal composite pilasters. Whereas Maruscelli's design had been luxurious and ornate, with "so many pilasters, *pilastretti,* and multiplications of bases and cornices," his was simple, and founded on the conviction that "pleasure stems more from good design than from materials or ornaments."[22] He stood by the design under criticism: "Nothing in this building pleased me more than being able to unite the loggie with a single order of pilasters, which create the appearance of real magnificence, as they seem to rise up to bear the cornice like so many giants."[23] Beneath the grandiose metaphors, however, there seems to run a deeper current of dissatisfaction. The *Opus* goes on to imply that an architect who is forced to work with details rather than massing is more of a tailor than a true creator; the giant order succeeds "in the way that a well-tailored suit of honest cloth looks far more handsome than an ill-cut suit of silk on the back of a rude knave *(homaccio)."*[24] When Borromini had the opportunity to illustrate the courtyard in Martinelli's guidebook of 1658, in effect he left the rude knave out; the print idealizes the courtyard by depicting the giant order and the loggie but omitting any trace of the awkward mass that should have loomed up behind them (Cat. 89c).[25]

The portion of the courtyard that was actually built during this campaign was relatively small, namely, eight bays along the east side and only two bays along the north (Cat. 81). Nevertheless, the pattern was set for what was to follow. The giant order was established. The arches of the *piano nobile* were closed to the weather in an ingenious way that emphasized the vertical thrust of the pilasters, left space for a small balcony-garden in each arch, and created the impression of evenhanded symmetry on the interior of the loggie.[26] Finally, the loggie embodied the principle that the major axes of sight and circulation were to be wider than any other passageways in the casa. Whereas in Maruscelli's project all the loggie around both courtyards were a constant 18 palmi wide, Borromini reserved this width for the loggia along the east side of the courtyards, the one a visitor would see on entering the main door. The others were reduced, at times to as little as 14½ palmi. As in many other features of the design, optical considerations took precedence over the absolute standards of the drawing board.

First Campaign: The First Courtyard (1641–44)

The first courtyard was the natural sequel to the construction of the functional and residential wings (Figs. 47–54). It was designed to be the ceremonial gateway to the casa, the place where most visitors would form their initial impressions of the building. Furthermore, since the oratory was still standing as an isolated block, it was a natural reflex to reach out and link it to the rest of the casa as soon as the opportunity presented itself. That opportunity came in April 1641, when financing was arranged to continue the sacristy corridor as far as the southern limit of the property. All subsequent planning followed upon this initial decision. The corridor led to the *portaria,* and the *portaria* to the main portal of the casa, which was designed in November 1641. The guest quarters on the *piano nobile* followed hard on the completion of the *portaria* on the floor below. As these rooms were built the oratory facade was finally brought to completion, and with the facade went the library, which was stationed behind its upper story and roofed in late 1642. All these upper rooms were useless without an adequate stairway, and so in August 1643 the loggia along the south side of the courtyard was finally built, and in conjunction with it the entrance to the grand *scalone* was begun. The staircase itself remained unfinished, and for two decades the oratory spiral substituted as the main route to the upper floors. When the building campaign was brought to a close in 1643, the courtyard still lay open on its western flank. Like the T-shaped wing at the rear of the casa, it was aesthetically incomplete, but nevertheless ready to function as a working unit.

A drawing for the first courtyard in the Victoria and Albert Museum exhibits the dynamics of Borromini's design (Cat. 66v, 66r).[27] The main lines of the space had been fixed in the early stages of planning (Cat. 39, 59), and they are simply taken over in enlarged form as the basic armature of the drawing. Borromini conceived of his task as one of fleshing out the bare bones of the structure, not only with ornamental details but also with larger motifs that would actively shape the space and introduce a rich array of new allusions into the architecture. In the area of the *portaria,* for instance, the basic shape including the room arrangements and the floor levels had been fixed since 1639. The drawing is mainly concerned with enriching these basic forms: round *seditori,* or messengers' seats, are added to the steps (Fig. 43), and the chambers are outfitted with fireplaces and other conveniences. Two proposals are shown for the *andito,* or corridor leading to the oratory, one for a groin vault on columns in imitation of a Roman thermal hall, another for a barrel vault over a complex system of superimposed pilasters. The second alternative was the one put into execution; a proposal for its elevation is sketched on the verso of the drawing, and an adaption of the same motif, designed with large areas of glazing to allow light into the side chapels of the church, is sketched on the bottom of the sheet. Finally, the sacristy wall, which had been left by Maruscelli as a barren, unpromising surface with problematic fenestration, is transformed into a cohesive organization of sculptural forms. The *nicchioni,* or pairs of large niches at either end of the wall (Fig. 49), are introduced ostensibly to solve a problem of asymmetry in the sacristy corridor, but also to fuse the wall and the loggie on either side of it into a single continuous motif "in the manner of a theater."[28]

All the pentimenti on the Victoria and Albert drawing point to the same underlying principle of design: free improvisation and enrichment of form within fixed overall limits. What happened to the courtyard is similar to what had already happened to the oratory: in each the inherited plan was kept with little physical change, but innovations of a psychological order altered the spectator's perception of space and structure. Although these innovations were explained as solutions to problems of alignment, lighting, or symmetry, in most cases the exuberance of the response far outstripped the gravity of the problem. The *nicchioni* were an overresponse to a small problem of asymmetry, just as the oratory facade and interior design had been overresponses to the problem of the thicker corner pier. The Victoria and Albert drawing gives the impression that Borromini actively sought such problems out and used them to justify the introduction of a large number of rich and exotic motifs.

This exuberance did not go entirely unchecked. The construction was closely supervised by a building committee and a *soprastante* who was supposed to keep the architect under watch.[29] There were some unpleasant exchanges between these men and the architect, and while the courtyard was under construction in 1642 the *soprastante,* Padre Isodoro Roberti, resigned over disagreements with Borromini.[30] Outside consultations were still used to check any major departures from the established design. The Victoria and Albert drawing itself was apparently used in the course of a consultation with G. B. Soria and Francesco Contini in November 1641, and its inscriptions rehearse the arguments Borromini used to justify motifs like the *nicchioni.* Borromini became extremely skilled at negotiating these encounters, but the need to defend every innovation gradually led him and Spada to formulate a special kind of language, which might be called a rhetoric of justification. This eloquent and persuasive argumentation often had to shift its tactics depending on the audience being addressed. In dealing with the Congregation at large it was necessary to justify every innovation in terms of structure or practical function, while for outside consultants the same innovations were described as borrowings from antiquity or respected architectural treatises. This rhetoric was occasionally put into writing as needed during construction.[31] It eventually came to pervade the text of the *Opus* when the manuscript was composed in 1647, and although it sometimes illuminates certain facets of the design, just as often it throws a veil over the architect's deeper motivations. The need to draw that veil aside will become clear in the following chapter on the building's imagery.

The new *forestaria,* or guest quarters, was located immediately above the *portaria* (Figs. 61–64). The space was designed both for the temporary reception of visitors and for the occasional accommodation of overnight guests.[32] Two rooms were designated for socializing prior to the services of the Oratory: a large square *camerotto* for cardinals, and a narrow gallery for the gentlemen of their suites.[33] Two adjacent *camerini,* each with a mezzanine, served as small apartments for those dignitaries who preferred not to return home after a late evening Oratory. Since these rooms were considered part of the public area, Borromini was freer to decorate them than he would have been with the private quarters, and he used them to demonstrate the optical qualities of his art. The cornices and vaults are made to cut across corners; the desired effect was to reduce the apparent length and width of the rooms in relation to their height, and thereby to improve their perceived proportions. In one of the small *camerini* one-quarter of a hidden spiral staircase was allowed to swell out into the room at cornice level, and internal symmetry was maintained by repeating this swelling in the three other corners.

These vaults gave to the rooms not only improved proportions and elegant shapes that foreshadowed Borromini's late style,[34] but also a subtle restatement of a familiar theme: the rooms tend to evoke the image of a Roman vault left standing after the corner columns had been removed.

As construction advanced, it finally became possible to complete the library,[35] which had remained unfinished for four years while the oratory stood isolated from the rest of the casa. Work on its walls was resumed in 1642 and on the shelves and ceiling in 1643; the furnishing was complete by 1644. In its original form the library consisted of a single large room, the *salone,* which was flanked by smaller chambers housing specialized collections. There were three private studies on the east; on the west were located the librarian's rooms, a small circulating library, a gallery of maps, a fireproof archive, and a cabinet for the collection of medals and antiquities that Spada intended to leave to the Congregation (Cat. 100). The *salone* towered over the neighboring annexes and its mass was originally visible protruding above the roof behind the upper story of the oratory facade (Cat. 99).

The library can best be understood as a compromise between an ideal model and a number of practical exigencies imposed by the patron and the site. The ideal model, nowhere explicitly named but everywhere apparent, was the library of the Palazzo Barberini, which had been finished about a decade before.[36] Like the library of the Filippini, it consisted of a main *salone* connected to a series of smaller annexes for manuscripts, medallions, rarities, *mappamondi,* and for the storage of overflow books. The Barberini *salone* was vaulted, but since the walls of the room were unbuttressed the vault had to be tied with visible chains. The walls were lined with shelving built in 1633 on the designs of G. B. Soria; it is familiar to users of the manuscript reference room in the Vatican Library, where it was transferred in 1902 (Fig. 133). Soria designed the shelves in two stories and used an architectural order of fluted Ionic columns to support the walkway that served the upper story; spiral staircases hidden in the corners connected the two levels. The one element of figurative decoration in the room was Bernini's bronze bust of Urban VIII, which stood in a walnut frame in the upper story. According to Tetius, the bust amply compensated for the absence of those inscriptions, pictures, proverbs, emblems, statues, and busts that usually decorated libraries. About sixty portraits of famous authors were kept in an antechamber outside the *salone;* pride of place among them went, by 1665 at least, to Galileo.

At the Casa dei Filippini, however, practical contingencies led to departures from the Barberini model. First and foremost, it was impossible to vault the Vallicella library since there was neither lateral buttressing nor adequate support from below. Instead it had to be given a wooden ceiling, and much that seems farfetched in the *Opus* chapter on the library, particularly the talk of an imitation travertine ceiling and the allusions to the stone coffering of Roman temples, can be explained as compensation for this basic loss.[37] Second, Borromini was instructed to reuse shelving salvaged from the old library, which kept the cost to half what the Barberini had spent but condemned the shelving to look archaic and dwarfed in the new space. Third, the fenestration of the room was set at levels dictated by the proportions of the oratory facade, and at first it seemed that the windows would be far too high. To compensate, Borromini enlarged the shelving system he had inherited; as it swelled in size, the forty-four Tuscan columns designed to support the upper ramp grew to enormous proportions, each 13½ palmi tall and 2 palmi thick. To save on wood and to increase the visibility of the lower shelves, Borromini changed the columns to giant balusters, equally tall but far more elegant and slender; the old *titoli,* or flat wooden scrolls, were then reused above the balusters to form a shaky parapet for the ramp. The marble bust of Baronius corresponded to Bernini's bust of Urban VIII, but it stood in less splendid isolation. It was surrounded by portraits of illustrious benefactors painted in grisaille on wooden roundels, with blanks reserved for future donors. At eye level there were engravings of illustrious authors, including Mohammed and a number of heretics; these modest prints were the analogue of the portrait gallery at the Barberini library, and were displayed "to fill the eye with charm and the intellect with erudition."[38] Images of the Virgin and S. Filippo were placed over the doors, and the program was completed by Romanelli's ceiling allegory of *Divine Wisdom,* surrounded by wooden stars alluding to the doctors of the church. A sensitive observer would have noted not only the religious nature of the iconography and of most of the titles on the shelves, but also the absence of opulent materials. The Vallicelliana would have seemed like a cardinal's library bled of color. There was parchment in place of the rich cordovan bindings that lined the Barberini shelves; the one bust was marble instead of bronze; all paintings were in grisaille; and even the coffered ceiling was given the tint of fictive travertine.

The campaign came to an end in the late months of 1643 and the start of 1644, when the library was completed and the loggia and staircase vestibule were built (Figs. 47, 55–57).[39] From the point of view of corporate sociology, the crucial date was August 1643, when a large part of the Congregation moved to the new quarters.[40] In spite of deep attachments, the building they left behind was a house without *penates*, since Filippo's relics had been moved nine years before. The casa that they now occupied was fragmentary and open on all sides to intrusion from the outside world; aesthetically, it was like a ship that had been launched before the hull was complete. But in practical terms it functioned well: supplies were laid in, meals began to be cooked and served, assemblies convened, guests received, and, most importantly, the Oratory could be held in a setting of proper dignity.

This building, incomplete and fragmentary as it was, is the casa described in the *Opus.* Borromini and Spada composed the original manuscript of this book in 1647, before further construction was undertaken.[41] The many rooms it describes in minute detail had all been built by 1647, particularly the oratory, *portaria,* kitchens, refectory, sala, square staircase, *forestaria,* and library. The features that evoke the most famous metaphors in the text were all products of the first campaign: the oratory facade that extends its arms in the form of an embrace, the pilasters that rise up like giants, the balusters that alternate like men and trees, and the columns with leafy bases and capitals that seem to grow like flowering stalks.[42] The elaborate precautions against theft which the text describes at length make sense only for an unfinished building, where the courtyards were still occupied by houses and the garden was still traversed by a public street.[43] As for the wings that remained to be built, the manuscript speaks of them either in the future tense or not at all. The main *scalone* with its special vault, the west wing, the gateway to the service court, and the garden with its fountains are all described as planned but not yet built. The oratory altar is still temporary. There is no mention of a pharmacy or any shops. There is still only "un poco di piazza" in front of the church; the new street along its right flank is still not opened; the Monte Giordano facade and clocktower are not mentioned at all. In a sense, an enterprise like the *Opus* was condemned from the start to be out of date, not only because of the length of time it took to finish the building, but also because of Borromini's habit of introducing improvised and unforeseen changes into the design as each new wing was begun.

Second Campaign: The Monte Giordano Wing (1647–50)

Between 1644 and 1647 work was suspended on the casa. In September 1644 Giovanni Battista Pamphilj was elected Pope Innocent X, and for the next few years he dominated the attentions of both Spada and Borromini. Spada had just begun his third term as Preposito of the Congregation when, in October 1644, he was compelled to relinquish this position and to become the papal *elemosiniere segreto,* a post that involved the administration of funds and bequests allotted to relief of the poor.[44] In addition, he became a valued architectural consultant. In 1645 he organized the commission convened to investigate the cracks appearing in the facade of St. Peter's, a group that included both Borromini and Maruscelli.[45] In the same year he became a consultant on the rebuilding of the Palazzo Pamphilj in Piazza Navona by the Rainaldi firm in conjunction with Borromini.[46] In 1646 he accompanied Borromini on a visit to inspect the basilicas of S. Giovanni in Laterano and S. Paolo fuori le mura, which led to Borromini's rebuilding of the Lateran for the Jubilee of 1650.[47] He collaborated with Borromini on the text of the *Opus* in early 1647.[48] Finally, in 1644 Innocent X entertained the idea of constructing a large family chapel to the east of S. Maria in Vallicella, but although he briefly considered a project submitted by Borromini (Cat. 39), the idea eventually was scrapped in favor of rebuilding S. Agnese in Piazza Navona.[49]

Work was resumed on the casa in May 1647, and during the brief campaign that followed attention was concentrated on the northwest corner of the building. This wing contained the *spetiaria,*[50] or pharmacy, and three shops on the ground floor; the upper stories were devoted to about twelve residential apartments of two rooms each.[51] Characteristically, construction stopped short at the edge of a small *vicolo* which was allowed to remain open for another decade. At the beginning of work Borromini found himself obliged to demolish part of a wall that Maruscelli had built on the site for legal reasons in 1629; in the process he resurveyed the building alignments and chose to depart from Maruscelli's orthogonal strictness in favor of what may be called the Collegio Romano principle,[52] whereby the obtuse angles of the final building are hidden by curved corners or concealed in the thickness of the walls (Cat. 80, 81).

During the course of the campaign, the Congregation encountered a serious legal problem that had repercussions on the design. The Filippini tended to keep their plans a strict secret,[53] so when the full extent of the new building was revealed in 1647, the public were surprised to see that the new plan overstepped the boundaries of the buildings just demolished (Cat. 14). The Boncompagni, the immediate neighbors to the north, demanded that the Congregation "pull back the corner of the fabric."[54] Naturally it refused to do any such thing. The dispute eventually came to focus on the small fountain that had been planned for the northwest angle of the casa, partly for ornamental reasons but also in part to stake out the last few feet of land that had been ceded by the city but left unoccupied by Borromini's concave design. The fountain was begun, contested, and finally left unfinished except for the large oval block of travertine still on the site; the full scope of the project is known only from a later print (Cat. 89a).

As the foundations were being laid, Borromini revised the design and introduced the *torre dell'orologio,* or clocktower, which, along with the facade below it, was one of the most important innovations in the entire building (Fig. 23; Cat. 89a, 98b).[55] The design he inherited from Maruscelli treated the whole west side of the casa as a unified image, with no concessions to the special optical conditions in which that image would be viewed (Cat. 23c). Borromini took the image and cut it into pieces. He isolated Maruscelli's left-hand projection, enlarged it from 71 to 93 palmi, and turned it into an independent facade commensurate in size with the piazza in front of it. He decorated it with a colossal order of pilasters, more overpowering in scale and finer in brickwork than those of the oratory projection. At its center he designed an element totally lacking in the earlier projects: a tall belltower, crowned with Filippini heraldry in wrought iron, and designed to dominate the view down the Via dei Banchi Nuovi. As these innovations are studied on the original plan of the wing (Cat. 80), they show the same process of design already encountered in the oratory and the first courtyard: improvisation wherever a foothold was offered, and optical enrichments that alter the way the building is perceived.

The Monte Giordano facade was Borromini's last contribution to the casa. Friction had been building between him and various members of the Congregation, and with the administration of the community out of Spada's hands, it reached a point where it could no longer be contained. Exactly what precipitated Borromini's departure is obscure: his last recorded payment is in July 1650, but in December 1650 his assistant Francesco Righi was paid, surprisingly, as the new architect.[56] In November 1650 Borromini refused to arbitrate in a dispute between the Congregation and their chief contractor, Defendino Peschal, over the value of work done on the Monte Giordano wing; inexcusably, he even refused to hand over the relevant "libro d'esse misure."[57] In 1651 and 1652 cracks began to appear in the oratory vault and the library wall above it; Borromini was not among the experts, who included Cortona, Arigucci, and Peschal, called in for advice.[58] In

October 1651 the Vaj bequest was announced and plans were made to transform the oratory altar in the face of opposition from both Spada and Borromini.[59] The definitive break came on August 23, 1652, when Camillo Arcucci, a nonentity who had furthered the Congregation's suit with the Mastri di Strade, was named architect "in place of Cavaliere Borromini, who has refused to be architect for our Congregation in the future."[60]

All this transpired while Spada was engaged in the service of Innocent X. After his return to the Congregation and reelection as Preposito in 1656, he attempted to have Borromini recalled. He played his hand in April 1657 by convening a meeting of the Four Deputies and informing them that a benefactor had offered an attractive loan to continue the building, but that for various reasons the loan was contingent upon Borromini's return. Spada placed three possible courses of action before the Deputies. One was to accept the loan and entrust the work to Borromini. The second was to entrust the work to Arcucci, dependable man that he was; in that case, however, Borromini would retaliate by abandoning work on the Lateran bronze doors,[61] to the pope's annoyance and to Spada's humiliation. The third was to postpone work until the Lateran doors were finished and then entrust it to Arcucci, but in that case the present offer of a loan would have to be declined. By a narrow margin the Deputies approved the first proposal and agreed to recall Borromini. The matter was then put before the Congregation at large. Spada explained the situation and reminded the padri that while they could vote on the financial side of the question their competence did not extend to the selection of the architect: if they accepted the loan they had to accept Borromini. The meeting was adjourned amid complaints about the rigid terms of the proposal; when it was reconvened on May 17, 1657, Spada suffered a stunning reversal: the Congregation rejected both the loan and Borromini by a vote of twelve to four.[62]

The Filippini were seldom indifferent to offers of finance, and the vote indicates a deep-seated resentment against their former architect. Coming when it did, it was only one among the many rebuffs that contributed to Borromini's psychological deterioration in the years immediately after Innocent X's death in January 1655. In 1655 the cupola of S. Ivo was criticized as structurally unsound.[63] In January 1656 complaints were lodged against the architect by the master masons of S. Agnese; Borromini deserted the workyard, spent his time browsing in the bookstalls of the area, and finally provoked the crisis of February 1657, when he resigned the commission amid attacks on his "intractable" and "inflexible nature."[64] The commission of architects took over the work in July 1657 included the now ubiquitous Arcucci. When in August 1657 the choice of the architect for the Apostles' Chapel at the Lateran fell on Felice della Greca, observers remarked that "Cavaliere Borromini looks as if he will die of chagrin"; and on September 2, 1657, Spada reported to the pope that "Borromini is not content, and it will require the intervention of the police to get the Lateran notes and drawings from his hands."[65] It appears that Borromini carried out the threat to abandon the Lateran doors, and then extended retaliation to Virgilio's brother Bernardino as well. By November 1657, however, "his passion had time to cool," and he effected a reconciliation at least with Bernardino, to whom he poured out a long tale of grievances and affronts upon his honor.[66] The break with Virgilio was not long in healing, but it may have been at this time that the *Opus* was permanently set aside; Borromini never delivered the drawings he had promised in the preface, and by 1658 he had begun to experiment with other channels for publishing his work.[67]

If Borromini had been given the opportunity to finish the casa, it might not have looked too different from the form in which it was finally built. The first courtyard was completed according to his plans, although it never received the fountain he wanted to place on its central axis.[68] The main *scalone* followed his designs in everything but decorative detail; even his chaining technique is used to secure the vault. The west wing shows a layout of rooms and corridors that was adopted after his departure, but its external appearance is largely what he intended it to be.[69] On the other hand, the garden courtyard was given a fountain and planting patterns of a quite different stamp from those Borromini had designed; furthermore, his plan to continue the giant order of pilasters around all four sides of the courtyard was never carried out, and the south side was thus deprived of his transparent screen of arches (Cat. 85g).[70] Figure 6 shows some of the finer nuances of planning that were ignored by his successors, particularly in the way the bulge caused by the *lavamani* and Maruscelli's pilasters-without-*membretti* were to be duplicated elsewhere in the design for the sake of balance.[71] These are small details, but they do bring out the unfortunate side of his premature dismissal—not that the casa was finished on totally different plans, but that the process of continuous improvisation and enrichment that characterized his way of working came to an abrupt halt.

Third Campaign: The West Wing (1659–62), Spada Chapel (1668 ff.), and East Wing (1669–75)

In 1658 Alexander VII issued a decree saying that all buildings that had benefited from the papal expropriation laws had to be finished immediately.[72] This pressure forced the Filippini to complete the long west wing[73] that stretched between the oratory and the Monte Giordano projection (Fig. 22). The architect in charge was Camillo Arcucci, who carried out his task of "putting Borromini's drawings into execution" without intruding much of his own personality into the design.[74] On the exterior he continued the combination of brick *cortina* and stuccoed rubble used elsewhere in the casa, and although he tried to impose a rhythmical grouping on the fenestration, the effect is lost in the vast expanse of the wing. The new arrangement of the residential suites, the relocation of the fourth-floor corridor, and the introduction of a new secondary staircase were probably all suggestions of the patrons. It was under Arcucci that both major courtyards were finally closed to the outside world and the danger of theft eliminated. The garden was laid out on his design, complete with fountain, paved *viali,* and barriers to protect the plantings. Arcucci became the executor of Borromini's designs for the main *scalone:* he installed the modello of Algardi's *Attila* relief over the third landing in 1660, and secured the barrel vault over the upper flights with the ingenious method of chaining that Borromini had invented for his palace projects of 1646–47 (Figs. 58–60).[75] It is one of the ironies of the casa that the very wing where Maruscelli's planning had begun and the very vaults that Borromini had hoped to turn into a showpiece of his structural technique were carried out by Arcucci's cold and anonymous hand.

By 1662 all impetus to expand the residential quarters had spent itself, and further work on the casa became ancillary to work on the church. The service courtyard remained unfinished; Borromini's "elbow" wing along its north side stopped short at the edge of the Vicolo del Corallo, which still traversed the courtyard and led to the back door of S. Maria in Vallicella. This situation was slowly remedied between 1662 and 1675. In 1662 the Marchese Orazio Spada offered to complete the Chapel of S. Carlo Borromeo.[76] The *vicolo* on which the chapel eventually stood was closed in 1663; Carlo Rainaldi was taken on as its architect in 1667; and in 1668 the chapel was begun in expanded form on his designs. Arcucci was retained for the design of the nearby campanile of S. Maria in Vallicella, which he began in 1666. Between 1669 and 1674 the east wing of the service courtyard was completed (Fig. 94). Only two stories high and containing a single apartment, it was the product of shrunken ambition; much of the wall built to seal the courtyard was a mere screen.

Between 1673 and 1675 a new thoroughfare, the Via della Chiesa Nuova, was opened along the east flank of the casa and a brick screen was built on Rainaldi's design along the east side chapels of S. Maria in Vallicella (Fig. 103; Cat. 102).[77] The street was important in both a legal and a symbolic sense: legally, because it repaid the many small debts the Congregation had incurred by encroaching on public land; symbolically, because the casa became an isola and the old house was at last set adrift. Rainaldi's screen completed the circle and brought work to a halt at the point where it had begun, under Filippo Neri's watchful eye, exactly one hundred years before.

Alterations (1651–1924)

Alterations were part of the adaptive process by which the Filippini settled into the casa and turned its eccentricities to their own uses. They began under Arcucci and continued throughout the mature life of the building. Inside the oratory the transformations began as early as 1651. In that year the Vaj bequest for a new high altar was announced; the model was approved over Spada's protests in 1652 and the altar built between 1653 and 1664, to the detriment of the centralized space that Borromini had attempted to create (Fig. 31).[78] It appears that the ground-floor windows on the north side of the oratory were sealed in the early 1650s.[79] Although steps were frequently taken to secure the vault, it was finally tied with three visible chains in 1788. In that year Romanelli's decaying fresco of the *Coronation of the Virgin* was replaced by Pietro Angeletti's *Divine Wisdom*.[80] When the casa was transformed into a tribunal in 1871 the porticoes at both ends of the oratory were walled up (Figs. 36, 37). They were reopened in the restoration of 1924, but a modern organ was built in the singers' loggia, blocking the natural light which the room was meant to receive from the west.[81]

The underground oratory (Fig. 30) never seems to have functioned in the way that was originally intended.[82] In 1711 the Congregation decided to rent it out, and in 1751 they allowed the tenant to raise the floor level. At some point the spiral staircase descending to this room was blocked and all acoustical connections with the oratory proper were sealed, although the two "rote di metallo" were left in place in the oratory floor.

The design of the oratory facade had been linked from a very early stage with the library, and the two elements reached their final shape together in 1665–67 when the west wall of the library, which stood over the center of the oratory vault and was thought to be threatening its security, was moved to the western edge of the building.[83] The small annexes to the west of the *salone* were sacrificed; the *salone* itself was expanded by a factor of one-half its original size, and its coffered ceiling was enlarged from five to seven bays (Fig. 65). Different materials and possibly a different color scheme were used to set the addition off from the original facade, and a small pendant room was built on the right to preserve the symmetry of the composition (Cat. 101). Although the alterations were carried out with some sensitivity, much of the three-dimensional quality and with it the verisimilitude of the original image were lost.

The first courtyard has been severely altered in order to reclaim spaces that Borromini originally left open to the weather (Figs. 47, 48; Cat. 115a). The documents are not entirely clear on the exact sequence of events, but it seems that between 1652 and 1660 the *piano nobile* arches on all three sides of the courtyard and the ground floor arches on the south and east sides were sealed with window-walls by Arcucci.[84] The recessed walls, balcony-gardens, and other subtleties used by Borromini in sealing the arches of the garden court were absent from Arcucci's design; his aim instead was simply to provide a well-lit and weatherproof passage for visitors between the front door and the *forestaria*. In 1871 the space between the two *nicchioni* was filled with a series of rooms one story high. Either in 1871 or in 1924 the *loggia scoperta* on three sides of the courtyard was converted into the closed corridor that now serves as the catalogue room and stacks of the modern Biblioteca Vallicelliana. In the restoration of 1924 the low structure between the *nicchioni* was removed and the ground floor arches opened once again, so that the present courtyard (Fig. 47) exhibits three different stages of the design: Borromini's open arches on the ground floor, Arcucci's closed arches on the *piano nobile,* and the modern closed corridor on the uppermost level. In 1924 the rooms over the sacristy were raised and transformed into the reading room of the Biblioteca Vallicelliana, and Borromini's elaborate balcony window, which had survived intact until that time, was needlessly removed (Figs. 49–52).

The garden courtyard was twice opened to rude intrusions from the secular world. In 1798–1800, during the Roman Republic, the casa was occupied by successive waves of Neapolitan and Jacobin troops; at one point in 1798 the main corridor along the east side of the courtyards was cordoned off and used as barracks for 666 men.[85] In 1871 the casa was confiscated and turned over to the Ministries of Public Works, of Grace and Justice, and of Public Instruction.[86] The sacristy, which had at first been destined for use as a courtroom, was eventually spared, but in compensation a structure of equivalent size was built in the three southernmost bays of the garden to house two tribunals and a number of smaller chambers (Fig. 83; Cat. 115a). The courtyard was thus reduced to a cramped square, five bays wide. The giant order of pilasters was duplicated with some care along the north wall of the new structure; the south wall absorbed Maruscelli's ramp and low pilasters, which had been adapted by Borromini but never entirely rebuilt (Fig. 81).[87] The courtroom structure was not removed in the subsequent restoration; it now houses the archives of S. Maria in Vallicella on the ground floor and part of the Instituto Storico per il Medio Evo on the *piano nobile.* In 1922–24 the ground floor rooms of the north wing, which had originally housed a shop, the pharmacy, and the *dispensa,* were converted to a public library, and the former shop under the clocktower was converted to the library entrance. The northwest staircase of the casa originally had not descended below the *piano nobile* (Fig. 26); at this time it was extended to the ground floor, given a doorway on the Piazza di Monte Giordano, and adapted as the entrance to the Instituto Storico.

In 1871 the "elbow" wing along the Via di Parione was assigned to the remaining Oratorians as their residence; either then or in 1922–24 the refectory and its adjacencies were severely altered.[88] The refectory itself was stripped of its furniture, the windows blocked, the pulpit removed, and the pulpit entrance converted to a doorway leading to the garden loggia. The low *portichetto* that ran along the eastern side of the refectory was removed and battered buttressing introduced to prop up the refectory vault. The Roman ruins in the grotto were buried when the cellars were waterproofed and rented out to a lumber dealer.[89] The *lavamani* area became almost unrecognizable: Borromini's fountains were removed, the floor level was raised, and the two niches flanking the refectory door were sealed; whatever illumination there had been from the north was blocked; the door to the square staircase was sealed; and finally a new doorway was opened under the window in the western niche (Fig. 85). The *sala di ricreazione* was stripped of its benches and fitted with shelving to hold the Orsini archives in the possession of the Archivio Storico Capitolino; Borromini's marble chimneypiece survives, inaccessible but intact.[90] The *piazza d'arme* room was deprived of its fountain and a doorway was pierced in its north wall; the room is now the vestibule and reception room of the modern Congregazione dell'Oratorio, and the door that enters it from the Via del Governo Vecchio is the belated fulfillment of a wish, expressed as early as 1641, for an entrance on the northern side of the building.[91]

5

Finance, Function, Imagery

On one level architectural history is simply the record of a building's construction, of the successive phases in which the design took shape, was given concrete form, and was subsequently altered. It tells the story of an outer shell. But on another level it is the history of the intangible elements that surround a building, such as the financial institutions that allowed or encouraged the shell to be built, the ephemeral life that formerly unfolded within it, and the language of corporate symbolism that the structure once spoke. On this level the building becomes a complex document which can shed light on broad issues of social history, and these in turn can illuminate the architecture and clarify some of its more puzzling features. The preceding chapters have been devoted largely to the outer shell of the Casa dei Filippini, and the building might now appear as a vast labyrinth of stark chambers and long corridors interspersed with a few ornate rooms. The present chapter attempts to counteract this impression by reconstructing something of the building's inner life. It is organized around three fundamental issues: how the casa was financed, how it functioned, and what it might have meant in terms of visual imagery.

Finance

Paradoxically, although the *Opus Architectonicum* depicts a Congregation obsessed with modesty almost to the point of stinginess, the residence the Filippini constructed became one of the most expensive buildings of papal Rome.[1] Records are fragmentary and it is difficult to calculate the exact cost; old estimates by the Filippini themselves are probably too high when they reach the figure of a million scudi for the entire complex: ∇170,000 for the church, ∇30,000 for its facade, and ∇800,000 for "the casa with annexes," which seems to include the large sums that went into the piazza and the houses surrounding it. A more realistic figure for the casa proper can be extrapolated from Spada's statement that between 1638 and 1644 he spent ∇100,000 on the building, with ∇30,000 going for demolition and ∇70,000 for new construction. These sums are more in line with what it cost to build a major residential structure; between 1581 and 1588 it had cost ∇166,550 to build a larger section of the Collegio Romano, with about the same proportions being spent on demolitions and new construction.[2] If the other parts of the casa are included at the same rate, namely, the sacristy and oratory built before 1638 and the Monte Giordano wings built after 1644, then the total cost may have been between ▽200,000 and ▽300,000. It is less than the old estimate of ▽800,000, but it is still an enormous sum. By way of comparison the Uffizi cost something like the equivalent of ▽400,000,[3] the Acqua Paola ▽396,476,[4] Maderno's nave and facade of St. Peter's ▽291,508,[5] the Palazzo Borghese ▽275,000,[6] the Acqua Felice ▽255,341 or more,[7] Sixtus V's Lateran Palace ▽172,884,[8] Borromini's reconstruction of the Lateran for Innocent X ▽127,563.06,[9] the Casa Professa of the Jesuits ▽100,000,[10] Borromini's wings of the Propaganda Fide something over ▽84,805,[11] the Gesù itself ▽70,000,[12] Clement VIII's Lateran transept ▽38,016,[13] and finally S. Carlo alle Quattro Fontane—cloister, casa, and church without the facade—a mere ▽18,939.[14] However approximate many of these figures might be, they do give the general order of magnitude, and they tell a quite different story from the much publicized claims to modesty, namely, that the Filippini were willing to engage in a building program as expensive as that of any wealthy patron.[15]

Part of the cost was simply due to the enormous size of the building, since it was the cubic mass of masonry that was always the greatest single expense. But part was also due to Borromini. He insisted on elaborate and expensive solutions to the so-called problems he kept discovering in the design. For his ornamental detail he insisted on work paid by *stima* and on supervised day-work *(a giornate),* which kept both quality and expense high.[16] One example shows how expensive his moldings and ornament could be: under Maruscelli a marble doorframe typically cost ▽76; one of Borromini's doorframes cost ▽700 "for the workmanship exclusive of material," and he records the cost in a spirit of pride.[17] Borromini habitually cut down bills that were submitted for his approval by craftsmen, but the very type of work was expensive, and during his tenure at the oratory it came to be remarked within the profession that "his buildings are beautiful but one pays for it."[18] Much of his later propaganda, particularly his desire to have the figures for S. Carlo published, was designed to counteract a reputation for extravagance that had been earned, with some justification, at the Casa dei Filippini.

The question naturally arises of how the casa was financed. There was no princely patron to bear the cost of expropriations or to provide an endowment, as Gregory XIII had done for the Collegio Romano or Odoardo Farnese for the Casa Professa. The Filippini had to raise the money themselves, and they began by approaching the problem conservatively. Their first principle was to avoid debt, and their second to alienate capital only when constrained to do so. In the 1620s all building expenses were paid out of surplus income, which averaged around ▽4,000 per year between 1617 and 1630. If extraordinary expenses, such as Filippo's canonization in 1622, consumed the surplus income in any given year then construction simply came to a halt. There was great reluctance to demolish houses, which seemed to be the equivalent of alienating capital without compensation. In 1627 the padri had been willing to alienate ▽10,000 of capital to build the piazza and the Strada Nuova, but only because the investment would produce new houses and new sources of income; it was more difficult to make this argument for the casa itself.[19]

A more dynamic and aggressive method of finance was gradually introduced by Virgilio Spada. Spada entered the Congregation in 1622 and assumed the important financial posts rapidly: auditor of the accounts in 1626, supervisor of the fabric in 1627, comptroller in 1629; he was thus in a position to influence policy long before he became Preposito in 1638.[20] Spada's approach to finances rested on four basic tenets. First, he introduced a new accounting system that put real property and intangible assets on the same footing and thus reduced the emotional impact of the demolitions: previously "the houses that were torn down could be seen with the eyes . . ., but the bonds and capital that were acquired were invisible."[21] Architectural drawings were used as financial tools to calculate the cost in lost rents for any wing of the future building (Cat. 14).[22] Spada's system can be seen at work during the internal disputes that divided the Congregation in 1633. He calculated the Congregation's average income over expenses for the past seventeen years and found it to be ▽4,000 annually. He knew also from Catalogue 14 that the Congregation stood to loose ▽2,700 a year in rents from the houses on the site, but he also thought they stood to gain ▽1,000 a year in rent from the shops which at that time were planned in the new casa and another ▽1,000 from renting the old casa out. Thus the real cost of demolition came to only ▽700 per year, which would reduce the annual surplus to ▽3,300. Some of Spada's predictions were more accurate than others: the Congregation gained far more than the ▽20,000 he anticipated over the next decade in bequests and pledges, and it may have received as much as ▽1,200 in annual rent from the old casa.[23] Nevertheless, apart from the question of accuracy, these accounts brought order to a subject formerly dominated by emotion, and without them the building could not have proceeded.

Second, Spada realized that if only current income was to be allotted to construction it would "make the building interminable,"[24] and so he found ways of putting the Congregation into debt. The first small step came in 1630, when current income *(avanzi)* ran short and an interest-free loan was accepted to buy building supplies. This loan opened the way to seeking finance in the capital market, which provided an instrument called the *censo* that was ideally suited to the Congregation's purposes.[25] A *censo* was a permanent loan made on real estate; the principal bore interest but was never itself repaid. A *censo perpetuo* bore interest in perpetuity and could be transferred from one creditor to another; a *censo vitalitio* was not transferable and the debt was extinguished upon the creditor's death. A similar distinction existed in public finance between *luoghi di monti non vacabili* and *luoghi di monti vacabili,* or transferable and nontransferable bonds. A *censo vitalitio* offered no liquidity but it could bring high interest rates; it would appeal to investors without heirs seeking a high return as long as they lived. It would also suit a cautious donor, since it could be viewed as an immediate gift of capital accompanied by a deferred gift of interest. Some benefactors lent the Congregation money in the form of a *censo perpetuo* but then assigned the *censo* to the Congregation in their wills, which was equivalent to a *censo vitalitio* except that it left the benefactor free to change his mind. In the world of Roman finance the distinction between creditor and donor was often blurred, and it was with men who stood somewhere in the middle ground that the Congregation preferred to deal. The *censo* helped them to find such men, and through the loans they obtained they were able to capitalize a small annual surplus into the large sums that the building required.

Third, Spada had enough insight into the dynamics of religious finance to prevent him from considering assets to be fixed and static. If a building cost money it also attracted money, especially in the form of bequests: there was "a competition to give and to bequeath . . . , and what God saw fit to send was more than we knew how to use." The building brought them to the notice of people like Ludovico Montoliveto, an ailing Piedmontese financier who saw the construction under way one day in 1639 and left the Congregation as his sole heir two weeks later. In a society where bequests revolved around masses for the souls of the dead, a large building promised "perpetuità."[26] Furthermore, Spada knew how to court bequests without appearing to solicit; as he said, "The more one flees, the more that comes one's way." Out of a daring mixture of need, permanence, worthiness, disinterest, and potential splendor, he helped to shape a public image, a "buon concetto," that held a strong appeal for the donors who financed the casa.[27]

Fourth, Spada used his own modest income to help break deadlocks in the decision-making process. In 1638 he paid the extra costs of converting the straight stairs to the saint's room into a more commodious spiral. Basically he paid the marginal costs of a change in plan, an act which unblocked a long chain of decisions that led to sweeping changes in the design of the service courtyard and eventually of the oratory facade (Cat. 40).[28] In 1641 he offered to pay the short-term interest on a loan of ▽4,000 needed to extend construction into the first courtyard; the offer was accepted and work was soon begun on Borromini's revised plan (Cat. 66r).[29] In each case the sums involved were small and disproportionately effective. They removed roadblocks and led immediately to drawings that rank among Borromini's most complex and intriguing creations. What Spada was willing to shoulder was not the cost of demolition or construction, but in effect some of the cost of improvisation.

By 1642 the Congregation was already becoming more cautious about taking loans, and after Spada resigned the office of Preposito in 1644 to take a post in Innocent X's administration, the financing of the casa lost much of its élan. In 1647 the Castellani bequest of ▽15,000 enabled work to begin on the Monte Giordano wing. Now each resident of the new wing agreed to share the expenses of outfitting his suite of rooms.[30] The documents fail to mention *censi,* but an interesting episode of 1650 reveals a new form of debt. It appears that the head contractor for the Monte Giordano wing and shops, Maestro Defendino Peschal, accepted deferred payment for his work and thus became a creditor of the Congregation. The exact amount he was owed could only be determined by accurate *misure e stime,* and here

Borromini did his patrons real financial harm by refusing to hand over the *libro delle misure,* since in effect he prevented them from verifying the exact amount of Defendino's loan.[31]

In 1648 the Congregation received one of the largest bequests in its history from Andrea Brugiotti, a self-made entrepreneur who had risen as a printer and accountant under the Barberini.[32] Brugiotti took pains to insure that his money would not go into the building. His will obliged the Congregation to convert all his property into *luoghi di monti* and to hold these bonds as a permanent endowment. They were expressly prohibited from alienating the capital or from mortgaging the income, which was to be kept free from liens and used for the needs of everyday life. The tenor of the will, with its prohibition of debt financing and of investment in building, ran counter to Spada's whole outlook on finance; it is a good index of the conservative temper of those twelve years when Spada was not directly involved in running the Congregation.

In October 1656 Spada was reelected Preposito and something of the old dynamism returned. The financial package he proposed in April 1657 is characteristic of his methods.[33] The cost of the remaining west wing of the casa was estimated at ▽21,000. The annual surplus at that time was about ▽1,900. If a *censo vitalitio* were secured, even at the high rate of 8 percent, the interest would still be only ▽1,680 and could be covered by the surplus. Better still, a benefactor named Pallamolla had just offered part of the sum needed, between ▽4,000 and ▽5,000, in the form of a *censo perpetuo* at the low rate of 5 percent. Pallamolla further hinted that he might offer as much as ▽10,000, and that he might leave the *censo* to the Congregation in his will, thus transforming it for all practical purposes into a *censo vitalitio.* If the surplus should somehow fall below the interest costs, then an anonymous donor, probably Spada himself, was ready to cover the difference.[34] Finally, new rents were just beginning to come in from one of the houses recently built in the piazza; this money (▽414.50) together with the annual income from a recent bequest (▽250.00) would offset the loss of rents caused by demolition (▽695.70). This is all pure Spada: the tendency to mortgage future income, the ability to turn creditors into partial donors, the willingness to view new construction as the financial equivalent of demolished buildings, and finally the attempt, although in this case unsuccessful, to use the levers of finance to reinstate Borromini as the Congregation's architect.

As it happened, the casa was completed by more conservative means. Alexander VII offered permission for a *censo perpetuo* of ▽21,000 in 1660, but the Congregation shied away from a debt of this size and financed Arcucci's west wing by cashing in ▽10,000 of its endowment, selling ▽3,000 worth of books, and taking a modest loan of ▽5,000 at 3½ percent.[35] The documents of these years repeatedly mention the sale of precious goods: of Borromini's marble balusters in 1658, of Algardi's golden chain of knighthood in 1662, and finally of a painting by Correggio to finance the expansion of the library in 1665.[36] As early as 1661 Spada had tried to break the Brugiotti will and invest the capital in real estate; the Congregation finally managed to do so in 1672–75, when some of his bonds were sold to finance the large rentable *appartamento* then being built along the eastern flank of the church.[37] From this time on the Congregation showed a propensity to transfer their endowment from bonds to real estate, particularly to the houses that went up around the casa in the eighteenth century. With each expansion of the piazza they drove out the other religious institutions that had invested in neighboring property, such as the Olivitani of S. Maria Nova, the hospital of S. Maria della Consolazione, the Cistercians of the Tre Fontane, the Lateran Chapter, S. Giacomo degli Spagnoli, and the Augustinians of S. Maria del Popolo.[38] The building program changed the financial structure of the Congregation. At the beginning of the whole enterprise they had been reluctant to invest in houses; by the late baroque era they were the dominant financial presence in the area and landlords of most of their environment.

In the end, the people who paid for the casa were of a different stamp from those who paid for the church. There the traditional patterns of patronage had still obtained, with the nobility and higher clergy assuming responsibility for individual chapels, and a single wealthy family, the Cesi, shouldering the main costs of construction and the expenses of the facade. The names Mezzabarba, Ceva, Caetani, Ruspoli, del Neri, and Donati are among those that occur as benefactors alongside Cardinals Cusano, Antoniani, and Federico Borromeo.[39] When it came to the casa, this kind of patronage ran dry. Both Ludovico Cesi, abbot of Chiaravalle, and his brother, Cardinal Pierdonato Cesi, had promised to finance a new house, but both died before they could fulfill their pledges, and no one stepped in to take their place. The list of gifts and bequests that actually paid for the building is remarkably lacking in great names.[40] Most of the money came from members of the middle class, from prelates in the papal service, doctors, widows, a groom and a cardinal's cook, and numerous foreigners who had made their careers in Rome. They left small sums, books and libraries, pictures and furniture, sometimes a few *luoghi di monti.* There are many bequests in which the donor has a house to leave but nothing else. The padri themselves often paid some of the expenses of their own rooms and left small amounts of money and property; occasionally their gifts were more substantial, like that of Padre Saluzzi for the completion of the oratory. The large sums came not from the nobility but from entrepreneurs and self-made men like the printer Brugiotti and the Turinese tax-farmer Montoliveto. Although piety and generosity played a part, one also gets the sense that the Congregation filled a void in the world of Roman philanthropy, and that the very lack of princely patronage appealed to men without titles or aristocratic roots, and attracted funds that had nowhere else to go.

Function

The documents convey the picture of a building that functioned on many separate levels simultaneously. It served as a receiving dock for goods and supplies, a storehouse for food, and a reservoir for water. It functioned as the residence of a congregation of as many as sixty men, to whom it offered certain standards of privacy and convenience. Finally, it provided the setting for a number of communal rituals and patterns of encounter that made up the fabric of everyday life, particularly those that centered on common meals, on the exercises of the Oratory, on the rich musical life that went on in the building, and on the reception of important guests.

Supplies   Supplies came to the casa along the Via di Parione, which now seems to be at the rear of the building but was then the main thoroughfare. They came mostly from the Congregation's own agricultural holdings, particularly from the area around Carbognano.[41] Beasts of burden laden with wood, wine, water, and food entered the third courtyard through the narrow Porta delle Carette, which was widened in 1675 to allow wagons to enter as well. Horses loaded with firewood descended a ramp at the northeast corner of the building and walked directly into the cellars of the north wing, where the wood was stacked. Charcoal was kept nearby, and wine was unloaded into a low grotto under the refectory basement, where it was stored among the remains of ancient walls. Fruits and vegetables were stored in the three levels of the *dispensa*: dry food, like apples, pears, and beans, in the mezzanine; food needing moisture, like cheese, oil, and greenery, in the cellar; and everything else at ground-floor level. Meat from the butcher was stored in a small compartment near the entrance to the courtyard and was cleaned next to the dishes in the *lavapiatti*. In general, goods were stored as close as possible to the places where they were used. The square staircase connected all three levels of the *dispensa* with the *piazza d'arme* room, where fruits and vegetables were washed and sorted before being served. Meat was kept closer to the kitchen hearth. Finally, wine could be hauled up directly from the cellar by a rope and bucket that descended to a well where the wine was cooled.[42]

Special arrangements were made for the water supply. When the Filippini first moved there, the Vallicella area was fed by numerous wells, of which the Pozzo Bianco was the most famous. Aqueduct water first reached the area in 1614, when Paul V extended the Acqua Paola from the Vatican across the Tiber to the Palazzo Orsini at Monte Giordano.[43] After it left the palace the water was still under Orsini control. Its route south can be seen in Cat. 14; for the most part it follows public streets through the area that would eventually become the casa, and then proceeds south to the Chiavica di S. Lucia, the main collector of the area. The Filippini contracted for five *oncie* of this water as early as 1614; they renewed the contract in 1620 and confirmed it again in 1633. As the new casa was built, the old hydraulic system was incorporated into it. Acqua Paola from Monte Giordano fed the fountain in the garden courtyard, then the *lavamani*, then the fountain basin in the service courtyard, from which some was diverted to a boiler in the kitchen and from there to the dishwashing room. Mixed with the runoff from the roofs, it was channeled through the privies installed between the side chapels of the Vallicella, and out to a vaulted sewer that Maruscelli had built in 1627–30 under the Strada Nuova. Acqua Paola was also supposed to be used for two public fountains, one at the northwest corner of the casa which was never built, and one in the piazza at the corner of the Strada Nuova.[44]

Several things were wrong with Acqua Paola: it was undrinkable, undependable, and always under low pressure. There was talk of supplementing it from other sources, either better Acqua Vergine or higher-pressure Acqua Paola from the Ponte Sisto, but apparently these plans came to nothing.[45] In the end the Filippini relied on wells and reservoirs. Two wells were kept from preexisting houses. The *lavamani* were designed with special reservoirs in the form of tulip blossoms to hold well water when the aqueduct gave out. Rainwater supplied the fountain in the *piazza d'arme* room. A water vendor occupied one of the shops under the *torre dell'orologio*. Finally a cistern was built underneath the service courtyard; it was marble-floored and vaulted to keep the water cool, and was partitioned into three chambers, each of which could hold a year's supply. Rainwater was funneled into one, and the favorite types of drinking water, Acqua Vergine and Tiber, were supplied on horseback to the others. Eventually the houses built around the piazza came to depend on a similar mixture of supplies: Acqua Paola that had already flowed through the casa, and wells for drinking water.[46]

Although it was practical and serviceable, the hydraulic system of the casa never quite lived up to Borromini's expectations. He planned one or more fountains for each courtyard and hoped to raise water as high as the *piano nobile;* he also proposed an extensive sewer system which would use fountain runoff to carry human waste from the residential wings and bring it to the Tiber. His imagination was stirred simultaneously by two ideals. First, he wanted to duplicate at the casa the kind of drainage system exemplified in the *cloaca maxima* and other ancient channels that were often found still functioning in the subsoil of Rome; and second, his vision was formed by the fantastic fountains, *giuochi d'acqua,* of villas in the Alban Hills, where water was available in abundance and under high pressure.[47]

Residence   The residential wings of the casa were among the first to be planned but the last to be built, and the changes that were gradually introduced into their design reflect demographic changes within the Congregation itself.[48] The 1620s and 1630s had been decades of expansion, with the number of voting padri reaching a peak of 27 in 1637, the year the oratory was begun. The early projects reflect the optimism of a growing organization. Maruscelli's caption project of 1627 provided a refectory for 60 people and living quarters for 70: twenty-seven apartments for the padri, of one and one-half rooms each, and forty-three single rooms for lay members. Even then the numbers were judged to be somewhat excessive: the mezzanine story was removed in Spada's critique of 1627, although it was restored when the rooms were actually begun in 1640. At that time Borromini planned accommodations for 56 to 60 people, and began by building small rooms for 12 padri in the "elbow" wing along the Via di Parione. In the 1640s, however, numbers fell off sharply. It was a Congregation of only 17 padri who voted to move to the new building in 1643; only 14 or 15 padri made the decisions on the Monte Giordano wing of 1647–50. Being so few, they could be more lavish in their use of space; in particular, they enlarged the standard apartment from one and one-half to two full rooms. By 1650 all the padri were comfortably housed, and some rooms for laymen were empty. The number of padri rose slightly in the 1650s, but there was still no overcrowding nor any real need for them to finish the west wing. When Alexander VII finally obliged them to do so in 1659–62 there were only about 16 voting padri, and they could afford to be generous in their allotment of the space. Whereas in 1627 this wing had been designed to house 31 people, it finally contained only nine apartments plus common rooms and the *scalone*. When the east wing of the casa was completed in 1669–74 it contained only a single apartment.[49]

From the outset these rooms were designed to provide comfort, quiet, and privacy to the men who lived in them. Rooms of "mediocre grandezza" were thought to provide a kind of psychological comfort; physical comfort came from the thick walls and vaults that insulated the rooms and protected them from fire, moisture, and noise.[50] With the exception of the top floor of the west wing, all rooms had windows on the street, hence shops were excluded from most wings to maintain an atmosphere of quiet, and the kitchen windows were sealed to prevent smoke from escaping into the rooms above.[51] Each major apartment had its own fireplace and chimney.[52] At the top of the square staircase, there was a general privy designed with great care by Borromini.[53] Although a heated bath had been planned at an early stage,[54] it is not known what arrangements were made for personal washing in the final building, beyond the *lavamani*. Of all the apartments, the most spacious were those on the *piano nobile* around the large courtyard; each had, besides the two basic rooms, a private garden on a small balcony overlooking the main garden. The description of Spada's apartment in the *Dialogo* of 1649 gives some idea of what could be done with this kind of space: it supposedly contained an audience room, bedroom, oratory, *camerino, saletta* serving also as a studio, *guardarobba* with a second bed for naps, a privy closet, and a gallery with fruit trees overlooking the garden; somewhere there was room for bookshelves, numerous little chests with Spada's collection of coins, cameos, medallions, and curiosities; and a collection of paintings by or at least attributed to Perugino, Palma Vecchio, Moretto, the Bassano family, Domenichino, and the Carracci school.[55]

The ideal behind these rooms came from the world of *famiglia* architecture, and it involved the conscious rejection of a more aristocratic ideal in which convenience was sacrificed to the demands of ceremony: "Often a man finishes a building and is dissatisfied with everything; he finds himself with a light-well for a courtyard, with dark rooms, steep stairs, and as in the Palazzo Farnese with not a room fit to sleep in."[56] Although Spada's criticism of the Farnese is exaggerated, it is true that advances in comfort and privacy made more headway in the institutional architecture of the seventeenth century than in traditional palace design.[57] While the

Palazzo Barberini was being built with rooms linked in sequence and affording little privacy, Maruscelli was designing the ingenious corridor system that made the casa such a private place in which to live. Furthermore, the sequence of courtyards at the casa gave the building a sense of penetralia. Although the living quarters overlooked the major thoroughfare of the area, to get to them the visitor had to negotiate a series of detours and barriers that kept intrusions to a minimum. The door was placed on the least convenient side of the building "to keep the casa free from intrusion."[58] There was a doorkeeper to contend with, whose spyholes were likened to gunports.[59] Inside the entrance a set of steps served as a psychological barrier *(ritegno),* and farther on wooden screens sealed the loggie and prevented circulation past the sacristy.[60] No sooner was the *scalone* finished in 1661 than a series of iron gates was installed at key points to prevent visitors from wandering around the upper floors.[61] Beyond these barriers the residential courtyard existed as an enclave apart, planted with greenery and citrus fruits on three levels, cooled by fountains, and providing sun terraces for solitary walks in the midst of the most crowded region of the city: "The terraces offer delights and a view beautifully adapted to the needs of men who are so absorbed in endless study and wearying exercises that they lack the time to go out in search of open air and refreshment of the spirit."[62] A place for priestly recollection, tinged with the ideal of *rus in urbe* and colored by memories of Filippo Neri's passion for rooftop heights,[63] these are some of the strands that interweave to give the residential courtyard its own particular character.

Dining, Oratory, and the Reception of Guests   Unlike the members of a monastic order, the Filippini led lives that were not rigidly structured in their daily routine. Each priest was bound to daily mass, recitation of the Divine Office, and a regular turn at the confessional; at the center of their activities was the Oratory of weekday afternoons and Sunday evenings. Otherwise their only major communal obligation was that of *convitto,* or common dining. Twice daily the refectory bell summoned the entire Congregation to the midday and evening meals. Padri and fratelli descended the square staircase into the *lavamani,* washed their hands at Borromini's fountains, took a napkin from one of sixty numbered boxes, and filed into the refectory where the padri sat at tables of four and the lay members at tables of six or seven. Food was served through the main door and the dishes cleared away through the side door; in addition to wine, cool cistern water was served and changed halfway through the meal to preserve its chill. Everyone ate in silence. A lesson was read from the pulpit, and when two-thirds of the meal was over, a padre would pose two so-called *dubii,* one case of conscience in the area of morals and one crux in the interpretation of scripture. Each padre would respond to the *dubii* in turn, and at the end the man who proposed them would present his own views. Since the padri remained seated during the *dubii* the oval shape of the refectory was designed to allow them to see and hear each other more clearly.[64]

After the meal the padri climbed the square staircase to the *sala di ricreazione* for an hour of conversation and general gaiety.[65] The room contained a fireplace designed in the form of a tasseled baldachin or tent (Fig. 91); in winter, when the evening meal took place after dark, the Congregation retired here for light and warmth. Periodically the General Congregation met here to vote on important issues, and one of the small chambers nearby was reserved for the accountant and his books. Twice a month the room witnessed the *congregazione delle colpe,* a session in which each person accused himself of minor offenses against his brethren, asked forgiveness on his knees, and was given penance by a communal Corrector. Compared to the prisons sometimes found in Roman monastic houses, this institution was an unusually mild and charitable way of dissipating the friction of communal living.[66]

At the center of this communal life, its principal purpose and its mainspring, was the Oratory.[67] Before Filippo's death in 1595 this devotion had evolved into two distinct forms, each of which continued on into the seventeenth century but with subtle shifts of emphasis. On the one hand, the greater Oratory held on weekday afternoons, which was Filippo's original Oratory, tended to ossify into conventional forms. As in its prime, it still consisted of four half-hour sermons with additional prayers and litanies. The language of the sermons remained direct and simple and the subject matter concrete. But there was no longer any informal improvisation or any speaking from the audience; sermons were all prepared in advance, delivered from a raised seat, and timed by an hourglass.

In contrast to the weekday Oratory, the Sunday Oratory, also called the *Oratorio vespertino* and the *Oratorio musicale,* underwent rapid development in the early seventeenth century. This particular form of the Oratory had originated as a popular offshoot of the normal devotion, with its roots in the outdoor gatherings held during the summer months in places like the portico of the Pantheon or on the slopes of the Janiculum. The audience, often as large as 3,000 or 4,000 people, included women and children, and there was much emphasis on vernacular singing. A gathering of this sort is described in a report of 1578 which the Oratorians sent to Gregory XIII:

> There is a sermon on feast days after Vespers. And after the sermon the fathers of the house go to Giulia street to the church of Santo Spirito de la Compagnia de' Napoletani, where more than three thousand persons gather. And there, since it is more comfortable, the people are allured by devotional music and by having boys recite some edifying things written by the fathers of the house. And then [the exercise] concludes with two discussions of compunctious and affective things.[68]

Even when held indoors during the winter months, in churches like S. Spirito de' Napolitani or eventually in the Vallicella, the Sunday Oratory kept much of its recreative and musical character. The number of sermons was reduced from four to one to allow more time for music before and after, thus contributing to the development of the oratorio as a musical genre. The music was usually composed in two structural parts with a pause in between for a sermon. In the early seven-teenth century the musical Oratory took shape in part under the influence of opera, for which the Oratory acted as a competitor during Carnival and a substitute during Lent, and also in part under the influence of the sacred *lauda,* which itself began to assume a more pronounced narrative and dramatic character. The *lauda* evolved into a dialogue between two solo voices, who alternated with a chorus of four to six voices reciting a narrative part and a final meditation; the voices were accom-panied by either a simple basso continuo or by a larger ensemble of instruments including violins, horns, lutes, harps, and an organ. By 1619, the date of Giovanni Francesco Anerio's *Teatro armonico spirituale,* there were dialogues being sung at the Vallicella which were sufficiently long and dramatic to be considered oratorios in everything but name. In his introduction to Anerio's collection, Orazio Griffi explained why the Oratory became musical:

> And to attain the desired aim so much more easily, and to draw, with a sweet deception, the sinners to the holy exercises of the Oratory, you [Filippo Neri] introduced Music there, seeing to it that vernacular and devotional things were sung, so that the people, being allured by song and tender words, would be all the more disposed to spiritual profit; nor was your idea in vain, since some, coming at times to the oratory only to hear the music, and then remaining, moved and captivated by the sermons and the other holy exercises that are done there, have become servants of God.[69]

Music brought people who would otherwise not have come; but the music quickly took on a life of its own, and received great impetus from the Oratorian Girolamo Rosini, a famed soprano who entered the Congregation in 1606 and who was Prefetto della musica from 1623–44. Rosini was often in demand at court and was in touch with the leading musicians of Florence and Mantua as well as Rome; it is early in his prefectship that the documents first begin to speak of a contrast between the present "musiche e sinfonie" and the "musiche semplici" of Filippo's day.[70] Under Rosini the emphasis was on vocal performance of great emotive force, an emphasis which was characteristic of progressive developments in Roman music and which also left its mark on the planning and the final architectural form of the oratory.

In the old oratory to the east of the Vallicella, where Cavalieri's *Rappresentatione di anima et di corpo* had been performed in 1600, musicians were not elevated above the audience in spite of the inconvenience this arrangement caused to the players of unwieldy instruments.[71] In the first decades of the Seicento, however, there was an increasing tendency to hide musicians, particularly those who sang or played from sheet music, in choirs shrouded with veils or screens.[72] Despite some resist-ance to this development within the Congregation, from Maruscelli onward all projects for the new oratory provided balconies for musicians on either side of the main altar (Cat. 20b, no. 5; Cat. 30–34). In the final design (Fig. 31; Cat. 85b) still more space was allotted to performers. Borromini provided the usual instru-mentalists' balconies and equipped them with cupboards and a small vaulted closet for storing books and scores; two small chambers for rehearsals during the sermon were installed in the nearby staircase and were later soundproofed.[73] The singers were elevated on a higher level still: the choir designed for them opposite the cardinals' loggia is an innovation found in none of the earlier projects. Finally, a pair of metal grilles was installed in the floor in order to provide an acoustic link with the underground oratory, which was supposed to hold overflow crowds during Holy Week and on important feasts.[74] All of these features were designed around the needs of the evening Oratory and its music rather than the ordinary weekday Oratory. The separation of singers from instrumentalists corresponded to the rise of different idioms for voice and instruments in early baroque music, and the upper choir, like the nascent *oratorio volgare* itself, encouraged an unprecedented exaltation of the singer's role.[75]

Borromini's new oratory was opened in August 1640 on a mildly austere note, perhaps in compensation for the very sumptuousness of the new room; for a short time there was a ban on *sinfonie* and elaborate instrumental accompaniment, though sermons and singing continued as usual.[76] The music immediately attracted connoisseurs. In a letter of 1640 the musicologist Pietro della Valle described how he listened to performances from the choir, where he socialized with musical friends and tried to interest Padre Rosini in his latest composition, a work formally entitled *Dialogo della purificatione* but informally called an oratorio; since there was still no organ, or at best only a wooden mock-up of one (Fig. 32), della Valle suggested "a little organ of my sort for the new oratory, which has been built so sumptuously."[77] When John Evelyn paid a visit to the new oratory in 1644 this is what he saw:

> This Evening I was invited to heare rare musique at the Chiesa Nova. . . . We went into the sacristia [by which he means the oratory], where the tapers being lighted, one of the Order, preach'd, after him stepp'd up, a child, of about 8 or 9 years old, who pronounc'd an Oration, with so much grace as I never was better pleased in my life, then to heare Italian so well spoken, and so intelligently. . . . This being finish'd began their motettos, which (in a lofty Cupola richly painted) were sung by Eunuchs, and other rare Voices, accompanied with Theorbas, Harpsicors, and Viols: so as we were even ravish'd with the entertainement of that Evening. . . .[78]

Two preserved librettos from around this date by the Sicilian poet Francesco Balducci may have been written for the Filippini; one of them, called *La Fede* or *Il sacrificio di Abramo,* shows developments in dramatic dialogue that mark it as an early example of true oratorio.[79] In 1645 J. N. Eritreo published a report of an evening performance in the oratory by the celebrated composer and castrato Loreto Vittori, who sang the part of the repentant Magdalen with the profoundest emotion, modulating his voice "like the softest wax" and moving Eritreo to tears.[80] In 1659 the English traveler Francis Mortoft visited the oratory frequently to hear "such sweete Musicke, that a man could not thinke his paines be il spent, if he should come two thousand mile, if he were sure to be recompensed with nothing else, but to heare such most melodious voyces." Among other things, Mortoft heard a composition by Giacomo Carissimi and "a kind of Comody acted by 5 little Boyes against the Maskaradoes."[81] In the following decades there were performances of oratorios by the composer Padre Cesare Mazzei, who joined the Congregation in 1647 and whose preserved librettos represent a return to some of the simplicity though not the brevity of the earlier *lauda* tradition.[82] In the later years of the seventeenth century there are notices of oratorios at the Vallicella sponsored by the highest aristocratic patronage, such as Christina of Sweden, Cardinal Ottoboni, Prince Francesco Maria Ruspoli, and by 1704 Clement XI, who subsidized oratorio at the Chiesa Nuova to compensate for the banning of secular entertainment during Carnival.[83] Between 1679 and 1682 Alessandro Scarlatti was active in Rome as a composer of oratorios, and when he returned to the city his first employment was as *maestro di cappella* at the Vallicella from 1703 to 1705. By that time oratorio had evolved into a sacred counterpart of opera and had taken on a distinctly operatic tone; it was even performed in palaces as a Lenten substitute for opera, when the sermon that used to come between the two parts of the musical composition would be replaced by a pause for refreshments.[84]

From the very earliest times the music at the Vallicella was a magnet that drew in important guests, particularly cardinals and the entourage of the papal court. In 1570 the composer Animuccia remarked that the Oratory had swollen "by reason of the concourse of prelates and the most distinguished gentlemen."[85] In 1575 Gregory XIII assigned the Congregation to the Vallicella because, as he said, no other church was as convenient for the court; after Filippo's death his disciple Tarugi remarked that the court had been the means by which the saint's reforming influence had been spread in Rome and beyond its walls.[86] If some courtiers came for reform, however, many more came simply for the music. In 1640 Pietro della Valle remarked that if it were not for the fine singing few would have ventured to go to church at night, through foul weather and bad streets, merely for the sake of doing good; whenever he himself attended an oratory or gave a performance in his own palace this same della Valle was quick to note that prelates, cardinals, ambassadors, foreign princes, and "the finest flower of the knights of court" were often in attendance.[87] Between fifteen and twenty cardinals heard each performance of Cavalieri's *Rappresentatione di anima et di corpo* in 1600, and at a normal Sunday Oratory there were usually four to six cardinals on hand.[88] Where these princes went, their entourages followed. In the 1620s the old oratory grew crowded with musicians and with cardinals and their retainers, the latter often quick-tempered noblemen jealous of precedence and licensed to bear arms. A document of 1625, which reports that "there were disturbances during the Oratory and some men went for their swords," describes the kind of incident that could and did occur under the circumstances.[89]

The Filippini were naturally ambivalent about this situation. From one point of view the visitors were a pestilent influence: they brought with them *servitù, corteggi, servili esercitii,* and other perils. While the Congregation lived in the old casa there were attempts to limit the influence of the visitors. They were not permitted in private rooms except Filippo's. For twenty-five years after Filippo's death gentlemen who had been his penitents continued to assemble in his private chapel, but no one was designated to meet them at the door and there was to be no official reception; after 1620 they were excluded altogether. In 1624 and 1625 the Congregation twice refused to build a private balcony in the old oratory for the convenience of cardinals and prelates, and further condemned the principle of secluded attendance at services.[90]

On the other hand, during the planning of the casa a more moderate point of view came to prevail, one that accepted courtiers as part of life and maintained that "the accidents of the world sometimes imposed a moral necessity to admit them."[91] Thus in Maruscelli's caption project (Cat. 20a, 20b) an entire courtyard is reserved for visitors, and rooms are provided on the *piano nobile* where they could socialize and look through windows giving onto the oratory below. Borromini took this trend still further. He moved the library to the first courtyard where it was within easy reach of outsiders. In the spacious cardinals' loggia he reintroduced the principle of secluded attendance, which had been emphatically rejected by the Congregation just a short time before. Face to face with the singers in the loggia opposite, elevated above preacher and audience alike, hidden behind screens and balustrades, cardinals enjoyed conditions in the oratory that approximated those of private performance. Furthermore, they set an example that dignitaries of lesser rank were quick to imitate. Throughout the 1640s noblemen were admitted to the singers' choir. Spada once argued against the practice of admitting prelates there, on the grounds that marquises, counts, and gentlemen would soon follow and the old disorders would soon return; but in spite of the accuracy of his warning, the practice continued and the choir was not locked against them until 1651–53.[92]

These magnates and their followers moved through the building in a way that resembled a secular reception in miniature. A padre was designated as the *ricevitore di forastieri* to meet them. After it had entered the door, the entourage began to break apart and continued to do so the farther it penetrated into the building. The *staffieri* and *palafrenieri,* servants and escorts, were left below in the *portaria;* the "gentil'huomini de SS.ri Cardinali" detached themselves upstairs and remained in a gallery at the entrance to the *forestaria;* as the Oratory began, the prelates and their retainers moved to the side arches of the carindals' loggia, while the central arch was reserved for the cardinals themselves. Impressive vistas that were normally closed were unsealed: one through the *forestaria* rooms to the altar at the far end of the oratory, another past the sacristy into the depths of the second courtyard, and a third down the length of the refectory and *lavamani* to the fountain in the *piazza d'arme* room. Dining with the Congregation was a special privilege, and a table was reserved at the head of the refectory for "cardinals, prelates and princes"; a chamber nearby was used for their service, which involved a variety of special vessels and frequent changes of plates. They heard the *dubii* and then ascended for an hour of recreation in a room that was designed to make them feel at home: the sala was decorated with portraits of the Oratorians who had been elevated to the rank of cardinal or bishop, and was heated by a fireplace that was thought worthy of a cardinal's palace. One supposes that the guests left, like the Duke of Mantua after a similar visit, "satisfattissimo" with all that they had heard and seen.[93]

Imagery

The issues of finance and function come together in the study of the imagery of the Casa dei Filippini. If either of these elements had been simple and straightforward, then the problem of imagery would not have arisen. If, for example, Cardinal Cesi had fulfilled his pledge of 1581 to finance a new residence, or if the Congregation had been a typical Counter-Reformational order, then the casa would probably not have looked very different from a number of other Roman religious houses, with a narrow expressive range focused mainly on the Cesi arms that it would have been obliged to bear.[94] Cesi died in 1586 before he could provide the funds, and in any case the Filippini felt strongly that they were a new phenomenon, with a role and a corporate personality quite distinct from those of the usual monastic order. Exactly what they were was another question. The Constitutions of 1612 gave juridical confirmation to their status as a congregation of secular priests and lay brothers living in common with personal property and without vows, but to put these concepts of canon law into architectural form was not an easy matter. It is the nature of architecture to make a positive statement, and yet the Filippini insisted on formulating their expressive program in negative terms: they were not secular magnates, not Jesuits, not Theatines, not a traditional monastic order; ornament must not exceed an ill-defined standard of modesty, nor fall below a minimum level of decorum. Whoever he might be, their architect was condemned in advance to steer a perilous course around these negative exemplars and to find some positive expression for a character that the Filippini themselves found difficult to articulate. He was also obliged to deal with the perennial problem of the court and the stance that should be adopted toward it. Wariness or familiarity, rejection or reform, *spernere mundum* or *spernere neminem,* these were the poles of oscillation around which the community divided in the 1620s, blocking the way to a coherent architectural imagery.[95]

Maruscelli's projects represented the first step out of this impasse. He managed to synthesize a new imagery by grafting two special residential types, a Milanese archepiscopal seat and a Roman *famiglia* palace, onto a classic Palladian convent. Like the Congregation itself, his project was a hybrid, and the Filippini accepted it as a faithful mirror of their self-image and their aspirations as they stood in 1627. When Borromini took over the commission ten years later, he introduced many basic changes into the Maruscellian framework; these innovations naturally embody his aesthetic creed, but they also constitute an imagery, that is, an expressive language based, like Maruscelli's, on the quotation of specific motifs that came from well-known contexts and brought an aura of acquired meaning with them. It is an imagery, however, that is not so easy to unravel. Borromini was more learned than Maruscelli, and consequently the range of his allusions is much broader. He was preoccupied with originality, and as a result there is a certain tension in his public statements between the need to justify the work in terms of precedent and the impulse to push beyond all known sources. Finally, the literary texts that surround his designs are themselves problematic. The *Opus Architectonicum,* in particular, is built around a special type of argument that explains every decision in simplistic functional terms. When it comes to sources, it mentions only antiquity and Michelangelo: antiquity is of course important, but not in so direct and immediate a fashion as the *Opus* would suggest; and Michelangelo is certainly there, but only as one of a broad range of sixteenth-century masters on whose example Borromini formed his style.

The *Opus* mentions four special motifs in the casa that were drawn from antiquity: the brickwork of the oratory facade, based on a ruin *(torrione)* outside the Porta del Popolo; the corner pilasters inside the oratory, intended to evoke the vaults of Roman thermal halls; the coffers of the library ceiling, which came from the stone coffering of Roman temple peristyles; and the flowery bases of the columns in the stairway vestibule, designed "after a curiosity *(bizzaria)* observed among the remnants of antiquity."[96] Indeed all of these motifs do derive from antiquity, but many came indirectly, through architectural books or through antiquarian research. Borromini certainly knew many actual examples of ornate flowery column bases, but his only extant sketches of them are based on a Renaissance manuscript, the so-called Codex Coner.[97] The passage in the *Opus* that links the library ceiling to stone coffers in the "Fora di Nerva Traiano" seems to be a literary topos drawn from Antonio Labacco's engraving of the temple of Mars Ultor of 1559.[98] The special type of fluting on the refectory fireplace and the special type of coffering used in one of Filippo Neri's chapels seem to have come to Borromini from the pages of Serlio, rather than from direct observation of the antique models; and in an analogous way the grand project for a Pamphilj chapel next to S. Maria in Vallicella came from one of Montano's reconstructions of antique tempietti (Figs. 128, 129).[99] Borromini certainly studied the ruins as profoundly as any contemporary, and details like the brickwork of the facade or the polychrome terra cotta of the entrance courtyard could have come to him only through direct observation. Nevertheless, there seems to have been a certain convenience and perhaps prestige in looking at antiquity in the pages of the classic treatises; the best expression of this attitude can be found in the title adopted by Borromini's friend Martinelli for his most famous guidebook: *Rome Researched [Both] on the Site and in the School of all the Antiquarians.*[100]

Michelangelo is cited in the *Opus* as the inventor of the giant order of the Capitoline Palace and as the "Prince of Architects" who "reformed the architecture of the great Basilica of St. Peter's,"[101] that is, as the person who transformed Sangallo's multiplicity of small orders into colossal pilasters, just as Borromini himself had transformed Maruscelli's project. It is not surprising that Michelangelo is mentioned while more recent architects are not; naturally Borromini had no wish to stress his debt to Francesco da Volterra for the basic scheme of the facade or to Girolamo Rainaldi for the skeletal structure of the oratory. But what is surprising is the frequency with which other sixteenth-century architects, those associated with what is now called the High Renaissance, are cited in a clear and recognizable manner throughout the casa. The *nicchioni* in the first courtyard are taken from Vignola's unfinished courtyard of the Palazzo Farnese in Piacenza (Figs. 130, 131).[102] The giant order itself, for all the talk of Michelangelo, was originally copied from Palladio's project for the Palazzo Iseppo da Porto in Vicenza; this becomes clear when one bypasses the rhetoric of the *Opus* and goes directly to Borromini's early drawing of the motif (Cat. 57).[103] The main ceremonial staircase of the casa, built by Arcucci on Borromini's design, attempts to duplicate the size and slant of the steps of Sangallo's grand staircase in the Palazzo Farnese, and thus to re-create some of the ease and luxury of ascent found in the model.[104] There are several fascinating spatial quotations from Renaissance exemplars. The apse-ended spaces that occur in several early drawings as well as in the cardinals' loggia of the oratory (Cat. 39, 40, 59, 85d), reflect a type of space common in sixteenth-century palace design, such as that in the vestibule of the Palazzo Chiericati in Vicenza or in the garden atrium of the Palazzo Farnese in Rome.[105] The room in which the *lavamani* fountains were installed is described as "full of niches" and is based directly on the archetype of this kind of Renaissance space, Bramante's first project for St. Peter's (Figs. 134, 135).[106] Finally, in one drawing Borromini toyed with using an antique motif and then replaced it with a Renaissance form. In his earliest proposal for the entrance corridor leading to the oratory (Cat. 66r), he drew an accurate miniature version of a Roman thermal vault resting on corner columns; when this part of the building was executed he reverted to a more typical kind of Renaissance atrium, like that in Sangallo's Palazzo Baldassini, which he enriched with an order of superimposed pilasters borrowed from Raphael's Palazzo Alberini-Cicciaporci (Fig. 44; Cat. 86k).[107] It is as though the great sixteenth-century masters had come to occupy a place in Borromini's canon of models alongside the ruins themselves, as the Moderns who came closest to the spirit of antiquity, and whose work provided a glass through which to view the lost designs of the Roman past.

None of this broad interest in the sixteenth-century masters and in the classic treatises emerges from the *Opus*. The reasons for this neglect seem to lie in the literary origins of the document and in the audience for which it was intended. Both the *Opus* and its companion piece, the *Dialogo,* were composed from material collected in the course of numerous meetings and outside consultations convened whenever Borromini proposed a change in the design. The texts still carry echoes of the old charges raised against innovation: "mere caprice," "pure caprice," "feature without precedent" *(cosa singolare).*[108] They still rehearse the old arguments pieced together to defend the novelties of the building, arguments which stress function, economy, and structural soundness but are silent on issues of style and imagery. In documents imbued with the rhetoric of justification that had grown up around Borromini's design there was no room to discuss what his innovations might have meant.

Most of the quotations in the Casa dei Filippini are from aulic architecture, and it is this general pattern that seems to supply the key to the building's imagery. The models are the Capitoline Hill, the palaces of the older aristocracy or of papal dynasties like the Farnese, and in the case of Piacenza the palace of an independent sovereign. Here the contrast with Maruscelli is striking. When Maruscelli went to the *Quattro libri* it was for the model of a convent; Borromini drew one of Palladio's grandest secular palaces out of the same book. As his nephew later put it, "He never undertook buildings that were not of the highest repute; to fabrics of low condition he never turned his talents, but only if they were temples or palaces."[109] Borromini was fascinated with aristocratic architecture, and Maruscelli's world of institutional building and *famiglia* design seems to have left him cold. Accordingly he directed his efforts to raising the social level of the casa, at outfitting it with the complement of spaces and features that had come to be considered characteristic of the design of an early-seventeenth-century palace. The giant order was introduced because it was "majestic" and the staircase was designed to appear "magnificent"; the round *seditori* (Fig. 43) lent "magnificence" to the entranceway, obviously not because of their lowly function as messengers' seats, but because they brought a borrowed aura with them from their former context, in this case the Palazzo Farnese.[110] The library was redesigned on the model of the library in the Palazzo Barberini and was moved to a more public part of the building. In general, majestic themes were clustered in places where visiting dignitaries were most likely to see them, such as the entranceway, the first courtyard, the refectory, and the recreation room. Out of the broad spectrum of functions the casa was designed to serve, Borromini selected one—the reception of important guests—and turned it into the leitmotif of his imagery, just as he had elevated the Sunday Oratory, the *Oratorio musicale,* over all other versions of the service and designed the new oratory around its needs. What is said explicitly of the main staircase, that it was meant to be "ample and magnificent, considering that it was more for visitors than for the padri themselves," applies implicitly to Borromini's imagery throughout the building.[111]

One might ask what the Filippini made of this fundamental shift in the meaning of their building, and why they were so slow to react. First, it seems that the mechanisms of patronage sheltered the architect from the basic conservatism of the majority of the Congregation. Many important decisions were relegated to the Four Deputies, and until 1644 the indefatigable Spada was always on hand to interpret the design in terms that the Congregation could accept. The rhetoric of justification had its effect, surrounding every change in the design with talk of practicality and function. Furthermore, few of the Filippini could cope with a design that unfolded only gradually. In 1637 most of the Congregation felt that they could get along without an overall model of Maruscelli's casa, but after the change of architects a consensus arose that a model would help to show where Borromini's casa was going. A model was antithetical to a design that proceeded by improvisation, and although he provided models of parts of the building, Borromini withheld the overall model until 1642, when the crucial phase of the work was past.[112] Then, too, the symbolic content of many of his details seems to have been below the threshold of perception of many Oratorians. The critical vocabulary of most of these men was primitive, and it constrained them to attack ornament when their real concern was with the social status that ornament expressed. At one point, for instance, some of the Filippini became convinced that the giant order of pilasters somehow misrepresented their corporate modesty, but when Borromini pointed out that he had used neither precious materials nor unusually expensive workmanship, they were at a loss to explain how or why the motif offended them.[113] One pictures an architect puzzling the majority of his patrons and talking circles around them, winning individual points but slowly adding to a fund of distrust and mute resentment.

As time passed and the design unfolded, a countercurrent of protest began to make itself felt within the Congregation. In 1639 Borromini was reminded of the modesty expected of the oratory facade. In 1641 there were proposals either to trim excessive ornament off the refectory fireplace—"so proud *(superbo)* in its carving and marble detail"—or, better, to give the fireplace away altogether.[114] It appears that neither this fireplace nor the oratory facade were given their full complement of ornament, at least as far as can be known from later prints (Fig. 90; Cat. 41). At first these were minor setbacks, but with time the cumulative import of the imagery became clear, and the Congregation showed themselves increasingly willing to be rid of Borromini. Imagery was one element, along with finances and difficulties of personality, that contributed to their adamant refusal in 1657 to readmit him to their service. In the following years the theme of the oversumptuous building recurs in the documents, and under Borromini's successor Arcucci the Congregation was even willing to go to extra expense to avoid the appearance of being "too luxurious."[115]

Both Oratorian architecture and Oratorian music seem to follow the same general development in the early seventeenth century. Music began as a lure for souls; gradually it grew more elaborate and its audience more aristocratic; by midcentury it was approaching a form of noble entertainment, being performed for cardinals and their entourages by the finest musicians of the city singing half-hidden "in a lofty Cupola richly painted."[116] There were occasional steps backward, moments of retrenchment and nostalgia for the simpler life lived in the days of Filippo Neri; the 1630s saw a short ban on *sinfonie,* and in the 1660s hope was revived that "the vanity of the music . . . [would] not distract the devotions of the oratory, for to some degree the Demon has won with our oratory of Rome, where we sweat blood to restrain the disorder of the music and daily we remain at a loss in this matter."[117] Just as its music had become operatic, the architecture of the Congregation's home became aristocratic. Borromini took a trend already latent in the second generation of Oratorians and gave it architectural expression slightly before it was due. What preoccupied the Congregation and alienated them from their architect was not the feeling of going in a totally wrong direction, but a sense of galloping too fast and of losing the reins. For thirteen years Borromini did indeed have his way on most issues. He transformed a conventional oratory into a delicately skeletal structure with an extravagant and beautiful ecclesiastical facade, he elevated the musical Oratory over all other versions of the devotion, and he outfitted what had started as a *famiglia* residence with the trappings of a noble palace. However, when one moves from the casa proper to the streets and piazzas surrounding it, Borromini no longer seems to exert this kind of control. In the matter of urban change, social patterns were more entrenched, finances more complex, and the time-scale immensely longer. Here the architect in his turn lost the reins to larger and less personal forces.

6

The Urban Context of the Casa

Institutional Urbanism

In the study of Roman urban history, the straight streets of the sixteenth century usually hold center stage. The Via Giulia, Lungara, Ripetta, Paolina, Condotti, Pia, and Felice have tended to rivet the scholar's attention, looming as the great achievements of the age and presaging the broad outlines of European urban development for generations to come. For all their importance, however, the great papal projects represent only one facet of Roman urbanism. To get a fuller picture, the historian must occasionally stray off the high roads of the Renaissance and make his way through more tangled undergrowth. Beneath the abstract patterns imposed by fiat from above, there was also an infrastructure of steady, persistent urban change generated around the construction of large buildings. While a smaller structure was generally confined by the contours of its particular isola, a larger building was often allowed to overstep the normal boundaries and become an active force in the shaping of urban space. It was a process abetted by two legal factors. First, the laws of expropriation were written to favor the expansion of large buildings.[1] Small proprietors could be forced to sell if they were bordered on two sides by a larger structure being built; the price was set at the estimated value of the property *(stima)* plus a surcharge *(augumento),* fixed at one-fifth for owner-occupied houses and one-twelfth for houses let to tenants; in special cases the surcharge could be abolished by papal decree and the property acquired at market value. Second, by an arrangement with the Mastri di Strade a property owner could often barter private land for public land.[2] He was always obliged to cede more land to the city than he took, and so the area in the public domain was slightly increased after each such transaction. But, in return, individuals and corporate patrons were allowed to adjust the shape of isole, to alter the alignment of neighboring facades, even to change the width and direction of streets. In short, public space came to be shaped according to private instincts.[3]

From an urban perspective the large buildings of Late-Renaissance Rome, particularly the institutional buildings of the Counter Reformation, tend to exhibit a recurrent life cycle. After an initial period of homelessness, the institution would secure a foothold, such as an old church or a group of modest houses, in a densely populated area. The church would be rebuilt and a suitable residence begun, but at this stage growth was still hesitant and early projects often were leaps in the dark, since the size and scope of the final building were seldom glimpsed at the outset. For a time the shape of the nascent building would be deformed by the irregular contours of the site: triangular and trapezoidal plans are common, and sometimes internal alignments are chaotic. As the building grew, it would shake off the deforming influence of the environment and begin to exhibit a new orthogonal discipline in its planning. At a crucial turning point it would begin to radiate its influence outward and take an active role in reshaping the environment. The surrounding street system would be rebuilt and neighboring structures redesigned to accommodate the institution's dominating presence. The process would continue until the building was encircled by its own dependencies or by other institutions as powerful as itself; only at that point would its growth be checked and equilibrium return to the area.

One institution that exhibits a classic version of this life cycle is the Collegio Romano, a large multifunctional building begun by the Jesuits in 1560 and completed, as far as its urban program was concerned, in 1728.[4] The Jesuits gained their initial foothold by a gift of property on the Piazza di S. Macuto, on a site that would now correspond to the church of S. Ignazio. Their first attempts to introduce some order into the area can best be studied on an anonymous plan of about 1560 that shows their earliest project for the building (Fig. 108).[5] The architect's first instinct was to regularize the western edge of the property by drawing a straight line down its entire length, from the Piazza di S. Macuto on the north to the Arco di Camillo on the south. This line became the benchmark of all future planning. It served as the baseline from which each wing on Figure 108—church, courtyard, and loggie—took its orientation. On the other sides of the property, however, the nascent building tended to be deformed by the contours of the environment. On the south, a broad new street was projected to run diagonally across the site, leaving an awkward trapezoidal garden. On the north and east, the building was adapted to the irregular perimeter of the property in the most haphazard fashion.

The turning point in the cycle came during the campaign of 1581–85, when the last concessions were made to the environment and the internal skeleton of the Collegio calcified along lines that predetermined future growth. Under the patronage of Gregory XIII, the Jesuit architect Valeriano completed what amounts to the southern half of the present building: the huge *cortile delle scuole,* the nearby dormitory wing, and the famous south facade that cuts obliquely across the site (Fig. 110). In one sense these wings, with their oblique alignments, still demonstrate the deforming power of the environment. But from another point of view they prove that the building had begun to take a more active stance toward its surroundings: the wings were built largely on expropriated land, public streets were shut, and the contours of several isole were drastically reshaped. By the end of the campaign the full outline of the building could be predicted, and from this point on its advance was inexorable. In 1626 the Jesuits began the northern half, including S. Ignazio and their own residential wings. In the project of 1560 (Fig. 108) the perimeter on the north and east had been left meandering and irregular; now it was made rigidly straight. The entire northeast corner was set on expropriated land. Wide streets were opened up along the new wings. In order to enhance the prestige of the building in relation to its surroundings, the Jesuits borrowed a device from the repertoire of secular palace design: they opened a street from the northeast corner as far as the Corso, and along its length they built a small oratory (Fig. 109, no. 848) with a facade set back from the normal building line.[6] To anyone approaching from the Corso the corner of the Collegio appears to jut out into this new street and to dominate it with its travertine mass (Fig. 111). Like the Baldassini and the Farnese before them, the Jesuits went so far as to recast the environment to influence the way their own residence was perceived.[7]

Nothing is so revealing of the urban life cycle as the creation of piazzas, spaces that are opened up in response to imagery on a building's surface. Before the Collegio Romano was begun there were already two modest piazzas in the area, the Piazza di S. Macuto on the northwest and the Piazza dell'Arco di Camillo on the south (Fig. 108). In the early stages of planning it seemed natural to design the building around these open spaces: hence in 1560 the church of the earliest project was designed to face the Piazza di S. Macuto, and in 1581 the main portal of the college wing was designed to open onto the Piazza dell'Arco di Camillo. In later stages of growth the situation was reversed: it was now the open spaces that were designed around the building. In 1659 the south piazza, the former Piazza dell'Arco di Camillo, was enlarged to form a broad, spacious urban corridor running the entire length of the facade. In 1727–28 the Piazza S. Ignazio was built to the north of the church on the design of Filippo Raguzzini. It was a fitting conclusion to the institutional life cycle: in all of Roman architecture there is no more vivid metaphor for an institution's power to carve out urban space than this small theatrical masterpiece.

At the start of the cycle, deference and dependence characterized the relation between the Collegio Romano and the urban fabric; by the end the Collegio was the dominant partner. In the course of growth, this complex building came to generate a variety of open spaces around itself, each tailored to some facet—college, residence, or church—of its eclectic program. When the process was over, the building was encircled by its own satellites or by institutions as powerful as itself: by the Dominicans on the west, by the Pamphilj and the convent of S. Marta on the south, and by the Oratory of the Caravita and other Jesuit property on the north and east. At that point its expansive potential was finally neutralized and equilibrium returned to the area.

The Casa dei Filippini

Once the patterns of institutional urbanism are understood, it becomes possible to study the Casa dei Filippini against its natural backdrop. Like most buildings of its class, it exhibits the familiar life cycle: initial foothold, deformed growth, internal calcification, dominance over the environment, creation of a ring of satellites, and

—finally—equilibrium. However, there are also a number of factors that complicate the picture and set the Casa dei Filippini apart from the more commonplace examples of the species. First of all, it stood in a unique relationship to a uniquely complex area of the city. Second, it was designed by a succession of architects, each of whom faced urban problems in a different way. Third, it remained active for a much longer time than most institutions: the equilibrium that was reached in 1745 was in a sense deceptive; in modern times the life cycle was reactivated and the casa became a pivot of urban change on an unprecedented scale.

The area in which the Filippini settled in 1575, their neighborhood in the broadest sense, can be described as a large, irregular wedge that has its point at the Zecca and its sides defined by the two major arteries of the Renaissance city. On the north the wedge was bounded by the Via di Parione or Via Papale, winding its way from the Zecca over Monte Giordano to Pasquino and S. Andrea della Valle; on the south by the Via del Pellegrino, following an equally sinuous course past the Chiavica di S. Lucia to the Cancelleria and the Campo de' Fiori.[8] These heavily traveled routes had been fixed in their course from the time of Sixtus IV. On the other hand, the physiognomy of the terrain inside the wedge remained fluid for a much longer time. This was an area of *vicoli,* small streets that provided local circulation between the major arteries and often took the form of short concentric arcs centered on the point of the wedge (Figs. 2–4). The *vicoli* were not irrevocably fixed; on the contrary, they grew or atrophied in competition with each other, and were often altered in the course of major construction in the area. The street now called the Vicolo della Cancelleria, for example, was abruptly closed when the Cancelleria was built in 1485. In recompense, the Vicolo Savelli, the street immediately to the west, grew prosperous and attracted two new palaces in 1480–90. In the ensuing years development shifted farther west, street by street. In 1503–10 the Palazzo Fieschi-Sora was built and a small piazza opened on the street now called the Via Sora. The next street, now called the Vicolo del Governo, may have been straightened in about 1500, when the Palazzetto Turci was built and a small piazza cleared at its northern tip; it is the straightest of all the *vicoli,* and in the early seventeenth century it was called simply the Strada Nuova. The next street, the Vicolo di Pizzomerlo (Vicolo dei Cartari), was the most important thoroughfare of the region, providing a link between the arteries of Parione and Pellegrino at the point of their widest divergence and then continuing south as far as the Tiber.[9]

It was between these last two streets that the Congregation gained its initial foothold in 1575. If growth had not been piecemeal, that is, if the Congregation had had the entire area bounded by these *vicoli* at its disposal from the very beginning, then it could easily have planned the church and casa without overstepping any urban boundaries. Unfortunately, both the Vallicella and the casa grew in hesitant steps; the awkward alignment of the medieval church was passed on to its successor, and consequently, as the building progressed the two neighboring *vicoli* came to act as barriers to expansion (Cat. 5, 15). When the church was enlarged and the transept added, the Vicolo di Pizzomerlo blocked its path on the northwest. When plans were afoot for a casa to the east of the church, the Vicolo del Governo became an absolute boundary which no project was allowed to overstep (Cat. 1a, 1b). The designs produced in these years are classic examples of deformed growth: caught between the desire for a rational plan and the demands of an irrational environment, the projects vacillate between a building designed from the inside out (Cat. 1a, 1b), and one designed from the outside in (Cat. 3). Furthermore, piecemeal growth caused a problem which was to plague the design for generations: because the new church began as a simple replacement for the old one, it came to face in the wrong direction. Other Counter-Reformational basilicas —the Gesù,[10] S. Andrea della Valle,[11] the Barnabite project for a church on the Piazza di Monte Giordano (Fig. 99)[12]—all had their facades directly on the main thoroughfare, the Via di Parione. In contrast, the Vallicella turned its back on this important artery, and although a system of alleys and rear doors alleviated the problem in practical terms (Cat. 4a, 5), they could never compensate for the loss in dignity and prestige. Filippo's Vallicella posed a two-edged problem to future architects: to acknowledge the Via di Parione in architectural terms, and to enhance a facade that stood in an urban backwater.[13]

The early projects for a casa to the west of the Vallicella show a further stage in the life cycle. There are still some concessions to the environment, but at the same time there are also attempts to reform and reshape it (Cat. 6a, 6b, 7a, 7b). The most interesting of these projects is Arconio's drawing of 1621–23 (Cat. 9). Here the internal skeleton of the building is still "soft" in the sense that the oblique alignment of the south facade sets the tone for the entire plan and no two wings meet at an angle of exactly 90 degrees. The oratory and its facade are made to face a piazza already in existence. On the other hand, a new street is projected along the east flank of the church to compensate the public for the loss of the Vicolo di Pizzomerlo.[14] The project is a strange mixture of adaptation and aggression. It would have gone a considerable way toward imposing order on the site, and yet it internalizes many local irregularities and fails to project its influence outward in any powerful way.

Maruscelli as Urbanist

The real turning point in the cycle of growth came with Maruscelli. In contrast to Arconio, Maruscelli laid out his design with a certain grand obliviousness to the demands of topography. He ignored ground levels, made crooked contours straight, and designed images like the west facade (Cat. 23c) that were coherent on the drawing board but could not easily have been perceived on the site. Although he originally thought of putting the oratory along the Via di Parione— that is, on the busiest side of the building—he soon moved it to a far more secluded corner (Cat. 12a, 12d, 14). He was deeply committed to a design organized around axes of vision; his enfilades imposed a strict orthogonal discipline on his planning, and one senses that he would have preferred to excise a crooked wing altogether rather than allow it to deform the design (Cat. 12a). It was under Maruscelli that the internal structure of the building hardened, and likewise under him that new patterns of urban space began to be opened up around it.

The idea of a piazza in front of the Vallicella facade did not originate with Maruscelli, but it was he who cast the design in its final form and who began to put it into execution. The earliest project for the Piazza della Chiesa Nuova is an anonymous drawing of 1604–12, which shows the space as a conventional square, each side equal to the width of the facade (Cat. 5). The square is left as a cul-de-sac with no connection to the Via del Pellegrino on the south, and only tenuous links to the surrounding network of *vicoli*. It was Maruscelli's achievement to take this initial design and integrate it more closely into the circulation patterns of the area. He planned a wide artery, the so-called Strada Nuova or Via Larga, that was to begin at the Via del Pellegrino and point at the center of the church facade; it was to cut through a built-up area for most of its path and emerge in the piazza at an oblique angle (Cat. 17c–e). The piazza itself was broadened from its initial width of 150 palmi to a width as great as 230 palmi on one drawing (Cat. 17e). It was now designed to accommodate a spacious avenue, later called the Via della Chiesa Nuova, that was to run along the right flank of the church and enter the piazza along its eastern edge. The two new streets and the piazza were envisaged as an integrated system, capable of carrying traffic between the arteries of Parione and Pellegrino as well as of providing room for maneuver in front of the church facade. But at the same time, the piazza was also designed to evoke a specific historical precedent, namely the Piazza Farnese, which itself took the form of a square broadened at the sides by the two streets flanking the palace and entered obliquely by a street, the Via dei Baullari, that pointed to the center of the palace facade.[15] In casting back to the Renaissance for patterns of urban space, Maruscelli was only acting in the spirit of his time. In exactly these years, 1626–28, the Barberini were also experimenting with a revival of Farnese themes, in particular, a similar piazza in front of their new palace.[16] And it was the Barberini pope, Urban VIII, who gave Maruscelli's project legal sanction in a bull of January 26, 1627.

The bull is a document of immense importance for the urban history of the area.[17] It authorized the construction of a generous piazza, measuring 150 by 200 palmi, that would be connected to the Via del Pellegrino on the south by a broad avenue 40 palmi wide. In clearing the street and piazza, the Congregation were empowered to purchase property at the assessed value alone, that is, by paying the *stima* without the usual *augumento*.[18] They were allowed to make fractional purchases of houses, taking what came within the domain of their improvements and leaving the remnants, no matter how small or how useless, to their original proprietors. The Congregation's privileges were to supersede prior privileges granted to any other institution. The terms of the bull were so generous that one naturally looks for political motivations behind the pope's gesture, and one finds them in the fact that in 1624 Urban VIII had installed the Governorato di Roma on the Via di Parione, not far from the Vallicella (Fig. 4; Fig. 2, no. 614).[19] Doubtless he hoped to harness the Congregation's building fervor to open up the area with broad, spacious thoroughfares. Whatever its immediate motivation, the bull remained in effect until the eighteenth century; it is a case where a legal instrument enshrined a particular visual form and preserved it long after it had become stylistically outmoded.

The street and part of the piazza were carried out under Maruscelli's direction between 1627 and 1630.[20] Demolition began at the Via del Pellegrino and proceeded northward, cutting through property that belonged partly to Antonio Cerri and partly to the Congregation. When the Strada Nuova was finished in 1630 it was paved and lined by several new houses, including a new Palazzo Cerri built on the designs of the architect Francesco Peparelli.[21] At the point where the street emerged into the piazza, Maruscelli built a sample of the plain, functional architecture that was supposed to line the entire periphery of the open space (Fig. 100, right edge); hardly one bay wide and one bay deep, this small building eventually set the pattern for the large *appartamenti* that went up around the church and casa between 1655 and 1745 (Figs. 9, 103). The piazza itself, however, was left incomplete when work stopped in 1630. Maruscelli had carried out the demolition of a cluster of buildings at its center, but he did not go so far as to clear the full rectangle authorized in Urban VIII's bull. The party walls of houses on the site marked the point where demolition had left off and came to form the outer boundaries of the piazza, which thus assumed the shape of a funnel, narrow at the southern end and broadening asymmetrically as it approached the church (Figs. 100–102, Cat. 17a). Doubtless an expedient of the moment, the funnel shape nevertheless provided an adequate, indeed, an interesting space from which the facade could be viewed, and it was not dismantled entirely until 1702.[22]

Borromini as Urbanist

If Maruscelli brought the casa to the point where it began to dominate its environment, with Borromini the whole cycle suddenly breaks step and the building seems to undergo a new phase of adaptivity to its surroundings. The plan of the casa was immediately relaxed. To gain interior space Borromini bent the north wing outward and made the northwest corner into an obtuse angle (Cat. 39, 59, 80, 81). He recognized the importance of the Via di Parione: he designed a separate facade for the Piazza di Monte Giordano (Cat. 89a); and when it came to plans for a Pamphilj rotunda, he instinctively sketched a facade on the northern side of the complex as well as on the south (Fig. 128).[23] Unfortunately, there is no evidence to show how he would have handled the design of the Piazza della Chiesa Nuova, which was the most important urban problem his architecture raised. When he gave the oratory a facade of its own, he broadened the backdrop of the piazza and rendered the old shapes—the square and the funnel—permanently obsolete. Yet there are no plans or sketches to show how he might have wanted the space to look, and in his later prints and drawings (Fig. 16, Cat. 89b, 90) he tends to isolate the facade entirely from its original context, leaving his urban intentions enigmatic.[24]

The Piazza di Monte Giordano is a much better index of Borromini's way of dealing with the urban environment.[25] Maruscelli had designed the exterior of his casa as a static image (Cat. 23c), and it did not seem to trouble him that his facade would have been splintered visually into fragments by the vast dimensions of the building, the narrowness of the street, and the changing levels of the site. It did trouble Borromini, and as a result he evolved a design that was both more realistic than Maruscelli's and more dramatic. He took Maruscelli's left-hand projection and cut it loose; a drawing shows him expanding its width from 71 to 94 palmi, creating an independent facade capable of standing alone in the piazza (Fig. 23, Cat. 80, 89a, 98b, 98c). The new image could be seen from afar, and was brilliantly designed to catch the diagonal view of the traveler approaching from the Ponte S. Angelo. The pilaster cluster at the corner would have seemed to jut out into the street, like the more ponderous corner pier of the Collegio Romano (Fig. 111), simultaneously asserting a dominance over the area and offering refreshment from a fountain that was designed to stand at the corner (Cat. 89a).[26] The facade itself was a strange hybrid, less than ecclesiastical in character but more than merely domestic, something between a full-fledged church facade and a side facade like that of S. Carlo alle Quattro Fontane. It was more complex than the strip patterns found, for example, on the Collegio Romano facade, which is its immediate model; but it was still less strictly logical than a clear-cut superimposition of orders, which the brick bands vaguely approach, like strips in search of a system.[27] It presented an unusual mixture of materials, from the travertine window frames and the dark rough brick of the central bays to the fine yellow brick of the giant pilasters at either end. Finally, it was a design based on camouflage, since the largest and most ornate window frames are placed a story higher than the most important rooms, a device that raises the center of gravity of the facade and prepares for the clocktower above it.

Other elements in the building expressed metaphors of growth, but the *torre dell'orologio* actually did grow, starting from nothing at all and rising to heights of 38 and then 56 palmi in the planning stages of 1647–48, and then still higher as different models for the iron crown were tried out in 1648 and 1649.[28] It became the most audacious of all the hybrid images in the casa, combining three classic types of Roman clock: the courtyard clock, the public clock, and the tower clock. There had been a courtyard clock in Maruscelli's project,[29] but the one Borromini chose for his model came from the Casa Professa del Gesù, which supplied him with the ironwork pattern for his earliest project, although the heraldic emblems used by the Jesuits, the Farnese *gigli,* were naturally transformed into the lilies of Filippo Neri (Figs. 105, 106).[30] Public clocks were relatively common, both on churches like S. Maria Maggiore[31] and S. Maria in Aracoeli,[32] and on institutional buildings like the Collegio Romano,[33] the Sapienza,[34] the Monte di Pietà,[35] the Lateran Hospital,[36] the Palazzo dei Mendicanti,[37] and the Capuchin convent on the Pincian;[38] but once again Borromini seems to have been thinking of the Casa Professa, which displayed a public clock high up on the corner facing toward the

Capitoline Hill.[39] But, for sheer visibility the most conspicuous type of clock was the kind installed on the face of a medieval tower; when he raised the Filippini's clock so high off the ground Borromini may have been following the example of the tower clock at the Palazzo Sforza-Cesarini, only a short distance from the casa (Fig. 3).[40] With two dials, the *torre dell'orologio* was both a private and a public clock; it was a demonstration of the effect of the impact of the eye on a malleable mass; it held a famous icon up to public view and crowned it with a canopy deriving from the *baldacchino* of St. Peter's. But in the end it is the medieval *torre* that emerges as the dominant element, giving the image a baronial stamp far removed from the original *famiglia* ideal.[41]

To judge from the example of the casa, Borromini was what might be called an indirect urbanist. He left no real plans for the space around the building, but instead he concentrated his efforts on the facades, clusters of imagery that later exerted their own influence on the contours of the urban fabric. One of these images, the Monte Giordano facade, fulfilled its space-shaping potential almost immediately. In 1661 Borromini himself, as architect of the Banco di S. Spirito, was able to rebuild the southern boundary of the piazza on a line already implicit in his earlier work (Cat. 97, 98b, 98c).[42] On the other hand, the oratory facade took much longer to exert its full influence, and the piazza around it did not assume its final form for roughly another century. It soon became apparent that the funnel shape was inadequate because its focus was too narrow (Fig. 101). The first step toward a new shape was taken in 1655, when the left half of the funnel was demolished, patches of private and public land exchanged, and a new property line established that was more nearly parallel to the oratory facade (Cat. 87).[43] The full facade was exposed to view for the first time in 1659, when a group of houses that had stood in front of the porter's lodge for two decades was finally demolished.[44] The eastern end of the piazza was completed in two stages: first in 1673–75, when a street was cleared along the right flank of the church,[45] and later in 1702, when the southeast corner was squared off (Cat. 105, 106a–c).[46] These operations amounted to nothing more than completing Maruscelli's old design (Cat. 17e), which was still given legal sanction in the bull of Urban VIII. The western end of the piazza was completed in 1743–45, when the last block of houses was finally demolished and rebuilt along a new property line.[47] The drawing for the new house, which shows all of the buildings of the piazza converging in a forced and unconvincing perspective, clarifies the "simetria quasi uguale"[48] that had become the Congregation's aesthetic goal (Cat. 112). Symmetry there might have been, of a compromised and wishful sort glimpsed fleetingly from the casa door, but from any other point of view the boundary of the piazza seems to meander and to lack the discipline of a guiding hand (Fig. 9).

Property and Design

Intertwined with the architectural life cycle of the casa was a demographic cycle, one that witnessed the uprooting of the earlier inhabitants of the site and the coming of a new group with its own culture and its own economy. Before the Filippini arrived the parish of S. Maria in Vallicella comprised 162 hearths.[49] Plans of the area show between 70 and 80 houses (Cat. 15); in 1627 about 29 of these belonged to corporations and about 44 to private individuals.[50] The inhabitants engaged in a wide range of economic activity; innkeeper, horsetrader, groom, herbalist, pharmacist, carpenter, jeweler, ironmonger, tinsmith, master mason, artist, cleric, schoolmaster, and dealer in used goods are some of the known trades.[51] They lived densely, and the ground floors of their houses were studded with shops to draw in the wealth that flowed along the Via di Parione and seeped down the smaller *vicoli.* In contrast to these people, the Filippini were a smaller and more coherent group, a single hearth, so to speak, numbering about sixty members in the year that the casa was planned.[52] Their economic base was founded on private wealth, *luoghi di monti,* rents, and the ability to attract bequests; often precarious, their income was nevertheless independent of entrenched patterns of local commerce. They were intent on living less densely than the indigenous population, and they enjoyed advantages conceded in Roman law to expansive organizations. Their advance was slow but inexorable, and eventually the displacement of the older inhabitants included removal even of their ancestral bones.[53]

The demographic cycle of an institutional building unfolded in a spirit of ongoing conflict between the old and the new inhabitants. Resistance tended to be most vigorous when the new group was searching for a foothold in an area. Ignatius of Loyola was sued when the Jesuits first began to expand on the site of what later became the Casa Professa;[54] the expansion of the Collegio Romano in 1581 provoked vigorous resistance from the local inhabitants;[55] the first Oratorians sent to the Vallicella were stoned and shot at, and in later years the Congregation was repeatedly brought to court by "tough and quibbling" men remembered with contempt for having tried to save their own homes.[56] Even after the building had been begun, there was a long period of uneasy coexistence between the two groups. Rent was precious, even from condemned houses, and there was a legal obligation to rebuild on the site of demolished property within six months.[57] As a result the casa was built in stages, and between 1621 and 1675 the expanding wings of the new building often stood only a few feet from the shrinking vestiges of old neighborhoods. When wells failed because of foundation digging, or when commerce was lost because a street was blocked, the Congregation had to lower rents to compensate for damages. In return they kept a surveillance on the condemned area, and could discourage certain forms of enterprise, such as new taverns.[58] As the building progressed, blocks of older houses came to stand impacted *(incastrate)* within courtyards that surrounded them on three sides, something like the medieval houses that still stood in the early nineteenth century between the wings of the Louvre.[59] One such house was allowed to stand in the entrance courtyard during the first year that the oratory was in use, and another abutted the sacristy until it partly collapsed in 1652.[60] The garden courtyard was still traversed by a public street in 1655 and was filled with houses that harbored "families of every sort of generation."[61] The extreme proximity of these people caused *soggettione,* a mixture of embarrassment, distraction, and annoyance that sometimes gave way to more substantial fears. Thieves had free access to the courtyard, and Borromini had to equip the loggie with traps to keep them from climbing to the *piano nobile.*[62] The interregnum of 1655 brought danger from civil unrest, and the *vicolo* leading into the courtyard had to be locked; 1656 was a year of plague; by 1657 all commerce had departed. Yet, characteristically, the last cluster of houses was not demolished until 1659, on the eve of the campaign to finish the west wing.[63]

Coexistence during construction was one thing, but after a building had been completed it was another matter. In Roman domestic architecture, it was the *bottega,* or shop, that symbolized coexistence between different social classes.[64] When shops were demolished to make way for a new building there was an intangible but acknowledged obligation to replace them, one analogous to the obligation to restore land to the city when a street was closed and occupied.[65] Shops were included in all of the early projects for the Casa dei Filippini;[66] they promised to generate rent and they were even sanctioned in the Congregation's chosen model of a *famiglia* palace (Fig. 118). However, an undercurrent of opposition to shops surfaced in 1627 when Maruscelli was told to strike them from his final project.[67] There was a feeling that the mezzanines above shops harbored promiscuity of the classes and represented a source of contamination. In a long and revealing discourse of 1639, Spada outlined the problems shops were expected to cause: distraction, indecency or scandal from the presence of women, overcrowding, screaming children, noise at night, family quarrels, and the threat of fire spreading among the rags of the poor.[68] Eventually a few token shops were built under and around the *torre dell'orologio* (Cat. 89a),[69] but elsewhere in the building the ground floor was used for storerooms on the model of those found in the Sapienza, a means of generating income without having troublesome inhabitants.

The kind of ideal coexistence that the Oratorians desired was eventually realized in the four large *appartamenti* that were built around the piazza and the church between 1627 and 1745.[70] As the casa advanced, the mechanisms used to finance it tended to develop a certain momentum of their own, and the chain of bequest, displacement, demolition, and reconstruction continued to operate in the houses around the piazza even after the casa itself was finished. Thanks to the expropriation laws and the bull of Urban VIII, each change in the contour of the piazza allowed the Oratorians to expand their property on advantageous terms. The uniform houses that went up around the church and casa came to form the Congregation's outermost ring of expansion. They included new shops, mezzanines, and apartments that offset the losses from demolished buildings.[71] In one sense the piazza was considered the financial equivalent of the old neighborhood, in another as its symbolic image, rebuilt, reordered, and held at a decorous distance (Fig. 9).[72]

All of these social and economic considerations left their stamp on the formal and aesthetic qualities of the piazza. At the beginning of the whole process, before much property had come under its control, the Congregation tended to think in terms of open spaces carved out of the built-up areas: the square and the funnel of the early projects were exercises in the organization of voids (Cat. 5, 17a, 17c–e, 38). At the end of the cycle, the Oratorians were landlords who planned in terms of property rather than space: their final project is an exercise in the organization of solid forms (Cat. 112). The two modes of perception, fundamentally incompatible as they were, nevertheless became entwined and confused: the earlier mode was frozen in the bull of Urban VIII and survived to shape the east end of the piazza, while the center and the west end tend to reflect the latter mode. This is the reason why the boundary of the piazza seems to meander and to lose all discipline the farther it moves from the Vallicella facade (Fig. 9). In the end, the piazza emerged as a compromise, successful when taken as the symbol of a demographic process or as a foil to the twin facades of church and oratory, but amorphous and uninspired when considered as a design in its own right.

Epilogue

As far as the Congregation itself was concerned, the Piazza della Chiesa Nuova was complete by 1745. It formed part of a comprehensive system of arteries that connected the Via di Parione with the Via del Pellegrino, entirely replacing the old network of twisting *vicoli*. A new and well-traveled route had been forged that ran from the Piazza di Monte Giordano along the side of the casa, through the piazza and the Strada Nuova to the Via del Pellegrino. Fountains were built or projected to punctuate its major turning points.[73] Seven images of the Madonna were placed on prominent corners as devotional guideposts.[74] Street lighting was in use by the early nineteenth century.[75] The surrounding property on three sides was owned by the Congregation or was built on surveying lines that the Congregation had helped to establish. The expansive potential of the institution, operative for 170 years, was finally neutralized, and there followed 140 years of absolute stability until other agents of change appeared.

After the dissolution of the Papal State in 1870, the Casa dei Filippini once again became the focus of urban change, and a new circulatory network was mapped out around it in the three principal master plans of modern Rome. In the Viviani Plan of 1873, the first *piano regolatore* of the Italian Republic, the Renaissance quarter was traversed by a broad new artery, the Corso Vittorio Emanuele, designed to connect the Quirinal and the new Via Nazionale on one side with the Vatican on the other.[76] The Corso Vittorio was built from east to west in two stages. The first tract, begun in 1884, simply followed the old winding course of the Via di Parione from the Gesù as far as S. Pantaleo; if it had continued on this route it would have skirted around the rear of the casa. When the second tract was begun in 1885, however, it parted from the Renaissance highway and veered south, cutting its own path through a heavily built-up area. The new route required extensive demolition, but it also exploited a series of older open spaces, in particular the long Piazza della Chiesa Nuova. It appears that the planners felt the magnetism of the twin facades; at a single stroke the former backwater around the Vallicella was opened up, and the casa became the crucial pivot at which the new boulevard turned to pursue its course to the Tiber (Fig. 1).

A new element was added to the scheme in the second *piano regolatore,* the Sanjust Plan of 1908, in which a north-south route was planned across the Renaissance quarter.[77] The artery was to begin at the Tiber on the south, cut northward until it entered the Piazza della Chiesa Nuova, continue along the right flank of the Vallicella, and finally proceed north until it rejoined the river in the neighborhood of the Tor di Nona. The new streets would have resembled the arteries that Maruscelli had mapped out by 1627 (Cat. 17e), but they were magnified to an enormous scale and would have extended far beyond the wedge in which Maruscelli's streets originally had been confined. No part of the project was carried out, but the idea of a broad boulevard pointing at the twin facades from the Tiber reappeared in the third *piano regolatore,* the Fascist master plan of 1931.[78] The avenue was to start at the Ponte Mazzini and cut through the dense area along the Via Giulia and the Via del Pellegrino; at one end the terminus would have been the Vallicella, and at the other—across the river on the site of the demolished Regina Coeli prison—a vast piazza with the Acqua Felice fountain installed on the hillside as its centerpiece. In contrast to the old institutional cycle, in which a building tended to become surrounded with dependencies, the new philosophy was to isolate famous monuments, "to free the trunk of the great oak from all that cramps and blights it."[79] Demolition for the new street was actually begun, causing havoc around the Via Giulia and coming within one block of the old Piazza della Chiesa Nuova by the time it was halted in 1940.[80] At that point a second and apparently definitive equilibrium descended on the area.

If the replanning of the Renaissance quarter of Rome came to focus on the Casa dei Filippini, it was in part due to the great size of the building and to its strategic location, but also in part to the pull of a strong architectural image. Once Borromini was allowed to give the oratory a facade of its own, every step followed in logical sequence, with the twin facades exerting their force on the eventual shape of the piazza, and the piazza attracting the grand boulevards of the Republican and Fascist planners. The final result was more sweeping and grandiose than anything in the repertoire of seventeenth-century town planning, but it was Borromini, the indirect urbanist, who set the process in motion by designing the oratory facade. Ironically, of all the elements of the casa, it was this capricious image, uncalled for by the program and ill-adapted to the site, that in the end exerted the greatest influence over the street pattern of the modern city.

7

Conclusion

The Casa dei Filippini is an unusually complex example of a common species, the multifunctional residence for the type of religious institution that sprang up in Rome in the wake of the Counter Reformation. Like most such buildings, its planning and construction had a spiritual dimension over and above the mere provision of a sound and comfortable place to live. In Counter-Reformational terms to build was to "edify," to communicate in a didactic way the peculiar values of a given institution.[1] The casa was accordingly the "temporal fabric" in which the life of the "spiritual fabric" was mirrored; it was meant to express the Congregation's dignity and modesty as well as the sense of "familiarità e domestichezza" that lay at the core of their communal life.[2] It was essential that it be built amid a "union of souls."[3] Planning was a slow affair. It took time to elicit the necessary consensus, then more time to create the mechanisms needed to raise sufficient funds, to acquire property and alter the urban landscape, and finally to judge architectural designs. Fortunately, time was on the Congregation's side. It prevented them from building a casa as amateurish and heavy-handed as any of the early projects, or from conforming to a standard monastic type ill-suited to expressing their unique corporate status. It meant that planning took place during a period of continuous expansion for the Congregation; the size and scope of the project were fixed just as the curve of growth changed direction, and there was no going back even after the institution had entered a phase of numerical decline. Finally it meant that construction was delayed until the more rigid conventions of Sistine and Pauline Rome had begun to thaw and a more expressive architectural language was available in which to formulate the building's imagery.

For all their stiff and wooden character, it was in the drawings of Paolo Maruscelli that this language was first spoken. His plans provided for a rational separation of functions, impressive vistas deep into the interior, and a decorous outer appearance designed to set off the Vallicella facade "like a jewel in a ring." In order to symbolize the unique status of the Congregation he grafted the type of Roman *famiglia* palace onto a basic Palladian framework and outfitted the result with ornament drawn from the archepiscopal palace of Milan. Maruscelli's project was the compromise that elicited the long-sought consensus. By fusing different architectural types it produced an adequate image for the Congregation, but it left the door ajar to more radical hybridization. Borromini would later open this door wide.

When a major residential structure was begun in seventeenth-century Rome, it was often understood that the patron or his advisors would really design the building, while the architect would be called in for matters of structure and ornamental detail. This division of responsibility was advocated at the Palazzo Barberini in 1624,[4] and it seems to have been what the Oratorians expected as well. Thus, Borromini's role at the casa was limited at the outset, and in recognition of this fact his most incisive metaphor for the casa came from the world of clothing: as he put it, his ornament was a well-tailored suit cut to fit a rude, oversized body of someone else's making.[5] Most of his work was directed at using ornament to change the spectator's perception of space and structure. The oratory was given an ecclesiastical facade based on principles of optical deception. Its interior was given a skeletal and centralized appearance and crowned with the image of a cupola more open and more daring than the actual structure could ever have allowed. The residential wings were outfitted with a variety of motifs drawn from the world of Renaissance palace design: a giant order, *nicchioni,* vestibules filled with niches, an atrium, a cardinal's library and fireplace, aulic stairs and *seditori.* Borromini built his imagery around a few important functions, such as the musical Oratory and the reception of distinguished guests; in so doing he elevated the social rank of the building, and effectively changed its dress to what might be called "pavonazzo" or "habito palatino," the level of attire expected from familiars of the court.[6]

The Casa dei Filippini was the commission that brought Borromini and Virgilio Spada together for the first time.[7] Both men were relatively young; a friendship was struck between them and eventually a tacit partnership was formed that exerted an enormous influence on the major commissions of the next two pontificates. In different senses the casa was a training ground for them both, and so it seems appropriate to ask what effect it had on their formation and on their subsequent careers.

For Spada the casa was a schooling in design.[8] He already had gained considerable architectural experience before entering the Oratory in 1622, but it was experience of a provincial sort acquired in the service of his father, Paolo Spada (1541–1631), in small towns in the Romagna. In 1619–21 he had submitted a design for a monumental fountain in Faenza; an awkward drawing of about 1621 for the Casino Spada at San Pancrazio near Ravenna has been attributed to him; at about the same time he was involved in the modernization of the family villa at Zattaglia. After he entered the Vallicella he continued to advise Paolo on the design of the convent of S. Francesca Romana in Brisighella, but from 1623 on his letters show a reluctance to leave Rome and a growing preoccupation with the one building now of overriding importance, the casa. Maruscelli's caption project of 1627, with all of the discussion and professional involvement that went into it, seems to have made a great impression on Virgilio; in the following year he submitted a design of his own for the Cistercian monastery at Brisighella which borrowed Maruscelli's main idea (the use of symmetrical projections to disguise an asymmetrical design, as in Cat. 23c) as the key principle of the design.[9] As the construction of the casa advanced, Spada acquired a broad knowledge of the technical language of the building trades. He came to know how contracts were drawn up and workmen paid, how vaults were chained and coffered ceilings hung from complicated truss-work, how foundations behaved during settlement, and how the warp in leaning walls could be measured. He learned to use archival research to supplement the usual tools of structural analysis, and he later put the lesson to use when he relied on a forgotten manuscript of Grimaldi's to probe the foundations of St. Peter's,[10] or when he went to old financial records to document chains in the vaults of the Villa Aldobrandini.[11] His years as Preposito taught him the science of architectural finance; when confronted in 1651 with Innocent X's proposal to demolish the *spina* of the Vatican Borgo, his first reaction was to compute lost rents on the basis of an account-drawing of the sort developed twenty-five years earlier at the casa.[12] From his experience at the casa, Spada developed the kind of personal diplomacy needed to manage the jealousies that tended to arise in the course of the *consulta* process, when individual contributions were submerged in the build-up of a design.

Most importantly, the casa taught Spada architectural criticism. Out of the literature of moral casuistry and the practice of the *dubii,* he developed a vocabulary for an involved hierarchy of errors, from simple structural "disordini," through a middle ground of "stroppie e dissonanze," "licenza," "sconcerto," and "neo contra la buona architettura," over the brink of "semplice barbarismo," to extreme flaws called "falsi e solecismi." He scanned modern architecture and found errors in a wide variety of respected models, from the facade of S. Susanna to the Collegio Romano, the Minerva Convent, and even the Vatican and Farnese palaces.[13] This implacable critical vision could also be turned on current projects, and even used to manipulate the *consulta* process and procure a change of architect. Much of Spada's experience at the casa can be seen at work in 1646 when he managed the design of the Palazzo Pamphilj.[14] In addition to the usual criticisms, at one point he drafted an extensive critique of Rainaldi's facade, raising "dubii," exposing what he considered "soligismi" and "errori intollerabili," and at the end advocating a general consultation; apparently he hoped to reenact the events of a decade before at the casa, when Maruscelli's so-called errors had been exposed and the commission had passed into Borromini's hands.

What made Spada so formidable as a critic was the way he combined the technical vocabulary of a *capomastro* with the unrelenting logic of a moral theologian. What he lacked was *disegno.* His few drawings for the casa (Cat. 19, 27, 79) are styleless diagrams with no inner spark. He was certainly capable of imaginative leaps, as a project like his mathematical villa for the Pamphilj family amply proves;[15] but he was simply incapable of putting knowledge or whimsy into elegant graphic form. "I pray you pay attention to the idea alone, and not to the botched drawing" was the note he attached to his earliest architectural project,[16] and the same theme continues throughout his designing career. If they had had nothing else to offer, Maruscelli and Borromini would have been indispensable for their drafting skills alone; like his brother Bernardino, Virgilio might have said, "My building needs an architect, a man with whom I can confer day by day, and whose drawings I can vary to some extent as they are put into execution."[17]

As for Borromini, the casa was the great prize of his early career, the building that launched him in the public eye. Throughout the 1620s he had been an obscure figure, known only to the other Lombards in Maderno's shop and to the artists for whom he had worked as draftsman at St. Peter's and the Palazzo Barberini. His appointment as architect of the Sapienza in 1632 was not destined to bring him work or fame for another decade. By 1634 he was offering his services without fee to two small and unpretentious groups, the Sodalizio dei Marchigiani and the new Spanish order of the Trinitarii Scalzi who had settled earlier in the century at the Quattro Fontane.[18] From 1634 to 1636 he was engaged on the house and cloister of S. Carlo alle Quattro Fontane, but it was the church there that would make his reputation, and until it was actually begun in February 1638, nine months after the oratory, no one had any inkling of its potential splendor.[19] It was the Casa dei Filippini that opened up Borromini's career, and furthermore it was an ongoing commission that occupied him for most of his early maturity. As the building progressed, it came to be a yardstick of his stylistic growth between the ages of thirty-eight and fifty-one. In particular, the two end projections of the west facade (Fig. 22) show where he started and where he stopped, bracketing his development from the tight precision of S. Carlo to the boldness of the Lateran giant order. The oratory facade appears to be the first in Borromini's *oeuvre* to follow an emphatically curved plan, and as such it stands behind a number of curved designs which he produced in the ensuing decade:[20] the Filomarino altar of 1639–42;[21] and the Sette Dolori facade of 1643–46.[22] The tendency towards severing horizontal links and accentuating the effect of sheer vertical rise, visible in the oratory facade and in the superbly abstract cluster of pilasters at the southwest corner of the building (Fig. 20), would become a leitmotif in the design of the Lateran nave.[23] The suggestion of hidden lighting and perforated structure seen over the entrances to the oratory (Figs. 40, 41) would reappear in grander form over the entrance to the Lateran and the high altar of S. Ivo.[24] The alternating balusters of the cardinals' loggia inside the oratory recur often enough in Borromini's work to be considered one of his trademarks,[25] but there are also a number of other interesting ideas that make an inconspicuous appearance in the casa and then resurface with some splendor in the later buildings. For instance, the plain stucco bands that are used in the rear staircase to create a subcurrent of symmetry in the design turn up again in the richer context of the Lateran stuccoes (Figs. 136, 137); and a principle first worked out in the saint's rooms at the casa, whereby a door and an opening above it are used to conceal the turns of a spiral staircase (Fig. 78), returns in monumental form in the spiral ramp designed for the Palazzo Carpegna in 1638–40.[26]

Borromini's fame rests to some extent on the marvelously intricate geometrical plans that stand behind the design of buildings like S. Carlo alle Quattro Fontane, S. Ivo, and S. Andrea delle Fratte. Buildings like the Casa dei Filippini, on the other hand, represent a different strain in his planning, one in which the design is worked out on top of a nongeometrical armature inherited along with the commission.

These are his constrained designs, and the oratory, which had to be hammered out on the basis of a plan which Maruscelli left behind, prepared Borromini for the ordeal of the Lateran, where he was obliged to proceed "without altering the plan, without moving walls, and without disturbance of any sort."[27] The early drawings for the Lateran are in fact elaborated on top of a plan of the medieval basilica, just as the first drawing for the casa (Cat. 39) is done over a copy of a Maruscelli drawing. It seems that the element of constraint was noticed in both buildings. It was physically apparent at the Lateran, where patches of the older walls were left visible "like relics" through oval apertures in the new fabric;[28] the overlapping of designs was never quite so obvious at the casa, and yet a number of later critics, who knew nothing of Maruscelli's existence, still split their verdict by praising the rational intelligence of the casa plan and deploring elevations and ornament that seemed to them the product of a more febrile mind.[29]

Although Borromini began his independent career at the oratory he went on to other things, and a good way to gauge his growth is to compare the Casa dei Filippini with the Propaganda Fide, the foremost institutional design of his later life. Borromini took over the Propaganda in 1646 and began to work in earnest on the half-finished building in 1652, the year Arcucci replaced him at the casa.[30] Over the next fifteen years he finished the remaining wings on the south and west, brought a measure of harmony to a courtyard that dated from three different campaigns, and replaced Bernini's Re Magi Chapel. In the functional wings he used a number of ideas that he had first encountered in Maruscelli's casa, such as the system of sunken corridors and *loggie scoperte,* or the one-story pilaster screen that makes an appearance in the courtyard on an early drawing.[31] As the design evolved, the Propaganda drawings begin to show revisions and enrichments that recall what happened at the casa. Niches come to terminate every major axis of vision; the mural masses of the chapel are reduced to a few "claw piers" shaped by the surrounding space; the theme of corner columns appears wherever major corridors intersect. The Propaganda facade fuses two motifs from the casa. Like the oratory facade, it deceives the sight and covers much more than just the chapel; but like the Monte Giordano projection, it is a "sliding facade" cut loose from the interior rhythms of the building and allowed to expand in response to the urban environment. Finally, inside the Re Magi Chapel ideas that were first stated at the oratory are reexpressed with a new maturity and assurance (Fig. 138). There had been an awkward contrast in the oratory between the slender porticoes at the two narrow ends and the heavy mural masses of the longer sides; the Re Magi Chapel is skeletal on all sides and at all levels. In the oratory, allusions to antique or Renaissance exemplars were to some extent applied to the surface of the building, like the final glazes on a work of art; in the Re Magi Chapel the lessons learned from antiquity, via Palladio and Raphael, lie deeper under the skin and permeate both space and structure.[32] The canted corners of the oratory look angular and ineffective next to the smoothly rounded corners of the Propaganda chapel, and the fictive oval oculus of the oratory vault lacks the dynamism of the Propaganda's interlocking ribs. In contrast to the precarious structural improvisations of the oratory, the Re Magi vault was never overloaded, and to the present day it stands unchained. Everywhere the Propaganda exudes the new elegance of the 1660s. What is missing, but had been present in the oratory, is the sense of struggle with an intractable commission and the excitement that came from using old conventions to carve out a new architectural style.

Borromini grew beyond the Casa dei Filippini, but in a sense it grew beyond him as well, or rather it had a life and a momentum of its own which he was able to harness but never entirely dominate. Borromini worked on the casa intermittently for thirteen years, Spada for thirty-five; but in all it took 170 years for the complete gestation of the building and its urban environment. The institutional mechanisms that produced the casa had been active before either of these men was born, and they continued to operate long after both were gone. Left to itself the institution could be tenaciously conservative, leveling, and slow; and if it briefly accommodated individuals of genius, it also outlived them and outlasted fluctuations of taste and style. It accepted Borromini's oratory and facade and his changes in the residence, but after he left it clung to forms that its financial structure sanctioned, and it later deposited these over the urban landscape as the curious products of a bygone age. At the dawn of the rococo, the Oratorians were still intent on building a piazza designed under Urban VIII as the revival of a Renaissance idea. In the end, it is the institutional dimension that makes it difficult to give a straightforward assessment of the casa. The building was at once modest and sumptuous, pedestrian and elegant, functional and courtly, familial and aulic, harbinger of a new style and watershed of Renaissance themes, in short, a reflection of deeper contradictions underlying art and society in the early baroque era.

APPENDIX I

Outline of Dates

1. Early History 1575–1622 (Chapter 1)

1575   Filippo Neri begins the rebuilding of S. Maria in Vallicella. Foundation of the Congregatione dell'Oratorio.

1577   The Congregation moves to houses on the east side of S. Maria in Vallicella, but Filippo remains at S. Girolamo della Carità.

1583   Filippo moves to the Vallicella.

1586–87   Projects for a casa to the east of the church. (Cat. 1–3.)

1594–1606   F. Rughesi's facade of S. Maria in Vallicella.

1595   Death of Filippo Neri.

1596   Birth of Paolo Maruscelli and Virgilio Spada.

1599   Birth of Francesco Borromini.

1611   Barnabite plans for a church of S. Carlo at the Piazza di Monte Giordano. (Chapter 1, n. 35.)

1621–23   Mario Arconio's project for a casa to the west of the church. Foundations of the sacristy. (Cat. 8, 9.)

1622   Canonization of Filippo Neri. Spada enters the Congregation at the age of twenty-seven.

2. The Casa under Maruscelli 1622–36 (Chapter 2)

1622   Maruscelli first appears in the documents. (Doc. 5.)

1624   Maruscelli's preliminary projects. (Cat. 12.)

1624–27   Maruscelli's caption project, which is criticized in Spada's notes. (Cat. 14, 20.)

1627   Maruscelli's final project, incorporating Spada's suggestions. (Cat. 23.)

1629   Sacristy begun. Demolition of the church of S. Cecilia and construction of a wall on its site.

1630   Sacristy vaulted.

1633–34   Sacristy *credenzoni*. (Cat. 24.)

3. Borromini: Oratory and Facade 1636–42 (Chapter 3)

1636   Borromini's participation in the building of the sacristy altar. (Cat. 28.)

1637 Jan.–May   Borromini, G. B. Mola, G. Rainaldi, and others are consulted on the design of the oratory. (Cat. 29–34.)

1637 May 10	Borromini is taken on as Maruscelli's associate. (Cat. 35, 37, 39; Decr. 103.)
1637 June 20	Maruscelli's last payment.
1638 Apr. 10	Spada elected as Preposito for a term of three years.
1638	Oratory vaulted. Decision to place the library over the oratory. Expansion of the oratory facade. (Cat. 40, 41.)
1638 Nov.	Contract for stuccoing the interior of the oratory. (Doc. 15.)
1639–40	Romanelli's fresco of the *Coronation* on the oratory vault.
1640 Aug. 15	Inauguration of the oratory.
1641 Apr. 6	Spada reelected Preposito for a second term of three years.
1641–42	Oratory facade completed. (Cat. 38, 66.)

4.   Borromini: Refectory Wing and Service Courtyard 1638–41 (Chapter 4)

1638	Library eliminated from the design of the service courtyard and service rooms rearranged. (Cat. 40.)
1638–39	Borromini's stucco and marble doorframes in the rooms around the saint's chapel, along with the oval spiral staircase.
1639	Refectory and *lavamani.* (Cat. 58, 59.)
1640	*Sala di ricreazione.*
1641 Aug.	Chimney of *sala di ricreazione* unveiled. (Cat. 61.)
1639–41	Rooms along the Via di Parione including *dispensa,* square staircase, kitchen, and three stories of residential rooms. (Cat. 84a.)
	Garden courtyard: two bays of north loggia, entire east loggia, alterations to south side of courtyard. (Cat. 57, 61–64.)
1641–43	Donati Chapel built near the saint's chapel. (Cat. 27, 65.)

5.   Borromini: First Courtyard 1641–43 (Chapter 4)

1641 Sept.–Nov.	Design of the entire courtyard, including *portaria,* entrance atrium to oratory, loggia, and south face of the sacristy. (Cat. 66.)
	Entrance portal to casa. (Cat. 67, 68.)
1641 Nov. 23	Consultation with Soria and Contini over the *nicchioni.* (Cat. 66.)
1641–42	*Forestaria* and right half of oratory facade. (Cat. 66.)
1642–43	Balcony window of the room over the sacristy. (Cat. 71–72.)
1642–44	Library and upper story of oratory facade. (Cat. 41, 76–78.)
1642 Nov. 15	Contract for the library ceiling. (Doc. 17, 19; Cat. 76.)
1643 Sept. 20	Contract for the library shelves. (Doc. 18, 19; Cat. 77.)
1643	Loggia between oratory and courtyard. Entrance vestibule to the main *scalone,* but not the *scalone* itself. (Cat. 70, 73.)
1643 Aug. 15	Most of the Congregation moves to the new casa.
1641–42	*Forestaria* and right half of oratory facade. (Cat. 66.)
1642–43	Balcony window of the room over the sacristy. (Cat. 71–72.)
1642–44	Library and upper story of oratory facade. (Cat. 41, 76–78.)
1642 Nov. 15	Contract for the library ceiling. (Doc. 17, 19; Cat. 76.)
1643 Sept. 20	Contract for the library shelves. (Doc. 18, 19; Cat. 77.)

1643	Loggia between oratory and courtyard. Entrance vestibule to the main *scalone,* but not the *scalone* itself. (Cat. 70, 73.)
1643 Aug. 15	Most of the Congregation moves to the new casa.

6. Interlude 1644–47

1644	Innocent X elected pope; Spada appointed to the office of *elemosiniere segreto.*
1644	Borromini's project for a Pamphilj Chapel to the east of S. Maria in Vallicella, with a project to duplicate the oratory facade. (Cat. 39, 79.)
1647	Manuscript of a "piena relatione della fabrica" by Borromini and Spada, later known under its published title *Opus Architectonicum.* (Cat. 84–86.)

7. Borromini: Monte Giordano Wing 1647–50 (Chapter 4)

1647 May	Design and foundations of the wing extending from the *dispensa* to the Piazza di Monte Giordano, with new features such as shops, a pharmacy, Spada's apartment, a belltower, and an enlarged Monte Giordano facade. (Cat. 80, 81, 84, 89a.)
1649	Maruscelli's death. (Appendix II.)
ca. 1649	Spada's *Dialogo.*
1650	Fountain project for the northwest corner of the casa. (Cat. 82, 89a.) Completion of the Monte Giordano facade.
1651	Shelving on the interior of the pharmacy. (Cat. 80.)

8. Interlude 1650–59 (Chapter 4)

1650	Dispute with the contractor Defendino Peschal; Borromini refuses to hand over the *Libro delle misure.*
1650 Dec.	Francesco Righi appears as the Congregation's architect. (Chapter 4, n. 56.)
1651–52	Cracks appear in the oratory vault. (Decr. 291–293.)
1651–53	Vaj bequest to transform the oratory altar: Camillo Arcucci's project, Spada's objections, Borromini's counterproject. (Cat. 48.)
1652 Aug. 23	Arcucci elected architect in place of Borromini.
1653–64	Rebuilding of the oratory altar. (Cat. 48.)
1655	Death of Innocent X and election of Alexander VII.
1656	Plague in Rome. Spada reelected Preposito on Oct. 21.
1657 Apr.–May	Spada's maneuver to recall Borromini as architect is defeated.

9. Arcucci: West Wing 1659–62 (Chapter 4)

1658 Sept. 2	Alexander VII orders the completion of all buildings which have benefited from the Gregorian expropriation law.
1659–62	Arcucci builds the west wing including the *scalone.* Garden laid out and fountain installed. (Cat. 73, 89b, 92–96.)

10.   Carlo Rainaldi: Completion of the Casa 1662–75 (Chapter 4)

1662 Dec. 11	Death of Virgilio Spada.
1663	Horatio Spada offers to finance the chapel of S. Carlo Borromeo.
1665–67	Expansion of the library *salone* and the oratory facade. (Cat. 100, 101.)
1666	Camillo Arcucci's campanile over the right transept of S. Maria in Vallicella.
1667 Feb. 25	C. Rainaldi appointed architect in conjunction with Giuseppe Brusati, who became C. Arcucci's adopted son in 1668. (Decr. 462; see L Neppi, *Palazzo Spada,* Rome, 1975, 207, n. 4.)
1667 Sept. 3	Borromini's death.
1668 ff.	Chapel of S. Carlo (Spada Chapel) by Carlo Rainaldi. (Cat. 102.)
1669–74	East wing of the service courtyard. (Cat. 102.)
1673–75	Rainaldi's screen wall along the east side chapels of the Vallicella. (Cat. 102, 103.)

11.   Architects 1667–1785

1667 Feb. 25	Giuseppe Brusati Arcucci under C. Rainaldi. (Decr. 462.)
1681–82	Marco Antonio Pinselli under Rainaldi. (Decr. 520, 521.)
1685	Tommaso Mattei under Rainaldi. (Decr. 532.)
1690	One Sig.re Felice "cum futura successione al Cav.re Rainaldi." (Decr. 543.)
1691	Rainaldi's death. Mattei and Sig. Felice share the post. (Decr. 544.)
1707	Proposal to remove Mattei. (Decr. 552.)
1711	Mattei deprived of annual salary but left with other emoluments. (Decr. 557.)
1725–45	Francesco Ferruzzi. (Cat. 113.)
1745	Antonio Ferruzzi and Giovanni Fiori. (Decr. 599.)
1749	Luigi Vanvitelli proposed if Fiori leaves the post. (Decr. 603.)
1785	Raffaele Fiori "nostro architetto" dies. Girolamo Masi appointed in his place. (Decr. 621, 626.)

12.   Alterations of the Casa 1651–1924 (Chapter 4)

1651–64	Oratory altar rebuilt. (Cat. 48.)
1653	Closing of some arches on the ground floor in the first court.
1660	Closing of some *piano nobile* arches in the first court.
1665–67	Expansion of the library *salone* and the oratory facade. (Cat. 76, 100, 101.)
1709	*Orologio* given a six-hour dial. (Cat. 89.)
1788	Romanelli's vault fresco in the oratory replaced by P. Angeletti's *Divine Wisdom.* (Chapter 3, n. 28.)
1798–1800	Occupation by foreign troops. *Orologio* given a twelve-hour dial once again. (Cat. 89.)
1871–72	Transformation of the casa into a tribunal: construction of a large courtroom building in the garden courtyard, numerous partition walls introduced into the oratory and the rest of the casa. (Cat. 115.)

1922–24	Restoration of the entire casa. Room over the sacristy enlarged and its balcony window destroyed. (Cat. 115.)

13. Piazza della Chiesa Nuova and the Urban Context 1604–1940 (Chapter 6)

1604–12	Earliest project for a piazza in front of the church. (Cat. 5.)
1621	Vicolo di Pizzomerlo closed as the sacristy is begun.
1627	Urban VIII's bull authorizing the piazza and the Strada Nuova. (Doc. 7.)
1627–30	Maruscelli's piazza projects. (Cat. 17.) Construction of Strada Nuova and funnel-shaped piazza under Maruscelli. (Cat. 19, 36, 38, 98a.)
1637	Isola di Pizzomerlo demolished as the oratory is begun. (Cat. 38.)
1655	License to enlarge the piazza: first departure from Maruscelli's funnel shape. (Cat. 87.)
1659	Isola dei Piatetti demolished. (Cat. 38.)
1660	Spada appointed Commendatore of the hospital and bank of S. Spirito.
1661	Piazza di Monte Giordano squared off. Via dei Filippini on the west side of the casa enlarged. Banco di S. Spirito begun. (Cat. 97.)
1663–67	Banco di S. Spirito taken over by Orazio Spada and continued as a family palace. (Cat. 97.)
1673–75	Via della Chiesa Nuova opened along the east flank of the church and casa. (Cat. 103.)
1702	Extension of Via della Chiesa Nuova and squaring-off of the southeast corner of the piazza. (Cat. 105, 106.)
1743	Final expansion of the piazza. (Cat. 111, 112, 114.)
1885	Piazza absorbed into the Corso Vittorio Emanuele.
1908	Sanjust Plan: projects for a street from the Tiber north to the oratory facade and from the right side of the casa north to the Tiber.
1931–40	Projected street from the Ponte Mazzini to the oratory facade; demolitions stop at the Via dei Banchi Vecchi.

14. *Opus Architectonicum* 1647–1725

1647	Manuscript of a "piena relatione della fabrica" by Borromini and Spada. (Cat. 84–86.)
ca. 1649	Spada's *Dialogo.*
1650–53	Drawings for the manuscript by three anonymous draftsmen. (Cat. 84–86.)
1658	Three prints of the casa by Domenico Barrière published in F. Martinelli's *Roma ricercata.* (Cat. 89.)
ca. 1660	Borromini's project for publishing his complete works beginning with the oratory and S. Ivo. Barrière engaged as his engraver. (Cat. 90.)
1667	Part of the material collected for the complete works is destroyed by Borromini before his death. Barrière's plates survive. (Doc. 28.)
1684	Some of Barrière's plates published in altered form by G. J. De Rossi. (Cat. 104.)
1725	*Opus Architectonicum* by S. Giannini, which includes the manuscript of 1647 and one Barrière plate of the oratory facade. (Cat. 110.)

APPENDIX II

Paolo Maruscelli

Paolo Maruscelli (1596–1649) is one of the many minor Seicento figures waiting to be retrieved from the obscurity that closed in after his death, a man whose career can be traced and whose professional personality can be glimpsed through the drawings and library he left behind. According to Baglione, Maruscelli was a native Roman, one of the few among the many Lombards and Florentines on the Roman architectural scene.[1] To judge from his ornamental style he may have come out of the ambient of Giovanni Battista Soria. His connections with the Oratorians began in 1622 and led to his first active commission, the Chiesa Nuova for the Oratorians of Perugia, begun in 1626. He made his name as an architect of sacristies and houses for religious orders, particularly the Filippini, the Dominicans, and the Theatines. His masterpiece was the reconstruction of the Palazzo Medici-Madama in 1642. Afterward his career was deflected toward engineering, and his last years were spent in forming a company to drain the Pontine marshes. His unexpected death was announced on October 23, 1649 in a notice that called him a "famoso ingegniere." There is enough evidence to discuss six of his most important buildings in detail.

1. Chiesa Nuova of Perugia (1626–65)

The chronology of the church can be summarized briefly.[2] The foundations were begun in 1626 and fully approved by Maruscelli the following year, although the steep inclination of the ground caused difficulty and raised some doubts about their solidity. The main nave was finished in 1632 and vaulted in 1634. The small church of S. Giovanni Evangelista, which stood on the site of the crossing, was abandoned in 1635, and the foundations of the two crossing piers near the tribune were begun in 1640–41. Work was interrupted by the War of Castro, but in 1645–46 the sum of ∇1,200 was donated for the facade and work was resumed on the the tribune. In a letter of May 19, 1646, sent from Rome, Maruscelli expressed his delight that the facade had finally been begun according to his design, although he questioned the estimated cost on the basis of Roman rates for the working of travertine. Construction dragged on long after Maruscelli's death, and the facade was only finished in 1665.

The commission was a provincial attempt to copy obvious Roman precedents, particularly the Gesù.[3] The shallow transepts are only slightly wider than the side aisles; connected chapels flank a barrel-vaulted nave; a circular space stands behind each of the four crossing piers. A few ideas from S. Andrea della Valle, such as the clustered pilasters of the nave and tribune, are grafted onto the basic scheme. The facade is one of S. Susanna's numerous descendants, bereft of Maderno's columns and rich sculptural ornament. One of the few original features of the design occurs on the exterior, where a dramatic cluster of brick pilasters over countersunk panels marks the point where the right transept protrudes into the neighboring street.

2. Theatine House at S. Andrea della Valle (1629 ff.)

Some work had been begun on the convent as early as 1602 under an architect named Giuseppe Calcagni.[4] New construction was planned in 1623, and in 1629 Maruscelli's name first appears on a license to lay out the building "contigua a detta Chiesa verso la piazza detta de Fornari," on land that formerly belonged to the Massimi family.[5] Sixtus V's nephew, Cardinal Alessandro Peretti Damasceni, had been the patron of the church up to his death in 1623;[6] his posthumous generosity is commemorated in the inscriptions of the sacristy that bear his name.

A substantial portion of the present convent was built according to Maruscelli's scheme, which is preserved in an autograph drawing.[7] His work includes the main piazza facade, the entrance courtyard with the fountain in the center and the sacristy at the far end, and the corridor with twin travertine doors that connects the sacristy and the church (Fig. 114). The drawing shows paired pilasters on all sides of the first courtyard; in the end they were reserved exclusively for the entrance loggia. In 1638 Maruscelli's work is described as "begun"; his wing along the left side of the building stopped after a single bay, where a clear break is still visible in the brickwork; it was continued down the Via del Monte della Farina sporadically in campaigns that began in 1664, 1668, 1695, and 1698.[8]

Maruscelli's plan exhibits characteristic flaws in fenestration. The windows on each side of the sacristy are aligned with the bays of two flanking courtyards, each of a different size and shape, an arrangement that threatened to upset the symmetry of window placement inside the room. Maruscelli responded with an unsatisfactory compromise in which the windows on one side of the room (south, nearer to top of sheet) are set closer together as they progress from left or right. This is the type of design which Spada would later characterize as "falsi e solecismi d'architettura."[9] In fact such problems were usually solved in the final building if not in the drawing. The present sacristy at S. Andrea exhibits a rational fenestration. Three of the north windows match the courtyard loggia and one is blind; the four windows on the south mirror the north windows symmetrically.

The twin travertine doors in the entrance corridor to the sacristy are the predecessors of doors designed by Maruscelli at the Vallicella in 1634, just as the two sacristies themselves are similar. The S. Andrea sacristy depends more on fine stucco detailing for its effect, that of the Vallicella on frescoes and gilding. The designer of the *credenzoni* and marble *lavamani* at S. Andrea is undocumented, although they are compatible with Maruscelli's decorative style.

3. S. Maria dell'Anima, Sacristy (1636–44)

The decision of the German congregation to build a sacristy dates from 1618, although construction did not begin until 1634.[10] L. Holstenius and J. Savenier supervised the commission and chose Orazio Torriani as architect. The foundations were laid in 1635, but in April 1636 Maruscelli replaced Torriani. Expenses had been high, but otherwise the circumstances of the change are obscure, and Torriani continued in his official post as architect of the church. Romanelli's vault fresco was executed in 1638. The sacristy doors were completed in the spring of 1642, and by August of the following year a congregation could be held in the room, although its use as a sacristy proper did not begin until November 1644, and the decoration dragged on even after that date.

The plan of the room is basically a rectangle with the four corners cut off to produce an elongated octagon. The leftover space at the corners is used for service rooms or corridors, through which the two deep altar chapels are indirectly lit. Whether the octagon is Torriani's idea, or whether it represents Maruscelli's attempt to reduce the size and cost of an earlier project, seems impossible to tell on the basis of the present evidence. Of the eight lunette windows in the vault, four are blind and one is lit only indirectly from a neighboring courtyard. The rich stucco ornament is Maruscelli's, particularly the motif of the cornucopiae and of the baldachin tassels. The device of splitting a string course to carry it around a square frame has parallels in Maruscelli's projects for the Filippini and in the Palazzo Madama facade.

4. *S. Maria sopra Minerva: East wing of the Convent (1638–42)*

Baglione mentions three projects undertaken by Cardinal Antonio Barberini at S. Maria sopra Minerva: the new sacristy, the translation and installation of the shrine of S. Catherine of Siena, and the novitiate wing of the convent bordering on the Piazza di S. Macuto.[11] He attributes only the last expressly to Maruscelli. In any case, the first two present no particular affinities with Maruscelli's style. The sacristy may be the work of Andrea Sacchi, author of the *Crucifixion* that decorates its high altar.[12] It communicates via an iron grille with the chapel built in a classicizing style around the chapel of the saint, which was transported from the Collegio dei Neofiti in 1637–38.[13]

The novitiate wing on the east side of the convent was begun in 1638 and originally extended for ten bays to the south of the Piazza di S. Macuto. It was bounded on the south by a simple travertine pilaster and on the north by an elaborate corner pier bearing the Barberini arms and a date of 1640–41.[14] The shops which originally occupied the ground floor are now walled up. Each room on the main floor was equipped with a mezzanine reached by a small private stairway. Large double-loaded corridors which now serve as reading rooms for the Biblioteca Casanatense ran the entire length of the building on the upper floors and were lit by huge windows that face the Piazza S. Macuto. Falda's print of 1665 shows a wing of similar design extending west from the piazza in the direction of the Pantheon, but this part of the convent was altered or rebuilt in the nineteenth century. The enormous vaulted hall of the original Biblioteca Casanatense was begun in 1719 to the south of Maruscelli's wing; its short side continues his facade, minus the top story, for three additional bays.[15]

In the evolution of Roman institutional architecture, the generous, well-lit corridors of the Minerva convent stand roughly between Antonio Casone's convent at S. Marcello al Corso[16] and Borromini's Propaganda Fide. Apart from this one element, the unremitting functionalism of the design makes it the plainest in Maruscelli's *oeuvre*.

5. *Palazzo Medici-Madama (1642)*

The rebuilding of the Palazzo Madama in 1642 for Ferdinando II de' Medici was Maruscelli's most important commission, although the circumstances under which he received it are still unknown.[17] He renounced much of the grandeur of the earlier sixteenth-century projects, particularly those of Giuliano da Sangallo, Antonio da Sangallo the Younger, and Cigoli, who all had envisaged a much larger block and a direct connection with the Piazza

Navona. Maruscelli's facade was a more ornate version of the Farnese, three stories high and nine bays wide, bounded at each end by heavy stone quoins.[18] The central window opened onto a balcony and was crowned by the Medici arms. Mezzanine windows protruded into an elaborate frieze that recalled that of the Farnesina. The facade continued back on the left side for nine bays, four of them elaborate and five simple in design, a division that corresponded to no internal caesura. The heavy facade ornament combined two princely themes: Hercules and the lion of Leo X.

On the interior Maruscelli incorporated at least three existing structures: the church of S. Salvatore in Thermis (S. Salvatorello), the medieval Torre dei Crescenzi, and parts of the Renaissance palace including two columnar loggie.[19] The loggia facing the main courtyard was given a balustrade and enriched with typical Maruscellian detail. The main staircase occupied two bays on the left side of the courtyard, where irregularly spaced windows were installed to light the landings between floors. The main ceremonial room of the palace was a grand *salone* on the *piano nobile,* modeled on that of the Farnese; it rose two stories in height and was lit by ten facade windows extending from the central balcony to the right-hand corner of the building.[20] The *salone* was subdivided into two levels in 1755 and the lower room decorated with scenes from Roman history by C. Maccari in 1880; Maruscelli's ornate window frames remain the only testimony to the former grandeur of the room.

A Falda print of 1665 indicates that no building activity had yet taken place at the rear of the palace, toward S. Luigi dei Francesi and the Dogana.[21] In 1755 Benedict XIV bought the building from the Medici heirs and commissioned the architect Pietro Hostini to adapt it as the seat of the Governor of Rome, complete with prisons and tribunals.[22] It underwent extensive restorations by the architect Servi in 1849–53, when Pius IX installed the Ministry of Finance, the Direction of the Lottery, and the Office of the Public Debt in the palace, and adapted the rear wing as the headquarters of the papal postal service. The Italian Senate moved to the building from the Uffizi in 1871. The initial adaptations were made by Ing. L. Gabet. Gaetano Koch's library behind the Torre dei Crescenzi was added in 1888–89. S. Salvatorello was demolished in 1905–7 and a modern wing constructed from Maruscelli's building to the Piazza di S. Luigi. In 1926 the angle toward S. Eustachio was rebuilt in a heavy style by the architect Nori and an annex was installed in the structures on the small triangular *isola* between the palace and the Sapienza to the south. The Renaissance loggia on the south was extended and Maruscelli's chapel above it was demolished to create a closed bridge between the two buildings, now called the Galleria dei Eroi. The irregular blocks of houses near the main facade were demolished when the former piazza was incorporated into the Corso del Rinascimento.

6.   *Alterations to the Palazzo Spada-Capodiferro (1633–49)*

Prior to Cardinal Bernardino Spada's purchase of the Palazzo Capodiferro in 1632, he lodged at the Palazzo Cupis in Piazza Navona and briefly entertained the idea of refurbishing it along the lines of a project by Maruscelli.[23] However, he soon diverted his attentions to the Palazzo Capodiferro. In 1633–34 Maruscelli apparently enlarged the narrow sixteenth-century entrance atrium into a more spacious atrium with two vaulted side aisles, "li doi vestiboli à botte con camere à canne [à cante ?]."[24] In 1636, acting as *sottomastro di strade,* he signed the license conceding the street along the left side of the palace, the Vicolo dell'Arco or dell'Arcaccio, to the cardinal. The arch which formerly spanned the *vicolo* next to the palace facade was closed; the first 165 palmi of the street became part of

Spada's *giardino segreto;* the next stretch became a covered tunnel under a room and a long gallery built by Maruscelli in 1636–37; the final stretch as far as the Via Giulia was left open as a carriage road to Spada's stables. The gallery was built with rough brickwork at the end facing the Via Giulia but was never extended farther; Maruscelli reinforced its structure in 1646.[25] In 1641–42 he supervised the renovation of the three left rooms alongside the main courtyard, a task in which Bernini and Borromini also participated to some undetermined extent. Following a suggestion of Bernardino's, the central arch at the left of the courtyard was opened and a vista created through the palace wing and the *giardino segreto* to the wall of the Casa Massari opposite, where Maruscelli and G. B. Magni created a display of perspective, partly architectural but mostly painted. It was replaced in 1653 by the well-known perspective colonnade executed by Francesco Righi on instructions from the mathematician P. Giovanni Maria Bitonti.[26] The central room was closed from the courtyard by the transparent gate still in place, made up of balusters similar to those used slightly later, in 1643, in the Vallicella library.[27] Maruscelli remained active in Bernardino's service until his death in 1649, being involved in—among other things—decorative work on the cardinal's telescope and on the library shelves.[28]

Virgilio Spada employed Maruscelli to design schemes for redecorating two of his family chapels in Rome, one in 1631–32 at S. Andrea della Valle (first chapel on the right), and another in 1634 at S. Girolamo della Carità (first chapel on the right); the extent of Maruscelli's actual work, however, is unknown.[29] In 1641–49 Maruscelli was in charge of restructuring the Palazzo Spada-Veralli opposite Piazza Colonna on the Corso.[30] Virgilio is known to have criticized Maruscelli's work on the Palazzo Spada-Capodiferro at least twice: once implicitly, when he condemned structural flaws in the gallery, and once explicitly, when he deplored the aesthetic qualities of some unspecified proposal Maruscelli had made.[31]

Minor Works

Several minor attributions may be attached to Maruscelli's name, although they do little to clarify his personality or style. He designed the last chapel on the left of S. Carlo ai Catinari in 1635; it is unclear, however, whether the documents refer to the entire chapel or simply to the altar.[32] He restored or rebuilt the church of S. Maria dell'Umiltà at the foot of the Quirinal in about 1642; several extant altars there resemble his altar in the Vallicella sacristy of 1636–37 (Fig. 72).[33] He allegedly was active in the design of the Collegio Germanico at S. Apollinare; work went on in that complex in 1624 and in 1632–37, but the extent and nature of Maruscelli's participation is unknown.[34] At an uncertain date he designed new organs in the transept of S. Maria sopra Minerva, and some gilt stucco decoration in or near the Lateran sacristy.[35] He was employed at S. Spirito dei Napoletani on the Via Giulia in 1642, though it is unclear in what capacity.[36] His name appears in the records of two professional associations, the Accademia di S. Luca (ca. 1630) and the Congregazione dei Virtuosi (1640).[37] He served in a consulting capacity on three known occasions: the design of S. Ignazio in 1627,[38] the commission charged with investigating Bernini's campanile of St. Peter's in 1645,[39] and the restoration of the Pamphilj palace in S. Martino al Cimino in 1647.[40]

Maruscelli concluded his career as a hydraulic engineer in the service of Innocent X. In 1646 he was awarded a contract to drain the Pontine marshes in the neighborhood of Terracina, Piperna, and Sezze within a term of fifteen years. He died unexpectedly in 1649 at the age of 53.[41]

Maruscelli's Library and Drawing Style

Maruscelli's library of 123 volumes was inventoried at his death, and the list survives to testify to an active intellectual life.[42] He owned most of the major architectural classics: three editions of Vignola, two of Vitruvius, and one copy each of Labacco, Du Cerceau, Serlio, Domenico Fontana, Viola Zanini, and at least two of the five volumes of Soria's edition of Montano. He certainly knew Palladio's *Quattro libri,* but seems to have owned only the commentaries on Caesar. He had extensive holdings in military science and fortifications, an interest he shared with Bernardino and Virgilio Spada.[43] Literature on hydraulics and regulation of the Tiber appears alongside engineering classics like Besson, Biringuccio, del Monte, and Ramelli. The standard handbooks on perspective were complemented by three editions of Euclid, in addition to Danti·'s learned commentary on Euclidian optics and Accolti's popularization of it. Maruscelli could consult Cartari and Ripa in matters of iconography, Petrarch and Ariosto for literary references, Galileo on the uses of the compass; G. B. della Porta provided a dose of popular science. The literature on religion included biographies of the founders of those orders or congregations for which the architect worked. Six dictionaries in at least eight languages attest either to linguistic ability or to projected travel, particularly in the Levant. In comparison with Maderno, who owned only twenty-four books, Maruscelli's library signals the redawning of an age of erudition in the profession. Presuming a reasonable amount of overlap, it may be the best preliminary guide to Borromini's vast but mysterious holdings.[44]

Nearly thirty of Maruscelli's architectural drawings are preserved. He was an impeccably neat draftsman, whose technique of ruled ink with pink and yellow wash over a pencil outline seems to have been formed in the orbit of Girolamo Rainaldi. He was not at home with graphite, and was not used to working out the minutiae of a design on the preliminary plans, which occasionally left him open to charges of errors in design. He found it easier to master a convention than to rethink it: light, for instance, always descends from the left in his elevations, regardless of compass direction (Cat. 23a, 23c). He is one of the few baroque architects to leave an explicit statement on how architectural drawings were used in practice, from the small-scale sheets which were meant to give a general idea of the project, to the "disegno maggiore" made to guide the workmen, to full-scale drawings used to carve individual components.[45]

What, in the long run, was the significance of this active and varied career? In the eyes of contemporaries Maruscelli was probably considered a success, and even after the affair of the oratory he went on to win the commission of the Palazzo Madama, one which would have outranked any of Borromini's domestic works in secular importance. For the patron who took an active role in the design, this reliable and transparent personality was the perfect architect. He could guarantee a rational plan and solid construction at reasonable expense. He offered an ornamental repertoire adapted to the entire spectrum of seventeenth-century patronage, from Theatine austerity to Medici splendor. And yet there remains a deep-seated anonymity about Maruscelli which the drawings, documents, and books fail to dispel, an anonymity which continues to cloak his work and even to emerge as the keynote of his achievement. In contrast to Borromini, whose proud boast was that he would never have entered the profession only to become a copyist, Maruscelli was a programmatic copyist. His buildings fused a variety of well-known sources to convey a clear image of the status and aspirations of his patrons, but in so doing his personality became too diffuse to deflect the course of architecture, and his range too broad and his quotations too literal to reflect a coherent personal style.

Notes

When a catalogue number is referred to both in the text and in the accompanying note, the text reference is to the illustration and the note reference is to the catalogue entry.

Introduction

1. *Ricordi dati dalla S.ta di Papa Innocentio X⁰ a Padri della Congregatione dell'oratorio l'ultimo anno di sua vita,* MS of 1654, AV, A.V.2 bis, 52 ff.

2. There is no treatment of the urban monastic residence in, for instance, Serlio's sixth book on houses (M. Rosci, *Il trattato di architettura di Sebastiano Serlio,* Milan, 1966; S. Serlio, *On Domestic Architecture,* introduction by M. N. Rosenfeld, New York, 1978). The convent plans included in the treatises of Ammannati and Vasari the Younger are idealized rural or suburban plans with no bearing on the realities of institutional building in crowded urban quarters (B. Ammannati, *La città,* ed. M. Fossi, Rome, 1970, Pls. XII–XIV; G. Vasari the Younger, *La città ideale,* ed. V. Stefanelli, Rome, 1970, Pls. 13 and 15).

3. P. Pirri, S.J., *Giuseppe Valeriano S.I. architetto e pittore 1542–1596,* Rome, 1970, 64; P. Pecchiai, *Il Gesù di Roma,* Rome, 1952, 298. Basic documentation on the Casa Professa is provided in P. Pirri, S.J., *Giovanni Tristano e i primordi della architettura gesuitica,* Rome, 1955, 263; P. Pirri, S.J., "La topografia del Gesù di Roma e le vertenze tra Muzio Muti e S. Ignazio," *Archivium Historicum Societatis Iesu,* X, 1941, 177–217; Passeri-Hess, 216; and Hibbard, *Licenze,* nos. 30 and 66.

4. V. Giustiniani, *Discorso sopra la musica,* 1628, in A. Solerti, *Le origini del melodramma,* Turin, 1903, 115 ff., where the phrase is used in the context of musical criticism.

5. Examples of saints' rooms preserved in this manner occur in the convent of S. Maria sopra Minerva (discussed below in Appendix II); in the Casa Professa del Gesù (P. Tacchi Venturi, S.J., *La prima casa di S. Ignazio di Loyola in Roma e le sue cappellette al Gesù,* 2nd ed., Rome, 1951); and in the Casa dei Filippini itself (Cat. 27 below). Cardinal Cesi wanted his family arms on the house he planned to build for the Filippini (Ponnelle and Bordet, 405–7); when Cardinal Francesco del Monte renounced this right it was considered exceptional: "Ha fabricato un monastero [S. Urbano ai Pantani] senza iscritione et senz'arme contento del teatro della sua coscienza" (*avviso* quoted in L. Spezzaferro, "La cultura del cardinal Del Monte e il primo tempo del Caravaggio," *Storia dell'arte,* 9/10, 1971, 60). Haskell came to similar conclusions for the patronage of painting by the religious orders, where he perceived a "clash sometimes hostile, sometimes so smooth as to be imperceptible, between two different types of patron, one with the spiritual authority that came from having a saint as founder, the other with the money" (*Patrons and Painters,* New York, 1963, 65).

6. *Opus,* V, 12ʳ; *Dialogo,* 183.

7. *Opus,* 3ʳ.

Chapter I

1. Ponnelle and Bordet, 68–165; Smither, *Oratorio,* 39 ff.

2. Throughout the text "Oratory" is capitalized when it refers to the devotion or to the group of priests who sponsored it, the Congrega-

tion of the Oratory; on the other hand, "oratory" is used in the lower case when it refers to the room in which the devotion was held. The genesis of the oratory as a Roman architectural type is treated in M. Lewine, *The Roman Church Interior 1527–1580,* unpublished Ph.D. diss., Columbia University, 1960.

3. Ponnelle and Bordet, 144, 166–73, 202–12, 253–56, 263–67; and the passage from Baronius, *Annali,* I, 160, quoted in Smither, *Oratorio,* 49.

4. Ponnelle and Bordet, 257–63, and 310 ff. A photograph of S. Orsola prior to demolition is published in *GR,* Ponte, IV, 13, and in Smither, *Oratorio,* 45.

5. Ponnelle and Bordet, 271–317.

6. Ponnelle and Bordet, 374.

7. Ponnelle and Bordet, 328 ff., 363–89, 431–45, 557–67; Gasbarri, 47 ff.; and P. Totti, *Ritratto di Roma moderna,* Rome, 1638, 227.

8. H. Jedin, *A History of the Council of Trent,* St. Louis, 1957, I, 439; Ponnelle and Bordet, 99–105.

9. The appearance of the area in antiquity is discussed in S. Platner and T. Ashby, *A Topographical Dictionary of Ancient Rome,* Oxford and London, 1929, 152 and 508 ff.; E. Nash, *Pictorial Dictionary of Ancient Rome,* London, 1968, I, 57 ff. and 393; Russo, "Piazza della Chiesa Nuova," 21–23; *GR,* Ponte, II, 5 ff., and III, 5–8. In the seventeenth century the ruins beneath the casa were identified as ancient sculptors' workshops on the strength of the quantities of marble that emerged from the foundation excavations as well as by the presence of metal tools and unfinished heads (R. Lanciani, *Storia degli scavi di Roma,* Rome, 1912, IV, 68 ff.).

10. The alignment of one large ancient building can be ascertained from a continuous Roman wall that appears to run under the left side of the church—or more precisely, under the balustrades of the left side chapels—and to continue through the middle of Borromini's oval refectory. It was discovered in two stages: first during excavations for the church in 1575 (Ponnelle and Bordet, 340), and then during foundation work on the refectory in 1638 (*Opus,* XXIV, 67^v).

11. *Opus,* I, 4^r.

12. The Via di Parione and the Via del Pellegrino are discussed in U. Gnoli, *Topografia e toponomastica di Roma medioevale e moderna,* Rome, 1939, 106–8, 205, 219 ff.; P. Tomei, *L'architettura a Roma nel quattrocento,* Rome, 1942, 15–19; T. Magnuson, *Studies in Roman Quattrocento Architecture,* Stockholm, 1958, 23–33; *GR,* Ponte, III, 48 ff., and IV, 62 ff.; *GR,* Parione, I, 6 ff., 94 ff., and II, 64 ff. The trades are listed in F. Martinelli,

Roma ricercata, 3rd ed., Rome, 1658, 475–85. The brick paving is mentioned in a document of 1587, "La Strada di Ponte sino alla chiavica di S. Lucia amatonata" (F. Cerasoli, "Notizie . . . di molte strade," *Bullettino Comunale,* XXVIII, 1901, 346 and 356). The Piazza di Monte Giordano is treated in R. Lanciani, *Storia degli scavi di Roma,* Rome, 1904, I, 114, and II, 232 ff.; *GR,* Ponte, II, 30–40; and F. Martinelli, *op. cit.,* 2nd ed. of 1650, 28, where it is described as the "piazza de' Regatieri slargata da Paolo III." The corporation of the *rigattieri,* which was installed in the church of S. Cecilia a Monte Giordano from 1595 to 1599, is discussed in G. Morelli, *Le corporazioni romane di arti e mestieri,* Rome, 1937, 251 ff.

13. Huelsen, *Chiese,* 224 ff.; Ponnelle and Bordet, 315; Hibbard, *Licenze,* no. 40 and Fig. 41.

14. AV, A.V.14, transcribed in Gasbarri, 211. The condition of the area prior to 1575 is studied in M. T. Russo, "Appunti sull'antica parrocchia vallicelliana," *Studi offerti a Giovanni Incisa della Rocchetta,* Rome, 1973, 89–115.

15. The best discussion of the church is Hess, "Chiesa Nuova," which supersedes E. Strong, *La Chiesa Nuova (S. Maria in Vallicella),* Rome, 1923, 50–65; there is further material in Ponnelle and Bordet, 339–47 and 404–19.

16. Hess, "Chiesa Nuova," Figs. 1 and 2.

17. Ponnelle and Bordet, 348–51, especially 351, n. 2.

18. Hess, "Chiesa Nuova," 355; *Dialogo,* 172.

19. Ponnelle and Bordet, 348–51 and 404–15, which remains the most perceptive treatment of Cesi's patronage; in addition, there is genealogical information on the Cesi family in E. Martinori, *I Cesi,* Rome, 1931, and some new letters in M. T. Russo, "I Cesi e la Congregazione dell' Oratorio," *Studi Romani,* XC, 1967, 101–63; XCI, 1968, 101–55.

20. Hess, "Chiesa Nuova," 355–59.

21. Ponnelle and Bordet, 414 ff.; Hess, "Chiesa Nuova," 359–61; Hibbard, *Maderno,* 43, 137 ff.

22. Ponnelle and Bordet, 408 ff. The caption document accompanying Fig. 124 (transcribed in Gasbarri, 211–21) provides the basic dates for the acquisition of property.

23. Cat. 1–3.

24. Ponnelle and Bordet, 378, 426, 482, 565 ff.

25. *Opus,* I, 4^r.

26. The principal document on the old casa is a poem composed by Padre Giacomo Bacci in 1643 on the occasion of the move to the new building (*L'a Dio del p. Bacci all'amata Vallicella nel partirsi per Monte Giordano, alla nova abitazione,*

Bibl. Vall., 0 57², fasc. 64, fols. 530ʳ–531ᵛ.)

27. Cat. 4 and 103. *Opus,* XXI, 57ʳ speaks of a "door for wagons and haulers *(sportaroli)* as used to exist in the first residence."

28. Cat. 77.

29. Ponnelle and Bordet, 120, 403 ff.

30. Doc. 10, clause 2; Ponnelle and Bordet, 347, n. 7.

31. Cat. 4.

32. D. Alaleona, *Storia dell'oratorio musicale in Italia,* Milan, 1945, 42.

33. Decr. 18 and 25, quoted below in Chapter 5, n. 71; and Decr. 118, quoted below in Cat. 40.

34. Cat. 103.

35. The three drawings showing the Barnabite project of 1611 are found in Bibl. Vall., 0 57², fol. 348, and in AV, C.II.8, nos. 107 and 108. The relevant documents are published in G. Incisa della Rocchetta, "La chiesa di S. Carlo sulla piazza di Monte Giordano," *Strenna dei Romanisti,* XXII, 1961, 43–48; see also *Dialogo,* 173; and Doc. 3.

36. House no. 37 on Cat. 14 and no. 42 on Cat. 15 were both purchased in 1611.

37. Russo, "Piazza della Chiesa Nuova," 37.

38. The dates of house acquisitions are given in the caption document accompanying Cat. 15 (transcribed in Gasbarri, 211–21).

39. Decr. 9, 34, 35 (the last quoted below in Cat. 39); Huelsen, *Chiese,* 225; Russo, "Piazza della Chiesa Nuova," 38; Gasbarri, 218, no. 51.

40. Cat. 6, 7.

Chapter 2

1. *Opus,* III, 8ʳ. The primary source for Arconio's career is Baglione, *Le vite de pittori, scultori, et architetti,* Rome, 1642, reprint 1935, 327–29. According to Baglione, Arconio lived to the age of sixty; if 1635 is indeed the correct date for his death (G. Eimer, *La fabbrica di S. Agnese in Navona,* Stockholm, 1970, I, 183), he would have been born in 1575. His known works are his own house in the Spoglia Christi area of Rome; a fresco over the portal of the nearby church of S. Maria in Campo Carleo (Nolli 121; Huelsen, *Chiese,* 319); completion of S. Isidoro, including the convent and high altar; the Merenda Chapel in S. Maria della Vittoria; the portal of S. Eufemia (Nolli 115); and the restoration of S. Urbano ai Pantani, including construction of a convent, under the patronage of Cardi-

nal Francesco Maria del Monte (Nolli 103; C. Ceschi, "S. Urbano ai Pantani," *Capitolium,* IX, 1933, 380–91; C. Frommel, "Caravaggios Frühwerk und der Kardinal Francesco Maria del Monte," *Storia dell'Arte,* 9/10, 1971, 10 and 14; and L. Spezzaferro, "La cultura del cardinal Del Monte e il primo tempo del Caravaggio," *Storia dell'Arte,* 9/10, 1971, 60). In addition, Arconio built the gateway and other structures for the Villa Sannesi on the Via Flaminia, as well as the garden portal for the same family in the Borgo. At some point he was in the employ of the Oratorians' powerful neighbor, Paolo Giordano. In 1627 he was one of the architects consulted on the design of S. Ignazio (Pollak, 148, reg. 411).

2. Doc. 4.

3. Cat. 8, 9.

4. Normally the term *misure* is used to refer to assessments of the value of work completed (Hibbard, *Maderno,* 377; Eimer, *La fabbrica di S. Agnese in Navona,* I, 212, n. 6). The reasons for interpreting Arconio's mistakes as errors of alignment rather than errors of assessment are outlined below in Cat. 9.

5. Doc. 5.

6. Maruscelli's career is discussed below in Appendix II.

7. Cat. 20.

8. Maruscelli's familiarity with Bolognese architecture is attested by a later document, dated 1647 (Eimer, *La fabbrica di S. Agnese in Navona,* I, 201).

9. The vistas follow these paths on Cat. 21: first, from 1 to 17; second, from 10 to 8; third, from 43 over 18, 20, 21, 22, and 23. An unpublished plan in the Albertina (Alb. 611) shows a precedent for this idea in S. Maria ai Monti, where a vista runs across the nave of the church to the end of the adjacent sacristy.

10. Decr. 10–12, 26, 27, 31. The bibliography on Spada is given below in Chapter 7, n. 8.

11. These notes are transcribed below in Cat. 20.

12. *Dialogo,* 183.

13. *Dialogo,* 183–86. Spada claimed to have invented the three-court layout of the casa, the *loggie scoperte,* and the sunken corridors (all of which are possible since they appear in Maruscelli's projects), as well as other features that should certainly be associated with Borromini, such as the giant order, the fourth floor vaults, and the loggie closed to the weather in the second courtyard.

14. *Dialogo,* 182.

15. Cat. 20; Hess, "Chiesa Nuova," 356 ff The role of the *consulta* in Jesuit practice is documented in J. Vallery-Radot, *Le recueil de plans*

d'édifces de la Compagnie de Jésus conservé à la Bibliothèque Nationale de Paris, Paris, 1960, 6 ff.; and P. Pirri, S.J., *Giuseppe Valeriano S. I. architetto e pittore 1542–1596,* Rome, 1970, 60 ff.

16. The advice offered by the consultants is discussed below in Cat. 20 and 23; the key document which illustrates the working of the *consulta* is Decr. 32,

17. Cat. 23.

18. Cat. 17.

19. Decr. 34, 35, 37 (the latter two quoted below in Cat. 39); Hibbard, *Licenze,* 100; Huelsen, *Chiese,* 224 ff.

20. Pollak, 431 ff., regs. 1699–1749; Decr. 42, 44–50, 52–54, 56, 57, 60, 71–73, 76, 77, 84–86, 94, 95, 97, 100.

21. Decr. 64, 66, 68, 69, 76.

22. Cat. 25, 66; Doc. 11, 12; Decr. 60, 69, 76, 77, 83.

23. Pollak, 436, reg. 1750; Decr. 63, 65, 69.

24. Cat. 24.

25. Decr. 84–86.

26. Cat. 27.

27. Cat. 28.

28. Maruscelli's work at S. Andrea della Valle is discussed in Appendix II.

29. *Opus,* XVII, 49[v]:

> Not forgetting to mention that in the corridors or portions of loggie which I found already built between the church and the sacristy on both floors, the molding *(cimasa)* ran under the impost of the vault without any apparent support, and the only protruding members were the pilasters supporting the footings *(peduccio)* of the vault. I was afraid that if the same articulation were continued, it would not only be boring, but would make the loggie appear too low. I decided to break it up by putting molding only at the footing of the vault, to leave the rest empty, and to put a pair of *membretti* next to each pilaster. It really seemed to me advantageous in making the loggie look decently high.

Although both systems of articulation can be found in Cinquecento architecture, Borromini's is somewhat more canonical (cf. the Farnesina, porch of S. Maria in Domnica, Sapienza). Maruscelli's system makes more sense at S. Andrea della Valle (Fig. 114), where a barrel vault covers a corridor without pilasters and the molding is continuous with the crowning motif of the portals. The articulation of the ground floor corridor at the Vallicella is repeated on the *piano nobile* in

the four bays completed by Maruscelli, although at present the shelves of the Archivio Capitolino obscure the contrast between his work and Borromini's. Borromini planned to duplicate Maruscelli's system on the west side of the sacristy (Fig. 6), but the more conventional *membretti* were used when this part of the casa was built by Arcucci in 1660.

30. A. Palladio, *Quattro libri,* Venice, 1570, II, vi, 30. Maruscelli's project is closer to the woodcut, which shows the building in reverse, than to the actual building, which was begun in 1560 and partly burned in 1630; see G. Zorzi, *Le opere pubbliche e i palazzi privati di Andrea Palladio,* Venice, 1965, 240–47; E. Bassi, *Il Convento della Carità,* Vicenza, 1971; and the remarks on the ambitions of the patrons in J. Ackerman, *Palladio,* Harmondsworth, 1966, 156.

31. L. Heydenreich and W. Lotz, *Architecture in Italy 1400 to 1600,* Harmondsworth, 1974, 297 and Pl. 322; W. Hiersche, *Pellegrino de' Pellegrini als Architekt,* Parchim i. M., 1913, 34–37 and Fig. 8; C. Baroni, *Documenti per la storia dell'architettura a Milano,* II, Rome, 1968, 243–72.

The so-called *canonica* incorporated a wing formerly used by the Spanish governor and his court (Baroni, 260, Doc. 759). It was intended to serve as the residence of visiting prelates, of Cardinal Borromeo himself, and of the entourage surrounding the cardinal, which Borromeo wanted to place under the direction of a disciple of Filippo Neri, Costanzo Tassone, in 1566 (Baroni, 265, Doc. 775; Ponnelle and Bordet, 272). The documents cited by Baroni (especially 261, Doc. 763) convey Borromeo's negative attitude towards ornament in the residence:

> I tell you I want no sort of ornament; therefore attend only to making it comfortable as a residence, not taking trouble with unnecessary beauty.

32. Ponnelle and Bordet, 271–79, 330–39, 374 ff.; *Opus,* I, 4[r].

33. Ponnelle and Bordet, 284.

34. Cat. 102.

35. The building is attributed variously to Venturi, Bolini, De Battistis, and Soria in the older guidebook literature, which is surveyed by H. Hibbard, *The Architecture of the Palazzo Borghese,* Rome, 1962, 73 ff., n. 6. Before the *famiglia* palace evolved as a separate type, it was normal for the retinue to live in the main family palace, often in rooms adapted "ad uso di celle de frati" (P. Tomei, "Un elenco dei palazzi di Roma del tempo di Clemente VIII," *Palladio,* III, 1939, 172, 221, and 224). The Palazzo della

Famiglia Borghese was hardly completed when it served as the model for a private residence, the Palazzo del Bufalo on the Piazza Colonna, begun in 1626 (Hibbard, *Licenze,* no. 141 and Fig. 50); the Barberini wanted to rival the Palazzo della Famiglia Borghese in 1626–28 (BV, Barb. lat. 4360, 54 ff.: "Delle stanze per la famiglia su la strada felice"); and the Ludovisi finally erected a very similar residence for their own *famiglia* between 1659 and 1664 on the west side of the Piazza Colonna (shown in a Lieven Cruyl view of 1664 in *Röm. Ved.,* II, Pl. 77). The sociological literature on the Renaissance *famiglia* is still slight, but there is at least one detailed study of a single retinue (L. Dorez, *La cour du Pape Paul III,* 2 vols., Paris, 1932) and one interesting overview (P. Partner, *Renaissance Rome 1500–1559,* Berkeley, 1976, 113–59).

36. Cat. 20, *List of preliminary ideas:* "Rooms for fathers on the *piano nobile . . .* similar to a room on the *piano nobile* of the new palace of Cardinal Borghese, specifically the one facing the courtyard in the middle of the loggia next to the stables."

37. Cat. 20a, caption no. 17.

38. AV, C.II.8, no. 162 (a ground floor plan measuring 48.8 × 37.4, with a scale of 100 p. = 15.3 cm.), and no. 161 (a *piano nobile* plan measuring 48.7 × 36.8). Both drawings are unlabeled and unpublished.

39. Ponnelle and Bordet, 377.

40. The ideal of the golden mean is discussed in Ponnelle and Bordet, 189 and 321, and formulated more cogently still in a letter of 1634 from Padre Bacci in Rome to Padre Pietro Bini in Florence, protesting Bini's attempt to introduce austere practices into the Oratorian community there:

> Here in Rome one hears that both of you have renounced your property to the fratelli, something which is against the Institute of the Saint and against the intentions of the Grand Duke, who does not want to increase the number of houses which have to go out and beg. In addition it is said that laymen have been urged to separate from their wives, a practice which, since it is extraordinary *(haver del trascendente),* is not the way of our Institute, which flees everything which is out of the ordinary *(ogni cosa che habbia del singolare)* even if it is in itself good. . . . Our way is this: we live as secular priests, with joy, having an ordinary life without anything exceptional *(singularità),* attending only to the simple word of God, to prayer at

its time, to frequenting the sacraments and encouraging others to do so too, provided they do so freely, keeping our own property, eating moderately but not austerely, and keeping rooms that are not sumptuous, but not poor either, as you have very well observed in Rome. (A. Cistellini, "I primordi dell'Oratorio filippino in Firenze," *Archivio Storico Italiano,* CXXVI, 1968, 209–11.)

41. *Opus,* V, 12^r.

42. Ponnelle and Bordet, 315–17.

43. Respectively Tassone, Tarugi, Borla, and Antoniano (Ponnelle and Bordet, 272, 279, 431–33, 525).

44. Decr. 18 and 25.

45. *Opus,* III, 8^r.

Chapter 3

1. *Dialogo,* 181. Three modern theories of how Borromini was introduced into the Congregation's service must be rejected at the outset, since each of them involves misdating some aspect of his work.

First, Hempel (49 ff. and 62) supposed that Borromini first met Virgilio Spada in 1632–36, while working on the Palazzo Spada-Capodiferro, which had just been purchased by Virgilio's brother, Bernardino. Borromini did indeed work on the palace, but the commonly accepted date of 1632–36 is erroneous. Borromini was not involved with the palace until 1641, and did not work there in earnest until 1650 (L. Neppi, *Palazzo Spada,* Rome, 1975, 149 ff.). Virgilio himself said that he did not know Borromini before the architect appeared at the Casa dei Filippini, and that he was actually Saluzzi's discovery (*Dialogo,* 182); this claim should be accepted at face value. Not only Borromini, but most of the other architects who worked on the Palazzo Spada worked first on the casa: Maruscelli is first documented at the casa in 1622 and at the palace in 1633; Arcucci began at the casa in 1652 and at the palace in 1658; Pinselli is mentioned at the casa in 1681 and at the palace in 1683 (Appendix I; Neppi, *Palazzo Spada,* 293).

Second, Bruschi ("Il Borromini nelle stanze di S. Filippo," *Palatino,* XII, 1968, 13–21) maintained that Borromini began his work at the casa in 1635–36 with the design of several ornamental doorframes in the area of the saint's rooms (Fig. 77). While these details are indeed by Borromini, an examination of circulation patterns in this part of the casa indicates a date of 1638–39, well after Borromini had begun the oratory (Cat. 27). Bruschi did perceive, however, that the design involved consultations with outside architects rather than a competition (20, n. 6).

Third, Haskell suggested that Borromini was chosen in 1637 after his plan for S. Carlo alle Quattro Fontane had become known: ". . . there can therefore be no doubt that the Oratorians were deliberately hoping for an architect whom their Carmelite brothers found admirable for his revolutionary qualities" (*Patrons and Painters,* New York, 1963, 76). In a forthcoming study of S. Carlo, I will argue that the complex was not only built gradually (residence in 1634–35, cloister in 1635–36, church in 1638–41), but also designed gradually, in a manner rather similar to the Casa dei Filippini. A key point in this argument is a passage in Fra Juan di San Bonaventura's *Relazione* (Pollak, 44 ff., reg. 225):

> The residence and cloister were already finished when Padre Giovanni, wanting to begin the fabric of the church, had Borromini make the design. . . . But the monks of this convent were repelled by the thought of building the church according to that design, which they did not want to accept.

The crisis between the monks and the architect, I would argue, came to a head in February 1638, and is reflected by the drastic changes which Borromini introduced on Alb. 171, when the original design for the church was severely reworked, a sacristy introduced for practical considerations, and the Barberini Chapel introduced in an attempt to attract Cardinal Barberini's support and patronage. According to this line of reasoning, neither the design for the church nor any of the early facade designs would have been known to anyone before the crisis of February 1638, which was nine months after Borromini had been chosen by the Filippini and the oratory begun.

2. Cat. 24, 28.

3. Pollak, 440, reg. 1787, and 425, reg. 1640; *Dialogo,* 182, n. 24. The *decreti* (101–103) which describe the circumstances surrounding the change of architect are quoted in Incisa della Rocchetta, *Dialogo,* 182, n. 23.

4. *Opus,* III, 8^r; VI, 13^r–14^r; 15^v.

5. *Dialogo,* 181.

6. Saluzzi was Preposito from 1617 to 1623 and again from 1632 to 1638. He died on Dec.

1, 1638 and left a legacy of ▽7,000 for the construction of the casa (Decr. 125; Gasbarri, 162, 199; *Dialogo,* 175, n. 11, and 176, n. 13).

7. Cat. 29–33. In addition, there are two drawings which stand outside the mainstream of development, namely, Cat. 34, which was unsolicited, and Cat. 35, which may possibly be a late drawing by Maruscelli.

8. Fra Juan di San Bonaventura, *Relatione,* 1650–52, in Pollak, 41, reg. 225.

9. D. Fontana, *Della trasportazione dell'obelisco,* Rome, 1590; E. Iversen, *Obelisks in Exile,* Copenhagen, 1968, I, 29 ff.; Hibbard, *Maderno,* 156 ff.; R. Wittkower, "S. Maria della Salute," *JSAH,* XVI, 1957, 3–10.

10. Hess, "Chiesa Nuova," 359; Ponnelle and Bordet, 414 ff.

11. The *consulta* of 1627 is discussed in Cat. 20 and 23, that of 1633–34 for the furniture of the sacristy in Cat. 24; there is a reference to the isolation of competitors in *Dialogo,* 184.

12. *Opus,* X, 35^v.

13. Borromini's *essatezza* is mentioned in Decr. 103; his role in the design of the sacristy altar is discussed in Cat. 28.

14. Spada used these words in a letter of 1630 to describe the situation of G. Finelli, whom he was trying to employ in the Spada Chapel in S. Andrea della Valle (M. Heimbürger Ravalli, *Architettura scultura e arti minori nel barocco italiano,* Florence, 1977, 77, n. 7); Borromini's explanation of his break with Bernini was similar: "I resented the fact that he got the honor for my work" (Doc. 28).

15. "Francesco Borromini, architect elected by the Congregation of the Four [Deputies]," in Decr. 105; this is reaffirmed in Decr. 350 and 351. The governing structure of the Congregation is discussed in Ponnelle and Bordet, 363 ff., and in Gasbarri, 47 ff.

16. On the Congregation's resistance to novelty see Chapter 2 above, n. 40; Chapter 5 below, n. 71 and n. 108; and Decr. 134, where it is decided that "non si innovo cosa alcuna."

17. *Opus,* 3^r.

18. The progress of construction is known from Pollak, 425 ff., regs. 1640–1656, and regs. 1787–1837, as well as from Decr. 101–155. The stucco contract is given in Doc. 15; according to Pollak, the work was carried out by Giovanni Maria Sorrisi between November 1638 and early 1640, and then it was subjected to an extensive critique by Borromini, which is given in Doc. 16. The physical isolation of the oratory for the first few years of its existence is discussed in Cat. 38.

The prelate invited to give the inaugural sermon in the oratory, Msgr. Alessandro Sperelli

(1589–1672; Decr. 153), eventually became involved in the dissemination of Borromini's style in the provinces. He was the patron of S. Maria del Prato in Gubbio, built in 1662 ff. as a full-scale copy of S. Carlo alle Quattro Fontane. Borromini knew of the church and provided at least one drawing, Alb. 1049, which bears the autograph inscription: "fatto p[er] al Sig. N . . . Cameriere del E.mmo Sig.re Card.le Carpegnia p[er] la chiesa che si fa in Agubi[o] simile a quella di S.to Car[lo] alle 4 fontane. 15 luglio 1665." Ulderico Carpegna had been bishop of Gubbio from 1630 to 1639, Alessandro Sperelli from 1644 to 1671 or 1672. Cf. C. Eubel, *Hierarchia Catholica,* Munich, 1913, IV, 183 ff.; M. Sarti, *De Episcopis Eugubinis,* Pesaro, 1755, 230 ff.; Anon., *Biografia di Monsignore Alessandro Sperelli,* Spoleto, 1872, 12 ff.; R. Schulze, *Gubbio und seine mittelalterlichen Bauten,* Berlin, 1915, Figs. 63–65; D. Pietro Baldelli, *Brevi cenni . . . Madonna del Prato,* mimeographed, ca. 1970. Construction documents for the church are to be found in the Archivio Storico di Gubbio, Fondo Congregazione di S. Francesco di Paola, X F/c 1 and X F/a 2.

19. The sixteenth-century oratory type is discussed in Lewine, *The Roman Church Interior, 1527–1580,* 1–49 and 72 ff.

20. *Opus,* VI, 16^r. The text mentions the collapse of one such vault in the Palazzo Alessandrino-Bonelli (Nolli 273). The palace was begun in 1585 (Hibbard, *Licenze,* no. 1), and was apparently originally designed to have a *salone* with a coffered ceiling, which is shown in a section drawing in the Accademia di San Luca, Fondo Mascarino, no. 2332; by the time of Ferrerio-Falda, Pl. 27, the *salone* is shown with a vault. The date of the accident mentioned in the *Opus* is not known.

21. The terminology comes from *Opus,* VI, 18^r and 19^v; and XV, 46^v–47^v.

22. Chains are faintly but quite definitely visible in Cat. 85b; according to Decr. 616, "the great chain put by Borromini where the crucifix stands above the musicians' choir" was rediscovered during repair work in 1759.

A structural explanation is usually advanced for an unusual feature of the east or entrance portico, namely, the stepped motif that partly fills the two small openings flanking the central arch (Fig. 34). In fact, the device contributes nothing to the strength of the portico; if it did, it would have been used in the west portico as well, which was considered the more perilous of the two (*Dialogo,* 207). Instead, the motif marks the point where two separate areas of design intersect, where the oratory and the entrance loggia meet each other, so to speak, back to back. Borromini was apparently critical of the way in which the stucco-worker Sorrisi left this awkward incongruity undisguised (Doc. 16, clause 6).

23. The comparison with S. Teresa was first made by R. Pommer, *Eighteenth-Century Architecture in Piedmont,* New York, 1967, 5; Pommer's remarks, though brief, remain the most perceptive analysis of the skeletal qualities in Borromini's architecture. There is further information on S. Teresa in Passeri-Hess, 216; L. Sebastiani, *Descrizione . . . Palazzo di Caprarola,* Rome, 1741, 110 ff. (where the church is correctly dated to 1621–26 but wrongly attributed to Martino Longhi the Younger); F. Fasolo, *L'opera di Hieronimo e Carlo Rainaldi,* Rome, 1961, 63–67 and Pls. 25–27; G. Eimer, *La fabbrica di S. Agnese in Navona,* Stockholm, 1970, I, 115 and Pls. XVIII.28 and XLII.60.

24. *Opus,* VI, 21^r.

25. *Opus,* VI, 20^r. The source of Borromini's famous image is something like Palladio's letter on the restoration of the Palazzo Ducale in Venice, where he claims that walls, like plants, should grow thinner and lighter as they rise. To the objection that man is thinner below and thicker above, Palladio replied that the human body was meant to be mobile, while buildings have to be stable; thus if a man holds his legs together he is easily pushed over (A. Magrini, *Memorie intorno la vita e le opere di Andrea Palladio,* Padua, 1845, 54 ff., with similar remarks in *Quattro libri,* Venice, 1570, I, 14 and 42). Maruscelli followed Palladio's advice that walls should grow thinner as they rise (Cat. 23), but Borromini did not (*Opus,* XV, 46^v).

In addition to the image of men alternating with trees, the *Opus* uses two other metaphors for the alternating balusters: they aid vision like a "carta forata" (?) and like the splayed jams of a gunport.

Originally there were alternating balusters in the porticoes at both ends of the oratory. Those in the musicians' choir were replaced by a solid architrave in 1652 ff., and the balusters themselves were sold in 1659 (*Dialogo,* 206; Decr. 358). Other instances of the motif in Borromini's work are listed in Cat. 49.

26. Doc. 15, clause 8.

27. John Evelyn, *The Diary of John Evelyn,* ed. E. S. de Beer, Oxford, 1955, II, 233.

28. The iconographical program was determined in April 1639, the time when Romanelli's vault fresco of the *Coronation* was begun (Cat. 40). The fresco was completed in June 1640; shown projected onto the plan by G. J. de Rossi

in 1684 (Cat. 104c); and removed in 1788, when a new fresco of *Divine Wisdom* was painted by Pietro Angeletti (Pollak, 446, reg. 1842; Decr. 624–627). Angeletti is better known for his *Apollo and Daphne* which decorates the vault above Bernini's statue group in the Villa Borghese (Thieme-Becker, I, 494).

29. *Opus,* VI, 18[r].

30. Such as the extraordinary analysis in E.-E. Viollet-le-Duc, *Entretiens sur l'architecture,* Paris, 1863, I, 266 ff.

31. L. Heydenreich and W. Lotz, *Architecture in Italy 1400–1600,* Harmondsworth, 1974, 297 ff.; Hibbard, *Maderno,* 121 and 201 ff.

32. *Dialogo,* 201–11; Cat. 48.

33. *Opus,* VII, 23[r].

34. The Oratory was held at various times in the church itself, in a stable in Padre Visconti's house, in rooms of the purchased convent of S. Elisabetta (Cat. 15, no. 7), and in the former sacristy adjoining the right transept of the church (Cat. 8), according to the documentation in Ponnelle and Bordet, 347; in Gasbarri, 215; and in Doc. 10, clause 2.

35. The Oratorio del SS. Crocefisso a S. Marcello is treated by J. von Henneberg, "An Early Work by Giacomo della Porta," *Art Bulletin,* LII, 1970, 157–71, and also by K. Schwager,

"Giacomo della Portas Herkunft und Anfänge in Rom," *Römisches Jahrbuch für Kunstgeschichte,* XV, 1975, 135; the Oratorio del Gonfalone is treated by L. Salerno in *Via Giulia,* 344 ff.; and the Oratorio della Caravita at the Collegio Romano is discussed below in Chapter 6, n. 6.

36. Giovenale Ancina, *Tempio armonico . . . ,* Rome, 1599. The frontispiece showing a church facade is illustrated in P. Damilano, *Giovenale Ancina musicista filippino (1545–1604),* Florence, 1956, Pl. III; and in Smither, *Oratorio,* 62, Fig. II.10. Curiously enough, the print shows a brick facade.

37. Expressed most clearly by Fra Juan di San Bonaventura, *Relatione,* in Pollak, 49 ff., reg. 225.

38. *Opus,* VII, 24[r].

39. Heimbürger Ravalli, *Architettura scultura e arti minori,* 37–42; K. Güthlein, "Die Fassade der Barnabiterkirche San Paolo in Bologna," *Römisches Jahrbuch für Kunstgeschichte,* XVII, 1978, 132–44.

40. *Opus,* VII, 24[r].

41. *Opus,* VII, 24[r]. The *ossatura* amounts to the part of a capital which could be drawn with compass and straightedge, omitting most freehand detail. Precedents for these bare capitals can be found on the columns in Michelangelo's Lauren-

Casa dei Filippini		Palmo	Roman foot
1647	Monte Giordano projection, fine work	8⅓	10½
1637	Oratory facade, lower story	7½	10
1637	Oratory projection, fine work	7½	10
1633	Maruscelli pilasters	6⅛	8¼
1638	Oratory facade, upper story	6	8
1637	Oratory projection, rough work	5	6½
1647	Monte Giordano projection, rough work	5	6 to 6½
Other buildings			
1510–20	Palazzo del Vescovo di Cervia	9	11½
1510	Palazzo Fieschi-Sora	8 or more	9 or more
1526	Palazzo Salviati-Adimari	8	10
1631	Palazzo Barberini, garden facade	7¾	9½
1516	Palazzo Baldassini	7½	9½
1644	Campidoglio, Palazzo Nuovo	7½	9⅓
1520–29	S. Maria di Loreto	7½	9
1563–66	Palazzo dei Conservatori	7	8⅔
1514	S. Maria dell'Anima	7	8⅔
1603	S. Susanna convent facade	6¾	9
1564	Sapienza, courtyard exhedra	6½	8½
1551	Villa Giulia facade	6	8
1599	Casa Professa del Gesù	5	6½
1598	Palazzo Mattei di Giove	4½	6
1568	Gesù, north side facade	4½	6
1581	Collegio Romano, south facade	4½	6

ziana vestibule (J. Ackerman, *The Architecture of Michelangelo,* New York, 1964, I, Pl. 17) which was kindly pointed out to me by C. Frommel, and on the background pilasters of Domenico Fontana's Cappella Sistina at S. Maria Maggiore.

42. Niche windows are found in the facades of S. Andrea in Via Flaminia and the Villa Giulia, and niche doors in the unexecuted project for the Gesù facade, as shown in Heydenreich and Lotz, *Architecture in Italy 1400–1600,* Pls. 275, 285, and 287. The Hadrianic vaults are discussed in A. Boëthius and J. Ward-Perkins, *Etruscan and Roman Architecture,* Harmondsworth, 1970, 254.

43. The terminology comes from Decr. 39, 40, 41, 104, 105, 127, 128, 129, 131, and 145.

44. Frommel, I, 8 ff., and Pls. 125 and 181a.

45. The preceding table gives some idea of the relative fineness of the brickwork found in the different parts of the Casa dei Filippini as well as in other sixteenth- and seventeenth-century buildings. It includes both the number of courses per palmo (22.3 cm.) and per ancient Roman foot (29.5 cm.), so that comparisons can be made with ancient models. However, in contrast to the situation in ancient architecture, the table makes it clear that relative fineness of brickwork is not a function of date but only of fashion and of the patron's budget.

46. Vincenzo Giustiniani (d. 1637), Discourse on Architecture, in the form of an undated letter in G. Bottari and S. Ticozzi, *Raccolta di lettere sulla pittura ed architettura,* Rome, 1822, VI, 112 ff.:

> The first way of doing the facade veneers of palaces and other noble buildings in Rome is in brick, either rough as they come from the kiln, or *arrotati a secco* and stuccoed with care, as one sees in the facade of the Collegio Romano, of the convent of the Gesù, and elsewhere; or *arrotati con acqua,* and stuccoed with greater care, as one sees in the facade of the Palazzo Farnese, in the flanking facades of S. Susanna, or in the modern structures of S. Maria Maggiore, and in other places I do not remember. This way is not generally used since it is of more than middling expense, even though it turns out to be beautiful and long-lasting, since it resists the influence of both air and fire, and for that reason the Jesuit fathers are accustomed to using it more than others, as men who exquisitely observe the beginning, the progress, and the end of all their actions.

47. *Opus,* VII, 25[r]; Boëthius and Ward-Perkins, *Etruscan and Roman Architecture,* 245–63, 275–78, and Pls. 125 and 146.

48. Benedetto Mellini, *Dell'antichità di Roma,* BV, Vat. lat. 11905, n.d. [1656 and after], fol. a:

> Il Palazzo dei Laterani si tiene communemente, che fosse nel sito, dove fu da Constantino Magno fabricata la Basilica del Salvatore, detta hoggi S. Giovanni in Laterano . . .
>
> Per discorre con qualche probabilità della grandezza di questo Palazzo, io osservo tre tempi: Il primo è della Republica, quando la Famiglia Laterana cominciò ad ingrandirsi, et a rendersi conspicua fra l'altre, et all'hora io stimo, che l'palazzo d'essa famiglia occupasse sito non così grande, come negl'altri due tempi susseguenti; del qual sito eran probabilmente quei vestigij, che l'anno MDCLVI furno scoperti dal Cavalier Fran.co Borromini Architetto della Basilica Lateranense: il quale nel voler fondare la nuova Cappella, che è in capo alla Nave de Padri Penitenzieri, scopri quaranta palmi sotto, i vestigij d'un grande edificio, con pilastri di terra cotta, e col pavimento di mattoni rossi, non essendo in quei tempi in uso per le fabriche private i marmi, i quali si mesero in uso in tempo, che introducendosi in Roma il lusso asiatico, diede la Republica l'ultimo crollo.

Opus, VI, 18[r] mentions a similar excavation under the Lateran, but implies a date of about 1646–47, just prior to the completion of the manuscript:

> . . . and lately (*ultimamente*) I observed this in an excavation conducted for the illustrious Marchese del Bufalo near the hospital of S. Giovanni in Laterano, where in a temple found underground there were piers (*pilastri*) in the corners which supported the vault.

Apparently the influence of ancient brickwork was also once apparent in the floor of the tempietto of S. Giovanni a Porta Latina, which was restored by Borromini in 1658; it was described in G. M. Crescimbeni, *L'istoria della chiesa di S. Giovanni avanti Porta Latina,* Rome, 1716, 67:

> . . . with unusual fantasy (*bizzaria*) the pavement is built of those enormous tiles of terra cotta which were in use among the ancient Romans, from the ruins of whose buildings they are daily quarried; and they are called *Tavolone;* and to make its appearance more

beautiful, there has been worked onto it a pattern or engraving *(un lavoro d'intaglio, o delineamento)* in imitation of the stucco pattern which ornaments the cupola, which is also lined up with the same octagon of the chapel.

49. The design of the side facade of S. Carlo seems to emerge after the heavy reworking of Alb. 171, which I assign to 1638 for reasons outlined above in n. 1. An important drawing for the side facade of S. Carlo, Alb. 292, has been mistakenly published as a drawing for the side projection of the oratory (Portoghesi, *Linguaggio,* Fig. xxxix, mislabeled as Alb. 337).

50. *Opus,* VII, 23^r; similar language is used in *Opus,* XXVIII, 79^v to describe the false bindings in the Biblioteca Vallicelliana.

51. The evidence for this reconstruction is presented in Cat. 41.

52. Hibbard, *Maderno,* 118–21 and Pl. 14b.

53. Hibbard, *Maderno,* 28–30, 40–43, and 68–70, which together provide a thoughtful analysis of the development of Roman facades.

54. Hess, "Chiesa Nuova," 361 and Figs. 9 and 10. The preliminary drawing for the print published by Hess is to be found in the Bibl. Ambrosiana, F 251 inf., D 95.

55. *Opus,* VII, 23^r.

56. As observed in A. Blunt, *Borromini,* Cambridge, Mass., 1979, 94.

57. Hempel mentions the curved facades of the Zecca, the Porta di S. Spirito, and the Palazzo di Pio IV on the Via Flaminia (70, n. 1). Borromini may have been aware of the curved facade of F. M. Ricchino's Collegio Elvetico in Milan, designed in 1627 or 1632 (Wittkower, 121; Eimer, *La fabbrica di S. Agnese in Navona,* I, 178 ff. and Figs. 96–99); but of course this is an institutional rather than an ecclesiastical facade. I hope to address the complex question of the influence of Cortona's SS. Martina e Luca on Borromini in another study.

58. *Opus,* VII, 25^r. The inventory of Borromini's possessions taken after his death in 1667 (*Ragguagli,* 162–76) lists several models in red wax and clay, including a wax "pezzo di modello" of the oratory facade.

59. Pietro Accolti, *Lo inganno de gl'occhi, prospettiva pratica,* Florence, 1625, 10 ff. Like much of Accolti's material, this particular proposition is taken from E. Danti, *La prospettiva di Euclide . . .,* Florence, 1573, 22. The principle of the arc of vision appears most clearly in a Bernini shop drawing of 1659 for the Piazza S. Pietro (Brauer-Wittkower, 81 ff., Pl. 162a); it shows the colonnade as curved in plan but flat in elevation, as though the circumference of a circle had been unrolled onto a flat plane. Maruscelli owned a copy of Accolti (Doc. 22); and Thelen (82, n. 2) felt that Accolti exerted an influence on the perspective of Borromini's drawings for the *baldacchino* of St. Peter's.

60. Blunt, *Borromini,* Cambridge, Mass., 1979, 30, gives a detailed analysis of these consoles, which are really a cross between a triglyph and a console, and their relation to the ornament on the attic of St. Peter's.

61. Cat. 41.

62. In some of the ornament on the facade of S. Susanna (Hibbard, *Maderno,* Pl. 13), and in Cortona's design of 1631 for the *cavallerizza* gate at the Palazzo Barberini (Thelen, C 64).

63. Borromini's drawings for the installation of the tomb of Urban VIII in St. Peter's (Thelen, C 35 and 36), which are strictly orthogonal elevations but still show the niche in perspective foreshortening, contain the germ of the idea used in the niche of the oratory facade.

64. Cat. 39, 79.

65. Cat. 98. Piranesi's idealized view of the facade, which omits the part of the projection to the left of the *bugnato,* is shown in E. Strong, *La Chiesa Nuova (Santa Maria in Vallicella),* Rome, 1923, Pl. XXXIII.

66. *Opus,* IV, 11^r.

Chapter 4

1. Cat. 38, 80.

2. C. Paola Scavizzi, "Le condizioni per lo sviluppo dell'attività edilizia a Roma nel sec. XVII: la legislazione," *Studi Romani,* XVII, 1969, 168.

3. *Opus,* III, 8^r.

4. Cat. 20; in *Dialogo,* 174, Spada speaks of "diversity of opinions" and a "great split among the spirits of the padri."

5. Cat. 39, 40, 58, 59; Decr. 127, quoted below in Cat. 40.

6. Cat. 27, 80.

7. *Opus,* XVI; Cat. 40, 58, 59, 84a.

8. The oval plan of the refectory was soon imitated in the refectory of the Hospice of the Trinità dei Pellegrini, shown in P. Letarouilly, *Edifices de Rome moderne . . .,* Paris, 1868, I, Pl. 9, room e. According to Decr. 253, the door to the "primo refettorio" at the Trinità dei Pellegrini was built under Spada's direction in 1650.

9. *Opus,* XXV; *Dialogo,* 185; Decr. 146, 166, 167; Cat. 61.

10. *Opus,* XX; Cat. 60.

11. According to payments in the Congregation's register of *Entrate et uscite,* 2855 (341), cc. 47 and 90, the *lavamani* fountains were installed rather later than might be supposed: Peschal was paid for "l'accomodamento fatto a' lavamani del refettorio" on July 13, 1647; and work was carried out on the water conduit on June 27, 1648 (a reference which I owe to the kindness of Lionello Neppi). In 1975 Borromini's one surviving fountain and a modern copy were reinstalled near their original location in the *lavamani* space.

12. *Opus,* XXII–XXIV; Cat. 84a.

13. *Opus,* XII, 39^{r-v}.

14. *Opus,* XIV; the shaft is now occupied by an elevator.

15. Decr. 152.

16. *Opus,* IV, 11^r; XXII–XXIV.

17. Compare the piers in the courtyard of the Palazzo del Bufalo a Piazza Colonna, begun in 1626 on the model of the Palazzo della Famiglia Borghese (Chapter 2, n. 35 above).

18. Cat. 27.II.

19. *Opus,* XIII, XV–XIX; Cat. 57, 61–64.

20. *Opus,* XV, 46^r; *Dialogo,* 183 ff. A warning against "aria colata" was given in 1647 at the Propaganda Fide (G. Antonazzi, "La sede della Sacra Congregazione e del Collegio Urbano," *Sacrae Congregationis de Propaganda Fide Memoria Rerum,* ed. J. Metzler, Rome-Freiburg-Vienna, 1971, 322, n. 85).

21. Decr. 152.

22. *Opus,* XIX, 53^r.

23. *Opus,* XIX, 53^r.

24. *Opus,* XIX, 53^r.

25. Cat. 89c.

26. *Opus,* XVIII.

27. Cat. 39, 66, 81.

28. *Opus,* X, 35^r.

29. *Dialogo,* 200.

30. Decr. 180, 182.

31. Decr. 146.

32. *Opus,* XXVI; see also Decr. 334 on lodging guests in the old casa in 1654.

33. Illustrated in Portoghesi, *Linguaggio,* Fig. 63.

34. Compare the plan of the campanile of S. Andrea delle Fratte (Alb. 114, illustrated in P. Portoghesi, *Roma barocca,* Rome, 1966, Fig. 164); the entrance vestibule of the Propaganda Fide (Portoghesi, *Linguaggio,* 385); and one of the Lateran ciborium projects (BV, Chigi P VII 9, fol. 6^r).

35. *Opus,* XXVIII; *Dialogo,* 188–93; Cat. 75–78, 86q–r, 99–101; Doc. 17 (ceiling contract), 18 (shelves), 19 (payments), 20 (medals), 23a–c (descriptions of interior); Pollak, 445 ff., regs. 1836, 1838–1841, 1843–1845. There is archival material in E. Pinto, *La Biblioteca Vallicelliana in Roma,* Rome, 1932, and in G. Incisa della Rocchetta, "Il salone della Biblioteca Vallicellana," *Palladio,* XXIII, 1973, 121–28.

In 1659–61 the "Libraria nuova da farsi" at S. Agostino was designed, especially in the arrangement of its annexes, on the model of the Vallicella library (Hempel, 175, Fig. 65).

36. A preliminary project for the Barberini Library is described in BV, Barb. lat. 4360, 26 ff; contemporary descriptions are given in Doc. 23d and in H. Tetius, *Aedes Barberinae,* Rome, 1642, 19 ff.; the original classification system is described in A. M. Bandini, *Commentariorum de vita et scriptis Ioannis Bapt. Doni . . . ,* Florence, 1755, xxx ff. According to Pollak, 330, reg. 930, Soria was paid ▽900 for the shelves in 1633; they are mentioned in their new location in J. Hess, "Some Notes on Paintings in the Vatican Library," in *Kunstgeschichtliche Studien zu Renaissance und Barock,* Rome, 1967, 178 ff. and Fig. 39. The exterior of the library on the south side of the palace is visible in the photographs published in A. Blunt, "The Palazzo Barberini," *Journal of the Warburg and Courtauld Institutes,* XXI, 1958, Pl. 23 c; Hempel, Pl. 4; and *Ragguagli,* 249, Pl. 4 (after Specchi, 1699).

37. *Dialogo,* 189, n. 38; Decr. 186, 187; and Cat. 40. The reference to the "forum of Nerva Traiano" in *Opus,* XXVIII, 77^r, seems to be a literary topos deriving from A. Labacco, *Libro . . . appartenente à l'architettura,* Rome, 1559, Pls. 7 and 8; it was also used by Martino Longhi the Younger in his *Discorso . . . delle cagioni delle ruine della facciata e campanile . . . di S. Pietro,* Rome, 1645, 10.

38. *Opus,* XXVIII, 79^v.

39. Cat. 70, 73.

40. *Dialogo,* 176; Decr. 189, 194.

41. Cat. 84–86.

42. *Opus,* VII, 23^r; XIX, 53^r; VI, 20^r; XI, 37^r.

43. *Opus,* X, 36^{r-v}; Decr. 403; see also Chapter 6 below.

44. Ehrle, "Spada," 4; *Dialogo,* 176, n. 13. The post of *elemosiniere* is discussed in G. Moroni, *Dizionario,* 1843, XXI, 155 ff. A document of 1651 calls Spada "Mag. Curs." or Master of the Post (E. Martinori, *Annali della Zecca di Roma,* Rome, 1919, fasc. 15, 45).

45. Ehrle, "Spada," 23, n. 105; Hempel, 91–

93; Thelen, *Disegni,* 14 ff., cat. 4.

46. D. Frey, "Beiträge zur Geschichte der römischen Barockarchitektur," *Wiener Jahrbuch,* III (XVII), 1924, 43 ff.; Hempel, 134–37; F. Fasolo, *L'opera di Hieronimo e Carlo Rainaldi,* Rome, 1961, 280 ff.

47. Hempel, 97. A project of Innocent X to repair the roof of S. Paolo fuori le mura is mentioned in A. Ciacconio, *Vitae et res gestae pontificum romanorum,* Rome, 1677, IV, 649; a document of 1664 June 28 mentions roof beams that had been stocked at the church for this purpose (ASR, Camerale I, Chirografi, busta 166, fol. 476 ff.). Alb. 704 is a plan of the basilica by Borromini; Alb. 705 is a fragment of a plan by Rainaldi, possibly in part by Borromini as well (R. Krautheimer, *Corpus Basilicarum Christianarum Romae,* Città del Vaticano, 1977, V, 136, Figs. 126 and 127).

48. Cat. 84–86.

49. Cat. 39.

50. Articles on pharmacies and on *elemosiniere segreto* in Moroni, *Dizionario,* 1854, LXVIII, 261–79, and 1843, XXI, 172, which mention the fact that it was one of the functions of the *elemosiniere* to dispense subsidized medicines to the poor through pharmacies. A pharmacy was included in the new wing of the Collegio Romano in 1629 (A. S. Harris, "Andrea Sacchi and Emilio Savonanzi at the Collegio Romano," *Burlington Magazine,* CX, 782, 1968, 249–57).

51. Cat. 80, 81, 84, 89.

52. *Opus,* II, 6^r; Cat. 9.

53. Decr. 146.

54. The lawsuit between the Boncompagni family and the Congregation is discussed in Cat. 82, 83, and 89a.

55. Cat. 80, 89a; see also Chapter 6 below.

56. *Ragguagli,* 213.

57. Decr. 277.

58. Decr. 291–293.

59. Cat. 48.

60. Decr. 310, 313, 314. Borromini became a *cavaliere* on July 16, 1652 (*Ragguagli,* 22).

61. Work on the Lateran doors lasted from August 1656 to June 1658. The drawings are catalogued in Thelen, *Disegni,* 55 ff., cat. 49; the dates are from R. Krautheimer and R. Jones, "The Diary of Alexander VII," *Römisches Jahrbuch,* XV, 1975, nos. 32, 33, 37, 40, 44, 84, 168, and 212.

62. Gasbarri, 82; Decr. 348–352. In Decr. 105 it had been stated that the selection of the architect was made by the Deputies rather than the Congregation at large.

63. *Ragguagli,* 151.

64. Hempel, 148; R. Wittkower, "Francesco Borromini: Personalità e destino," *Studi sul Borromini,* I, Rome, 1967, 23 and 29 ff.; G. Eimer, *La fabbrica di S. Agnese in Navona,* Stockholm, 1970, II, 428, n. 113.

65. Krautheimer and Jones, "The Diary of Alexander VII," 200 and nos. 123 and 130.

66. The relationship between Borromini and Cardinal Bernardino Spada is vividly illustrated by three important documents published in L. Neppi, *Palazzo Spada,* Rome, 1975. The first shows the two men on cordial terms a few days before Borromini's rejection by the Oratorians on May 17, 1657; the second shows the difficulties that immediately ensued; the third shows that a reconciliation had taken place by November 1657.

a. Letter of Bernardino to Virgilio Spada, dated May 13, 1657:

> Borromini was the one who found the two examples in Palladio, one antique and the other modern. Of the other two examples produced by me that of S. Eusebio, which is to be seen on the street going from S. Antonio to the Porta San Lorenzo, is not by Martino Longhi, as I maintained, but by Onorio Longhi his father, who was a more flexible person than him *(che fu persona più elastica di lui),* while the other example of the Sala Regia is by Daniele da Volterra, according to what I maintained, but Borromini says that Daniele was executing the designs of Michelangelo, and that it is by Michelangelo (Neppi, 168, n. 153).

b. Letter of Bernardino to Francesco Righi, undated, but written prior to the death of Domenico Castelli on October 13, 1657 (date from *Ragguagli,* 54 ff.):

To Righi,

To clear up every doubtful point, I am putting these few lines on paper, so that you might show them to Cavalier Borromini, and go to tell him, that my building needs an architect, with whom I can continually confer as I did with him, and also vary in part the designs that have been done as they approach the point of being put into execution; that you (Righi) are dear to me for supervising, and for insuring that what I established with him is put into effect, but that decisions need to be taken in conference with Borromini himself; that if yesterday he had sent a message that he was not feeling well, or was busy, even for weeks, I would not have minded, but would have conferred with you over some things which could easily be referred to him. But to say that he would not come because of my relatives, and because of S. Giovanni in Laterano, this is the sort of thing that makes me think I could no longer use him, since these are things that have no time limit, aside from the fact that it appears to me a kind of oblique resentment, with which I have nothing to do and yet the penalty lands on me. But the thing which is most important is that he does a great injustice to my relatives, if one means by them those who have a hand in S. Giovanni in Laterano, since he was always helped by them in dealing with the Pope and with everyone, by their taking endless troubles *(con pigliar mille brighe);* and padre Virgilio never comes to my house, and the two of us never treat of his affairs together; on the contrary on Thursday we were deliberating on how to announce to the Pope his latest explosion *(ordegno),* and [we thought of saying to the Pope] that he has been put upon and made suspicious by someone with little sense or much ill-will, that we did not know what to do with him but just attend to keeping his friendship and esteeming his talents. I repeat, [tell him] that I need an architect; that the building is not well this way; that I would rather have him alone than all the others together; that I have never dealt with any except Cavalier Bernini and Vincenzo de la Greca, and with the late Maruscelli, and with old Rainaldi, and with Castelli, and recently with Pietro da Cortona on the occasion of some painting. If Cavalier Borromini will continue, it would give me the greatest pleasure; if not he should tell me, or name someone in his stead, whom I will value, as I will value you in the *misure,* in doing plans, in supervising the master mason and similar things. If he does not want to continue it will be necessary for me to take one of three men mentioned above, or young Rainaldi (since I knew his father), since I know no one else, and I do not know if padre Virgilio my brother knows anyone else either, though I will tell my need to him. Fine days are being lost; I want to be all set right after the Holy Days (Neppi, 283, Doc. 42).

c. Letter of Bernardino to Monsignore Mario Alberici of the Congregazione di Propaganda Fide, dated November 7, 1657:

Ill.mo e Rev.mo Signore,

Since it was communicated to me by padre Virgilio my brother that the Pope would be pleased if Cavalier Borromini would take up the charge of matters at S. Giovanni again, notwithstanding the fact that due to his malady the design of certain ironwork was given to someone else whom I do not know, yesterday I spoke twice with the Cavaliere, and I listened at length to his various grievances growing out of pure matters of honor, which I suppose are familiar to your Reverence, especially since he told me that he had gone over them fully with you several weeks ago. The conclusion is that he commends himself fully to your Reverence, and will do whatever you desire in this particular matter, not only for the great esteem in which he holds your authority and advice, but also since he feels bound by the affection and sympathy which you showed him; all of which, combined with this little stretch of time in which his passions could cool, was a forceful motive to resolve the matter. Whenever your Reverence should give him the command, I assure you that you will find him most ready to serve the Pope and your benignity, which I remember and on this occasion I confirm my desire to serve you (Neppi, 283, Doc. 41).

67. By 1661 Virgilio Spada and Borromini were working in cooperation on the Banco di S. Spirito on the Piazza di Monte Giordano (Cat. 97); the publication enterprise is discussed below in Cat. 90.

68. *Opus,* X, 36^v.

69. Cat. 92–97.

70. Cat. 64, 85g.

71. Cat. 84.

72. Scavizzi, "Attività edilizia," 170 ff. The papal decree is reflected in Decr. 355, 357, and 359.

73. Cat. 73, 92–96.

74. Decr. 350. Camillo Arcucci's exact dates are unknown. In 1646 he was noted in a list of Sottomastri di Strade (*Ragguagli,* 22), the post in which he came to the Congregation's attention in 1652 (Decr. 310, 313–14). In 1658 he was recorded at work for Cardinal Bernardino Spada; the garden theater at the Palazzo Spada, with its herms and pinecones, was carried out by Arcucci and his adopted son Giuseppe Brusati Arcucci in 1664–67 (Neppi, *Palazzo Spada,* 208, especially n. 8). He was also responsible for the facade of the Palazzo Gottifredi-Grazioli and Palazzo Pio

da Carpi (Thieme-Becker, 1908, II, 73; *GR,* Parione, II, 151–54; D. de Rossi, *Studio,* Rome, I, 1702, Pls. 116–118).

75. This vaulting technique appears in the Palazzo Pamphilj *salone* of 1646 (*Opus,* XV, 46^v–47^r); in the Palazzo Falconieri of 1646 ff. (Tafuri, *Via Giulia,* 445 ff.); and in the staircase of the Palazzo di Spagna of 1647 (Hempel, 129 ff.). The technique was later given canonical textbook form in J. F. Blondel, *Cours d'architecture,* Paris, 1777, Plate vol. VI, Pls. LXXXIV–LXXXXVII.

76. Cat. 102.

77. Cat. 102, 103.

78. Chapter 3 above; Cat. 48, 85, 104.

79. Cat. 85.

80. Chapter 3 above, n. 28; Decr. 613–616, 622–627.

81. Cat. 115.

82. *Opus,* VI, 15^r; Decr. 560, 561, 604.

83. Cat. 76, 100, 101.

84. Cat. 85.

85. Gasbarri, 103–9; Decr. 630, 631.

86. Gasbarri, 125–30; Cat. 115; Emilio Re, "L'edificio dei Filippini dal 1870 ai giorni nostri," *Studi Romani,* VI, 1958, 680–84.

87. Cat. 62–64, 85g.

88. Cat. 115.

89. The grotto may have fallen out of use as early as 1684: see Decr. 484 and 530.

90. Photo in Hempel, Pl. 46; Portoghesi, *Linguaggio,* Fig. 60; *GR,* Parione, II, 51.

91. Decr. 159 and 162 deal with the entrance at the rear of the building, along the Via di Parione.

Chapter 5

1. J. Delumeau, *Vie économique et sociale de Rome dans la seconde moitié du XVIe siècle,* Paris, 1957, II, 653–945 is fundamental for the institutional background. The basic sources for the Congregation's finances are Gasbarri, 54–57, and 253–70, and *Dialogo,* 171–80.

2. P. Pirri, S.J., *Giuseppe Valeriano S. I. architetto e pittore 1542–1596,* Rome, 1970, 55, n. 5, and 71, n. 43.

3. L. Heydenreich and W. Lotz, *Architecture in Italy 1400–1600,* Harmondsworth, 1974, 322.

4. Delumeau, *Vie économique,* 765 ff.

5. Delumeau, *Vie économique,* 764; the sum seems rather low.

6. H. Hibbard, *The Architecture of the Palazzo Borghese,* Rome, 1962, 62.

7. L. von Pastor, *History of the Popes,* St. Louis, 1952, XXII, 303, n. 4.

8. R. Lanciani, *Storia degli scavi di Roma,* Rome, 1912, IV, 139.

9. ASR, Archivio Spada, vol. 192, 411–43. The document is a generic accounting of all Lateran expenses up to 1651, which total ∇116,530.09½; on the front page Spada computes a total of ∇11,032.96½ of additional expenses. In a *scandaglio* or summary of remaining expenses for the church drawn up by Borromini on March 25, 1656, it is estimated that it would cost ∇43,475.58 to finish the building, including ∇40,000 for the facade (Alb. 373–78).

10. P. Pecchiai, *Il Gesù di Roma,* Rome, 1952, 300.

11. G. Antonazzi, "La sede della Sacra Congregazione e del Collegio Urbano," *Sacrae Congregationis de Propaganda Fide Memoria Rerum,* ed. J. Metzler, Rome-Freiburg-Vienna, 1971, 327, n. 113, where the expenses from 1655 to 1665 are recorded.

12. Pecchiai, *Il Gesù,* 300.

13. Lanciani, *Storia degli scavi,* IV, 185.

14. Pollak, 43.

15. The high cost cannot be attributed to inflation, which, according to Delumeau, *Vie économique,* 745, reached its peak in Rome between 1570 and 1609; after 1610 Italy entered a recession which lasted for most of the century, accompanied by a mild decline in prices.

16. Doc. 32.

17. Doc. 11; *Opus,* VI, 22^r.

18. Pollak, 48.

19. Gasbarri, 54–75; Decr. 8, 16, 19, 24; Doc. 10; *Dialogo,* 174.

20. Ehrle, "Spada," 4; Decr. 10–12 and 26–29. Spada also composed an unpublished treatise on monetary policy which exists in at least five manuscript copies: BV, Chigi C III 64; BV, Cod. Ferrajolus 365; Bibl. Vittorio Emanuele, Fondo Iesuitico, n. 114; Bibl. Casanatense, in index; and British Library, MS. Add. 12,489. It is undated but consists of notes and documents collected under Innocent X and prepared in final form for Alexander VII; possibly it was composed after Spada took charge of the hospital and bank of S. Spirito in 1660. It deals with certain endemic problems of the bimetallic system in Rome and the cities of Bologna, Ferrara, and the Romagna: abundance of gold on the Roman exchange, the disappearance of certain coins from circulation, and the relative prices of gold and silver. It advo-

cates a unified currency for the papal states and a mild debasement of some coin issues, to prevent the intrinsic value of the metal from becoming greater than the face value, a phenomenon that encouraged the disappearance of these coins. Although it shows Spada's characteristic acuity, the treatise does not deal with the financing of construction.

21. *Dialogo,* 175 ff.

22. Cat. 14. Spada produced a similar account-drawing in 1652 to calculate the cost in lost rents of demolishing the *spina* of the Vatican Borgo; it is illustrated by Ehrle, "Spada," 87, Pl. VII.

23. The issues that arose in 1633 are discussed in Doc. 10. In Doc. 29 of about 1644 the old casa is said to be bringing in ∇1,200 in rents, although in 1650 it was to be put up for only ∇100 in rent; the most expensive shop on the Piazza di Monte Giordano was to rent for ∇50 (Decr. 244, 261, 265, 278, 434).

24. Doc. 9.

25. Delumeau, *Vie économique,* 783 ff. and 870 ff., treats *luoghi di monti* and *censi* but does not discuss the various types of *censi* or their use to finance construction. The present discussion is based principally on Decr. 349 and on Decr. 8, 16, 159, 184, 185, 384, 391, 395, 404, 405, and 476. The use of the *censo vitalitio* is mentioned in Pollak, 43, in the documents that deal with the financing of S. Carlo alle Quattro Fontane.

26. *Opus,* V, 12^r, which was mistranscribed as "proprietà" in the 1725 edition of the book.

27. *Dialogo,* 176–80, for all the quotations in this paragraph.

28. Decr. 120, 130; Cat. 40.

29. Decr. 159; Cat. 66.

30. Gasbarri, 170; Decr. 210, 257, 260.

31. Decr. 244, 262, 263, 267, 275, 277, 305.

32. Gasbarri, 263–65.

33. Decr. 348–352 of 1657 describe the financial mechanisms of the *censo vitalitio* and *censo perpetuo* in detail.

34. According to Decr. 360, Spada identified himself as the donor when similar terms were offered in 1659.

35. Decr. 365, 384, 391, 395, 404, 405.

36. Decr. 358, 412, 447.

37. Decr. 393 394, 476, 501, 609, 610.

38. Decr. 480, 481, 492–494, 497, 505, 507, 510, 547, 575–582; see also Chapter 6 below.

39. Hess, "Chiesa Nuova," 363–67; Ponnelle and Bordet, 404–19; Cat. 27.III.

40. Gasbarri, 258–67; Decr. 87, 124, 257, 469, 514; *Dialogo,* 171–80.

41. Gasbarri, 255.

42. *Opus,* XXII–XXIV; Cat. 84.

43. Hibbard, *Maderno,* 200 (for the extension of Acqua Paola to the *banchi* area).

44. Gasbarri, 83; Decr. 67, 163, 171, 265, 269–271, 400, 529; Doc. 8; Cat. 89, 114; *Opus,* IX, 32^r; XXIII.

45. Gasbarri, 83, cites a drawing of 1614 for bringing water from the Ponte Sisto area (Bibl. Vallicelliana, 0 23, p. 120); and a drawing of 1706 shows a conduit system apparently designed for the same purpose (AV, C.II.8, nos. 112 ff.).

Plans to tap the Acqua Vergine are mentioned in *Opus,* XXIII, 65^r; this would have become possible after April 1647, when Borromini was charged with extending the conduits as far as the Piazza Navona (Hempel, 93, n. 2; *Ragguagli,* 102; the conduit plan is in BV, Vat. lat. 11257, fol. 149).

46. *Opus,* XXII–XXIII; Decr. 506, 529, 587; Doc. 13.

47. Cat. 74; *Opus,* XIV, 43^r; Pollak, 146 ff., regs. 402–403 (on S. Ignazio); see also Thelen, C 16, p. 21. A similar proposal was made in 1642–43 for the drainage of the Propaganda Fide (Antonazzi, "La sede della Sacra Congregazione e del Collegio Urbano," *Sacrae Congregationis de Propaganda Fide Memoria Rerum,* 316).

48. The only constant index to the size of the Congregation is the number of padri who are recorded as voting at the meetings of the Congregazione Generale. In 1627, when the entire Congregation numbered about sixty members, there were twenty-seven voting padri, amounting to about 45 percent of the total. The number of voting padri recorded in the *decreti* of 1637 is twenty-seven, whereas in 1643 there are only seventeen, in 1650 fifteen, and in the 1660s between thirteen and sixteen.

49. Cat. 20, 92–95, 102; Decr. 125, quoted below in Cat. 40.

50. *Opus,* XV, 45^r–47^v.

51. *Opus,* XXIII, 63^v.

52. Cat. 95; *Opus,* XIV, 43^r.

53. *Opus,* XIV.

54. Cat. 20a; *Dialogo,* 201; Doc. 20, which describes Spada's coin and curiosity collection while it was still in his old rooms in 1644; and BV, Chigi E V 147, Testamenti varii, fol. 117^v, which lists the paintings.

56. *Dialogo,* 184.

57. Hibbard, *Maderno,* 32.

58. Decr. 162.

59. *Opus,* IX, 33^r.

60. *Opus,* IX, 34^r; *Dialogo,* 188; Cat. 25, 26.

61. Decr. 403, 419–421, 563.

62. *Opus,* XVIII, 51^{r-v}.

63. Ponnelle and Bordet, 398 and 404.

64. Gasbarri, 47–54; Ponnelle and Bordet, 385–89; *Opus,* XXI. Spada's own collection of literature on *dubii* and cases of conscience is mentioned in Doc. 20.

65. *Dialogo,* 199.

66. Gasbarri, 51–54; Ponnelle and Bordet, 386 ff.; *Opus,* XXV. A prison is included in the project for the convent of S. Andrea della Valle mentioned in Appendix II, n. 7 below.

67. The major sources for Oratorian music are D. Alaleona, *Studi sulla storia dell'oratorio musicale in Italia,* Turin, 1908, reprinted as *Storia dell'oratorio musicale in Italia,* Milan, 1945 (references are to the reprint); Ponnelle and Bordet, 389–402; Gasbarri, 306–23; and especially Smither, *Oratorio,* which surveys all previous work and provides a great deal of new information on which the present summary is based. The following are also helpful: M. Bukofzer, *Music in the Baroque Era,* New York, 1947, 1–70; C. Palisca, *Baroque Music,* Englewood Cliffs, 1968, 1–54; H. M. Brown, "How Opera Began: An Introduction to Jacopo Peri's *Euridice* (1600)," in E. Cochrane, ed., *The Late Italian Renaissance 1525–1630,* London, 1970, 401–43; H. Smither, "The Baroque Oratorio. A Report on Research Since 1945," *Acta Musicologica,* XLVII, 1975, 50–76 (this reference courtesy of Prof. E. Lowinsky).

68. Von Pastor, *History of the Popes,* XIX, 585 ff., quoted in Smither, *Oratorio,* 53.

69. Smither, *Oratorio,* 121.

70. Decr. 25.

71. Conditions in the old oratory are described in Decr. 18 and 25.

72. "Con panni o con gelosie," as reported in Pietro della Valle, *Della musica dell'età nostra . . . ,* January 1640, in A. Solerti, *Le origini del melodramma,* Turin, 1903, 171.

73. *Opus,* VI, 16^r and XI, 37^v; Decr. 335, 410.

74. *Opus,* VI, 15^r.

75. Bukofzer, *Baroque Era,* 13–16.

76. Decr. 154; Smither, *Oratorio,* 160 ff.

77. A. Solerti, "Lettere inedite sulla musica di Pietro della Valle a G. B. Doni," *Rivista Musicale Italiana,* XII, 1905, 289 and 292; Smither, *Oratorio,* 174 ff.; and on the organ in the oratory: Cat. 48.

78. John Evelyn, *The Diary of John Evelyn,* ed. E. S. de Beer, Oxford, 1955, II, 233, with other visits on 277, 283 ff., and 291.

79. Alaleona, *Oratorio musicale,* 141.

80. J. N. Eritreo, *Pynacoteca altera,* Cologne, 1645, 217, quoted in Alaleona, *Oratorio musicale,* 139.

81. Francis Mortoft, *Francis Mortoft: His Book. Being His Travels Through France and Italy 1658–1659* (The Hakluyt Society, 2nd ser., LVII), London, 1925, quoted in Smither, *Oratorio,* 162 ff.

82. Alaleona, *Oratorio musicale,* 144.

83. Smither, *Oratorio,* 259.

84. Bukofzer, *Baroque Era,* 241 ff.; D. Poultney, "Alessandro Scarlatti and the Transformation of Oratorio," *The Musical Quarterly,* LIX, 1973, 584–601. The date and circumstances of Scarlatti's appointment are given in a series of lengthy *decreti* of January 5 to 9, 1703, in AV, C.I.9, 166 ff.

85. Ponnelle and Bordet, 267.

86. Ponnelle and Bordet, 315 ff.

87. Pietro della Valle, *Della musica dell'età nostra,* 176; A. Ziino, "Pietro Della Valle e la 'musica erudita.' Nuovi documenti," *Analecta Musicologica. Studien zur italienisch-deutschen Musikgeschichte,* IV, 1967, Documents 3, 6, and 10 on pp. 106 ff.

88. Opus, VI, 19^r; Alaleona, *Oratorio musicale,* 42; and the remark of Emilio de' Cavalieri in a letter of 1600–1601:

> I forgot to say what the priests of the Vallicella told me, and this is great. Many prelates among those who came to Florence saw a *rappresentatione in musica* that I have done this carnival at their Oratorio, for which the expenditure was six scudi at the most. They say that they found it much more to their taste, because the music moved them to tears and laughter and pleased them greatly, unlike this music of Florence, which did not move them at all, unless to boredom and irritation.

The passage is given by C. Palisca, "Musical Asides in the Diplomatic Correspondence of Emilio de' Cavalieri," *The Musical Quarterly,* XLIX, 1963, 352; and by Smither, *Oratorio,* 82.

89. Decr. 25. The musicians themselves might carry swords, for instance Dorisio Isorello (Alaleona, *Oratorio musicale,* 42) or the nobleman Pietro della Valle, who was briefly exiled in 1636 for using his sword to kill a papal servant (A. Solerti, "Lettere inedite," 279).

90. Decr. 18 and 25; Ponnelle and Bordet, 404; and G. Lunadoro (G. Leti), *Relatione della corte di Roma,* Venice, 1664, 103 ff.:

> The Cardinal of Florence, who later be-

came Pope Leo XI and who was extremely well-versed in social etiquette, used to stand in a place set apart when he attended a comedy or similar event, behind a screen sheltered from people's view.

91. *Opus,* XXVI, 71^r.

92. A. Solerti, "Lettere inedite," 289. The question of who might be admitted to the singers' choir is taken up in Decr. 198, 302, and 331.

93. The *ricevitore di forastieri* is mentioned in Decr. 331 and in *Opus,* IX, 32^r. The way an entourage moved through the building, as well as the vistas unsealed for them, comes from *Opus,* VI, 19^r; IX, 34^r; X, 36^r; XXII, 61^r; XXVI, 71^r. Useful references on the sociology of receptions are: Lunadoro (Leti), *Relatione della corte di Roma,* 102 ff.; F. Sestini, *Il maestro di camera,* Venice, 1664, 69 ff., especially 87; and O. Walker, *Of Education,* Oxford, 1673, 219–28, where much of Sestini's material is summarized in English. Comparative material from England is to be found in H. M. Baillie, "Etiquette and the Planning of the State Apartments in Baroque Palaces," *Archaeologia,* CI, 1967, 167–99; and most brilliantly in M. Girouard, *Life in the English Country House,* New Haven and London, 1978, 145 ff. According to Lunadoro (Leti), 131, "It is said that the first place at the dining table is the one which has a view straight down to the door through which the food is carried by the pages," which accords with the information on dining given in *Opus,* XXI; XXII, 61^r; XXV, 70^r. A proposal to give the refectory fireplace away to Cardinal Barberini is recorded in *Dialogo,* 197–200, while the Duke of Mantua's undated visit is mentioned in Alaleona, *Oratorio musicale,* 47.

94. Ponnelle and Bordet, 405–7.

95. Gasbarri, 47–54; *Opus,* V; Ponnelle and Bordet, 583, where the full rubric of Oratorian spirituality is given: "Spernere seipsum, spernere mundum, spernere neminem, spernere se sperni."

96. *Opus,* VII, 25^r; VI, 18^r; XXVIII, 77^r; XI, 37^r.

97. Thelen, C 1–5.

98. A. Labacco, *Libro appartenente à l'architettura,* Rome, 1559, Pls. 7 and 8; see also Thelen, 88, n. 1, and C 78, as well as *Dialogo,* 189 ff., n. 38.

99. S. Serlio, *Tutte l'opere,* Venice, 1619, III, 58^r for the S. Costanza vault patterns, and 54^r for the pilaster design. The influence of Serlio's S. Costanza woodcut on Borromini was first noted by L. Steinberg, *Borromini's San Carlo alle Quattro*

Fontane. A Study in Multiple Form and Architectural Symbolism, New York, 1977 (revised Garland Press edition of a 1960 dissertation), Appendix A of Chapter 4. The recurrence of this motif in an obscure part of the Casa dei Filippini was first noted by A. Bruschi, "Il Borromini nelle stanze di S. Filippo alla Vallicella," *Palatino,* XII, 1968, 21 and Fig. 11. The classic statements of Montano's influence on Borromini are in A. Blunt, "Introduction," *Acts of the Twentieth International Congress of the History of Art,* III, Princeton, 1963, 6, and in Blunt, *Borromini,* 41 ff. The Montano source for the Pamphilj chapel in Borromini's drawing is identified in Cat. 39.

100. Fioravante Martinelli, *Roma ricercata nel suo sito, et nella scuola di tutti gli antiquarij,* Rome, 1644, 1650 and 1658.

101. *Opus,* 3^r; XIX, 53^r.

102. The comparison with the palace at Piacenza was made by Portoghesi, *Linguaggio,* 30 and 55. The palace was begun in 1558 on the design of Vignola and executed in part by G. Rainaldi; work stopped in about 1593. See L. Heydenreich and W. Lotz, *Architecture in Italy 1400–1600,* Harmondsworth, 1974, 272 ff., and Passeri-Hess, 216.

103. The comparison of Borromini's giant order with Palladio is made by Portoghesi, *Linguaggio,* 28 and Fig. 397; the drawing is analyzed in Cat. 57 below; the references to Michelangelo's Campidoglio are made in *Opus,* XIX, 53^r, as well as in *Dialogo,* 184, where Spada surprisingly claims the invention for himself.

104. Arcucci's staircase is discussed in Cat. 73 and 92–96. The Farnese steps average 12 cm. in height and 58 cm. in depth, including a lip of about 3 cm. along the front edge. The steps of the casa also average 12 cm. in height; they extend 47 cm. in depth and have a lip of 4.5 cm. In both buildings the steps have a marked upward slope of about 1 *oncia* per step. Borromini's terminology for steps is given in a drawing for the Propaganda Fide (Alb. 894, illustrated in Portoghesi, *Linguaggio,* Fig. cxi): width is *larghezza di pedata,* lip is *agetto del cardine,* and slope is *pendenza.*

105. The principles of this kind of spatial configuration, in which apses and niches cut into the masonry mass and reduce it to what has been called a "filigrane wall" or a series of "claw piers," are discussed in the following studies: L. Heydenreich, "Spätwerke Brunelleschis," *Jahrbuch der Preussischen Kunstsammlungen,* LII, 1931, 1–28; J. Ackerman, *The Architecture of Michelangelo,* London, 1961, I, xxvii ff.; M. Gosebruch, "Vom Pantheon Vergleichlich-Unver-

gleichliches," *Römische Quartalschrift*, 30. Supplementheft, 1966, 388–409; C. Frommel, "Bramantes 'Ninfeo' in Genazzano," *Römisches Jahrbuch*, XII, 1969, 137–60.

Apse-ended and niche-filled spaces passed from the designs of Bramante, Raphael, and Peruzzi into the woodcuts of Serlio (*Tutte l'opere*, IV, 175^r) and Palladio (*Quattro libri*, II, 13, 25, 26, 44, 47, and III, 46), who incorporated an apse-ended vestibule into the Palazzo Chiericati in Vicenza (*Quattro libri*, II, 6; J. Ackerman, *Palladio*, Harmondsworth, 1966, 103). Vignola appears to be the designer of the apse-ended atrium in the garden wing of the Palazzo Farnese in Rome of about 1560 (Ackerman, *Michelangelo*, London, 1961, II, 84; Frommel, II, 144 ff. and Pls. 47b, 56a, 56b, 56d; K. Schwager, "Giacomo della Portas Herkunft und Anfänge in Rom," *Römisches Jahrbuch*, XV, 1975, 135, n. 144 and Fig. 18).

Between Vignola's death in 1573 and Borromini's early work, apsed spaces, though still found in some Mascarino projects (J. Wasserman, *Ottaviano Mascarino*, Rome, 1966, Figs. 85, 92, and 168), play an insignificant role in Roman architecture.

106. It is difficult to specify exactly how Borromini might have known Bramante's first project: the version of Bramante's plan in the Codex Coner reduces the niche-filled vestibules to a very small scale (T. Ashby, "Sixteenth-Century Drawings of Roman Buildings Attributed to Andreas Coner," *Papers of the British School at Rome*, II, 1904, Pl. 31); while the plan in Serlio omits them altogether (*Tutte l'opere*, III, 65^v, after UA 20).

107. Cat. 66; the Palazzo Baldassini atrium is illustrated in Frommel, III, Pl. 11b, and the motif from the Palazzo Alberini-Cicciaporci in Pls. 3c and 6d.

108. Decr. 146 (quoted in Incisa della Rocchetta, *Dialogo*, 199, n. 54) of 1640 mentions "the paper *(scrittura)* drawn up by His Reverence [Spada] and signed by the architect which demonstrates the impossibility of building the recreation room in a rectangular shape." The accusations about "mere caprice," etc., are found in *Opus*, VI, 20^r; XXI, 58^v; and *Dialogo*, 196.

109. Doc. 28.

110. *Opus*, XIX, 53^r; XII, 39^r; IX, 34^r. The Farnese *seditori* are illustrated in Frommel, III, Pl. 43a.

111. *Opus*, XII, 39^r. There are further remarks on the outfitting of palaces in J. Connors, review of M. Heimbürger Ravalli, *Architettura scultura e*

arti minori nel barocco italiano, Florence, 1977, and of L. Neppi, *Palazzo Spada*, Rome, 1975, in *JSAH*, XXXVIII, 1979, 193–96.

112. Decr. 102, 122, 128, 176, 178. Pollak, 441, reg. 1790 records a payment of ∇10 to Gasparo Berti for the purchase of "cartoni" for a model of the fabric, which was delivered in January 1642.

113. *Opus*, XIX, 53^r.

114. Decr. 128, 166, 167; *Dialogo*, 200.

115. Decr. 383, which records a decision of 1660 not to use a marble column found in the foundations for the new stairs but to purchase travertine "per non rendere detta scala troppo fastosa."

116. John Evelyn, quoted above in n. 78.

117. Letter of the Roman Oratorian Padre Mario Sozzini to the Florentine Oratory, quoted in Smither, *Oratorio*, 259.

Chapter 6

1. C. Paola Scavizzi, "Le condizioni per lo sviluppo dell'attività edilizia a Roma nel sec. XVII: la legislazione," *Studi Romani*, XVII, 1969, 160–71.

2. This principle is clearly spelled out in a license of 1655 for the Piazza della Chiesa Nuova, transcribed in Cat. 87.

3. A similar view is expressed in P. Partner, *Renaissance Rome 1500–1559*, Berkeley, 1976, 167:

> Probably the best way to look at Roman urban growth is not to consider it as a series of grandiose plans with wide urban aims, but as a series of smaller developments, each of which was sponsored by some powerful man or family, and each of which then produced new requirements for urban communications and facilities.

4. In spite of an extensive bibliography there is no good architectural study of the Collegio Romano. Documentation on the college is provided in the following monographs: E. Rinaldi, S.J., *La fondazione del Collegio Romano*, Arezzo, 1914; R. Villoslada, *Storia del Collegio Romano dal suo inizio (1551) alla soppressione della Compagnia di Gesù (1773)*, Rome, 1954; E. Beltrame Quattrocchi, *Il Palazzo del Collegio Romano e il suo autore*, Rome, 1956; and especially P. Pirri, S.J., *Giuseppe Valeriano S. I. architetto e pittore 1542–*

1596, Rome, 1970. Early plans are published by Rinaldi, without source, and by J. Wasserman, *Ottaviano Mascarino and his Drawings in the Accademia Nazionale di San Luca,* Rome, 1966, Figs. 35 and 36. There is an extensive survey of Jesuit architectural practice, with some information on the college, in J. Vallery-Radot, *Le recueil de plans d'édifices de la Compagnie de Jésus conservé á la Bibliothèque Nationale de Paris,* Paris, 1960. The pharmacy of the college is documented in A. Sutherland Harris, "Andrea Sacchi and Emilio Savonanzi at the Collegio Romano," *Burlington Magazine,* CX, 782, 1968, 249–57. Some information appears in sources primarily concerned with the church of S. Ignazio: Hibbard, *Maderno,* 232–34; Hibbard, *Licenze,* nos. 22 and 155, and Fig. 30; Thelen, 39–44 and C 32–33; J. Connors, review of Thelen, in *JSAH,* XXXV, 1975, 146; D. Frey, "Beiträge zur Geschichte der römischen Barockarchitektur," *Wiener Jahrbuch für Kunstgeschichte,* III (XVII), 1924, 11–13; Pollak, 144–58; and L. Montalto, "Il problema della cupola di Sant'Ignazio di padre Orazio Grassi e fratel Pozzo a oggi," *Bolletino del Centro di Studi per la Storia dell'Architettura,* XI, 1957, 33–62. Two important sources for the construction of the south piazza, in the Piazza del Collegio Romano, are O. Pollak, "Antonio del Grande, ein unbekannter römischer Architekt des XVII. Jahrhunderts," *Kunstgeschichtliches Jahrbuch der K. K. Zentral-Kommission,* III, 1909, 133–61; and Frommel, III, Pl. 36c. In addition there is a group of drawings in the Chigi papers in the Vatican: BV, Chigi P. VII. 9, fol. 90^v (plan); fol. 91^r (sewer system); fol. 131; Chigi P. VII. 13, fols. 33^v–34^r (lines of vision along the corners); fol. 35^r (lines of vision of the entire piazza); fol. 37^r (plan of S. Maria in Via Lata, a duplicate of the plan in the church archives illustrated in L. Cavazzi, *La diaconia di S. Maria in Via Lata,* Rome, 1908, 246 ff.); fols. 38^v–39^r (lines of vision between the college and the monastery of S. Marta). There is information on the north piazza, the Piazza di S. Ignazio, in E. Rossi, *avvisi* in *Roma,* VIII, 1929, 371 ff.; H. Hager, "Puntualizzazioni su disegni scenici teatrali e l'architettura scenografica del periodo barocco a Roma," *Bollettino del Centro Internazionale di Studi di Architettura Andrea Palladio,* XVII, 1975, 124 ff. and Fig. 51; and M. Rotili, *Filippo Raguzzini e il rococò romano,* Rome, 1952, 51 ff.

The Collegio Romano assumed its present shape in the course of three building campaigns each of which can be linked with the name of a major donor: Vittoria della Tolfa, Gregory XIII, and Cardinal Ludovico Ludovisi. In 1560 the Je-

suits were given land for their college, which had been housed in the Palazzo Salviati since its founding in 1551, in the area to the east of the Piazza di S. Macuto on property owned by Vittoria della Tolfa. It is difficult to determine how much was actually built at this point aside from the church of the SS. Annunziata, which stood on the site now occupied by the transept of S. Ignazio (foundations laid under Giovanni Tristano, S.J., in 1562, inaugurated in 1567, demolished in 1650). In the second campaign of 1581–88 the south half of the present college was built on the design of Giuseppe Valeriano, S.J.; it included the large *cortile delle scuole,* about 400 rooms including eleven *aule scholastiche* and a frescoed *aula magna,* the east facade as far as the present monumental portal, and the famous south facade, which is often mistakenly attributed to Bartolomeo Ammannati. (Pirri's arguments in favor of an attribution to Valeriano seem conclusive: Ammannati was not in Rome when the facade was built and never mentions it in his extensive correspondence with the Jesuit General Acquaviva; the documents connect Valeriano's name with the drawings and a wooden model as well as with the supervision of construction; all sixteenth-century sources attribute the facade to Valeriano, while Ammannati's name is not suggested until Baglione in 1642, who qualifies his attribution as one based on hearsay; finally the college has nothing in common with Ammannati's work but is repeated almost literally in the Jesuit college in Naples, designed by Valeriano in about 1584. Against these arguments the reassertion of Ammannati's authorship by M. Fossi, *Bartolomeo Ammannati architetto,* Florence, n.d., 140–47, carries no weight whatsoever.) In the third campaign of 1626–85 Cardinal Ludovico Ludovisi sponsored the construction of S. Ignazio, which eventually replaced the original church of the SS. Annunziata, and the northern wing of the college, which served as the Jesuit residence and contained a new pharmacy and refectory. The church and possibly also the residence were designed by committee, in which the dominant figure was the Jesuit architect Orazio Grassi.

5. Uffizi A 4180. The drawing carries an old attribution to B. de' Rocchi; it still does not show the church of the Annunziata in its final location, which was selected in about 1561.

6. The documents for the Oratory of the Caravita, begun in 1631 and inaugurated in 1633, are in Pollak, 243, regs. 834–837. The oratory stands in part on the site of the church of S. Nicolo de Forbitoriis, demolished in 1631

(Huelsen, *Chiese,* 398). The opening of the Via della Caravita, the street that runs into the northeast corner pier shown in Fig. 231, was recorded in Cassiano dal Pozzo's diary written in about 1642: "Con occasione della fabrica della chiesa di S. Francesco Saverio [*i.e., the Oratory of the Caravita*] fatto un taglio et apertasi la nuova strada che va da piazza Sciarra per andar alla Ritonda . . ." (G. Lumbroso, *Notizie sulla vita di Cassiano dal Pozzo,* Turin, 1874, 180).

7. Frommel, I, 23 ff.

8. Sources for the Via di Parione and the Via del Pellegrino are given in Chapter 1 above, n. 12; some documentation is provided in Russo, "Piazza della Chiesa Nuova."

9. The cross-streets are hardest to chart in the formative period of the late fifteenth and early sixteenth centuries. All of the following are shown with varying degrees of accuracy by Bufalini (1551), Duperac (1577), and Tempesta (1593), which should be supplemented with Cat. 5, 14, 15, 17a–e, 18, 38 for the area eventually occupied by the casa. Proceeding southwest from the Zecca:

a. *Vicolo del Pavone* (Nolli 517). The street was part of a larger route (Vicolo della Campanella, del Pavone, Sugarelli, del Cefalo) which extended from the Via di Panico all the way to a ferry on the Tiber. Its presence is indicated on Bramante's sketch for the Piazza dei Tribunali (Frommel, Pl. 146b). It is mentioned in 1569 in connection with the house of Pietro Aldobrandino (R. Lanciani, *Storia degli scavi di Roma,* Rome, 1912, IV, 179) and again in 1587 when it was paved ("La strada del vicolo del Pavone che si fa adesso," in F. Cerasoli, "Notizie circa la sistemazione di molte strade di Roma nel sec. XVI," *Bollettino Comunale,* XXVIII, 1901, 347).

b. *Vicolo Sforza-Cesarini* (the Piazza is Nolli 568). Possibly opened or systematized in conjunction with the Palazzo Borgia-Sforza-Cesarini (Nolli 569), which it flanks. Paved in 1587 (Cerasoli, "Notizie," 347), it was 30 palmi wide south of the Piazza Sforza, but narrow and irregular to the north (Doc. 29).

c. *Via dei Filippini-Calabraghe-Cellini* (Nolli 659). It was the only cross-street of the area not to be paved in 1587 (Cerasoli, "Notizie"). The Vicolo di Calabraghe on the south was only 19 palmi wide; the northern stretch is well documented in Cat. 15.

d. *Via di Pizzomerlo-dei Cartari* (Nolli 658). It was the most important cross-street of the area, one of the few that extended to the Tiber. It was paved in 1587 "da Pizzomerlo alla chiavica . . . dalla chiavica . . . in Strada Giulia" (Cerasoli,

"Notizie," 346 ff.). Its level was adjusted when a door was opened in Filippo's chapel in the Vallicella in 1605 (Hibbard, *Licenze,* no. 43). Permission to close the upper half of the street was granted in 1621 (Decr. 4), but it is well documented in Cat. 5, 14, and 15. The lower reaches near the Tiber are shown in a series of plans by Antonio del Grande for the Carceri Nuovi (BV, Vat. lat. 11258, fols. 125, 133, 137, illustrated in *Via Giulia,* 364 ff., Figs. 273–276).

e. The following small alleys branching off the Via di Parione did not extend to the Via del Pellegrino:

e.1. *Vicolo del Corallo.* The original course of the street is identified as no. 3 on Cat. 15; it was truncated by the building of the Vallicella transept in 1588 (Cat. 8) and closed altogether when the casa was completed in 1668–75. The stretch north of the Via di Parione leading to the Piazza del Fico (Nolli 590–91) remained more important (*GR,* Ponte, III, 64). Paolo Maruscelli lived on the street (Doc. 22), but the exact address is unknown.

e.2. *"Vicolo che da Pozzo Bianco portava in Parione"* (Cat. 15, no. 2). The alley was closed after the construction of the Vallicella; cf. Cat. 8.

e.3. *Via dell'Arco della Chiesa Nuova.* The old casa, purchased from the Monastery of S. Elisabetta in 1581–82, was located on this street; several houses still have crossed shields on Renaissance window frames, and part of a *bugnato* corner exists in one of the exterior walls (Cat. 15, no. 8). The Barnabites described it in 1611 as follows: "Vicoletto dietro l'habitatione di detti Preti dove si fanno mille sporcitie, e non si passono carozze, il quale posson commodamente chiudere . . ." (Fig. 97, no. 7). The arch which gives the street its modern name was built in 1675 (Cat. 103).

f. *Vicolo del Governo* (Nolli 654). The street runs in a straight line from the Palazzo Nardini-del Governo to the Via del Pellegrino. It may have been laid out when the Palazzetto Turci and the house with diamond graffiti (no. 52) were built in 1500 ff. (*GR,* Parione, I, 98). It was still called Strada Nuova in 1604–11 (Cat. 5, and Fig. 97, no. 27). Borromini seems to mention it in *Opus,* I, 4^v when he says that there was little room to expand to the east "rispetto a certe strade molto apportune."

g. *Via Sora (Nolli 652) and Vicolo Sora.* In 1491 and 1509–10, the Palazzo Fieschi-Sora was described as close to the Pozzo Bianco, which implies that the small Vicolo Sora, the street that points at the palace door, was then in existence. Presumably the Piazza Sora was cleared and the Via Sora systematized when the west facade of the palace was begun ca. 1503–10 (Frommel, II, 180–88).

h. *Vicolo Savelli* (Nolli 650). The early wing of the Palazzo Fieschi-Sora (Frommel, II, 186) and the Palazzo Caccialupi (*GR,* Parione, I, 100 ff.) were built on this street in 1480–90, implying that it was then more important than the Via Sora.

i. *Vicolo della Cancelleria.* Blocked by the Cancelleria garden at an uncertain date.

j. *Vicolo dei Leutari.* The street originally led to the side door of S. Lorenzo in Damaso, but was given another outlet of some sort in 1541 (*GR,* Parione, I, 102). Until the demolitions of 1885 it emerged into the Piazza delle Cancelleria, which itself was opened up by Cardinal Francesco Barberini in 1673 (ASR, Presidenza delle Strade, busta 28, chirograph of July 20, 1673).

k. *Via dei Baullari-del Gallo* (Nolli 640, 707). Possibly opened with an alignment on the portal of the Palazzo Farnese in 1517; partly incorporated into the Piazza Farnese in 1535 (Frommel, I, 23). The stretch between the piazza and the Campo dei Fiori was paved in 1587 and is partly visible in a drawing of 1554–60 (Cerasoli, "Notizie," 347; *GR,* Regola, II, 8, 61, 86; J. Ackerman, *The Architecture of Michelangelo,* London, 1961, I, Fig. 42b).

l. *Strada and Piazza del Paradiso* (Nolli 628, 630). Paved in 1587 ("La strada che va dalli Massimi all'Orologio di Campo de Fiori, per il Paradiso," in Cerasoli, "Notizie," 346); partly visible in a sixteenth-century drawing (Frommel, Pl. 98d).

10. P. Pirri, S.J., "La topografia del Gesù di Roma e le vertenze tra Muzio Muti e S. Ignazio," *Archivium Historicum Societatis Iesu,* X, 1941, 177–217.

11. Hibbard, *Maderno,* 146–55. A plan of the Piazza di Siena, later Piazza di S. Andrea della Valle, exists in BV, Chigi P.VIII.13, fol. 50; old photographs, taken before the demolitions of 1885, appear in A. Bianchi, "Le vicende e le realizzazioni del piano regolatore di Roma capitale," *Capitolium,* X, 1934, 37 and 39.

12. These projects are documented above in Chapter 1, n. 35.

13. The awkward orientation of the building was underlined in 1641, when there was a proposal to shift the main entrance from the south side of the casa to the Via di Parione. The proposed location was acknowledged to be more convenient, but it was rejected in order to keep the casa free of *soggettione* (Decr. 159 and 162).

14. *Opus,* II, 6^r: ". . . a new street to be made along the east flank of the church to restore to the public a street which had to be closed on the side of Monte Giordano."

15. Ackerman, *Michelangelo,* I, 87 ff.; II, 69–84; Frommel, I, 23; *GR,* Regola, II, 52 ff.

16. Thelen, Fig. 50; Hibbard, *Maderno,* Pl. 92b. The best exposition of Farnese influence on the Palazzo Barberini is in Hibbard, *Maderno,* 82.

17. Doc. 7.

18. Decr. 367 and 371, which confirm "il privilegio, che habbiamo, per non pagar l'augumento."

19. *GR,* Parione, I, 94 ff.

20. Cat. 17–19.

21. G. Baglione, *Le vite de pittori, scultori, et architetti,* Rome, 1642, 376; *GR,* Parione, II, 58 ff. Photographs of three drawings of the Palazzo Cerri are to be found in the Fototeca of the Bibliotheca Hertziana: one elevation proposes six shops instead of the present ten windows to be found on the ground floor; two late seventeenth-century plans show proposals for rebuilding the entrance atrium and the staircase. Prior to the restoration of 1974, the atrium was decorated with Borrominesque stucco motifs, possibly deriving from ornament in the oratory and in the Propaganda Fide.

22. Cat. 38, 105–6.

23. Cat. 39.III. Inscription no. 1 is particularly relevant.

24. Possibly some information on the amount of viewing space which Borromini envisaged in front of the oratory facade can be deduced from the radius which he used in drawing its curve. In the Windsor drawing of 1638 the radius is about 200 palmi (Cat. 41); in the revised drawing of 1660 the radius is reduced to 150 palmi (Cat. 90). In the bull of 1627 the depth of the piazza had been fixed at 150 palmi (Doc. 7).

In several other designs Borromini was careful to ensure that the center of vision fell inside the available viewing space. The fireplace in the Palazzo Barberini (C 51) was designed with volutes which converged on the papal throne at the other side of the *salone* (J. Connors, review of Thelen in *JSAH,* XXXV, 1976, 145). The radii used to draw the curve of the Propaganda Fide facade are limited to the width of the adjacent street (Alb. 889, illustrated in Portoghesi, *Linguaggio,* Fig. cix).

The concept of an "arc of vision" is discussed

above in Chapter 3, n. 59.

25. Cat. 80, 81, 89, 97.

26. See n. 4 above, and Cat. 82.

27. The Collegio Romano facade is discussed above in n. 4. The clearest example of superimposition of orders in Borromini's work occurs in the Propaganda Fide chapel, discussed in Chapter 7 below, n. 32. Patterns of brick bands are ubiquitous on the side walls of Roman buildings, reaching some complexity in, for example, the work of Maderno (Hibbard, *Maderno,* Pls. 12c and 141b).

28. Cat. 89.

29. Cat. 20h, caption no. 11. The basic treatise on Roman clocks and clocktowers is by the antiquarian Padre Giacomo Pouyard, printed in F. Cancellieri, *Le due nuove campane di Campidoglio,* Rome, 1806, 131–87.

30. The Casa Professa clock is possibly by Girolamo Rainaldi, though it is not discussed in the only treatment of the building, P. Pecchiai, *Il Gesù di Roma,* Rome, 1952, 295 ff.

31. *Röm. Ved.,* II, 26 ff., Fig. 9, and Pls. 64 and 65.

32. *Röm. Ved.,* II, Pls. 5 and 7.

33. Ferrerio-Falda, unnumbered plate with elevation of the Collegio Romano facade.

34. *Opera* I, Pls. II and III.

35. Thelen, 24 ff. and C 21; Hibbard, *Maderno,* Pls. 89a and 89c.

36. G. B. Mola, *Breve racconto,* 1663, ed. K. Noehles, Berlin, 1966, 78, fol. 125; the facade and presumably the clock date to 1636.

37. Not yet shown in a fresco by Nebbia (*Via Giulia,* 71), but visible in a Van Wittel view of 1682 and in old photographs (*GR,* Regola, III, 81–83).

38. Pollak, 165 ff., regs. 523–548. The clock is shown in views by Domenico Castelli (ca. 1644), Vasi (1757), and Pinelli (1834), and illustrated in C. D'Onofrio, *Scalinate di Roma,* Rome, 1974, Figs. 184 ff.

39. This clock seems to have been in existence until 1931, when this wing of the Casa Professa was set back in order to enlarge the Via delle Botteghe Oscure; it is faintly visible in an old Gabinetto Fotografico Nazionale photograph (G 751). There may have been some sort of clock at this point as early as 1587, to judge from the following notice: "dal corridore di S. Marco all' Orologio del monastero delli Padri del Gesù" (F. Cerasoli, "Notizie," *Bull. Comm.,* XXVIII, 1901, 348).

40. Tempesta also shows a similar clock on a medieval tower in the Palazzo Orsini dell' Orologio in the Campo de' Fiori.

41. The wrought-iron volutes of Borromini's *torre dell'orologio* seem to have influenced Bernini's project of 1667 for the *terzo braccio* of the colonnade of St. Peter's (Brauer-Wittkower, Pl. 64).

42. Cat. 97.

43. Cat. 87.

44. The so-called Isola dei Piatetti, mentioned in Decr. 356 and 359.

45. Cat. 103.

46. Cat. 106.

47. Cat. 111, 112.

48. Cat. 112.

49. Ponnelle and Bordet, 339.

50. This information is deduced from the long caption (transcribed in Gasbarri, 215–21) that accompanies the site plan shown in Cat. 15.

51. Gasbarri, 215–21; other trades are mentioned in Decr. 15, 17, 102, 288, 587, and 612. See also F. Martinelli, *Roma ricercata,* Rome, 1658, 475–85; and G. Morelli, *Le corporazioni romane di arti e mestieri,* Rome, 1937, 251 ff. (on the *rigattieri*).

52. Fluctuations in the size of the Congregation are discussed above in Chapter 5, n. 48.

53. Decr. 126.

54. Pirri, S.J., "La topografia del Gesù," 187 ff.

55. Pirri, S.J., *Giuseppe Valeriano,* 55 ff.

56. Ponnelle and Bordet, 343; *Opus,* XXI, 57^v, where the proprietor of a house on the site of the refectory is described as "huomo duro assai e cavilloso."

57. Scavizzi, "Attività edilizia a Roma," 165.

58. Decr. 6, 15, 47, 584, 585.

59. D. Pinkney, *Napoleon III and the Rebuilding of Paris,* Princeton, 1958, 10 ff. and 52, Pl. 12.

60. House no. 51 on Cat. 14 (Decr. 178, 179); and house no. 42 or 43 on Cat. 14 (Decr. 307).

61. Decr. 341, 349. The street is shown between houses no. 36 and 41 on Cat. 14.

62. *Opus,* X, 36^{r-v}.

63. Houses no. 26, 40, and 41 on Cat. 14 (see Decr. 349 and 360). The plague of 1656 is discussed in Gasbarri, 80–82.

64. Frommel, I, 90 ff., is the basic treatment of Renaissance *botteghe.*

65. Doc. 10, clause 5.

66. Decr. 15, 32, 37, 138.

67. Decr. 32.

68. The matter of shops is discussed in Decr. 138–140.

69. Cat. 89.

70. These buildings are discussed in Cat. 87, 98, 103, 106, 112, and 114.

71. Decr. 349.

72. A similar instance of this phenomenon oc-
curred in 1665, when Alexander VII gave the
Congregation of the Propaganda Fide the right
to acquire the houses and shops bordering on its
isola in order to safeguard "l'honorevolezza
dovuta al predetto Palazzo, Chiesa e Collegio"
(G. Antonazzi, "La sede della Sacra Congregazione e del Collegio Urbano," *Sacrae Congregationis
de Propaganda Fide Memoria Rerum,* ed. J. Metzler, Rome-Freiburg-Vienna, 1971, 330, especially n. 125).

73. Decr. 163; Cat. 82, 89, 111, 114.

74. The following street icons are documented:

a. Mosaic icon on the *torre dell'orologio,* 1657.
In 1629 there had been a debate on whether or
not to install the Madonna of S. Cecilia on the
corner of the new *casa* (Decr. 38). In 1648 the
Congregation decided against such an image
(Decr. 227), but in 1657 one was installed on
Spada's initiative (Decr. 354), apparently on the
design of Pietro da Cortona (P. Aringhi, *Memorie
. . . Virgilio Spada,* Venice, 1788, 54). The icon
appears in the prints of Barrière and Falda (Cat.
89a and 98b); it was restored in 1688–89 (Decr.
536, 539, 540).

b. Icon on the northwest corner of the *casa*
(Fig. 23), installed on Nov. 27, 1756 by the
sculptor Tommaso Righi and the painter Antonio
Bicchierai; in 1932 it was embellished with a
wrought-iron lamp salvaged from a demolished
house on the slopes of the Capitoline; the lamp
was removed in a subsequent restoration (G.
Scarafone, "L'edicola mariana di Piazza dell'
Orologio e i suoi autori," *L'Urbe,* XL, n.s. 2,
1977, 17–21; Decr. 608).

c. Icon on the northwest corner of the *appartamento* to the east of the church, at the intersection of the Via di Parione and the Via della
Chiesa Nuova. Installed by "devoti" in 1716
under the inscription of 1675 (Decr. 568, 570).

d. Icon of S. Filippo and the Virgin on the
corner of the Vicolo Sora and the Piazza della
Chiesa Nuova. Installed by "devoti" in 1755,
destroyed in 1885 (Decr. 605).

e. Icon shown in the Vasi print of 1758 on the
corner of the Piazza della Chiesa Nuova and the
Strada Nuova (Cat. 114).

f. Icon of the Virgin on the corner of the Strada
Nuova and the Via del Pellegrino. Installed by
the Congregation in 1629 (Russo, "Piazza della
Chiesa Nuova," 42, n. 50).

g. Icon of Filippo and the Virgin on the corner
of the Via del Pellegrino and the Arco di S.
Margherita. Attributed to Filippo della Valle

(1697–1768) under the patronage of Cardinal
Ottoboni (vice-chancellor 1689–1740) (*GR,*
Parione, II, 68 ff.).

75. N. Nicolai, *Sulla presidenza delle strade,*
Rome, 1829, II, 111.

76. M. Zocca in F. Castagnoli, *Topografia e ur-
banistica di Roma,* Bologna, 1958, 559 ff., 577 ff.,
and 699; Bianchi, "Piano regolatore," 33–43;
GR, Ponte, III, 14; and especially S. Kostof, *The
Third Rome 1870–1950* (exhibition catalogue),
Berkeley, University Art Museum, 1973. The
monthly progress of demolitions for the Corso
Vittorio can be followed in *Notizie degli scavi,*
1884–90, particularly 1887 for the Piazza della
Chiesa Nuova.

77. E. Sanjust de Teulada, *Relazione presentata
al Consiglio Comunale di Roma,* Rome, 1908, 14,
Part I, nos. 11 and 12; M. Zocca, *Topografia
. . . di Roma,* 616–19; *Via Giulia,* 149, and Pl. LV
following 148; S. Kostof, *The Third Rome,* 46 ff.

78. Governatorato di Roma, *Piano regolatore di
Roma 1931,* Milan and Rome, n.d. [1931], 53,
no. 17; *GR,* Trastevere, I, 36 ff.

79. Mussolini's discourse of 1925, quoted in
the *Piano regolatore di Roma 1931,* 7: "Voi con-
tinerete a liberare il tronco della grande quercia
da tutto cio che ancora l'aduggia."

80. M. Zocca, *Topografia . . . di Roma,* 664 ff.;
GR, Regola, III, 18.

Chapter 7

1. Doc. 10 and Decr. 128 both warn against
the danger of giving "poca edificatione a'
secolari."

2. Decr. 31; Ponnelle and Bordet, 574.

3. Decr. 31.

4. Pollak, 258 ff., reg. 855; P. Waddy, "The
Design and Designers of Palazzo Barberini,"
JSAH, XXXV, 1976, 151–85.

5. *Opus,* XIX, 53^r.

6. The adverse reaction on the part of the Congregation to this sort of dress, which was imposed on Spada when he assumed a post in Innocent X's *famiglia* in 1644, is documented in
Ehrle, "Spada," 5 ff., n. 21. See also L. Neppi,
Palazzo Spada, Rome, 1975, 127, n. 28.

7. *Dialogo,* 182; see also Chapter 3, n. 1 above.

8. Bibliography on Virgilio Spada: Ehrle,
"Spada"; L. Montalto, "Il problema della cupola
di Sant'Ignazio da padre Orazio Grassi e fratel
Pozzo a oggi," *Bollettino del Centro di Studi per la*

Storia dell'Architettura, XI, 1957, 44–48; Incisa della Rocchetta, *Dialogo;* Thelen, *Disegni;* Neppi, *Palazzo Spada;* and M. Heimbürger Ravalli, *Architettura scultura e arti minori nel barocco italiano. Ricerche nell'Archivio Spada,* Florence, 1977.

9. Heimbürger Ravalli, *Architettura, scultura e arti minori,* 15–17 and Figs. 12–16.

10. The key document on the affair of the St. Peter's campanile is V. Spada, *Discorso . . . sopra i disordini della facciata della chiesa, e portico di S. Pietro,* BV, Vat. lat. 11899. Bibliography: S. Fraschetti, *Il Bernini,* Milan, 1900, 162–69; Ehrle, "Spada," 21–28 and 77 ff. (with extracts); Hempel, 91–93; Brauer-Wittkower, 37–43; Thelen, *Disegni,* 14–17, cat. no. 4; H. Millon, "An Early Seventeenth Century Drawing of the Piazza S. Pietro," *Art Quarterly,* XXV, 1962, 236 ff., n. 2. The related text by Martino Longhi, *Discorso . . . delle cagioni delle ruine della facciata e campanile . . . di S. Pietro,* Rome, 1645, is published in facsimile in A. Pugliese and S. Rigano, "Martino Lunghi il giovane architetto," in M. Fagiolo, ed., *Architettura barocca a Roma,* Rome, 1972, 115–28.

11. Ehrle, "Spada," 11.

12. Ehrle, "Spada," Pl. VII.

13. *Dialogo,* 181, 183, 184, 196, 199, 204 ff.

14. F. Fasolo, *L'opera di Hieronimo e Carlo Rainaldi (1570–1655 e 1611–1691),* Rome, 1961, 310.

15. The program for the villa is to be found in BV, Vat. lat. 11258, fol. 14^{r-v} along with a plan sketched in ink by Virgilio and more professional drawings which have been attributed to Girolamo Rainaldi and Alessandro Algardi (*ibid.,* fol. 15, and Vat. lat. 11257, fols. 201^v–202^r). The attribution to Virgilio is confirmed by Heimbürger Ravalli's discovery of a more extended version of the program and of another sketch plan in the Archivio Spada (vol. 235, pp. 631–34, and vol. 186, pp. 1083–89). The project is undated, but certain internal references seem to indicate a date of 1644–45. On the one hand, it must come after Innocent X's coronation on September 15, 1644; on the other hand, Spada punningly refers to himself as "spropositato," which would appear to indicate that he had already resigned his office as Preposito of the Filippini, which occured in June 1645 (Incisa della Rocchetta, *Dialogo.* 176, n. 13). Bibliography: P. Portoghesi, "Intorno a una irrealizzata immagine borrominiana," *Quaderni dell'Istituto di Storia dell'Architettura dell' Università di Roma,* 6, 1954, 12–28; P. Portoghesi, *Cultura,* 224–26 (transcription) and Figs. 163, 164, 175;

Thelen, *Disegni,* 11 ff., cat. no. 2f–g; Heimbürger Ravalli, *Architettura scultura e arti minori,* 271–74 and Figs. 182–185.

16. Heimbürger Ravalli, *Architettura scultura e arti minori,* 32, n. 4.

17. Neppi, *Palazzo Spada,* 283.

18. Thelen, C 40–65, C 58–64, C 75–76; *Ragguagli,* 131 ff. and 81.

19. Chapter 3, n. 1 above.

20. The facade drawn on the earliest stratum of Alb. 171, the first project for S. Carlo alle Quattro Fontane, is an extremely mild curve; the drawing is discussed above in Chapter 3, n. 1.

21. The possible range of dates for Borromini's design for the SS. Apostoli altar is 1635–42: the Theatines conceded the chapel to Filomarino in 1635; Calandra signed the mosaic of the *Annunciation* in 1636 (in Rome), and in December 1636 Filomarino was promising to send the painting (i.e., the mosaic) to Naples; the two Filomarino portraits are dated 1641 and 1642 and the inscription 1642; finally, the altar was finished and dedicated in 1647 (F. Strazzullo, *La Chiesa dei SS. Apostoli,* Naples, 1959, 57 ff.). Within this range two scholars have preferred an early date of 1636, on the basis of a harmony which they perceive between the mosaic and the overall design (A. Gonzales-Palacios, "Giovanni Battista Calandra, un mosaicista alla corte dei Barberini," *Ricerche di Storia dell'Arte,* 1–2, 1976, 211–40; and A. Nava Cellini, "Per il Borromini e il Duquesnoy ai S.S. Apostoli di Napoli," *Paragone* [Arte], 329, 1977, 26–38). The older view placed the design rather later, about 1638–42, and saw it as a reflection of the oratory facade; it noted that the mosaic is rather small for the space that it has to fill (Hempel, 86 ff.; and Portoghesi, *Linguaggio,* 61). From a stylistic point of view, the late date is more convincing; it is reinforced by a document of July 20, 1639 in which the four capitals and bases are ordered from a *scarpellino* according to Borromini's drawings (ASR, not. Fonthia, vol. 3166, fols. 456^r ff., a reference which I owe to the kindness of Jennifer Montagu).

22. *Ragguagli,* 119 ff.

23. As is evident from comparison of the three early Lateran projects (Portoghesi, *Linguaggio,* Figs. xlii–xliv), with the final elevation shown in the drawing in Stockholm (P. Portoghesi, *Roma barocca,* Rome, 1966, Fig. 144).

24. The light source over the high altar of S. Ivo was to include mirrors to reflect eastern light downwards (*Ragguagli,* 227 ff.); the final effect can be seen in a print of 1720 (*Opera* I, Pl. XXXI), but the aperture was blocked during res-

torations of 1802–4 (R. Pacini, "Alterazioni dei monumenti borrominiani e prospettive di restauro," *Studi sul Borromini,* I, Rome, 1967, 334–38).

25. Cat. 49.

26. *Ragguagli,* 95 ff. and 214 ff.; Portoghesi, *Linguaggio,* Fig. 150.

27. Passeri-Hess, 362.

28. F. Martinelli, *Primo trofeo della S.ma croce,* Rome, 1655, 134; C. Rasponi, *De Basilica et Patriarchio Lateranensi,* Rome, 1656–57, 85.

29. The classic statement of this view is in P. Letarouilly, *Edifices de Rome moderne,* Liège, 1849, I, 253:

> On doit vivement déplorer qu'une oeuvre d'une conception aussi belle soi déparée par une foule d'extravagances. . . . Mais abstenons-nous de parler des élévations de ce vaste édifice, cherchons plutôt à les oublier, pour ne conserver d'autre impression que celle de la beauté et du mérite incontestable de ce plan.

Quatremère de Quincy admired the uncommon intelligence in the distribution of the rooms (*Encyclopédie métodique,* 1788, quoted in de Bernardi Ferrero, xxiv); Milizia condemned the exterior but praised the good judgment of the habitation (*Memorie degli architetti antichi e moderni,* 1768, and *Roma delle belle arti del disegno,* Bassano, 1787, quoted in de Bernardi Ferrero, xviii ff.); and Bottari thought that Borromini was "mirabile" in planning the building, "sapere ben compartire una fabrica, sicche torni vaga e comoda," which he knew through the prints of the *Opus* (*Dialoghi sopra le tre arti del disegno,* Naples, 1772, 165).

30. The dates of the Propaganda Fide have been documented in detail by Msgr. G. Antonazzi, "La sede della Sacra Congregazione e del Collegio Urbano," *Sacrae Congregationis de Propaganda Fide Memoria Rerum,* ed. J. Metzler, Rome-Freiburg-Vienna, 1971, 306–34. Bernini's facade and oval chapel were designed and built in 1634; and in 1644, on his advice, the north facade of the old Palazzo Ferratini was consolidated and reinforced. Gaspare de Vecchi designed the east dormitory wing on the Via Due Macelli in 1639; it was carried out between 1640 and 1645 (de Vecchi died in 1643 or 1644); his southeast corner is shown with an inscription dated 1642 in a later drawing by F. Righi (Alb. 899). Borromini was appointed architect in 1646; his first plan was presented and criticized in 1647; his revised plan, including a new chapel to replace Bernini's, was presented in 1652; and

after many delays work finally began on the south wing, the one adjacent to S. Andrea delle Fratte, in 1652. Demolition and other preparations for the east wing were under way in 1655, but most of the work seems to have been done in 1660–62. The structure of the chapel was complete in 1664, and the stuccoes were done in 1665.

The facade first appears on Alb. 898 as a design five bays wide and two stories high. It was expanded to seven bays on Alb. 889. Falda's print of 1665 (*Nuovo teatro,* Rome, 1665) shows a facade seven bays wide and two stories high, with an open loggia on top. The open loggia was then filled by a third-story attic, which is first shown in a print of 1666 (M. G. de Rossi and L. Cruyl, *Prospectus Locorum Urbis Romae,* Rome, 1666, frontispiece).

31. *Loggie scoperte* and sunken corridors are shown on Alb. 902; the curved pilaster screen appears on Alb. 887a, 888, and 889a, where an inscription describes it as "Alta solo il primo ordine" (Hempel, 159 ff., Figs. 56, 58, and 59).

32. The plan of the Re Magi Chapel is based on Palladio's Redentore, while the elevation shown in Alb. 906 (Hempel, Pl. 108) began as a close copy of the facade of Palladio's Palazzo Valmarana in Vicenza (*Quattro libri,* II, 17), including at first even the balustrade and bulging cornice of the model, which were omitted in the final design. The cushion-like pilaster bases of the chapel are adapted from a similar motif in the Villa Madama, which Raphael in turn had borrowed from the Arco di Portogallo (J. Shearman, "Raphael as Architect," *Journal of the Royal Society of Arts,* CXVI, 1968, 388–409); Borromini copied one of the Raphael bases in a beautiful elevation drawing, Thelen's C 80 (J. Connors, review of Thelen, in *JSAH,* XXXV, 1976, 146).

Appendix II

1. G. Baglione, *Le vite de pittori, scultori, et architetti,* Rome, 1642, 181: "Paolo Marucelli Romano"; an *avviso* on Maruscelli's death is in *Roma,* XVI, 1938, 121.

2. Documents from the church archive are published by Ettore Ricci, d.O., *La Chiesa dell'Immacolata Concezione e di San Filippo Neri (Chiesa Nuova) in Perugia* (Deputazione di Storia Patria per l'Umbria. Appendici al Bollettino, No. 10), Perugia, 1969, 7 ff.; Ricci cites the MS by Carlo Baglione, d.O. (d. 1726), *Memorie della Chiesa*

Nuova di S. Filippo Neri.

3. AV, C.II.8. Autograph plan by Maruscelli which corresponds to the church as built.

4. S. Ortolani, *S. Andrea della Valle* (Le Chiese di Roma Illustrate, 4), Rome, n.d., 6 ff.; Hibbard, *Maderno,* 155.

5. Hibbard, *Licenze,* nos. 120 and 160. F. Martinelli, *Carbognano illustrato,* Rome, 1695, 58 ff.: "Girolamo Piscioletti da Carbognano . . . parentò con li Massimi, avando dato una sua sorella al padre di Marcantonio de' Massimi, che alhora habitava, dove è stata fatto il convento di S. Andrea della Valle."

6. G. Moroni, *Dizionario di erudizione storico-ecclesiastica da S. Pietro,* Rome and Venice, LII, 90 ff.; C. Eubel, *Hierarchia Catholica,* Munich, 1913, III, 50.

7. ASR, Dis. e Map., cart. 85, fol. 481: 67.4 × 48.1, ink with yellow and blue-gray wash; illustrated in Hibbard, *Licenze,* Fig. 45. An alternative project of uncertain date exists in ASR, Dis. e Map., cart. 84, fol. 479; it shows a single large trapezoidal court at the rear of the building, with long uninterrupted corridors running down all the wings. The rooms are identified by a caption that outlines the program of the convent in summary form. The major rooms and services mentioned are the following: sacristy, *cappelletta, camerine* for confessions, loggie with open arches facing a cloister, two stories of rooms and one of mezzanines, oratory with room above for the General Chapter, refectory with library above, kitchen with service rooms and *dispensa,* recreation room, staircase, and prison.

8. P. Totti, *Ritratto di Roma moderna,* Rome, 1638, 373. The licences are in ASR, Presidenza delle Strade, busta 46, c. 75^{r-v}; busta 47, cc. 88^{v}–89^{r}; busta 54, c. 14^{r}; and busta 55, c. 30^{r}.

9. *Dialogo,* 181; *Opus,* VI: "finestre senz' ordine e regola alcuna."

10. J. Schmidlin, *Geschichte der deutschen Nationalkirche in Rom S. Maria dell'Anima,* Freiburg im Breisgau, 1906, 511 ff.; J. Lohninger, *S. Maria dell'Anima. Die deutsche Nationalkirche in Rom,* Rome, 1909, 116–22.

11. Baglione, *Le vite de pittori, scultori, et architetti,* 181.

12. Bellori, Life of Andrea Sacchi, Rouen MS 2506, Montbret 171: "rinovando il vecchio e cadente Convento della Minerva verso il Collegio Romano, Andrea lo dispose con quel bello, e comodo uso di fabrica . . . distribui gl'ornamenti della Sagristia" (quoted by M. Piacentini, "Architetti romani minori nel 600," *Palladio,* IV, 1940, 29–31). A full treatment of the complex is given in A. S. Harris, *Andrea Sacchi,*

Princeton, 1977, 79–81 and Pls. 77–84.

13. Pollak, 182, regs. 623–631.

14. Pollak, 206, regs. 729–730. Since Urban VIII was crowned on September 29, 1623 (Eubel, *Hierarchia,* IV, 1935, 17), a date of September 29, 1640 to September 28, 1641 may be deduced from the inscription: "URBANI VIII/ PONT.OPT.MAX./ANNO XVIII." A drawing by Borromini's assistant Righi (Alb. 899) records a similar corner by Gaspare de Vecchi at the Propaganda Fide, dated 1642.

15. G. B. Falda, *Nuovo teatro,* I, Rome, 1665, unnumbered plate. The Mastri di Strade issued the following license on Nov. 20, 1692:

> Concediamo licenza alli Rev. PP. di S. Maria sopra Minerva di due fili per rifare il muro delle facciate della fabrica nuova del loro convento cioè la facciata verso la Piazza detta della Guglia di S. Macu[to], e la facciata della strada, che va da detta Piazza alla Rotonda, incontro al Seminario Romano nel Rione della Pigna, senza occupare sito del publico, et a filo della fabrica vecchia . . . (ASR, Presidenza delle Strade, busta 53, c. 65^{r-v}).

The date of the Casanatense foundations is recorded in connection with discoveries of Egyptian antiquities in the Serapaeum (R. Lanciani in *Storia degli Scavi,* 1883, 244).

16. Baglione, *Vite,* 339. The facade inscription on the Via del Corso is datable to 1623–24; the rear wing of the convent is authorized in a license of Nov. 29, 1659 (ASR, Presidenza delle Strade, busta 45, cc. 131^{v}–132^{r}).

17. The guidebook attributions were first sifted by O. Pollak, "Architektenmärchen," *Kunstgeschichtliches Jahrbuch der K.K. Zentral-Kommission,* IV, 1910, Beiblatt, 163–74. The basic study is D. Gnoli, "Il Palazzo del Senato già Madama," *Nuova Antologia,* August 1, 1926, 249–64; V. del Gaizo and others, *Il Palazzo Madama sede del senato,* Rome, 1969, contributes nothing beyond photographs of the inaccessible interior. Plans by the Sangallo family are in Frommel, P1.177b–d. Cigoli's unbuilt project for Cosimo II is described in Baldinucci, *Notizie de'professori di disegno,* 1812, IX, 120 ff.: ". . . fece un modello in tal proportione, che si con' duceva il palazzo colla facciata fino à mezo essa piazza, incrostandolo tutto di bozze di travertini" (quoted in Pollak, "Architektenmärchen," 171).

18. There is a drawing of the facade in the Lanciani Collection in the Palazzo Venezia, 52.162, ink and brown wash over graphite, 22.2 × 35.9 cm. It appears to be an elevation drawn

by Falda for the print in Ferrerio-Falda, Pl. 11, which corresponds exactly to the drawing but reverses the direction of light. The drawing is reproduced by E. Bentivoglio, "Un palazzo 'barocco' nella Roma di Leone X," *Architettura*, XVIII, 1972, 204, with the mistaken assertion that it shows traces of Borromini's style.

19. F. Sabatini, *La chiesa di S. Salvatore in Thermis*, Rome, 1907; the garden loggia and south court of the Renaissance palace appear in C. Huelsen and H. Egger, *Die römischen Skizzenbücher von Marten van Heemskerck*, I, 4, fol. 5^r and II, 29 ff., fol. 48^r. A comparison of the drawings with the plan in Ferrerio-Falda, Pl. 12, suggests that Maruscelli left the Renaissance loggia intact in his rebuilding.

20. Stockholm drawings, Nationalmuseum, Sammlung Tessin, Nr. THC 3211–3213. An inscription on the "2.0 Piano" plan (THC 3212: "vano per l'altezza della sala") proves that the *salone* was originally two stories high, as in the Palazzo Farnese.

21. Falda, *Nuovo teatro*, I, unnumbered print of S. Luigi dei Francesi.

22. Two plans in the Coll. Lanciani, 52.163 and 164, show the state of the palace in 1826, when the *salone* had already been subdivided into three smaller rooms on the *piano nobile.*

23. L. Neppi, *Palazzo Spada*, Rome, 1975, 122, n. 8, which quotes a letter of Bernardino to Virgilio Spada of March 12, 1650:

Sono 18 anni [i.e., 1632] ch'io trattai del Palazzo Cupis et in quel tempo mi valevo del Maruscelli Architetto presso del quale erano la pianta di detto e d'alcun altro palazzo, con occasione massime di un notabile rassettamento ch'io intendevo di farvi dentro e fuori. Mori pochi mesi or sono il Maruscello, onde ho mandato a chiamare il figliolo.

Spada told his brother that the Palazzo Capodiferro would be better and cheaper (n. 9).

24. Neppi, *Palazzo Spada*, 134–40. Since neither this alteration nor any others by Maruscelli appear on the plan in Ferrerio-Falda, I, n.d., Pl. 33, it must be assumed that this print reflects a sixteenth-century drawing rather than the state of the palace when it was published in ca. 1655.

25. Neppi, *Palazzo Spada*, 270, Doc. 25, and also 134–40.

26. Neppi, *Palazzo Spada*, 147; 175–82; and 271 ff., Docs. 29, 30.

27. Cat. 77, 78. Neppi, *Palazzo Spada*, photograph on p. 184.

28. Neppi, *Palazzo Spada*, 126 and 128, n. 35.

29. Neppi, *Palazzo Spada*, 125 ff., n. 19; and 134, n. 13; M. Heimbürger Ravalli, *Architettura scultura e arti minori nel barocco italiano. Ricerche nell'Archivio Spada*, Florence, 1977, 75 ff.

30. Neppi, *Palazzo Spada*, 144, n. 82.

31. Neppi, *Palazzo Spada*, 290, Doc. 47, section 16:

[Bernardino] fece una galleria sopra un vicolo, che tira a strada Giulia, e fatta che fu, convenne non solo rifondarla, ma crescere notabilmente la grossezza delle muraglie, perche essendo sciolta, benche non vi sia volta se non nella parte inferiore, minacciava rovina.

The second complaint is in an undated letter of Virgilio to Bernardino quoted in Neppi, *Palazzo Spada*, 134:

Il pensiero che già propose il Maruscelli, quale quando non gostasse un soldo ad ogni modo nol farei, parendomi tanto ignobile, e tanto fuori d'architettura che sii più il danno che risulta da un prospetto così brutto, che l'utile del poter sboccar nelle loggie, tanto maggiormente mi pare inutile, quanto che porta la perdita d'una stanza, e gosta qualche centinaro di scudi.

32. S. Ortolani, *San Carlo a' Catinari* (Le Chiese di Roma Illustrate, 18), Rome, n.d., 20; G. B. Mola, *Breve racconto*, ed. Noehles, fol. 164.

33. Baglione, 1642, 310; F. Titi, *Descrizione delle pitture*, Rome, 1723, 327, where the facade is attributed to C. Fontana. The inscriptions flanking the high altar are dated 1643 and 1647. Altars are shown in A. Cicinelli, *S. Maria dell' Umiltà*, Rome, 1970, Figs. 24, 25. Cf. Cat. 28.

34. The history of this building is still quite obscure. According to A. Steinhuber, *Geschichte des Collegium Germanicum Hungaricum in Rom*, Freiburg im Breisgau, 1895, I, 367, the new building was constructed in 1632–37 at a cost of ▽43,000 plus ▽20,000 in debts; no information is given on the architect. According to the article in Thieme-Becker by F. Noack (XXIV, 1930, 187) Maruscelli's work at the college dates to 1638. There are some building licenses in Hibbard, *Licenze*, nos. 122 and 174–176. The monograph by C. Mancini, *S. Apollinare* (Le Chiese di Roma Illustrate, 93) is uninformative. The entire complex is shown in three sets of plans: the first set comprises Borromini's drawings for the Piazza di S. Agostino (Hempel, Figs. 62–64); the second, an eighteenth-century plan (ASR, Dis. e map., cart. 88, fol. 595); and the third, four plans

of the nineteenth century (ASR, Dis. e map., cart. 85, fol. 483).

35. Mola, ed. Noehles, fols. 114 and 153.

36. *Via Giulia,* 397, 406, Fig. 32.

37. Noack, Thieme-Becker, XXIV, 1930, 187.

38. Pollak, 148, reg. 411.

39. Ehrle, "Spada," 23.

40. G. Eimer, *La fabbrica di S. Agnese in Navona,* Stockholm, 1970, I, 201.

41. The project was conceived in 1642 (*avviso* in E. Rossi, *Roma,* XVI, 1938, 121). Innocent X's *motu proprio* awarding the job to Maruscelli is in ASR, R.C.A., not. P. A. Severus, vol. 1881, c. 849^r. The contract contains twenty-three clauses and discusses the "societas super negotio Paludum Pontinarum" which Maruscelli was to form. Further *avvisi* are in *Roma,* XVII, 1939, 175, including the announcement of Maruscelli's death.

42. Doc. 22.

43. Heimbürger Ravalli, *Architettura scultura e arti minori,* 157–88.

44. Maderno's library is documented in Hibbard, *Maderno,* 98 and 103. Cortona owned 222 books, in all, but fewer architectural and technical books than Maruscelli (K. Noehles, *La chiesa dei SS. Luca e Martina,* Rome, 1970, 365–67). The 1667 inventory of Borromini's possessions mentions at least 459 books, including 123 folio volumes on architecture, but gives no titles (*Ragguagli,* 163–76).

45. Ricci, *Chiesa . . . in Perugia,* 46 letter of May 19, 1646 to the Oratorians of Perugia:

Prima di metter mano a cosa alcuna bisogna fare un disegnio maggiore della facciata, perche quello che già fece era piccolo e fu fatto solo per dare sodisfatione di vedere a presso a poco quello doveva essere; e per ciò havendosi a far l'opera, è necessario prima farvi altra diligenza, et in oltre fare il disegno a pezzo per pezzo di tutte le cornici, base, et altre cose necessarie in grande della giusta misura che devono essere.

Documents

The archives of the Congregazione dell'Oratorio di Roma were originally housed in rooms adjacent to the *salone* of the Vallicella library. After the dissolution of the Congregation in the years following 1871, part of the archives, particularly papers relating to legal and financial matters, were taken and incorporated into the Archivio di Stato; a detailed index is provided by A. M. Corbo, *L'archivio della Congregazione dell'Oratorio di Roma e l'archivio della Abbazia di S. Giovanni in Venere: Inventario* (Quaderni della Rassegna degli Archivi di Stato, 27), Rome, 1964; a selection is presented along with many other useful documents in M. del Piazzo, *Ragguagli borrominiani,* Rome, 1968. The more important documents, as far as this study is concerned, remained at the Vallicella. Recently an index has appeared of these holdings: G. Morello and F. Dante, "L'Archivio della Congregazione dell'Oratorio di Roma alla Chiesa Nuova," *Ricerche per la Storia Religiosa di Roma,* 2, 1978, 275–362; the index makes it clear that a considerable amount of unexploited material remains, particularly for the quantitatively oriented historian, in matters of economics and finance. For the historian of art and architecture the key source material is to be found in the *Libri dei decreti,* particularly the five volumes that cover the period 1616–1800 (C.I.6 to C.I.10). The *decreti* are the minutes of meetings of the Congregation, either the Congregation of the Four Deputies (CDep), or the Congregation at large (CGen); they are frequently cited and sometimes transcribed in the standard literature, such as Ponnelle and Bordet, Hempel, Hess, Russo, Portoghesi, Bruschi, and Pacini; in addition, a summary of their contents is given in the chapter on the building in C. Gasbarri, *L'Oratorio romano dal cinquecento al novecento,* Rome, 1962. Many important excerpts from the *decreti* have been published by Marchese G. Incisa della Rocchetta, particularly in the edition of Virgilio Spada's *Dialogo,* but also in numerous other publications (a full list of which is given in *Studi offerti a Giovanni Incisa della Rocchetta,* Rome, 1973, xi–xxvi); thanks to his generosity I consulted the *decreti* up to 1666 in the transcripts which he prepared for publication in the *Archivio della Società Romana di Storia Patria,* CII, 1981. Throughout my text the abbreviation Decr. refers to the numbering system used in this publication. Reference should also be made to the *schedario* covering 536 works of art at the Vallicella compiled by Lionello Neppi for the Soprintendenza delle Gallerie in Palazzo Venezia, which contains an immense amount of valuable documentation from the *decreti* and other sources. Although focused more on painting and sculpture than on architecture, it forms the basis for much of the information presented in Hess's analysis of the chapels of S. Maria in Vallicella. The documents that follow, for the most part from the Archivio di Stato or the Vallicella Archives, are intended to supplement this material.

In the following transcriptions abbreviations are usually spelled out in full if they are obvious; if not, letters have been added in square brackets. Italics identify passages or words added in the margins or between the lines of the original text. The punctuation is my own; u is distinguished from v; *scudi* and *baiocchi* are abbreviated by using the symbol ∇ and a decimal point. Many documents, especially payments for routine or unspecified work, have had to be sharply abridged; however, summaries and exact references are given so that the material can be found by anyone who wants to pursue it further.

1.   1585 May (ultimo giorno)
     AV, C.I.26 (unpaginated).
[The Filippini] cupientes eorum aedes, et oratorium pro comoda, et congrua ipsius Congregationis et illius patrum habitatione ampliare, et construere nuper duas domos eorum habitationi, contiguas ad moniales olim Monasterij sanctae Helisabet, ad ven. Monasterium S.ti Iacobi dele Moratte de urbe nuncupatum in Regione Trivij existen[tem] Annis prox. retroactis translatas . . . etc.

2.   1587
     AV, C.I.26 (unpaginated).
Payments for work on the casa and on the loggie over the chapels of S. Maria in Vallicella.
Loggie et lavoro disfatto et rifatto verso ponente sopra le cappelle a mano manca a l'intrar della chiesia, summa ∇51.39
Loggie . . . le . . . a mano dritta a l'intrar la chiesia disfatto et rifatto il tetto[?]   60.19
Lavori fatti nella libraria   7.26
Tagliature et levature delli ornamenti della facciata dinanzi dove son fatte le bottege 25.60
Lavoro fatto nelle bottege summa ∇17.40 et in tutto le altre stantie di sopra computatoci li sopradetti∇17.40 summano   73.27
                                      ∇238.63

3.   1611
     ASR, CRM, Oratorio dei Filippini, vol. 140, cc. 390^r ff.
Copy of a document drafted by the Oblates of Milan (Barnabites) in which they outline their plan to erect a church on the site of the Osteria della Spada in the Piazza di Monte Giordano, and in which they attempt to refute the Oratorians' case against them. One of the many arguments produced by the Oratorians to block the new church was allegedly the following:
4.o Dicono di più che per esser tanto stretti, et scomodi di stanze dove al presente stanno, et

anco esser humidi, e di cattiva aria, pretendono allargarsi intorno su la piazza di Monte Giordano, e far il convento, et oratorio loro dall' altra parte della chiesa, pretendendo di voler chiuder la strada del Corallo, et abbandonare il lor convento dove adesso habitano, e vi hanno habitato per tanto tempo sotto pretesto di haver fatto il disegno del convento già molto anni sono.

The Oblates allege that there will be no competition with S. Maria in Vallicella since their church will be a *chiesa collegiata;* that the Oratorians can easily expand to the east; that there is no *mal aria* in this densely inhabited part of Rome and that in any case S. Filippo lived here until the age of 84; that the Oratorians can always inhabit the house of Cardinal Baronio which they now rent out for∇400; and finally that the glory of their S. Carlo demands that their church be built not "in qualch'angolo, o luogho indegno, o vero sottoposto al fiume, o altre miserie, ma si bene in quel luogho dove maggiormente illustrerà questa città si con la dovotione, e concorso del medesimo santo com'anco con la magnificenza della fabrica, che si pretendi di fare . . ."

Documents on this subject continue to c. 399^r, including Paul V's brief of March 26, 1611 (c. 392^{r-v}) and the affidavits of witnesses that as early as 1605 it was common knowledge that the Oratorians wanted to buy a house in the Piazza di Monte Giordano with the intention of transferring their residence there (c. 393^{r-v}).

4.   1620 September 7
     AV, C.I.32 (unpaginated).
Valuation of the Casa dei Rusconi (Fig. 123, no. 22) by F.Breccioli, M.Arconio, and C. Maderno.
Fù stimata la casa grande delli Signori Rusconi nella strada di Parione da Filippo Breccioli et Mario Arconio, e perche non erano detti periti

d'accordo nelle stime elessero amicabilmente per terzo perito Carlo Maderni il quale valutò il sito di detta casa∇25 la canna et il sito della casetta dietro posta nella piazzatta di [*crossed out:* Monte Gior] S.ta Cecilia a Monte Giordano valutò il sito ∇18 la canna come per gl'atti del Bonelli notaio di camera [*added in margin:* mi pare che vi fusse presente al voto del Maderni anche Domenico Castelli].

5. 1622 (day left blank)
AV, C.I.32 (unpaginated).
Valuation of the house of Pietro Colutio and Laetitia Cocciani by G. A. de Pomis, D. Maderno, H. Torriani, and P. Maruscelli. Cf. Decr. 13, Cat. 14.
Fù stimata la casa di Pietro Colutio et Lettitia Cocciana sua moglie posta nella strada che da Monte Giordano va all'novo oratorio della Chiesa Nova, furono periti per parte delli Padri Gio. Antonio de Pomis, il quale stimò il sito∇18 la canna, et per parte delli padroni della Casa Domenico Maderni il quale stimò il sito∇30 la canna, fù eletto 3.o perito Horatio Torriani il quale stimò il sito ∇20 la canna, fù anche eletto 4.o perito Paolo Maruscelli il quale retificò la stima del Torriani come per gl'atti del Amadei notaio A.C.

6. 1625 (?) November 24
AV, C.I.32 (unpaginated).
Valuation of the Casa dei Rusconi by P. Maruscelli.
Fù stimata la casa delli SS.ri Rusconi nella piazzetta di S.ta Cecilia dove habitava il parocchiano da Paolo Maruscelli perito comunemente et amicabilmente eletto dalle parti, il quale valuto il sito di detta casa∇18 la canna.

7. 1627 January 26
ASR, CRM, Oratorio dei Filippini, vol. 160 (unpaginated).
Copy of the decree of Urban VIII authorizing the Congregation to open the Strada Nuova.
Rmo. Cardinale Cammerlengo, e Mastri di Strada.
Desiderando li Preti della Congregatione dell' Oratorio esistenti nella Chiesa di S. Maria in Vallicella di questa nostra Città di Roma per commodo publico come per ornamento di detta Loro Chiesa, e di questa Città aprire una strada del Pellegrino di larghezza di p. 40 e quel più, che bisognerà ad arbitrio di detti Preti, e a suo tempo fare una piazza avanti detta chiesa di canne 20 in circa in longhezza e di larghezza di canne 15 in circa, acciò possino mettere in essecuzione tal'

opra, abbiamo deliberato di concederli l'infrascritte grazie . . . [legal language] . . . sforziati tutti i Padroni delle case, che faranno di bisogno per l'apertura di detta strada, come per la detta piazza, e loro fabrica da farsi a suo tempo, et in specie delle due Isolette dette del Piatteto e Pizzomerlo, et altre ancorche spettassero così per l'utile, come per il diretto dominio, o altra raggione, a qualsivoglia persona, quanto si voglia privillegiata, etiam Chiese, Collegi, luoghi pij a vendere a detti Padri le dette case, et Isolette con tutti i loro membri, raggioni, pertinenze per li prezzi da stimarsi da due Periti. . . . [legal terms for choosing the *periti* according to the bull of Gregory XIII] . . . Et affincche la strada da farsi come sopra si mantenghi perpetuamente dritta, et uguale per maggiore ornamento della Città, vogliamo et ordiniamo, che persona alcuna, etiam privilegiata, e qualificata come sopra non possa fare Ponti, tavolati, ferrate di cantina, mettere colonne, fare ringhiere, cordonate, scalini, o altrimente fabricare in detta strada senza consenso di detti Preti, ne in essa fare innovatione alcuna per causa di porte, o fenestre senza prima pagare a detti Preti quello, che a voi parerà giusto per il commodo che riceveranno da detta strada, e piazza, ne mastri di strada, o altri possono in detta strada o piazza cedere, o vendere Ius ad alcuno di vendervi o farvi botteghe, o altro. Voi dunque per essecuzione delle presenti assisterete alla detta opera, sino alla suo totale perfettione volendo Noi, e decretando . . . [legal language excluding loopholes].
Dato nel nostro Palazzo di S. Pietro il di 26 gen.o 1627 Urbanus PP. VIII

8. 1630 May 7
AV, C.I.32 (unpaginated).
Misura e stima of the Strada Nuova by Paolo Maruscelli. Among other pieces of work the following are specified:
Per haver cavato il fosso e fatto la chiavica murata con suo massiccio, sponde e volta incollata dentro div.o palmi 1¼ che porta l'acqua delli cortili alla chiavica sotto la strada del Pelegrino . . . palmi 74½∇18.62
Sommario
Tutta la terra cavata e portata via per abbassare tutta la strada, e far la selciata avanti le case delli padri, e del Signore Antonio Cerro e quad[ra]ta insieme canne 62:577 quale a giulij 33 la canna ∇206.50
Sommano insieme tutte le sopradette partite ∇585.15
Paolo Maruscelli m.o

9. 1633

ASR, CRM, Oratorio dei Filippini, vol. 160 (unpaginated).

Copy of a request made by the Oratorians to Cardinal (Antonio) Barberini for permission to use income on their capital in continuing the casa; copy sent to Cardinal Bernardino Spada.

Eminentissimo Signore,

Poiche consta alla Sacra Visita chi li Preti della Congregatione dell'Oratorio di Roma non fanno spese sopra le forze e bisogni loro, non pare, che se li dovessero legar le mani, di non poter spendere almeno quei pochi avanzi, che si vanno facendo ogni anno detratte tutte le spese ordinarie e straordinarie restando ordinariamente in cassa qualche migliaro di scudi; poiche il limitare, o sminuire i detti avanzi saria un rendere la fabrica quasi immortale oltre il danno notabile, che ne seguirebbe per la perdita di tempo che fariano i membri già fabricati, e saria anco un' disanimare, tanto i benefattori di càsa, quanto gl'esterni vedendo la fabrica caminare tanto lentamente, e se per fare la strada inanzi alla Chiesa buttando, e donando al publico tanta quantità di case, la qual strada non era però di tanta necessità potendo bastare un poco più di piazza, la sacra Visita diede licenza a i suddetti Preti l'anno 1627 all 29 di Gennaro, di spendere per la nuova strada e piazza ∇10,000 di capitale; quanto è più raggionevole, che per servitio della Chiesa e casa si possino spendere nella sacristia, et habitatione de sudetti gl'avanzi che si fanno ogn'anno, senza toccar cosa alcuna del capitale. Però si supplica humilmente V. Em.za che continuando verso la sudetta Congregatione i suoi favori resti servita rappresentare all'Emin.mo Sig.re Card.le Vicario, et a chi meglio le parerà l'angustie, e necessità di detta Congregatione che il tutto si receverà per gratia da V. Em.za. Etc.

10. 1633

Bibl. Vall., Cod. O 57², fasc. 64, fos. 524^r–526^v.

Report to the Sacra Visita of Urban VIII representing the views of the majority of the Congregation in favor of continuing the building program, against the minority opposed to the new casa.

Havendo già tanti anni sono la Congregatione dell'Oratorio di Roma havuto animo, e trattato di fare la sua habitatione verso Monte Giordano, per essecutione di questa sua volontà in piena Congregatione fù risoluto nemine discrepante con tutti li voti affirmativi, che si comprassero le case, che facevano di bisogno per fare detta habitatione, et Oratorio verso la piazza di Monte Giordano, come consta per il decreto fatto in

Congregatione Generale a di 6. di Maggio 1611. come nel 3.o libro de decreti fol. 133.

A quest'effetto fù per ordine, e decreto dell' istessa Congregatione nel 3 libro di decreti fol. 169 [a di ii di dicembre 1613] ottenuto un Breve dalla felice memoria di Papa Paolo V di poter' accomprare tutte le case delle due isole, che sono poste fra la Chiesa, et Casa di detti padri, et la suddetta piazza di Monte Giordano, le quali essendo state accomprate per la maggior parte.

L'anno del Signore 1621 a di 20 di Ottobre fù proposto, e risoluto dalla maggior parte, cioè con voti secreti 19 bianchi per l'affirmativa, e 7 neri per la parte contraria, che quanto prima si cominciasse la sacristia da fabricarsi nella parte del Vicolo tra la chiesa, e Monte Giordano secondo il modello approvato dall'Architetto, e dall' istessa Congregatione come si vede per più decreti dell'anno 1621 à di 20 di Ottobre, et a di 24. del med.o mese, et anno.

Fù per tanto dato principio alla nova Sacristia con saputa di Mons.re Viceg[eren].te di quel tempo, il quale diede anco licenza al Padre Preposito di benedire la prima pietra. E perche vi restavano ancora alcune case da comprare del Sig.r Teodosio de'Rossi per compimento delle stanze necessarie per uso di detta sacristia fù proposto ultimamente cioèo dell'anno presente 1633 a di 6. di lug.o se era bene fare una procura speciale in persona del P. Procuratore della Casa di poter'accomprare le dette case ad effetto come sopra; e fù risoluto che si facesse, come fù fatta con l'intervento, e consenso di tutti li Padri ad 16 di lug.o 1633. Dal che si può vedere, che la mente della Congregatione persiste nella determinatione fatta, e continuata per tanti anni di fare la sacristia, Oratorio, et habitatione verso Monte Giordano; e questo per molte ragioni, et inconvenienti, che ne seguirebbono facendosi altrimente.

Prima: perche tutte le case, o la maggior parte è stata accomprata per vigore del Breve suddetto a stima di periti senza l'aug[umen].to della Bolla con obligo di servirsene per detta fabrica; il che non seguendo saria tenuta la Congregatione a restorare i Venditori d'ogni danno, et interesse; anzi essendo alcune di quelle state donate a questo fine, bisognaria restituirle con scommodo, e detrimento *notabile*. Inoltre a questo med.o effetto fù ottenuta la chiesa, che fù di S.ta Cecilia conforme al decreto fatto dalla Congregatione Generale nell'anno 1623 a di 22 di Genn.o come nel libro 3.o de decreti a fol. 16 et demolita per ordine della Sacra Visita, fù anche chiuso /*fol. 524ᵛ* / il Vicolo, che passava da Parione a Pizzomerlo per concessione della fel. me. di Papa

Gregorio XV e furono parimente tenuti indietro i Padri Bernabiti, e quelli della Comp.a di S. Carlo, quali disegnavano di fabricar Chiesa, dove sta hoggi l'hostaria della Spada onde furono apportate per parte della Congregatione molte dottrine, et in particolare quella di San Bonaventura, che prova, che i luochi de'i Religiosi devono havere una certa distanza fra di loro per ovviare all'emulationi, e disordini, che sogliono avvenire in simili casi. Hora ritrovandosi già fatta la sacristia con stanze, e loggie da quella parte, troppo gran disordine danno, e scandolo ne seguirebbe con mormoratione de gli'interesati, e di tutto il popolo, che restarià sopramodo scandalizato della Congregatione, la quale ne restarià tal volta con carico grave di coscienza, quando s'intermettesse l'opera.

2.o Nel sito che si ritrovano al presente può vedere ognuno, che non vi è in tutta Roma loco pio, o religioso più male alloggiato, senza commodità di potersi allargare, poiche si trovano angustiati da ogni parte dalla gran frequenza dell' habitato, di modo che etiamdio con spesa grandissima non saria possibile potersi dilatare, dove all'incontro dall'altra banda vengono à godere della commodità della piazza di Monte Giordano, di quella di Pizzomerlo, e della strada di Parione, che in quella parte resta assai larga; assicurandosi inoltre dall'inondatione del Tevere, dalla quale ne patirono gran danno l'anno 1598.

A questo disegno, e risolutione comune, già in parte notabile messa in essecutione, alcuni sotto diversi pretesti, e colori di pietà si oppongono; Prima, che essendo morto il Santo Padre nella casa al presente habitata, et havendo in quella data l'ultima benedizione a suoi figli, par cosa ragionevole, e pia di honorare la sua camera, con fermarsi, dove hoggi si trovano.

Al che si risponde, che la camera propria del Santo, nella quale morì, e dipoi fù ridotta in Cappella saranno ben da 14. anni, che nella . . . coronatione [?] di Papa Paolo V entratovi un raggio di quelli, che sogliono tirarsi all'aria in simile allegrezza, si abbrugiò tutta con perdita notabile di argenti, e parati pretiosi, e per esser cosi rovinata, e consumata dal fuoco, fù quel sito semplicem.te coperto a tetto, ne mai più circa quel luoco si è fatta alcuna dimostratione. Vi resta in piedi un altra cameretta, nella quale soleva dir messa, et havendo anche in essa havute estasi, e visioni, la quale hora serve per Cappella di Casa, e questa si potrà facilmente trasportare dall'altra parte, e collocarsi in loco decente, come pure si potria fare di quella poca parte di muro abbrugiato rimasta nell'altra camera, quando sia

in essere di potersi trasferire.

2°[*sic*] Oppongono che nel testamento di S. Filippo si trova, che lascia▽300 da impiegarsi nell'oratorio; e sebene non specifica il luoco preciso, si produce nondimeno un decreto della Congregatione de i quattro sotto Baronio, dove si dice, che i ▽300 lasciati dal /*fol. 525ʳ* / Santo, si devono spendere nella fabrica della Sagristia, che in tanto doverà servire per Oratorio.

A questo si risponde, che il vaso destinato per la sacristia, come sopra, non è riuscito buono ne per l'uno, ne per l'altro. Non per oratorio, per non esser capace a bastanza, massime per il concorso delle feste, dove per rispetto delle Musiche, et altri essercitij spirituali concorre gran gente, e per la gran folla son'occorsi disordini, e disturbi notabili. Ne tampoco è buono per Sacristia poiche riesce assai oscuro, essendo coperto da un canto dalla Tribuna, e chiesa, e dall'altro dalle case circonvicine, in modo che gode poco, o niente di sole, e l'aria non può giocare, onde resta alquanto humido, e di poco grato odore, e con tutto che vi sia sotto la volta della cantina è stato necessario farvi un tavolato alto un palmo da terra. Anzi havendo il p. Angello Velli, che immediatamente successe al p. Baronio, proposto di fare un'oratorio capace dalla parte, che al presente si habita, la Congregatione reietto il partito, non ostante che un personaggio di qualità si fosse offerto di fabricarlo a tutte sue spese. E questo fece la Congregatione perche disegnava di trasferirsi dall'altra parte verso Monte Giordano *come testificano molti Padri di Casa, che furono presenti.*

3°Dicono, che al Santo non piacevano le fabriche magnifiche, et che lui ha dato esempio di questo habitando in piccole celle.

Qui si risponde, che il Santo volse, che s'ingrandisse la Chiesa più di quello, che disegnavano gli Architetti, cosi è anco da credere, che a proportione havesse voluto anche la sacristia. Quanto poi all'habitatione, i Padri non pretendono di fare fabrica sontuosa; et il disegno della casa, che si è fatto, non arrivarà di gran longa alla grandezza, nobiltà delle fabriche antiche, e moderne di molti religiosi mendicanti, collegij, e luochi pij di Roma. E tanto più si rendono degni di essere compatiti i Padri dell'Oratorio in questa parte, quanto che non havendo altra casa, ne altro ricovero, fuorche questo di Roma, restano privi di ogni sorte di esalatione, e respiro, quando venghino impediti di potersi accomodare di qualche honesta stanza, che al più si riduce ad una mediocre camera con un camerino.

4°Fanno difficoltà nella spesa, che sarà eccessiva, e necessitarà la Congregatione ad indebitarsi. Al che si risponde, che stante il Decreto fatto dalla Congregatione come al libro 4 (Decreti adi 6 settembre 1630) et osservato inviolabilmente che non si possino spendere in fabriche senon gli avanzi dell'entrate, già si è provisto ad ogni disordine, che potesse avvenire.

5°Dicono, che si piglia gran paese *del publico* dalla parte di Monte Giordano. Si risponde, che conforme al chirografo di N.S.re Papa Urbano, et alla pianta sottoscrita dalli Mastri di Strada, et approvata in detto chirografo, è assai più quello, che si dona al publico, che quello che si riceve, dando la Congregatione nel stretto, e ricevendo nel largo con avantaggio del Publico */fol. 525ᵛ/*. oltre all'ornato che apporterà alla Città la fabrica. Ne tampoco si ha da temere, che sia per diminuirsi molto l'habitato, poiche oltre le molte botteghe, che si faranno intorno à detta fabrica, restaranno anche le case al presente habitate da Padri.

Finita poi, che sarà la fabrica piacendo al Sig.re restarà la Congregatione con la medesima entrata, o poco meno, poiche tutte le case di Monte Giordano rendono hoggidi∇2700 di entrata e nella nova fabrica si cavarà di botteghe circa un migliaro di scudi d'entrata, et altri mille si cavaranno dalle case hoggidi habitate da Padri. In modo che al più si farà scappito di∇700 d'entrata, quali difalcati dalla somma di∇4000 che avanzano agn'anno, restarà sempre la casa con avanzo di∇3300 d'entrata l'anno, oltre l'entrata delle spese ordinarie e straordinarie della Casa. E quando ben restasse con minor'entrata, e senza avanzi, ne anco saria ragionevole lasciare di provedere di Sacristia, Oratorio, et habitatione necessaria per Congregatione. Però quando non lo facesse per se stessa, pareria cosa conveniente, che i superiori l'astringessero a fare le suddette spese per levare ogni occasione di attendere a tesaurizare con poca edificatione de'i secolari. Si lascia da parte, che tra heredità sicure, censi vitalitij, case, et altri beni fra X anni in circa sono per ricadere alla Congregatione più di∇20,000.

Per conto poi delli pesi, e delle doti delle cappelle, et altri oblighi di messe non è stata fatta alienatione di rilievo, senon certa meza casa di ∇39 di entrata, la quale fù buttata a terra in virtù della licenza ottenuta dalla Sacra Visita *ut per far la strada nova* oltre che, occorrendo, si potra surrogare un'altra casa equivalente. Che vi sia poi una messa quotidiana, senza il suo fondo. Si risponde, che è errore, ma sibene una, a due messe l'anno, delle quali non si è trovato il fondo, credesi o per essere cosa minima, overo che si dichino non per obligo, ma per mera gratitudine.

Quanto poi alli gettiti fatti, quello della strada nova è stato fatto con licenza della Sacra Visita, la quale ha concesso facoltà di poter alienare ∇10,000 di capitale a questo effetto, e quello della sagristia è stato fatto legitimamente per vigore del Breve di Papa Paolo V di felice memoria, e per causa di pietà, utilità, e necessità con saputa di Mons. Vicegerente di quel tempo, il quale diede anche licenza al Superiore della Congregatione di poter benedire la prima pietra. Ne si può dire, che questa sia alienatione, non vi essendo traslatione di ragioni, ne [*or* e] dominio di terza persona. Le parole dell'estravagante ambitione sono queste:

[*There follows a legal definition of alienation, citing* Navarro, De Alienatione rerum ecclesiarum, *and* Suarez, De excommun. Papae reservatis disp. *The document continues on fol. 526ʳ.*] Ne meno si può dire, che vi sia deterioramento, o danno alcuno poiche la fabrica della nova Sacristia succede in loco delle case demolite, il prezzo delle quali dato che ascenda a otto, o dieci mila scudi, il valore della Sagristia con li membri annessi eccederà la somma di∇15,000 oltre quello, che si cavarà dalle due cantine cavate sotto la detta sagristia e stanze, e anco quello, che si cavarà dal partamento, che al presente serve di sacristia.

Poiche dunque il sito di Monte Giordano è stato accomprato a fine di fabricarvi l'habitatione, sacristia, et Oratorio, e la Congregatione tuttavia persiste in volersi trasferire da quella parte, per le ragioni dette, e per li grandi inconvenienti, che ne seguirebbono, essendosi già fatta spesa notabile nella sacristia, e disegnando con gli avanzi di tirare inanzi l'opera incominciata senz'aggravar nessuno, non par cosa conveniente debbano essere impediti di non proseguire. Massime che non si farà cosa di novo circa la fabrica, o altro negotio grave, che non si proponga al solito in piena Congregatione, e passi per suffragij secreti, come si è fatto sempre, essendosi ciò, che la maggior parte risolve.

Però si potria mettere in consideratione alli emin.mi Sig.ri Cardinali, che desiderando la pace, e quiete della Congregatione, restassero serviti di far'intendere a Padri, che seguitassero a vivere come hanno fatto per il passato, acquietandosi tutti alle resolutioni della Congregatione. Supplicandoli insieme a non voler dare più orecchie a quelli, che si oppongono al senso commune, et alla maggior parte della Congregatione.

11.   1634 May 4

AV, C.I.32 (unpaginated).

Misura e stima signed by Paolo Maruscelli for work done by two *scarpellini,* Flaminio Statera and Domenico Chenna, in the sacristy and adjacent corridor. The items of greatest importance are the two matching black marble doors in the corridor, shown in Fig. 69. According to the document, the doors ("Porta di marmo bigio" and "un altra porta simile") cost ▽76.44 each, for a total ("le due porte di biscio nella loggia insieme") of ▽152.88; on the other hand, the "porta di biscio in chiesa" cost ▽59.97. The total *misura,* including these three doors and other minor work, amounts to ▽241.57.

12. 1634 September 17
AV, C.I.32 (unpaginated).
Misura e stima signed by Paolo Maruscelli for a total of ▽67.97 worth of work done by the *scarpellini* Flaminio Statera and Domenico Chenna in and around the sacristy. The document mentions the following specific features of the building:
camerino sopra il lavamano.
stanzino secreto sopra detto lavamano.
porta della scala che sale alla loggia sopra le cappelle della chiesa.
3 camere a canto la sagrestia.
scalini di marmo dell'altare della sagrestia.
stanza dell'ampolline.
scalino di trevertino che ricorre sotto le base della chiesa a canto la porta della sagrestia.
le 8 base delli pilastri della loggia.
nicchia di marmo biscio al lavamano.
vaschetta del vaso di africano.

13. 1636 October 14
AV, C.I.32 (unpaginated).
Misura e stima by Paolo Maruscelli for work on houses along the Strada Nuova. The following specific features of the buildings are mentioned:
la casa grande a canto, verso il Pellegrino.
bottega dove lavorano li falegniami.
muro comune con il forno.
muro incontro al detto che divide la bottega dal cortile grande.
il pozzo comune con Rutilio Marsigliano nel cortil grande.
The total value of work measured amounts to ▽791.38.

14. 1638 October 13
AV, C.I.32 (unpaginated).
Scarpellino's bill for work at the casa including plumbing for the new refectory, amounting to a total of ▽3.65.

15. 1638 November
AV, C.I.32 (unpaginated).

Contract for the stuccoing of the oratory interior.

Capitoli e patti da osservarsi dalli sottoscritti Capomastri stuccatori per l'opera di stucco da farsi a manifattura solamente di detti Mastri per stuccare l'oratorio novo della Congregatione del detto Oratorio della Chiesa Nova in S.ta Maria Vallicella con li capitoli e patti, che qui sotto saran dechiarati.

P.a Saranno obligati, sicome si obligano, fare detta opera di stucco di marmo a loro sola manifattura, con darsegli dalli Padri tutta la calce, pozzolana, polvere di marmo, legnami per fare li ponti, schifi, zappe, pale, et il resto dell'ordegni da mettersi a spese, e fatture di detti Mastri come anco il fare li ponti per loro commodità, e disarmare tutte le volte di detto et altro cosi di patto.

2.o [*Extent of stucco-work*] Sarann' obligati stuccare tutto il suddetto oratorio con polvere di marmo come sopra: le facciate di dentro, volte, portici, cori, stanzini, grossezze de muri, de vani, di porte, finestre, con capitelli Ionici, pilastri, cimase, cornicione, cartelloni, telari di finestre, cuchiglie, fascie, quadri nelle volte, et altra sorte di lavori conforme mostran per li corpi delli suoi agietti secondo sarann'ordinati dall'Architetto.

3.o [*Adherence of stucco*] Tutte le colle di stucco di marmo tanto sopra muri, come sopra pilastri, volte, et altri luochi saranno ben fatte con sue liccature [?] sotto adrizzate con li regoli senza crepature, ne scanti, ma dritte a piombo il tutto a contentamento dell'Architetto, e Deputati.

4.o (*Ionic capitals*) Tutti li capitelli Ionici, che andaranno in detto Oratorio saran fatti conforme mostra per la abbozzatura con tutti li suoi membri che si vede, secondo gli sarann'ordinati, saranno con ogni diligenza ben fatti da buon'Intagliatori a sodisfattione come sopra.

5.o [*Cornice and horizontal string courses*] Il cornicione che va attorno detto Oratorio architravato conforme la sua mostra, qual' è liscio con una stampa intagliata se così parerà per quattro faccie resaltato sarà ben fatto, polito, senza crepature, et similmente le cimase sopra li pilastri all' imposta della volta come anco quelle girano attorno all'oratorio all'imposta delli archi, et quelli delle nichie' et il tutto andarà liscio, conforme li modeni, et ordini da darsegli dall'architetto.

6.o [*Windows*] Tutti li telari, o recinti di fenestre attorno gli otto finestroni di detto Oratorio con cornici in cima, seraglio in mezo, come anco quelli di mezanili sopra gli archi delle finestre, e nel portico all'entrata de detto Oratorio saranno ben fatti secondo li modeni da darsegli dall'architetto con una stampa o più bisognando, secondo l'ordine di detto architetto se così parerà.

7.o [*Wall thickness*] Saranno anco obligati incollare e stuccare le grossezze de muri di detti finestroni con pilastri, cimase sopra con suoi archi sopra secondo li modeni, come sopra da darsegli dall'Architetto.

8.o [*Vault*] Saranno'anche obligati stuccare il voltone di detto Oratorio di longezza palmi 81 largezza palmi 55, quale andarà stuccato sopra li suoi agietti già fatti con fascie, che fan costole a uso di cuppola, con un intavolato liscio che rigirano attorno dalle bande di detta in mezo della quale farà un'ovato di vano palmi 50 e palmi 25 in faccia palmi 4 incirca con un' ornamento attorno con un festone a fronde doppie ricco di lauro con un'intavolato dentro e fuora con doi stampe intagliate di dentro, se così parerà, con sua fascia attorno, secondo il modeno, et ordine da darsegli dall'Architetto, quale sarà ben fatta con ogni diligenza a sodisfattione, come sopra.

9.o Sarann'anche obligati stuccare le doi cuchiglie traforate nelli vani d'archi piccoli a capo d'oratorio largo l'uno palmi 7 alto palmi 3½ incirca con sue scannellature, volute ben fatte, secondo l'ordine dell'Architetto.

10. [*Musicians' loggia*] Saranno anche obligati stuccare sopra gli agietti fatti, li muri, volte, archi del coro sopra l'altar maggiore de musici di longezza p. 44 larghezza p. 9 con suoi compartimenti con fascie, con intavolato dalle parte, e quadri conforme li costole delle cuppole, et similmente li sotto archi di detto coro di dentro, e di fuora, con sfondati dentro, come anco stuccare li suoi finestroni di detto oratorio, secondo ordinarà, e secondo li modeni dell'Architetto.

11. [*Coretti*] Saranno anche obligati stuccare li muri, e volte delli doi coretti longo l'uno p. 11½ largo p. 9¼, andaranno stuccati sopra li suoi agietti de pilastri, fascie, capitelli, volte pian sopra con spartimento del quadro nel mezo con intavolato attorno, con cornice architravata all' imposta indorata liscia secondo il modeno dell' Architetto.

12. [*Altar area*] Saranno anche obligati stuccare li doi vani dalle parti dell'altar maggiore, et il vano di mezo di detto altare con suoi muri, volte, tavola, pilastri, fascie, et altro sopra li suoi agietti con partimenti delle volte, il tutto secondo l'ordine dell'architetto con un spirito santo nel mezo della volta sopra detto altare con raggi doppij secondo gli sara ordinato.

13. [*Three stanzini in southwest corner*] Saranno anche obligati stuccare li tre stanzini con suoi muri, volte, ovati a otto fascie di p. 9 l'uno e p.

6 con nicchiarelle a quadri il tutto liscio, ben fatti come sopra.

14. [*Cardinals' loggia*] Saranno anche obligati stuccare tutto il coro grande a piè di detta chiesa con pilastri, fascie, recinti di gusci, cimase, sottoarchi, capitelli, volte . . . [blank in the text] . . . doi nicchioni dalle parti, il tutto conforme il coro incontro, et secondo gli ordini da darseli.

15. [*Entrance loggia*] Saranno obligati stuccare il portico sotto detto di palmi 50 largo palmi 16 all'entrare di detto oratorio, con pilastri, recinti de gusci, fascie, capitelli, cimase, volte a vela liscia, simile all'altre, con grossezze de muri de vani di porte, e finestre, nell'arco d'una finestra un'ovato traforato per dar lume, il tutto secondo l'ordine come sopra.

16. [*Payment for unforseen changes in the design*] Tutti li sopradetti lavori di stucco nominati, come sopra, e non nominati, che andassero fatti, sarà il tutto ben fatto con ogni diligenza a sodisfattione dell'architetto, e Deputati, et al paragone d'ogn' altri fatti in Rome; come anco sia in arbitrio dell'Architetto di mutare, sminuire, et accrescere in parte detti lavori detti di sopra, in modo tale che non faccino mutatione eccessiva et in caso di accrescimento eccessivo, il tutto promettono stare a quello sarà giudicato da Ministri Deputati da detti RR. Padri senza replica alcuna, et a quello stare quanto sarà giudicato. Et in evento, che un'istessa opera bisognasse farla doi volte per ordine dell'Architetto, li detti RR. Padri sian' obligati pagarla per quello che sarà.

17. [*Fee*] E tutti li sopranominati lavori, e non nominati che andassero fatti come si è detto di sopra detti Mastri promettono, e si obligano farli per prezzo di ▽450 da pagarsegli di mano in mano andaran facendo detta opera, e secondo sarà ordinato da Ministri Deputati da detti RR. Padri.

18. [*Date*] Saranno anche obligati fare tutta la suddetta opera come sopra in termine di mesi otto cominciarsi il di [blank] Novembre 1638 altrimente mancando.

16.   Undated (ca. 1640)
AV, C.II.7 (unpaginated).
A critique of the stucco work done by G. M. Sorrisi according to the above contract; autograph pencil script by Borromini.
Oratorio Novo.
Lavori di stucco che non sono statti fatti li quali sono di meno di quelli che si sono convenuti nelli Capitoli et Patti fatti con M.o G.Maria Sorise per l'oratorio nuovo che a fatto fare l'RR. PP. della Cong.n di detto oratorio in S.ta Maria in Valicella come qui sotto.

Cap.o IV [*Ionic capitals*]

Manchano quattro capitelli in fiancho al'Altare quali non si sono fatti e più li otto che si sono fatti nel entrata del oratorio sono di minore fatura asai di quello che era la mostra conforme li patti et modello.

Cap. V [*Cornice and horizontal string courses*]

Il cornicione architravato atorno l'oratorio per 4 faccie con una stampa intagliata resaltato qui mancha la stampa intag.ta atorno le 4 faccie in lunghezza di palmi ducentosetantadua incircha.

Cap. VI [*Windows*]

Li seragli delle 8 finestre gia erano fatte le mostre delli cherubini con sue ale che fingono per serag[li]o. E più nelli mezzanini sopra li archi che riguardono l'oratorio et al entrata di detto erano fatte le mostre delli suoi agetti con li frontispitii sopra al n.o di otto delli quali li due mezzanini che riguardavano l'oratorio si sono levati et è restato il muro piano liscio et alli altri che sono n.o sei non si sono fatti li detti frontispitii e più mancano in detto una stampa intagliata o più le quale non si sono fatte che sareb[be] statto a farne un solla stampa una longhezza di palmi cento quaranta quattro in circha et se ne fussero fatte due sarebbe statto una lunghezza di palmi ducentottantotto le quale non si sono fatte.

Cap. VIII [*Vault*]

Il festone atorno la pittura nel voltone doveva avere l'intavolato dentro et fuori si è fatto solo di dentro verso la Pittura di fuori non si è fatto però mancha detto intavolato.

/verso of sheet/

Cap.lo X [*Musicians' loggia*]

Che li sottoarchi del coro di dentro et di fuori siano con suoi sfondati dentro li quali non si sono fatti e mancano al incontro ancora.

Cap. XI [*Coretti*]

Li capitelli non si sono fatti et sono n.o quattro e più non se è fatto un spartimento a quadro nel mezzo delle volte con suo intavolato però mancha.

Cap. XIII [*Should read XII: Altar area*]

Dice la volta a vella sopra l'altare con partimenti in detta con uno Spirito S.to nel mezzo della detta con raggi doppi. Manchano li spartimenti et il S.to S.to et li razzi quali non si sono fatti.

Cap. XVI [*Payment for unforseen changes in the design*]

Sono obligati a perfettionare l'opere e dove acrescere et diminuire come se fa per aggiustare le cose pur che non mutino faccia.

E più si ricorda che non si sono fatte le conchiglie nelle volticelle delle due Nicchie laterale al oratorio pero, se si deve pagare il lavoro che si

è acresciuto si deve anche sciemare il lavor che si è manchato.

17.   1642 November 15

ASR, CRM, Oratorio dei Filippini, vol. 140, cc. 203ʳ ff.

Contract between the carpenter Simone Roscialli and the Congregation for the library ceiling. (Cited in *Ragguagli,* 93, no. 133, and Pls. XXVIII–XXIX; transcribed in M. T. Russo, "Origini e vicende della Biblioteca Vallicellana," *Studi Romani,* XXVI, 1978, 31–33.)

1. Promette e si obliga con la presente Mastro Simone Roscialli falegname di fare il soffitto della libraria della nuova fabrica della Chiesa nuova, conforme il modello di legno e cera fatto dal Signore Francesco Borronino [*sic*] architetto, e conforme la mostra, che si vede posta nel medesimo luogo della libraria, tutta a spese sue, così di robba, come di fattura cioè legnami, chiodi, ferri, intagli, mettitura *in opera,* e qualsiasi altra cosa, così per armatura di dentro, come per ornamento di fuori, in maniera che resti il lavoro fornito, e perfettionato di tutto punto senza il *colore di travertino* [crossed out: *in maniera*] *talmente che non sia inferiore in conto alcuno alla mostra posta in opera anzi l'intaglio della gola si conviene che sia più ressentito.*

2. E di più si obliga di fare sopra di esso il solaro rustico da caminarvi sopra, tutto di tavole di castagno ben drizzate, e che sigillino l'una con l'altra. *nel qual solaro debba fare tre chiusini nelli tre quadri di mezzo che col suo incastro quali penetrino la soffita commes.i [?] in maniera che non si cognoschino, e sijno 3 palmi di vano per ogni verso, e nelli 15 fondi de i quadri le tavole siano incastrate a mezzo della tavola con meno di un oncia d'incastro per il largo, e sopra gl'incastri debba porre un regolo largo mezzo palmi in circa con chiodi dall'una e dall'altra parte cioè chiodi cappoccioni ben ribattuti* [crossed out: *e detti quadri debbano essere sostentati da nove . . . per il meno*]

3. E promette fare detto soffitto scorniciato, et intagliato tutto d'albuccio bene stagionato almeno di tre anni e di grossezza in tutt'i membri almeno conforme la mostra già fatta, ben forte e sicuro a giuditio dell'Architetto di detta Congregatione, e con l'armatura dentro, forte et atta a sostenere detto soffitto, e cornicione a giuditio dell'Architetto, e fra una corda e l'altra debba porre de'i cassarecci habili a sostenere il peso di detto solaro, e soffitto per caminarvi sopra *sodamente* dichiarandosi *però* che bastarà di porre tre cassarecci per tavola *mentre le tavole siano grosse e fidate.*

4. *E di più si obliga di fare il ponte tutto a spese sue*

eccetto i legnami che si darà.

5. E tutto detto lavoro promette darlo finito [*crossed out:* dentro sei mesi, cioè] per tutto Maggio 1643.

6. All incontro i Padri di detta Congregatione, e per essi il Padre Preposto si obliga di pagarli scudi [*crossed out:* sette] *sei* cento cinquanta contanti a scudi venti la settimana, mentre vi lavori con tanti huomini, che possa finirlo nel tempo sudetto.

7. Et inoltre promettono li detti Padri di darli in pagamento in fine del lavoro, ducento delli tavoloni, che sono accatastati inanzi all'Oratorio, cominciando a levarli dalla cima, e seguitando a numerare, e levarli sino al compimento, quali però non possa porli in opera senon sino al numero di cento, mentre servino in cosa, che non ricevi pregiuditio dal non essere stagionati, a guiditio dell'Architetto della Congregatione.

8. E di più promettono darli parimente in pagamento piane settecento nuove, di quelle, che sono risposte nel Cortile della cucina quali li deveranno esser consegnate nel principio del lavoro, caso che se voglia servire per il ponte, ma non se ne possa servire per porre in opera per esser verdi, e bisognandone alcune per mettere in opera se li daranno [*crossed out:* in conto] delle stagionate in conto delle [*crossed out:* cinque] *sette* cento.

9. Et inoltre promettono darli ottanta travicelli di castagno che dicono havere nuovi, che sono sotto la loggia della cucina.

10. E se per fare detta soffitta i Padri havessero tavole, travicelli, o altri legni, che potessero servire, e volessero darli al detto Mastro Simone, sia il detto Maestro Simone obligato a riceverle in conto delli scudi *seicento cinquanta* a stima dell' Architetto.

11. E se i Padri si contentassero, che il solaro di sopra in luogo di tavole nuove di castagno, fosse fatto di tavole vecchie, e che esse glie le volessero dare, il detto Mastro sia obligato di pigliarle, e scontare nel prezzo quella, che ad esso mastro sarebbero gostate le tavole nuove, che sparagnarebbe, a giuditio, e stima dell' Architetto, come sopra.

12. Et inoltre si obligano detti Padri di accomodare al detto Mastro Simone tutti quei legnami grossi, che stanno otiosi nella fabrica di detti Padri, perche se ne possa servire nel ponte per detta soffitta, quali però dovrà portare, et accommodare a spese sue, e reportarli dove si levano.

13. E si conviene, che nei quadri del soffitto si facci a sodisfattione dell'Architetto un'ottangolo, o altro lavoro di cornice [*crossed out:* piana]

[*crossed out:* non . . . senza intaglie*] proportionata e di* [*crossed out:* grossezza]*altezza e largehzza circa al rilievo all'altri quadri, che hanno fornamento,* benche nel modello, o nella mostra non stia espresso e designato.

14. E per osservanza di tutte le suddette cose, così il detto Maestro Simone in nome proprio, come il Padre Preposto in nome della Congregatione obligano se medesimi, beni, et heredi respettivamente in forma della R. Cam.a, et in ogni altro meglior modo.

15. E per maggior sicurezza de Padri il detto Maestro Simone promette di far accedere come principale, e principalmente obligato il solido Mastro Paolo Malagigi in termine di [*crossed out:* tre] *otto* giorni, e di celebrarne pub.co Instro. et in tanto questa vaglia come Instro. rogato questo di 15 novembre 1642.

Io Virgilio Spada Preposto della Congregatione dell'Oratorio promette e mi obligo a quanto di sopra.

Io Francesco Rigucci. [*Witness signs for the carpenter with a cross.*]

Io Francesco Borromini fui presente a quanto di sopra manu propria.

Io Vaio Vai fui presente a quanto di sopra manu propria.

18.   1643 September 20

ASR, CRM, Oratorio dei Filippini, vol. 140, cc. 205^r ff. Duplicate copy on cc. 207^{r}ff.

Contract between the carpenter Simone Roscialli and the Congregation for the library shelves. (Transcribed in M. T. Russo, "Origini e vicende della Biblioteca Vallicellana," *Studi Romani,* XXVI, 1978, 33–34.)

1. Si obliga il detto Maestro Simone di far di nuovo dieci pezzi di scanzia della forma, materia, e qualità delle già fatte, poste di nuovo nella libraria nuova, cioè di albuccio di dentro, di noce di fuori, con cornici *cassetti,* titolo, vasi, et ogni altro membro, come sono fatte, eccetto nella misura, quale devrà esser circa otto oncie per pezzo, meno delle fatte.

2. E di più si obliga di fare le testate alle già fatte ne'luoghi, ove bisogna et in effetto resarcire, aggiustare, et accommodare quelle, che ci sono o con l'aggiongere legnami, o col levare, in maniera che tutti apparischino della medesima larghezza, e qualità.

3. Parimente si obliga di porre una tavola a tutte le scanzie così fatte, come da farsi sopra il luogo de'i legij, o cassetti, longa quanto tutta la scanzia è larga, quanto il ripiano di esso legio, fermata sopra la cornicetta nel luogo, ove si farà la gionta, della quale si dirà appresso; e detta

tavola sarà della qualità dell'altre, coperta per di fuori di noce, come l'altre.

4. A tutte le scanzie fatte, e da farsi nel luogo, dove si congionge il pezzo superiore all'inferiore, devrà fare una gionta di noce senza intagli e cornici *alta palmi 1½ o quanto bisognarà.*

5. Dalle cornici di dette scanzie fatte devrà levare l'ultimo regoletto, e riportarlo nelle scanzie, dove manca, valendosi della cornice che restarà per porre sopra le colonne, che giraranno intorno la libraria, dove, e come vorrà detto Maestro Simone. E perche le cornici suddette non bastaranno, devrà esso aggiongerne tanta, che basti della medesima qualità di noce, e modenatura, girando anche dove sono le porte vere, e finte.

6. Si obliga anche di fare tutte le colonne, che bisognaranno per il portico che sono numero quarantaquattro intorno le scanzie di noce, con ordine Toscano, con le debite diminutioni, con architrave, capitello, base, piedestallo, conforme il profilo fatto dal Signore Francesco Borromini Architetto, il tutto fatto al tornio eccetto la cimasa del capitello, et architrave, che vanno quadrati, et isolati, con questo, che la colonna dal *limoscappo* [?] sino sotto al collarino, sia d'un pezzo intiero, senza giunte, o tassello, o altra magagna, alte fra tutt'i membri senza la cornice palmi 13½ in circa, e piantarle immobili nel marmo posto nell'ammattonato.

7. Sopra le dette cornici devrà porre i titoli, come stavano prima, con li vasi fra uno e l'altro, facendo di nuovo tutti quelli titoli, e vasi, che mancaranno gl'intiero ornato del portico, anche sopra le porte, conforme che li dettarà detto Signore Francesco.

8. Dentro al portico devrà ricorre un travicello di castagno dall'una e dall'altra parte del portico anche sopra le scanzie, alto mezo palmo; e l'uno e l'altro dalla parte, che si vedrà, haverà forma d'un'architrave, conforme il profilo già disegnato, sopra un fusto dal detto Signore Francesco Architetto, sopra de' quali abbracciando anche il sito delle scanzie, devrà farvi un solaro con eguali tavole di olmo *o albuccio di tavole interzate* di oncia 1½, di buona grossezza, con spessi chiodi, ben lavorate sotto e sopra, incollate insieme fusto per fusto da una colonna all'altra, e fra un fusto e l'altro coperta la fissura con un falsetto [?] scorniciato da tutte due le parti a gusto dell'architetto, e che tutti tendino al punto, e tanto alli travicelli, quanto alle dette tavole devrà dare il colore di noce, et accanto la muraglia devrà parimente ricorrere un travicello per sostentar dette tavole.

9. Alle 4 cantonate devrà fare quattro scale lumache di castagno ben lavorate con cordone, e di fuori ornate di noce, conforme le scanzie senza però porticella da chiuderle, devendo stare del continuo aperte, et in far queste, si devrà regolare, conforme che li dirà il detto Architetto.

10. Et inoltre premette di fare le scanzie per la parte superiore della libraria con sei divisioni, conforme il profile già fatto, di tavole d'albuccio, interzate di dentro, e coperte le grossezze di noce di fuori, conforme quelle da basso, con le testate di noce semplici, e con quattro traverse per ogni scanzia, di dieci in dodici palmi, e le altre a proportione, riempendo di scanzie tutte le muraglie anche dove vanno le scale lumache, eccetto dove sono le finestre, e sopra la porta della Ringhiera.

11. E tutti li suddetti lavori si obliga farli a tutta robba, e fattura sua, così di legnami, come di ferramenti, eccetto le serrature, e chiavi, e di adoprare legnami buoni, ben stagionati, e ben lavorati a giuditio de'Periti, senza tasselli, magagne, o altra imperfettione e di dar fine al lavoro per tutto il mese di Novembre prossimo del corrente anno.

12. All'incontro si obligano i Padri di darli la meza scanzia, che resta vacante, acciò si servà del legname, e lavori di essa per il lavoro da fare, come più parerà al detto Mastro.

E di più si obligano darli un tavolone di noce, longo sopra palmi 20 delli quattro compri in Pelestrina.

E di più alcune tavole di noce, già vedute da esso, non molto stagionate, che sono sopra la loggia delle cappelle.

E di più tavoloni di albuccio numero nove, che sono in sue mani.

E di più due masse di mozzature [?], et avanzi di tavole di noce, che sono ammassate in doi luoghi nella loggia sopra le cappelle.

E per compimento del prezzo di detti lavori si obligano darli ▽400 moneta, da pagarseli ▽50 contanti ora, ▽50 fra un mese, e ▽300 per tutto Marzo prossimo 1644 *e così ambe le parte obligano se suoi beni et heredi in forma della R.C. . . . et in ogni altro meglior modo Roma 20 settembre 1643.*

[Added at the end of the contract in another hand:]

Anzi in luogo di colonne tonde con piedistalli et architravi si obliga di fare balaustri conforme il già fatto tutti di noce senza veruna magagna et all'incontro i Padri si contentono di acrescere il prezzo delli ▽400 altri ▽10.

Io Virg.o Spada preposito della Congregatione prometto e mi obligo in nome della Congregatione a quanto di sopra.

Io simone rossano affermo e mi obligo a quanto sopra mano propria.

19. No date (ca. late 1643)
ASR, CRM, Oratorio dei Filippini, vol. 140,

cc. 209^r–211^r.

Payments to Simone Rosciani for carpentry work in the library.

Supplement to documents of April–December 1643 in Pollak, 445, regs. 1838–41.

Lavori di legname e tutta robba fatti da Maestro Simone Rosciani per la nova libraria sopra l'oratorio della Congregatione dell' RR. Padri della Chiesa Nova mrs.e [?] et armati da me sottoscritto per ambi le parti e stanzini acapo la detta libraria verso la strada.

[*An itemized bill amounting to* ▽132.48 is endorsed by Gio. Maria Bolina. There follow various sums of money with the following totals:]

soffitto della libraria	▽740.00
porte e fenestre della libraria	130.00
scanzie della libraria	100.00
. . . . . .	
fattura del cancello detto abass.	15.00
Havuto per l'antiporta o sia cancello nel corritore delli appartamenti nobili	15.00
Havuto per il soffitto della libraria	650.00
et più per cancelli di detta	40.00
et più per porte e finestre al piano della libraria	
	820.00
Et per diversi altri lavori fatti di piu per la libraria di quello ch'era obligato	70.00
Per le scanzie della libraria	400.00
	1290.00
Et per il cancello del primo [?] piano	15.00
Et per lavori di più nel soffitto della libraria	15.00
	1320.00

20.   1644 August 30

ASR, 30 Notai Cap., Uff. 28, Testamenti 1657–67, not. N. Rignanus, vol. 6, c. 400^{r-v}.

First testament of Virgilio Spada, made at the age of 48. (Cited but not transcribed in *Ragguagli,* 107 f.) The following excerpts are of interest for the Casa dei Filippini.

Lascio per ragione di legato alla medesima Congregatione la mostra grande d'orologgio da contrapesi, acciò se ne servino in libraria, o dove parerà alli Padri.

Lascio per ragione di legato alla medesima Congregatione dell'Oratorio tutte le medaglie antiche e moderne di metallo, oro, argento, e piombo, intagli, camei, monete antiche, et ogni altra curiosità antica, e moderna, che soglio tenere in camera mia, raccolti in dodici studioletti, e tre libretti più o meno che siano, e fuori di essi, in una credenza sopra il camino della mia camera, et in altri luoghi i quali si ponghino nel camerino della libraria, che fa cantone sopra l'oratorio verso la piazzetta. . . .

Lascio parimente alla medesima Congregatione tutt'i miei libri stampati, e manoscritti, con le scanzie; avvertendo che ve ne ponno essere alcuni dell'em.mo Sig.re Card.le Spada, al detto del quale si debba credere: con questo che il Padre Preposto con la Congregatione de'quattro pro tempore li diano a goder tutti ad un Padre di casa quale si diletti de' casi di coscienza ad elettione loro, convenendo, che in una Congregatione com'è questa di Roma ci sia sempre più d'uno versato in queste materie per rispondere con fondamento alli dubij, che ogni giorno posson occorrere. . . . Avvertendo però, che li monoscritti fatti da me si potranno dare alla luce del foco, essendo cose imperfette, indigeste, mal copiate, e fatte solo per mio studio. E le scritture, lettere, o manuscritti, che non appartengono a studij litterarij, si deveranno dare al mio herede, per il che si debba stare alla distintione che ne farà il Sr. Card.1 Spada. E se ci sarà alcun libro o stampato, o manuscritto, che non sia in libraria, si possi ritenere per la libraria di Congregatione.

21.   1648 April 30–August 3

ASR, CRM, Oratorio dei Filippini, vol. 140, cc. 120^{r-v}.

Payments to Gasparo Alberti for the mechanism of the clock in the *torre dell'orologio.*

Io Gasparo Alberti ho ricevuto dalla congregatione dell'Oratorio per mano del Padri Silvio Bilancetti ▽12 di moneta a bon conto di quello che mi promese per fattura dell'horologio di detta Congregatione et me ne son servito per pagamento li lavora . . .[?] di detto horologio . . .

[*The same Gasparo Alberti receives payments up to August 3, 1648.*]

22.   1649 December 5

ASR, Tribunale dell'A.C., not. Jacobus Simoncellus, vol. 6612.

An inventory of Paolo Maruscelli's possessions including his library, drawn up in his house on the Vicolo del Corallo after his death "ab intestato." The word order of some of the following 123 titles has been rearranged to conform to a standard format, and additional bibliographical information has been provided in parentheses. (Cited but not transcribed in *Ragguagli,* 214.)

/c. 502ᵛ/

(Domenico Fontana), *Fabriche di Papa Sisto,* foglio reale	▽1.50
Calepino, *Sette lingue,* foglio, Venetia	1.20
Idem, *5 lingue,* foglio, 1550	.70
(Agostino) Ramelio, *Machine,* foglio tutto figurato, Parigi	5.00
(Federico) Comendino, *Euclide,* volgare, Urbino (1575)	1.50
Pomidoro, *Giometria,* foglio, Roma	.40
Fiamelli, *Principe diffeso,* foglio, Roma	.30
Vignola, *Architettura,* foglio reale, Rome	.40
Anon., *Essequie di Papa Pauolo 5.o,* foglio figurato, Roma	.30
(Lorenzo) Sirigatti, *Prospettiva,* foglio reale, (Venice, 1596)	.60
(Iacobus) Besson mattemat., *Machine,* foglio reale figurato, Roma	.30
(G.B.Montano), *Scelta di varij tempij antichi,* foglio figurato, Roma	1.00
Carlo Ghetti [?], *Fortifichatione,* foglio, Vicenza	1.40
Antonio Labacco, *Architettura,* in foglio reale	.50
Vignola, *Prospettiva,* foglio, Roma	.60
Durero, *Simetria,* in Venetia, foglio figurato	1.00
(G.B.) Montano, *Architettura,* in foglio figurato	.40
Floriani, *Fortificatione,* foglio, Macerata	1.00
Jacques Androuet Du Cerceau, *Prospective,* Paris, foglio figurato, francese	.50
2 depositi varij, in foglio figurato, Roma	1.00
(Vittorio) Zonca, *Machine et defisij,* Padova, foglio figurato	.60
Vignola, *Architettura,* Spagnola, foglio figurato	.40
Bernardo Radi da Cortona, *Varij disegni d'architetti anat . . . , de porte,* foglio	.50
	21.60

/c. 503ʳ/

Piero Accolti, *Ingano del'occhio prospettiva,* Fiorenza, foglio (1625)	.50
Melzi, *Regole militare, Sopra la Cavall.a,* Aversa, foglio figurato	1.40
Sarti, *Fortificatione,* foglio, Venetia	.40
Clemente de Clementibus, *Encijclopedia romana,* foglio figurato	.20
Vignola, *2 architettura,* Roma, 1648	.80
Vitruvio, *2 architettura,* Venetia, 1566, ant. 1524	1.40
Tomeo accademici, *Amore prigioniero in Delo,* Bologna	.20
(Ed. Zamberto or Fine), *Euclide. latino antico,* stamp. Paris	.40
(Luigi) Colliado, *Praticha manuale dell'artigliaria,* Milano, 4.0 (1606 or 1641)	1.00
Bartolo Sassoferato, *Tiberiade,* Roma, 1587, 4.o	.30
(Giovanni Battista della) Porta, *Fisonomia,* volgare, Vicenza 1615, 4.o	.60
Fiocchi, *Indurdatione alla fede,* Rome, 4.o	.60
(Gioseffe) Viola (Zanini), *Architettura,* Padova, 1629, 4.o	.60
Guido Ubaldo del Monte, *Le machine,* Venetia, 1615, 4.o	.60
Cosimo Bartolidi, *Da mesurare,* Venetia, 1589, 4.o	.20
Vite di Santi Toscani, Fiorenza, 1593, tom. 1 e 2, 4.o	.60
Vita di S. Filippo Neri, Roma, 1622, 4.o	.20
Vita di S. Eligio, Roma, 1629, 4.o	.20
Trattato utilissimo in Conforto de Cond(emna)ti a morte per via di giustitia, 4.o	.10
	▽31.50

/c. 503ᵛ/

Salarie del appaltura, Roma, 1635, 4.o	.10
Misure delle acque corenti, Rome, 1628, 4.o	.10
Galileo, *Compasso,* Padova, 1640, 4.o	.60
Breccioli, *Sopra l'innondatione del Tevere,* Urbino, 1647	.10
Agostino Ferentilli, *Discorsi universale per le 6. eta e 4. monarchi,* (Venice, 1570)	.30
Pellicciari, *Avertimenti militari,* Venetia, 1619, 4.o	.40
P. Massimo, *Machine,* fig.o, 4.o	.40
Orgio Melfetano, *Discorsi militari,* Lucca, 1615, 4.o	.40
(Egnatio Danti), *Prospettive di Euclide,* Fiorenza, 1573, 4.o	.20

P. Giovacchino, *Profetie,* Padova, 1625, 4.o   .30
Francesco Partizi, *Giometria,* Ferrara, 1587, 4.o   .20
[?]ierone e del Porta, *Spiritali,* Urbino, 1592, Napoli, 1606, 4.o   .60
Sarti, *Simitria, Di fortificationi, Regole,* Venetia, 1630, 4.o   .30
Brecciolini, *Pietra del paragone,* 4.o   .30
Giorgio Basta, *Governo della Cavall.a,* Venetia, 1612, 4.o   .20
Ruscelli, *Precetti della militia moderna,* Venetia, 1605   .10
Orlandino, *Indrudatione delli Bonbardieri,* Roma, 1602, 4.o   .10
Nobilita della pittura, Roma, 1585, 4.o   .10
P. Marsilio Onorati (dell'Oratorio), *Vita di Giesu Christo*   .30
(Bartolomeo Crescentio, *Nauticha,* Roma, 1607, 4.o   1.00
(Cesare) Ripa, *Iconologito,* Padova, 1630, 4.o   .60
                                                                                                                  ∇38.20

/c. 504ʳ/
Polidoro, *De Re* [?] *Inventoribus,* Fiorenza, 1587, 4.o   .40
Serlio, *Architettura,* Venetia, 1600, 4.o, lib. 7.0   .30
Ars delineandi, Roma, 1631, 4.o   .20
Acchademia de Pittori, Scult. et Archit., Pavia, 1604, 4.o   .30
Biringoccio, *Pirotech(n)ia,* 1554, 4.o   .80
Cosmografia universale, 1619, 4.o   .20
(Girolamo) Cataneo, *Fortificationi,* brevio, 1608, 4.o   .60
(Vincenzo) Cartari, *Imagine delli dei,* Padova, 1608, 4.o   .60
Fiamelli, *La riga mattematica,* 1605, Roma, 4.o   .20
Fiamelli, *Principe christiano gueriero,* Roma, 1611, 4.o   .30
Gentiliani, *Instrutt. e del artiglieria,* 1606, 8.o   .10
Messia, *Selva di varie eletione,* Venetia, 1597, 8.o   .20
Christf. Messisbogo (Christoforo di Messisbughi), *Libro che insegna a cuccinare,* Venetia, 1557 .10
Ludovico Ariosto, *La cassaria,* comedia, Venetia, 1556, 8.o   .10
Casteldurante, *Tesoro di Sanita,* Venetia, 1611, 8.o   .10
Giardino di essempij, Venetia, 1618, 8.o   .20
Zucca del doni [?], Venetia, 1589, 8.o   .20
Rossello, *Secreti,* Venetia, 1619, 8.o   .10
Apuleo, *Asino d'oro,* Venetia, 1614, 8.o   .10
Calmo, *Lettere,* Venetia, 1580, 8.o   .10
Dittionario francese etaliano a moreg [?], 1584   .10
Vocabolario Spagniolo etaliano, Venetia, 1608   .10
                                                                                                                  ∇43.60

/c. 504ᵛ/
Rosaccio (?), *Mondo elementare,* Trivigi, 1604, 8.o   .10
(Gio. Battista della) Porta, *De miracoli e maravigliosi effetti da la natura,* 8.o, 1556   .10
Petrarca, *Del dolce Giolito,* Venetia, 1554, 8.o   .20
Panig.a[?], *Dichiaratione dei salmi di David,* Venetia, 1586   .20
Catechismo, Piacenza, 1596, 8.o   .10
Dittionario Italiano e turchesco, Roma, 1641, 8.o   .10
Vita di S. Bruno, Roma, 1622, 8.o   .10
Suriano, *2 Miracoli di S. Domenico*   .10
Viaggio al Santo Sepolcro, Ronciglione, 1615   .05
Miracoli della Madonna della Quercia, Todi, 1631   .05
Ricci, *Introdutione di meditare,* Roma, 1611, 8.o   .05
Vitruvio, *Architettura,* Fiorenza, 1522, 8.o   .20
P. Clavio, *2 Aritmetica,* volgare, Roma, 1586, 8.o   .30
Filippo Venuti, *Ditionario,* 1589, 8.o   .20
Ditionario Galesino, Venetia, 1602, 8.0   .10
Caffari, *Gramatica,* Venetia, 1605, 8.o   .10
(Andrea Palladio), *Comentario di Cesare,* latino, Venetia, 8.o   .10
Galateo, Fiorenza, 1606, 8.o   .05

Vita di S. Nilo, Roma, 1628, 8.o .05
Rimedio di conservare il vivo, 8.o .05
Colloquio dittionario otto lingue, Venetia, 1627 .20
Clement. Grienburgerio, Euclide, *Sex Primo,* Roma, 1629 .10
∇46.20

/c. 505^r/
Comentario Julij Cesare, Lud., 1558, 16.o .05
Fioretti di S. Francesco, Venetia, 1601 .05
Terentias, Venetia, 1601 .05
Difesa della fortificatione Italiana, Roma, 1639 .05
Da trenta tra comedie et altri libretti imp. .60
Arte da venire a dio, Venetia, 1608 .05
P. Alfonso Rodriguez, *Trattato del oratione* .05
∇47.30

---

23. 1659–83.
ASR, Cartari-Febei, vol. 185.
Descriptions of Roman libraries by Carlo Cartari, prefect of the Sapienza. The visits were made in order to collect ideas for the shelving and organizational system of the Sapienza library; up to 1665 they often took place in the company of Borromini. Although the document describes many libraries, the selections which have been included here relate to only two: the library of the Vallicella and its immediate model, the library of the Palazzo Barberini. (Cited and discussed in *Ragguagli,* 132; 135, no. 205; and 229 ff., no. 205.)

Library of S. Maria in Vallicella
23a. 1659 June
ASR, Cartari-Febei, 185, 71^v.
Cited in *Ragguagli,* 230; partly transcribed by Incisa della Rocchetta, *Dialogo,* 191, n.42.
Di Giugno MDCLIX viddi la libraria della Chiesa Nuova, è voto anche capace; gl'ordini sono dui; tanto il primo, quanto il secondo hanno le scanzie contigue al muro, essendo sostenuto il largo cornicione da colonne tornite, dal d . . . sino in testa, che rendono più spatiosa la libraria e fanno bella veduta. Vi è un libro in foglio stampato dell'indice di detta libraria; vi è memorie in pietra al Card. Baronio con il suo ritratto di chiaro scuro, vi sono altri ritratti simili di persone, che hanno lasciato alla detta libraria. Vi sono [*crossed out:* diversi] moltissimi ritratti d'huomini illustri stampati, di grandezza di mezo foglio, di buon'intaglio, però vi sono diversi heretici, anzi anco quello da Mahometto ,se bene questo lo tengono coperto con altra carta; stanno nel primo ordine, sopra il luoco dove si puol studiare in piedi. Vi è un bizzaro soffitto, et al muro son finti certi pilastri, che lo sostentono; il tutto è disegno del Padre Virgilio Spada e del Cavalier Bormini.

23b. 1660 March 2
ASR, Cartari-Febei, 185, 90^{r-v}.
Fully transcribed in *Ragguagli,* 229 f.

23c. 1667 October 15 and 1676 May 8
ASR, Cartari-Febei, 185, 92^r.
Cited in *Ragguagli,* 230, and in Incisa della Rocchetta, *Dialogo,* 191, n.42.
Li 15 di ottobre 1667 viddi di nuovo la libraria della Chiesa Nuova, la quale si era ingrandita con l'aggiunta della libraria segreta, essendoci levato il muro tramezo che offendeva la volta dell'Oratorio, sopra la quale era posato. Vi si lavoravono le scanzie per detta aggiunta. Erano bibliotecarij il Padre Diotalevi et Padre Belluci. Da questo intesi, che detta libraria haveva di dote annua ∇100, ma hora per il calo de'monti era ∇90.
Li viii di Maggio 1676 di nuovo la viddi, condottovi da Padre Porta secondo bibliotecario; era già posta in ordine, col compimento di tutte le scanzie, anche nel sito dove prima era l'archivio, o forse libraria segreta. Non mi seppe dire il numero de'i libri, molti pero erano duplicati. Confermo che l'entrata era di circa ∇90.

Library of the Palazzo Barberini
23d. 1665 January 31
ASR, Cartari-Febei, 185, 110^r–111^v.
Cited in *Ragguagli,* 231.
All'ultimo di Gennaro 1665 andai assieme con il S. Abbate Buratti e sig. Cavalier Bormini a veder la libraria del S. Cardinale Francesco Barberini alle Quattro Fontane, per considerar le scanzie, in ordine a quelle da farsi per la Sapienza, essendosi concertato con il S. Carlo Moroni bibliotecario. È situata in cima del palazzo, non havendo altra fabrica sopra di se, onde dalle due fenestre che sono in capo alla libraria, si vede Roma con vaga prospettiva. Avanti che si entri nella libraria, si trova una camera, che può dirsi piccola, ornata con diversi

quadri di letterati illustri, ma disposti con poca simetria. Tra questi il più bello, cioè di migliore è quello del Galileo, che pare certamente vivo, et è fino al busto, vicino all'ingresso. Vi viddi di' viventi il ritratto del Padre Ughelli, e di dui altri, essendo costume di non esporre simili ritratti se non dopo la morte. Ve è il ritratto di Giaccomo Mazzoni, a sedere, in tela d'imperatore, e questo è il più gran quadro che vi sia. Saranno in tutti circa sesanta. Il vaso della libraria è assai lungo (ma minore di quella della Sapienza) e largo a proportione; è però assai bassa, che in riguardo della lunghezza riesce sproportionata. È in volta, la quale è mantenuta da diversi ferri, che sono a traverso la libraria, con certi cannelli lunghi dorati, che sembrono d'ottone. Si entra in detta libraria dalla destra prima camera, e la porta riesce in mezo, si che chi entra vede libraria alla destra et alla sinistra. Le fenestre sono solamente nella facciata lunga incontro all'ingresso, et altre dui sono a capo la libraria, che vengono ad' essere alla parte destra, quando si entra, si che la facciata alla sinistra, e quella lunga, dove e l'ingresso, restono senza fenestre. A capo la libraria tra le due fenestre, ma in mezo le scanzie del secondo piano, è una nicchia ovata, dentro la quale è la statua a busto di Papa Urbano */fol. 110ᵛ/* fatta di metallo; ma poco si gode, si perche il lume delle due fenestre dà in faccia a chi vi guarda, come anche perche la detta statua, oltre l'esser divenuta oscura, conforme fù il metallo con gli anni, ha anco per fodera del nicchio e per ornamento di fuori il legname di noce che tutt' assieme, come ho detto, rende oscurità; e meglio sarebbe stato, o di indorare la statua o d'indorare il legname di noce. Li quattro muri di detta libraria sono ricoperti dal pavimento sino alla volta di belle scanzie di noce, e queste sono tutte ripiene di libri di diverse forme e di belle ligature, anche in gran parte in cordoano di levante, ornato d'oro etc. L'architettura di dette scanzie è tale. Sono undici ordini. Il primo serve come di piedistalla a tutta la machina delle scanzie, e viene in fuori più degli altri, havendo avanti le ramate che se chiudono con catenaccetti e con serrature dorate. Seguono altri quattro ordini di libri di diverse grandezza, cioè in folgio et in quarto; a questi soprasta un'altro ordine di libri piccoli, e la sua simetria quasi una cornice, nella quale termina il primo piano. Questa cornice posa sopra colonnette scannellate di noce, quali posono sopra il primo ordine detto, che fa base, o piedestallo, e questo sporge tanto in fuori degli altri, che vi si potrebbe ponere il libro e studiarvi, quando per altro non fosse troppo. A queste colonnette corrispondono li pilastrini scannellati,

che con la debita distanza dividendo li partimenti delle scanzie, rendono vaga e ricca veduta, havendo i suoi maschietti [?] dorati alle ramate. */fol. 111ʳ/*

Sopra il dett'ordine, che rassembra [?] cornice, e il corritore di legno, largo dui palmi, che dà commodità alli libri del secondo piano, quali giungono, come dissi, fino alla volta e terminano le scanzie con certi vasi di [*crossed out: legno*] noce intagliati. Avanti questo corritore è parapetto di ferri lavorati, e con palle d'ottone. Al secondo piano non sono ramate. Le scanzie di questo piano sono interrotte dalle finestre, nel muro in faccia all'ingresso et in quello a capo la libraria, se gli altri dui muri sono seguite. Di questo piano si ascende per dui lumache, fatte in dui angoli della libraria, dalla parte delle fenestre, dui delle quali danno [*crossed out: adito a*] sito per dette scalette. Osservai, che non vi sono le cartelle, come nelle altre librarie che indichino le materia, ma invece di queste vi sono li numeri alla Romana. Il piano superiore ha le scanzie di un palmo e mezo. Dimandai al S. Moroni il numero de'libri; non seppe dirmelo. Gli domandai se li stamparebbe l'indice, come già se ne stampa la p . . ., ma parve non vi fosse inclinatione. E essendo dunque piena la detta libraria, ne essendovi sito da ingrandirla, vedemmo un'altra camera privata che anche quasi era piena; e percio il S. Cardinale haveva fatte principiare alcune altre scanzie di noce, che in due fila sarebbono lunghe quanto la libraria. Sono queste a foggia [?] di tavole, per conservarvi libri da due parte, in dui ordini in foglio et uno in quarto, e potervi anche scriver di sopra, come si vede in altre librarie. In detta libraria vi sono mappamondi. Contigua vi è una gran camera di MSS. pretiosi. Vi è il Museo di medaglie e curiosità rare. Si puol dunque conchiudere, che */fol. 111ᵛ/* dandosi il primato, senza dubio, alla Vaticana, questa in secondo luogo sia la più bella e la più copiosa libraria di Roma.

24.   1661 March 26
Bibl. Vallicelliana, Cod. O 57², fol. 529ʳ.
Camillo Arcucci lays out the design of the garden and presents a model for the fountain.
Adì 26 Marzo 1661 sabbato fù scoperta una colona al secondo pilastro per andare al Refetorio, sabbato essendo sopra alla fabricha il P. Cesare Spada e Gio. Antonio Tanovello e il medemo giorno il Sig.re Camillo Arcucci tirò li fili per fare li spartimenti del giardino e portò il modello della fontana il detto sabbato.

25.   1662 September 23
ASR, Osp. di S. Santo, not. S. Sebenicus, vol.

343, bound libretto following c. 542.

Second testament of Virgilio Spada with related documents, including the following inventory of Spada's own writings on p. 29^r. (Cited but not transcribed in *Ragguagli,* 214.)

Nota de i manoscritti, legati in libri, e libretti, che trovo questo giorno 30 Agosto 1662 nella mia libraria della Chiesa Nuova, et appresso di me, quali si daranno al mio herede, eccettuati quelli, che notaro in corpo, e trovandosene di vantaggio, si dovranno parimente al detto mio herede, o almeno ne dovrà esso disporre, conforme che dalla materia raccogliera convenire.

Composti da me, che non meritano altra luce, che quella del fuoco.

4 volumi in foglio di casi di conscienza a cento per volume con appendice in fogli volanti, intitolati centurie.

15 libretti in 4.o di cento sermoni per libro

. . .

Trattato di monete in foglio francese.

Sopra la medesima materia più discorsi.

2 libretti in foglio grande della medesima materia, ma sono particelle del primo, e si ponno brugiare.

Discorso sopra alcuni peli nella facciata, portico, e Basilica di S. Pietro nel 1644.

Discorso ecconomico al Marchese Rodolfo mio nipote.

. . . . . .

Relatione de i Castelli Mondaldeschi, hoggi di casa Panfilia.

. . . . . .

Noti sopra medaglie antiche *cosa di poco, o niun rilievo*

. . . . . .

Volume di scritture relative a me, et a cose mie in foglio.

. . . . . .

Stato della casa dell'Archihosp.le di S. Spirito, fatto nel 1661. *Il compagno è nell'Archivio di S. Spirito.*

Libro in foglio di curiosità sopra le 7 chiese.

Libri ne i quali ho io havuto parte, e vi e mescolato del mio.

. . . . . .

4. Congregationi de Propaganda Fide.

5. Congregationi sopra diversi negotij, passati per mie mani, cioè Notarij, Acque, Porte, Strade, etc.

6. Congregationi sopra elemosine, carestia, Anno Santo.

. . . . . .

12. Per la fabrica del Castello di S. Martino.

. . . . . .

16. Scritture intorno la fabrica di S. Pietro.

17. Spese nelle fabriche di S. Pietro, e disordini, osservati da me.

18. Scritture intorno la fabrica di S. Gio. Laterano.

19. Due gran tomi di disegni con alcuni dei miei.

. . . . . .

Libri manuscritti, nelli quali non ci ho faticato se non il raccogliere qualche scrittura.

. . . . . .

Libro grande de disegni del Campanile di S. Pietro.

Tomo grande dello stato delle chiese di Roma, fatto nella Visita d'Urbano VIII.

26.   1685 June 10

Florence, Bibl. Naz. Centrale, Cod. Magliab. II II 110, fol. 36^r and fols. 170^r–171^v.

A biographical sketch of Borromini, drafted by his nephew Bernardo and later revised by Filippo Baldinucci (d. 1696) for publication in the sixth volume (1728, posthumous) of his *Delle notizie de'professori del disegno.* The manuscript was long considered to be a rough draft by Baldinucci himself (Hempel, 6, n. 1; and Passeri-Hess, 361, n. 2). However, Bernardo's authorship was simultaneously recognized in 1967 by Thelen (*Corpus,* 96, n. 1) on the basis of the handwriting and by Wittkower ("Personalità e destino," 34–36) on the basis of style, internal evidence, and the consistent anti-Bernini bias. Thelen transcribed the first half of the biography and several lines from the second half. For the sake of completeness these sections are repeated in the following transcription of the entire document, and Thelen's orthographical conventions are retained throughout. A transcription is also provided of the questionnaire sent by Baldinucci from Florence, to which Bernardo's text closely adheres.

(Filippo) Baldinucci et (Antonio Francesco Marmi), et al. *Memorie di pittori scultori e architetti autogr.*

/fol. 33^r/ Nota per aver le cognizioni, che si richieggono nel descrivere le vite de i Pittori, della quale se ne potria fare più copie per darle a questo, e quello.

Intorna alla Nascita Bisogna:

Il Ritratto

Patria

Padre, Madre, fratelli, parenti

Anno, mese, e giorno

Nome, casato, sopranome

Suo stato e qualità de Nascita

Qualità di tempi

Intorno alla Vita:
  Progresso
  Genio fantasia
  Studi maestri
  Accidenti della vita
  Stravaganze, facezie, burle dette, e fatte da lui
ad altri; da altri a lui.
  Maniera di dipingere
  Disegni
  Opere, dove, quando
  Se publiche, se private
  Se da giovane, se da vecchio
  Se fù Accademico
  Se fù scapigliato, se ritirato
  Se sano, se ammalato, se allegro
  Se malinconico, se litterato o sciente d'altro,
che di una sola professione
  Se ci sono scritture, o poesie di suo
  Gl'amici, le conversazioni
  Se ebbe moglie, e chi
  Se ebbe figlioli
  Se lascio roba
  Se fù secolare, se ecclesiastico
  Dove abitò, suoi viaggi
  Se ebbe servitù di Principi
  Suoi allievi
  E simili altri Particolari, i quali sovvengono col
pensarci
Intorno alla Morte:
  Quando segui
  Dove
  Di che età mori
  Dove sepolto, come
  Se vi è epitaffio
  Se fece Testamento
  Se lascio roba
  Se gl'allievi li sopravissero/*fol. 170*ᵣ /
      A dì 10 Giugnio 1685
        Nottitia
[*Thelen's   transcription:*] Il.   Sig.re Francesco
Boromino nacque l'anno 1599—nella terra di
Bissone al lago di lugano diocese di Como(.) il
suo padre si chiamaua il Sig.re Gio. Domenico
Castelli Boromino di detto locho. staua al se-
ruitio di Architetto delli Sig.ri visconti di milano
—la sua madre si chiamaua la Sig.ra Anastasia.
Cosi alleuato sino all' età di noue anni incircha
fu da suo padre mandato a milano a inparare a
lauorare di intagliatore di pietra nella quale professione si auanzò tanto che riuscì bon maestro(.)
arriuato all'età di sedici anni incircha—li uenne
uoglia di andare á roma per le grande Cose che
di quella cità sentiua a dire. e così fatto risolutione Con altri suoi amici di trasferirsi a roma
senza parlarne con li suoi genitori.facendo il tutto
segretamente(.) agiustato e stabilito il tempo di

partire—andiede da certi che teneuano denari á
censo dal suo padre—dicendogli che li pagasse li
frutti decorsi poichè suo padre ne aueua
bisogno(;) et il bon debitore li pagò li frutti et
egli li fecie la riceuta a nome di suo padre et con
detti denari andiede á roma [*added by Bernardo:*
questo delli denari così me fu detto(;) così io lo
dico ma non lo so di certo]—arriuato a roma
andiede ad abbitare al uicolo del agniello a sant
giouanni delli fiorentini in un apartamento della
Casa della compagnia della pietà de fiorentini
quale apartamento lo teneua in affitto misier
leone garouo capomastro scarpellino del suo
paese e suo parente—ricouerato in detta Casa
andiede poi per ordine del mede(si)mo misier
leone á lauorare a sant pietro—per intagliatore di
pietra nella qual chiesa lauorò molto tempo e
quando ere l(')ora di merenda li altri intagliatori
andauano chi a merenda e chi giocaua a piastrella
et egli si ritiraua in detto tempo destramente da
loro et andaua per detta chiesa á disegniare di
figure et di architettura et tutto il tempo che
poteva avanzare atendeva a disegniare con grandissima diligenza et polizia(:) et accorgendosi di
ciò Carlo maderni suo parente per uia di donna
li daua da fare e da tirare disegni in polito per
lui—
   morì poi papa Gregorio XV—et fu asunto al
ponteficato Vrbano VIII il quale ordinò al
maderni molti lauori per s. pietro et oltre di ciò
li ordinò di fare li disegni per un palazzo del
prencipe Barberino suo fratello(,) il quale
palazzo fu cominciato dal detto maderni—et il
boromino faceua tutti li disegni di detta fabricha
et lasiò afatto la professione de intagliatore di
pietra per il molto dafare che haueua per il detto
maderni—il quale conosiendolo molto diligente
e acutto di ingenio et per la grande sua atione che
nel disegniare haueua fatto—et per la grande
pratica del fabricare che in si longo tempo
haueua praticato che diuentò peritissimo doue
che il maderni essendo assai vecchio lassiò tutta
la Cura del detto palazzo et delli altri lauori di
s. pietro al boromino—godendo di hauer un gio-
vine simile suo parente che facesse li disegni et
l(')opere in suo luogo nella sua uechiaia(;) et per
misuratore si seruiua del Breccioli e per dire
qualchi cossa delli lauori di marmo che lauorò il
Boromino nel principio e nel mezzo del pontificato di urbano fra li altri lauori sono di sua mano
quelli Carubini di marmo spiritosi e uiuaci che
sono dalle parti delle porticelle con /*fol. 170*ᵛ /
pannini e fistoncini—et anche il carubino sopra in
mezzo al arco sopra dette porticelle per di dentro intorno a sant pietro et anche é di sua mano
quel carubino che è nel mezzo del arco sopra il

basso rilieuo del attila flagellum dei—

fu suo disegno et suo inuentione la Cancellata di ferro dauanti alla capella del Santissimo in detta chiesa di Sant pietro—

et il palazzo delli barberini fu tutto fatto con suo disegnio et ordine(.) morì poi il maderni et papa urbano in luogho del maderni deputò il Signor. gio. lorenzo Bernino—famoso Scultore —e questa deputatione del bernino per architetto di sant pietro fu perchè il papa quando era Cardinale era statto più uolte a uedere a lauorare di scoltura il Bernino nella sua Casa a Santa maria maggiore et per quella conosienza lo deputò per Architetto di sant pietro(;) il quale trouandosi di hauer hauto quella caricha e conosiendosi di ciò inabbile per essere egli scultore—e sapendo che il boromino haueua fatto per il maderni la fabrica á Sant pietro—et anche per il mede(si)mo haueua manegiato e seguito il Palazzo delli Barberini—lo pregò che in tale occasione non l(')abandonasse promettendogli che hauerebbe riconosiuto con una degnia ricompensa le molte sue fattiche(;) così il Boromino si lasiò uincere delle sue preg(h)iere—e seguitò. e promise *(il Boromino)* che hauerebbe continuato a tirare auanti le fabriche già incomiciate per detto ponteficato come già egli era informato del tutto —et il Bernini atendeua alla sua scolture(;) et per l(')architettura lassiaua fare tutte le fattiche al boromino(.) et il bernino faceua la figura di architetto di s. pietro e del Papa—et infatti il bernino in quel tempo in tal profesione era inocentissimo(.) tirati che furono del Boromino, a bon termine le fabriche di quel pontificato(,) il Bernino tirò li stipendij e salarij tanto della fabrica di sant Pietro Come del Palazzo Barberino et anche li denari delle misure—e mai diede cosa alcuna per le fatiche di tanti anni al boromini— ma solamente bone parole et grande promisione(.) e uedendosi il boromino deluso e deriso lasiò et abandonò il Bernino—con questo detto(:) non mi dispiacie che abbia auto li denarij, ma mi dispiacie che gode l(')onor delle mie fatiche—

[*here Thelen's transcription ends*] et che il bernino fosse inocente nel architettura [*inserted above line:* in quel tempo] si uerifica perche abandonato che fu da Boromino (,) e douendo seguitare a fare la figura di Architetto di s. pietro per non parer un stiuale seguito(;) et occorse che papa urbano uolse che si facesse li Campanili alla faciata di Sant pietro—et il bernino fecie il disegnio et lo comincio a mettere in oppera(.) e quando fu alla mita del altezza comincio il gran peso senza proportione a fare crepare la faciata per ogni parte (.) doue che successe la morte di

urbano e fu asunto al pontificato inocenzo X(,) il quale uedendo tanto lacerato la fabrica della faciata di s. pietro(,) e il campanile non era alla mita del altezza(,) e dubitando che se si finiua a seguitar di alzare si saria tirato dietro la faciata(.) e cosi fecie congregatione de architetti i quali risolseri che si demolisse(.) altrimente aueria tirato a tera la faciata(.) e cosi fu demolito(,) con tanta grande spesa in fare e poi disfare per inperitia—epure con tutto questo grande errore e danno della fabrica di S.pietro(,) tanto a continuato a stare nella medema carica con li medemi salarij e stipendij sino al fine della sua uitta—gran fortuna(.) */fol 171r/* et il Boromino in tempo del medemo Papa urbano piantò e fecie la bella chiesa é tempio della sapienza(,) et la prosequi in tempo di inocenzo X.o(,) et la fini in tempo di Alessandro vii—fecie anche in tempo di urbano—la bella chiesa é conuento di sant Carlo alle quatro fontane et la faciata di detta chiesa— et nel pontificato di Inocenzo X.o fecie la bella chiesa di Sant Giouanni Latterano—la chiesa di santa agniesa in piazza nauona—ma poi si sdegnió con il prencipe don Camillo panfilio doppo alla morte di papa inocenzo—e non fini di stabilire detta fabricha di s.agniesa(.) poiche la faciata dal cornicione del primo ordine in sú, non e suo disegno(,) ma era diferente et aueua assa piu del grande come si uede nel suo modello—il tempio per di dentro e tutto suo(,) ma li stuchi non e fatto con ordine suo(.) il lanternino non e suo— fecie e misse in bona simitria il palazzo delli sig.ri falconieri(.) fecie per li medemi sig.ri falconieri la capella maggiore di mezzo nella chiesa di sant gio.' de fiorentini(,) con li depositi quali non ebero il finimento da lui mediante la morte— fecie il portone del palazzo del prencipe giustiniano et mese alchune altre cose con bon ordine —fecie la noua fabricha del conuento oratorio et orologio delli padri della congregatione del oratorio di sant filippo neri(.) fecie la noua fabricha del Collegio di propaganda fide con la chiesa e facciata—fecie la crocie tribuna cupola é Campanile di sant Andrea delle fratte per li sig.ri del Bufalo(,) quale non e finita ma ui e il modello(.) fecie per la sig.ra duchessa di latera la chiesa e monastero di monache della madonna de sette dolori sotto sant pietro montorio con la faciata quale non e finita(,) ma ci e il modello(.) fecie per il Cardinale spada la Capella in sant girolamo della Carita—et la bella prospettiua nel palazzo di detto Cardinale—fecie per il Cardinale filomarino la Capella della santissima Anonziata in una chiesa in napoli—detta uolgarmente da quel popolo la capela del tesoro—fecie la scala a chioccola al palazzo del Cardinal Carpegnia a fontana di treve(,) e fecie li fondamenti del recinto di detto palazzo [*inserted above line:* et altre cose]—é perche delli molti studij e pensieri fatti per diuersi personaggi—et altri disegni di tempij e fabriche secondo che li ueniuano nel pensiero —quali acio non restassero sepolti aueua determinato di farne un libro et darli alla lucie con stamparli(,) tanto quelli messi in opera qua(n)to quelli non messi in opera per diuersi acidenti(,) et li altri soi pensieri per fare uedere il molto del suo sapere(.) e cosi prese domenicho Bariera intagliatore de rami—al quale li diede li disegni della sapienza(,) e li fiece intagliare la pianta giumetrale et in prospettiua(.) li fiece intagliare l'alzata per di dentro et per dauanti et per di dietro—et anche li fiece intagliare la faciata del oratorio de s.filippo—con lorologio(,) nelli quali rami spese da quatro cento scudi in circha(,) come delle riceute apare apresso al nepote di detto boromino [*which is written over the erased word* caualiere]—fatte dal detto Bariera—et li detti rami sono in mano del nipote del boromino [*which is written over the erased word* caualiere]. fu questo homo fatto Caualiero da papa inocenzo X.o il giorno di santa anna che fu al di 26 di luglio 1652—uisse anni sesantotto e mori alli doi di agosto lanno 1667. e uolse essere sepolto incognito e senza pompa ma priuatamente—e volse andare nella sepoltura di Carlo maderni /*fol. 171ᵛ*/ che sta nella chiesa di s.t giouanni de fiorentini—per essere suo parente e maestro. e diede cento Doble per ragione della sepoltura alla figlia di detto Carlo Maderni. La sua morte dichano che seguisse in questo modo. lui pattiua di umore malinconico—o come diceuano li medici di umore ipocondrico—staua in quelli suoi ultimi giorni con una uista stralunata che rendeua terrore a chi lo miraua(,) con molto afanno di stomacho—lo consolo piu uolte il patre oratio callera suo parochiano e' confessore—e lui sofriua tutto—ma qualche uolta uinto dal afanno si inpatientiua(,) e mentre staua in questo essere l(')andiede auistare il suo nipote(,) et egli mostro di gradire la uisita(.) poi si licentio il detto nipote et egli andiede a mettersi a cena(,) perche non staua al letto(.) et doppo cena quello che lo seruiua sparechio et doppo andiede al letto(.) doppo hauer riposato al quanto si suelio et domando il lume(,) dicendo uoler scriuere(.) et quello

che lo seruiua li disse che il medico li aueua inposto che lo lasiasse riposare—e riplicando doi otre uolte che li portasse il lume—et egli sempre si scusaua che aueua ordine dal medico di lasiarlo riposare—e cosi uinto dalla collera ouero dal male [*crossed out:* o puro che per mezzo di quello

che lo seruiua li fosse dato da soi emoli (*inserted:* cosa) per farli uoltare il ceruello] inpatientito disse(:) io non posso dormire(,) non sono sentito(,) non mi uogliono dare il lume(,) non posso scriuere(.) e cosi pilio un spadino che aueua a capo al letto tra le candele benedette et sello cacriase[?] nella panza(,) et si pasase da parte aparte(.) e cosi casco dal letto con la spada in corpo—corse quello che era al seruitio al rumore —e uide il caso corse a chiamare il barbiere di notte(.) ritorno et asieme con il barbiero(.) lo misero al letto—li leuarono la spada dal corpo che era passato nella schina—e campo 24 hore doppo la ferita(,) et in dette hore ebbe tempo di fare il suo testamento—e lasio a quello che faceua li fatti soi che non li uolse dare il lume scudi 500(;) [*crossed out:* che si chiama f . . .] a un altro che li facieua qualche seruitio li lasio scudi 100(;) al seruitore niente(;) alla serua scudi 25—lasio tutta l(')argentaria al cardinal Carpegnia con due colane doro et doi mila scudi di denari contanti et altri legati pij et per l(')anima sua(.) lasio erede il nipote—fu huomo grande e grosso di bella presenza(.) uistiua alla romana anticha di robba fiorata(.) nel uiuere era parchisimo—non intraprese mai negotij che non fossero di somma reputatione—e dimostrare il ualore—alle fabriche di bassa conditione non ui aplicaua—se non erano tempij ouero palazzi—non uolse mai misurare ne sotoscriuere misure fatte da soi giouani— dicendo che non conueniua al architetto di fare altro che disegniare et ordinare che le fabriche caminano bene—e non di intrigarsi nelli interessi tra Capimastri e padroni delle fabriche—non uolse mai disegniare a concorenza(,) et essendo pregato dal Cardinale spada che uolese disegniare a concorenza [*crossed out:* li risposo] per l(')ouera del re di francia(,) li rispose che li disegni erano li soi figlioli e che non uoleua che andassero a mendicando a concorenza con li altri —faceva li modelli delle fabriche di creta e di cera di propria mano di qualsiuoglia opera che intraprendesse a fare—pochi giorni auanti di morire brugio tutti li disengni che egli aueua determinato di dare alla stampa dubitanto che non andassero in mano delli emoli soi doppo la sua morte [*crossed out:* e questo e quanto posso dire (?)] [*added in margin:* . . . si uede che fusse huomo casto](.) fu huomo disinteressato—non stimo mai in alcun tempo il denaro(,) e dalli padroni delle fabriche non uolse mai cosa alcuna per poter con magior liberta operare a modo suo —da Inocenzo X.o—si che prese quello che li diede

27. 1851 April 23
AV, C.II.3 (unpaginated).
Report of Girolamo Romani, architect and engineer, on structural problems besetting the library and oratory, including the following: (1) The west wall of the library was leaning 2 oncie out of plumb. (2) A lesion 150 palmi long had appeared in the vaults of the loggie in the second court. (3) Foundation settlement had caused lesions in the staircase, including a crack running up the entire wall behind the Attila relief. Furthermore:

L'aula della Biblioteca presenta un'avvallamento assai sensibile nel suo mattonato talche teso un filo nella sua larghezza di palmi 52 si è trovato un'avvalamento nel mezzo del mattonato di once dieci del passetto romano; avvallamento notabilissimo, e che dimostra un cedimento grande nella sotto posta volta che forma la copertura dell'Oratorio. Passando nel sottoposto Oratorio ho osservato, che precedentemente alla presente epoca si pretese di riparare mediant catene, un alto cedimento che mostro in allora questa volta e si vedono le vechie crepaccie stuccate; ma prova evidente della inconvenienza, ed inutilità di quel restauro sono le nuove lesioni che nonostanti le catene di ferro si mostrano in tutti della volta descritta; e considerando, che a queste lesioni corrisponde il cedimento del sopraposto mattonato della Biblioteca, ne segue certa conseguenza lo stato pericoloso della descritta volta, e la necessità di una sollecita riparazione.

La facciata dell'Oratorio presenta esternamente forti lesioni quasi verticali che sempre piu concorrono a dimostrare le cose esposte.

28. Various dates, ca. 1579–1656
ASR, Archivio Spada, vol. 496.
Described in M. Heimbürger Ravalli, *Architettura scultura e arti minori nel barocco italiano. Richerche nell'Archivio Spada,* Florence, 1977, 191–94. I first examined the document through a microfilm kindly provided by William McGuire.

The volume is a collection of documents, in particular, contracts with the various types of building trade, which resemble modern specifications. They regulate the quality of work and of materials in minute detail; on the other hand, they remain generic and provide little new information on the progress of work or on the evolution of the design. Many of the documents relate to the Casa dei Filippini; a few were drawn from older files relating to the construction of S. Maria in Vallicella; some relate to other buildings such as the Palazzo Cerri or the Palazzo Falconieri.

They were assembled in order to create a kind of legal handbook and price list which would be of use in drawing up future contracts. Although they provide few new dates or facts, they are informative about the organization of work, particularly the work of the *muratore* and the *scarpellino.*

The *capomastro muratore,* master mason, is the general contractor responsible for the outer shell of the building: foundations, walls, partitions, and roof. He directs a crew of workmen whom he hires and pays; he is in turn paid as work progresses according to the *misura e stima* of the architect; at the end there is a *saldo* or final payment. Building materials *(robba)* are sometimes supplied by the Congregation but more often by the mason, who is reimbursed at preestablished rates. In the former case the contracts stress the economical use of the materials provided; in the latter the accent is on the quality of the supply. The mason is responsible for the demolition of existing structures at his own expense. He is entitled to keep whatever bricks and stone can be salvaged, but must turn over roof beams, iron, and pieces of dressed stone *(conci)* to the Congregation. All antiquities, in particular marbles, gold, lead, and statues, revert to the Congregation; the mason is reimbursed for the effort of excavation; in the case of blocks of travertine or peperino, half of the stone may be kept by the mason as his excavation fee. Strict clauses regulate the quality of foundations, which cannot be laid at night or in times of extreme heat or cold. Work is supposed to come up to an accepted standard "according to the use of Rome," or "according to the best ancient and modern usage." Fine brickwork *(cortina di mattoni arrotati a secco,* cc. 16 ff.) merits a special clause regulating indices of quality such as flush surfaces and horizontal joints. The cost of vaults is calculated at fixed multiples of the rate for walls, increasing as the span increases. The mason is paid at fixed rates for the installation *(mettitura in opera)* of decorative details carved by the *scarpellino* and his shop.

The *scarpellino* or skilled stonecutter is responsible for details such as string courses, doorframes, capitals, and moldings. Unlike a pure sculptor, he is tied to the construction site; most contracts allow him to set up his yard no more than 10 *canne* away. He usually supplies his own travertine and there are standard formulas which regulate its quality ("qual travertino sia sinciero, saldo e bianco non poroso, ne spongoso, senza giunte, tasselli e tradimenti, ne imbosinato [?] con lo stucco." cc. 144 ff.). The same standards apply whether a piece is to go near eye level or high above the ground; the facade of St. Peter's and S. Ignazio are once named as paradigms of *diligenza* and *esquisitezza* (cc. 156 ff.). The *scarpellino* hires his own men but is not entirely free to pay them in any way he wishes. The contracts specify that they are to be paid *a giornate,* by time, and directly supervised by the master; the system of payment *a cottimo,* which seems to mean letting out details as unsupervised piecework with no quality control, is expressly forbidden (c. 159ᵛ; Decr. 109, 115; Pollak, 444, reg. 1829; Hibbard, *Palazzo Borghese,* Rome, 1962, 106ff.).

Several contracts end with a clause concerning unforseen types of work. In the case of the *muratore* the detailed *capitulationi* in force at the Dominican convent then in construction (1638–42) at S. Maria sopra Minerva are mentioned as a standard of arbitration (cc. 16 ff.); in the case of the *scarpellino,* the model is the *capitulationi* in force at the Palazzo Barberini (cc. 144 ff. and 148 ff.). Thus the documents maintain the distinction implied in *Opus,* XIX, 53ʳ between the masonry body of the building, which the contracts put on the same legal level as a monastic structure, and the ornamental dress, which is put on the same level as an aristocratic palace.

The following checklist includes documents that can be dated and linked to a specific building or phase of construction.

Old documents

a. (1579) Expenses of the Chapel of Vincenzo Lavaiana. The chapel was the fourth on the right, taken over by the heirs of Mons. Diego di Campo in 1598 (Hess, "Chiesa Nuova," 364 ff.). According to the document, Cesare Nebbia was paid for the altarpiece and Domenico Fontana for the stuccoes. (cc. 229 and 231.)

b. 1581 January 3 and August 13. Receipts from Horatio Giusti of Montepulciano, *scarpellino.* Also included is a document (dated Dec. 10, 1580, according to Heimbürger Ravalli) on the tomb pavement of the Vallicella, witnessed by Horatio Giusti and G. A. Dosio. (cc. 128 ff.)

c. 1594 March 21. Contract for the facade of S. Maria in Vallicella, between Mons. Angelo Cesi and Mastri Domenico de Marchesi and Domenico de Guidici, *scarpellini,* according to the design of Fausto Rughesi. (cc. 130 ff.)

Documents on the Piazza and the Casa

a. 1627 December 13. Work to be done by the carpenter Simone Roncalli on the house rebuilt at the corner of the Strada Nuova. (c. 169.)

b. (1627) Demolition expenses for the Piazza della Chiesa Nuova: ▽10,900 worth of property affected, offset by ▽5,200 worth of property or

materials salvageable, for a total cost of ▽5,700. Followed by a document disputing some estimates of the worth of salvaged materials. (cc. 236–240.)

c. (1627) Latin document on a house belonging to S. Maria del Popolo, apparently located in the Piazza della Chiesa Nuova. (c. 245.)

d. 1629 August 22. Decreto on the Strada Nuova and its houses. (cc. 248 ff.)

e. 1637 May 27. Estimate of the value of a house and its division between two parties. Sergio Venturi is the *terzo perito* after Maruscelli and Domenico Attaccanti; the house, which is illustrated by three plans, is no. 69 on Cat. 15. (cc. 227 ff.)

f. 1637 August 18. Agreement on the supply of pozzolana and stone for the oratory. (c. 181.)

g. 1637 October 25. Agreement for the supply of bricks, arranged by Padre Marsilio Honorati, then *soprastante alla fabrica.* (c. 183.)

h. 1638 October 24. Agreement with Giovanni Somazzi, *scarpellino,* on the new *scala lumaca.* (c. 163.)

i. (1638) *Scarpellino* contract for finishing the oratory. (cc. 148 ff.)

j. (1638–42) Mason's contract for the remainder of the "fabrica dell'Oratorio." (cc. 16 ff.)

k. (1639) Mason's contract for the new refectory, with notes on prices and technical matters by Borromini in pencil in the margin. (cc. 4 ff.; copy with alterations cc. 22 ff.)

l. 1641 August 11. Contract with Felippo Rodriquez, carpenter, for the pair of walnut doors in the sacristy corridor. (cc. 173 ff.)

m. (1647) Contract with Defendino Peschal, *muratore,* for the Monte Giordano wing. (cc. 111 ff.)

n. 1647 January 19. *Scarpellino* contract for the stonework of the Monte Giordano wing (a revised version of the *scarpellino* contract of 1638 above). (cc. 144 ff.)

o. 1648 May 5. Assessment of travertine worked by Lomazzi but not put into place. (c. 213.)

p. 1649. Assessment of work by Luca Berrettini, *scarpellino.* (cc. 215 ff.)

q. 1651 March 18. *Misure* totalling ▽12,981.96 for work by Defendino Peschal, *muratore,* on the Monte Giordano wing. (cc. 207 ff.)

r. 1656 June 10. *Scandaglio* of work to be done on a bay of the cloister, totalling ▽1,540.82. (cc. 220 ff.)

Documents Relating to Other Buildings

a. (1627) Mason's contract for the Palazzo Cerri on the Strada Nuova. (cc. 48 ff.)

b. (Before 1645) Mason's contract for the Palazzo Carpegna. (cc. 71 ff.)

c. 1646 January 28. Contract with Antonio Fontana, *muratore,* and with the *scarpellini* Luca Berrettini and Matteo Albertini for the Palazzo Falconieri. (Related to documents summarized by M. Tafuri in *Via Giulia,* Rome, 1973, 445 ff.) (cc. 56 ff.)

d. 1646 November 17. Assessment of work by Defendino Peschal on the cupola of S. Maria in Vallicella, totalling ▽754.92. (cc. 199 ff.)

e. 1650 September 15. Mason's contract for the Palazzo Giustiniani. (cc. 105 ff.)

f. Undated mason's contract for the Palazzo Barberini. (cc. 62 ff.)

g. Undated mason's contract for a building of the Duchessa di Latera. (cc. 70 ff.)

h. Undated mason's contract for the Sapienza, at the end of which Borromini copied the names of five or six of the signatories in pencil. (cc. 80 ff.)

i. Undated mason's contract for S. Girolamo della Carità. (cc. 90 ff.)

j. Undated mason's contract for the Carcere Nuove. (cc. 94 ff.)

k. Comparative table of rates "a tutta robba ecceto la calce bianca" for various buildings, including the Palazzo Falconieri (no entries), Palazzo Cerri (no entries), Chiesa Nuova Orologgio, Palazzo Falconieri (?), Sapienza, Palazzo Giustiniani, Case nuove incontro la facciata, Cardinale Spada, Palazzo Carpegna, Palazzo Barberini; on the verso: refettorio, oratorio. (cc. 238–239.)

29. Late 1644.

ASR, Archivio Spada, vol. 235, *Miscellanea di negotij passati per mani mie sub Innocentio PP. X,* fols. t–x added at the beginning of the volume.

The document is the rough draft of arguments for and against five possible ways in which Innocent X might choose to show his affection for the Vallicella. It can be dated obviously after Innocent X's election on September 15, 1644, but more importantly before Camillo Pamphilj's elevation to the cardinalate on December 12, 1644 (C. Eubel, *Hierarchia Catholica . . . ,* IV, 27), which is discussed in the last sentence as a future possibility. The document is in Virgilio Spada's hand; in the transcription below I have omitted canceled passages when they seemed to add nothing to the sense of the text.

Pressuposto che N. S. Papa Innocentio X vogli lasciare nella nostra congregatione o chiesa alcuna memoria della devotione che la sua ecc.ma casa hà portato al nostro Santo Padre, mi sovvengono 5 pensieri.

Prima. Una cassa d'argento e gioie sopra la cassa di ferro dov'è il corpo del santo.

2. Una cappella corrispondente a quella del Santo Padre.

3. Una cappella grande sfondando et allargando quella de Glorieri.

4. L'ornato de la tribuna della chiesa.

5. L'ornato dell'oratorio col fare *come* un Pantheon per la sua ecc.ma casa.

Sopra ciasched'uno di questi pensieri trovo diverse difficultà quali rappresento perche si possi da ciasc'uno de Padri discorrere per vedere se siano *di rilievo ò* superabili, e quale di questi pensieri si habbi per il megliore, ò per il meno cattivo e sovvenendo altro pensiero ad alcuno potrà rappresentarlo a Padri a fine di *considerarlo* per portare a N. S. cose diggerite.

Circa il primo pensiero della cassa d'argento considero più cose.

Primo. Che è forse minor impresa di quello che hà in animo S. Santità.

2. Che è cosa nascosta, e conseguentemente non ottiene l'intento d'una publica demonstratione della sua devotione al Santo dal quale riconobbe il Zio ch'egli applicasse alla professione ecclesiastica.

3. Che si leverebbe forse l'occasione ad un Gran Prencipe di far detta opera conforme che altre volte destinò e non so che si sia mutato di volontà, anzi hà voluto le misure et il modello del luogo.

4. Che è verisimile che Papa Innocentio vogli nell'opera da farci collocarvi il corpo del Card. Girolamo suo zio e forse farvi la propria sepultura.

Al secondo.

Della cappella corrispondente a quella del Santo Padre.

Bisogna presupore che non può esser maggiore almeno in larghezza di quella di San Filippo e la raggione è che a mano manca vi è la tribuna che non si può toccare conforme che è alla capella di S. Filippo e non potendo la mano dritta esser maggiore della mano manco, verrà ad esser eguale à quella di S. Filippo, e per capella d'un Papa è troppo piccola massimamente se vi andasero depositi convenienti ad [*crossed out:* sepolcro d'] un Papa.

Al 3.o

Del sfondare la capella de Glorieri a fine che serva per reporvi il S.mo Sacramento o almeno per communicare le feste.

Presupongo che l'apertura sia quella della cappella presente mà poi si slarghi quanto è tutto il braccio della croce della chiesa [*crossed out:* e che dai lati dove hora è il confessionario del P. Marsilio et la porta ch'entr . . . ? nella casa vecchia si faccino due porte che entrino nella medesima cappella] e sia longa da quanto sarà largo.

Dico che privarà la chiesa della porta laterale che si era designata di fare o almeno converrà farla col robare sito alla detta capella [*crossed out:* non vi restando alcuno luogo da fare tal porta], e la privatione di essa sarebbe di gran scommodo alla chiesa poi che quelli ch'habitano e che passino di parione non potrebbero intrare in chiesa senza un gran circuito per andare a ritrovare la faciata.

2.o Si perderebbe la commodità di quella spatiosa strada che si era designata di fare da parione alla facciata, poiche il sfondato della detta capella con la grosezza di muri arivarebbe forse [?] al refetorio vecchio, e la detta strada non si potrebbe fare che di la dalla capella e conseguentemente nel[?] luogo dal detto refettorio vecchio e delle cucine, e non terminarebbe nella piazza avanti la chiesa mà fra le strettezze di quei vicoli che però in tal caso si voltarebbe [?] il pensiero ad un poco di piazza fra la capella e la strada di Parione.

3.o La spesa de i gettiti sarebbe grandissima poiche tutta o quasi tutta l'habitatione vecchia fra il sito della capella e strada o piazza che s'inviscerà [?] in detta habitatione andarebbe per terra e cavandosene più di ▽1200 d'entrata con le botteghe sarebbe un gran danno per la Congregatione . . . [?] converebbe far instanza del . . . [?] mentre facesse gagliarda spesa nella capella.

4.o Il Servitio che noi speriamo per le communioni in pratica credo certo che riuscirà disservitio perche per grande che si facci la cappella la ballaustrata intorno l'altar di essa cappella non sarà mai maggiore di quella dell'altare maggiore, e sarà forse simile a quella a punto del Coronatione mà con questo svantaggio che dove hora per accostarsi alla ballaustrata non ci è alcuno impedimento ma tutta la larghezza della chiesa . . . [?] all Hora [?] converra entrare et uscire per l'apertura [?] della cappella quale ben spesso sarà occupata da 4 o 6 donne, e chi si vorrà communicare, ò ci sarà communicato, si fermarà facil-

mente in detta cappella a far le sue devotioni in maniera che mi pare di prevedersi una grande e continua angustia in accostarci alla communione.

5.o Si perderà la bella vista che era per riceversi dall'ingresso in chiesa per la porta dove hora stà il confessionale del Pre. Marsilio poiche a dritture si vedera una gran longhezza terminata de la statua del Santo.

6.o Si perderebbe facilmente un luogo per confessionario poiche quello del P. Marsilio si sarebbe potuto pore dove è hoggi la porta che entrava nella casa vecchia e Dio [?] sa se vi potrà restare.

7. La lontanza del luogo della Congregatione da la sagrestia difficulta il trovare chi vadi volentieri a fare la charità et hoggi senza tal difficultà la chiesa patisce di questo piu che d'altra cosa.

Al 4.o

Dell'ornare la tribuna.

1. Li SS.ri Cesi forse ne riceverebbero disgusto havendo altre volte voluto premurosamente [?] che si levassero le arme Borromee.

2. L'ornato che maggiormente spicca si fà con le colonne tonde, e questa levarebbero il luogo a i Padri per cantare i vespri.

3. Fra le pitture da i lati, corretti, e memorie de nostri Cardinali vi resta poco luogo da ornare mass.e [?] non potendosi cingere il teatro con colonne tonde come si è detto.

Al 5.o

Dell'ornare l'oratorio nuovo.

1. Potrebbe essere che dispiacesse che non stà continuamente aperto, et esposto.

2. L'altare non potrebbe esser di gran ornato altrimente levarebbe il sito quale è essenziale all' Oratorio.

3. Il maggior ornato che si potesse far sarebbe fra un pilastro e l'altro col andar facendo sepolcri con statue a gl'heroi di quella casa e si potrebbe cominciare da quello del S.r Card. Girolamo e del Papa regnate per seguitare conforme che da quella casa ne nascevanno, essendo cappace di 8 et anche X quali facendosi ricchi e ornati di statue havrebbe quel vaso del grande e del regio. Mà se l'ecc.mo S. D. Cammillo divento ecclesiastico [*crossed out:* sarebbero] [*crossed out:* restarebbero questo vaso non egualmente àrrichito] cessarebbe l'occasione di tanti depositi.

Catalogue of Drawings

An asterisk (*) in front of a bibliographical entry indicates that it contains an illustration of the print or drawing under consideration.

The following principle is followed regarding translation of the Italian: if the document is available in some other publication, the author has translated it into English; if the document is published here in a note or catalogue entry for the first time, it is left in Italian.

1. Martino Longhi the Elder. 1586.

Projects for the completion of S. Maria in Vallicella, and for a casa to the east of the church.

1a. AV, C.II.8, no. 5. 78.0 × 59.3. Ink and wash over graphite.

Inscriptions (clockwise from upper left):

Sagrestia Larga p. 42 longa p. 60. Stant . . . basa per servitio dela sacrestia. . . . con credenza. Cortile. Refectorio longo p. 65 largo p. 35. Aria scala. Ambulatoria. Cuocina p. 27. Stantia per la cuocina. Camera. Camera. Sala per ospiti. Camera. Andito.

1b. AV, C.II.8, no. 4. 85.7 × 96.0. Ink over graphite, with details at the top of the sheet shaded in pink wash.

Inscription (in faint pencil in the upper corner of the large shaded room; script resembles Girolamo Rainaldi's): Casa del Cava[lie]re Aretino.

The dating and attribution of the drawings were established by Hess in his study of the Vallicella: the church facade shown on both plans corresponds exactly to Longhi's project of 1586–88 (Hess, Fig. 9). Eight side chapels of the church are shown in the form established by Matteo da Castello in 1575,

prior to the addition of side aisles and semi-circular apses in 1586–88. The tribune, transepts, and adjacent chapels are projected in a form close to what was actually built between 1588 and 1593.

Longhi's projected casa is laid out around a large square courtyard, seven bays to a side, which abuts the east flank of the church and is aligned with its axis. His casa was to extend east as far as the Vicolo del Governo. The present Via dell'Arco della Chiesa Nuova was to be closed and the Palazzetto Turci destroyed and replaced by a wing of six shops with mezzanines. Eight shops are projected without mezzanines along the Via di Parione; the upper floors of this wing were doubtless reserved for members of the Congregation, who could descend to the refectory via a spiral staircase. The south wing of the building is reserved for public rooms: an oratory (?) measuring 45 × 60 palmi on the left, and guest rooms and the main staircase on the right. The entire wing is set back slightly to enhance the adjacent church facade; a columnar portal marks the entrance,

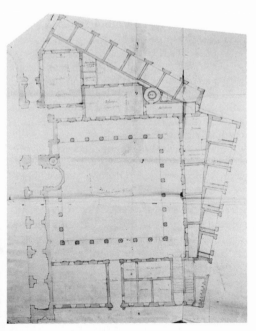

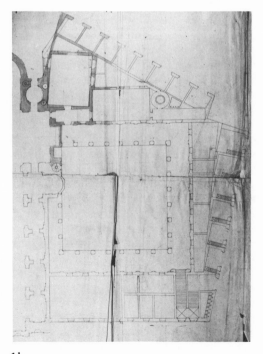

1a   1b

and the regular fenestration is disrupted only by the pair of staircase windows on the right.

Cat. 1b shows an identical project with minor revisions: the large room colored pink is slightly realigned to conform more closely to the extant buildings on the site (Cat. 8).

Bibl.: *Hess, "Chiesa Nuova," 357, Fig. 4 (detail of Cat. 1b).

2. Martino Longhi the Elder. 1587.

Project for completing S. Maria in Vallicella, and for a casa to the east of the church.

AV, C.II.8, no. 7. 84.5 × 65.5. Ink and wash with graphite pentimenti. Scale: 50 p.
Inscriptions (clockwise from lower left):
Cortile per il lume delle capele. Del Sig.r Pineli. Beatio della Crozze. Segrestia. Stanza per il lava mano. Refetorio. Cortile per lume del Refettorio et Segrestia. Stanze per le Bote. .e. Botege. Stanza per servire al Refetorio. Busola. Cuzzina. Stanza per la Cuzina. Saquatore. Botege. Cortile. Entrata per il cortile per le caroze. Lochi comunj. Scala. Botege. Dispensa. Entrata. Stanza per confesare. Cortile. Stanza per il portina[ro].

The casa occupies the same area as in the preceding projects, but the size of the courtyard has been reduced from seven to a mere three bays square. The refectory and sacristy are both displaced to the south, while extra rooms are provided for eight of the nine shops on the Via di Parione. Neither these shops nor the eight in the east wing have mezzanines; presumably the upper stories were to be entirely devoted to the living quarters of the Congregation. The oratory is considerably larger than in previous projects: 62 × 78 palmi, as opposed to 45 × 60 palmi on Cat. 1b. It is provided with an entrance from the courtyard as well as from the piazza, but is lit inadequately by two windows on the south.

The date is once again implied by the rendering of the Vallicella side chapels: the rectangular additions proposed on the present drawing were carried out in a somewhat different form, as semicircular apses, in 1586–88. The light-wells left between the chapels were planned to compensate for the

darkening effect of the new building. Agostino Pinelli, who is mentioned in one of the inscriptions, carried out the decoration of the Chapel of the Assumption (fifth on right) in 1587 (Ponnelle and Bordet, 418, n. 6).

Bibl.: *Hess, "Chiesa Nuova," Fig. 5.

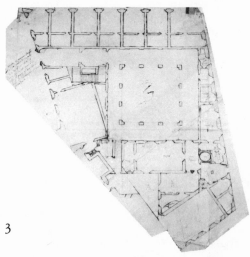

3

3. Anonymous. Ca. 1587.

Project for a casa to the east of S. Maria in Vallicella.

AV, C.II.8, no. 6. Irregular shape with maximum dimensions 53.5 × 57.5. Ink and light beige wash over stylus and graphite.
Inscriptions (counterclockwise from upper left):
. . . questa pianta si caverano stanzie per letti n.o 22 grande di 25 palmi et n.o 52 de p. 20 et n. 16 mezzanini che in tutto serano n.o 90 senza il piano a tera et la libreria et Guardaroba et camera di ricreazzione.

Cortile. Saquatorio. camino. cuozzina. cortile. Logia. per inbandire. Stanza del forno et dispensa. Forno. Dispensa. Dispensa segreta. Speciaria. Stanza per la specaria.

The present drawing reduces the size of the projected casa, which now extends only as far as the Via dell'Arco della Chiesa Nuova and no longer involves the demolition of the Palazzetto Turci block. The transept of the church and part of the fifth side chapel (completed 1587) are shown at the left edge.

Unlike the previous projects, the three-bay courtyard is here aligned with the Via di

Parione rather than with the axis of the church. On the other hand, the oratory is drawn at right angles to the flank of the Vallicella, creating a certain amount of confusion in the disposition of the inner rooms where these conflicting alignments meet.

Some work was carried out on the old casa in 1589–92, probably consolidation of the existing structures after the damage incurred by the expansion of the chapels in 1586–88 (Ponnelle and Bordet, 413, n. 6). Plans for a new building on the site, even one of modest scope such as the present drawing envisages, seem to have been shelved by the time these repairs were undertaken.
Unpublished.

4. Anonymous. Late 16th century.
Projects for a covered entrance to the old sacristy-oratory and to the transept of S. Maria in Vallicella.

4a. AV, C.II.8, no. 26ʳ. 29.1 × 43.4. Ruled ink.
Inscription: S.M. IN VALIC[ELLA].

4b. AV, C.II.8, no. 26ᵛ. Variant of Cat. 4a.

The porticoed entrances shown in these crude drawings appear to be connected with the large room to the right of the Vallicella apse (Cat. 8), which doubled as oratory and sacristy for the old residence (Doc. 10, clause 2). The projects propose to exploit a small public alley (Cat. 8, "Habitatione vecchia"; Cat. 15, no.2) as a rear entrance to

4a

the transept of the Vallicella. They also propose two additional doors opening onto the alley: one to the oratory-sacristy and another of uncertain purpose which might be the casa door. The projects may have been entertained when the transept and tribune of the church were finished in 1588–93, or they may correspond to later projects now only dimly known, such as the plan of P. Angello Velli (Preposito 1596–1611) for a new oratory somewhere in the old casa area (Doc. 10, clause 2). However clumsy the draftsmanship, and however devoid of architectural pretension the drawings may be, they are the earliest known elevation projects for an oratory facade.
Unpublished.

5. Anonymous. 1604–12.
Project for the Piazza della Chiesa Nuova.
AV, C.II.8, no. 97. 57.2 × 42.9. Ink and wash on paper that has browned considerably.
Inscriptions (top to bottom):
S.ta Cecilia. Monte Giordano. Casa dove abita li R[everen]di Padri della Cong[regatio]ne del Oratorio. S.ta Maria in Valicella. Casa dove abita Monsig[no]r Manfredi [?]. Piazza di Pizzo Merlo. Isola del piatetto. Scala che ascende undeci scalini. Casa delle Monache delle Murate. Casa delli Monachi di S.ta Maria Nova. Il Barbiero. Barb . . . [?] S.re Giovanni Ca . . . [?] pitore. Strada Nova. Strada che va al Palazzo del Ill.mo et Ecelen.mo Sig.re Ducha di Sora. Isola di S.to Stefano. Strada che va alla chiavica. Il fornaro. Casa del Tudesco dove sta il sartore. Casa della . . . abiara. Casa di M. Antonio Salegia [?] Casa del Buccha. Case di M. Paullo. Casa del . . . Sig.re Felice Salvatorij. Del Ill.mo et Eccelle. Sig.re Ducha di Sora. Dove sta Monsig[no]re Baratto. Sitto et casa del Sig.re Curcio [?].

The drawing envisages a square piazza based on the width of the Vallicella facade. Eight houses opposite the church are slated for total or partial demolition; a slice is shaved from the Isola dei Piatetti to the left, while a street is projected through the old convent on the right to connect the Filippini residence with the piazza. The square remains a cul-de-sac with no outlet to the south. North-south circulation is still provided by the old street network, particularly

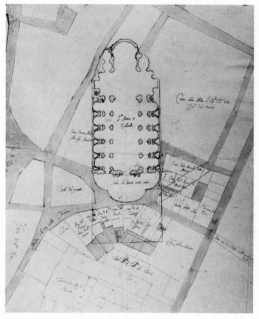

5

the Via di Pizzomerlo ("street which leads to the Chiavica") and the Via Sora (confusingly called the "Strada Nuova"; cf. Ch. VI, n. 9g).

The project for stairs of trefoil shape (eleven steps) in front of the church facade was altered when the steps were begun in more compact form on Jan. 9, 1612 (Gasbarri, 224; Hibbard, *Licenze,* no. 67; Fig. 102, Cat. 17a–e, 38, 87, 98a, 99, 111, 113). The house "where Mons. Baratto resides" was purchased by the Congregation in 1606 from G. Mignanelli (Gasbarri, 219, no. 66a). The drawing may even precede this purchase by a few years and reflect the negotiations of 1604 with Cardinal Aldobrandini to select the site for the proposed Strada Nuova, a street to connect the piazza with the Via del Pellegrino on the south. *Bibl.* *Strong, *La Chiesa Nuova (Santa Maria in Vallicella),* Rome, 1923, Fig. III (dated ca. 1550).

6. Anonymous. Date uncertain: either 1586–88 or 1611–21.

Project for a casa on the west side of the church.

6a. Ground floor plan.

AV, C.II.8, no. 8. 57.3 × 70.3. Ink and light beige wash.

6b. *Piano nobile* plan.

AV, C.II.8, no. 9. 56.6 × 34.2. Ink and deep rose wash. Scale: 150 p.

The projected casa is organized around two large courtyards of nearly equal size: 5 × 6 bays, and 5 bays square. The ground floor is given over entirely to functional spaces: 25 shops with mezzanines, kitchen with oven and sink, refectory, vestibule, and larders with mezzanines in the east wing. There is neither a sacristy nor an oratory, both of which presumably were to remain on the east side of the church. The upper floor is devoted to living accommodations: 8 large and 33 small single rooms, 17 rooms with *camerino,* and 5 rooms of irregular shape, all serviced by double-loaded corridors. Two large staircases connect the ground floor with the *piano nobile,* and a third staircase ascends from the *piano nobile* to an additional story not represented by any plan.

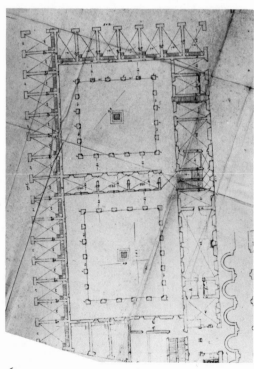

6a

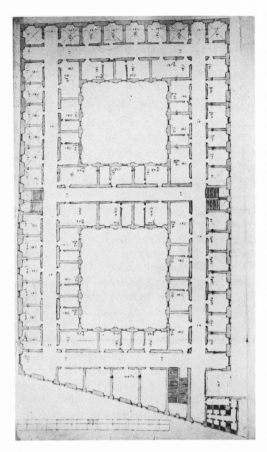

6b

The evidence for dating is contradictory. On the one hand, the side chapels of the Vallicella are still shown without the connecting passageways that were built in 1586–88. On the other hand, the likeliest time for a casa of this size and location to have been considered is between 1611 and 1621, after the decision to expand to Monte Giordano had been taken and before the foundations of the sacristy were laid. The 17th-century date is more probable than one during Filippo's own lifetime (d. 1595), and it is possible that the draftsman was simply ill-informed of the plan of the church, as his rendering of the crossing piers seems to indicate.
Unpublished.

7. Anonymous. 1611–21.
Project for a casa on the west side of the church.

7a. Ground floor plan.
AV, C.II.8, no. 15. 44.6 × 33.0. Red chalk, ink, and olive wash. Scale: "Canna di Palmi Cento."
Inscriptions (right to left):
Muro de la chiesa. Strada tra la chiesa et il convento. Oratorio. Spetiaria. camera per lo spetiale. Hospitio. lavamano. Refettorio. Strada Papale. Cortile Principale comune. Cortile secondo privato. Dispensa. dispensino. cam[e]ra per il coco. cam[e]ra per il forn[a]ro. Cocina. Loggie. bottege. Piazza di Monte Giordano.

7b. *Piano nobile* plan.
AV, C.II.8, no. 16. 45.7 (maximum height) × 28.5. Ink and olive wash.

The project resembles Cat. 6, but is far more amateurish in conception and execution. The entrance to the casa is located at the Piazza di Monte Giordano, and the ground floor is occupied by a refectory, pharmacy, kitchen, infirmary, and twenty-four shops. The oratory occupies a secluded position in

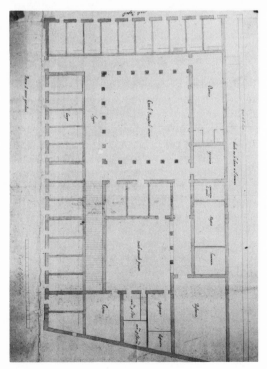

7a

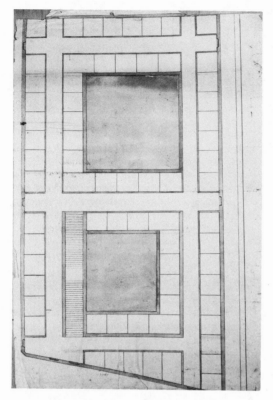

7b

the right wing; no sacristy is indicated. Sixty-nine rooms line the double-loaded corridors of the upper floor. The south facade is bent to avoid unnecessary demolitions, and a public street runs between the casa and the left flank of the church, which are connected by a bridge near the oratory. This urbanistically timid project was probably entertained shortly after the decision to expand toward Monte Giordano; it predates the permission granted in 1621 to close the Via di Pizzomerlo (Decr.4).
Unpublished.

8.   Attributed to Mario Arconio. 1618–21, probably 1621.
Site plan prior to the construction of the casa.
AV, C.II.6, Pls. A or I–II. 45.5 × 35.5. Ink and yellow wash over light stylus lines. Scale (along axis of church): 100 p. = 7.4 cm.

Inscriptions:
Piazza di Monte Giordano. Chiesa di S.ta Cecilia. La Cong[regatio]ne possiede q[uest]e Isole *segnate di giallo* e tutte le case che sono attaccate alla chiesa. Strada di parione. Vicolo fra la casa e chiesa che si desidera chiudere. Habitatione vecchia de Padri. Piazza di pizzomerlo.

The drawing distinguishes between property already in the possession of the Congregation (yellow) and property still in private hands (white). In so doing it furnishes evidence for dating: most of the houses colored yellow had been purchased by 1618, while most of the remainder were acquired between that date and 1621 (Gasbarri, 216–19; and Cat. 15). An inscription alludes to the plans under way in 1621 to close the Vicolo di Pizzomerlo (Decr. 4), and appears to link the drawing with the building campaign directed by Mario Arconio between 1621 and 1624. The sheet served as the basis for his project for the new casa (Cat. 9), which included an outline of the older houses on the site and omitted the Vallicella facade in a manner identical with the present drawing. The idea of showing houses awaiting demolition was later taken up by Maruscelli (Cat. 13, 14) and through him transmitted to Giannini's 18th-century edition of the *Opus* (Fig. 5).
Bibl.: *Hempel, 65, Fig. 16.

9.   Attributed to Mario Arconio. 1621–23.
Project for a casa on the west side of the church: ground floor plan.
AV, C.II.6, Pls. F or XI–XII. 44.6 × 31.0. Ink and green wash.
Inscriptions:
Strada di Parione. Oratorio.
Caption on the following page of the MS:
A.   Chiesa
B.   Prima entrata
C.   Scala principale
D.   Cortile
E.   Sacristia con due altre stantie per suo servitio
F.   Refettorio
G.   2. Cortile
H.   Cisterna
I.   Altra Bocca della Cisterna per la cocina
K.   Cocina
L.   Dispensa
M.   Stantia del lavator delle mani

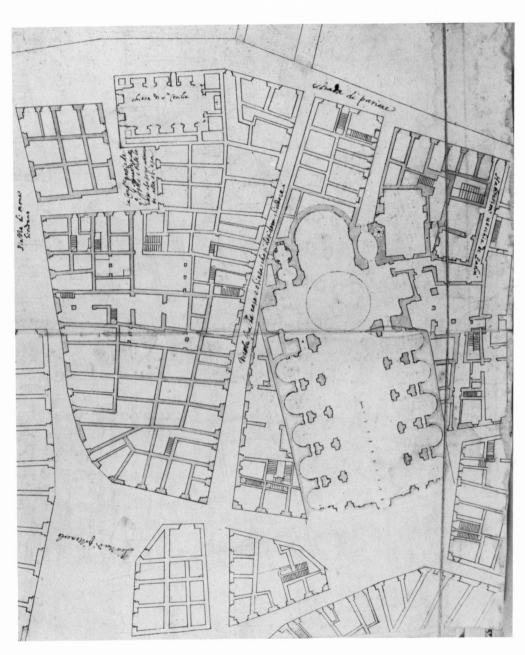

8

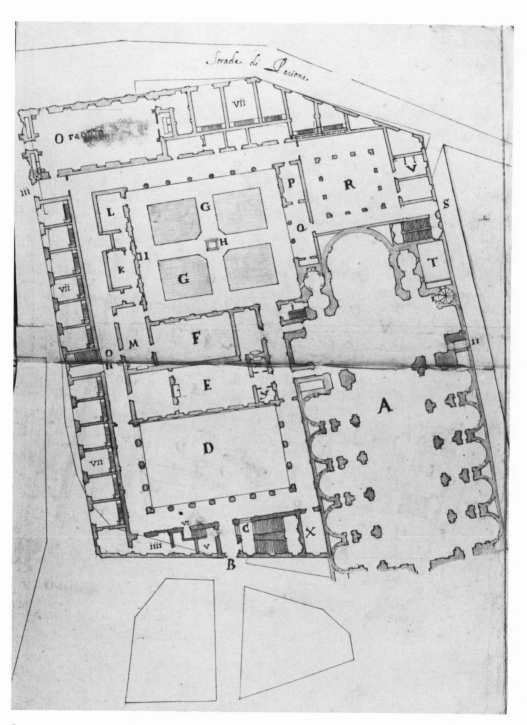

N. Transito che va a basso alla Cantina
O. Scala per il Refettorio
P. Spetiaria
Q. Loggia
R. 3 Cortile
S. 2da Entrata per le cose di fuora
T. Cortiletto
V. Stalletta
X. Altro Cortiletto
Y. Per le Caraffelle
Z. Per il lavatore delle mano per la Sacristia
i Scalette per il Choro della Musica
ii Porticella
iii Entrata che serve per l'oratorio
iiii Sala con due Camere per forestaria, et audentia
v Stantia del Portinnaro
vi Scala per il granaro
vii Botteghe

The project envisages a new oratory with a full ecclesiastical facade on the site of the church of S. Cecilia. Five shops with mezzanines occupy the Via di Parione to the north, and twelve the Via dei Filippini to the west. The south facade of the casa is set at an oblique angle to the axis of S. Maria in Vallicella, and although it is partly absorbed in the south wing, some of the angle is transmitted throughout the entire building: the sacristy meets the side of the church obliquely, and the northwest corner of the casa is an angle of less than 90 degrees. These misalignments provide the principal evidence for the dating and attribution of the project.

Mario Arconio (1575–1635?) was the Congregation's architect during the first campaign of 1621–24. The walls of the sacristy were begun in October 1621 under his direction (Decr. 4–7; *Opus*, III, 8ʳ). They were left incomplete in 1623 (Decr. 16), and were found in 1624 to be based on surveying errors, "errore nelle misurare" (Decr. 19). When Maruscelli replaced Arconio in 1624 he immediately resurveyed the walls (Decr. 19–21), and all of his own projects show them at right angles to the axis of the church. This evidence, though somewhat slender, seems to indicate that the walls of Arconio's original project were aligned obliquely with the church, as in the present drawing. An allusion to a project of this sort occurs in the opening pages of the

Opus: "In laying out the first lines [of the Casa dei Filippini] difficulties were encountered which often occur in new buildings on densely inhabited sites, particularly that of departing from the right angle. . . . This problem arose in laying out the Collegio Romano, which has no right angles, although the defect is concealed in the thickness of the walls" (II, 6ʳ). The identification of the present drawing as Arconio's project is reinforced by a document of 1622, which speaks of using the site of S. Cecilia for "the fabric and the oratory": none of the other extant projects shows an oratory on the site of S. Cecilia.

There are certain later *termini ante* also implicit in the project. The northwest corner of the casa was laid out at right angles to the axis of the church in 1629 (Decr. 35–38, 137; cf. Cat. 39). The present drawing still shows this angle as less than 90 degrees. In publishing the drawing as an anonymous competition entry of 1637, Hempel overlooked the evidence of the alignments as well as the more obvious *termini* first pointed out by Bruschi: neither the sacristy service rooms of 1632 nor the sanctuary of S. Filippo of 1634 appears on the drawing. *Bibl.:* *Hempel, 66, Fig. 17; Bruschi, "Il Borromini nelle stanze di S. Filippo alla Vallicella," *Palatino*, XII, 1968, 19, n. 4 (possibly prior to Maruscelli's work on the sacristy in 1624 ff.).

10. Anonymous. 1621–24.
Project for a casa on the west side of the church: ground floor plan.
AV, C.II.8, no.11. 63.3 × 71.0. Ink.
Inscriptions (bottom to top, left to right):
Prima entrata. Saleta per l'aud[ienz]a de forastieri. Camera per l'aud[ienz]a de forastieri. Camera per il portinaro. P[rim]a scala grande. Camera per il portinaro. cortiletto. Primo cortile. Retro sacristia (34 × 37 p.). Sacrestia (68 × 37 p.). Per le caraffine (15 p.). lavamani della sacristia. corridore avanti la sacristia. Oratorio (52 × 106 p.). 2ª scala per il refettorio. Stanza da lavar le mani (57? × 22 p.). Refetori[o](68 × 35 p.).

A close variant of the preceding project, possibly a revision of it. The south front of the casa and the sacristy are both drawn at right angles to the church, while the northwest corner of the building remains less than

a 90 degree angle. The Vallicella apse appears shorter than in the preceding project, while the service courtyard is one bay longer, and an extra shop has been added to the Monte Giordano wing.
Unpublished.

11.   Anonymous. 1621–29, possibly 1622.
Project for a casa on the west side of the church: ground floor plan.
AV, C.II.6, Pl. E or IX–X. 45.3 × 37.0. Ink with colored wash (yellow for church, pink for casa), pinpricks. Scale: 100 p. = 9.5 cm.
Inscriptions:
Refettorio longo p. 79½ largo 37. [Lavamano] 25 × 37. Cucina 59½ × 37. Cortiletto 52. Dispenza 57½ × 37. Giardino longo p. 150 largo p. 124½. Oratorio longo p. 110½ largo p.50. Sag[resti]a longa p. 80 larga p. 54. Chiostro longo p. 110 largo p.67.

The project envisages a casa with nineteen shops, seven on the north and twelve on the west, all equipped with mezzanines. Aside from the sacristy, which occupies the same site as in Arconio's project, the major functional rooms of the building line the north wing. The oratory is placed directly behind the Vallicella apse and is entered from a street proposed along the right flank of the church. It has a modest three-bay ecclesiastical facade and is equipped with a small stairway behind the chapel of S. Filippo to service the musicians' *coretti*. Despite its nine window bays, the oratory stands too close to the massive apse to be adequately lit.

The architect devoted particular attention to the symmetrical appearance of the west and south facades, and in so doing presaged future projects by Maruscelli (Cat. 23c) and Borromini (Cat. 29). A problem was created by the position of the two entrances to the building: they were aligned with the central axes of the two courtyards but did not fall in the center of their respective facades. Symmetry was achieved on the west by duplicating the steps and portal of the entrance on an ordinary shopfront, and on the south by adding a pilaster strip and creating a projection on the left side.

The project would have been obsolete after the final decision, taken in 1629, to

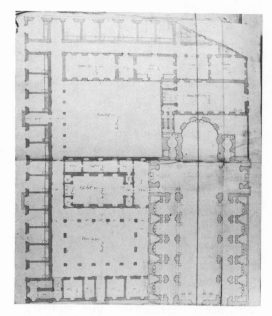

11

locate the oratory in the south wing (Decr. 37). In addition, the drawing proposes a corridor 24½ palmi wide between the church and sacristy, which would have been obsolete after Maruscelli's 18-palmi corridor was finished in 1631 (Decr. 60). At the other extreme, the project follows Arconio's foundations for the sacristy, laid in 1621. The graphite lines inside the church may indicate an even more precise date. They appear to describe a temporary arrangement of seats or wooden barriers (with the pulpit pier singled out from the others) for a ceremonial event, such as the canonization of S. Filippo in 1622 (shown in a contemporary painting in Hess, "Chiesa Nuova," Fig. 13, and in Incisa della Rocchetta, "La Chiesa Nuova nel marzo 1622," *Oratorium*, III, 1972, 39).
Bibl.: *Hempel, 67, Fig. 18 (as a competition project of 1637); *Bruschi, *Palatino*, XII, 1968, 14, Fig. 1 (detail) and 19, n. 5 (prior to 1636, possibly Maruscelli's first project).

12.   Attributed to Paolo Maruscelli. 1624.
Preliminary projects for a new casa: plans sketched in outline.

12a.   AV, C.II.8, no. 24ʳ. 52.2 × 39.2.

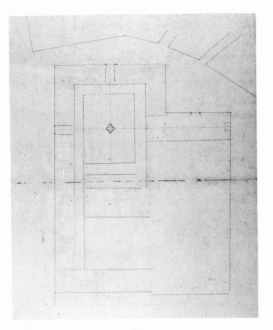

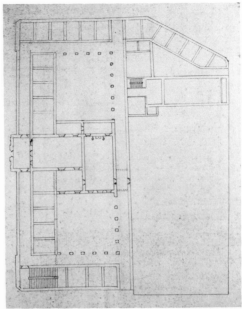

12a

12d

Ink, graphite, and red chalk. Scale: 100 p. = 7.2 cm.

12b.   AV, C.II.8, no. 24^v. Red chalk.

12c.   AV, C.II.8, no. 13. 43.0 × 29.0. Ink over graphite, pinpricks.

12d.   AV, C.II.8, no. 14. 43.0 × 28.7. Ink over graphite and stylus incisions, pinpricks.

The projects are linked together by medium, style, and technique, all of which point to Maruscelli as the author. The sharp steel pen over graphite, and the paper prepared in such a way that light foxing occurs with time, are elements that recur in all of Maruscelli's secure drawings (e.g., Cat. 20b). The dotted *visuali* drawn through the courtyard on Cat. 12a emphasize one of his characteristic architectural idioms. The layout of the rooms behind S. Maria in Vallicella on Cat. 12d corresponds to his definitive plan (Cat. 21, nos. 20–25, 30, 31, 33). The perimeter of the casa is given a small extra facet at the upper right corner, an idiosyncrasy that occurs only on Maruscelli's drawings.

The building proposed on Cat. 12a avoids the inconvenience of a bent north wing by ceding a large triangular plot of land to the public (the quandary is explained in *Opus,* II, 6^r). The oratory occupies the area behind the church later destined for the refectory (Cat. 21, no. 22); direct access was provided to the piazza on the north and indirect access through a vestibule to the courtyard on the west. Staircases, internal partition walls, and the slanted stretch of the street which led to a rear door in the church are sketched in faint red chalk.

Cat. 12d proposes a drastic rearrangement of the area at the center of the casa. Two L-shaped loggie of nearly identical size (5 × 5 and 5 × 6 bays) are arranged symmetrically around a complex of rooms which includes a sacristy that is turned 90 degrees on its axis, and an oratory that is entered through a vestibule protruding into the public street. Apparently Arconio's sacristy foundations still permitted a shuffle of this sort. The fenestration along the north side of the first courtyard confirms the attribution to some extent, since it exhibits the same errors in planning as Maruscelli's project for the Theatine residence at S.Andrea della Valle (explained in Appendix II).

The four projects document Maruscelli's

first attempts to design a casa within the limits of certain fixed data: the location of Arconio's sacristy foundations, and the street pattern of the surrounding area. They document the beginning of the oratory's migration south from the Via di Parione but they do not yet show it in its final resting place in the southwest corner of the building. Unpublished.

13.   Attributed to Paolo Maruscelli. Ca. 1624.

Project for a casa: outline superimposed over a site plan.

AV, C.II.6, P1. B or II–IV. 44.6 × 31.5. Ink with pink and yellow wash. Scale: 100 p. = 7.0 cm.

The plan recapitulates the basic data of earlier site plans. It includes a spiral staircase in the left transept of S. Maria in Vallicella which is not shown on any other drawing. The lower reaches of the staircase were removed at an uncertain date to make way for the entrance to Maruscelli's sacristy (Cat. 21, no.10); the upper reaches, which were described in *Opus,* XII, 40ʳ ("a spiral staircase left intact, which leads from the *piano*

nobile over the main vault of the church"), still exist in the present building.

The projected casa, which is shown in outline, resembles Maruscelli's later projects in size and shape but still fails to treat the west facade as a single coherent image: the projection added at the northwest corner is considerably larger than the southwest projection, perhaps out of respect for its position on the Piazza di Monte Giordano.

A similar plan of the church by Maruscelli, without the spiral staircase and without an accompanying casa project, exists in AV, A.V.14, fol. 11ᵛ, bound to the "Dichiaratione della Pianta" which relates to Cat. 15. Unpublished.

14.   Paolo Maruscelli. 1624–27, probably February 1624.

Project for a casa: ground floor plan superimposed over a site plan.

AV, C.II.6, P1.G or XIII–XIV. 56.9 × 42.5. Pen and yellow wash, graphite shading, light graphite reworking. Scale: 200 p. = 14.5 cm.

Inscriptions:

Top left:

17—∇100		Speziaria del corallo
18—∇110		Magazzino del Salviati
19—∇ 30		casa che tiene il speziale del Corallo
20—∇105		Casa ove sta il Roviglio
21—∇ 62		Casa che era del Roviglio verso il vicolo della sagristia
22—∇352		Casa d[ett]a del Rusconi con boteghe tre
23——		Casa de Canonici di S. Lorenzo in Damaso
24—∇ 69		Rimessa che tiene il salad.o et apartam[ent]o sopra
25—∇ 48?		Casa ove e una . . . di . . . [*damaged*]
26—∇		Case del Paganino
27—∇ 40		Casa che habita Cosimo formaio nel vicolo della sag[risti]a.
28—∇ 15		Casa ove habita M[as]tro Defendino
29—∇ 55		
30—∇ 55		Case che riescono nel vicolo dietro la capella del s[an]to
1041		

Top center:

31—∇ 44	Gioielliero
32—∇ 40	falegname
33—∇ 30	Stagnaro
34—∇ 90	Dove stava il . . .
35—∇ 70	. . . Ragatiere

```
36—▽100        Mariotto ragatiere
37—▽ 20        Mastro di scola
38—▽  9.60     m——ta galliacra [?]
39—▽ 38        Crispoldo [?] Abbaoio [?] note
40—            (damaged) Monsu . . . francese [?]
41—▽212.50
42—▽ 90        Centillo ragatiere
43—▽120        dov'era la corona
44—▽ 78        un procur . . . [?]
45—▽ 80        dove stava il S.o Badino
   1157.10
```

Top right:
Casa della Toretta

```
                             46—
                             47—▽ 66
                             48—▽ 43
                             49—▽ 36

Liscicarolo a pizzomerlo     50—▽150
Casa incontro il Baronio     51—▽150
Casa del Baronio con boteghe tre   52—▽281
. . . della . . . [damaged] del
vescovi sopra il S . . .     53—▽ 50
                                776.
                              1157.10
                              1041.
                              2974.10
```

Upper right corner:
Le lettere dell'alfabeto dichiarano le officine della nova fabrica per mezzo della tavoletta a piedi di questa. Li numeri sparsi nella pianta servono per sapere che case rispondino a ciasched' una officina, e ch'fitto si perdi col privarsi di esse per mezzo della di contro tavoletta.

Labels on the plan, from top to bottom:
Chiesa di S. Cecilia
Piazza di monte giordano
sito dell'habitatione ove hora stanno i Padri
sito della chiesa
strada da farsi
Isola del Pizzomerlo
Isola del Piatetti
Facciata della chiesa

Bottom center:
Tutto il colorito di giallo e la fabrica da farsi il tinto di lapis sono recinti di case circonvincine che restano il pontegiato e il recinto delle case che devono gettarsi a terra
Scala di palmi romani 200

Bottom right:
(The letters of the caption do not always correspond to the correct rooms on the plan; additional confusion is introduced by the severe damage to the sheet at this point.)

a   Porta principale
b   camere alla porta per tratenere forastieri
c   camera del portinaro
d   Oratorio
e   scale principali
f   cortili
[g] sagrestia con camerini
[h] camere per serv[iti]o di sagrestia
[i] Porta che entra in chiesa [*damage*])
[n] [re]fetorio
[o] commodita per il refetorio
p   in ocas[ion]e de Prencipi [*does not appear on the plan*]
q   cucina
r   [*should read* q]   commodita per cucina
    [*should read* r]   stalla
    [*should read* s]   luoghi communi
    [*should read* t]   cortile rustico con porta per spezzaroli
u   Dispensa
x   Dispensino

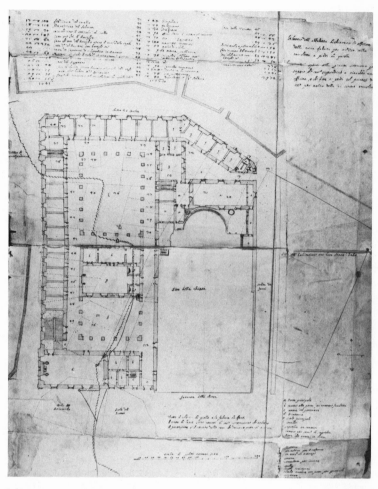

14

The plan combines two features: Maru-scelli's project for a new casa, and a financial survey of property in the area. Houses subject to demolition are shown in outline, and a table of the rents received by various proprietors is included to facilitate calculation of the demolition costs for any given part of the new building. This financial information provides certain broad limits for the date of the drawing. The houses already purchased in 1621 to begin the east end of the sacristy are omitted altogether (casa del Capitolo di S. Pietro, mentioned in 1621, Decr. 4; casa di Madonna Laetitia Cocciani, mentioned in 1622, Decr. 13, and Doc. 5, with a *stima* of 1623 in Pollak, 431, reg. 1700). Several other houses are described as though their

purchase had already taken place: "the house which belonged to Roviglio" (no. 21, bought from Agostino Rovelli around October 1617, Decr. 1), and the "so-called house of Ruscone" (no. 22, bought around April 1621, Decr. 3). On the other hand, the drawing was executed before the demolition of S. Cecilia in 1629. It still shows the Casa della Toretta (no. 46) which was purchased between 1627 and early 1630 (Decr. 33, 44, 45) and finally destroyed in March 1630 (Pollak, 432, reg. 1707).

The Congregation first called in Maruscelli in 1624, at a time when two problems had brought construction to a standstill—first, reduced income due to the purchase of houses, and second, surveying errors in Arconio's sacristy (Decr. 19–21). The present drawing tackles both problems simultaneously. It clarifies the financial obligations that further demolitions would involve, probably on the basis of Spada's new accounting system (*Dialogo,* 175). And it presents a project for a new casa that rectifies Arconio's mistakes. In the disposition of rooms, the drawing is nearly identical to Maruscelli's caption project of 1627 (Cat. 20), although the fenestration is less sophisticated and follows no predictable pattern: the windows in the two west projections are not symmetrically arranged; those in the sacristy fail to align with the adjacent courtyard loggie; chaos prevails on the south facade. Either the drawing stands at the very beginning of Maruscelli's designs, or he simply allowed the administrative aspect of the project to predominate over the aesthetic. Holes in the corners of the sheet may indicate that the drawing had been tacked up for discussion or display long before Spada inserted it into the *Opus* manuscript "as a curiosity" (IV, 10^r).

The following pentimenti in faint graphite were introduced onto the sheet at some later date: (1) A square staircase occupies the north wing, its west flight aligned with the east loggia of the garden court. (2) The corridor between the church and sacristy is sealed by two lines, and then a third line is drawn to suggest the position of the present wooden screen-door (cf. Cat. 66). (3) Steps are drawn under caption no. 52 to indicate a difference in level between the *portaria* and the first court. (4) There is an attempt to adjust the windows in the south wall of the sacristy. (5) The measurement 16 palmi is added to the north loggia of the garden court, and 18 palmi to the corridor between the church and sacristy. (6) The outline of several houses slated for demolition (19, 20, 36, 41, 50, and 51 among others) is reinforced with a sharp pencil, guided by pinpricks, as though the drawing has been copied. The first five pentimenti correspond to innovations introduced by Borromini. The marks were apparently made by someone interested in updating and copying the plan. One candidate remains Sebastiano

Giannini, who collated the drawing with Fig. 6 to produce the plan in his edition of the *Opus* in 1725 (Fig. 5).
Unpublished.

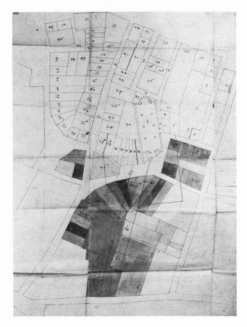

15

15.   Attributed to Paolo Maruscelli. Late 1626–27.
Old S. Maria in Vallicella with adjacent streets and houses.
AV, A.V.14. 73.1 × 52.7. Ink with orange, beige, and purple washes.

The plan is attached to a lengthy caption document that lists eighty-one houses in the area and summarizes their financial history. The text was written in 1627 by a professional scribe, and kept up to date thereafter with marginal notes, often in Spada's hand, added between 1628 and 1648 (no. 70, p. 59^r). The combined plan and document form an inventory of the Congregation's holdings along with the acquisitions needed to complete the Piazza della Chiesa Nuova and the Strada Nuova. They form a complement to Cat. 14, which provides a similar financial overview for the casa.

Although the drawing is usually dated prior to the destruction of the old Vallicella in 1575, points of style link it to Maruscelli. The crisp pen technique on paper that has lightly foxed, and the use of bright purple (caption no. 67) and beige (nos. 68, 76) washes are typically his. The outline of a piazza and Strada Nuova corresponds exactly to one of his projects (Cat. 17e). Although there seems to be no reason to date the actual drawing any earlier than the document it accompanies, it obviously does record information from older sources, such as the disposition of the medieval church and the street layout immediately behind it. *Bibl.:* Ponnelle and Bordet, 339; *Strong, Fig. II (detail, dated ca. 1550); Hess, "Chiesa Nuova," Appendix II, 363–67, draws on the accompanying caption document; *Gasbarri, 211–21, and second unnumbered plate (dated 1575); *Russo, "Piazza della Chiesa Nuova," *Studi Romani,* XIII, 1965, p. 27, n. 15, and Fig. III (dated prior to the construction of the new church).

16.   Mario Arconio or Paolo Maruscelli. Date uncertain.
     Houses around S. Maria in Vallicella: site plan.
     AV, C.II.8, no. 96. 64.8 × 43.0. Ink.

This crude drawing shows the blocks of houses eventually occupied by the casa. The area of the church is left blank. While the internal structure of the houses resembles the site plan attributed to Arconio (Cat. 8), the external outline of the blocks resembles the plan attributed to Maruscelli (Cat. 15). There seems to be no basis for determining whether the sheet is a preparatory study for or a copy after one of these drawings. It makes a minor contribution by showing the side door of S. Cecilia in greater detail than is available elsewhere (Cat. 8).
Unpublished.

17.   Paolo Maruscelli. Late 1626.
     Projects for the Piazza della Chiesa Nuova and the Strada Nuova.

17a.   Site plan in outline form.
     AV, C.II.8, no. 99. 42.5 × 57.5. Ink (In Fig. 102 lines have superimposed on the drawing to clarify Cat. 38).

17b.   Site plan with colored wash.
     AV, C.II.8, no. 98. 57.9 × 43.1. Ink over stylus, with yellow, beige, and purple washes. Scale: 150 p. = 11.4 cm.

17c.   Alternative projects for the street and piazza.
     AV, C.II.8, no. 100. 43.3 × 57.4. Ink and wash; piazza sketched in pencil; street in pencil, ink, and red chalk. Scale: 100 p. = 7.1 cm.
Inscriptions:
     ▽6000. ▽1300. ▽1200. Natione tedesca. Girolamo Maziotti. Gio. Pietro Salati ▽1500. Vinc[enz]o Bocca ▽2420. Clemente Agnelli ▽1400. ▽2000. ▽1600. Cong[regatio]ne dell'Oratorio [*houses tinted gray*]. Ecc.mo S.re Duca di Sora [*yellow*]. S.re Antonio Cerro [*purple*].

17d.   Narrow project for the piazza.
     AV. C.II.8, no. 101. 43.2 × 57.9. Ink and wash. Scale: 100 p. = 7.1 cm.

17e.   Wide project for the piazza.
     AV, C.II.8, no. 102. 42.2 × 56.4. Ink and wash. Scale: 100 p. = 7.1 cm.

The drawings encompass a large area between the church, the Chiavica di S. Lucia, and the Via del Pellegrino. The outline plan in Fig. 102 shows the property that would be affected by the proposed urban transformations; the drawing appears to be the master sheet from which the other plans were taken. Cat. 17b provides information that would have been useful in planning demolitions: built-up areas are filled with colored wash, while courtyards and alleys are left blank. A square piazza, identical with the one projected on Cat. 5, has been faintly incised with a dry stylus. Cat. 17c offers numerous overlapping alternatives for the proposed Strada Nuova. One economical route, drawn in red chalk, is only 30 palmi wide and almost entirely avoids the Cerri and Sora properties on the right. The proposals drawn in ink are closer to subsequent projects and to the executed street: they are wider (41–43 palmi), more damaging to the Cerri and Sora properties, and they meet the church facade at a less oblique angle. Two piazza projects are sketched in pencil: the narrower is the traditional square based on the width of the Vallicella, while the wider is based on the principle of a street passing along the east flank of the church

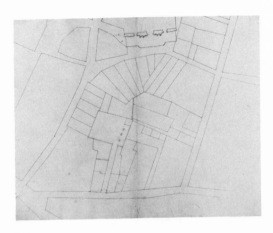

17a

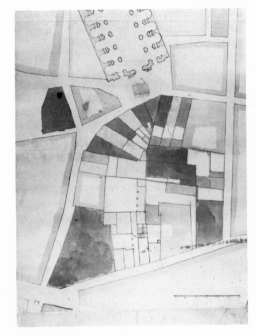

17b

17c

17d

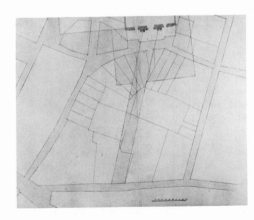

17e

and emptying into the piazza, an idea explored in the two projects that follow.

Cat. 17d shows the Strada Nuova in its final form: it cuts heavily into the Cerri and Sora properties, and widens gradually from 39 to 41 palmi as it approaches the Vallicella facade at an oblique angle. The drawing shows a projected casa, 193 palmi wide, which is the cause of several alterations in the shape of the piazza. In compensation for the public thoroughfare closed by the proposed building, a new street is opened along the right flank of the church and incorporated in a somewhat irregular way into the square piazza. Faint pencil lines suggest a further enlargement of the piazza which would make its left side run parallel to the Strada Nuova.

Cat. 17e is a handsome finished drawing which appears to come at the end of the series. It projects a piazza of regular contours and generous dimensions, about 155 × 235 palmi. The street along the flank of the church is 40 palmi wide and balanced by a 40-palmi enlargement of the piazza on the opposite side. However, in spite of the definitive appearance of the drawing, the piazza was executed in a different, far more economical form which is shown on Cat. 17a and explained in Cat. 38.
Unpublished.

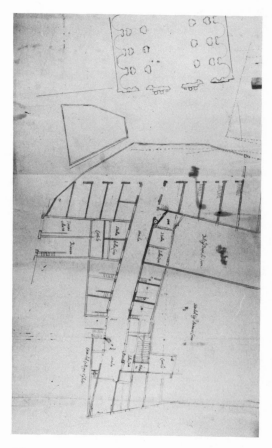

18

18.   Anonymous. Ca. 1627.
Project for the Piazza della Chiesa Nuova and the Strada Nuova.
AV, C.II.8, no.103. 80.0 × 41.6. Ink with red and yellow wash over pencil.
Inscriptions:
Del Sig. Duca di Sora. Sito del Sig. Antonio Cerro. Stalla della Casa. Cortile. Entrata della Casa. Strada. Arco. Arco. Strada. Arco. Stalla dalla casa. Cortile. Vermicellaro. Rimessa. Casa del Collegio Englese.

This crude project envisages a Strada Nuova flanked by eight shops which front on a piazza of indefinite shape. The line of shopfronts is not parallel with the Vallicella facade, and the new street is crooked, although a dotted line through the Cerri property suggests a somewhat straighter alternative. Three proposed arches traverse the street at its southern end.

The drawing does not correspond to the site as it is known from Maruscelli's detailed plans (Cat. 17). To assume, with Russo, that it shows a preexisting alley later enlarged into the Strada Nuova is to ignore the project character of the drawing and to overrate its topographical accuracy.
Bibl.: *Russo, "Piazza della Chiesa Nuova," Pl. VI.

19.   Virgilio Spada. 1629–30.
Proposed pavement levels of the Strada Nuova: section diagram.
AV, C.II.8, no. 109. 24.8 × 43.3. Ruled ink over graphite. Scale: 10 canne = 6.7 cm.
Inscriptions:
[1] Stato della strada secondo che di presente a proporre[?]. Piano del S.Duca di Sora.
[2] Piazza. Stalla del S.Duca di Sora. Casa del

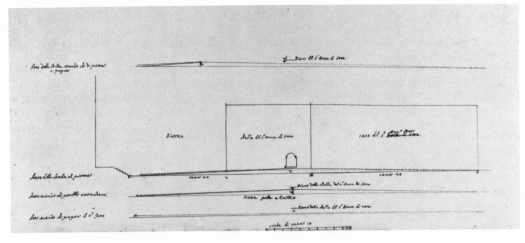

19

S.Ant[oni]o Cerri. Stato della strada al presente. canne 20. canne 20.

[3] Stato secondo che potrebbe accomodarsi. Linea posta a livello. Piano della stalla del S.Duca di Sora.

[4] Stato secondo che propone il S.Cerri. Piano della stalla del S.Duca di Sora.

The drawing illustrates a dispute between two adjacent property owners on the Strada Nuova: the Duca di Sora and Antonio Cerri. At the time of the drawing (inscription no. 2) the slope of the terrain entirely favored Sora; it reached its maximum height of 6 palmi above the level line at the door of the Sora stables, to the disadvantage of the Cerri palace next door. Cerri proposed (inscription no. 4) making the street entirely level, which would have left the Sora threshold stranded 6 palmi above the pavement. The drawing presents two compromise solutions. One (inscription no. 3) would have lowered the street level slightly; the other (inscription no. 1) would have transferred the peak of the street level to the middle of the piazza, minimizing although not entirely eliminating the disadvantages to both parties.

The dispute between Cerri and Sora seems to have run its course between 1627 and 1629, and Maruscelli was able to supervise the final paving of the street in 1630, although which solution he adopted is unknown (Russo, "Piazza della Chiesa Nuova," n. 45; Doc. 8). Some of the same personalities emerge in another affair of 1630, when Virgilio asked the Theatines for permission to outfit a Spada Chapel in S. Andrea della Valle on a site that had already been ceded to Antonio Cerri. Maruscelli served as an intermediary in the negotiations, which were broken off in 1632 (Heimbürger Ravalli, *Architettura scultura e arti minori . . . ,* 75–79).

The handwriting of the inscriptions on the present drawing is Virgilio's; it is the only element that permits the attribution of an otherwise styleless diagram.
Unpublished.

20. Paolo Maruscelli. 1627.

Project for a casa: 4 plans and 4 sections with caption numbers.

20a. Ground floor plan.
Lost, but reconstructed in Cat. 21.

20b. *Piano nobile* plan.
AV, C.II.6, Pl. D or VII–VIII. 43.2 × 28.9. Ink and pink wash.

20c. Mezzanine story plan.
Alb. 280. 27.4 × 26.2. Ink and pink wash.

20d. Third story plan.
Alb. 279. 36.4 × 25.7. Ink and pink wash.

20e–h. Four sections, all lost.

Inscriptions:

The set of eight drawings was originally accompanied by a list of captions that identified the functions of 98 rooms on the plans and 36 rooms on the elevations. Three versions of this document are preserved in the Vallicella archives (C.I.26): (1) A rough draft on two loose folded sheets; the text abruptly stops after item 10 under the heading *Spaccato delle Loggie, e camere a canto segnato E.* (2) A fair copy of the complete text, with further additions and corrections. This is the version transcribed below, along with some loose notes which list the preliminary ideas that went into the project, and then enumerate some criticisms of it. These notes stem directly from Spada: a rough draft, dated 1627, is preserved on two loose sheets written in his autograph but nearly illegible hand. (3) A professional scribe's copy of the above version, limited to the captions.

In Spada's hand:

1627

Distribut[ion]e delle stanze conforme la pianta del Maruscelli

In the hand of a professional scribe:

Pianta al piano terreno larga palmi 18 alta palmi 30 segnata A. [Cat. 20a]

1. Portaria, et entrata principale della Casa verso la piazza di Pizzomerlo. larga p. 18.
2. Stanza per il portinaro a soffitto alta p. 15, longa p. 17, larga p. 13.
3. Salotto per audienza a soffitto alto p. 15, longo p. 30, largo p. 22.
4. Camere numero 3 a soffitto per il medesimo effetto con mezzanini sopra in volta, alte p. 15 et una longa p. 22, larga p. 17, le altre due longhe p. 24, larghe p. 15.
5. Oratorio alto alla cima sotto la volta p. 71, longo p. 100, largo p. 50.
6. Scala principale alta p. 25 e piu larga p. 13, e sotto la scala commodita per Musici, e per l'oratorio in tutto p. 50, larga p. 28.
7. Cortile primo longo p. 97, largo p. 65.
8. Sacristia longa p. 79, larga p. 45, alta p. 67.
9. Stanzini per lavamano ciascuno largo e longo p. 12, alto p. 15.
10. Transito della sacristia in chiesa largo p. 12, longo p. 19.
11. Luogo da sonare le campane.
12. Luogo per le caraffine largo p. 6½ longo ad libitum.
13. Luogo per fare aqua maggiore di quello che hoggi e in casa p. 6.
14. Per la tavoletta dei nomi.

15. Stanze numero 3 per servitio della sacristia larghe p. 24, longhe p. 32 . . . alte p. 25, l'ultima delle quali si puo ammezzare.
16. Scala per servitio di casa, chori, et organi larga p. 4½.
17. Loggia intorno al cortile, et giardino larghe p. 18, alte p. 30 [*inserted by Spada:*] La loggia designata a longo delle stanze della Sacristia, fa mal'effetto, perche leva il lume vivo a dette stanze, e leva lume, et aria alla medesima sacristia, e non giova a cosa nessuna, pero per parere del Sig.r Gaspar de Vecchi, e del Soria non vi sta bene.)
18. Giardino longo p. 133 largo p. 97.
19. Cortile per dar lume alla Cappella del santo longo p. 47, largo da capo p. 25, da piedi p. 20.
20. Entrone per andare in Refettorio, e sue officine largo p. 16.
21. Lavamano longo p. 36, largo p. 20.
22. Reffettorio per 60 bocche longo p. 85, largo p. 36.
23. Bottigliaria e servitio per forastieri largo p. 10.
24. Dispensa longa p. 30 larga p.24.
25. Stanzino per boccali, e bicchieri col mezzanino sopra longo p. 15, largo p. 13.
26. Stanza dietro la Cappella del Santo la quale si scorta, et si allarga, resta longa p. 14 larga p. 11.
27. Transito per passar dietro la Tribuna.
28. Cortile con cisterna longo p. 40 largo ragguagliato p. 35.
29. Scala per il Refettorio larga p. 6.
30. Cucina longa p. 41, larga p. 36.
31. Stanze due con li soi mezzanini per servitio di cucina, et per il cuoco, larghe p. 21 la maggiore longa p. 20 l'altra p. 14.
32. Cortile rustico per la cucina col pozzo e scala non segnata per andar in cantina, il cortile e triangulare largo nella base p. 56, e longo p.90.
33. Porta rustica per cavalli, e some.
34. Lochi communi.
35. Stalletta per un par di cavalli col mezzanino sopra.
36. Tinello per le botti l'inverno longo p. 48 largo p. 22.
37. Stanza per la dispensa longa e larga p. 22.
38. Granaro longo p. 45, largo p. 28, si puo amezzare.
39. Forno la stanza e longa p. 28, larga 22.
40. Stuffa longa ragguagliata p. 18 larga ragguagliata p. 10.
41. Stanze numero 3 per servitio del forno longhe p. 28 l'una, e larghe p. 22.
42. Altra scala per tutta la casa larga p. 5.

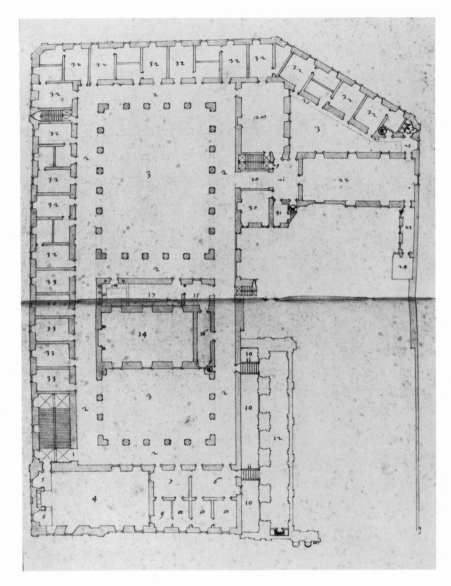

20b

43.   Porta nella piazza di Montegiordano che corrisponde in mezzo del Giardino

Tutte le altre stanze non signate con numero possono servire o per infermaria, o speciaria, o per botteghe le quali sono ciascuna longa p. 28 largh. p. 22.

Piano Nobile signato B. [Cat. 20b]
1.   Scala principale larga p. 13.
2.   Logge larghe p. 18 alte p. 35.
3.   Aria del Cortile e giardino.
4.   Vano dell'Oratorio.

5.   Chori dell'oratorio uniti insieme sopra l'altare larghi p. 12.
6.   Sala per foresteria longa p. 40, larga p. 24.
7.   Salotto per forastieri con finestre nell'Oratorio longo p. 32, largo p. 24.
8.   Stanze numero 3 per forastieri longhe l'una p. 24, larghe due p. 20, una p. 14½.
9.   Stanza per forastieri che guarda nell'oratorio longa p. 24, larga p. 14½.
10.   Vano sopra le Cappelle.
11.   Scale due per salir alla loggia nuova sopra le capelle.

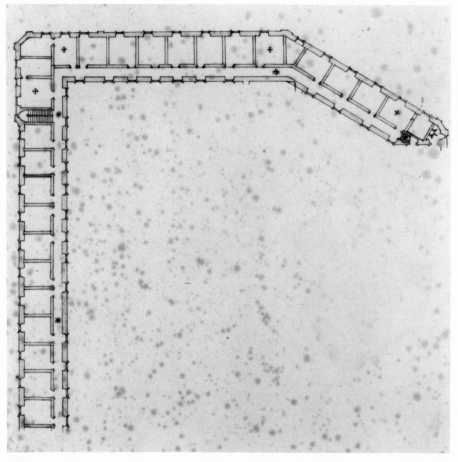

20c

12.   Loggia nuova sopra le cappelle.
13.   Muraglia fra la sudetta loggia, et il cortile sopra le capelle, quale dovera essere aperta a arconi, se bene adesso pare unita.
14.   Vano della sacristia.
15.   Cappella di casa longa e larga p. 22.
16.   Stanza per servitio della cappella longa p. 45, larga p. 12.
17.   Cortile pensolo nel quale si possono fare due stanze per il predicatore.
18.   Lochi communi.
19.   Scala sopra la scala signata al pian terreno numero 16 che va alli chori, et alla cuppola.
20.   Entrone per andare alla libraria, largo p. 16.
21.   Ricetto avanti la libraria sopra il lavamano longo p. 36 largo p. 22.
22.   Libraria longa p. 100, larga p. 38.
23.   Siti per camerini per la libraria.

24.   Camera con altra di sopra simile per la libraria, o per Archivio.
25.   Camerino, overo transito per la libraria.
26.   Lochi communi.
27.   Corridore per servitio di alcune stanze acanto detto corridore coperto di sopra largo p. 6.
28.   Sala grande per le Congregationi longa p. 65, larga p. 38.
29.   Scala dal lavamano alla ricreatione larga p. 6.
30.   Stanza per la ricreatione del'Inverno longa p. 30, larga p. 25.
31.   Stanza della ricreatione per i fratelli l'inverno col suo mezzanino sopra longa p. 17, larga p. 13.
32.   Stanze numero 14 col suo Camerino longa la stanza p. 30, larga p. 22. Il camerino longo p. 22, largo p. 14½, alto 22.

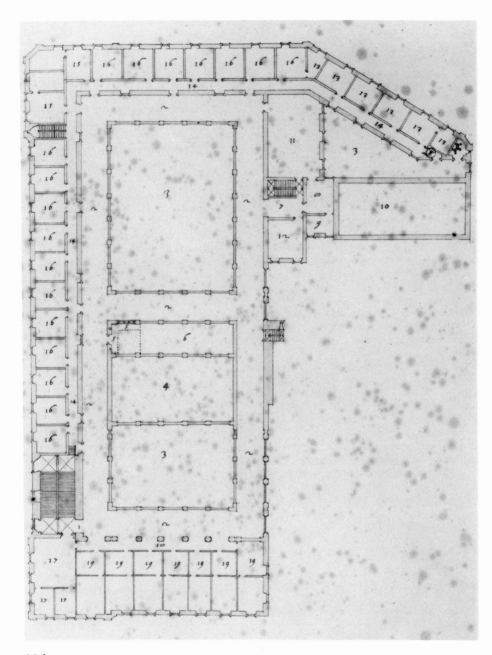

20d

33.   Stanze numero 5 senza Camerino longhe p. 30, larghe p. 22.

Piano del mezzanino sopra il piano nobile segnato C [Cat. 20c]
Stanze col suo Camerino numero 4 segnate con una + longhe l'una p. 24, larghe p. 22.
Tutte le altre sono stanze sole senza Camerino longhe p. 24, larghe p. 22, alte p. 15.
Corritore avanti le dette stanze signato con una * largo p. 8, alto p. 15.

Ultimo Piano Signato D. [Cat. 20d]
1.   Entrata della scala alla loggia scoperta.
2.   Loggie scoperte sopra le altre loggie.
3.   Aria dei Cortili.

4. Sottotetto sopra la sacristia, che potra servir a diversi usi di Casa.

5. Lochi communi.

6. Aria del cortile pensolo, overo sopra il sito detto per le stanze del predicatore.

7. Entrone per andare alla sartoraria, et guardarobba.

8. Sartoraria longa p. 26, larga p. 21.

9. Camera per il guardarobba longa p. 21, larga p. 14.

10. Guardarobba longa p. 100, larga p. 40, alta p. 19.

11. Sito per speciaria quando non si volessero servire delle stanze sudette del primo piano longo p. 65, largo p. 40, alto p. 19. Non e giudicato al proposito mettendo in servitu tutta la Casa.

12. Stanza per il fuoco delli fratelli quando la signata al pian nobile non bastasse longa p. 31, larga p. 24, alta p. 19 [*inserted:*] (e bastante la sudetta al pian nobile.)

13. Stanze numero 4 con doi Camerini per gl'infermi quanti non si volessero servire delle stanze sudette del primo piano per maggior commodita del servimento longhe l'una p. 24, larghe p. 18, alte 19.

14. Corritore avanti le camere largo p. 8.

15. Camere numero 2 con i soi camerini una longa p. 26, larga p. 24, il suo camerino longo p. 26, largo p. 14, l'altra longa p. 24, larga p. 19, il suo camerino longo p. 26, largo p. 16, alto p. 19.

16. Camere senza camerino numero 18 longhe l'una p. 23, larghe p. 22, alte p. 19.

17. Saletta con due stanze puo servire per il predicatore. La sala longa p. 40, larga p. 32, alta p. 19. Le stanze longhe l'una p. 20, larghe p. 15, alte p. 19.

18. Loggia coperta larga p. 8.

19. Stanze numero 7 doppie longhe p. 28, larghe p. 22, e le minori longhe p. 22, larghe p. 18, alte p. 19.

Spaccato delle loggie, e Camere acanto segnato E. [Cat. 20e]

1. Stanze a pian terreno in volta alte sotto la volta p. 30.

2. Loggia a pian terreno largo p. 18, alta p. 30.

3. Stanze al pian nobile in volta alte p. 22.

4. Loggia al pian nobile in volta alta sotto la volta p. 34.

5. Mezzanino a soffitto alto p. 15.

6. Andito per i Mezzanini largo p. 8.

7. Stanze a soffitto nel piano superiore alte p. 19.

8. Corridore a soffitto per dette stanze largo p. 8.

9. Loggia scoperta.

10. Sottotetto.

Spaccato dell'Oratorio e loggia contigua signato F. [Cat. 20f]

1. Oratorio alto sotto la volta p. 71.

2. Loggia a pian terreno alta p. 30.

3. Loggia al pian nobile alta p. 34.

4. Camere doppie signate nella pianta dell'ultimo piano numero 19, alte p. 19.

5. Loggia coperta larga p. 8.

6. Loggia scoperta.

7. Sottotetto.

Spaccato della sacristia Camere, e loggie contigue segante G. [Cat. 20g]

1. Sacristia alta p. 67.

2. Sottotetto avvertendo che si puo fare l'incavallatura, che serva per transito.

3. Camere per servitio della sacristia a terreno alte p. 30.

4. Loggia a terreno verso il giardino alta p. 30.

5. Cappella, et appresso a quella cortile pensolo e stanze per il predicatore alt. p. 24.

6. Loggia al pian nobile alta p. 34.

7. Loggia scoperta, overo Cortil pensolo.

8. Loggia scoperta.

Spaccato del Refettorio Lavamano libraria et scala signata H. [Cat. 20h]

1. Scala da basso in alto.

2. Lavamano alto p. 30.

3. Refettorio alto p. 35.

4. Andito per servitio del Reffettorio alto p. 18.

5. Mezzanino alto p. 15.

6. Ricetto avanti la libraria alto p. 34.

7. Libraria alta p. 35.

8. Sartoraria alta p. 24.

9. Guardarobba alta p. 19.

10. Sottotetto.

11. Loggia coperta sopra tutti i tetti per l'Horologgio, e campana del Reffettorio che si sonara dal cortile di basso rustico.

List of preliminary ideas:

Libraria grande quant'e la nostra una volta e mezzo.

Reffettorio per 60 bocche e longo p. 8 piu di quello di S. Salvator in Lauro, piu stretto p. 2, piu alto p. 2.

Oratorio grande quanto il presente una volta e mezzo, e longa quanto la chiesa dello Spirito S.to de Napolitani meno un palmo, e piu largo p. 3.

Camera e Camerino come quella del p. Giovanni Severano.

Stanze per padri del piano nobile in volta

longhe p. 30, larghe p. 22, alte p. 22, simili ad una stanza nel piano nobile del palazzo novo del S.r Cardinale Borghese a man dritta sopra le stalle, et e quella di mezzo verso il cortile nella loggia contigua a dette stalle.

Le camere per padri a soffitto sono in altezza, longhezza, e larghezza quasi come quella del p. Girolamo Rosino.

La loggia e larga come quella della casa professa del Giesu ov'e la porteria e piu alta p. 2.

La sacristia e piu longa di quella del Giesu p. 5, piu larga p. 5, piu alta p. 10.

Cucina e per doi terzi del nostro reffettorio.

Sala per le Congregationi quanto sara il reffettorio.

Gl'Anditi nel 2.o piano, e ne mezzini sono della larghezza et altezza come quelli inanzi al p. Fausto dalla banda della finestra.

Il Giardino riuscira longo, e largo quanto e la meta del giardino maggiore della Minerva pigliando tutti i doi quadri da una fratta all'altra a mano manca nel entrare di detto giardino.

Il primo Cortile sara di longhezza, e larghezza quanto e un quadro del sudetto giardino maggiore della Minerva nell'entrare a man dritta il p.o.

Camere col suo Camerino per padri

n[umer]o 20

Camere doppie numero 7 per i padri in tutto

numero 27

Camere per padri senza Camerino

numero 23

Camere per fratelli nel mezzanino

numero 24

Camere

In tutto numero 74

Crossed out in version no. 2 and omitted from the professional copy, version no. 3:

Tenendosi la fabrica piu bassa riuscira la casa piu ariosa, e levando via i mezzanini restano camere in tutto numero 74 (50?) che sono davanzo, o che alcune altre piccole stanze che sono sopra i lavamani per i sacrestani—et l'appartamento per i forastieri—

Criticisms based on Spada's rough notes:

Considerationi sopra il disegno

P.o A ciascuna camera il suo camino nel pian nobile verso il giardino e nel pian'ultimo nella facciata.

2.o Dei spaccati apparisce migliore e piu utile, e di minor spesa il segnato con + quando non si voglino mezzanini. i quali veramente non sono necessarij.

3. Per andare alla guardarobba si pensa di

poter far girar il corridore sopra il fianco della volta segnata numero XI, quale e per la ricreatione et detta sala per la ricreatione si crede doversi tener alta circa p. 38.

4.o Bisognera haver avvertenza ai mezzanini sotto la stanza del'ultimo piano segnate 7–8–9–12 dovendoseli andare dalla scala, che vi sta a canto.

5.o Sopra l'oratorio le stanze maggiori converria fossero verso tramontana.

6. La loggia inanzi la sagristia al 3.o piano si giudica non potersi errare in farla alta p. 18 et a questa misura tener la gronda del tetto.

7. Al Refettorio multiplicar le finestre dalla parte del cortile, e col fare sopra finestre nelle lunette, come col farne 4 ad un piano.

8. I luoghi communi staranno bene nel luogo disegnato per scala nel cortiletto acanto alla capela di Todi poi che in loco di quella scala gia se n'e fatta un'altra dall'altra parte.

9. Il primo branco della scala maggiore si crede che starebbe meglio farla larga quanto la loggia facendo prima 3 scalini nel imboccatura, e per un piano con altri 3 scalini, e questo per maggior grandezza, come per non ingrossare il muro dell'Oratorio superfluamente.

10. La scala del 2.o piano o riesce nana, salendo a doi branchi, o si dovra fare a un branco solo.

11. Tirare inanzi il tetto della sagristia a drittura, presupposto, che non ci vadino loggie ne coperte, ne scoperte; et il sito sopra la loggia che restara coperto, potra servire per doi stanze, oltre l'andito di mezzo.

The two loose sheets of paper which contain the rough outline of the above critique also contain several nearly illegible criticisms by Spada that were not incorporated into the final draft:

Ci [?] unire [?] una cisterna con pozzo che delli [cancelled: vecchie(?)] logge si possa tirar l'acqua in . . . da i canali.

Il tinello mi parerebbe meglio nelli 3 stanze nel cortile rustico per la commodita di maneggiar li botti nel cortile senza imbrattar la loggia e far un scalino che le bestie cariche possino andare in cantina.

Non vedo come di sopra si possi andare all'4 stanze sopra il cortile rustico.

La scala principale non servira mai per ch'ognuno si valera della p . . .

Nel cortile rustico ci vuole . . . che riguarda [?] in refettorio.

Una tavola [?] + e palmi [?] 18 il vano e palmi 2 perche un vano . . .

Only three drawings are preserved out of the original set of eight. The missing ground floor plan can be reconstructed from a variety of sources (Cat. 21). First, it appears to have been identical with another ground floor plan drawn up by Maruscelli without any caption numbers. Furthermore, it was copied in pencil by Borromini (Cat. 37a and 39), and although this copy was subsequently erased and reworked, many of the caption numbers still remain legible on it: these are underlined in the reconstruction in Cat. 21. The document itself often supplies the exact shape and dimensions of a room, which allows its unambiguous location. The few rooms for which some uncertainty still exists have been entered on the reconstruction in parentheses; the location of three rooms (11, 12, 14) still remains undetermined.

The absolute dimensions of the casa are identical on all three preserved drawings.

East-west width of casa plus church
           24.7 cm. = 335 palmi
North-south length of casa
           32.8 cm. = 470 palmi
Scale   1 : 320

The building is organized around three courtyards and three principal enfilades: one running along the left flank of the church (Cat. 21, nos. 1–17), a second crossing the transept of the church and ending in the sacristy (nos. 10–8), and a third crossing the garden court and ending in the refectory (nos. 43–18–20–21–22–23).

The oratory (no. 5) is located in the southwest corner of the building. Its fenestration, later considered a major problem (*Opus*, VI, 13^r) is indeed erratic. The basic rhythm is set by the windows behind the altar, two of which are open and one blind. The spacing of these windows is repeated along the south wall of the room, there with two adjacent windows open and the third one blind. The two apertures in the north wall align with the adjacent courtyard loggia, in disregard for the principle of symmetry across the room. In the upper left corner a door connects the oratory with the

first landing of the staircase, overlooking a considerable difference in level.

The sacristy (Cat. 21, no. 8) is located in the position established by Arconio's foundations. Three service rooms are attached to its north flank (no. 15), and the whole complex is separated from the garden court by a loggia two stories high. The sacristy was to be lit almost exclusively by windows in its south side; the architect was pessimistic about the usefulness of the windows with a northern exposure (Cat. 20b, no. 17: "Light well in which two rooms may be built for the preacher").

The functional services of the building tended to cluster around a small courtyard in the northeast corner (Cat. 21, no. 32). The recreation room was stacked directly over the kitchen; both needed fireplaces and could share a common chimney (Cat. 20b, no. 28; Cat. 21, no. 30). The library (Cat. 20b, no. 22) is located over the refectory and *bottigliaria* (Cat. 21, nos. 22, 23), even though the presence of the Vallicella apse on the south and the inadequate exposure on the north would have conspired to make these rooms the darkest in the building. (Cf. the comments in *Opus*, XXIV, 67^v–68^r). The *piano nobile* rooms of the "elbow" wing were serviced by a narrow corridor cantilevered out into the courtyard (Cat. 20b, no. 27).

The plan of the third story (Cat. 20d) presents some inconsistencies of level. The corridor (no. 14) that services the rooms of the north and west wings opens directly onto the adjacent *loggia scoperta* (no. 2), despite a difference in level of about 2 palmi. There seems to be no means of access to either the attic over the sacristy (no. 4) or the *guardarobba* (no. 10).

According to *Opus*, III, 8^r and IV, 10^r, Maruscelli designed the sacristy without bothering to draw up a complete plan for the entire casa; thus by implication the present project would date to 1637, when Maruscelli was forced to put the sacristy in the larger context of the oratory and the rest of the casa. In fact, the project must be dated 1627, a decade earlier. Spada's criticism of the project, which provides a firm *terminus post*, is dated 1627. Furthermore, a series of

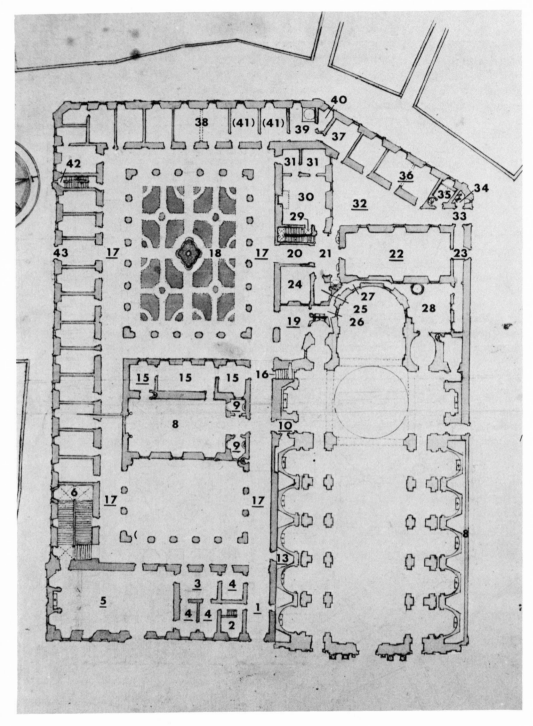

decreti describe in some detail the events of the summer of 1627, when a new plan "not only of the sacristy but of the entire casa" was drawn up and submitted to the scrutiny of several outside professionals, including Gaspare de Vecchi, G. B. Soria, and apparently also Girolamo Rainaldi (Decr. 30, 32, 37). The gist of these accounts is that Maruscelli's drawings were put on display in the summer of 1627, discussed in the presence of the consultants and many of the padri, approved with some changes, and finally registered with the Mastri di Strade. The criticisms and recommended changes were recorded in Spada's notes, transcribed above, and incorporated into a new set of presentation drawings, Cat. 23a–c.

Bibl.: Connors, "Early Projects for the Casa dei Filippini in Rome," *Oratorium,* VI, 1975, 107–11.

21.   Paolo Maruscelli. 1627.

Project for a casa: ground floor plan (caption numbers added to the photograph).

AV, C.II.8, no. 10. 55.0 × 42.7. Ink with pink (casa) and yellow (church) washes, pinpricks. Scale: 200 p. = ca. 14 cm.

The plan represents a project identical with the one in Cat. 20, and hence has been used as the basis for reconstructing the lost ground floor plan of the caption set (Cat. 20a). The decorative compass in the upper left hand corner of the present sheet indicates that it served as a formal presentation drawing.

Bibl.: *Hempel, 67 ff., Fig. 19 (attributed to Maruscelli as a competition drawing of 1637); *Gasbarri, 4th unnumbered plate.

22.   Paolo Maruscelli ? 1627.

Two cross-sections of the casa.

AV, C.II.8, no. 21. 33.5 × 42.8. Graphite.

The sheet contains two north-south sections of the proposed casa, one cutting through the entire west wing, the other through the oratory, sacristy, and two courtyards. The casa is the same absolute length (32.8 cm.) as on Maruscelli's caption project (Cat. 20), but it already incorporates some of Spada's criticisms of 1627, particularly the instructions to reduce the height from four to three

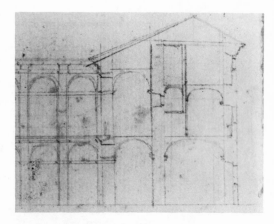

22 (detail)

stories. The drawing is unfinished and in one aspect tentative: the corridor system shown in the north wing is still in the experimental stage between the lost section drawings of the caption project (Cat. 20f–g) and the much larger presentation drawings that follow (Cat. 23a). If the attribution is correct, it is one of Maruscelli's few drawings entirely in pencil, although not a skillful exercise in that medium.

Bibl.: *Heimbürger Ravalli, *Architettura scultura e arti minori nel barocco italiano,* Florence, 1977, 194 and Fig. 143 (as an undated and anonymous drawing with a tentative suggested attribution to Maruscelli).

23.   Paolo Maruscelli. 1627.

Final project for the casa.

23a.   Two north-south sections.

BV, Vat. lat. 11257, fol. 196ʳ. 46.2 × 131.0. Brown ink and gray wash over graphite, on two sheets of paper pasted together to the left of zero on the scale. Scale: 150 p. = 35.6 cm.

23b.   East-west section through the second courtyard.

BV, Vat. lat. 11257, fol. 195ʳ. 45.7 × 108.5. Brown ink and wash over graphite, on two sheets of paper pasted together at the second arch from the left. No scale, but drawn to the same scale as Cat. 23a.

23c.   West facade elevation.

BV, Vat. lat. 11257, fol. 197ʳ. 46.0 × 135.0. Brown ink and gray wash over graphite, on two sheets of paper pasted to-

23a

23b

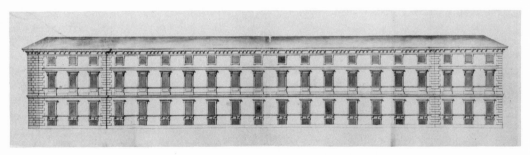

23c

gether between the tenth and eleventh bays from the left. No scale, but drawn to the same scale as Cat. 23a.

The drawings incorporate many of the suggestions outlined in Spada's notes of 1627 and represent Maruscelli's final pro-

ject, on the basis of which work was begun in 1629 (Cat. 20; Ch. 2).

Cat. 23a shows two sections of the proposed casa, one cutting through the two major courtyards. The oratory and sacristy are shown as vaulted halls of nearly identical size; both stand at the same level and both support a series of rooms serviced by a double-loaded corridor over their vaults. Throughout the building, the rooms of the first two stories are vaulted, while those of the third story are covered by flat ceilings and are reached by a system of sunken corridors. As the term "loggia scoperta" implies, the uppermost level of the loggia is open to the weather, although a confusing convention of draftsmanship makes it appear roofed at first glance. The grand *scalone,* housed in a vaulted chamber, rises to the *piano nobile* in two long flights after a short flight of five steps. The cornice between the two loggia stories in the smaller courtyard appears to cut across the sacristy windows; vague shading here indicates that the problem had been recognized but not solved. The large courtyard at the right is one bay longer on the *piano nobile* than on the ground floor, and an extra narrow bay has been inserted between the last two arches of the upper loggia. An elevated ramp 8½ palmi wide crosses the courtyard at this point and leads to a small access door 5 palmi wide. This ramp is shown in section to the right of the sacristy and its service rooms; although unprotected from the weather, it provided a useful transit across the center of the casa (*Opus,* XIII, 41^r). The roof of the service rooms slopes down to the level of the springing of the loggia arches; the space above is devoted to a light-well for the sacristy.

The section in Cat. 23b cuts through the large courtyard in the fourth bay from the north. An entrance portal had formerly been planned at this point (Cat. 21, no. 43), but it was suppressed when the courtyard was expanded from an odd (seven) to an even (eight) number of bays. The complex of long vaulted rooms on the right of the drawing can be identified with the help of the captions listed in Cat. 20. On the ground floor, beginning at the courtyard and proceeding from left to right, the drawing shows a loggia, *entrone, lavamani, refettorio,* and *bottigliaria.* On the *piano nobile:* loggia, *entrone, ricetto, libraria.* On the third floor: *loggia scoperta, entrone, sartoria, guardarobba.* At roof level, the caption gives indications of a *sottotetto* and a "loggia coperta sopra

tutti i tetti per l'Horologio, e campana del Reffettorio che si sonara dal cortile di basso Rustico" without precise location. The length and height of the three principal rooms may be scaled from the drawing; they agree with the dimensions indicated in the caption document:

	Length	Height	Width (from Cat.20)
Refectory	85	35 p.	36
Library	100	35	38
Guardarobba	100	19	40

Each of the upper rooms is 2 palmi wider than the one below it: the wall thickness diminishes 1 palmo for each story it rises, a practice recommended by conventional theory but later disapproved by Borromini (Palladio, *Quattro libri,* I, xi, 14; *Opus,* XV, 46^v). The library floor is five steps higher than the adjacent vestibule, and the *guardarobba* floor fourteen steps above the level of its vestibule. This cumulative increase in height is finally absorbed by the low ceiling of the *guardarobba.*

Cat. 23c shows the long side facade of the casa organized into a visually coherent unit: a pair of three-bay projections flank a central section of fourteen bays. Pentimenti in the pencil underdrawing show that the windows of both projections have been moved away from the center: the windows of the right projection 1.5 cm. (6 palmi) farther to the right, and those of the left projection 0.9 cm. (3¾ palmi) farther to the left. The left corner of the facade is canted and built of drafted masonry to emphasize its urban importance (cf. Cat. 20b, 21). The drawing takes no account of the drop in ground level from left to right (contrast Fig. 22) and irrationally maintains the convention of a light source on the left.

Although no elevations transmit a picture of the south front of the building, the eventual site of Borromini's curved facade, it can be reconstructed from available data (Fig. 13). Plans show a three-bay projection at the left corner, followed by a portal, four window bays, and another portal next to the church (Cat. 21). The section drawing in Cat. 23a shows small attic windows which should cause periodic interruptions in the series of consoles supporting the roof; these interruptions continue in a vestigial way around the rest of the building, even where there are no attic windows to accommodate (Cat. 23c; cf. Fig. 118).

Some dimensions scaled from the drawings, when contrasted with those of Cat. 20, provide a vivid illustration of Spada's instructions to reduce the overall height of the building.

spond approximately to the elevations shown on Cat. 24b and 24c.

AV, C.II.8, no. 37. 29.0 × 43.0. Scale: 20 p. = 8.1 cm.

24b. Anonymous.
Elevation project with alternating wide and narrow bays.

AV, C.II.8, no. 42. 27.2 × 42.7. Ink and wash over graphite.

	Cat. 20 (caption project)	Cat. 23 (final project)
Length of casa	455 palmi	455
Oratory height	71	62
Oratory width	50	50
Sacristy height	67	62
Sacristy width	45	45
Ground floor loggia height	30	30
Ground floor loggia width	18	18
Piano nobile loggia height	35	30
Piano nobile loggia width	18	18
Piano nobile room height	22	22
Piano nobile room width	22	20 or 22
Piano nobile room length	30	28½

In its final form Maruscelli's casa measures 73 palmi from the ground to the cornice under the roof, exactly the height of the Vallicella facade entablature over the inscription. The relationship of casa to church thus follows established usage: the roof line of the Casa Professa meets the Gesù facade at an analogous point.
Bibl.: * Connors, "Early Projects for the Casa dei Filippini in Rome," *Oratorium,* VI, 1975, 107–11, Figs. 1–3; * Heimbürger Ravalli, *Architettura scultura e arti minori nel barocco italiano,* Florence, 1977, 194 ff. and Figs. 140–42 (as undated and anonymous drawings, with Maruscelli's name tentatively suggested).

24. Various architects. Mid-1633–April 1634.
Projects for the sacristy *credenzoni.*

24a. Anonymous.
Plan of the sacristy (ink) with a plan for the system of chests (pencil). The dimensions inked in along the north wall corre-

24c. Anonymous.
Elevation project similar to Cat. 24c.

AV, C.II. 8, no. 41. 19.9 × 40.7. Presentation drawing, ruled ink over graphite with two shades of blue wash.

24d. Carlo Buzio
Elevation project: bays of equal width separated by paired pilasters; large cartouche over north door.

AV, C.II.8, no. 45. 31.0 × 43.5. Ink and gray wash over graphite. Scale: 20 p. = 16.0 cm.
Inscription:
Carolus Butius Architectus Mediolanen f[ecit]

24e. Anonymous.
Two half-projects for *credenzoni* along the entire north wall, differing only in details from the executed version.

AV, C.I.6, Pls. V–VI. 27.7 × 42.5. Ink and pink wash. Scale: 20 p. = 7.9 cm.

24b

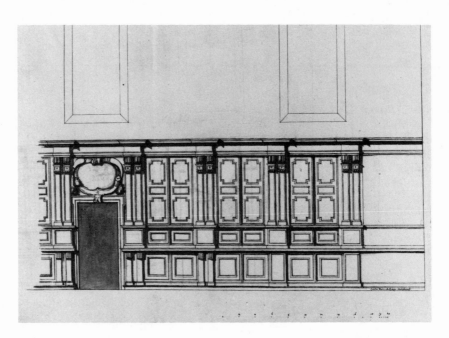

24d

24f. Anonymous.

Elevation project of a single bay. The design of the cabinet doors and the ionic pilasters is identical with the executed version. The balustrade shown on the original sheet and the ornate parapet shown on an attached flap would have protected the ledge used to adjust the sacristy windows; neither was executed.

AV, C.II.8, no. 47. 42.2 × 28.5. Ruled ink and wash, flap pasted along upper edge.

24g. Anonymous.

Elevation project, with no provision for north door.

AV, C.II.8, no. 46. 27.5 × 54.1. Ink and wash, water stains on right. Scale incomplete.

24h. Anonymous.

Elevations and profile of a single chest of drawers.

AV, C.II.8, no. 38. 26.3 × 46.3. Ruled ink over graphite. Scale: 5 p. = 15.2 cm.

24i. Anonymous.

One bay in perspective.

AV, C.II.8, no. 43. 37.6 × 24.6. Ruled ink and blue wash.

24j. Anonymous.

Elevation project for the south wall, with chests arranged *en ressaut* around the paired pilasters of the sacristy.

AV, C.II. 8, no. 44. 20.7 × 48.1. Ink and pink wash over pencil. Scale: 30 p. = 16.9 cm.

24k. Anonymous.

Elevation project: unfinished graphite underdrawing.

AV, C.II.8, no. 49. 43.2 × 56.4. Scale incomplete.

24l. Anonymous.

Elevation project unlike anything executed.

AV, C.II.8, no. 39. 19.1 × 24.5. Presentation drawing in ruled ink and brown wash.

24m. Anonymous.

Schematic outline elevation.

AV, C.II.8, no. 40ʳ. 22.5 × 38.3. Ruled ink.

24n. Anonymous.

Schematic outline, identical to Cat. 24m but shown in perspective.

AV, C.II.8, no. 40ᵛ.

24o. Francesco Borromini.

Elevation of three bays, lower part not strictly orthogonal; profile of a chest.

Alb. 323. 21.0 × 30.7. Graphite.

24p. Francesco Borromini.

Elevation of two bays with emblems of heart and star; consoles at the bottom of the drawing are not strictly orthogonal.

Alb. 324. 20.4 × 24.1. Graphite.

The basic structure of Maruscelli's sacristy imposed certain limits on the design of its furniture. Apertures had to be left for the main entrance, north door, high altar, and the doors of the small unlit storage rooms at the west end. The high level of the window sills, 20¼ palmi above the floor, allowed the chests to run without interruption along the north and south walls; one drawing proposes a balustrade or parapet to ensure the safety of the route along the top used to adjust the sacristy windows (f). The basic design of the furniture was reached in Cat. 24e, and subsequent drawings tend to concentrate on refinements of detail, such as the design of the chest doors or the articulation of the pilasters *en ressaut.*

According to Decr. 74 and 78–82, the Congregation had collected various *credenzoni* designs by September 1633, when it asked Taddeo Landi to select the best and "make a model of two types." When the final choice was made in April 1634, it involved a preference for pilasters rather than columns, "in conformity with the above-mentioned model." None of the present drawings shows columns, which suggests that this was the group made available to Landi for his model.

The attribution of the drawings poses more difficult problems. At least two (b and e) are by the same hand, although the style does not completely coincide with that of the most likely candidate for authorship, Maruscelli. The one signed drawing (d) is by an outsider, Carlo Buzio, a Lombard architect better known for his work at Milan cathedral (Wittkower, *Gothic vs. Classic*, 45–65). Two pencil drawings in the Albertina (o and p) pose the problem of Borromini's participation, which is unrecorded before 1636 (Cat. 28) and unlikely in 1633, when the *credenzoni* were designed; yet the drawings are autograph, and in fact show features of design similar to the oratory facade. Either Borromini was in contact with Landi at this early date or the designs are for some other, unidentified *credenzoni*. The fictive wooden lanterns installed above the *credenzoni* in the actual sacristy have concave sides similar to Borromini's balusters in the oratory. However, they are not shown in the 1725 edition of the *Opus* (Fig. 25), and they may represent a later revival rather than an authentic specimen of the architect's style. Unpublished.

25. Anonymous. Late 1633–early 1634.
Project for a wooden corridor screen with door.
AV, C.II.6, Pl. XXXVIII. 43.5 × 28.4. Ink and brown wash over graphite; sheet folded in half and sewn to manuscript at the center.

A crude project, possibly by the carpenter Taddeo Landi, for one of the pair of screens that enclose a stretch of corridor between the church and the sacristy. Two central panels, picked out with dotted lines, are hinged to open as leaves of a door. The corridor was lit only through the large glazed area occupying the upper half of the project, which was enlarged still further in the executed version (Fig. 69).

The corridor in question was roofed in late 1633 and furnished with Maruscelli's marble doors in May 1634 (Decr. 69; Doc. 11); it is likely that projects to seal it from the weather, such as the present one, should date from that time. Borromini was familiar with the function and design of this type of screen (C 10 of 1620–22), but he contributed nothing to the present project and later criticized the asymmetrical placement of the screens around the sacristy door (Cat. 66, section 2).

The drawing was copied in a reduced format by one of the anonymous draftsmen of the *Opus* manuscript (Cat. 86 1). Unpublished.

26. Anonymous. Date uncertain.
Project for a wooden screen with door, exact location uncertain.
AV, C.II.8, no. 50. 42.0 × 28.2. Ink and brown wash over pencil.

The large project for a wooden screen and door presents diverse problems according to the way the dimensions ambiguously inscribed on the sheet are read. If the lower width is 18 palmi, then the drawing is a variant of the preceding project, though a somewhat impractical one since the door handles are located 7 feet off the ground. If the width is read as 13 palmi, then the drawing is ill-proportioned but could fit in any one of the arches of the loggia, either on the side of the courtyard or on the side of the church. (The dimensions of these arches, 13 × 21 palmi to the impost of the vault, are taken from Cat. 23a, 57a, and 66^r). It could represent the door to the narrow stairway wedged between the casa and the fifth side chapel of the Vallicella (Fig. 6; Cat. 39), which was removed when the stairs were altered by Borromini in 1641 (Cat. 66^r). Unpublished.

27. Virgilio Spada. October 1634.
Project for the sanctuary behind the Cappella di S. Filippo: *piano nobile* plan.
AV, C.II.8, no. 33. 61.8 × 24.6. Ruled ink. Scale: 30 p. = 7.4 cm.
Inscriptions:
Loggia di sopra. Anticamera del santo. Capella del Santo. Andito da basso. Dispensa. mezzanino. dispensino.
  1. Andito fra la chiesa, e la sagristia
  2. porta verso la chiesa
  3. porta verso la sagristia
  4. porta delle camere nove sotto l'andito
  5. porta hoggi finta, qual dovra servire per andare alla capella
  6. scala commoda, e luminosa, e dritta
  7. Camerotto avanti la capella per le congregat[ion]i, e per tenerci il confessionario, e tutto quello ch' habbiamo del S.to Padre, e serv' d'anticamera alla Capella del santo, sara in volta,

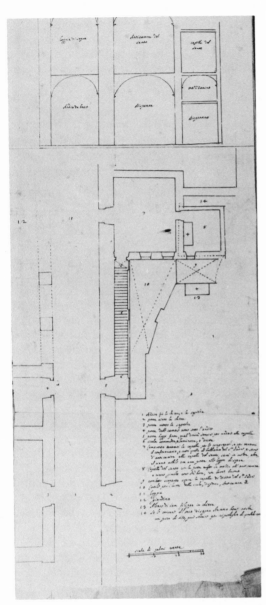

27

11. loggia
12. giardino
13. Altare di San filippo in chiesa
14. Se le misure del mio disegno stanno bene resta un poco di sito, puo servire per ripostiglio di qualch' cosa.

Filippo Neri moved from S. Girolamo della Carità to S. Maria in Vallicella in 1583 and lived the rest of his life in a small apartment in the old casa (Ponnelle and Bordet, 402 ff.). After his death in 1595 two rooms were venerated in his memory. One, the saint's bedchamber, was accidentally burned in 1620 but the other, a private chapel, was preserved as a relic, and by 1633 objections were raised against abandoning it. In October 1634 the Congregation decided to transfer the chapel stone by stone to a site destined to be enveloped by the new casa. Building operations and embellishment continued for nine years, from 1634 until 1643. A few of the doorframes and stucco designs in the small complex of rooms are unquestionably Borromini's work, but problems arise over their exact date. If early, that is, 1634–36, then the details in question assume great importance as Borromini's first contributions to the building (Bruschi). If late, that is, 1638–43, they revert to the role of interesting curiosities. The evidence is tangled but does seem to lean in favor of the second, less exciting alternative, particularly when patterns of circulation are taken into account as a means of dating doorways.

Figs. 73 and 74 provide a guide to the complex nomenclature used in this part of the building. The main rooms on the *piano nobile* are the Anticamera del Santo (25) and the Cappelletta, or transported chapel (31). Those on the ground floor are the Sala Rossa (5) and the Cappella Interna (10). The chapel inside the church is known as the Cappella Esterna (16), that is, "external to the casa."

Phase I—1634–36: Maruscelli.
Decr. 87–93, 96, 98, 99; Pollak, 430 ff., regs. 1688–97. Fig. 79.

The Congregation made its initial decision

alta al piano nobile con una porta nelle loggie di sopra.
   8. Capella del santo con la porta [a fer] in mezzo all'anticamera e riesce giusto come sta hora, con lume buono
   9. Cortiletto scoperto sopra la capella di dietro del S.to Padre
   10. Cortile per i lumi della scala, dispensa, anticam[e]ra

to transfer the chapel in 1634 on the basis of a drawing "fatto da p. Virgilio," which may be identified with the present sheet on the basis of handwriting as well as style (compare Cat. 19). The plan incorporates the chapel into Maruscelli's project with little disturbance. It occupies space on the *piano nobile* previously designated as a recreation room and it is given the adjacent antechamber for the storage of relics (Fig. 74, nos. 25, 31). This location was accessible from both the church and the planned casa, but still isolated enough to minimize incursions into the Congregation's domestic privacy. It was also close to the body of the saint, which rested in the Cappella Esterna (16) inside the church. It was accessible from the ground floor via a new staircase described as "commodious, bright, straight," but which was in fact unusually steep (Cat. 27 shows thirty-seven risers and Cat. 39 thirty-two risers for the 32 palmi ascent, implying heights of 10 *oncie* to a full palmo for each riser).

The site was cleared in late 1634 (by demolishing houses 28 and 29 on Cat. 14) and the actual chapel was dismantled and transported by January 1635, together with pieces of the vault beneath it, a stairway, and charred fragments of Filippo's former room. The architect in charge was presumably Maruscelli. His style is visible in four doorframes inside the complex: two simple frames in the Sala Rossa (6, 7), one in the Cappella Interna (12), and an elaborate frame at the top of the new staircase (24, Fig. 79). One further doorway was approved in December 1634 but apparently was not executed at this time (30; cf. Cat. 56). Work was probably complete by the time the anticamera vault (25) was frescoed by Cortona in April 1636.

Phase II—1638–39: Borromini.
Decr. 118–121, 127, 130, 134, 135. Cat. 51–56; Figs. 77–80.

The changes introduced in this phase were the direct result of larger decisions affecting the building as a whole. Maruscelli's project had been designed so that the rooms behind the Vallicella apse could serve as a temporary bridge between the old and the new

casa. In September 1638 Borromini transferred these rooms elsewhere and thus severed the link with the old building. In compensation, a makeshift route of catwalks and wooden bridges was proposed, passing behind the apse of the church, through the Anticamera del Santo, and down the stairway to the sacristy (28–27–26–25–24–23–1). These stairs had been designed for occasional visitors and were now considered too steep and narrow to accommodate the increased traffic flow. Hence, Spada proposed their replacement with a more commodious spiral, which was built at his personal expense in late 1638 and extended to the upper floors in February 1639. The new route was heavily traveled for four years, even to the point of distracting priests saying mass in the Cappelletta (31, 32); it probably declined in importance when the Congregation moved to the new casa in 1643.

Borromini's relocation of the refectory (8) in 1638 also had repercussions on the ground floor rooms underneath the transported chapel. Originally the Sala Rossa (5) was an appendage to Maruscelli's refectory, and was entered through a door in its northeast corner. This door was effectively blocked in 1638 and the entrance shifted to the south wall, where Borromini installed a pair of fanciful new doorways (Fig. 77). One (3) opened onto the corridor leading to the sacristy, and the other (4) onto the small courtyard from which it was possible to pass into the saint's chapel in the church (18, 16). Thus the orientation of the Sala Rossa was shifted from the north to the south, while its function was changed from secular to sacred.

In summary, Borromini's one structural contribution to this phase of building activity was the spiral stairway with the adjacent system of superimposed corridors (Cat. 51). If the argument from circulation patterns is correct, the two fanciful stucco doors of the Sala Rossa date from the same period. The evidence for dating the elaborate marble doorframe of the Cappelletta (30, Fig. 80) to 1638–39 is discussed in Cat. 56. Finally, although there is no solid evidence for their date, the Borrominian stucco patterns found on the *piano nobile* (24, Fig. 79; S. Costanza-Serlio vault pattern in 31, illustrated in Bruschi, p. 21) may belong to this phase and represent an attempt to enliven Maruscelli's more conventional style.

Phase III—1641–43: Borromini and an unknown architect.

Decr. 161, 164, 165, 168, 169, 180, 191, 202, 205, 206, 308; Cat. 65.

In 1641 the Congregation granted the small chapel (14) behind the Cappella Esterna (16) to Giulio Donati, who agreed to finance its decoration as his own sepulchral chapel (illustrated in Bruschi, 20, Fig. 9; and *GR*, Parione, II, 33). Owing to the minuscule size of the chapel, Donati was also granted the room immediately behind it, the so-called Cappella Interna (10), which had housed the charred fragments of Filippo's bedchamber (11) since 1635. Previously this room had been linked to the Cappella Esterna in the church by a small passageway (13) for which Maruscelli had provided a decorative marble doorframe (12). In 1641 Borromini closed the passageway and sealed the doorframe with a stucco niche, making the whole composite design into a reliquary for a chair that had belonged to the saint (Fig. 75). At the same time a low corridor (19, Fig. 77) was built across the small courtyard; it provided covered access between the church and the Sala Rossa at the cost of some damage to one of Borromini's stucco doorframes.

Work on the Donati Chapel continued until 1643 when the two family tombs were installed. The designs bear only a loose relation to Borromini's style, and the name of the architect remains undocumented. Guercino's altarpiece was installed in 1644; presumably Borromini's work on the altar and coffin of the saint was complete by that time (Cat. 65). In 1643 the commission for the vault fresco of the Sala Rossa was awarded to the Sienese painter Niccolo Tornioli (*Opus*, VIII, 31ʳ), who procrastinated on the work and left it to be completed posthumously in 1652 by students of Pietro da Cortona.

Bibl.: The present drawing is unpublished. Studies of the entire complex: Bruschi, *Palatino,* XII,

1968, 13–21; Incisa della Rocchetta, "Il santuario filippino della Vallicella," *Quaderni dell'Oratorio,* II, n.d., 1–20; Incisa della Rocchetta, "La Cappella di San Filippo alla Chiesa Nuova; II–L'anticamera del Santo e la cappelletta privata di s. Filippo; III–La 'sala rossa' e la cappella interna di s. Filippo," *Oratorium,* III, 1972, 46–52, 74–101.

28.   Francesco Borromini. Late 1636.
   Project for the sacristy altar(?).
   Alb. 910. 37.7 × 18.2. Graphite. Scale: 10 palmi in Roman numerals.

The attribution of the drawing to Borromini is entirely secure on the basis of graphic style alone: the same severe accuracy of line, and the same precision of shading and rendering of freehand detail recur in the drawings for the Palazzo Barberini, such as Thelen's C 49 and 50, dating to 1629–30. The use of Roman numerals in the scale also points to an early date, since this convention does not seem to occur on Borromini drawings after 1643, although it is relatively frequent before that, as the list at the end of this entry shows. The drawing represents an altar standing under an arch 15 palmi wide and 29½ palmi high, which are exactly the dimensions of the arch at the west end of Maruscelli's sacristy. Two anomalies support the hypothesis that the altar here is indeed that of the sacristy. First, although the drawing is by Borromini, the ornament up to the pediment level is not entirely typical of him, while it does agree with Maruscelli's style. Second, although the square frame would suggest a painted altarpiece, the stepped base just above the altar is clearly intended for a statue.

The following chronology can be established for this part of the building. The altar itself was completed under Maruscelli's direction in September 1634. There is no information about the type of altarpiece that was intended at that date, although Maruscelli's plans (Cat. 20b and 21) show a flat backdrop rather than a niche, suggesting a painted altarpiece or at most a relief. In October 1635 three members of the Boncompagni-Corcos family offered to decorate the chapel; the principal donor, Pietro, was to pay for Algardi's statue, while the brothers

Agostino and Hippolito agreed to provide ▽200 in cash and a pair of columns, and the Congregation agreed to supply certain *marmi mischi*. In April 1636 the statue was being blocked out in Algardi's studio on the Lungara. In November 1636 the Congregation presumably began to think about the installation of the statue, and issued instructions "not to touch anything, neither more nor less, not the pilasters, nor the arch, but everything should stay as it is at present, and this so as not to ruin the architecture and order of the sacristy." In December 1636, Borromini and the carpenter Taddeo Landi were paid for "various drawings and models done for the saint's chapel in the sacristy" (Pollak, 431, reg. 1699); in Aringhi's life of Landi there is more information on these drawings:

> [Landi] made an appropriate drawing of the altar of the sacristy, where he knew how to adjust the ornaments of *marmi mischi* with the two columns around the statue of the saint with wonderful proportion, which gave architects really something to think about, as at present can be seen, since everyone asserts that it would not have been possible to adjust and beautify *(aggarbare)* the ornament in a better way for the site than this brother had done to the design already established *(al disegno già ritrovato).*

The following hypothesis may explain what was going on. Maruscelli's altar was designed in 1634 before a statue was envisaged, and so it had to be adapted to Algardi's *S. Filippo Neri,* commissioned in 1635 and carved in 1636. In late 1636 the lay brother Taddeo Landi offered several proposals for rearranging the altar. At first the Congregation were hesitant about major changes, but eventually they changed their minds and allowed Landi to excavate a niche for the statue. Landi's proposals, which caused some stir among professional architects, may in fact have been drawings by Borromini such as the present one; in any case, Borromini was paid for the help he supplied to Landi. The present drawing would be an early proposal for accommodating the statue. It suggests advancing the rectangular frame to provide more depth, and keeping the columns and capitals that are already there but adding a cartouche and other ornament to the pediment, which is not too far from the ornament around the *piano nobile* windows of the oratory facade. Shortly afterward Borromini and Landi proposed the more radical idea of dispensing with the rectangular frame and introducing a niche, which was to be hollowed out of the sacristy wall, as shown on Fig. 6. The statue was given a more recessed base, and the ornament was arranged to accommodate the upper curve of the niche (Fig. 72). The ornament looks like Maruscelli's; Borromini would have done the drawings; Landi did the work and got much of the credit. Payment was made to Borromini and Landi in December 1636, a very short time before Borromini was invited to participate in the consultations that eventually brought him the commission for the oratory. The drawings for the sacristy altar may have been the crucial thing that brought him and his talents as a designer to the Congregation's notice.

Unpublished. The documentation for the altar comes from Decr. 85, 86, 94, 95, and 100. The basic article on the statue is J. Montagu, "Alessandro Algardi and the Statue of St. Philip Neri," *Jahrbuch der Hamburger Kunstsammlungen,* XXII, 1977, 75–100, which quotes the *decreti* in full and includes the passage from Aringhi, quoted from Strong, *La Chiesa Nuova,* Rome, 1923, 127.

Roman Numeral Scales

The device apparently originated in Maderno's workshop for drawings of special importance (cf. the project of 1623 for S. Andrea della Valle, illustrated in Hibbard, *Maderno,* Fig. 46b). Scales with Roman numerals appear frequently on Borromini's own early presentation drawings, including five projects for the Casa dei Filippini:

1627	Iron window grating in St. Peter's. C 21.
1631	Palazzo Barberini. C 64.
1632–42	S. Ivo, plan with Barberini bees. ASR, Università, vol. 198, no. 122 (Portoghesi, *Cultura,* Fig. 58, detail).
1634–36	S. Carlino, plan of convent library. Berlin 1049 (Portoghesi, *Linguaggio,* Fig. xxiii).

1636   Casa dei Filippini, project for the high altar of the sacristy (Cat. 28).

1638–43?   S. Lucia in Selci? Altar with reliquary casket. (Portoghesi, *Linguaggio,* Fig. xxvi).

ca. 1638   Unidentified casino project, similar in plan to the Casino Ludovisi. Oval *lumaca* and curved corner pilasters are close to similar features of 1638 in the Casa dei Filippini. AV, C.II.8, no. 151 (Portoghesi, *Disegni,* Fig. 54).

1638   Palazzo Carpegna plans. Alb. 1014a, 1017a, 1018, 1019b (Portoghesi, *Linguaggio,* Figs. xc–xcii, xciv); Alb. 1023 (Tafuri, "Borromini in Palazzo Carpegna," *Quaderni dell'Istituto di Storia dell'Architettura dell' Università di Roma,* 79/84, 1967, 89, Fig. 8).

1637–38   Casa dei Filippini, oratory altar (Cat. 48).

1638–39   Casa dei Filippini, oratory facade window (Cat. 46).

1638–39   Casa dei Filippini, oratory facade window (Cat. 47).

1639–40   S. Carlino, altar. Alb. 210 (Hempel, Pl. 16.2; Steinberg, *Borromini's San Carlo alle Quattro Fontane,* New York, 1977, Fig. 64).

1639–40   Casa dei Filippini, plan (Cat. 59).

1641   Casa dei Filippini, *portaria* and first courtyard (Cat. 66).

1641   Casa dei Filippini, main portal (Cat. 67).

1643 ff.?   Cloister of S. Maria dei Sette Dolori? Alb. X 1. Actual cloister (Muñoz, *Roma barocca,* Milan and Rome, 1928, 249) executed by G. B. Contini in 1662 (*Ragguagli,* 119).

29.   Francesco Borromini. Early 1637.
Preliminary project for the oratory: ground floor plan.
Alb. 283. 36.7 × 53.7. Graphite.

The present drawing stands at the beginning of a series of seven projects for the oratory by various architects. The fenestration here is drawn much more scrupulously than on Maruscelli's plan of 1627, and the rhythmic arrangement of pilasters on the interior is more carefully thought out. It is important to notice that the basic logic of the fenestration is still the same as that established by Maruscelli, that is, it is designed from the outside in, taking its key from the placement of windows in the projection behind the

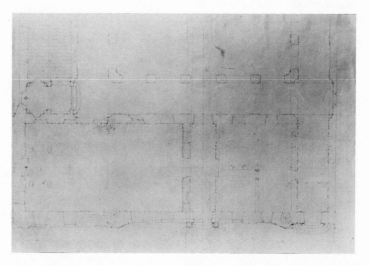

29

altar (as explained in detail in Cat. 20). Beyond the fenestration, however, the project does depart from Maruscelli in several important ways. It provides an entrance corridor to the oratory by sacrificing some of the space formerly devoted to the *portaria* and audience rooms. The floor of both the corridor and the oratory are sunk several palmi (five risers) below the level established for the rest of the casa. The corridor is aligned with the center of the first courtyard but consequently not with the center of the south facade. In compensation, a projection is designed to eliminate some of the surplus wall at the left (compare Cat. 11), while a five-bay facade, articulated by pilasters, is designed around the corridor and its columnar portal. Originally the facade was recessed but still flat; a later pentimento transforms it into a single continuous curve.

The innovations on the interior of the oratory are a pulpit on the north wall and a ciborium supported by four columns over the altar. The main stairway in the courtyard has been rearranged so that the landing is reached after a short flight of three steps "which invite ascent" (*Opus,* XI, 37ʳ). The first long flight is now on the right; and the space gained on the landing is used for a chapel with columns in the four corners. The logic of the thick corner pier influences the fenestration of the west wing through the flights of the staircase; it fails, however, to make any impact on the fenestration of the oratory. To judge from the width of the pilasters in the courtyard, the giant order has not been introduced (contrast Fig. 6).

Features characteristic of Borromini, such as the curved pilasters which make their appearance in the courtyard, loggia, and entrance corridor, confirm an attribution already secure on the basis of graphic style. *Bibl.:* Hempel, 70; *Portoghesi, *Linguaggio,* Fig. xxxiv.

30. Anonymous. Early 1637.
Project for the oratory: ground floor plan.
AV, C.II.8, no. 30. 26.7 × 57.0. Ink and light yellow wash over graphite. Scale: 100 palmi.
Inscription: Chiesa.

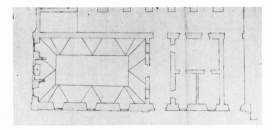

30

The drawing appears to stand between Borromini's preliminary project for the oratory (Cat. 29) and subsequent projects by other architects (Cat. 31–33). It adopts the entrance corridor of the former, but does not yet show the altar loggia of the latter. The project makes no significant contribution to the problems at hand, particularly that of fenestration. It envisages a vault pattern similar to Maruscelli's sacristy: a small rectangle is drawn within the larger rectangle of the room, and the windows are set into lunettes evenly spaced around it. There is no attempt to create a coherent pattern on the south facade, and to avoid conflict with the loggia the entire north wall is left windowless. Unpublished.

31. Giovanni Battista Mola. Early 1637.
Project for the oratory: plan and two sections.
AV, C.II.8, no. 31. Pen with green, yellow, and pink wash over graphite. Scale: 10 canne (100 p.) = 19.0 cm.
Inscription:
Jo[hanne]s Ba[ttista] Mola fec[? *or* Inv.]

Despite its graphic sophistication, this drawing makes little progress in solving basic problems of fenestration. The oratory is treated as a duplicate of the sacristy, with pairs of pilasters separating three window bays on each long side. No attempt is made to align the window bays with the arches of the loggia or to express the logic of the thicker corner pier. The one innovation in the project is the pair of service closets and musicians' *coretti* that flank the altar of the oratory and reduce the length of the room from 88 to 80 palmi.

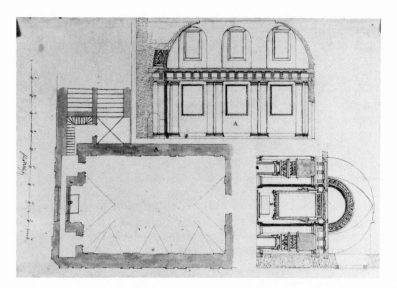

31

The severe Doric order, the ornament of the doorframes and balconies, and the cluster of pilasters at the southwest corner on the exterior all recall the Lateran hospital, built on the designs of Giovanni Battista and Giacomo Mola in 1636.

Bibl.: *G. B. Mola, *Breve racconto . . .,* 1663, ed. K. Noehles, Berlin, 1966, 25, Fig. 10 (considered as a competition entry of 1635–36). A survey of G. B. Mola's career is given by Noehles on pp. 20–27.

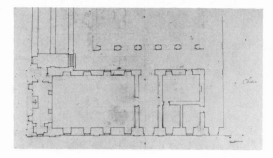

32

32. Attributed to Girolamo Rainaldi. Early 1637.
    Project for the oratory: ground floor plan.
    AV, C.II.8, no. 28. 28.7 × 40.9. Ink over graphite. Scale: 100 p.
Inscriptions—
    recto: Chiesa
    verso: Fabrica Pianta e Dichiarate

33. Attributed to Girolamo Rainaldi. Early 1637.
    Project for the oratory: ground floor plan.
    AV, C.II.8, no. 29. 28.9 × 43.0. Pen and dark brown wash over graphite. Scale: 100 p. = 14.7 cm.
Inscription: Chiesa.

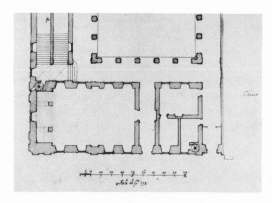

33

This drawing and the preceding one appear to be variants of the same project: Cat. 32 is drawn in outline and shows uncertainty about details like the spiral staircases, while Cat. 33 is a finished presentation drawing with some pentimenti on the left side of the design. Both drawings incorporate features from the preceding projects, especially the entrance corridor, but they also record significant advances in the oratory design. The altar canopy proposed by Borromini on Cat. 29 and the musicians' *coretti* proposed by Mola on Cat. 31 have been merged into a single new feature: a columnar loggia at the west end of the oratory with a nearby spiral staircase to service the upper galleries. The loggia has the effect of shortening the room from the original length of 100 palmi (Cat. 21) to 78 palmi, which it remains in subsequent projects and in the final building.

Cat. 33 is the first project to work out a solution to the problem of the thick corner pier as explained in *Opus,* VI, 14^r: the shallow niches on the interior of the oratory and a pilaster on the exerior correspond to the corner pier and disguise the fact that the interval between windows is greater at this point than elsewhere in the room. The basic rhythm established on the south facade (projection on the left, five bays bounded by pilasters and aligned with the courtyard, *portone* on the right) persists in most subsequent facade projects, including Borromini's.

A tentative attribution of Cat. 33 to Girolamo Rainaldi may be made on the basis of the script, the characteristic use of wash, and the idiosyncratic manner of marking the scale, which is identical to the scale on the Rainaldi drawing for S. Teresa in Caprarola in BV, Vat. lat. 11257, fol. 156. A document of 1629 indicates that a Sr. Girolamo, the architect of the Jesuits, had already served as a consultant on the Maruscelli projects of 1627 (Decr. 37, 32). Cat. 32 is difficult to attribute on any other basis than the script, which is identical to the handwriting on Cat. 33.
Unpublished.

34. Anonymous. Mid–1637.
Project for the oratory: ground floor plan.
AV, C.II.8, no. 32. 19.6 × 27.0. Ink and pink-orange wash over graphite.
Inscriptions:
Cortile. Loggia. Vestibolo A. Oratorio. Stanza da raggionare e sopra per li musici B. Porteria. Chiesa.
Attached document (AV, C.II.8, no. 32 bis):
Considerationi da farsi sopra l'acclusa Pianta.

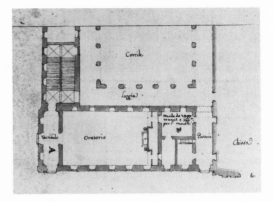

34

La fabrica della Chiesa Nuova, per se stessa conosciuta tanto per l'edifitio di dentro, quanto nel frontespitio di fuora ben proportionata, et con buona regola d'architettura proseguita; non pare che permetta hora nel novo Oratorio, che si fabrica, in che si move da mero zelo et affetto, e non da alcuna particolar passione di tacere, e non proponere le qui di sotto brevemente accennate considerationi a gloria de Dio, et del Glorioso S. Filippo, e non da altro particolar fine, o pensiere incitato.

Si propone dunque primieramente il far l'Oratorio secondo la qui acclusa Pianta, con esser voltato l'altare alla parte della chiesa, poiche così si verrebbe a levare una probabile inconvenienza delli doi corridori vicini, et porte attaccate conforme a quel che hora principiato si vede, poiche nel prospetto mai farà bene, si come all'incontro caminarebbe benissimo facendo il corridore, o vestibolo segnato con la lettera A nel cantone, et in questa maniera proportionatamente accompagnarebbe l'altro della portaria, et la facciata con bella vista caminarebbe unita.

Secondo, è da considerare, che tutto l'ornamento con li resalti, o altro finalmente poi entrarà per fianco ad un corridore, e fianco all'oratorio facendosi nella maniera incominciata, ma in questo pensiere, che si propone non solo s'accompagnarebbe la portaria, ma anco si potrebbe fare la porta dall'altra banda, che venisse in mezzo all'oratorio, et così verebbe ad havere doi entrate, ambedoi lodevoli nel medemmo modo di quello del Padre Gravita, ornandole di fora con le sue porte, e così verebbe ad essere il tutto alli suoi veri dritti con buona raggione d'architettura.

3° Sopra il vestibolo si potrebbe fare il luogo delli Sig.re Cardinali, et altri Sig.ri, quali per la scala senza altro giro potrebbono salire a diritura senza ponere tutto il claustro a soggettione, et quando si volessere far entrare per la portaria, tanto caminarebbe bene il presente disegno, e con maggior fondamento di raggione.

4° È da considerare, che per li musici, vi si richiede sempre una stanza di dietro al coro, non molto lontana acciò nel tempo delli sermoni possino provare le cose da cantarsi, qual stanza nel modo cominciato non puol esservi, se non lontana, et con scommodo, ma ponendosi in essecutione, secondo questo pensiere e disegno accluso potrebbe per li musici servire la stanza dietro segnata lettera B. cioè per dissopra, et il disotto servirebbe per servitio della portaria, per raggionare, o altro.

Quinto se si considera bene il modo con il quale hora è cominciata l'oratorio, oltre a molte cose, che si potrebbono dire etc. essendo l'altare situato nell'angolo soggetto alle doi strade viene ad esser sottoposto alli romori del passaggio delle genti, carrozze, carrette, et anco al sentire parole oscene imparticolare nel tempo dell'estate, nel quale l'Oratorio si fa hore 23 et le feste la mattina, oltre che nelli giorni de lavoro ne s'aggiunge il romore dell'artigiani, e così non seguirebbe l'intento d'esser luogo retirato, et destinato alli divini essercitij, ma ponendo in essecutione il presente disegno si ponerebbe rimedio a tutti questi inconvenienti poi non verebbe ad essere tanto soggetto, più commodo tanto a chi verrà all'oratorio, quanto alli Padri, che in un passo dalla portaria si verrebbono a trovare in Chiesa senza passar per tutto l'oratorio, quale molte volte essendo pieno di gente a pena possono passare per andare al luogo del sermone, o all'altare, si come si prova adesso con manifesta esperienza.

Quando poi li Padri si risolvessero a far ponere in essecutione il presente disegno potrebbe il tutto fare con poca spesa, e se ridurrebbe il cominciato a questo disegno accluso (benissimo) e sopra di ciò è necessaria una manifesta consideratione poiche molte volte il pentimento dapoi esser compita una fabrica è vano, et delli doi mali, è prudente cosa elegere il minore, e mutar il conseglio in megliore, e sagace cosa, et atto di manifesta prudenza considerabile, essendosi tutto questo detto, e proposito per mero scrupolo, che si fa quello che lo propone, quale non havendolo detto si pensarebbe di ciò haverne da render conto a Dio, conoscendo più molti che uno, oltre a che facendosi la debita consideratione, questo pensiere si crede non sia per esser biasmato da chiunque remirarà quanto qui brevemente si dia, et fondatamente si propone.

Sottoponendo però il tutto ad ogni più saggio, e prudente conseglio di persona dotta, et nella professione dell'architettura vero intelligente.

The present drawing, which appears to have been unsolicited, was submitted after the foundations of the oratory had been begun. In the accompanying document the author criticizes the project under way on several counts: the altar is within earshot of the noise and profanities of a major intersection; the musicians have insufficient room for rehearsals near their balconies; cardinals will have to walk through the casa to get to their loggia; and the architectural membering along the south facade makes no sense. He then proposes to remedy all these flaws in a single maneuver: the altar is shifted to the east end of the oratory, while the entrance vestibule is moved to the west end and given two doors on the model of the Oratory of the Caravita (1631–33; see Chapter 6, n. 6). A door on the west opens onto the vestibule and the oratory; two doors on the south, opening onto the vestibule and the *portaria,* are arranged symmetrically around seven central bays.

The foundations that were begun early in 1637 incorporated a wider interval between the two central windows of the oratory (Cat. 39). This interval, which embodied a long-sought-after solution to problems of fenestration, is naively ignored in the present unpublished project.

35. Anonymous (possibly Paolo Maruscelli). Mid–1637.

Project for the oratory: ground floor plan. AV, C.II.8, no. 23. 28.9 × 43.0. Graphite. Scale: 50 p. = 10.5 cm.

The plan incorporates the major innovations that had accumulated between Cat. 28 and Cat. 34: the oratory is 78 palmi in length, and space is reserved for an altar loggia on the west and an entrance corridor on the east. The wide gap between the two middle windows corresponds to the thicker corner pier of the courtyard.

The present handling of the graphite medium is foreign to Borromini but similar to Maruscelli's style: the lines are faintly drawn with an unsharpened pencil, and the hatching strokes do not run strictly parallel (compare with Cat. 22). The convention used for the scale recurs occasionally on Maruscelli's plans (Cat. 17b). During the brief partner-

ship between the two architects which ended in June 1637, Maruscelli was probably left in the dark about Borromini's revisions in the plan. This project may reflect his attempt to cope with the foundations as he saw them being built, and with hints of uncomprehended details like canted corner pilasters. The drawing is unfinished; the curved southwest corner and the pathetic articulation of the oratory facade play no role in the final design.
Bibl.: *Portoghesi, *Disegni,* 14, cat. no. 31, Fig. 31.

36. Pompilio Totti. 1638.
View of the Vallicella area and the Strada Nuova.
Ritratto di Roma moderna, Rome, 1638, 225. Engraving.
Inscriptions:
Santa Maria alla Valicella detta la Chiesa Nova. Strada Nova.

Although published in 1638, the print shows none of the construction begun around the oratory in 1637. It is, however, one of the few attempts to render the visual effect of Maruscelli's Strada Nuova, which points obliquely at the church facade (Cat. 17a–e, 38). The large building at the right edge of the print is the Palazzo Cerri, followed by the Sora stables (Cat. 19) and by a building which does not conform to the one-bay structure shown in later sources (Cat. 98a). The rooftop view of the "belle habitationi" (Totti, 228) on the left side of the Strada Nuova does little to supplement the slight information otherwise available on these dwellings (Doc. 13; *Dialogo,* 177). The house attached to the left flank of the church is the Casa del Baronio (Cat. 8, 14; Decr. 51), destroyed in about 1641 to construct the new *portaria.* The print still shows the Vallicella cupola with a blind drum, before Cortona's oculi were pierced in 1649 (Decr. 238).
Bibl.: * Strong, *La Chiesa Nuova (Santa Maria in Vallicella),* Rome, 1923, Pl. IV.

37. Francesco Borromini. 1636–37.
Copies of Maruscelli's plans and sections.

37a. Copy of Maruscelli's lost ground floor plan, Cat. 20a.
Alb. 285, first stratum. Cf. Cat. 39.

37b. Copy of Maruscelli's *piano nobile* plan, Cat. 20b.
Alb. 278. 35.3 × 28.3. Graphite.

37c. Copy of Maruscelli's mezzanine plan, Cat. 20c.
Alb. 282. 29.1 × 27.4. Graphite.

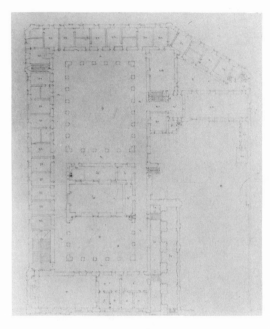

37b

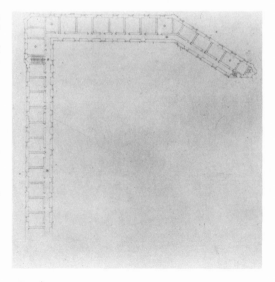

37c

37d.   Copy of Maruscelli's third-story plan, Cat. 20d.

  Alb. 281. 34.0 × 26.2. Graphite.

37e.   Copy of Maruscelli's north-south sections, Cat. 23a.

  Alb. 900. Graphite. Scale: 100 p.

37f.   Copy of Maruscelli's east-west section, Cat. 23b.

  Alb. 901. Graphite.

Both Maruscelli's original plans (Cat. 20a–d) and Borromini's copies (Cat. 37a–d) show a building of identical absolute dimensions: 32.8×24.7 cm. The copies may have been made with the help of the numerous pinpricks that appear on the originals. In spite of the mechanical nature of the task, the copies clearly show Borromini's hand in the fineness of the graphite line, the precision of molding profiles, the characteristic way of marking the scale, and the freehand touches that appear in the capitals and keystone grotesques. Furthermore, the copy of the ground floor plan was partly erased and reused as the basic armature for Borromini's famous early project, Cat. 39.

It is difficult to ascertain the exact date at which Borromini was supplied with his predecessor's drawings: presumably after his earliest work for the Congregation in late 1636 (Cat. 28) but before his own project was accepted in May 1637 (Decr. 103). Copying was often part of the standard *consulta* process: Borromini himself was frequently entrusted with the task in Maderno's shop, although he later spoke of the copyist's role with some disdain (C 32; Connors, review of Thelen in *JSAH*, XXXV, 1976, 146; *Opus,* Preface, 3[r]).

Bibl.: *Portoghesi, *Linguaggio,* Fig. xxxvi (Cat. 37b, attributed to Maruscelli); Portoghesi, *Disegni,* 12, Cat. no. 26 (Cat. 37d, as a possibly nonautograph Borromini drawing which may date from the period of initial collaboration between Borromini and Maruscelli).

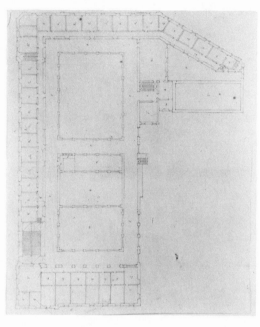

37d

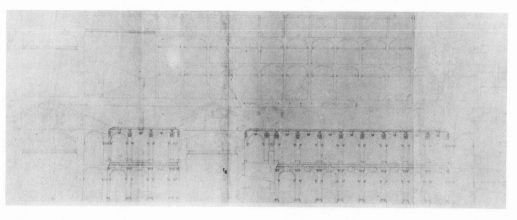

37e

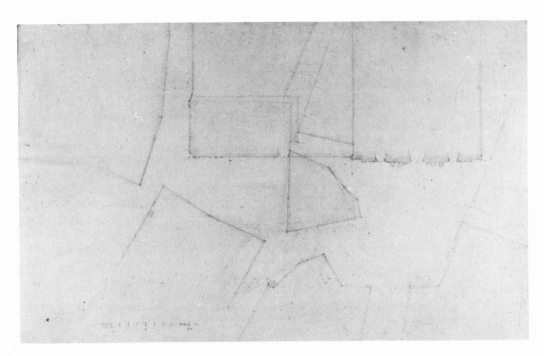

38

38. Francesco Borromini. 1637–41, probably 1637.

Measured plan of the Piazza della Chiesa Nuova. (Fig. 101, detail.)

AV, C.II.8, no. 104. 28.4 × 42.9. Graphite. Scale: 100 p. = 7.2 cm.

The drawing represents a measured survey of the piazza area as it appeared between 1637 and 1641. The obliquely aligned Strada Nuova and the funnel-shaped piazza were the result of Maruscelli's efforts between 1627 and 1630 (Cat. 17). Although the scale of the drawing matches that of Maruscelli's casa projects, it renders distances and angles more accurately and appears to be based on measurements taken from the site. At least one of the dimensions it records is confirmed by other sources (the gap of 7 palmi between the Vallicella facade and adjacent houses on the right is mentioned in 1604: Hibbard, *Licenze,* no. 37). Since the drawing is concerned with building rights and property lines, the flat facade shown on the oratory is probably a schematic rendering and not an alternative to or a predecessor of the curved facade.

The Isola di Pizzomerlo, which the drawing omits, was demolished early in 1637 (Decr. 102), while the Isola dei Piatetti, which it shows intact, was acquired in 1638, trimmed in 1641 and again in 1650, and demolished altogether in 1659 (Russo, "Piazza," 43, n.52; Cat. 66; Decr. 265, 266, 359, 360). The fact that this latter block of houses is still shown protruding into the *portaria* has two striking implications. The first is that the two halves of the oratory facade were built at separate times: the left half and portal by December 1638 (Pollak, 446, regs. 1846–51); the right half, here drawn with a dotted line, late in 1641, when the *portaria* was under construction (Cat. 66). Accordingly the library stood in a fragmentary state until the rooms below it were complete; the contract for its ceiling was not signed until November 1642 (Doc. 17). The second implication is that the undemolished *isola* prevented the use of a rope as radius in laying out the curved facade, which in fact consists of straight segments rather than a single continuous arc.

Faint pencil marks near the upper left corner of the drawing indicate that Borromini was planning to expand the oratory projection 22 palmi northwards along the Via dei Filippini. This suggests that he was already planning a similar and symmetrical expansion of the Monte Giordano projection toward the south, an idea that is not worked out in extant projects until 1647 (Cat. 80). *Bibl.:* *Portoghesi, *Linguaggio,* Fig. xxxiii; *Portoghesi, *Disegni,* 12, cat. no. 25, Fig. 25 (dated 1637 and considered prior to projects for a curved facade).

39.   Francesco Borromini. 1636–37; early 1637; and late 1644.
   Plan of the Casa dei Filippini in three stages.
   Alb. 285. 46.7 × 37.9 (original sheet) plus 29.8 × 12.5 (sheet added along right edge). Graphite. Scale: 200 p.
Inscriptions relating to the circular chapel on the right:
   [1.] S.Sta. vole un Altare solo e che si entri della strada di Parione nel tempio et che si passi nella facc[ia]ta dava[n]ti dove sara l'altra entrata compagnia di quella del oratorio.
   Ricordo che N.S. vol vedere l'scritture delle stanze variate l'una del'altra et a [*or* o ?] promesso di portare [?] il libro proprio dove a[?] voltato [?] il foglio.
   Non si fara questo diseg[n]o per che S.Sta mi desse che voleva [?] fabricare a Sta. Agnese.
   [2. *Above chapel:*] colonne con [?] catene
   [3. *To the right of the rotonda:*] camere [?]
   [4. *Below rotonda:*] cortile
   Other inscriptions below the facade and inside the rotunda have been erased.

Three different strata on the sheet, executed over a span of at least seven years, represent successive phases in the planning of the casa: first, a copy of an earlier ground plan by Maruscelli; second, Borromini's first presentation project for the entire complex; and third, a project for a Pamphilj chapel added to the Vallicella transept.
   I. Borromini's copies of Maruscelli's entire set of caption drawings appear to date to early 1637 (Cat. 37). The copy that forms the first stratum of the present sheet is particularly valuable, since it records a lost drawing (Cat. 20a). Although partly erased, it preserves some of the original caption numbers and can be used to reconstruct the missing drawing (Cat. 21).
   II. Subsequently Borromini reused this copy as the basic armature for a presentation

project of his own. He adopted Maruscelli's general layout, including one feature that was already out of date (the loggia along the south side of the garden court had been suppressed in 1627: Cat. 20, 23a; Chapter 2). He incorporated the two straight staircases which Maruscelli had built in 1633–34 along the left flank of the church: one leading to the *piano nobile* corridor (Chapter 2, n. 29), and another leading to the Anticamera and Cappelletta del Santo, which are themselves shown on the *piano nobile* level. This second staircase was replaced by a more commodious spiral in October 1638 (Cat. 51) and thus provides a *terminus ante* for the dating of this stratum. A more exact clue to the date may be found in the rendering of the sacristy altar: the plan shows a project similar to Cat. 28 but still does not include the large niche in which Algardi's statue was installed in late 1636 or early 1637 (Cat. 28, Fig. 72). Borromini was officially accepted as architect on May 10, 1637; it would seem likely that his project or one deriving from it was in the Congregation's hands by that date or shortly thereafter (Decr. 103).
   The changes Borromini introduced into Maruscelli's project affect the interior disposition of the oratory, the fenestration, the relative proportions of the stairs and loggie, and the location of specific rooms in the rear service courtyard.
   First, the plan shows the oratory in its final size and form. It incorporates many of the features proposed in earlier consultation drawings, particularly those by Girolamo Rainaldi (Cat. 32, 33). The room has been reduced in length (100 to 78 palmi) but expanded in width (50 to 55 palmi) and height (floor level sunk by six risers or 4 palmi). The entrance corridor of earlier drawings has become an entrance loggia, matched by an altar loggia at the opposite end of the room. Although the two loggie are different in size (9 × 44 palmi on the left, 16 × 50 palmi on the right), they are designed to appear identical to a person standing in the center of the room.
   The fenestration of the oratory follows the logic first demonstrated on the drawings attributed to Girolamo Rainaldi (Cat. 32, 33) and explained in detail in *Opus,* VI,

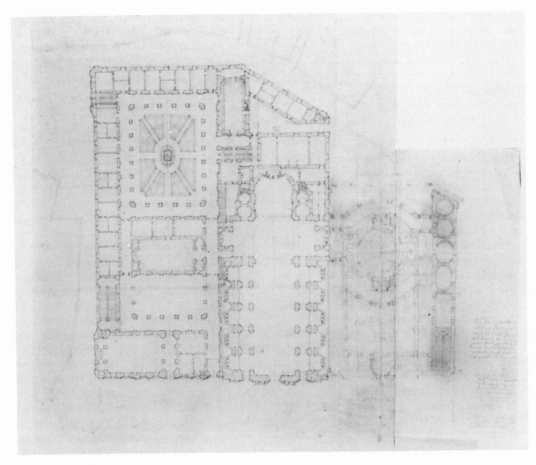

39

13^r ff.: a wide interval between the two central windows reflects the thick corner pier of the courtyard loggia. The interval is disguised on the interior by two niches and on the exterior by the left edge of the curved facade. The same logic is extrapolated to other parts of the building: the windows of the north and west wings reflect the thicker corner piers of the two courtyards with equal insistence.

In plan the oratory facade has reached its final form: five bays drawn along a curve with a radius of 190–200 palmi, flanked by two flat bays and bounded by *bugnato* pilasters at either end. However, since the library has not yet been moved to its final position over the oratory, the facade probably differed in elevation from the present one, although no drawings record its appearance at this early stage (cf. Cat. 41).

The problem of the fenestration of the sacristy is also considered on the drawing, although the solution it proposes differs from the one described in *Opus,* X, 35^r. The sacristy windows, four open and one blind, are aligned with the arches of the courtyard loggia, and the courtyard itself is expanded 8 palmi to the west. There is no trace of the fictive windows advocated in the *Opus* passage.

The project introduces changes that tend to make the main staircase more inviting. It is extended to occupy the full width of the first courtyard; landings are introduced in each flight; each step is slightly higher but also much longer; and the first landing is reached after a short flight of three steps (later reduced to two) "which from a distance invite ascent" (*Opus,* XI, 37^r). The scales on Cat. 23a and 39, combined with the fact that the first story is 32 palmi high (*Opus,* XV, 45ʳ), allow an exact measurement of these changes:

that it would be better to try to camouflage the defect rather than spend ▽700 in demolishing and rebuilding the wall. By the

	Cat. 21 (Maruscelli)	Cat. 39 (Borromini)
Number of risers	62	57
Average height of riser	6 *oncie*	under 7 *oncie*
Width of step	18 *oncie*	21 *oncie*

The drawing also proposes alterations in the relative proportions of the loggie. While those that surround the first courtyard remain 18 palmi wide, elsewhere in the casa this width is reserved for the major axes of sight and circulation. The less frequented loggie along the north and west sides of the garden court are reduced to 15 palmi in width; further alterations of the same sort occur in the final building (Cat. 66r, 81).

Finally, the drawing proposes a total revision in the distribution of rooms in the third courtyard. Originally four services were located in this part of the building in stacked pairs: the kitchen (Cat. 21, no. 30) and the congregation room (Cat. 20b, no. 28), which shared a common chimney; and the refectory (Cat. 21, no. 22) and library (Cat. 20b, no. 22), which were placed in the shadows behind the Vallicella apse. The present drawing reverses the respective positions of these two pairs of rooms, possibly out of a desire to provide the refectory with greater privacy (*Opus,* XXI, 57ʳ; *Dialogo,* 199) and the library with adequate light. The location proved somewhat cramped for the refectory and its adjacent vestibules and staircase. Expansion was impossible to the south, where the Sala Rossa and Anticamera del Santo had been standing since 1634 (Cat. 27). Hence the drawing proposes a small expansion of 3 palmi to the north (indicated by a faint dotted line protruding into the Via di Parione) which transforms the northwest corner of the building into a slightly obtuse angle (explained in *Opus,* II, 6ᵛ and XX, 57ʳ). However, Borromini was not entirely free to maneuver on the north side of the building, since the north wall had already been started in 1629 during Maruscelli's tenure. In 1639 the Congregation realized that this wall would not suit the new oblique alignment proposed by Borromini, but felt

time this wing came to be built in 1647, considerable portions of the old wall were in fact uprooted and replaced (Cat. 80, 81; Decr. 35, 37, 38, 137).

III. Prior to his election as Pope Innocent X, Cardinal Giovanni Battista Pamphilj had expressed the wish to be buried at the Vallicella (Eimer, *S. Agnese in Navona,* I, 36, n. 8), and after his election, in November 1644, Borromini received instructions to study the church to see if "without ruining the old design it would be possible to make enough space to build a fine chapel for the Pamphilj" (*Ragguagli,* 212). The project for a Pamphilj chapel is discussed at some length in a memorandum by Virgilio Spada (Doc. 29) that can be dated between September 15 and December 12, 1644. Apparently it was considered as one of five possible ways in which Innocent X might wish to show his esteem for the Vallicella, the others being: first, to encase the iron casket holding the saint's body in a bejeweled silver casket; second, to construct a chapel to the east of the tribune, on the site of the later Spada Chapel, matching the Cappella di S. Filippo; third, to adorn the tribune with columns and other ornamentation; and last, to convert Borromini's oratory into a Pamphilj "Pantheon."

The alternative of a large Pamphilj chapel is discussed in terms that match exactly a diagram that seems to have been drawn by Spada (Cat. 79). The chapel would be attached to the east or right transept of the church, with two smaller side entrances and a large central entrance taking the place of the existing Glorieri Chapel (with D'Arpino's altarpiece of the *Coronation of the Virgin* removed). The new chapel is modeled on the Sistine and Pauline Chapels in S. Maria Maggiore, as befitting a papal project. In his memorandum Spada outlines the many difficulties such a project might be expected to cause. The side street then projected along the east flank of the church would have to be foregone or moved still further east. The old casa, which brought in ▽1,200 in rents, would have to be demolished. The new chapel would not open onto the existing Piazza della Chiesa Nuova, although a small piazza might possibly be opened up for it facing north, toward the Via di Parione (in the space marked by an X in dotted lines on Cat. 79). The line of sight projected since Maruscelli's caption project across the Vallicella transept, terminating in Algardi's statue of S. Filippo in the sacristy (shown with a dotted line on Cat. 79), would be lost. Finally, the altar balustrade of the new chapel (sketched on Cat. 79 with a dotted line) would be no wider than the present Glorieri Chapel balustrade, and the entrance to the new chapel would be blocked by the half-dozen women who usually stopped there to make their devotions at communion time.

Borromini took some of these criticisms into account when he sketched his own project for a Pamphilj chapel on Cat. 39; on the other hand, both the drawing and the inscription give the impression that he was working more for the pope than for the Congregation. Borromini envisaged the chapel as a massive rotunda pierced by an entrance and three altar chapels on the main axis, and by smaller niches—one would suppose for tombs—on the diagonal axes. Sixteen columns are arranged in pairs around the interior to create a circular aisle 5 palmi wide. The extreme thickness of the rotunda wall (15 palmi) and the presence of three spiral staircases indicate plans for a structure two stories high. Two systems of support are possible for the cupola: either it could rest on the ring of columns, buttressed by the rotunda wall; or more likely it was meant to rest directly on the wall itself, and the ring of columns was designed to support a balcony at *piano nobile* level. Examples of both solutions occur in G. B. Montano's *Libro secondo. Scielta di varii tempietti antichi,* ed. G. B. Soria, Rome, 1624, Pl. 6, 7, 58, and 61, which show the vault resting on the columns, and more appropriately Pl. 46, the immediate source for Borromini's design (Fig. 129), which shows the vault resting on the wall. The rotunda is placed directly on the axis of vision that crosses the transept and runs through the sacristy, thus avoiding one of the criticisms raised by Spada; on the other hand, it has a narrow entrance from the church, and is much less of a dependency of the Vallicella than the one sketched on Cat. 79. Rather than being a freestanding structure, it is conceived as the center of a complex which extends to the Vicolo del Governo on the east and the Via di Parione on the north and duplicates some of the features of the casa, such as the curved facade and the main *scalone,* which are repeated in mirror symmetry. The rotunda is buttressed on two sides by loggie that follow its circular plan. The east wing is taken up by a series of rooms "varied from one another" in five different shapes—rectangle, oval, octagon, hexagon, and circle—which suggest crypts rather than functional spaces. According to the inscription, Innocent X had time to inspect the project and to criticize it; as a result, Borromini changed two of the three projected altars into entrances, and attempted to create a dignified prospect on the north by sketching concave wings that meet the convex curve of the loggie, and by drawing a series of colonnettes with chains as the southern boundary of a triangular piazza facing the Via di Parione. Apparently Spada was right when he suspected (in Doc. 29) that Innocent X would want the greatest possible public exposure for the chapel.

The last of the five possible papal projects discussed in Spada's memorandum was to turn Borromini's oratory, which had been finished for about four years, into a Pamphilj "Pantheon" by installing tombs between the pairs of pilasters, beginning with the tombs of Cardinal Girolamo Pamphilj and of the pope himself; in this manner the oratory could take as many as eight or ten tombs. On the other hand there were certain disadvantages: the pope might want his Pantheon open to the public more continually than the oratory normally was; and not much could be done to ornament the oratory altar without cutting into space needed for the devotion, something that eventually happened anyway when the altar was rebuilt in the years following 1652 (Cat. 48).

The memorandum ends with Spada's perceptive comment that a mausoleum would not be of much use to the Pamphilj if Don Camillo Pamphilj, the pope's heir, were to be elevated to the cardinalate instead of remaining a layman and founding a dynasty; Camillo was in fact made a cardinal on December 12, 1644, although he renounced this position on January 21, 1647 (Eubel, *Hierarchia Catholica . . .* , IV, 27). In the end, the Oratorians got none of Spada's five suggested embellishments; as Borromini's inscription states, the idea of a papal chapel at the Vallicella was eventually set aside in favor of the rebuilding of S. Agnese in Piazza Navona, which was begun in 1652. *Bibl.:* *Hempel, 72 ff., 94, and Fig. 21 (dated 1638–39, with a partial transcription of the inscription); *Portoghesi, *Linguaggio,* Fig. xxxv; *Portoghesi, *Disegni,* 13 ff., cat. no. 29, and Fig. 29 (with a full transcription of the inscription); *Studi sul Borromini,* Rome, 1967, I, Fig. 24; *Hager, "Carlo Fontana's Project . . . ," *Journal of the Warburg and Courtauld Institutes,* XXXVI, 1973, 329, n. 63 and Fig. 47a (detail).

40.   Francesco Borromini. Summer 1638.
      Project for the casa: ground floor plan.
      Alb. 284. 42.5 × 27.4. Graphite.
Inscriptions:
      S[an] F[ilippo]
      SS. ASUN[ta]
      S[anta] C[ecilia]
      Porteria. Spezzaria. Dispensa.

The drawing shows the entire casa in outline, with intense reworking of selected areas, in particular the refectory and the oratory. Although it is usually considered an early design and dated prior to Cat. 39, in fact the sequence should be reversed: the present drawing was begun as a copy of Cat. 39, and is the later of the two projects by over a year. The correct sequence should be Alb. 283, then 285, finally 284. The two areas of reworking on the present drawing deal with a single problem that arose in the summer of 1638: the relocation of the library from its original position at the back of the building to its present position above the oratory; the events are described in de-

tail in Decr. 112, 115–119, 125, 127, and 129, which are quoted in Incisa della Rocchetta, *Dialogo,* 189, n. 37 and 177, n. 14, and in Incisa della Rocchetta, "Biblioteca," 126.

The chain of revisions shown on the drawing began with the attempt to provide the refectory with sufficient space. The stairway and *lavamani* originally planned immediately to the south of this room were eliminated, and the refectory was extended as far as the Sala Rossa, which had been standing since 1635 (Cat. 27). The enlarged refectory was redesigned as a polygonal room with fifteen tables, a seating capacity of sixty-one, and an elevated pulpit in the center of the right wall. It was given an entrance vestibule to the north which began as an octagon (with one angle determined by the bend in the "elbow" wing and the others by symmetry), was then redrawn as an oval, and finally ended as a more elongated oval with eight apertures for doors and windows. The adjacent staircase was planned in three flights but then reduced to two to provide space for a corridor. The dimensions of the staircase were largely dictated by circumstance: the landings followed a predetermined pattern of fenestration, and the width of the flights was fixed at 7 palmi by a decision to reuse steps from a staircase then being dismantled (Decr. 120; Cat. 27, 51; the staircase, which formerly led to the Anticamera del Santo, is erased on the present drawing).

The enlargement of the refectory had repercussions throughout the building. Circulation patterns had to be altered in the rooms already built around the saint's chapel (Cat. 27, Phase II). The rooms formerly located behind the Vallicella apse were erased from the drawing, since access to this area was blocked and the new staircase too distant to be of use. The kitchen was shifted to the "elbow" wing and the congregation room moved over the refectory, but in the process the library was displaced, and it proved difficult to relocate because of its peculiar needs, such as ample height and fireproof vaults both above and below (*Opus,* XXVII, 75^v, 77^r; Cat. 77). The drawing singles out two large vaulted rooms

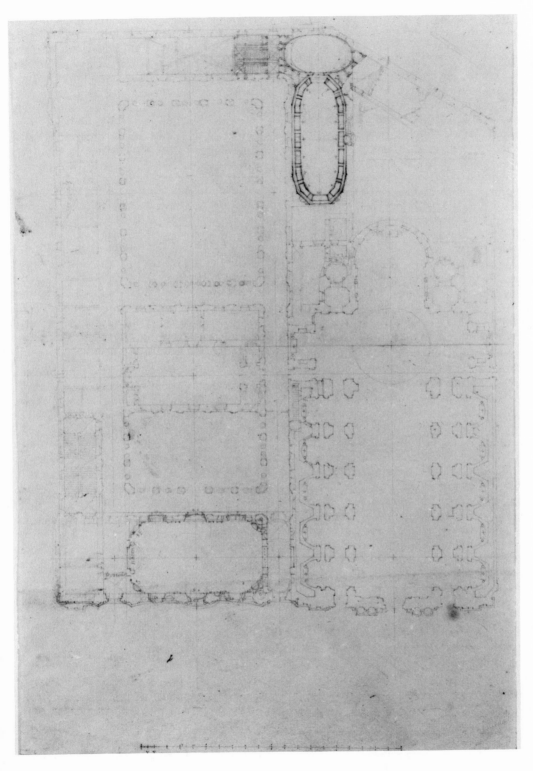

—the *spezzaria* and the *dispensa*—as potential substructures, but the final choice was to place the library over the oratory (Decr. 115; *Opus,* XXVIII, 75^r; *Dialogo,* 188 ff.). The conflicting implications of this move are worked out at the bottom of the sheet.

The reason for centering the library in the south wing was that the upper story of the oratory facade could be easily raised to conceal the room's added height. The alterations which the drawing proposes in the design of the oratory (displacement toward the center, canted corners, thickened walls, reduced number of windows) represent an attempt to provide adequate support for the weight of the library vault. The reworkings of the oratory facade tend to expand its apparent width in response to the increase in height, first in an extreme and unrealistic way (the brick pilaster cluster drawn at the left end of the casa is supposed to match a similar cluster of travertine pilasters on the Vallicella facade), and then in a more moderate fashion (twin portals and strongly canted pilasters emphatically include a full seven bays in a manner similar to the prints of 1660—Cat. 90; Fig. 16). Finally, the alterations in the courtyard (paired columns replacing the former single piers) represent an attempt to cope with the new fenestration of the oratory and of the library.

In summary, the expansion of the refectory led to the displacement of the library and to its eventual migration to the south wing, which in turn brought about a momentary shift in the proposed location of the oratory and an attempt to redesign the facade and the courtyard loggie. This chain of events was worked out on the drawing by August 1638, when permission was granted to put the library over the oratory (Decr. 115, 116). Approval for some of the other proposals came only later (Decr. 127, 129), and the most drastic revisions were finally rendered unnecessary by the decision to cover the library with a wooden ceiling instead of a vault (*Opus,* XXVIII, 77^r). With this great reduction in weight, no alterations were needed in the plan of the oratory, and only small changes were introduced in the elevation of the facade (Cat. 41).

The inscriptions on the drawing appear to propose statues of S. Filippo and S. Cecilia in corner niches analogous to those later introduced at the Lateran (BV, Vat. lat. 11257, fol. 258). The Assumption was approved as the subject of the altarpiece in April 1639 (Decr. 132, 133); when finally executed by Raffaello Vanni in 1664, it included images of both of these patrons of the oratory (Decr. 431; Fig. 31).

Bibl.: *Hempel, 71 ff., Fig. 20 (dated prior to Cat. 39); *Portoghesi, *Linguaggio,* 53 ff., Fig. xxxii; Portoghesi, *Disegni,* 13, cat. no. 28 (casa and oratory dated to 1637, refectory area reworked ca. 1640).

41.   Francesco Borromini. August 1638.

Elevation project for the final stage of the oratory facade.

Windsor 5594. 40.4 × 33.8. Graphite. Scale: 100 p. = 15.4 cm. A strip about 3.5 cm. wide has been added along the right edge, apparently by Borromini, since the drawing on the strip seems to be autograph.

Usually Alb. 291 (Cat. 90) is considered a preparatory sketch for the oratory facade, and the Windsor drawing a presentation project drawn up after the sketch but before construction began in mid-1637. In fact the situation is much more complex. The Windsor drawing should be dated to August 1638, about a year after the beginning of construction; it records a major change in the design of the facade which was made at that time to accommodate the library in a new position over the oratory. The Albertina drawing, on the other hand, is not a preliminary sketch but a revision of the design for publication in 1660, twenty-two years later than the Windsor drawing.

The transfer of the library and the decisions this move involved are discussed above in Cat. 40. According to the documents, the move involved a change in the design of the oratory facade, which had already been in construction for a year: ". . . Padre Spada thought that everything could be settled by building the library on the site of the oratory facade, since the walls of that facade could be raised as much as was necessary, since they were of a different

41

order. . . ." (Decr. 115). An increase in the height of the facade would necessarily involve an increase in its width, but any drastic change, such as those indicated on Cat. 40, was ruled out by the fact that the first story of the facade (or at least of the left half of the facade) had already been built. Borromini solved this dilemma by making what had originally been a five-bay facade into a seven-bay facade. The reasons for thinking that Borromini had originally intended the facade to be a five-part image are as follows. The curved part of the facade, as well as the fine brickwork and the powerful entablature, only extend for five bays. In the *Opus* (VII, 23^r) it is stated that the facade proper ends at the exact middle of the oratory; the text then goes on to liken the facade to a five-part image, namely "the human body with open arms embracing everyone who enters, a body which is divided into five parts, that is the breast in the center and arms each of which consists of two linked parts. . . ." Furthermore, *Opus,* VII, 27^r says explicitly that the facade proper had a different type of basement grille from the grilles designed for the casa, and in the present building these special grilles extend no farther than the five curved bays. Finally, a perfect model for the kind of facade Borromini was aiming at is found at S. Giacomo degli Incurabili (Fig. 122), where the facade proper is built of travertine and flanked by bays of rough brickwork and brick *bugnato* strips on either side. The reconstruction in Fig. 14 shows what this early design looked like: in fact the lower story of the facade was physically no different from what it looks like now (except in matters of ornamental detail), but what are now considered the outer bays of the facade were then considered by the architect as mere flanking bays not belonging to the main image. As for the upper story of the facade, it was originally lower (the *decreto* quoted above said that it had to be raised) and narrower (on the Windsor drawing the roof line seems to continue, still faintly visible, underneath the outer bays of the present upper story). These two pieces of evidence appear to rule out what at first might seem to be an obvious precedent for the facade, namely, the block-

facade of the type found in S. Bibiana or S. Gregorio Magno (or the pseudo-block-facade found at S. Luigi dei Francesi), in which the upper story is fully as wide as the lower story. On the contrary, the evidence seems to indicate that the upper story of the oratory facade was originally three bays wide, articulated by four columns, and probably linked to the wider lower story by volutes, like most Roman facades of the Gesù, Vallicella, or S. Susanna type.

When Borromini was told to put the library behind the upper story of the oratory facade in August 1638, his first reaction was the drastic expansion in width shown on Cat. 40, and his second reaction seems to be shown in a faint underdrawing on the present sheet, where there are traces of Ionic capitals and an entablature across all of the flanking bays on the left side of the building; he may also have experimented with other changes on the right edge of the original sheet, which he then chose to cut off and repair. His final solution was much simpler: volutes were added at the library level to link the former flanking bays into the central image, which now became a seven-bay facade. The grandiose entrance portals that appear on the drawing are used to reinforce the impression of a wider facade; the right portal was carried out in a more progressive form in 1641 (Cat. 68); the left portal was never carried out, and even on the drawing it is shown as blind in plan and lacking the five steps that lead up to its counterpart. A curved facade would have been unconventional enough, but the new facade was partly curved and partly straight, an extraordinary hybrid which Borromini's propagandist Martinelli tried to defend in his guidebook of 1658: ". . . Borromini created a new order, uniting the lines of the curved facade *(Frontespitio orbicolato)* with those of the straight, which form a third species as unusual as it is thoughtful. . . ." (quoted below in Cat. 89, where the context makes it clear that *frontespitio* is to be translated as "facade" and not, as Hempel thought, "pediment").

The present drawing still shows ornamental details which differ from those carried out in the final building. The central portal of the oratory has two spiral columns, "con un tronco che vi giri intorno al modo di quelle del Tempio di Salamone" (Decr. 110, 113), which were discussed in May and July 1638 but replaced by straight shafts in the final building. The upper story is shown with four large columns which were in the end omitted; their capitals, originally modeled on the capitals of the Sforza Chapel in S. Maria Maggiore (as indicated by the inscription on Thelen's C 82, scale 4a), became much more heraldic in the final design; whatever type of ornament had been originally shown on the main frieze was erased from the drawing and omitted from the building. The four windows flanking the central balcony are more conventional than those designed in Cat. 46 or those carried out in the final building; the balcony door is more ornate and heraldic; and the balcony balusters do not yet alternate. The drawing shows a crown in the central niche which would have been somewhat inappropriate for Filippo Neri, who was not a martyr; the crown, palm fronds, and lilies over the entrance portal in the final building must be symbols of S. Cecilia, to whom the oratory technically is dedicated. The emblems of Filippo Neri which were to adorn the skyline of the facade were never executed, and the dove (a reminder that the Oratory was a service of the inspired word) was later moved down from the pediment to the illusionistic coffers of the balcony niche. The final decision on all of these matters seems to have been taken in January 1639, about six months after the drawing was done (Decr. 128).

Some of the unexecuted decorative elements of the drawing reappear in Barrière's print of 1660 (Fig. 16), in particular the symmetrical portals, the heraldic ornament of the balcony niche, the salomonic columns of the main door, and the straight columns of the upper story.

Bibl.: *Portoghesi, *Disegni,* 16, cat. no. 39 and Fig. 39; *Blunt, *Supplements to the Catalogue of Italian and French Drawings,* in E. Schilling, *The German Drawings . . . at Windsor Castle,* London and New York, n.d., 53 ff., Plate 72; *Blunt, *Borromini,* Cambridge, Mass., 1979, 94 ff., Fig. 69.

42. Francesco Borromini. October–December 1638.
Molding profiles and columns framing a doorway, possibly for the main portal of the oratory.
Alb. 318. Graphite.
Unpublished.

43. Francesco Borromini. 1638.
Sketch for an unidentified altar.
Alb. 317^{r-v}. 17.3 (right edge) × 13.2. Cropped along right edge. Graphite.
Inscriptions on verso:
Porta del oratorio. Capitello composito alto pm 2 . . .
Base e zoccolo sotto cioe . . .
la basa alta pm 1 il zoccolo . . .
½ in tutto p. 1 . . .
colonna p. 18 . . .
21

Cat. 42 and the inscriptions on the verso of Cat. 43 appear to refer to the main portal at the center of the oratory facade, which was executed between October and December 1638 (Pollak, 446, regs. 1846–51). The altar on the recto measures 11 × 15¾ p. and thus is too small to be associated with the sacristy altar shown in Cat. 28; it remains unidentified.
Unpublished.

44. Francesco Borromini. 1638.
Projects for iron window grilles.

44a. Grille for a window of the oratory facade: elevation sketch and plan. Verso: molding profiles and a freehand oval.
Alb. 326^{r-v}. 18.0 × 6.8. Graphite.
Inscriptions:
recto: St. filipo orat[orio] / tre / sei.
verso: D. Castelli et . . .
Bibl.: Hempel, 84, n. 1.

44b. Oratory facade grille. Verso: sketch of one side of a window frame.
Alb. 327^{r-v}. 13.6 × 6.8. Graphite.
Inscriptions:
Oratorio C . . . [?] 4⅓ 10⅓.
Bibl.: *Hempel, Pl. 40.2 (recto); *Portoghesi, *Linguaggio,* Fig. xlvi (recto); *Steinberg, *Borromini's San Carlo alle Quattro Fontane,* New York, 1977, Fig. 172.

44c. Oratory facade grille.
Alb. 328. 19.1 × 8.4. Graphite.
Bibl.: Hempel, 84, n. 1.

44

44d.   Oratory facade grille.
   Alb. 329. 19.3 × 8.5. Graphite.
Bibl.: *Hempel, 84, n. 1 and Pl. 40.3; *Portoghesi, *Linguaggio,* Fig. xlvii (mislabeled as Alb. 239); *Steinberg, *Borromini's San Carlo alle Quattro Fontane,* New York, 1977, Fig. 173.

44e.   Window grille.
   Alb. 330. 16.9 × 8.1. Graphite.
Unpublished.

44f.   Window grille.
   Alb. 320. 7.7 × 20.4. Graphite.
Inscription (not autograph):
   St. Philippo e . . . [?]

Of the four windows in the oratory that face the piazza, two occur in niches and are thus curved in plan, while the other two are flat. This difference posed a problem in the design of the window grilles, all of which had to appear identical from the interior of the room. Borromini's solution was to downplay the horizontal elements. His design began as a pattern of 3×7 hearts, which was then reduced to 3×6. In the upper left corner of Cat. 44a he experiments with inverting the pattern; in Cat. 44d he arrives at the final solution by omitting the upper half of each heart, thus combining abstraction of form with economy in the use of iron.

Cat. 44e and 44f may be designs for the grilles of the slit windows that light the small closets in the southwest corner. Other grille studies are preserved in the Albertina (308, 331, 332, 333^{r-v}), but they appear to be for the side facade of S. Carlino. Similar diamond-shaped grilles were used in the later phases of the casa, particularly in the Monte Giordano projection of 1649 and the long west facade, executed in 1660 after Borromini's departure.

45.   Francesco Borromini. Early 1639–41.
   Project for the doorframe in the balcony niche at the center of the facade.
   Alb. 305. 25.1×17.0. Graphite. Scale: 10 p.

Apparently Borromini was still at liberty in early 1639 to alter some of the facade ornament (Decr. 128). The present drawing began as a rendering of the balcony doorframe at a stage close to Cat. 41. The curves on either side of the door were then enriched with palm branches, and the angular *orecchie* transformed into the more sinuous forms of the executed version. The original

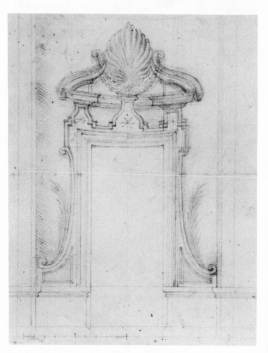

45

coat of arms, which may have caused some offence, was replaced by a stylized palmette wedged between two volutes which echo the large volutes at either end of the facade. *Bibl.:* Hempel, 84, n. 3; *Thelen, *70 disegni,* 15, cat. no. 25, Fig. VI.

46.   Francesco Borromini. 1638–39.
   Project for the upper windows of the oratory facade: elevation with two half alternatives.
   Alb. 306. 26.2 × 19.2. Graphite. Scale: 10 p. (Roman numerals, cf. Cat. 28.)
Inscription:
   Si dara l'Agetto solo nelli doi risalti che portano su il frontespito il resto della cornice seguitera [?] l'agetto del' Imposta la quale non pasara fuori alli pilastri.

The drawing shows the large upper windows of the facade at a stage close to Cat. 41. However, the vertical lines that flank the window seem to indicate pilasters rather than the columns formerly proposed, and the inscription appears to offer instructions on how much these pilasters should protrude. The plain keystones of Cat. 41 are here transformed into angels' heads and wings. In the final design, these decorative elements were omitted in favor of a simple star under a projecting cornice.
Bibl.: Hempel, 84, n. 3; Thelen, *70 disegni,* 15, cat. no. 24. Engraved in *Studio,* I, Pl. 92 (Cat. 107h).

46

47.   Francesco Borromini. Ca. 1638–39.
   Project for the upper windows which flank the oratory facade.
   Alb. 307. 22.4 × 17.5. Graphite. Scale: 10 p. (Roman numerals, cf. Cat. 28.)

The drawing is close to the upper windows in the two flanking bays of the facade as they appear in Cat. 41 and in the final building, although the decorative stars were never executed. It also resembles the window frames projected on Alb. 292 for the side facade of S. Carlo alle Quattro Fontane, to which the tiny square frame in the lower right-hand corner of the sheet also refers. (Alb. 292 is illustrated in Portoghesi, *Linguaggio,* Fig. xxxix, but mislabeled as Alb. 337 and wrongly assigned to the Casa dei Filippini.)
Bibl.: Hempel, 85, n. 2.

47

48. Francesco Borromini. 1637–38, revised October–November 1652.

Altar loggia at the west end of the oratory: plan and elevation. Project for installing four columns in front of the loggia.

Alb. 294. 50.2 × 34.0. Graphite. Scale: 30 p. (Roman numerals, cf. Cat. 28.)

Inscription:

venire avanti con questa colonna quanto bisognia p[er] confrontarsi [?] con l'angolare [?] p[er]che piu viene avanti piu locho [*or* quello che ?] resta per il sito del Altare resta piu magnifico.

In its original state the drawing showed a project for the altar loggia in plan and elevation. The shell motif inserted into the arch on the left marks the first hesitant appearance of the musicians' *coretti* in Borromini's design (cf. Cat. 20b, no. 5). This pair of balconies was built in late 1638 to 1639 on a more generous scale, with convex fronts that projected out on brackets (Cat. 85a, 85c; Doc. 15, clause 11). In order to connect the balcony on the left with the spiral staircase on the right, Borromini moved the altar forward and installed a wooden floor, or *transito,* behind it (contrast Cat. 39 with Cat. 85a; cf. Decr. 472). The altar itself was built only in the form of a full-scale wooden model, which is shown in Fig. 32 and is also known from Spada's description of it in 1652 (*Dialogo,* 207). It was decorated with fictive organ pipes in allusion to S. Cecilia (*Opus,* VI, 18^v), as well as with putti, festoons, and a crown. The Assumption of the Virgin was chosen as the subject of the altarpiece in 1638 (Cat. 40; Decr. 133).

The drawing was reworked in 1652 in conjunction with efforts to rebuild the oratory altar on a more lavish scale. In the latter half of 1651 a bequest of ▽3,000 was accepted for this purpose from the estate of Vaio Vaj; the gift was unusually attractive because the masses which it endowed could be said elsewhere than in the oratory, which lacked a sacristy and was ill-suited to anything but preaching (Decr. 294–299). Since Borromini was no longer in the active service of the Congregation, a model of the new altar was solicited from his replacement, Camillo Arcucci (Decr. 313–315). Spada attempted to block the proposed al-

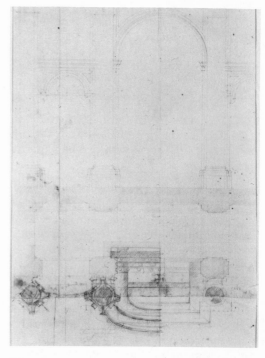

48

terations: in October 1652 he delivered a verbal critique of the design, which he expanded and submitted in written form on November 10, 1652 (text in *Dialogo,* 203–7). Basically he felt that the expenses would be high, that the acoustics would suffer, and that the alterations could never be made to harmonize with the extant design. At the same time, Borromini aired a compromise proposal which incorporated some of the proposed embellishments but attempted to minimize the aesthetic damage to the room.

The proposals of both architects are sketched at the bottom of the present sheet, where they overstep the Roman numeral scale and spread onto a strip of paper appended along the lower edge. The faint compass-drawn circles represent Arcucci's project: they show four alabaster columns installed in a straight line, tangential to the central piers but sunk into the canted pilasters at either end. The darker freehand circles represent Borromini's counterproposal, in which the columns are brought forward and rotated 45 degrees. Those at the two ends no longer cut into the canted pilasters;

those in the center create a more generous space for the altar (cf. inscription); and the four capitals echo the concave plan of the two *coretti*. This counterproposal was worked out in October or early November 1652, between the time of Arcucci's model and Spada's memorandum, which mentions it in passing (*Dialogo*, 204 ff.).

Neither the counterproposal nor the memorandum had more than a delaying effect. Arcucci's model was shown to three other architects—Arigucci, Cortona, and Rainaldi—and was approved with minor alterations on January 22, 1653 (Decr. 317, 320, 322, 323). Work proceeded slowly, and Vaj's heirs showed a constant reluctance to pay their share. Under the direction of Luca Berrettini, a marble cutting shop was established in 1654–55, the *coretti* were rebuilt, and the piers of the loggia revetted; finally in 1659 the four alabaster columns were installed and the former balustrade of the musicians' loggia was replaced by a solid architrave. The altar itself was under construction in 1660–62. After being declined by Cortona and Lazzaro Baldi in 1663, the commission for the altarpiece was finally executed by Raffaello Vanni in 1664. Arcucci had also planned a statuary program consisting of a crucifix flanked by four angels with instruments of the passion, which was in part designed to conceal the mismatch between the four alabaster columns and the webbing of the vault. At first, temporary effigies on wooden panels were installed but they were not replaced either by the marble statues originally intended or even by the stucco images which the Congregation requested in 1667. The panels are still visible in a print of 1684, though not in Giannini's prints of 1725 (Fig. 28; Cat. 104b). Ironically, the prolonged legal disputes with the Vaj heirs caused the Congregation finally to reject the endowment in 1672.

(Summary in *Dialogo,* 201–3 and 208–11; Decr. 336, 340, 358, 363, 364, 368, 369, 378–381, 406, 413, 431, 435, 436, 439, 464, 470, 471, 616.)

Bibl.: Hempel, 74, n. 4; Incisa della Rocchetta, *Dialogo,* 208–9; *Portoghesi, *Linguaggio,* Fig. xxxvii; *Portoghesi, *Disegni,* 15, cat. no. 38, Fig. 38 (dated ca. 1640 with pentimenti ca. 1650).

49.   Francesco Borromini. 1638.
Sketch of the stucco ornament of the altar loggia.
Alb. 295. 21.3 × 18.6. Graphite.
Inscriptions:
Archo Altare di S. Filipo. oratorio. cantorino.

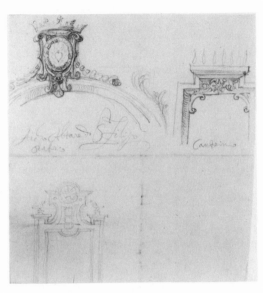

49

The sketches of stucco ornament on the upper half of the sheet were carried out in slightly modified form between November 1638 and midsummer 1639 (Doc. 15). The altar arch is shown with a large shield and crown that would have penetrated up into the balustrade zone. The motif was executed on a smaller scale (Fig. 32) but was destroyed when the altar was remodeled in 1652 ff.; its twin is still preserved on the Cardinals' loggia opposite (Fig. 34). The balusters sketched over the choir on the right still fail to alternate. Presumably the idea of alternating balusters (*Opus,* VI, 20^r) was introduced as the stucco work was under way in late 1638 or early 1639. It was repeated by the architect four times within five years, and then became something of a trademark:

ca. 1641	Campanile of S. Carlo alle Quattro Fontane. (Shown on a drawing of ca. 1667 by Bernardo Borromini, Alb. 183^r.

Bernardo dismantled the original triangular campanile and replaced it with one of four sides in 1667–70. Cf. Hempel, 179, and *Röm. Ved.,* II, Pls. 69, 70.)

Late 1641–1642   Balcony of oratory facade (Cat. 41).

1642   Naples, Filomarino altar in SS. Apostoli (Hempel, 86).

July 1644   Cloister of S. Carlo alle Quattro Fontane (Hempel, 37; Pollak, 77, reg. 241).

1664 ff.   Falconieri Chapel in S. Giovanni dei Fiorentini (*Ragguagli,* 268).

1667–76   Balcony and upper balustrade of the facade of S. Carlo alle Quattro Fontane, the latter probably by Bernardo Borromini.

The balustrade over the altar loggia in the oratory was removed and sold in 1659 (Decr. 358; *Dialogo,* 206, no. 4).

The drawing of a door with Falconieri arms on the bottom of the sheet appears to be contemporaneous with the other sketches. Orazio Falconieri purchased a Renaissance palace on the Via Giulia in July 1638, but recently published documents seem to indicate that work began only in 1646, not in ca. 1640 as Hempel supposed (Hempel, 51; Tafuri in *Via Giulia,* 445 ff.). *Bibl.:* *Hempel, 295, n. 1 and Pls. 41.2–41.4 (details); *Portoghesi, *Linguaggio,* Fig. xliii.

50.   Francesco Borromini. Date uncertain.
Project for a decorative grille.
Alb. 320^r. Graphite.
Inscription by Bernardo Borromini:
St. [Agne] Philippo . . . Chiesa [?] Nova [?]

The lilies, hearts, and stars link the project with the oratory, although it eludes more precise specification. The ornament and intersecting pointed arches suggest a decorative screen designed to allow for the passage of sound but not of sight, which would have

been appropriate for wooden grilles like those of the musicians' balconies (Fig. 32). Unpublished.

51.   Francesco Borromini. October 1638–November 1639.
Project for two spiral staircases of the casa.
Alb. 289. 45.5 × 34.1. Graphite.

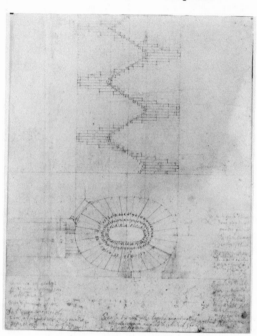

51

Inscriptions:
       4
     5 2
  3 1

[1.] Scala che va della loggia avanti alla Sagrestia all anticamera avanti la cella del s[an]to Chiesa Nova.

[2.] Questa scala tiene due girate e' quattro quinti. In tutto si sono scalini 56.

Et ogni scalino [*written over two erased lines*] sara alto oncie sei e minuti 4 dicho pm. ½ m[inu]ti 4.

E p[er]che d[et]ti scalini fuori restaranno debo[?] . . . rispetto alla sua lung.a si . . . [*five undecipherable lines*].

[3.] lumacha del oratorio p[er] ri . . . al primo giro . . . ⅚ resta di parapetto p. 4½. Del detto coro piccolo [*written over an erased line*] sino al piano del [coro ?] grande sono p.m 15¾ resta p. 5 di parap[et]to.

[4.] Scalini [*fraction erased*].

[5.] [*Steps numbered 1 to 57 in plan; 20 steps equals one complete rotation; on the 56th step:*] qui si sperdera un scalino Pianti . . . [?]

The staircase was extended from the *piano nobile* to the *loggia scoperta* between February and June 1639 (Decr. 130; Pollak, 446 ff., regs. 1852–53). Borromini concealed one full turn of the spiral behind a door and oval aperture which now houses a bust of Blessed Giovenale Ancian (Fig. 78). The inscription under the bust reads "Ioannes Iuvenalis Ancina / Unus Ex Sociis / S. Philippi Nerii / Episcopus Salutiarum." (1545–1604, bishop of Saluzzo 1602–4; cf. Gasbarri, 150 ff.).

According to inscription no. 3, the drawing was reused to gauge the measurements of the spiral staircase in the oratory, which ascends from the basement to the *cantoria (coro piccolo)* and musicians' loggia. This stairway was under construction in November 1639 (Pollak, 447, reg. 1854). Unpublished.

52.   Anonymous.
Project for a spiral staircase.
AV, C.II.8, no. 34. 43.5 × 28.6. Ink, wash, and graphite. Scale: 5 p. = 11.5 cm.

This crude drawing shows a spiral staircase of circular plan 9 palmi in diameter. Eleven steps are needed to complete one full turn, while each step drawn in ink is seven-eighths of a palmo high. In the pencil section sketched at the top of the sheet, the steps have been reduced to six-eighths of a palmo, which is still less commodious than the steps one-half palmo high in Borromini's oval *lumaca* (Cat. 51).

Of the eight spiral staircases remaining in the casa, four would appear too small for the dimensions indicated on the present drawing: the two spirals in the area of the *spetiaria* in the north wing, the spiral in the *portaria-forestaria*, and the spiral in the kitchen. The spirals in the oratory, recreation room (southwest corner, from *piano nobile* up), preacher's apartment, and over the left transept of the church all remain possible candidates (Fig. 6; Cat. 5; *Opus*, XII, 40^r). Unpublished.

53.   Francesco Borromini. 1634–41, probably 1638.
Sketch for a door and oval window for the Sala Rossa.
Alb. 660. Graphite.
Cf. Cat. 54.
Bibl.: *Hempel, 80, n. 5 and Pl. 41.5; *Portoghesi, *Linguaggio*, Fig. xlii; *Bruschi, *Palatino*, XII, 1968, 16, Fig. 5.

54.   Francesco Borromini. 1634–38, probably 1638.
Sketch for a door and oval window for the Sala Rossa.
Alb. 661. Red chalk.

The drawings were correctly identified by Bruschi as projects for the pair of fanciful doorways in the south wall of the Sala Rossa (Fig. 77; nos. 3 and 4 on Fig. 73). Although he assigned them an early date, 1635–36, there is evidence that the doors in question were not introduced until the second phase of operations on the saint's rooms in 1638–39. The corridor to the sacristy, indicated by the parallel vertical lines that flank the design on Cat. 53, was not installed until Borromini's spiral staircase was built in 1638. Furthermore, there was no need for doors in the south wall of the Sala Rossa until Borromini's relocation of the refectory blocked its north door in 1638. Once installed, the door on the right opened onto the small courtyard for three years. It was truncated in 1641 when a low corridor was built to connect it to the Cappella Esterna in the church (cf. discussion in Cat. 27).

Hempel knew both drawings but wrongly interpreted them as projects for the doors in the transept of the church, such as the portal which leads into the sacristy (Fig. 71). In fact, the transept doors are pastiches. They were executed in marble up to the cornice level in 1634 on Maruscelli's design (Doc. 11; Pollak, 435, reg. 1745). Later, black stucco volutes and gilt stucco ovals were added above this point, apparently on the model of Borromini's doors in the Sala Rossa. The exact date of this transformation is unknown: a Regnart print of 1650 still shows the north transept doors in their original state (*GR*, Parione, II, 19; Hess,

"Chiesa Nova," Fig. 14), while a print of 1721 shows the stucco volutes and oval for the first time (*Studio*, III, Pl. 20).
Bibl.: Hempel, 80, n. 5; Bruschi, *Palatino*, XII, 1968, 16.

55.   Francesco Borromini. 1634–39, probably 1638–39.
Door to the Cappelletta di S. Filippo: five pediment sketches.
Alb. 74. 18.0 × 25.2. Graphite.
Cf. Cat. 56.
Bibl.: Thelen, *70 disegni*, 15, cat. no. 22 (dated 1636); Bruschi, *Palatino*, XII, 1968, 14; Incisa della Rocchetta, "Cappella—II," 75.

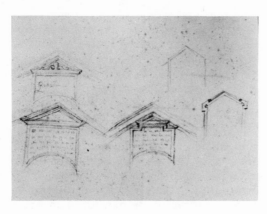

55

56.   Francesco Borromini. 1634–39, probably 1638–39.
Door to the Cappelletta di S. Filippo: measurement of the *scarpellino's* work.
Alb. 315. 26.1 × 19.2. Graphite.
Inscriptions:
inscrittione larg[a] p. 2¾ alta reg[uaglia]ta p. 2 con fondo di un giglio della medema pietra della inscrittione lung[o] p. 1¼ larg[o] ½ reg-[uagliat]o p[er] doi . . . [?] della med[ema] pietra d . . . [?] p. ½
Brocatello gira p. 24½ larg[o] ⅙
Bro . . . [?] dove sone le . . . de un pezzo reg[uaglia] to p. 1½ 1½
Lettere ducento con le stelle le piccole sono ⅛ le grande sono ⅙ e sono [numero ?] 16
Soglia della . . . [?] bigio lung[a] p. 7¾ larg[a] 1
Pavimento lung[o] reg[uagliato] p. 5½ larg[o] 2⅔
Soglia . . . [?] istello di . . . e campo nero fodre [?] di peperi[no] dui pezzi p[er] li stipiti lung. p. 10 ½ larg. 1¼ ¾

. . . [?] del Arch . . . lung. p. 8 alt. 3 grosso 1½
A 1663 [*last digit partly erased*].

Both drawings relate to an elegant green marble frame around the door which leads from the Anticamera to the Cappelletta del Santo (Fig. 80; located at no. 30 on Fig. 74). Cat. 55 contains preliminary sketches for the project, while Cat. 56 appears to postdate the door and to contain notes for the *misura e stima* by which the *scarpellino* was paid (Thelen). The attribution of the doorframe to Borromini, already evident from the style, is thus confirmed by the drawings as well as by a passage in *Opus*, VIII, 31ᵛ.

The date poses a more difficult problem. In December 1634 the Congregation approved a design for a marble door "which will serve for the transported chapel" (Decr. 92); the designer is not mentioned, but at that time Maruscelli was still the official architect. The door itself bears the misleading date 1635, which only refers to the time when the chapel was moved; the dated inscription was not even composed or inserted until 1639 (Decr. 135). In August 1636 two and a half loads of saligno marble were purchased "for the Chapel of S. Filippo," which can refer however to any one of the numerous chapels of the saint, particularly the high altar of the sacristy (Pollak, 431, regs. 1698–99). Finally in May 1639 the inscription was inserted into the doorframe "on the occasion of the ornaments carried out in the anticamera" (Decr. 134, 135). Of the three possible dates for the door—1634, 1636, or 1639—the last seems most probable. The "ornaments" mentioned in the document of 1639 most likely refer to the door, since the other ornamental work in the room—the cornice and vault fresco—had already been carried out in 1636 (Decr. 98). It is more likely that the door and its inscription were installed simultaneously rather than three or five years apart. Finally there was more reason to install an elaborate doorframe in 1638–39 than there had been previously, since the Anticamera had just become part of a frequented route between the old casa and the sacristy (Cat. 27).

Along with the travertine portal of the casa and the black marble portal of the ora-

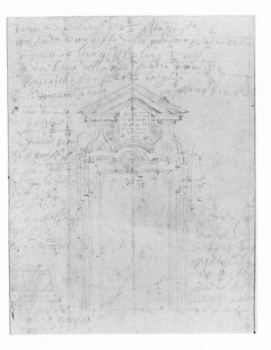

56

tory, the present door was one of three slated for illustration in the manuscript of the *Opus* (VIII, 31ᵛ).

Bibl.: Hempel, 80, n. 4; Thelen, *70 disegni,* 15, cat. no. 23 (dated 1636); Bruschi, *Palatino,* XII, 1968, 14; Incisa della Rocchetta, "Cappella— III," 75.

57. Francesco Borromini. Early 1639.
Project for the pilaster elevation of the garden court.
Alb. 301. 52.2 × 41.5. Graphite. Scale: 10 p.

Inscriptions:
[1.] Vetriate finte [*upper left arch*].
[2.] vetriate reali [*rectangular openings in the same arch*].
[3.] questo avera la proportione del ordine toscano il quale deva essere li sett . . . il basi . . . et capitelli.
li pilastri . . . si si . . . fare p[er] anco[?] del . . . [lower right edge, torn and partly illegible].

The drawing shows three bays of the loggia which was constructed in 1639–41 along the east side of the future garden courtyard; the full results of this campaign are shaded on Cat. 81. In part the loggia served a struc-

tural function: it was designed to buttress the vaults of the adjacent refectory and recreation room, although it never properly bonded with them and repairs were soon necessary (*Dialogo,* 185). The design of the giant order, arrived at here several years before it was carried over into the first courtyard, shows the influence of both Palladio and Michelangelo. The immediate source is the *Quattro libri* woodcut of the Palazzo Iseppo da Porto in Vicenza (II, 10). However, pentimenti at the lower left corner of the sheet convert the low pilaster base into a high pedestal inspired by the giant order of the Palazzo dei Conservatori. The proposed change would have involved lowering the pavement of the loggia and the courtyard by 4 palmi, until it reached the level of the sunken floor of the refectory. This drastic measure, which would have had repercussions on floor levels throughout the casa, could only have been considered early in 1639, when the refectory was just beginning; it was rejected, although the comparison to Michelangelo stuck and eventually overshadowed the immediate Palladian source (*Opus,* XIX, 53ʳ; cf. Cat. 66, inscription no. 2). Thelen's dating of the sheet

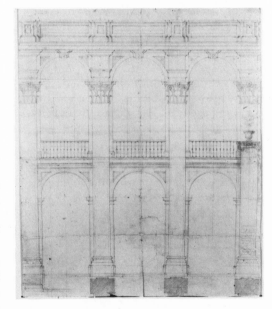

57

(1647, based on an earlier project of 1640) neglects the implications of these pentimenti, and appears to rest on the erroneous assumption that this wing of the loggia was built in 1647.

While the lower story of the loggia was to remain open to the weather, the upper story was closed in the ingenious way described in *Opus,* XVII, 49[r] and *Dialogo,* 186 ff., and indicated on the present drawing by the references to "real" and "fictive" windows. The flower pot and Ionic capital at the extreme right edge mark the awkward juncture between the giant order and the single-story pilasters that formerly lined the south side of the courtyard (Cat. 62–64). An inscription prescribes the Tuscan order for these shorter pilasters, although the drawing represents them as eight modules high rather than the usual seven (Palladio, *Quattro libri,* I, xiv).

Bibl.: Thelen, *70 disegni,* 16 ff., cat. no. 28.

58. Francesco Borromini. Late 1638–early 1639.
    Project for an oval refectory.
    Alb. 287. 45.3 × 28.8. Graphite.

The drawing represents a transitional stage between the rectangular and polygonal refectories shown on Cat. 39 and 40 and the final oval refectory, which was approved in January 1639 (Decr. 129) and is shown in Cat. 59. Although no longer polygonal, the refectory and the square staircase still intrude on the space eventually devoted to the *lavamani.* Eight tables are shown in the upper half of the oval in an attempt to gauge its seating capacity, although a final decision about their form was not made until late in 1641 (Decr. 172).
Unpublished.

59. Francesco Borromini. November 1639–January 1640.
    Plan of the casa.
    Alb. 286. 42.7 × 26.5. Total width of casa along south facade: 13.4 cm.; total length along west facade: 32.3 cm. Graphite. Scale: 200 p. in Roman numerals.

The plan was traced in outline from Borromini's early project of 1637 (Cat. 39),

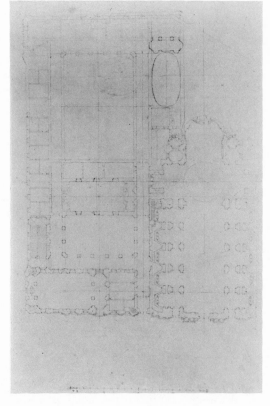

59

which it matches exactly in dimensions. It was updated by the omission of several features removed or dismantled in 1638: the kitchen-library wing behind the Vallicella apse (Cat. 40), and the narrow stairway to the saint's room (Cat. 27.II). It shows the oval refectory and the *lavamani* in their final form, which was approved in decisions of January and November 1639 (Decr. 129, 143). The main innovations proposed on the drawing concern the size and shape of the *piazza d'arme* room to the north of the *lavamani,* and concomitantly the alignment of the north wall of the casa on the Via di Parione. This street originally changed direction at the northeast corner of the church of S. Cecilia (Cat. 8). In subsequent projects (Cat. 21, 39, 40) the bend was displaced 10 palmi farther east, and on the present drawing it is moved 10 palmi more in the same direction, so that the *piazza d'arme* room is fully incorporated "nel quadro principale e gionge sino all'angolo del detto gomito" (*Opus,* XXIII, 63ʳ). In addition, the north wall of the casa is moved a short distance farther north (6 palmi on the present drawing, 3 palmi in the final building) to provide extra room for the refectory wing. As a result of this revision, the northwest corner of the casa was no longer a perfect right angle, although the imperfection was considered imperceptible on the site (Decr. 137; *Opus,* II, 6ᵛ; Cat. 80, 81).

When the *lavamani* area was under discussion in November 1639, there was still no talk of a partition wall between it and the *piazza d'arme* room, and none is shown on the present drawing (Decr. 143: "si lasci aperto, con alcuni pilastri"). A thin partition was introduced when these rooms were built, in or shortly after January 1640 (Decr. 145; Fig. 6); it effectively sealed the refectory from the place where food was prepared, but created problems of lighting (*Opus,* XX, 55ᵛ–56ʳ).

The atrium or east entrance vestibule to the oratory makes its first appearance on the present drawing, where it is carved out of the area formerly devoted to the *portaria* and audience rooms. It is shown at the same sunken level as the oratory, in accordance with a decision of April 1638 to lower floor levels throughout the south wing (Decr. 108). The door jambs shown at the east end of the vestibule were eliminated to improve lighting in September 1641 (Decr. 170; Cat. 66).
Bibl.: Hempel, 73.

60. Francesco Borromini. November 1639.
Elevation sketch of the *lavamani* area.
Alb. 1276. Ink.

The sketch shows the south wall of the *lavamani* area, with a more elaborate project for the refectory door than the one actually executed. Alternative projects are shown for the two niches which flank the central door: the simple design on the left is closer to the executed niches, while the more complicated design on the right reflects the wall opposite, where Borromini experimented

with "certe riquadrature et ovati" to increase indirect illumination (*Opus,* XX, 55ᵛ). At the extreme right of the sheet the niche that protrudes with a bulge into the adjacent loggia is shown in section. The drawing must have been done when the basic decisions on the design of the *lavamani* were taken in November 1639; by January 1640 the second floor of the wing was already under discussion (Decr. 143, 146). Unpublished.

61. Francesco Borromini. 1640–41.
Working plan of a single bay of the second courtyard; sketches for the first courtyard.
Alb. 299ʳ⁻ᵛ. 41.2 × 52.3. Graphite.
Inscriptions (recto, on the large working plan):
[1.] Agetto della cornice del tetto.
[2.] Si farano crociere [?]
[3.] Si ricorda la misura p[er] il camin dalla Sala.
(On the sketch plan of the first courtyard:)
[4.] del mezzo della porta del oratorio che riescie nel cortile al vivo del muro compreso . . . la loggia son p[almi] settantad[ue].
[5.] del vivo del fianco . . .
(Verso:)
[6.] zoccolo pm. 1⅙
[7.] Fine del Architrave della porta del Oratorio verso il cortile.

The sheet originally served as a large-scale working plan of the northeast corner of the second courtyard: it shows the northeast corner pier, one and a half bays of the adjacent eastern loggia, and sketches for the fireplace in the adjacent *sala di ricreazione.* The keystones and roof cornice lines indicate that the plan was taken at the level of the *piano nobile* rather than of the ground floor. The drawing was subsequently reworked on the site, folded in quarters, and covered with sums and notes. The dimensions penciled onto the sheet confirm the above identification: in particular, the width of the loggia (18 palmi) excludes any possibility that the plan might have been done for the first courtyard (cf. Cat. 66 and 80).

The fireplace sketches show the first steps in the evolution of the chimneypiece from a more conventional design to one in which the piers follow the ovoid curve of the man-

tle. They provide grounds for dating the
sheet after January 1640, when the *sala* was
begun, and before August 1641, when the
chimneypiece was unveiled (Decr. 146,
166).

The remainder of the sheet is devoted to
sketches of the first courtyard. A plan on the
recto shows half of the courtyard prior to
the introduction of the *nicchioni* in late 1641
(Cat. 66; Decr. 174, 175). Three sketches
on the verso show projects for the door
leading from the center of the courtyard
into the oratory, along with profile sketches
for the flanking pilaster bases. Of the three
sketches, only the second at all resembles
the executed door (Cat. 70).

Bibl.: Thelen, *70 disegni,* 17, cat. no. 29 (dated
ca. 1641–42).

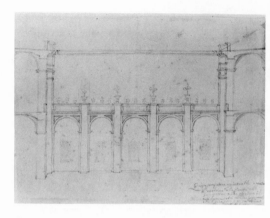

62

62.　Francesco Borromini. 1639–41.

Project for the south side of the garden
courtyard, version with low pilasters: elevation sketch.

Alb. 302. 19.9 × 26.3. Graphite.

Inscription:

Questa prospettiva aggiustarebbe a coprire il
disordine delle finestre della sagrestia senza
offendere il suo lume et si uscirebbe inpian
. . . alla loggia sopra a un . . . dori . . . [corri-
dore ?] largo p. 6.

Cf. Cat. 64.

Bibl.: Portoghesi, *Disegni,* 15, cat. no. 36.

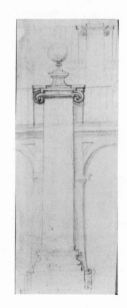

63.　Francesco Borromini. 1639–41.

Sketches of the low pilasters at the south
side of the garden courtyard.

Alb. 300^{r-v}. 26.7 × 9.4. Graphite.
Cf. Cat. 64.

Bibl.: *Hempel, pl. 41.1 (recto); *Portoghesi,
Linguaggio, Fig. xli (verso).

63

64.　Francesco Borromini. 1639–41.

Project for the south side of the garden
courtyard, version with low pilasters: sketch
plan.

Alb. 303. 13.3 × 21.8. Graphite.

Inscriptions:

Si potrano fare delli contraforti sopra il dritto
delli muri che traversarano [?] le stanze dalla
sagrestia p[er] rinforzare la volticella del cori-
dore.

64

64bis

64 bis.   Gilles Marie Oppenort. 1692–99.
View of the southeast corner of the garden courtyard.
Stockholm,   Nationalmuseum,   THC 5121.
Cf. Cat. 64.
Bibl.: *Portoghesi, *Roma barocca*, rev. ed., Bari, 1978, 178 (attributed to N. Tessin). The attribution of the sheet to Oppenort was kindly communicated to me by Börje Magnusson.

The above drawings represent Borromini's attempts to deal with problems in the design of the area between the sacristy and the garden courtyard. The structures here had to fulfill three requirements: first, to harmonize with the rest of the courtyard; second, to provide a passage across the middle of the casa at *piano nobile* level; and third, to allow adequate light into the sacristy. Maruscelli had originally designed a two-story loggia which satisfied the first two requirements but not the third (Cat. 20). In his revised project he eliminated the loggia and substituted a screen of blind arches, one story high, attached directly to the service rooms that line the north side of the sacristy (Cat. 23). The roof of these rooms was kept as

low as possible in order to allow the maximum of light into the sacristy; it is shown with a single pitch on Cat. 23a but was apparently built with a double pitch when the rooms were actually constructed in 1633 (*Opus*, XIII, 41^v; Decr. 73, 76). Passage between the east and west wings of the building was provided by an open ramp, 8 palmi wide, atop the screen of blind arches (Fig. 25; Cat. 23a).

When the giant order was introduced into the courtyard, Maruscelli's low pilasters and ramp, which had already been built along its southern end, no longer harmonized with the new design (Cat. 57). Borromini devised two alternative solutions to the problem. In the first provisional solution of 1639–41, Maruscelli's low pilasters were raised 4 or 5 palmi, changed from Tuscan to Ionic, and capped with flowerpots (Cat. 63 shows "Porta Pia motifs" as an alternative). The ramp was narrowed from 8 to 6 palmi and a buttressed "volticella" was proposed to protect it from the weather (Cat. 64). The pitched roof over the sacristy service rooms was converted to a *loggia scoperta*, which was waterproofed first in 1641 and again in 1645 (Decr. 157, 204; *Opus*, XIII, 41^v). Access to this area was to be provided via the two staircases sketched on Cat. 64.

Borromini's second, more drastic alternative was first mentioned in Decr. 158 of 1641, then discussed at greater length in *Opus*, XIII, 41^v–42^r and shown on Cat. 85g. He wanted to continue the giant order along the south side of the courtyard, where it would form a transparent screen for most of its height. The project satisfied the requirements of illumination and of unity of design, but it failed to provide a convenient passage across the casa. Maruscelli's ramp would have been destroyed and cross-traffic shifted to the *loggia scoperta* over the service rooms, which could only be reached by descending 11 palmi (about 15 steps) on one side of the building and climbing the same height at the other. The project was still unexecuted by the time Borromini left the commission in 1650.

In 1659 ff. the west wing of the casa was completed by Camillo Arcucci (Cat. 92–95). Maruscelli's open ramp was preserved and finally equipped with the necessary iron railings. The *loggia scoperta* over the sacristy service rooms was replaced by a pitched roof (Decr. 397, 400, 417). The new arrangement is visible on an interesting drawing in a sketchbook by Gilles Marie Oppenort now in Stockholm (Cat. 64 bis) which, it may be assumed, dates to the period of this artist's Italian sojourn, 1692–99 (Thieme-Becker, XXVI, 31 ff.). It depicts the southeast angle of the garden court, including the sacristy (shown in section), the sacristy service rooms with their pitched roof, and Maruscelli's screen of arches and walkway, which is protected by iron railings attached to freestanding Ionic capitals of about waist height. In all of these features Oppenort agrees with the print in the *Opus* of 1725 (Fig. 25); his view is more picturesque, however, in that it shows vines reaching up to the level of the *loggia scoperta*. Of the two other sketches on the same sheet the one on the upper left, a shell fountain, has yet to be identified; the one on the upper right, a rustic fountain with four superimposed basins, may possibly be Arcucci's fountain of 1661 in the garden courtyard of the casa (Doc. 24), which is not recorded in any other print or drawing.

The arrangement shown by Oppenort continued to function until approximately 1871, when the whole area was drastically altered by the construction of a large courthouse in the three southern bays of the garden (Figs. 81, 83; Cat. 115a–115d). The open ramp was reinforced by iron struts and turned into a closed corridor. The roof over the sacristy service rooms was once again waterproofed and turned into a *loggia scoperta,* though without convenient means of access. Behind these alterations a few surviving remnants of the original system can still be seen: Maruscelli's ramp, and the open arches of the screen that once formed the southern boundary of the courtyard (Fig. 81).

Bibl.: Portoghesi, *Disegni,* 14, cat. no. 34 (with the mistaken assertion that the two staircases descend to the ground floor).

65.   Francesco Borromini. Ca. 1641.
Projects for the systematization of the Donati Chapel near the body of S. Filippo.

65a.   Altar project.
Bibl. Vall., 0 57², fol. 361ʳ.
Inscription: piano sotto alla cassa del Santo.

65b.   Plan of locale.
Op. cit., fol. 361ᵛ.
Inscriptions: cassa. alta p. 4 luce.

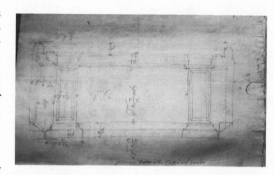

65a

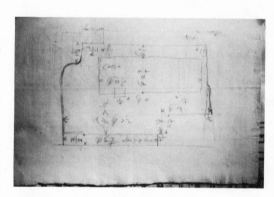

65b

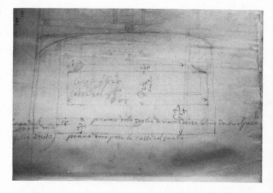

65c

65c. Section of altar.
Op. cit., fol. 360ʳ.
Inscriptions:
    vano del paliotto. cassa larg[a] p. 2¾. cassa del
S[an] to p. 8⅙ p. 2½ scarzo [?]. piano della
soglia di marmo verso l'altare adietro al pr[i]n-
c[ipa]lle [?]. linea del matonato della capelle adietro. piano dove possa la cassa del santo.

The drawings deal with the last in a long
series of translations, depositions, and sys-
tematizations of the body of S. Filippo before modern times:

1595	Death and burial under the presbytery of S. Maria in Vallicella.
1595–99	Body immured in a chamber over the right transept of the church.
1599–1602	Body deposited in a cypress casket lined with velvet, which is kept in the same chamber.
1602–38	Body and cypress casket together are deposited in a larger walnut casket, which is on display under the altar in the Cappella Esterna (Fig. 73, no. 15).
1638	Body is temporarily hidden in order to thwart D. Anna Colonna Barberini's request for a relic. Finally it and the cypress casket are deposited together inside an ironbound casket displayed in the Cappella Esterna.
1642–43	The Cappella Interna (Fig. 73, no. 16) is transformed into a sepulchral chapel for the Donati family.
1922	Recognition of the body, which is removed from both the cypress and ironbound caskets and deposited in its present coffin of glass and bronze.

The present drawings show plans to sys-
tematize the Donati Chapel so that its altar
would be located in close proximity to the
saint's body, which had been displayed
under the altar of the Cappella Esterna since
1602. The drawings deal particularly with

the problem of slight misalignment and difference in floor level between the two chapels. They imply that Borromini was involved in the more routine architectural
aspects of the Donati Chapel project in
1641–43; however, his connection with its
interior decoration still remains tenuous (cf.
Cat. 27.III). The "cassa del santo" shown in
plan and elevation is apparently the iron-
bound casket first fabricated in 1638. The
drawings offer no evidence for Borromini's
authorship of a perforated and decorated
wooden coffin, admittedly close to his style,
which is now on display in the Sala Rossa
(Strong, Pl. 32; Bruschi, 16, 18, Fig. 7,
where the coffin is attributed to Borromini
and dated prior to 1638; Incisa della Rocchetta, "Cappella—III," 94, where a duplicate of the coffin at the Tor de' Specchi is
mentioned).
Bibl.: Portoghesi, *Cultura,* Fig. 28 (Cat. 65a);
Bruschi, "Stanze," 21, n. 16. Full literature on
the rooms of S. Filippo is cited above in Cat. 27.

66. Francesco Borromini. September–
November 1641.
Project for the completion of the *portaria*
and first courtyard.
Victoria and Albert Museum, E 510–
1937ʳ⁻ᵛ. 39.7 × 53.9. Graphite. Scale in
Roman numerals: 100 p. = 21.6 cm.
Inscriptions on recto:
    [1. *Left side of courtyard:*] no[n] facendo divis-
ione s'invitano li medemi ornamen[ti] co[n] li
pilastri . . . overo . . . desdicevole sta . . . senza
difesa e pocho grata alla vista anzi quasi intolera-
bile.
    [2. *Right side of courtyard:*] facendo divisione
non si e obligato a cosa nesuna . . . nella
nicchia[?] . . . delli Greci e Romani si ved . . . di
esempio in [?] Vitruvio Paladio Serlio et altri
Autori.
    [3. *Inside door of oratory:*] se si trovassero p[er]
casa sei colonne di granito o altro che potessero
servire sen[on] si faran[no] di matoni ma bisognera farle poggiate al muro p[er] poterle in-
catenare co[n] esso [?] accio sian[o] sicure.
    [4. *Between first two chapels of S. Maria in Val-
licella:*] fondamento . . . di . . . [*two indecipherable
lines*] . . . in tutto.
    [5. *Above scale:*] muro del oratorio.
    [6. *Below scale:*] entrata. mezzo del oratorio.
    [7. *Lower right corner:*] Anche p[er] il fond-
[amen]to del tramezzo.

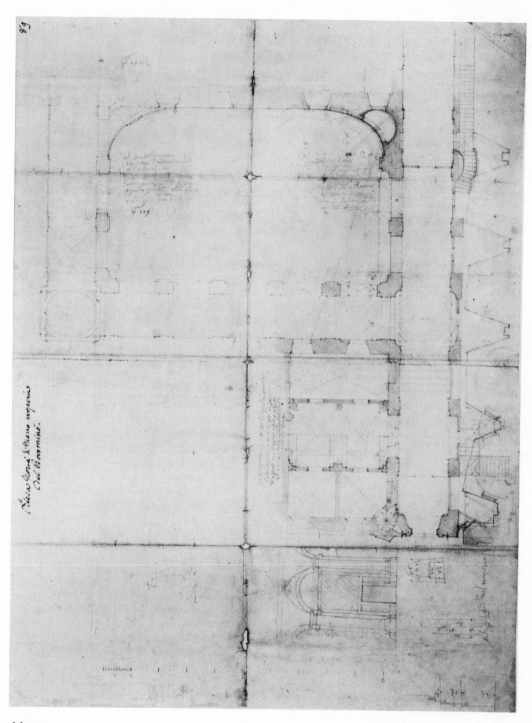

66 recto

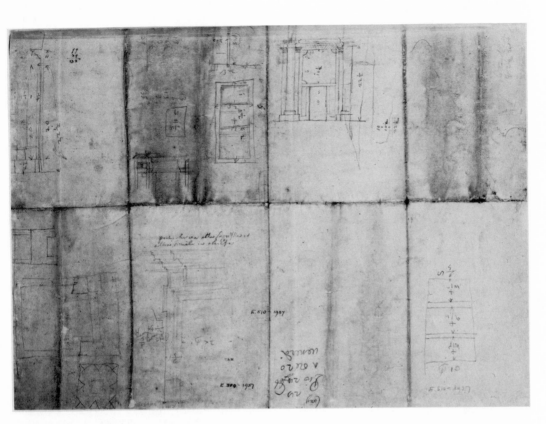

66 verso

[8. *Left edge of sheet in Bernardo Borromini's hand:*]
Chiesa Nova di mano propria del Boromino. 89.

Inscriptions on verso:
[9. *Upper right corner in red chalk:*] le tavole
. . . p. 2½ reg[uaglia]te larg . . .
[10. *Left center in pencil but not by Borromini:*]
porta che va alla sagrestia et altra simile in chiesa.
[11. *Bottom center:*] Cong[regatio]ne Pio 28
feb a ore 20 venerdi.

The drawing originally showed a plan of the
first courtyard and *portaria* at a stage close to
Cat. 59, which was then reworked to alter
three interconnected aspects of the design:
first, the *portaria;* second, the juncture between the courtyard and the sacristy; and
third, the wall of the casa which adjoins the
west flank of S. Maria in Vallicella. The
changes in each of these areas will be
analyzed in turn.

1. *Portaria.* Originally, both Maruscelli
and Borromini planned only two entrances
for the oratory, one from the courtyard, and

one directly from the street (Cat. 21, 39).
The third entrance was first introduced by
Borromini on Cat. 59 in late 1639. It took
the form of a narrow closed vestibule,
carved out of the area formerly allotted to
audience chambers and the porter's lodge,
and joined to the oratory through a door
pierced in the *muro maestro* already built at
the eastern end of the oratory (contrast Cat.
39 with Cat. 59). The vestibule received no
direct illumination, and so in September
1641 the Congregation decided to dispense
with one of its doors and turn it into an open
atrium (Decr. 170). The present drawing
and its pentimenti reflect the situation both
before and after this decision.

The drawing records two proposals for
the design of the atrium. One alternative,
reminiscent of an ancient thermal hall (*Opus,*
VI, 18[r]), envisaged a groin vault resting on
six granite columns. The second alternative
called for a barrel vault and a corridor ar-

ticulated by superimposed pilasters. A single bay of this solution is sketched on the verso of the sheet; it did not depend on a chance find of columns, and it became the alternative that was finally executed (Cat. 86k). In the finished building the atrium was flanked by four small chambers (*Opus,* IX, 32ᵛ mentions "tre camerini" plus the porter's room). The drawing, however, shows only three: possibly the large vaulted room with a fireplace shown to the north of the atrium was designed either for the fratelli of the oratory, or for the *palafrenieri* who remained below while their masters ascended to the *piano nobile* (*Opus,* XXVI, 71ʳ). In accord with a decision of April 1638 (Decr. 108), the entire *portaria* area is designed to be on the same level as the oratory. Six steps span the difference of 4 palmi between the *portaria* and the first courtyard; a railing at the top is proposed to restrict entry further into the casa; and the *seditori* make their first appearance in the form of a quarter circle drawn at the right side of the lower steps (*Opus,* IX, 34ʳ).

2. *Nicchioni.* The drawing was folded in the manner of what Thelen calls a "pocket sheet" (C 57, p. 70), and then apparently taken to the site and used by Borromini to explain his design during a consultation with two outside architects, G. B. Soria and Francesco Contini (Decr. 174). The *nicchioni* were used to solve a problem inherited from Maruscelli: they disguised the extra bay added to the closed corridor between the church and sacristy, and this extra bay in turn assured symmetry around Maruscelli's twin marble doors, which are sketched on the verso of the sheet and identified in inscription no. 10. Inscription no. 1 dismisses an alternative solution, sketched on the left side of the courtyard, as an offense against the rules of architecture. Inscription no. 2 justifies the *nicchioni* on the authority of antique and Renaissance authors, possibly marshaled to convince the two outside consultants. Nothing on the drawing corroborates the claim made in Decr. 174 and *Opus,* X, 35ᵛ that the *nicchioni* improved the lighting of the small rooms at either end of the sacristy: the window of the small chamber on the right remained a constant 5 palmi

wide even after the alterations, while the small chamber on the left was planned and built without windows altogether. Finally, the blind windows which were designed as twins to the actual windows of the sacristy, and which solved the problem explained in *Opus,* X, 35ʳ⁻ᵛ, make their first appearance on the present drawing.

3. *Area between the casa and S. Maria in Vallicella.* The drawing proposes solutions to three problems of circulation and illumination in this area. First, it shows an awkward attempt to shift the entrance to the narrow stairway built by Maruscelli in 1634 between the sacristy corridor and the church. Before the completion of the main *scalone* these stairs offered the most convenient route to and from the living quarters of the casa (Decr. 195; *Opus,* XII, 40ʳ). The *nicchioni* solution and the enlargement of the sacristy corridor threatened to seal the stairs from public access, so that the entrance had to be moved from its former location (Cat. 39) to a new one farther south (Fig. 6; Cat. 66ʳ).

Second, the drawing attempts to deal with the problem of lighting the chapels on the west side of the Vallicella. The new casa was expected to block light from the west, and so compensatory efforts were made to keep this part of the building as translucent as possible. A sketch at the bottom of the recto shows a solution for a single bay of the east wall of the loggia: the lower part of the bay is walled up with a small door in the center; the upper part appears to be glazed; the lunette appears to be open. A similar solution is shown on Cat. 85a; the open lunettes appear to be prescribed in an obscure decree of September 1641 (Decr. 171: "si muri, poi, fra un pilastro e l'altro con mattoni in piano").

Third, the drawing shifts to the *piano nobile* in an attempt to deal with the problem of access from the casa to the open loggia over the side chapels of the church (Cat. 20b, nos. 11 and 12). (The loggia is now occupied by the Biblioteca Romana of the Archivio Capitolino). It proposes a stairway that begins in the center of the three-bay gallery next to the *forestaria,* and ascends fifteen risers over the semi-dome of the first side chapel of the Vallicella. This stairway corresponds exactly to the description in *Opus,* XXVI, 72ʳ; it is replaced in the present building by a modern stairway that follows the same route. The gallery itself was to be lit by a single window, located in the oratory facade immediately above the entrance portal of the casa (Cat. 41); this window is sketched on the verso of the sheet (upper half, second folded compartment, shown inverted with the edge of the curved facade on the left and the brick *bugnato* on the right).

Only one of the other sketches on the verso can be identified with certainty (lower half, bottom of the first folded compartment). It shows a preliminary scheme for the vault of the guest rooms above the porter's lodge, complete with the ingenious spiral staircase embedded in the corner (*Opus,* XXVI, 71ᵛ).

Inscription no. 8 seems to indicate that Borromini's nephew Bernardo included the present drawing as the eighty-ninth sheet in a set, and that he was anxious to assert its autograph quality. The museum records tell only that the drawing was purchased with two unrelated drawings for £75 on June 18, 1937 from a Dr. H. Burg.

Unpublished. Kindly brought to my attention by Rolf Ermeller.

67. Francesco Borromini. Late 1641, revised ca. 1648.

Project for the entrance portal of the casa. AV, C.II.6, Pl. XXXV. 32.4 × 25.3, with a strip of 3.3 cm. added on the left. Graphite. Scale (in Roman numerals, cf. Cat. 28): 30 p. = 20.2 cm.

Cf. Cat. 68.

Bibl.: *Portoghesi, *Linguaggio,* Fig. xl; *Ragguagli,* 94.

68. Francesco Borromini. November 2, 1641.

Project for the entrance portal of the casa: one elevation sketch and six profile studies. Alb. 304. 21.4 × 15.8. Ink.

Inscription: Die 2 Novembris 1641.

The main portal of the casa is first depicted in relatively conventional form on the Windsor drawing of 1638 (Cat. 41). It is shown in a more highly evolved stage on Cat. 67, which was drawn originally as a presentation project for the door: the oval window was set on the same plane as the flat strip in the enframing pediment. The design was further refined in the ink sketch shown in Cat. 68: the oval window was recessed and the enframing members undercut in order to emphasize vertical continuity between the jambs and the upper zone. This area of the casa first came under discussion in April 1641, and was in construction between September and November of that year (Decr. 159, 162, 170; Cat. 66.3); the inscription on Cat. 68 appears to indicate the date when the portal was begun.

After the presentation drawing (Cat. 67) had served its purpose, it was folded into six parts in the manner of Borromini's "pocket sheets" (Thelen, C 57, p. 70). Sometime after 1647 Spada inserted it into the manuscript of the *Opus,* where it remains the only autograph drawing by the architect. Shading was added to the upper portion, and the members around the oval were redrawn to emphasize the undercutting of the moldings. The revisions are somewhat clumsy: either Borromini was being overemphatic for the benefit of a printmaker, or they were done by another hand altogether.

The revised drawing was copied twice: once by the third draftsman of the *Opus,* Anonymous C, who used pinpricks to reproduce the exact dimensions of the door and who imitated even the Roman numerals of the scale (*Opus* MS, Pl. XXXIV; Cat. 86j); and a second time by Giannini in 1725 (Cat. 110.XIII).

Unpublished.

69. Francesco Borromini. Date uncertain.

Plan of the facade of S. Maria in Vallicella.

Alb. 659. Graphite.

Inscriptions:
facciata Chiesa Nova. [*Left portal:*] alta luce p. 19. [*Center portal:*] Alta luce p.m 28¼.

The plan omits the door and corner pilasters at the right side of the facade. There are no grounds for dating the sheet. Possibly Borromini became interested in the dimensions of the church doors when he was designing

67

the doors of the oratory (clear height of 22 palmi on Fig. 156) and of the casa (20 palmi on Cat. 67).
Unpublished.

70. Francesco Borromini. 1641–43.
   Elevation project for the door to the oratory from the first courtyard.
     Alb. 313. 22.9 × 18.9. Graphite.

The door shown here is a simpler variant of the outer entrance portal to the oratory as it was projected on the Windsor drawing (Cat. 41). It lacks the salomonic columns and elaborate upper moldings of the exterior door but performs the same dual function: the lower part opens onto the entrance loggia of the oratory, while the upper window provides illumination for the light box immediately inside. The difference of 4 palmi between the level of the courtyard and the level of the oratory accounts for the difference in clear height between the two doors. The preliminary sketches on Cat. 61 of 1640–41 grapple with the problem of dual function without approaching the final form of the door. The loggia along the south side of the first courtyard was completed in the summer of 1643, and the door presumably was finished by that time as well. The drawing appears to have been taken up by Giannini in 1725 as the basis for *Opus,* Pl. XXXV.
Bibl.: Thelen, *70 disegni,* 16, cat. no. 26 (dated ca. 1640).

71. Francesco Borromini. 1642–43.
   Window of the room over the sacristy: four elevation sketches and a molding profile.
     Alb. 311. 18.2 × 25.5. Graphite.
Inscriptions:
Si fara questo p[er] non tocare il tetto et romp-[e]re la cornice. Questa. questo.
   Cf. Cat. 72.
Bibl.: *Hempel, 74, n. 1 and Pl. 44.1; *Portoghesi, *Linguaggio,* Fig. xlviii; *Portoghesi, *Disegni,* 15, cat. no. 37 and Fig. 37.

72. Francesco Borromini. 1642–43.
   Window of the room over the sacristy: plan and elevation.
     Alb. 310. 16.3 (center of sheet) × 14.6. Graphite. Scale: 15 p. (marked along the baseline of the elevation).

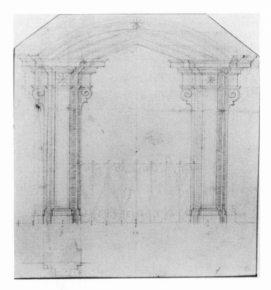

72

Three of the four sketches on Cat. 71 derive from the Porta Pia; they combine the triangular and segmental pediments of Michelangelo's gateway with its polygonal arch in a variety of ways. The fourth and largest sketch omits the polygonal element and draws more heavily on Giacomo della Porta's window in the central bay of the Palazzo dei Conservatori. The window in this version is fully as wide as the pair of real and fictive windows in the sacristy below (Fig. 50; this device was introduced on Cat. 66^r and is explained in *Opus,* X, 35^{r-v}). Its pediment breaks the cornice line and rises into the area of the roof. In the end, the lower and narrower version sketched at the left was preferred; it was redrawn in orthogonal elevation in Cat. 72, where pentimenti show the architect's efforts to narrow the opening still further. In the executed window, the triangular pediment of the drawing was simplified, while the molding profiles were made more intricate (*Opus,* Pls. LI, LIII), and the iron balustrade was built on a curved plan (Fig. 51).

   Documents do not provide an exact date for the window, but they do indicate that the roof, on which its height depends, was built by March 1642, and that the loggia along the south side of the courtyard, which figured in decisions about the window's width and placement, was under way in August 1643 (Decr. 181, 195). Although the window survived the later transformation of the casa into a tribunal (1871 ff.), it was destroyed in the restorations of 1922–24. *Bibl.:* Hempel, 74, n. 1.

73.   Francesco Borromini. 1643
   Project for the entrance vestibule to the main *scalone.*
   Alb. 314. 25.2 × 19.7. Graphite.
Inscriptions:
   [1.] Verso la scala si fara Architrave fregio et cornice assieme Alta p. 3½ overo p. 3¾ questa [quanta ?] . . . p. 3½ questo [quanto ?]
   [2.] sodo rilevato e non sf[og]ato [?]

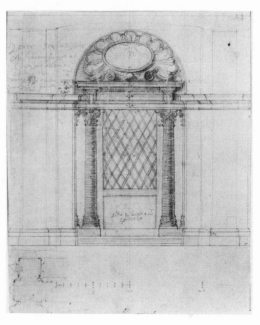

73

Maruscelli's main stairway had no entrance vestibule and had been criticized as relatively uninviting (Cat. 20, 23). In his earliest consultation project, Borromini altered the design so that the first long flight ran along the courtyard rather than along the street; thus space was created on the landing for a vestibule and an adjacent chapel or sacristy (Cat. 29; Decr. 299). The theme of corner columns appears for the first time in this drawing; it recurs in the Victoria and Albert project for an oratory vestibule (Cat. 66^r, with antique shafts ca. 18 palmi high), and again finally in the staircase vestibule as executed (Figs. 56, 57). The present drawing shows columns with shafts 14 palmi high resting on the flowery bases described in *Opus,* XI, 37^r. They support a flat entablature, which in turn supports the floor of two small chambers designed as rehearsal rooms for the musicians. Access to these rooms was provided via the oratory spiral staircase, and indirect light through two oval windows facing north (Fig. 55) and east (Fig. 56). The heavily reworked shell motif that enframes one of these ovals on the present drawing was left unexecuted. The plan of the vestibule area is shown in a sketch at the lower left corner of the sheet: the space closer to the courtyard is given a diamond coffer and four corner columns; while the space closer to the street is given a door to the oratory on the left, a window in the center, and a door to a storage room for benches on the right (*Opus,* XI, 37^{r-v}).

The entrance vestibule was presumably constructed in mid-1643 together with the adjoining loggia along the south side of the courtyard (Decr. 178, 179, 195); the *scalone* itself, however, was left incomplete until the west wing of the casa was built under Camillo Arcucci in 1659 ff. (Cat. 93–96). The juncture between these two campaigns can be seen in the present staircase; the flat architrave, described in inscription no. 1 on the present drawing, is by Borromini, while the elaborate moldings of the upper zone are Arcucci's work, similar to the moldings around the Attila relief and elsewhere in the staircase. Even before the *scalone* was in use, however, the columnar vestibule served as a ceremonial gateway to the guest quarters of the casa; the main route to the *forestaria* between 1643 and 1660 led along the courtyard loggia, through the entrance vestibule, up the spiral stairway of the oratory, and back along the same loggia at *piano nobile* level (Decr. 195).

The present sheet bears some resemblance to the drawings that were promised but not provided to illustrate *Opus,* XI, 37^v: a plan of the staircase, elevation of its entrance vestibule, and section of its second

flight together with a section of the musicians' choir of the oratory. It was evidently unknown to Giannini, however, whose print of the vestibule (Fig. 57) appears to derive from the building as it stood in 1725.
Bibl.: *R. Pacini, "Alterazioni dei monumenti borrominiani . . .," *Studi sul Borromini,* I, Rome, 1967, 355, Fig. 26 (detail); Thelen, *70 disegni,* 16, cat. no. 27 (1640, reworked 1645–47).

74. Francesco Borromini. Date uncertain.
Projects for an unidentified fountain: nine plans and five elevation sketches.
Alb. 336. 25.7 (right edge) × 39.3. Graphite.
Inscription: Si fara Questa.

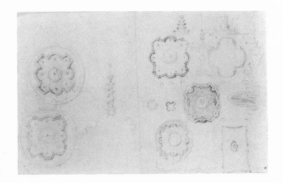

74

Five of the nine plans are variations of a common fountain type, in which a small circular basin stands at the center of a more complex basin, which in turn is placed at the center of a large round basin, or *pescheria.* Of the other four plans, the one at the upper right is closer to a fountain type characteristic of Giacomo della Porta; the small octagon resembles the wellhead of the cloister of S. Carlo alle Quattro Fontane; the adjacent plan resembles the plan of a Corinthian capital; and the plan located in a courtyard on the lower right loosely resembles a project for the garden fountain of the casa (Cat. 39). The elevations on the right half of the sheet show the circular centerpiece common to all the larger plans; the spiral column on the left introduces a motif more common to villa architecture (C. D'Onofrio, *La Villa Aldobrandini di Frascati,* Rome, 1963, Figs. 78, 79, 86, 90).

There is no firm evidence for assigning the sheet to the Casa dei Filippini, beyond a general similarity of proportion between the garden courtyard and the sketch on the lower right. If the number 30 inscribed under one of the plans can be taken as a measurement in palmi, then the basin would be slightly larger than the one projected on Cat. 39, which measures 21 × 35 palmi. Several fountains are mentioned in the *Opus* (36^v, 51^v, 41^r) but unfortunately none of them is described in detail: one was projected for the center of the first courtyard, another for the *piano nobile* of the garden court, and several others for the garden itself. A garden fountain was under consideration in 1641 (Decr. 163), but none is shown in Barrière's print of 1658 (Cat. 89c). The garden was in fact laid out under Arcucci in 1661, and lead conduits for several fountains were installed in 1677 (Decr. 394, 513; Doc. 24). A rustic fountain consisting of four superimposed basins with dolphins supporting the top basin is shown on the same sheet as a sketch by Oppenort of the garden courtyard (Cat. 64 bis); there is the possibility that this is Arcucci's fountain, which is not recorded elsewhere. The present fountain with a single rustic basin was installed in the center of the reduced courtyard after 1871; nothing is known of its ancestry.
Bibl.: *Hempel, 79, Pl. 42; *Portoghesi, *Linguaggio,* Fig. xlix; Portoghesi, *Disegni,* 14, cat. no. 33; *Blunt, *Borromini,* Cambridge, Mass., 1979, 49 ff., Fig. 40.

75. Francesco Borromini. 1642.
Partial plan of the library: one short end and two bays of a longer side.
Alb. 297. 41.1 × 29.4. Graphite.
Inscriptions:
Pianta delle scanzie del 2do piano. [*Not autograph.*] Libraria Chiesa Nova.
Cf. Cat. 76.
Unpublished.

76. Francesco Borromini. 1642.
Plan of the library and its coffered ceiling.
Alb. 288. 23.6 × 36.9. Graphite. Scale: 60 palmi.

The plan juxtaposes two interconnected elements of the design: the upper story of the oratory facade and the library *salone* which stood directly behind it. The facade is drawn with two separate curvatures, the shallower of the two corresponding to the lower story of the facade and the deeper to the upper story. The *salone* is lit by nine windows and connected to the exterior balcony by a door in the middle of the south wall (Fig. 67). The coffered ceiling outlined on the plan was described in detail in the carpenter's contract of November 15, 1642 (Doc. 17). Since the room could not support a vault, the ceiling had to be waterproofed by giving the roof a steep pitch and by interposing a layer or "floor" of tight-fitting chestnut boards between the roof and ceiling (Doc. 17, clauses 2, 3, 11, which explain the expression "mattonare il soffitto" used in *Opus*, XXVIII, 77ʳ). Although the carpenter was guided by both a model and a mock-up of the ceiling, not all of its details were fixed at the outset: the octagons suggested in the contract (clause 13) were later changed to stars. The swelling volutes of the central bay are still not shown on the present drawing, and Romanelli's grisaille painting of *Divine Wisdom* appears to have been painted originally on a simple square panel and only subsequently adapted to the volutes. According to the contract, the ceiling was to be finished by May 1643; the beams were tinted, presumably the color of travertine, in December 1643 (Pollak, 445, reg. 1841; *Opus*, XXVIII, 77ʳ).

The ceiling was enlarged in 1666, shortly after the extension of the library *salone* (Cat. 100). The westernmost bay, which originally had consisted of square coffers, was converted to volutes to match the former central bay, and two new bays were added at the western end. Symmetry of a sort was retained but the strong central accent was lost. Two of Giannini's prints confuse the design by showing a ceiling with either four or eight bays (Fig. 27 and *Opus*, Pl. XLVIII), instead of the original five bays or the seven which existed in his day and in the present room.
Unpublished.

77.   Francesco Borromini. 1643.
Project for the library shelves.
Alb. 296. 40.5 × 27.3. Graphite.
Inscriptions: 1 2
                             3
[1.] Piano sotto al soffito.
[2.] long. p. 102⁷/₁₂, [larga] p. 57¹/₁₂.
[3.] Libraria Chiesa Nova.

Inscribed dimensions:
Lower story of bookshelves, from bottom to top: 2¹/₆, 2, ²/₃, 1, 1¾, ¾, 1⁷/₁₂, 1¹/₃, 1¹/₆, 1¹/₆ [*total:* 13½ palmi].
Upper story, from bottom to top: 2¹/₈, 1¾, 1¹/₅, 2¹/₁₂, 1¾, 1¼, 7 [*distance from top shelf to top of window*] [*total:* 17¹⁹/₁₂₀ = *about* 17¹/₆ palmi].
Ledge below window: 3¾.
Clear height of window: 13.

The decision to put the library behind the upper part of the oratory facade (Cat. 40) caused problems with the shelving system on the interior. On the one hand, the Oratorians insisted on salvaging the shelves from their old library, which amounted to seven tiers of wooden boards totaling about 10 palmi in height. On the other hand, the windows in the new room were inordinately high; the room measured 19 palmi from the floor to the window sills, and 32 palmi from the floor to the top of the windows (scaled from the Windsor drawing, Cat. 41). The problem was to prevent the old shelves from being dwarfed in the large new room. Borromini's solution was worked out on the present drawing, incorporated into a contract signed with the carpenter on September 20, 1643 (Doc. 18), and explained in detail in *Opus*, XXVIII, 75ʳ–79ᵛ.

First he supplemented the old shelving with three additional tiers, bringing it to a total height of 13½ palmi. He then added a second story of six new tiers (the "sei divisioni" of Doc. 18, clause 10), which added a further 10 palmi of shelving. Access to this second story was provided by four spiral staircases in the corners of the room; they ascended to a narrow wooden ramp that ran around the entire library; decorative carvings from the old shelves were reused as a parapet ("corona") for this precarious route (Figs. 65–67). Borromini had at first intended to support this ramp with forty-four Tuscan columns of walnut, and provision for these was written into the carpenter's contract. But then he became aware of just how huge these columns would be: 13½ palmi high and 2 palmi thick, according to "la debita proportione conforme le regole d'architettura" (*Opus*, XXVIII, 78r; cf. Palladio, *Quattro libri*, I, 17). Worried about the visibility of the lower shelves and problems of supplying wood, he abandoned the colonnade for a series of tall, lithe balusters that supported the walkway without obstructing vision. A postscript added to the contract instructs the carpenter to follow the example of a trial baluster which was by then in place. (The problem of the sources of the balusters is treated in *Dialogo*, 190 ff., n. 40.)

In their final form the shelves were adequately proportioned to the exceptional dimensions of the room, with space for a third story to accommodate growth in the collection. The gap between the ramp and the windows was narrowed still more by lowering the window sills 3¾ palmi without altering the glazed area; outfitted with benches and tables, these narrow ledges became study alcoves, interrupting the upper story of shelving every few feet. In contrast, the shelving of the lower story was continuous except for interruptions at the three doors. Fictive bookbindings by the lay brother G. A. Iannarelli provided visual continuity at the corners, simultaneously deceiving *(ingannare)* and pleasing the eye (*Opus*, XXVIII, 79v; *Dialogo*, 191, n. 42; payments to a G. A. Jacomelli for "figure e libri finti" between April and June 1644 are recorded in Pinto, *La Biblioteca Vallicelliana*, 68, n. 2). Filippo's own books were assembled and put in a special case opposite the balcony door in 1654 (Decr. 338, 427).
Bibl.: Hempel, 81.

78. Francesco Borromini. 1643.
Project for the doors of the library *salone:* two half-alternatives.
Alb. 325. 19.0 × 13.3. Graphite.
Inscriptions:
P[er] la libraria RR. PP. Chiesa Nova.
fu fatta questa meta in opera.
soglia.
p. 7½ con li batenti . . . verso le loggie.

Since the *salone* of the library was entered from closed spaces at either end (from nos. 7 and 12 on Cat. 100), its doors were not required to seal out noise or weather, and could thus be designed as wooden screens, "la porta traforata" (*Opus*, XXVIII, 76r). The carpenter responsible for the library shelves and ceiling, Rosciani, was paid for various doors in 1643 (Doc. 19; Pollak, 445, regs. 1838–41). Of the two alternatives shown on the present drawing, the one on the right was finally put into execution. The design is close to a similar *cancello* at the Palazzo Spada, the one which stands at the center of the left side of the courtyard and at present allows a view into the perspective colonnade; it was installed under Maruscelli's direction in 1641–42, although it appears that both Borromini and Bernini were active in some unidentified way in this wing of the palace (Neppi, *Palazzo Spada,* 147).

The door at the western end of the library was boarded up in 1647 when some of the small nearby annexes were used as residential rooms (Decr. 214); it was removed altogether in 1665 when the *salone* was expanded to its present size. The door at the eastern end is still in place (Fig. 65).
Bibl.: *Hempel, 82, Pl. 40.4 (cropped).

79. Attributed to Virgilio Spada. Late 1644.
Critique of a project for a chapel adjoining the east transept of S. Maria in Vallicella.
Bibl. Vallicelliana, Cod. 0 57², fol. 364. Graphite.

The project is discussed in Cat. 39.III above. The attribution to Virgilio Spada is based on the close fit between the drawing and the project discussed and criticized in Doc. 29, which is in Spada's hand; since the plan itself is amateur and schematic, a secure attribution would not have been possible on the basis of graphic style alone.
Bibl.: Portoghesi, *Disegni,* 13 (cautiously attributed to Virgilio Spada).

80. Francesco Borromini. May 1647.
Project for the north wing and the Monte Giordano projection.
BV, Vat. lat. 11257, fol. 152. 31.1 ×

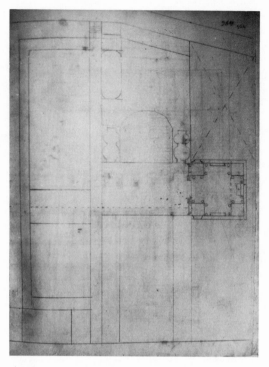

79

44.5. Graphite. Damage along bottom of sheet. Scale: 100 p. = 14.4 cm.
Inscriptions—recto (reading counterclockwise):
p[al]mi 18 il vivo. Giardino. 18 il vivo. sp[e]t-[iar]ia. spe.tia. Strada Papale. fond[amen]to [?]. Sala. Anticamera. Camera. Camera. p[al]mi 71½ il [risalto] gia fatto ... p[al]mi 37 della cima delli pilastri che gira[no] sotto la volta. Piazza di Monte Giordano. p[al]mi meglio 80 [?].

verso (from Thelen):
A di 20 Aprile. Secondo fondamento nella Strada Pappale. fondo pm. 36 della soperficie del zoccolo detto, grosso reg[uagliato] pm. 7 lungo pm. 22½ reg[uagliato] si defalca pm 14½ tra un fondamento e l'altro dove si fa un archo sopra al muro Auto fondo dal piano del zoccolo pm. 20 senza la imposta.
A di 14 Maggio 1647 Fondamento incontro alla Nave vicino alla Nave grande fondo pm. 42¾ con un stracc[i]o sotto al muro della chiesa grosso pm 5, longo 10, alto 12.
si defalcha una morsa di muro vecchio in fiancho al fondamento lungo pm 14, largo pm 3 reg[uaglia]to, Alto pm 11 questo va per doi altri stracci che crescano lungo il fondamento pm 13, larghi 11½ si crescie una resegha in testa al fondamento. Alta pm 7½ lunga 11½, grossa 5½.

In January 1647 the Congregation voted to continue work on the north wing of the casa. They altered the original design by enlarging the individual suites from one and a half to two full rooms. They decided to build a clocktower in May 1647, ordering adequate foundations to be laid, but not committing themselves to any specific design. These foundations are the subject of the present drawing, and their documented date agrees with the date of May 14, 1647 inscribed on the verso (Decr. 210, 212–218).

The angle of the northwest corner of the casa presented a recurrent problem to successive architects. Arconio had designed this angle as less than 90 degrees (Cat. 9). Maruscelli converted it to a perfect right angle, and when he began the north wall of the casa for legal reasons in 1629, he accordingly set it perpendicular to the axis of the Vallicella (Cat. 21). Borromini's revisions in the refectory area caused him to realign the north wall and to make the northwest angle of the casa slightly greater than 90 degrees (Cat. 39, 59). Since Maruscelli's wall was no longer suitable, its demolition was discussed in 1639, but then deferred until the new building campaign of 1647. The inscriptions on the present drawing, which refer to a "second foundation" and to the demolition of old masonry fragments, record technical data relevant to these demolitions. The drawing itself, however, shows a solution that differs from Borromini's earlier proposal. Unlike Cat. 39, it allows the two exterior walls of the casa to meet at a 90-degree angle, and the two wings of the loggie on the interior of the casa to meet at an angle considerably less than 90 degrees. The north wing of the building thus expands in width as it progresses from west to east, providing the extra space needed for the refectory without any distortions visible from the street. In the long run, this solution was discarded in favor of what was considered an imperceptible distortion in the angle on the piazza (Cat. 81).

The pentimenti along the left edge of the casa record the expansion of the Monte Giordano projection from its initial width of

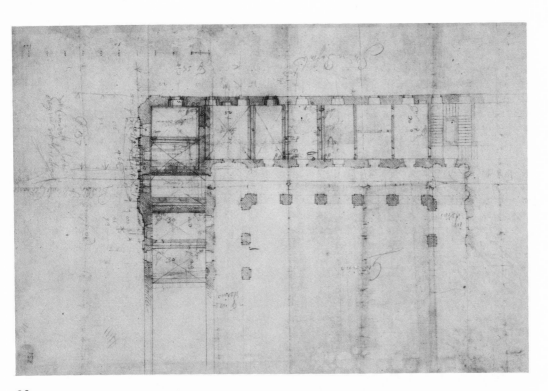

80

71 palmi—identical with the projection "already done" at the other end of the building —first to 80, then to 86, and finally to 93 palmi, which is close to its final width. (The present Monte Giordano projection is 21 meters or 94.1 palmi wide; the present oratory projection is 15.9 meters or 71.3 palmi wide.) Several factors encouraged this expansion: it created a facade of sufficient breadth to dominate the urban environment; it moved the clocktower into the center of the future piazza; and it brought the tower's inner face into line with the loggia and made it more easily visible from the courtyard. It also had the incidental effect, stressed by Thelen, of enlarging the space available for Spada's apartment on the *piano nobile* (cf. Cat. 81). Although this enlargement is first worked out in detail in the present drawing, a similar and symmetrical enlargement of the oratory projection had already been hinted at in a drawing of 1637–41 (Cat. 38).

The *spetiaria,* or pharmacy, mentioned in the inscriptions was eventually installed in the north wing on the axis of the courtyard. The two faint sketches on the verso of the sheet appear to be designs for the decoration of its vault. The shelving for its interior was discussed in 1650 and approved in 1651 (Decr. 261, 285–287); it is visible in the eighteenth-century engravings of the *Opus,* along with a doorframe that is undocumented but is distinctly Borrominian in design (Pls. LIII–LVI; Fig. 25; Cat. 89c). *Bibl.:* Ehrle, "Spada," 14 (unidentified); *Portoghesi, *Cultura,* Fig. 23; Thelen, *Disegni,* 40–42, no. 30; Incisa della Rocchetta, *Dialogo,* 201, n. 56.

81.   Francesco Borromini. 1647.
   Project for the north and west wings.
   AV, C.II.8, no. 22. 37.3 × 43.4. Red chalk (entire south and east loggia, two bays of north loggia) and graphite. Scale: 100 p. = 14.5 cm.

The drawing uses a color convention to distinguish the parts of the casa already built (sacristy service rooms, refectory, east loggia, square staircase, and two bays of north wing, all shown in red chalk) from those under consideration (north and west wings, shown in graphite). It is drawn to the same scale as the previous project (Cat. 80), from which it incorporates the enlarged projection, a full 93 palmi wide. It offers a different solution, however, for accommodating extra space around the refectory. Unlike the Vatican drawing, the branches of the loggia meet at strict right angles, whereas the northwest corner on the piazza is made greater than 90 degrees. This solution is already shown on earlier plans (Cat. 39, 59), described in the *Opus* as a "cosa insensibile" (II, 6ᵛ), and disguised in the present building by the curved corner pilaster and the oval fountain base, which appears here for the first time.

Like the Vatican plan, the present drawing tends to shift from one floor to another without warning. The apse-ended *lavamani* and the short flight of the square staircase are appropriate only to the ground floor, but the rooms drawn to the west of the staircase are located instead on the *piano nobile* (Cat. 115b). Thus the rooms labeled A and B in the lower left corner of the drawing could refer either to the shops on the ground floor or to the area of Spada's apartment on the floor above (*Dialogo,* 201: "Io ebbi due stanze, al primo piano, una sotto l'orologgio, l'altra, contigua, verso l'oratorio").

The building campaign of 1647–50 stopped immediately to the right (south) of the Monte Giordano projection, at a point where a small public street still entered the courtyard (Fig. 15; Decr. 341). A staircase was built here when construction was resumed by Arcucci in 1659 ff.; it is not mentioned in the *Opus* or shown on any of Borromini's plans, presumably because it did not figure in his project (Cat. 92–95).

When the courtyard was complete, its dimensions deviated slightly from those indicated on this drawing and the preceding one (in palmi):

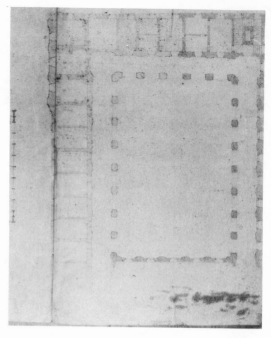

81

Bibl.: *Portoghesi, *Linguaggio,* Fig. xxxi; *Portoghesi, *Disegni,* 14, cat. no. 30 and Fig. 30; Incisa della Rocchetta, *Dialogo,* 201, n. 56.

82.   Francesco Borromini. 1650.
Project for the northwest corner and the fountain at the Piazza di Monte Giordano.
Alb. 290. 16.6 × 20.6. Graphite. Scale: 10 p.

The plan shows the extreme northwest angle of the casa, with a project for a fountain at the intersection of the Piazza di Monte Giordano and the Via di Parione. The giant pilasters measure a full 7 palmi in width, in agreement with the finished building and in contrast to the 5 or 5½ palmi shown on earlier plans (Cat. 80, 81). The curved corner pilaster is drawn in two versions: first as a shallow curve with a radius of 9½ palmi, then as a more pronounced curve with a radius of 7 palmi. Three con-

	Cat. 80	Cat. 81	Present building
East loggia:	16.5 (inscribed 18)	16.75	16.5
North loggia:	15	14.5	14.2–14.7
West loggia:	15 (inscribed 18)	16	16.5–17.0

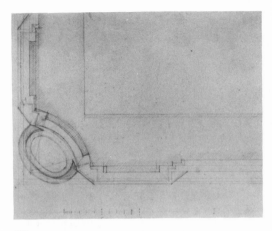

82

centric ovals indicate the basin, base, and pedestal of a fountain that had been planned since 1641 and was begun in 1650. The basin rim *(muricello)* was to measure 6 × 9 palmi and to stand 1 or 2 palmi high. Work was suspended on the fountain in July 1650, due to opposition from the Boncompagni family, who owned the palace across the Via del Governo Vecchio and who resented the way the new wing occupied former public land (Decr. 163, 265, 269–271). The only part of the fountain to be executed was the base, a large oval block of travertine with a plugged hole at the center which still stands on the site (Fig. 23); the design for the rest of the fountain, a figure standing on a pedestal and pouring water from a vase, is recorded in Barrière's print of 1658 (Cat. 89a).
Bibl.: *Portoghesi, *Linguaggio,* Fig. xxxviii; *Portoghesi, *Disegni,* 15, cat. no. 35 and Fig. 35.

83. Attributed to Camillo Arcucci. July 20, 1652.
License to build a *muricciolo* along the north wing of the casa on the Via di Parione.
ASR, CRM, Cong. dell'Oratorio, vol. 145, fol. 8. Ink and wash. 42.5 × 48.9. Scale: 50 p. = 6.2 cm.
Inscription on verso:
Copia licentiae et plantae pro RR. Padribus Congregationis Oratorij l'altra pianta originale vedi [cancelled-nello spartimento] nell' . . . loro fra le altre piante di fabriche anzi legata tra l'altre a . . .

License on recto:
Copia. Noi Gregorio Serlupi et Giacinto del Bufalo di Roma, e suo distretto Mastri di Strada. Concediamo licenza alli molto RR. Padri della Congregatione di S. Maria in Vallicella di potere fare il muricciolo, seu banchetta attaccato alla loro nova fabbrica per la parte di Parione, principiando doppo la cantonata verso la piazza di Monte Giordano, e seguitare sino all'altra cantonata che risvolta verso la porticella accanto la tribbuna di detta chiesa, con uscire fuori dal vivo del zoccolo di detta fabbrica palmi sei parallelo a detta fabbrica, conforme è segnato nella Pianta, che viene a pigliare parte del sito che detti RR. Padri hanno donato al pubblico nel tirare la linea della loro fabbrica con attondare dalla parte di sopra verso Monte Giordano, e morire a niente con l'altezza di detta banchetta, et unire con la selciata, che è nella cantonata per la fontana conforme nella pianta qui sotto segnata A, e nel mezzo dove fa angolo segnato B deve scantonarsi detta banchetta a segno, che nell'angolo detta banchetta non sia più larga di palmi 2½, e nell'altro cantone verso la porticella della chiesa segnato C debba tondarsi e morire al resalto della cantonata conforme è segnato nella pianta, nella qual' banchetta concediamo anco licenza di poter' mettere le colonnelle conforme è segnato nella pianta alte da terra palmi 2 in circa, il tutto conforme al'infrascritta pianta, e con l'asistenza del'Arcucci nostro sottomaestro di strade, e per tal conto commandiamo non siano molestati che tale è mente nostra data sotto il di 30 luglio 1652. G. Serlupi Maestro di strada. Giacinto del Bufalo Maestro di strade.

Inscriptions (from right to left):
Vicolo del corallo. Case de particulari. Vicoletto della porticella della Chiesa Nova. Habbitatione delli RR. PP. della Congregatione dell-'Oratorio. C. Sito dato al Publico. Strada di Parione che va verso Monte Giordano e Banchi. Vicolo che non ha riuscita. De Particulari. Vicoletta verso il fico. Palazzetto delli Sig.ri Avila. Sito dato al Publico. De particolari. De Sig.ri Boncompagni.

In building the north wing of the casa, the Oratorians had ceded a considerable amount of land to the public domain, which is marked by a red line on Cat. 83. One way of reasserting their claim over some of this land, at least symbolically, was to build a *muricciolo,* or pedestrian sidewalk, along their side of the Via di Parione. They deliberated the matter on June 21, 1652; a license was granted by the Mastri di Strade on July 30; the work was finished on August 31. The present license shows that the *muricciolo* was 6 palmi wide except at the bend in the building, where it narrowed to a width of 2½ palmi; it was separated from the street proper by sixteen colonnettes; it is shown in a Falda view of 1665, where it seems to be slightly raised off the street level (Cat. 98c). The street itself varied from 55½ palmi at its widest to 30 palmi at its narrowest. Both the narrow width and the claim over what seemed to them public land annoyed the Oratorians' neighbors to the north, the Boncompagni, who brought suit against the *muricciolo* on August 10, 1652 on the grounds that the street was now too narrow for their coaches to make the turn into their palace door. The Oratorians blocked their suit by producing affidavits from several veteran coachmen, including the Duke of Altemps's coachman, that it was easy enough to make the turn even with a six-horse carriage. In addition, they seem to have had the Mastri di Strade on their side; the *sottomaestro* delegated to oversee the case, Camillo Arcucci, appears to have been particularly helpful, and on August 23, 1652 he was taken on by the Congregation as Borromini's replacement (Decr. 309, 310, 312, 313, 314).

Besides objections to the *muricciolo*, the Boncompagni pointed out that the Monte Giordano corner did not stand on the line of the demolished buildings but projected 7 palmi farther west into the public land of the Piazza di Monte Giordano, which was just enough to block the line of sight from the portal of the Boncompagni palace through the piazza and down the Via dei Filippini. They were powerless to do anything when the Monte Giordano facade was built in 1647–50, but they did bring suit in August 1652 against the fountain that Borromini had planned for the corner of the building (Cat. 82, 89a); the fountain base was put into place, but the fountain itself and the basin designed to catch the water were abandoned. Six years later Pietro Boncompagni resumed work on the facade of his palace; a license granted by the Mastri di Strade on October 30, 1658 conceded: ". . . che nella facciata che ha principiato ad adornare con-

tigua l'altra sua casa già adornata nella strada, e Piazza di Monte Giordano possa far porre in opera l'adornamento della porta, con farci la sua ringhiera sopra a similitudine, et misura già fatta, con porre più avanti detta porta le sue due colonne di granito, et accompagnar la selciata avanti per facilitar l'ingresso . . ."; in addition he was allowed to use 1½ palmi of public land to straighten the new facade, which incorporated a neighboring house belonging to the chapter of St. Peter's (ASR, Presidenza della strade, busta 45, fols. 104ᵛ–105ʳ).

Bibl.: The drawing is listed in Corbo, *L'archivio della Congregazione dell'Oratorio di Roma e l'archivio della Abbazia di S. Giovanni in Venere. Inventario,* Rome, 1964, 145.

84–86.   Three anonymous draftsmen in the employ of Virgilio Spada.

Drawings of the casa sewn into a manuscript description of the building by Virgilio Spada and Francesco Borromini, called a *Piena relatione* by the authors but commonly referred to as the *Opus* manuscript.

AV, C.II.6. Published by Sebastiano Giannini as the *Opera del Cav. Francesco Boromino Cavata da Suoi Originali cioe L'Oratorio, e Fabrica per l'Abitazione De PP. dell'Oratorio di S. Filippo Neri di Roma (Opus Architectonicum Equitis Francisci Boromini),* Rome, 1725.

Although the manuscript is always dated 1648, many internal references in the text indicate a date between 1646 and early 1647 for its composition. A passage at the beginning refers to the establishment of the Congregation at the center of Rome "70 or more years ago": 1575 (the date of the founding of the Vallicella) plus 70 brings the date to 1645 or later. The oratory vault was finished "8 years ago and not a crack has appeared since" (VI, 18ʳ): the scaffolding was removed in mid-1638 (Doc. 15 and Cat. 40), and 8 years brings the date to 1646. One passage (XV, 46ᵛ) mentions work recently carried out at the Palazzo Falconieri, which was under way by March 1646 (Tafuri, *Via Giulia,* 445 ff.); another (XV, 46ᵛ–47ᵛ) discusses a vault of the Palazzo Pamphilj which was carried out in April 1646 (Fasolo, *L'opera di Hieronimo e*

Carlo Rainaldi, 306); while a third (XI, 37ʳ) mentions a vault in the Palazzo di Spagna, which was begun after January 1647 (Hempel, 129–33). In another passage (XXIII, 65ʳ) there is talk of bringing the Acqua Vergine to the casa via conduit; this hope would have been realistic only after April 1647, when Borromini began the task of extending this aqueduct from Trevi to the Piazza Navona (*Ragguagli,* 102).

On the other hand, the manuscript fails to mention any of the important features introduced into the design after May 1647: the Monte Giordano facade and clocktower, Spada's apartment, or the pharmacy and the shops at the northwest corner of the casa. It uses the future tense to describe the parts of the casa that were not built before mid-1647: the oratory altar (VI, 18ᵛ), the main *scalone* (XI, 37ʳ; XXVI, 71ʳ; IV, 11ʳ), the residential rooms of the west wing (XVII, 49ᵛ), the fountains of the first and second courtyard (X, 36ᵛ; XIII, 41ʳ), the street along the eastern flank of the church (II, 6ʳ), and the carriage door of the third courtyard (XXIII, 64ᵛ).

The date of 1648, first proposed by Hempel (61) and repeated by all subsequent scholars, is too late by a small but significant amount. It was based on the assumption that the oratory vault was finished in 1640, which is really the date it was inaugurated (Decr. 153–155), two years after completion. Furthermore it was based on a reading of the printed text of 1725 rather than the actual manuscript; Giannini confused matters by deleting most of the future tenses, by introducing a reference to the Monte Giordano clocktower which is not in the original, and by adding the date of May 10, 1656 to his preface. What is important about the new date of 1646–47 is that the manuscript was completed before the Monte Giordano campaign was begun in May 1647.

The two prefaces may have been added to the text at a slightly later date. In them, Borromini—speaking directly—assumes a tone hostile to the Congregation. This may indicate a date of around 1650, when he was no longer active in their service; on the other hand, he still does not call himself

"Cavaliere," a rank to which he was elevated on July 16, 1652 (*Ragguagli,* 22, 161).

84. Anonymous A after Francesco Borromini. 1650–53.
Plans of the casa.

84a. Plan of the entire casa.
Opus Ms, Pl. XV. 35.2 × 25.2. Pen and light yellow wash over stylus, pinpricks, torn along upper fold and lower right corner, bound to MS upside down. Scale: 100 p. = 7.4 cm.
Fig. 6.

84b. Plan of oratory and *portaria.*
Opus Ms, Pl. XVI. 22.5 × 31.3. Pen and light yellow wash, pinpricks. Scale: 100 p. = 13.9 cm.

Cat. 84a (Fig. 6) is in part a record of the wings built under Borromini's direction in 1637–50, and in part a project for completing the building. On the one hand, it shows the oratory, first courtyard, refectory, and service rooms along the Via di Parione exactly as they were built in 1637–44; the kitchen wing and rear staircase in particular correspond in minute detail to the description given in *Opus,* XX–XXV. The Monte Giordano projection is shown in its expanded form, corresponding to the design revisions of 1647 (Cat. 80, 81). The plan accurately records a decision of May 20, 1650 to double the size of the northwest corner shop by opening a door to an adjacent room, which was then outfitted with a mezzanine staircase and a street door of its own (Decr. 261). This decision provides a *terminus post* for the drawing; a *terminus ante* resides in the fact that the high altar of the oratory, which was transformed in the years following 1653 by the addition of four alabaster columns (Cat. 48), is still shown in its original form.

On the other hand, the drawing also shows the unbuilt wings of the casa in project form. The long west wing, eventually built by Arcucci in 1659–62, is shown with a schematic arrangement of rooms and fifteen window bays instead of the sixteen actually built. The corridor on the left side of the sacristy is articulated by pilasters without *membretti,* designed to match an idiosyncrasy of Maruscelli's corridor on the other side; when the corridor was carried out in 1659 it was given normal pilasters with *membretti.* A niche of Borromini's *lavamani* bulged out into the adjacent loggia (Portoghesi, *Linguaggio,* Fig. 288); the plan shows four such bulges at other corners of the loggia, all introduced into the design for reasons of symmetry. On the east side of the building there is no wagon door into the service courtyard; the Vallicella transept has two street doors rather than the single door built in 1666; and the Chapel of S. Carlo is not yet shown in its expanded form of 1667 ff. (Cat. 102).

There are indications that the drawing is a mechanical copy of a lost plan by Borromini. The absolute dimensions of the casa —24.7 cm. along the bottom including the church and 32.9 cm. along the left side— correspond precisely to the dimensions of the casa on all the early plans, both those by Maruscelli (Cat. 20b, 21), and those by Borromini (Cat. 39, 40, 59). Numerous pinpricks on the sheet seem to indicate the means of transfer.

Cat. 84b is an exact plan on a larger scale of the south wing of the casa, including the oratory, *portaria,* and adjacent loggia. It is more accurate than the previous plan in several small details. It records the oblique lighting for both spiral staircases found in the present building, and it shows the extra quarter-circle introduced into a corner of the porter's lodge for reasons explained in *Opus,* IX, 33^r. It shows that the floor level of the oratory was a step higher than the original floor level of the entrance atrium (Fig. 44); however, it also erroneously introduces an extra riser into the staircase at the right, which connects the *portaria* area with the first courtyard. On the left the drawing shows the columnar entrance vestibule of the main *scalone* but fails to show the *scalone* itself; thus it stops at exactly the point where construction left off in 1644.

Cat. 84a was copied by Giannini and collated with the site plan of the area on Cat. 14 to produce the well-known engraving which opens the *Opus* of 1725 (Fig. 5; cf. Cat. 110.II).

Bibl.: Cat. 84a is unpublished. Cat. 84b: *G. Incisa della Rocchetta, "L'oratorio borrominiano nella descrizione del p. Virgilio Spada," *Quaderni dell'Oratorio,* 13, n.d., p. 3.

85.   Anonymous B. 1652?–53.
Oratory: sections and facade elevation; project for the second courtyard.

85a.   *Opus* MS, Pl. XVII–XIX.
East-west section through oratory and adjacent entrance vestibule.
31.3 × 60.6. Two sheets pasted together with damage along all folds; not sewn into the volume, but loosely inserted in the correct position following fol. 15^v. Scale: 20 p. = 5.1 cm.

85b.   *Opus* MS, Pl. XX.
Section through the west end of the oratory, behind the altar.
Drawn on the same sheet of paper, measuring 32.2 × 44.2, as Cat. 85c. Scale: 20 p. = 5.2 cm.

85c.   *Opus* MS, Pl. XXI.
Section through the west end of the oratory, in front of the altar.
Drawn on the same sheet of paper as Cat. 85b. Scale: 20 p. = 5.2 cm.
Fig. 32.

85d.   *Opus* MS, Pl. XXII.
Section through the entrance and cardinals' loggie at the east end of the oratory.
Drawn on the same sheet of paper, measuring 32.1 × 44.5 cm., as Cat. 85e. Scale: 20 p. = 5.2 cm.

85e.   *Opus* MS, Pl. XXIII.
Section through the east end of the oratory, in front of the entrance and cardinals' loggie.
Drawn on the same sheet as Cat. 85d. Scale: 20 p. = 5.2 cm.

85f.   *Opus* MS, Pl. XLIV–XLV.
Oratory facade elevation.
31.5 × 42.6. Heavily damaged along center fold; remounted. Sheet not sewn into the volume and incorrectly inserted after fol. 77^v; Scale: 100 p. = 18.0 cm. (implying a total width of 192 p. for the casa).

85g.   *Opus* MS, Pl. XXXIII.
Second courtyard: project for rebuilding

85a

85b

85c

the south wing as described in *Opus,* XIII, 41ᵛ–42ʳ.

44.4×32.0. The drawing occupies one half of a larger sheet, which was originally folded and inserted in the MS following fol. 29ᵛ; the blank half of the sheet is numbered in the pagination as fol. 30. Inserted after fol. 42ʳ and Pl. 31 in the present edition. Ink and brown wash over graphite, stylus, and pinpricks. Scale: 100 p. = 17.6 cm.

Stylistic features are the basis for attributing these seven drawings from the *Opus* MS to a single hand: all are drawn in the same relaxed perspective with the same careless rendering of details; all share a common medium of biting brown ink thinned and used over graphite as a wash. Despite their amateurish appearance, the drawings betray an insider's knowledge of design and structure, particularly the views of the oratory. Several of them accurately depict obscure features of the underground oratory, such as the corner piers (Fig. 30). One drawing (Fig. 32) shows Borromini's original wooden model for an oratory altar: it was a small structure surmounted by fictive organ pipes alluding to S. Cecilia (*Opus,* VI, 18ʳ); the crown held aloft by angels above the altarpiece of the *Assumption* was part of an iconographic program terminating in the *Coronation* of the vault (Cat. 40). Another drawing (Cat. 85b) shows the small chains immured over the hexagonal corner chambers and the "gran catena" immured above the altar (Decr. 616). Another (Cat. 85d) shows that the door at the eastern end of the room was an unexpected addition and had to be cut into moldings that were not designed for it (Cat. 59). Finally, the long section through the oratory and *portaria* (Cat. 85a) shows not only the correct number of steps at each change in level, but also the system that had been worked out on Cat. 66ʳ for allowing light into the side chapels of the Vallicella.

If the drawings are accurate on all these minor points, then by implication they should also be accurate on one further point that cannot be so easily tested, namely, the way in which they show the ground floor windows of the oratory as closed. When the graphic evidence on this point is set forth in

85d

85e

85f

85g

detail, however, it turns out to be full of contradictions:

1637	Cat. 39 shows all eight windows open.
1638	Cat. 41 shows the four facade windows closed.
1641	Cat. 66^r is incomplete but does show two of the north windows as closed.
1650–53	Fig. 6 shows all eight windows open.
1652?–53	The present drawing shows all eight windows closed.
1665	Cat. 98a and 99, by Falda and Cruyl, show the four facade windows as closed.
1684	Cat. 104a and 104c show all eight windows as closed.
1721	Cat. 109 shows two windows open and two closed in each wall.
1725	Figs. 15, 16, 27 and 28 show all eight windows closed.
1871	Cat. 115a shows three south windows and two north windows open, the rest closed.
1871–1924	Figs. 36 and 37, photographs taken while the oratory served as a tribunal, show three doors in the north wall and several facade windows open.
Present building:	All four facade windows are open and all four north windows are sealed so thoroughly that there is no trace they ever existed.

Without doubt some of these contradictions are due to the nature of the evidence: Borromini's early plans tend to depict the windows as open in order to demonstrate the logic of the thicker corner pier; views of the facade, on the other hand, tend to depict the windows as closed in order to emphasize the device of the facade window niches and to strengthen the illusion of an ecclesiastical interior. Given this situation, it seems almost impossible to chart the exact sequence of events with certainty. Possibly the oratory was built with all its lower windows open in 1637 when the logic of the corner pier was an issue; possibly the windows in the north wall were filled in 1652–53 when cracks appeared in the oratory vault and when the arches of the adjacent loggia were sealed (Decr. 311, 316, 319–322, 325, 327–329, 387, 388); possibly some of these apertures were opened again as doors in 1871 and closed again in 1924. If this hypothesis is correct then the present drawings can be dated after 1652, since they show the ground floor windows as closed. On the other hand, they still fail to show the rebuilt high altar of 1653 ff. (Cat. 48). However, given the shaky nature of the evidence, it seems better to leave the *terminus post* open, although the *terminus ante* is securely fixed.

The final drawing in the set, Cat. 85g, appears to be based on a project by Borromini for rebuilding the south side of the garden courtyard; it is discussed in Cat. 64.

Bibl.: *G. Incisa della Rocchetta, "L'Oratorio borrominiano nella descrizione del p. Virgilio Spada," *Quaderni dell'Oratorio,* 13, n.d., p. 5 (Cat. 85a), p. 7 (Cat. 85c), p. 9 (Cat. 85e), pp. 10–11 (Cat. 85f); Incisa della Rocchetta, *Dialogo,* 214, n. 4, and 206, n. 6 (Cat. 85c); *Ragguagli,* 94, (Cat. 85a).

86.   Anonymous C. After 1647.
Details from the casa.

86a.   *Opus* MS, Pl. XXIV.
Elevation of balusters in the oratory.
23.2 × 32.6. Ink with blue and brown wash over graphite.
The plans sketched in pencil beneath two balusters contradict the elevations above them. Ink border.

86b.   *Opus* MS, Pl. XXV.
Wooden grille of cardinals' loggia.
23.3 × 33.2. Ink and brown wash over graphite; additional ornament sketched in pencil. Ink border.

86c.   *Opus* MS, Pl. XXVI.
East portal of the oratory.

33.2 × 23.3. Ink and light brown wash over graphite, with molding profiles in graphite. Ink border.
Cf. Cat. 110.XXXIII.

86d. *Opus* MS, Pl. XXVII.
Plan of oratory facade.
23.2 × 33.1. Brown ink and blue wash over graphite; wash stippling; part of Vallicella facade added at right. Ink border. Scale: 40 p. = 6.9 cm.

86e. *Opus* MS, Pl. XXVIII.
Capitals and pilaster bases of the two stories of the oratory facade.
33.2 × 23.1. Pen and gray wash over graphite. Ink border.

86f. *Opus* MS, Pl. XXIX.
Oratory facade: elevation of the curved portion only.
33.2 × 22.6. Ink with brown and yellow wash. Ink border.

86f

86g. *Opus* MS, Pl. XXX.
Niche window from the lower story of the oratory facade.
33.2 × 23.3. Pen and blue wash over graphite. Ink border.

86h. *Opus* MS, Pl. XXXI.
Basement window grilles.
33.2 × 23.2. Brown wash, ink stippling over graphite. Ink border.

86h

86i. *Opus* MS, Pl. XXXII.
Three window frames from the oratory facade.
33.2 × 23.2. Pen and yellow wash over graphite. Ink border.

86j. *Opus* MS, Pl. XXXIV.
Main portal of the casa. Exact copy of a Borromini drawing, Cat. 67 (*Opus* MS, Pl. 26).
33.4 × 23.1. Ink and blue wash over graphite; pinpricks. Ink border. Scale (Roman numerals): 10 p. = 6.6 cm.

86k. *Opus* MS, Pl. XXXIX.
Portaria: plan and section.
33.0 × 23.2. Ink and blue-green wash over graphite. Ink border. Erroneously sewn into the manuscript after fol. 36^v.

86l. *Opus* MS, Pl. XXXVI.
Wooden screen with door: reduced copy of Cat. 25 (*Opus* MS, Pl. 29).
33.3 × 23.2. Pen and blue wash over graphite. Ink border.

86j

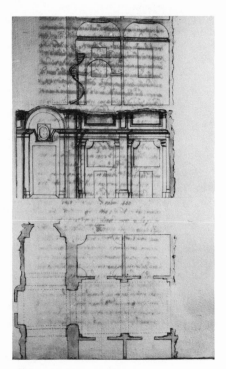

86k

Dimensions of screen on the present sheet: 27.1 × 16.7 cm. Dimensions of screen on Cat. 25: 39.5 × 23.8 cm.

86m. *Opus* MS, Pl. XL.

First courtyard: plan and perspectival view looking north. The plan correctly shows no windows in the left *nicchione,* in contrast to the elevation. Vanishing lines still visible.

33.1 × 23.3. Ink with blue and brown wash over graphite. Ink border.

Fig. 50 (detail).

86n. *Opus* MS, Pl. XLI.

Second courtyard: elevation of one long side.

23.2 × 33.0. Ink and blue wash over graphite. Scale: 60 p. = 8.1 cm.

86o. *Opus* MS, Pl. XLII.

Lavamani fountain: perspectival view, section and plan.

33.1 × 23.3. Ink with blue and yellow wash over graphite. Ink border.

86p. *Opus* MS, Pl. XLIII.

Chimneypiece in the *sala di ricreazione:* plan and elevation.

32.5 × 23.2. Damage along lower edge. Ink with brown and yellow wash. Ink border.

86q. *Opus* MS, Pl. XLVI.

Library: perspectival section.

23.2 × 32.8. Ink with brown and blue wash over graphite; pencil vanishing lines still visible. Ink border.

The section cuts lengthwise through the room at a point slightly forward of center. Although the bookshelves are accurately depicted, the boxes (for codices ?) on the right are not recorded in any other source. The roundels attached to four pilasters were intended for grisaille portraits of benefactors: six out of a possible total of twelve were executed, and three are preserved (*Dialogo,* 192 ff., n. 44; *Opus,* XXVIII, 78^v).

The draftsman introduced serious distortions by rendering the central bay as wider than any of the others and inserting two windows where none was present. The bust of Baronius, installed over the central balcony door in 1644, is omitted (Pollak, 446, regs. 1843–45).

86q

On the library shelves, cf. Cat. 77.

86r. *Opus* MS, Pl. XLVII.
Library ceiling, prior to expansion of 1666.
23.1 × 32.5. Ink and blue wash over graphite. Ink border. Unfinished.
Cf. Cat. 76.

These eighteen drawings from the *Opus* MS form a coherent group on the basis of style and graphic technique. All were done on paper of identical format framed by a black ink border. Many adopt a convention of "ragged edges" to indicate sections through a wall or breaks in the design. Although the draftsman at first sight appears more professional than Anonymous B, his weaknesses become evident in the freehand detail and rendering of perspective. He remains anonymous, although he does seem to have worked for Spada on at least one other occasion, namely, the repair of a coffered ceiling between approximately 1646 and 1651 (BV, Vat. lat. 11258, fols. 5^r–6^r and 8; assigned in Thelen, *Disegni*, 38, cat. no. 21–29b–c, to the Lateran, although the dimensions indicated on the drawing exclude the coffered ceilings of both the Lateran nave and transept). Beyond the connection with the *Opus* MS of 1647, the drawings offer no internal evidence for a precise date. Spada's note on the flyleaf of the manuscript seems to fit these drawings more than any of the others: "ne ho fatti fare alcuni da altri ma poco a proposito."
Bibl.: *Incisa della Rocchetta, "L'Oratorio borrominiano nella descrizione del p. Virgilio Spada," *Quaderni dell'Oratorio,* 13, n.d., p. 16 (Cat. 86g); p. 17 (Cat. 86h).

87. Anonymous. March 2, 1655.
License for rebuilding a house in the piazza along an altered property line.
AV, C.II.8, no. 105. Ink with red and yellow wash.
An official copy of the license with a crude sketch of the plan is to be found in ASR, Presidenze delle Strade, busta 45, fols. 15^v–16^r.

Inscriptions:
Antonio, del Titolo della Sant.ma Trinita de'-Monti, Prete, Card.le Barberino, della S.ta R.a Chiesa, Camerlengo.
In virtù della presente, e per l'autorità del nostro offitio, concediamo licentia alli molto RR. PP. della Congregatione dell'Oratorio di S. Filippo Neri di Roma, di poter proseguire la fabrica che fa cantone nella Strada Nova da loro aperta, nella piazza avanti la loro Chiesa di S.ta Maria in Vallicella, e seguitare al medesimo filo della stessa fabrica principiata in detto cantone, segnato nella pianta A sino l'altro cantone B da farsi verso la strada de Cartari, che con la rivolta deve pigliare il filo delle case di detta strada, lassando in benefitio del publico in detta piazza il triangolo segnato C colorito di giallo con incorporare il triangolo D colorito di rosso, che è minore in quantità di quello si lassa al publico, e ne viene maggior ornamento alla città, terminando le diritture delle case nelli suoi cantoni senza far'resalti, e comodo per le carrozze e piazza avanti detta chiesa et oratorio. Che è conforme il chirografo della felice memoria di Urbano VIII, spedito sotto li 26 Gennaro 1637 [sic, *should read* 1627; *cf. Doc.* 7], che concede loro, il poter far piazza in longhezza di canne venti e

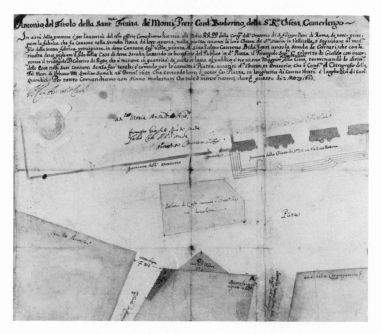

87

larghezza di canne quindici. Per tanto coman-
diamo non siano molestati che tale è mente nos-
tra, dato questo di 2 Marzo 1655.
Il Card. Antonio Cam.o
Francesco Maria Antaldi [?] Aud.re
Francesco Gottifredi Mastro di Strade
Felice Cessi [?] Mastro di Strade
Vincentio . . . [?]
　　Facciata dell'Oratorio. Porteria. Facciata della
Chiesa di S.ta M. in Vallicella. Isoletta di case
avanti l'Oratorio che va demolita. Piazza. Case de
Particolari. Resta larga p.mi 31½. 26½. Vicolo
de Cartari. C: Casa de Padri. Botteghe principi-
ate de PP. Strada Nova fatta dalla Cong.ne dell'
Oratorio. Case della Congregatione.

The license allows the Congregation to demolish the house located between the
Vicolo dei Cartari and the Strada Nuova
and to rebuild its facade along a straight line
running between points A and B. In compensation for ceding the triangle marked C
to the public, the Oratorians were permitted
to occupy a smaller plot of public land
marked D. The license signals a departure
from the funnel-shaped piazza laid out by
Maruscelli in 1627 (Fig. 101), and a step in
the direction of the long, narrow, and relatively symmetrical piazza of future projects

(Cat. 112). The work of demolition and
reconstruction began shortly after the license was issued, and the new house took
two years to complete. It was five bays wide
and apparently four stories high, matching
the design of the house Maruscelli had built
across the Strada Nuova (Fig. 100). In 1657
its rent yield was calculated at ▽414.50. It
was raised one story in 1744, and appears in
its final form in Fig. 9 (Decr. 349, 589, 590;
Doc. 12).
Bibl.: Russo, "Piazza della Chiesa Nuova," *Studi
Romani,* XIII, 1965, Pl. VII.

88.　Anonymous. Date uncertain.
　Project for a house on the Piazza di S.
Maria in Vallicella.
　AV, C.II.8, number uncertain. 28.3 ×
42.8. Ink and pink wash over graphite.
Scale: 100 p.

A project for reconstructing part of the
block bounded by the Strada Nuova and the
Vicolo dei Cartari. Inaccurate in proportions and amateur in draftsmanship, the
sheet presents contradictory evidence for
dating. The schematic outline of the Isola di
Pizzomerlo may indicate a date prior to its

destruction in 1637; the roughly square piazza may either refer to Maruscelli's projects of 1626 or to the piazza as executed after 1702; or, finally, the house under construction may be associated with the license of 1655, although the house built in 1655–57 on this site had five bays on the piazza rather than the six shown here. Unpublished.

89. Domenico Barrière after Francesco Borromini. 1658.

Three ideal views of the casa.

89a. *Torre dell'orologio.*

Fioravante Martinelli, *Roma ricercata nel suo sito, et nella scuola di tutti gli antiquarij,* 3rd ed., Rome, 1658, 79.

12.4 × 8.9 (plate mark). Etching.

89b. Oratory facade.

Op. cit., 83.

12.4 × 8.9 (plate mark). Etching.

89c. Garden court looking north.

Op. cit., 86.

8.8 × 12.3 (plate mark). Etching.

Inscription on all three plates:

Dom. Barrière delin. et sculp.

The first edition of Martinelli's *Roma ricercata* dates to 1644, the second to 1650; at this stage the text describing the Casa dei Filippini is still brief:

> . . . calendo nella piazza de'Regatieri slargata da Paolo III andarete à visitare la sontuosa e devota Chiesa di santa Maria della Vallicella de'Padri dell' Oratorio, con entrata in sagrestia, oratorio, e casa nobilmente fabricate con disegno del Sig. Francesco Borromini, e riverire il miracoloso corpo del glorioso S.Filippo Neri, come anche la camera, nella quale visse (ma non in questo sito) e mori, ornata con molto splendore e religione. [P. 28.]

The third edition of 1658 gives a much more elaborate description of the casa and the surrounding area. The route which Martinelli traces begins at the Palazzo Farnese, passes along the Via dei Pellegrini to the Ponte S. Angelo, and then winds back to the Piazza di Monte Giordano. Thus Martinelli begins his description and his illustrations at

89a

89b

89c

what we would consider the back of the building:

> ... scorgerete in quella parte, che risguarda la strada de' Banchi la nuova faccia della casa delli Padri dell'Oratorio, sopra la quale s'erge un torre con imagine della gran Madre di Dio terminata con l'ornamento d'Horologio dal nobile ingengo del Sig. Cavalier Francesco Borromini, come si vede nel seguente disegno. [Cat. 89a.]
>
> Avantaggiatevi a seconda della detta casa, e trovarete l'Oratorio delli detti Padri, dalla cui facciata, architettata in forma d'abbracciamento humano, par siate invitati a contemplare la sua vaga inventione. Ma acciò che questo luogo sacro, nel quale con frequenza d'atti religiosi s'honora la Maestà di Dio, non restasse privo del Frontespitio dovutogli come a casa Celeste per regola di vera architettura, ha composto la prudenza del Borromino un nuovo ordine, unendo le linee del Frontespitio orbicolato insieme con quelle del retto, che formano un terza specie, tanto inusitata, quanto giuditiosa per rendere più maestevole la fronte del tempio di Dio, come appare nel seguente disegno. [Cat. 89b.]
>
> Viene abbracciata la detta sagrestia da due cortili, li cui portici, e loggie sono sostenute con un solo ordine composito, e non da più, come e stata solita operare l'architettura fin' hora: inventione al certo, che rende più magnifica la fabrica, e più ammirabile l'ingegno del Borromino suo sutore, dal quale sono stato honorato del suo disegno seguente. [Cat. 89c.]
>
> Questo luogo si chiama Pozzo Bianco; entrate nella strada nuova, dove a man sinistra è la casa di Monsignor Cerri ... [Pp. 78-89.]

The three prints show various parts of the casa in the order in which a visitor was likely to encounter them. The first is an idealized view of the *torre dell'orologio*. It shows Borromini's project for a corner fountain which was begun in 1650 but immediately abandoned when the Boncompagni family contested its legality (Cat. 82). It shows the Madonna della Vallicella, which had been installed on the clocktower in 1657, but it also shows the two flanking *candelieri* which were not executed until late 1660 (Decr. 354, 387, 389). Although Arcucci's long west wing was not begun until 1659, the year after the print was published, it is already depicted as though it were complete (Cat. 92–96).

The idea of a clocktower, which is still not mentioned in the *Opus* MS, was provisionally accepted in May 1647; the masonry structure itself, an assembly of flat, concave, and convex surfaces, was built between April and July 1648 (Decr. 218, 227–230). At first a limit of 38 palmi was set to its height; in the end it rose to 56 palmi exclusive of ironwork. Giannini's engravings of 1725 preserve two early projects for the design. The first (Fig. 105) is the closer to the Casa Professa model (Fig. 106); something like it was actually tried out on the site in July 1648, when three bells marked with Filippo's image were positioned, unsuccessfully, along the front edge of the tower (Decr. 222, 229). Decorative details of this project are still close to those of the oratory facade; the second project, on the other hand, is closer to some of the forms found in Borromini's Lateran of 1646–49. A design for the metal superstructure of the clocktower was approved in August 1648, and a lead model approved in January 1649 (Decr. 230, 234, 235). In its final form the superstructure consisted of four iron volutes supporting three bells, a cross, a copper star and banner, and an iron heart (Decr. 239).

The clock began to work on November 21, 1649; its mechanism, still preserved in the Museo di Roma, is inscribed "Gaspar Albertus Pisauren. F. 1649" (Doc. 21; A. Pernier, "Documenti inediti . . . ," *Capitolium,* X, 1934, 429). It is variously represented with a dial of six or twelve hours according to a changing fashion which can be charted as follows. The original clock had twelve hours and a single hand, conforming to standard seventeenth-century practice (Cat. 89a; cf. Thelen C 21 and Hibbard, *Maderno,* Plate 52a). At the end of the century fashion shifted to a six-hour dial, "la mostra di hore sei in sei alla Romana" (D. Martinelli, *Horologi elementari . . . ,* 83), and the Oratorians altered their clock to conform to this usage in 1709 (Decr. 554). The six-hour dial was kept throughout the eighteenth century; it is a good index to those prints in the *Opus* of 1725 that were drawn from the actual building (cf. also the crude view on Alb. 293^{r-v}), as opposed to those that were taken from Borromini drawings (Fig. 105). In 1798, under the influence of the French occupation, usage shifted back to a twelve-hour dial, this time with two hands instead

of one (Decr. 628); it is this dial that appears in the oldest photographs as well as in the present building.

Finally the print shows the shops that were incorporated into the Monte Giordano facade in 1649–50. Resembling narrow doorways rather than the usual Roman *bottega,* the shops were inconspicuous and hard to rent. Small signs were allowed in 1650 and were again under discussion in 1664; they are not shown on the print. A high rent of ∇50 was charged for the corner shop because it occupied two rooms and faced two streets. Only the eighteenth-century occupants of the shops are known, a water vendor and a tailor (Decr. 243, 244, 256, 257, 261, 265, 278, 434, 587, 612).

Barrière's second print shows the oratory facade in an idealized and isolated state, detached from both the Vallicella on the right and the remnants of Maruscelli's projection on the left. In some respects the print is the heir of the Windsor drawing of 1638 (Cat. 41): it shows the four niche windows of the lower story as blind, and adds a portal on the left to balance the portal on the right and to create the illusion of a normal ecclesiastical interior behind the facade. It shows a skyline adorned with an array of torches, stars, and a heart that recalls the Windsor drawing but has here spread to include the two flanking bays. A draftsman's convention is used to distinguish the rough brickwork of the bays added to the design in 1638 from the finer brickwork of the five central bays. A podium raised four steps from the ground demarcates the facade in a manner similar to Maderno's steps in front of St. Peter's (Hibbard, *Maderno,* 161 and Pl. 55); the design of the podium later underwent modification and was not executed until 1745 (Cat. 113). The degree of idealization makes it seem likely that the print, like others in the series, was based on a drawing furnished by Borromini himself; it looks forward to the more dramatic revisions of the design recorded in a drawing of 1660 and a number of prints which descend from it (Fig. 16.; Cat. 90, 91, 104a).

The third and final print shows the garden courtyard in an idealized rendering. On the one hand, it includes features that were not yet in place by the date of publication. In 1658 the garden was still occupied by houses and traversed by a public street (Decr. 341, 349, 360); the *viali* were not laid out and the fountain was not installed until 1661 (Doc. 25; Decr. 394, 397, 407, 408). The west wing of the courtyard was not begun until 1659 (Cat. 92–96). On the other hand, the print omits features that were already in place by 1658. The upper stories of the casa are not shown, although they were conspicuous from the chosen vantage point. In the actual building each bay was closed on the *piano nobile* level by a thin weather-wall set flush with the inner face of the piers (Cat. 57). The advantages of this arrangement are described at length in *Opus,* XVII and *Dialogo,* 186 ff., but nevertheless the print fails to show these walls. Instead, it emphasizes the majestic qualities of the giant order, a point on which Martinelli's text also dwells.

The print of the courtyard manages to include all eight bays of the side wings by combining a close viewpoint with the high degee of foreshortening typical of more distant perspectives. This device is found in several earlier Borromini drawings (C 51, 68–70; cf. Thelen, 79 ff.), and its presence here lends weight to Martinelli's assertion that the print is based on a drawing which he received from the architect. Similar techniques of foreshortening and idealization are used in many of the prints and drawings connected with Borromini's publication enterprise, particularly those of S. Ivo, but possibly also of the Palazzo Falconieri (Cat. 90).

The illustrations of the courtyard in the *Opus* of 1725 represent a return to realistic depiction. Opus, Pl LIII reduces the foreshortening and reinstates the suppressed upper stories, although it retains the fiction of open bays on the *piano nobile*. Fig. 25 and *Opus,* Pl. LIV shed this last vestige of Barrière and simply reproduce the state of the courtyard as it stood in 1725.

Bibl.: Schudt, *Le guide di Roma,* Vienna and Augsburg, 1930, 251 ff., nos. 230–255; D'Onofrio, *Roma nel seicento,* Florence, 1969, 189 (illustration of Cat. 89a). Martinelli is studied extensively in Huelsen, *Le chiese di Roma,* Florence, 1927, xliii–xlv.

90.   Francesco Borromini. Ca. 1660.
Oratory facade revised for publication.
Alb. 291. 43.0 × 30.3 cm. Graphite. Two scales: (1) 100 palmi (at bottom); (2) 85 palmi (unnumbered, immediately beneath left half of facade).

Inscriptions:
[1. *Above scale 2:*] Accrescimento nella Pianta nel mezzo mezzo Pilastro. meta della faciata.
[2. *Under scale 2:*] Scala agiustata per il diseg-[n]o novo di darsi alla stampa a rag[io]ne di p[al]mi 91 . . . lasciare [?] un palmo piu delli . . . qui sopra [?]
[3. *To the right of inscription no. 2:*] Agiustai [?] p[r]imo [?]
[4. *Above left half of plan:*] meta della facciata vecchia
[5. *Above scale 1:*] 78 modoli
[6. *Below scale 1:*] modoli N.o 80 p[er] coppiare questo disegno
[7. *Below right half of facade:*] modoli . . . p[er] redure il disegno . . . accompag . . .

The drawing is one of the most complex and famous in Borromini's *oeuvre*. Usually taken as a sketch of 1637 for the oratory facade, it is in fact a revision of the facade design produced in connection with the publication enterprise of ca. 1660. The two scales and their related inscriptions help to clarify the architect's procedure and intentions.

The drawing began as a ruled orthogonal elevation of the facade at a stage close to the Windsor drawing (Cat. 41) in size and proportions, but more advanced in decorative detail. Originally it had been transferred to the sheet with the aid of scale 1 (inscribed "80 modules for copying this drawing"). When measured on this scale, the dimensions of the facade agree completely with the Windsor drawing and the actual building: about 160 palmi for the seven principal bays, hence the expression "80 modules" for half of that length. This original elevation was also accompanied by a plan labeled "half of the old facade," meaning half of the facade which had been built about twenty-three years before. This plan was drawn along a relatively shallow curve with a radius of 200 palmi, as in the Windsor drawing.

In the next stage of reworking the scale of the entire building was enlarged by one-

90

third, and the curve of the facade deepened in two ways: first, by the graphic device of redrawing the elevation in more dramatic foreshortening, and second, by the geometrical device of shortening the radius of the plan. Measured on scale 1, this radius was reduced from 200 to 150 palmi, that is, from an amount equivalent to the width of the entire casa to a smaller amount equivalent to the width of only the seven principal facade bays. Evidently Borromini's primary intention was to show a detached and completely symmetrical facade, with no residue of either the church on the right or of Maruscelli's projection on the left (as in Cat. 89b, the Barrière print of 1658). The new, narrower facade was redrawn with a shorter radius. Then, as if in compensation for the loss of 50 palmi on the left, Borromini enlarged the whole composition once again by adding scale 2 ("scale adjusted for the new drawing to be published"). The result was a freestanding seven-bay facade that measured 200 or 210 palmi in width on scale 2. Thus, the revised facade had grown to be as wide as the entire south wing of the actual building. Final pentimenti increased its height and width on the right, while the central axis was shifted a short distance to the left. Alterations tending to increase the dramatic and sculptural effect of the curve continued far beyond the point where the drawing could still have been of use to an engraver.

The publication enterprise of 1660 is known primarily from the account of Borromini's career given by his nephew Bernardo in 1685:

> So that the many studies and projects for various patrons, as well as spontaneous designs for buildings and temples, would not remain buried, [Borromini] planned to compose a book out of them and publish it, both executed projects, those left undone due to some mishap, and other ideas, all to demonstrate the great extent of his knowledge.
>
> So he employed the engraver Domenico Barrière, and gave him drawings of the Sapienza. He had him engrave the geometrical plan, a per-

spective, a section, and elevations of the front and rear facades, and also the facade of the Oratorio di San Filippo, along with the clocktower. He spent about ∇400 on these plates as appears from Barrière's receipts, which are in the possession of Borromini's nephew, as are the plates themselves. . . .

> A few days before his death he burned all the drawings which he had planned to publish, out of fear that they would fall into the hands of his rivals after his death [Doc. 26.]

Although this account gives no date for the enterprise, several types of evidence point to the year 1660. First, the engraved plates for the Sapienza survived into the eighteenth century, when they were used by Sebastiano Giannini as the basis for plates II to IX of his *Opera* of 1720. These plates show S. Ivo neither as it was finally built nor as it looked in Giannini's day, but rather as it appeared in April 1660. They include details not finished or installed until that time, such as the Chigi cupola stuccoes and the arms of Leo X (*Ragguagli,* 226 ff.); they also show features rendered obsolete soon thereafter, such as the round bases with stars on top of the exhedra, the floor paving pattern, the high altar, and the balustrade at the rear of the building (*Ragguagli,* 138 ff. and 226 ff.). Plates VIII and IX recall the large half-model refurbished for Alexander VII in 1658 (*Ragguagli,* 138). Although the plates are unsigned they are close in style to Barrière's known work, especially in their forced perspective and their rendering of details like clouds; furthermore there exists an ink drawing of the cupola of S. Ivo that seems to be by Barrière and seems to show how he reworked material supplied to him by Borromini (Portoghesi, *Linguaggio,* Fig. lvi). Finally, Barrière's fee is recorded on a Borromini drawing of 1662 for the Propaganda Fide (Alb. 914^v): "danari pagati al Sr. Domenico Bariere p[er] l'intag[lio] della Sapienza."

Aside from Giannini's plates of S. Ivo, the other main vestige of the publication enterprise is the present drawing, which can be dated to 1660 on the basis of several stylistic features. The canted pilaster at the extreme right of the plan, (Cat. 40) although foreshadowed on an earlier drawing, is very close to a similar device used in 1660–62 at the Propaganda Fide. The Filippini heraldry on top of the facade has been merged with the Chigi acorns of Alexander VII (1655–67); a study for this ornament exists on the verso of a drawing for S. Ivo (Cat. 91) that can be dated firmly to 1659–60.

The destruction of the material assembled for publication just before Borromini's suicide in 1667 may be one reason for the almost total absence of uncommissioned or fanciful projects in his extant graphic work. Fortunately the destruction was incomplete. According to Bernardo Borromini, the engraved plates were still in his possession in 1685, and the engraver G. G. de Rossi seems to have had access to them for his *Insignium Romae Templorum Prospectus* of 1684 (Cat. 104). In 1720 Giannini used the plates of S. Ivo, and in 1725 either the present drawing, or more likely a drawing or engraved plate that descended from it, was used as the basis for Pl. V of the *Opus Architectonicum* (Fig. 16). Unlike de Rossi, Giannini did not reverse the print or drawing in front of him and did not attempt to redraw it as an orthogonal elevation; he retained the dramatic perspective of his source as well as smaller details like the semi-oval ramp in front of the main door and the four columns of the upper story. One element in Giannini's print does not appear in the present drawing, however, namely, the pair of spiral columns flanking the main portal; they may have been borrowed from a source such as the Windsor drawing (Cat. 41).

In addition to the material on S. Ivo and the oratory, a drawing of the Palazzo Falconieri (built between 1646 and about 1656) may represent one last vestige of the publication enterprise. The drawing is Alb. 1059, illustrated by Tafuri in *Via Giulia,* 455, Fig. 373. It shows the palace from a vantage point in the Farnesina gardens across the river, appearing reversed, idealized, sharply foreshortened, and populated by small genre figures. It strongly resembles some of Barrière's prints, for example Cat.

89c, and may be the only extant example of the type of drawing Borromini supplied to his engraver. Unlike the material mentioned above, however, the Falconieri drawing was not used by any later printmakers. *Bibl.:* *D. Frey, *Die Architekturzeichnungen der Kupferstichsammlung der Öster. Nationalbibliothek,* Vienna, n.d. (ca. 1920), Pl. 3; *Hempel, Pl. 38; *Frey, *Architettura barocca,* Rome-Milan, n.d. (ca. 1925), Pl. cxvii; *Portoghesi, *Cultura,* Fig. 25; *Portoghesi, *Linguaggio,* Fig. xxx; *Portoghesi, *Disegni,* 16 ff., no. 40 and Fig. 40; *Koschatzky, Oberhuber, and Knab, *I grandi disegni italiani dell'Albertina di Vienna,* Milan, 1972, 64, Fig. 32; Blunt, *Supplements . . . Windsor,* London, n.d., 53 ff.

In all of the above literature the drawing is considered explicitly or implicitly to be an early idea or a preliminary sketch for the Windsor drawing (Cat. 41). The one exception is Thelen, *70 disegni,* 28, no. 70, who considers the design a "Facciata ideale" sketched in 1666–67 in preparation for a plate of the *Opus Architectonicum.*

91.   Francesco Borromini. 1659–60.
    Sketches of ornament for the revised oratory facade.
    Alb. 515ᵛ. Graphite.

The lines sketched below the ornament correspond to the straight and curved segments

91

of the pediment of the oratory facade; the ornament itself, particularly the acorns growing through wreaths and the Porta Pia motif, is quite similar to the ornament sketched on Cat. 90. The device of a heart within a star apparently was taken over into Barrière's print (Fig. 16; Cat. 104a). The sketch is found on the verso of a drawing for the Chigi stucco ornament of the cupola of S. Ivo, which was begun in September 1659 and completed in April 1660 (*Ragguagli*, 225–27). Both recto and verso are quick sketches; it seems unlikely that they would be separated by any great length of time. Unpublished.

92

92.   Camillo Arcucci. 1659.
Project for completing the west wing: plan and elevation.
AV, C.II.8, no. 18. 18.2 × 31.2 cm. Ruled ink with pink and gray wash, pentimenti in dark brown ink. Scale: 100 p. = 8.7 cm.
Inscription: 2.° Piano Nobile.
Cf. Cat. 95.
Unpublished.

93

93.   Camillo Arcucci. 1659.
Project for completing the west wing: plan at *piano nobile* level.
AV, C.II.8, no. 17. 11.2 × 41.4. Ink with graphite flap.
Inscription: 3.0 Piano. [*This is erroneous as far as most of the plan is concerned; however, the third floor corridor is traced in room B, and the flap at the left shows the third floor flight rather than the second.*]
Cf. Cat. 95.
Unpublished.

94

94.   Camillo Arcucci. 1659.
Project for completing the west wing: elevation.
AV, C.II.8, no. 19. 30.8 × 49.9. Ink and wash over graphite. Scale: 100 palmi (unnumbered) = 13.3 cm.
Inscription: Sito della scala.
Cf. Cat. 95.
Unpublished.

95.   Camillo Arcucci. 1659.
Project for completing the west wing: six plans.
AV, C.II.8, no. 20. 78.5 × 50.4. Ruled

ink over graphite. Scale: 100 palmi = 17.1 cm.
Inscriptions (from top to bottom):
Pianta della Fabrica dalla banda di Montegiordano, dall'Orologio fino all'Oratorio.
IV. Piano.
III. Piano.
II. Piano nobile. Va nel 3.o Piano. Camino. Sala . . . [?] Mezzanini. Di Sagrestia.
Piano' terreno. Di Sagrestia.
Fondamento.

In 1657 Spada assumed that regardless of who the executant architect might be, the west wing of the casa would be built on Borromini's designs, "trattandosi di porre in esecuzione i disegni di lui" (Decr. 350). Borromini's drawings for the west wing do

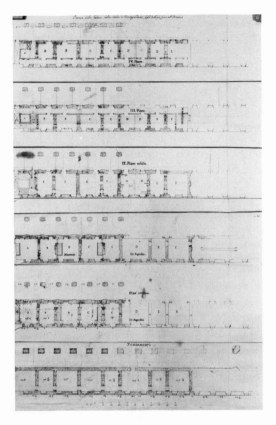

95

not survive, but there is some evidence to show that Arcucci departed from them on two important points when he executed the wing in 1659–62. First, Borromini planned no general staircase near the Monte Giordano projection. One is shown on an early plan as a vestige of Maruscelli (Cat. 21, 39), but it is eliminated in all of his later drawings (Cat. 59, 80, 81) and is not mentioned in the *Opus*. Arcucci reintroduced a staircase at this point; it traversed the three upper floors of the casa but originally did not descend to the ground floor (Fig. 26). In 1924 it was continued to the street and now serves as the entrance to the Istituto Storico per il Medio Evo. Second, Borromini planned to place all corridors on the inside of the building and to have the residential rooms on all floors face the street, just as he had done in the north wing of 1647–50 (implied in *Opus*, XV, 47ᵛ). When Arcucci built the west wing he followed Borromini's arrange-

ment on the third floor but reversed it on the fourth floor, where the rooms all face the courtyard and the corridor now runs along the street. The difference between Borromini's north wing and Arcucci's west wing is apparent not only in later plans and sections (Figs. 25, 26; Cat. 15c, 115d), but also in the position of chimneys along the rooftop (Fig. 83).

Arcucci worked out the system of fenestration on Cat. 92 and 94. As in Borromini's original plan of 1637 (Cat. 39), the four windows at the right reflect the logic of the thicker corner pier, a point emphasized by the dotted lines on Cat. 93. This pattern is duplicated for symmetry at the left end of the wing, and the remaining windows are grouped to form a mild crescendo at the center. At first Arcucci planned seventeen bays; in Cat. 94 a strip of paper pasted down the center reduces the number to sixteen, as in the final building (Fig. 22). Pentimenti on Cat. 92 show Arcucci experimenting with several innovations: the top windows are raised into the level of the roof, basement windows are cut into the *zoccolo,* and mezzanine windows are introduced into the first seven bays on the left; the letter P is used to indicate a street door in the first, third, and fifth bays on the left. Most of these changes were incorporated into the finished elevation in Cat. 94. The upper windows on this latter drawing were numbered from 1 to 48 in pencil, possibly as part of a calculation made in May 1659 of the amount of travertine needed to complete them (Decr. 362); the finial on the Monte Giordano projection still lacks the star installed in late 1660 (Decr. 389).

The disposition of rooms was established in Cat. 92, 93, and 95. The *piano nobile* and the two upper floors were each outfitted with three apartments of two rooms each, labeled B, C, and E; another room, D, was reserved for sacristy storage on the ground floor and used as a *sala* on the *piano nobile.* The wing appears to have been built in conformity with the drawings; modern plans show the same disposition of rooms and differ only in the addition of numerous thin partitions (Cat. 115a–d).
Unpublished.

96.   Anonymous. 1660.

Section of small staircase connecting the *scalone* with the third floor corridor.

Bibl. Vallicelliana, Cod. O 57², fol. 358ᵣ. Ink and graphite.

Inscriptions:

Piano della loggia.
3.o Piano.
Piano del 3.o branco della scala grande.
di [oncie ?] 8 [?] alti. 1½ largo.

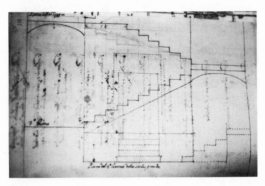

96

This crude section shows the small staircase that connected the main *scalone* with the corridor system of the upper floors. It is shown in eighteenth-century prints (Figs. 26, 54) and was still in use in 1871 (Cat. 115c), but it was suppressed apparently during the restorations of 1924. The sealed doorway that led to the staircase is still visible under the *Attila* relief (Fig. 59). The present drawing must be imagined as facing south and cutting through the wing at a point near the letter "d" in "Via *d*ei Filippini" on Cat. 115c. It shows six steps ascending from the landing of the main *scalone* up to the level of the third floor corridor, and a further nineteen steps ascending up to the level of the *loggia scoperta*. The small staircase was apparently built along with the main *scalone* in 1660; the *Attila* relief was installed above its entrance by October of that year; and in 1662 the door was given a *cancello* to prevent outsiders from wandering into the residential wings (Decr. 383, 385, 419, 420).

Borromini began the main *scalone* in ca. 1643 but left it unfinished; it is still described in the future tense in the *Opus,* and it is difficult to judge how much of it was complete when Borromini left the commission in 1650. The length and width of the staircase housing was apparently fixed on his designs (Fig. 6; Cat. 39). The vault that spans both upper flights was designed by Borromini but carried out by Arcucci, who used his predecessor's chaining technique, complete with "Porta Pia" merlons, to compensate for the lack of lateral buttressing (Fig. 60). The number and dimensions of the risers were apparently up to Arcucci, but since all other variables were fixed his margin of maneuver was limited and his final staircase probably was close to what Borromini would have built. Its four flights contain 107 risers; the two flights shown on Borromini's early plan (Cat. 39) contained 54 risers, which would have made a total of 108. Possibly Arcucci inherited a drawing like the one that survives for the staircase of the Propaganda Fide (Alb. 904) to guide his calculations on the size and height of the steps; his own contribution came to the fore only in the design of moldings and the frame for the *Attila* relief (Fig. 59; cf. Cat. 73).

Unpublished.

97.   Carlo Fontana. 1661.

Plan of *isola* to the west of the casa.

ASR, Archivio Spada, vol. 370, no. 71. 68.4 × 41.5. Ink and wash over graphite. Scale: 100 palmi.

Inscriptions:

—*verso:* Pianta di tutto il sito delle piazze, strade, e case di tutta l'isola a Monte Giordano dove presentem[en]te e il Palazzo de i Sig.ri Spada.

recto: Case de Particolari. Case de particolari. Case Particolari. Convento. Dell'Emm.o Card. Sforza.

Captions:

AB   Piazza di Monte Giordano
B   Strada che da la sud[det]ta Piazza va in Parione
C   Strada che da d[et]ta va al fico
D   Strada che dalla sud[det]ta piazza va in Banchi
E   Strada che viene alla piazza ava[n]ti alla Chiesa nova
F   Piazza ava[nti] come sopra e Oratorio
G   Strada che va alla Chiavica d[et]ta Cala Braghe

97

H Piazza Sforza
I Strada che va alla chiavica
K Vicolo d.o [?] le stalle di Sforza dietro l'Isola della Spada
L Piazzetta del feracochio ind[et]to vicolo
1 Il colore torchino l'ostaria della Spada
2 Il colorito di verde casa dell' [*blank*]
3 Il colore di fior di persico habbia il Barbiere delli RR. PP. di S.o Agostino e
4 Il colore rosso habbia il fornaro della Sforza [?]
5 Il colore pavonazzo scuro abbitano il facchino
6 Il colore di acquarella della Mad[onn]a SS.ma della Consolatione e Concettione
7 Il corole [*sic*] di fior di persico di SS.ri [?] Bon Giovanni
8 Il colore ranciato delli sud. [?] abbita il feraccochio
9 Il colore torchino scuro del Gio. de' Genovesi
10 Il colore Gialla della Sig.ra Tilla
11 [*blank*]
C. Dove sonno li C. dinchiostro sonno cortili nelle sud[det]te case.

The drawing is essentially a site plan of the irregular block of houses between the Piazza Sforza on the south (marked H near the top of the sheet) and the Piazza di Monte Giordano on the north (marked AB near the bottom). Faint pencil marks indicate proposals to revise certain property lines. One, drawn parallel to the casa, slices through seven houses to define a new street 36 palmi wide; to judge from maps, not much of this project was carried out (Fig. 2). Another, drawn at right angles to the casa, delineates a new southern boundary for the Piazza di Monte Giordano (the line passes between nos. 1 and 3, slightly above the letters AB). This line marks the position of the facade of the Banco di S. Spirito and thus provides an indication of the date and function of the drawing.

Spada was appointed Commendatore of the Hospital of S. Spirito by Alexander VII on March 15, 1660. In January 1661 he proposed moving the headquarters of the associated bank from the Piazza dei Banchi to the Piazza di Monte Giordano and installing it in a new building on the site of the old inn coincidentally named the Osteria della Spada (no. 1 on the present plan; its history is narrated by U. Gnoli, *Alberghi ed osterie di Roma nella rinascenza,* Spoleto, 1935, 135 ff.). In March 1661 Spada proposed that the Congregation join with the bank to buy the houses shown on the present plan and regularize the street running along Arcucci's west wing, then nearing completion. Borromini provided facade drawings for the new bank as well as proposals for moving a messengers' stable from the Sforza property to the new building; his assistant Righi was involved in some work on the site. Alexander VII supported the project and in early 1661 even considered moving the Dogana to the Piazza Sforza, after some of its functions had been displaced by the construction of the Bibliotheca Alessandrina in 1659. The directors of the bank, however, were strongly opposed to moving out of the center of the Banchi area. They were overruled and work was begun between June and August 1661; but after Spada's death on December 11, 1662 the opposition gained ground and one of Spada's relatives, Marchese Orazio Spada, was forced to purchase the unfinished palace for ▽25,649.00 on August 18, 1663. For some reason, the hospital was still concerned with ironwork and glazing in the palace in 1666–67. The extent of Borromini's involvement in the building is still uncertain. Falda was still unsure of the facade design in 1665 (Figs. 98b, 98c); most of the present exterior dates from a late-nineteenth-century restoration. (Decr. 392, 393, 394; Ehrle, "Spada," 7 ff., especially nn. 25–27; *GR*, Ponte, III, 59 ff.; *Ragguagli,* 125 ff. and 224 ff.; Ponti, *Il Banco di Santo Spirito,* 87–92. Three Borromini elevations for the facade and plans and elevations for the Stanza dei Cursori are found in ASR, Archivio Spada, vol. 370, nos. 72 and 76, published by M. Heimbürger Ravalli, Pls. 31–33 and 36–38. Another elevation, Alb. 1160, is illustrated in Hempel, 177, Fig. 67, and in Portoghesi, *Linguaggio,* Fig. cxxii. On the Dogana, cf. Decr. 393; *Ragguagli,* 225 ff.; and Martinelli's remarks in D'Onofrio, *Roma nel seicento,* 217.)

Heimbürger Ravalli rightly attributed the present drawing to Carlo Fontana on the grounds of graphic style. It is not unusual to find Fontana working as draftsman and assistant to other architects on some of the major Chigi projects of the period (cf. Ost, "Studien . . . S. Maria della Pace," *Römisches Jahrbuch,* XIII, 1971, Figs. 16, 17, 23).

The main ideas proposed on the present drawing—namely, that the Piazza di Monte Giordano should be reshaped by a swap of private for public land and that the front and sides of the Banco di Santo Spirito should run at right angles to the casa or parallel with it—were incorporated into a license issued by the Mastri di Strade on August 22, 1661; an official copy is to be found in ASR, Presidenze delle strade, busta 45, fol. 170^r–v.

Bibl.: *Heimbürger Ravalli, "Dìsegni sconosciuti del Borromini per il Banco di Santo Spirito e per Palazzo Spada," *Paragone* (Arte), 275, 1973, 57–63, Pl. 39.

98. G. B. Falda. 1665.
Views of the two piazzas.

98a. Piazza della Chiesa Nuova.
Il nuovo teatro delle fabriche, Rome, I, 1665, Pl. 8. 17.0 × 29.0 (plate mark). Engraving. Fig. 100 (detail).
Inscriptions:
Piazza Chiesa e Oratorio di Santa Maria in Vallicella.
1. Chiesa di Santa Maria in Vallicella.
2. Oratorio de Sacerdoti della Cong.ne di S. Filip. Neri.
3. Piazza ampliata da Nostro Sig. Papa Alesandro Settimo.
Per Gio. Jacomo Rossi in Roma alla Pace con P. del S.P. Gio. Batta. Falda di. et f.

98a

98b

98c

98b. Piazza di Monte Giordano looking east at the *torre dell'orologio.*

Op. cit., Pl. 11.

Inscriptions:

Piazza di Monte Giordano Ampliata da N. S. Papa Alessandro VII.

1. Casa delli PP. dell'Orat.o di S. Filip.o Neri.

2. Palazzo de Sig.ri Scarinci.

3. Palazzo de Sig.ri Spada.

4. Strada da monte giordano a Pasquino.

98c. Piazza di Monte Giordano looking south at the Palazzo Spada.

Op. cit., Pl.12.

Inscriptions:

Altra veduta della Piazza di Monte Giordano Ampliata da n. Sig. Papa.

1. Casa delli PP. del'Oratorio di S. Filippo Neri.

2. Palazzo de Sig. Spada.

Per Gio. Jacomo Rossi in Roma alla Pace con Priv. del S. P. Gio. Batta. Falda fece.

Falda's prints are based on those of Barrière (Figs. 89a, 89b), but at the same time they depict the casa and its surroundings with greater realism. His view of the oratory facade, like Barrière's, shows only seven bays, but it does so without entirely idealizing the image. His view of the Piazza della Chiesa Nuova conveys an accurate impression of how it looked between 1630 and 1673, when Maruscelli's funnel-shaped piazza was still in existence (Fig. 101). The four-story house shown at the extreme right marks the point where the Strada Nuova opened into the piazza; judging from the plan shown in Cat. 105, it was hardly more than a shop one bay wide and one bay deep with a few small rooms above. The house was raised one story and incorporated into a larger building in 1702; it appears thus in old photographs (Fig. 9). The print next shows what looks like a rubble wall; this had been a party wall between two houses (nos. 80 and 81 on Cat. 15), which was exposed to view when one of the houses (no. 80) was demolished in 1628. Further to the left, across the Vicolo Sora, stood a block of low "casuccie" (Decr. 366) that came within 7 palmi of touching the corner of the Vallicella facade. The Congregation tried to acquire these houses in 1659 and again in 1673, when they were finally demolished and a broad new street, the Via della Chiesa Nuova, was cleared along the flank of the church (Decr. 366, 367, 371; Cat. 103). Falda is also accurate in showing the unpaved surface of the piazza and the lack of any podium in front of the oratory facade (Cat. 113).

Falda's two prints of the Piazza di Monte Giordano contradict each other in their rendering of the Banco di S. Spirito (then Palazzo Spada): Cat. 98c shows a columnar portal and shops which are lacking in Cat. 98b. They also disagree on the number of stories in the house at the northwest corner of the casa. Furthermore, Cat. 98c shows Arcucci's side wing with either fifteen or seventeen window bays, depending on the story, the correct number being sixteen. However, Cat. 98b provides an accurate

rendering of the Palazzo Boncompagni-Corcos, the major neighbor of the casa to the north (*GR,* Ponte, III, 60 ff.; here labeled Pal. Scarinci and on Nolli 580 Pal. Camerata).

Bibl.: GR, Ponte, III, 59 and 61 (Cat. 98b–c).

99.   Lieven Cruyl. February 1665.

View of the Piazza della Chiesa Nuova (reversed).

The Cleveland Museum of Art, Dudley P. Allen Fund, 43.267. 40.1 × 50.9. Pen and wash.

Inscriptions:

[1.] Prospetto della Chiesa di S. Maria in Vallicella vulgo Chiesa Nuova.

[2.] L. Cruyl delin. Romae mense Febr. 1665.

The view is taken from the top of the house at the southwest corner of the piazza; however, the stylized roof terrace shown in the foreground appears to be an artist's convention rather than a realistic depiction of the house prior to its rebuilding in 1743–45 (cf. *Röm. Ved.,* II, Pls. 78, 91). The rendering of the oratory facade is occasionally capricious: Cruyl's four-column portal, his exaggerated curvature, and some of his window frames do not correspond to the actual facade, and he persists in showing all lower windows of the oratory as though they were sealed. On the other hand, he accurately represents the appearance of the library and the skyline of the facade prior to the expansion of the *salone* in October 1665 (Cat. 100, 101). The width of the Via dei Filippini to the left of the casa is exaggerated, but the drawing provides the only view of the side facade of the Banco di S. Spirito of 1661 ff. In other details, such as the state of the paving of the piazza and the appearance of the houses along its eastern edge, the drawing agrees with Falda's print of the same year (Cat. 98a).

Bibl.: *Egger, *Röm. Ved.,* II, 41 and Pl. 99; *Hess, "Chiesa Nuova," Fig. 15. On the artist, cf. Ashby, "Lieven Cruyl e le sue vedute di Roma (1664–70)," *Mem. Pont. Acc. R. di Archeologia,* Ser. III, I, 1, 1923, 221–29.

100.   Anonymous. 1665.

Project for expanding the library *salone:* plan and partial elevation (caption numbers added).

99

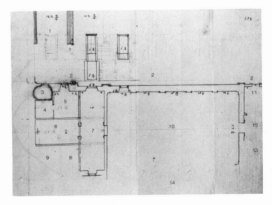

Bibl. Vallicelliana, Cod. 0 57², fol. 354.
Ink and graphite. Scale: 100 palmi.

The lower half of the drawing provides an accurate plan of the library and its annexes between 1642 and 1665; the upper half shows a crude project for the expansion of the *salone,* which took place in 1665–67.

The oratory facade is not indicated on the drawing, but if it were, the central balcony would be located at no. 14. The main *salone* (10) and three small annexes to the east (11, 12, 13) served for general reading and study, while the annexes to the west served a number of specialized functions: librarian's rooms (4 and 5), circulating library (6), gallery of maps (7), archive (8), and finally a small museum (10) for the collection of medals and antiquities which Spada intended to leave to the Congregation (Doc. 20). Some of these rooms were allotted to padri as living quarters between 1647

100

and 1660 (Decr. 214, 391, 396). Until the main *scalone* was built in 1659–62, the principal route to the library had been up the spiral staircase (3); afterward it was up the *scalone* (1), through a portal flanked by columns to the *loggia scoperta* (2), and through another door into the entrance vestibule (7) which also doubled as the map gallery (*Opus,* XXVIII, and *Dialogo,* 192 ff., especially n. 45).

The plan shows that the wall at the west end of the *salone* (between 10 and 7) was thinner than the wall at the east end, an indication of the care Borromini had taken not to strain the oratory vault below. Nonetheless, widening cracks were observed in September 1665 and outside consultants urged moving this thin wall to the outer edge of the building, thus enlarging the *salone* at the expense of the smaller annexes. The operation was begun in October 1665; an extension of the coffered ceiling of the *salone* was authorized in February 1666, of the bookshelves in December 1666, and finally of the brick floor in November 1667 (Decr. 446–451, 453–455, 457, 459, 460, 465).

The elevation sketch on the upper half of the sheet is an amateur project for this expansion. One window of the old *salone* is shown in ink, bookshelves in pencil. Two additional windows are projected, one in pencil where the former spiral stairs had emerged, one in ink over the entrance to the former map gallery. A professional would have begun by working out the design on the south side of the room, where the oratory facade imposed stricter limits on the fenestration. The only possible solution was the one adopted in the final building: no new windows on either the north or south wall of the *salone,* and three new apertures in the west wall to match the three already existing in the lower stories (Figs. 20, 22). *Bibl.:* *Incisa della Rocchetta, "Il salone della Biblioteca Vallicelliana," *Palladio,* XXIII, 1973, 123.

101.   Anonymous. 1665.
Project for enlarging the oratory facade in conjunction with the library.
Bibl. Vallicelliana, Cod. 0 57², fol. 351. Ink.
Inscriptions:
    gionta che si fa alla libraria. facciata dell'Oratorio. Chiesa . . .[?]

The enlargement of the library was carried out with more sensibility to Borromini's de-

101

sign than is usually supposed. The new exterior sections were given pilaster strips to match the articulation of the original facade; the section at the left was balanced by a smaller pendant on the right (Decr. 453, 454); the dark color indicated by the ink hatching was intended to make the additions less conspicuous. The new window at the upper right was balanced by a blind window at the upper left (Fig. 12); equal care was taken with the inner face overlooking the courtyard (Fig. 60).

Hess attributed the drawing to P. Sebastiano Resta on grounds of handwriting and of his known artistic activity at the casa. Resta did enter the Congregation in 1665 (Gasbarri, 181), but his main activity is later in the century and his name is absent from the *decreti* which deal with the enlargement of the library.
Bibl.: *Strong, Pl. XXXIV (attributed to Borromini); *Hess, "Chiesa Nuova," 360, Fig. 16; *Portoghesi, *Cultura,* Fig. 27 (attributed to V. Spada, who died in 1662); *Ragguagli,* 254 (attributed to V. Spada).

102.   Carlo Rainaldi. 1667–74.
Project for the curtain wall along the east flank of S. Maria in Vallicella.
AV, C.II.8, no. 35. 43.2 × 79.0. Ink over graphite, with pink, beige, and dark brown wash.
Inscription on verso:
    Pianta della strada aperta nel fianco orientale della nostra Chiesa nel 1675.

Marchese Orazio Spada offered to undertake the patronage of the Chapel of S. Carlo Borromeo in January 1662. The *vicolo* that

102

occupied the site was closed in May 1663. Carlo Rainaldi was taken on as associate architect in February 1667; his associate on the site was Giuseppe Brusati Arcucci, nephew of the Arcucci who built the west wing in 1659–62 and who designed the campanile of the church in 1666. Old houses on the site of the chapel were finally cleared in 1668. Work on the short wing needed to close the service courtyard of the casa went on simultaneously with the chapel. A donor appeared in 1669, probably P. Ascanio Belluzzi, the Oratorian who inhabited the rooms upon their completion in 1675 (Decr. 422–424, 462, 467–469, 504, 514).

The Chapel of S. Carlo originally had been intended as a twin to the Chapel of S. Filippo Neri. At the patron's request the site was extended and the structure made into a generous tripartite sequence of vestibule, chapel, and altar (cf. Cat. 109 in contrast to Figs. 5 and 6). The final east wing of the casa was limited in width by the extended chapel and in length by the *portone* arch; its height was kept to less than half of Borromini's wing of 1638–40. The terrace above the new rooms was shielded from the street by a screen wall, a device Rainaldi borrowed from his father's work at the Casa Professa (Fig. 94).

Rainaldi was also responsible for the design of the brick screen along the east flank of the Vallicella, which was probably executed along with the opening of the Via della Chiesa Nuova in 1673–75 (Cat. 103). His design solved problems of lighting that had eluded earlier architects: triangular spaces were left between the chapels to illuminate them from the sides. The elevation which is proposed on the present drawing

was altered to some extent in execution. The paired pilasters, borrowed from the opposite side of the church, were converted into simple framing bands. Each tall window was divided into two separate apertures, one for the chapels and one for the loggia immediately above. Only one of the two transept doors was executed; the corridor behind the second door, the one on the right, was used to install a stairway to the campanile in 1674 (Decr. 489).

Bibl.: Fasolo, *L'opera di Hieronimo e Carlo Rainaldi,* Rome, 1961, 365, n. 39.

103a. Anonymous. March 2, 1675.

License to build an arch over the *vicoletto* entering the Via della Chiesa Nuova.

AV, small cartella.

Inscriptions:

Concediamo licenza alli molto Reverendi Padri della Congregatione dell'Oratorio in Santa Maria in Vallicella di poter coprire con arco, e volta il vicoletto traversale, che è tra le case nuove, che essi Padri vanno fabricando per tutta la longhezza dal cantone della nuova strada da' medemi aperta, segnato nella qui sotto pianta con littera A sino all'altro cantone vecchio del vicoletto, che rivolta segnato con littera B a tutta la larghezza che porta il detto vicoletto traversale, con lassare al piano della strada il passo libero, inherendo anche al Chirographo di Nostro Signore Papa Clemente X.mo, segnato sotto li 15 di Novembre 1673 . . . , et esibito avanti Monsignore Thesoriero negl'atti de Cancellieri della Rev. Camera Apostolica li 28 detto. Havendo noi riconosciuto, che unendo con detto arco le loro fabriche fatte nella nuova strada, con l'altre che fanno nella Piazza rende ornamento e magior'comodità alla citta, e di verun pregiuditio al publico. Pertanto commandiamo non siano molestati, che tale . . . questo di 2 marzo 1675.

Bartolomeo Capranica Maestro di Strada
Mutio Massimi Maestro di Strada
Il Barto . . . Capran . . .

Chiesa. Strada aperta di nuovo. Piazza. Vicoletto traversale. Vicoletto. Case che si fabricano. regis. a fol. 110.

103b. Anonymous. July 6, 1677.

License to build two *muriccioli* under the arch flanking the Via della Chiesa Nuova.

ASR, CRM, Cong. dell'Oratorio, vol. 136, fol. 134. 27.3 × 41.7. Ink with pink and gray wash over pencil. Scale: 100 p. = 5.5 cm.

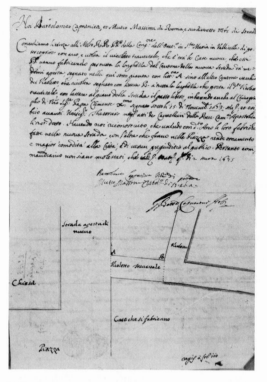

103a

License on fol. 132:

Noi Marchese Prospero Maccarani, et Prospero Boccapaduli di Roma, e suo distretto Mastri di Strade.

Per tenore della presente, e per l'autorità dal Nro. officio concediamo licenza alli molto RR. PP. della Congregatione dell'Oratorio in Santa Maria in Vallicella di poter fare due muriccioli dalle parti dell'arco nel vicoletto traversale, che è tra le case nuove fabbricate da detti molti RR. PP. e sbocca nella strada nuovamente dalli medemi aperta, e questi siano in longhezza di tutto l'arco, et di larghezza palmi tre non portando pregiuditio al pubblico, et il tutto si faccia con l'assistenza del Sig. Tommaso . . . [?] architetto, e nostro sottomaestro deputato per tanto. Commandiamo niuno sij per tal causa molestato. Dal li 6 luglio 1677. Prospero Maccarani Maestro di strada. Prospero Boccapadule Maestro di strada.

Inscriptions on drawing:

Chiesa di S.ta Maria in Vallicella e S. Filippo Neri de PP. dell'Oratorio detto della Chiesa Nova. Piazza. Strada Nova fatta da PP. Vicolo fabricato chiuso con arco sotto. Case fabricate e alzate da PP. Case fabricate e alzate da PP. Vico-

letto. Casa della Sig.ra Olimpia Teresia de Palzari. Strada dal Pellegrino al Governatore. Palazzo del Governatore di Roma. Piazza del Duca di Sora.

A wide street along the right flank of the church and casa had been planned ever since the Via di Pizzomerlo was closed in 1621; it was shown on Maruscelli's plans (Cat. 14), predicted in Spada's *Dialogo* (p. 195), and finally begun in September 1673. The street was opened up in two stretches: first from the Via di Parione as far south as the *portaria vecchia* (a point just outside the second chapel on the right side of the church), and from there south to the Vicolo Sora. The street was ready for the Holy Year of 1675, closed to traffic with a chain on April 30, 1675, and paved as far south as the Vallicella steps in 1677 (Decr. 480, 481, 492, 493, 496, 497, 499; inscription given in Gasbarri, 234, n. 176).

The west side of the new street was lined with a large rentable structure, described as an *appartamento,* which was built in four units, three of them between the Via di Parione and the arch, and the fourth between the arch and the Vicolo Sora. According to the documents accompanying Cat. 103b (in vol. 136, fols. 127–142), these units cost ▽6,703.73, ▽3,701.28, ▽4,134.63, and ▽5,057.83, in addition to ▽2,754.34 worth of salvaged material from demolished structures on the site; these figures add up to ▽22,351.81, but somehow the total recorded in the documents is slightly higher, ▽25,279.38. When the foundations were being excavated many pieces of antique sculpture were discovered and entrusted to the sculptor Ercole Ferrata for appraisal; they are mentioned in an entry of September 11, 1673 in the diary of Carlo Cartari. The master mason in charge of building the new *appartamento* was Carlo Morelli and the architect Giuseppe Brusati Arcucci. In elevation the building was modeled on the house already standing in the center of the piazza opposite the oratory facade, erected in 1655 (Cat. 87). In November 1674 a dispute arose over the height of the new building: Arcucci and Padre Ascanio Belluzzi wanted to include a mezzanine story on the top, while Carlo Rainaldi objected on

FACIES EXTERIOR ORATO RII PP S PHILIPPI NERII

104a

the grounds that the proportions of the design would be upset and the neighboring houses deprived of light and air. The outcome is not known, and it is unclear whether the new building was five stories high from the beginning, or was raised to that height in 1748 (Decr. 487, 499, 602, 609). It is the only one of the four *appartamenti* surrounding the Piazza della Chiesa Nuova to have escaped the demolitions of 1885 (Fig. 103).

On Cat. 103b colored washes were used to show simultaneously the actual state of the piazza in 1677, which was still the funnel left by Maruscelli (Cat. 38), as well as the ideal state authorized in Urban VIII's bull of 1627 but not carried out until 1702 (Cat. 105, 106).

Bibl.: Cat. 103a is unpublished. Cat. 103b and the accompanying documents are mentioned in Corbo, *L'archivio della Congregazione dell'Oratorio di Roma e l'archivio della Abbazia di S. Giovanni in Venere. Inventario,* Rome, 1964, 42. Further documentation is provided in Corbo, "Apertura di una strada alla Chiesa Nuova nel 1673: ritrovamenti archeologici e polemiche," *Commentarii,* XXIII, 1972, 181–85.

104. Giovanni Jacomo de Rossi. 1684.
Three engravings of the oratory.

104a. Idealized view of the oratory facade, after Barrière's engraving of 1660.
Insignium Romae Templorum Prospectus . . . , Rome, 1684, Pl. 31.

104b. West end of the oratory: plan and elevation.
Op. cit., Pl. 32.

FACIES INTERIOR, AC ALTARE ORATORII PP S PHILIPPI NERII

104b

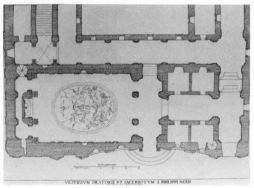

VESTIGIVM ORATORII PP SACERDOTVM S PHILIPPI NERII

104c

104c.   Plan of the oratory and *portaria.*
Op. cit., Pl. 33.

In the first edition of his book, which appeared in 1683, de Rossi included plates of three Borromini buildings: the Lateran (adapted directly from the plates in Cesare Rasponi's *De Basilica et Patriarchio Lateranensi Libri Quattuor,* Rome, 1656, colophon 1657); S. Carlo alle Quattro Fontane (apparently based on a Borromini plan like Alb. 173 but omitting the geometrical armature: Portoghesi, *Linguaggio,* Fig. xvii); and S. Agnese. By 1684, however, de Rossi had discovered the Barrière plates of S. Ivo and the oratory, which at that time were still in the possession of Bernardo Borromini; de Rossi immediately used this new material for a second and enlarged edition. He redrew the Barrière prints as strict orthogonal elevations and sections, and in the process he reversed them, a fact that is most apparent when the angels at the crown of the oratory facade in his print (Cat. 104a) are compared with the same feature in the Barrière-Giannini print (Fig. 16). In general, de Rossi's prints are stiff and clumsy, but the oratory engraving does preserve most of the main features of the original Barrière source, namely the canted corner pilasters, the portal at the left side of the facade, the fiction of sealed window niches, the rougher treatment of the brickwork of the two end bays and of the pediment, and the abundance of ornament along the skyline.

De Rossi's view of the west end of the oratory (Cat. 104b) shows the high altar as it appeared in his day. The *coretti* dated from 1654–55, the four alabaster columns from 1659, the altar from 1660–62, and the altarpiece from 1664. The four angels and crucifix were apparently painted effigies on wooden panels (Cat. 48).

De Rossi's plan of the oratory and *portaria* is crude and inaccurate in many respects: the oratory facade is shown with canted end pilasters; all oratory windows are shown as sealed; the rendering of the courtyard is incomprehensible. However, the print does contain the only record of Romanelli's vault fresco of the *Coronation,* which was painted in 1639–40 but replaced by Pietro Angeletti's *Divine Wisdom* in 1788 (Chapter 3, n. 28).
Bibl.: *Strong, *La Chiesa Nuova (Santa Maria in Vallicella),* Rome, 1923, Pl. XXXVIa; *De Bernardi Ferrero, Pls. 29–31.

105.   Anonymous. 1702.
Houses at the southeast corner of the piazza: site plan and project for rebuilding.
AV, small cartella. Ink and wash. Scale: 100 palmi.

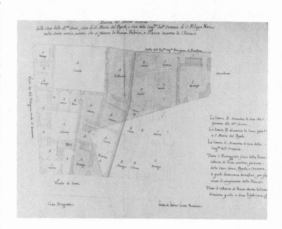

105

Inscriptions:
Pianta del Piano Terreno delle case delle SS.re Cerosi, case di S. Maria del Popolo, e case della Cong.ne dell'Oratorio di S. Filippo Neri nello stato antico, avanti che si facesse la nuova Fabrica, e Piazza incontro la Chiesa.
Stalla dell'Ecc.mo Sig. Principessa di Piombino.
A. Bottega. Bottega. Cortile. Gallinaro. Stanza. Passo. Stanza. Stanza. Entrone. Cortile. Osteria. Bottega. Rimessa.
B. Stanza. Cortile. Stanza. Stanza. Bottega. Entrone.
C. Stanza. Cortile. Bottega. Stanza. Bottega.
Vicolo di Sora.
Casa Brugiotti.
Stradone.
La littera A. dimostra le case che spettano alle SS.re Cerosi.
La littera B. dimostra la casa spett.e a S. Maria del Popolo.
La littera C. dimostra le case della Cong.ne dell'Oratorio.

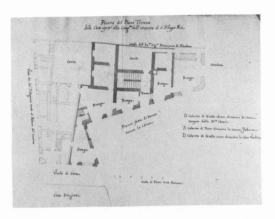

106a

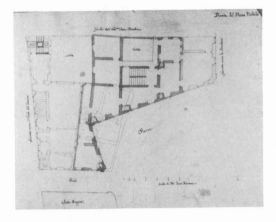

106b

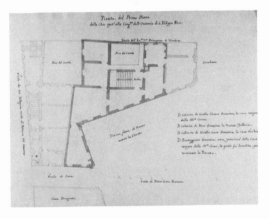

106c

Tutto il punteggiato furoi della linea colorita di rosso, contiene porzione delle case, Cerosi, Popolo, e Oratorio, le quali doveranno demolirsi per formare il compimento della Piazza.

Tutto il colorito di rosso dentro la linea dimostra quello si deve rifabricare.

Cf. Cat. 106.
Unpublished.

106. Anonymous. 1702.
Projects for squaring off the southeast corner of the piazza.
AV, small cartella. Ink and wash. Scale: 100 palmi.

106a. Ground floor plan.
Inscriptions:
Pianta del Piano Terreno delle Case spett.i alla Cong.ne dell'Oratorio di S. Filippo Neri. Stalla dell' Ecc.ma Sig.ra Principessa di Piombino. Cortile. Cortile. Bottega. Bottega. Bottega. Entrone. Bottega. Bottega. Stradone. Vicolo che dal Pellegrino tende al Palazzo del Governo. Vicolo di Sora. Piazza fatta di nuovo avanti la Chiesa. Casa Brugiotti. Il colorito di giallo chiaro dimostra la casa compra. dalle SS.re Cerosi. Il colorito di nero dimostra la nuova Fabrica. Il colorito di giallo scuro dimostra la casa vecchia.

106b. *Piano nobile* plan.
Inscriptions:
Fienile dell' Ecc.ma Casa Piombini. Cortile. Cortile. Facciata verso il Vicolo del Governo. Vicolo. Isola Brugiotti. Piazza. facciata verso lo Stradone.

106c. Second floor plan.
Inscriptions:
Pianta del Primo Piano delle Case spett.i alla Cong.ne dell'Oratorio di S. Filippo Neri. Fienile dell' Ecc.ma S.ra Principessa di Piombino. Aria del Cortile. Aria del Cortile. Scala. Vicolo che dal Pellegrino tende al Palazzo del Governo. Vicolo di Sora. Casa Brugiotti. Piazza fatta di nuovo avanti la Chiesa. Stradone. Il colorito di Giallo chiaro dimostra la casa compra dalle SS.re Cerosi. Il colorito di nero dimostra la Nuova Fabrica. Il colorito di Giallo scuro dimostra la Casa Vecchia. Il Punteggiato dimostra una porzione della Casa compra dalle SS.re Cerosi, la quale fu demolita per terminare la Piazza.

In 1700 the celebrated doctor Giovanni Maria Lancisi (1654–1720) became official physician of the Congregation; in 1702 he proposed to build his residence at the southeast corner of the piazza and at the same time to carry out the old project for a square piazza, shown in Maruscelli's drawings (Cat. 15, 17e), and authorized in Urban VIII's bull of 1627 (Doc. 7). Cat. 105 shows a site plan of the old houses to be demolished: house C corresponds to house no. 81 on Cat. 15, houses B and A are shown unnumbered on the same early drawing. Cat. 106a–c show the definitive project for the new Casa Lancisi: they provide the well and light-court stipulated in the documents and in general attempt to make rational use of an irrational site (Decr. 546, 547; on Lancisi cf. Gasbarri, 89 ff., and *Bibliografia Romana*, I, Rome, 1880, 146–49).

The plans elucidate some of the puzzling features of these buildings shown in nineteenth-century photographs. Fig. 9 shows the Casa Lancisi on the extreme left; the shadow in the foreground of the photograph indicates that the house was built around a right angle, as the present drawings propose. Fig. 11 shows the rear facade of the Casa Cerosi along the "Vicolo che dal Pellegrino tende al Palazzo del Governo." The narrow side of this building along the Vicolo di Sora, seen in shadow just to the left of the oratory facade on Fig. 11, appears to be made up of two separate structures, a fact confirmed by the present drawings. Unpublished.

107.   Alessandro Specchi. 1702.
Details of the oratory facade and the *sala di ricreaztione.*
Domenico de Rossi, *Studio d'architettura civile,* I, Rome, 1702.

107a.   *Op. cit.,* Pl. 85. 32.5 × 22.2 (plate mark).
Main portal of the oratory.

107b.   *Op. cit.,* Pl. 86. 32.5 × 22.2.
Details of a.

107c.   *Op. cit.,* Pl. 87. 32.5 × 22.2.
Window of the cardinals' loggia over the main portal of the oratory.

107d.   *Op. cit.,* Pl. 88. 32.5 × 22.2.
Details of c.

107e.   *Op. cit.,* Pl. 89. 36.5 × 23.3.
Facade window.

107f.   *Op. cit.,* Pl. 90. 32.5 × 21.3.
Central niche of facade.

107g.   *Op. cit.,* Pl. 91. 32.5 × 21.3.
Details of f.

107h.   *Op. cit.,* Pl. 92. 41.3 × 20.5.
Upper facade window.

107i.   *Op. cit.,* Pl. 97. 43.6 × 31.8.
Chimney of the *sala di ricreazione,* plan and elevation.

(107 continued)   Carlo Quadri and Antonio Barbey. 1702.

107j.   *Op. cit.,* Pl. 93. 36.0 × 20.0.
Main portal of the casa.

107k.   *Op. cit.,* Pl. 94. 36.2 × 24.8.
Portal from the atrium into the oratory. The bust of a Caesar is fancifully substituted for Bolgi's bust of S. Filippo Neri shown in Fig. 36.
Cf. *Opus,* IX, 32^r; *Opus* MS, Pl. 17; Decr. 111, 253.

107l.   *Op. cit.,* Pl. 95. 30.8 × 16.2.
Sacristy portal, here wrongly attributed to Borromini.
Cf. Doc. 11.

107m.   *Op. cit.,* Pl. 96. 34.5 × 19.2.
Door of the cardinals' apartment on the *piano nobile.*
Bibl.: *De Bernardi Ferrero, Pls. 75–87 (facsimile).

108.   Assistant of Domenico de Rossi. 1711.
Garden courtyard: three bays of the loggia in perspective.
Domenico de Rossi, *Studio d'architettura civile,* II, Rome, 1711, Pl. 7. 38.2 × 26.2. Engraving.
Bibl.: *De Bernardi Ferrero, Pl. 95 (facsimile).

109.   Assistant of Domenico de Rossi. 1721.
Plan of the casa.
Domenico de Rossi, *Studio d'architettura civile,* III, Rome, 1721, Pl. 22. 61.4 × 42.4 (plate mark). Engraving.

The three volumes of Domenico de Rossi's *Studio* appeared between 1702 and 1721 at intervals of roughly a decade; during this period a certain evolution seems to have

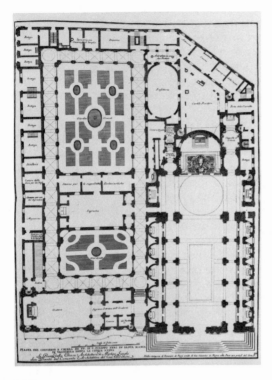

109

1661–62, complete with the balustrades or grilles that were installed between the piers of the loggia to keep people from walking on the plants (Decr. 394, 397, 402, 407, 408; Doc. 24). The plan is the first to record three new features of S. Maria in Vallicella: the Spada Chapel begun in 1663, the heraldry of the Oratorian Cardinal Leandro Colloredo (1639–1709) on the pavement over his tomb in the presbytery, and the polygonal exterior revetment that Carlo Rainaldi gave to the chapels along the right side of the church in 1667–74 (Cat. 102; Gasbarri, 182; Strong, 78).

The way in which the plan renders the first courtyard is more problematic. The arches are shown sealed in a way that may correspond to a decision taken in 1652–53 (Fig. 48; Decr. 319, 327, 328, 387, 388). No other source documents a garden in the first courtyard, and in any case, if one ever existed, it was paved over in 1761 (Decr. 618). The staircase that is shown descending from the Via dei Filippini to the basement under the sacristy is not recorded on other plans but is present in the building today.

The plan is manifestly inaccurate in only one respect. The rooms of the west wing of the casa are correct in number but distorted in their relative proportions (Cat. 95, 115a). The evidence is at present too contradictory to judge whether the plan accurately renders the fenestration of the oratory as it stood in 1721 (Cat. 85).

Bibl.: *Hess, "Chiesa Nuova," Fig. 12 (which is confused with the plan in the *Opus* of 1725); *De Bernardi Ferrero, Pl. 120.

taken place in the publisher's goals and working methods, one which involved a shift from the rendering of ornamental details to larger overall renderings of entire buildings. The last volume of the *Studio* shows signs of competition with Giannini's volume on S. Ivo, which came out the year before; furthermore, de Rossi may have known that Giannini's next volume would be on the Casa dei Filippini and for that reason have included a detailed plan of the casa based on his own fresh survey of the building (Cat. 109).

De Rossi's plan is one of the few that do not seem to derive in some way from the original projects of Maruscelli and Borromini, and in many respects it is more accurate than any of its predecessors. It correctly shows pilasters with *membretti* in the corridor to the east (plans like Figs. 5 and 6 are the pilasters without *membretti* in the corridor to the east (plans like Figs. 15 and 16 are inaccurate in this respect). The garden in the second courtyard apparently represents the one laid out by Camillo Arcucci in

110.   Sebastiano Giannini. 1725.
   Prints of the entire casa.
   Opera del Cav. Francesco Boromino Cavata da Suoi Originali cioè L'Oratorio, e Fabrica per l'Abitazione De PP. dell'Oratorio di S. Filippo Neri di Roma . . . , Rome, 1725. Accompanied by a Latin translation entitled *Opus Architectonicum Equitis Francisci Boromini.*

A full treatment of the plates in Giannini's *Opera* would be too lengthy to include here, but a summary may be given of the kinds of conclusions that are possible from an analysis of the internal evidence. Giannini began his enterprise of publishing the *Opera,* or complete works of Borromini, in 1720 with his volume on S. Ivo alla Sapienza. Plates II to IX of this book are based directly on the prints of S. Ivo prepared by Borromini and Barrière in 1660, as discussed above in Cat. 90. The rest of the plates derive from a variety of sources: from Giannini's enlargement and updating of the Barrière group; from drawings by Borromini or his assistant Righi; and finally, though to a very limited extent, from the building itself as it appeared in 1720. Giannini's second volume on the Casa dei Filippini, which appeared in 1725, was based on the same kind of sources, but in addition he now also had access to the manuscript by Spada and Borromini in the Vallicella archives, commonly known as the *Opus* manuscript (C.II.6 in the current numbering of the archives, discussed above in Cat. 84–86). Giannini took his text directly from this manuscript. He worked hurriedly and made many mistakes of transcription; he omitted countless short phrases and one longer passage on the Palazzo Pamphilj; he changed the text wherever it referred to an illustration, adding interpolations that emphasize his own particular interest in *modinature,* elaborate molding profiles; he introduced a reference to the Monte Giordano clocktower although none occured in the original; and finally he added a date into his edition, May 10, 1656, which appears in no known source, and which has misled scholars into thinking that he was working with a lost manuscript that represented a further stage in the evolution of the text. On the contrary, Giannini used the manuscript now in the Vallicella archives, and in addition adapted many of its drawings as the basis of his engraved plates. This fact can best be demonstrated by sorting his prints into a few basic groups, and then indicating some of their sources.

1. *Plans.* Plate II (Fig. 5), the famous, widely reproduced plan of the casa, was created by superimposing two drawings of the *Opus* manuscript. The dotted lines showing demolished houses on the site were taken from Cat. 14, whereas the plan of the casa was taken from Fig. 6 (Cat. 84a). The

inscriptions on the print were transcribed from the former drawing, with changes in tense where appropriate. Giannini tried to update the plan of the casa but in fact introduced many new errors into his print, such as the distorted renderings of the Spada Chapel, the north staircase, the northwest corner shops, the sacristy windows, and the pilaster rhythms on the north interior wall of the oratory. Consequently the plan has no independent value as a record of what the building looked like in 1725. Plate III is a plan of the west half of the building, basically copied from Plate II but slightly corrected to conform to the plan in de Rossi's *Studio* III.

2. *The oratory facade.* Plate V (Fig. 16) is either the original or a faithful copy of Barrière's engraving of the oratory facade of 1660, which showed the facade in an idealized, freestanding state, seven bays wide, and considerably enriched with decorative ornament, as discussed in Cat. 90. Plate VI (Fig. 15), on the other hand, is an orthogonal elevation of the facade as it stood in Giannini's day, complete with the library extension of 1665; possibly it represents an updated version of something like the Windsor drawing (Cat. 41). Several of Giannini's prints are enlargements of details from Barrière (Plates X, XI, XX); others show details from the actual facade (Plates VII–IX, XIV–XIX, XXI–XXVI). Three prints of facade details seem to come from drawings by the draftsman Anonymous C of the *Opus* manuscript (Plate XII from Cat. 86g and 86h; Plate XIII from Cat. 86j; and Plate XXVI from Cat. 86e); they take over the peculiar conventions of shading and the use of a "ragged edge" to abbreviate pilasters that characterize Anonymous C's work. One print, Plate IV, is a bizarre concoction of Giannini's own; it combines Barrière's idealizing tendencies with a rather literal view of the facade as it stood in Giannini's day to produce a hybrid quite foreign to Borromini's or to anyone else's intentions. Giannini's final plate (LXVII) is a characteristic eighteenth-century *veduta* of the casa from the southwest, showing it more or less as it looked in 1725.

3. *The west facade.* In order to understand

Giannini's large fold-out elevation of the west facade (Plate XXVII, Fig. 22), it is helpful to make a distinction between the engraver's conceptual model and his factual sources. In this case Giannini's conceptual model is without doubt Maruscelli's original facade drawing (Cat. 23c), just as his long sections through the casa (Figs. 25 and 26) are modeled on Maruscelli's sections (Cat. 23a or possibly Cat. 37e). By going back to the Maruscelli drawings Giannini missed the point of Borromini's innovations, which had the effect of splitting off the Monte Giordano facade from the casa; as usual, Barrière gives a much better idea of the idealized state in which Borromini wanted the building to be seen (Cat. 89a). once Giannini had settled on his basic conceptual model he redrew the facade on the basis of other factual sources; his plate represents the west facade as it stood in his day, including the six-hour clock dial and the expanded library. Three other prints, Pls. XXVIII, XXIX, and XXXII, are simply enlarged details from the basic image. Two prints, however, Pls. XXX and XXXI (Fig. 105), show a twelve-hour clock dial and appear to be based on lost drawings by Borromini, as discussed in Cat. 89.

4. *Doorframes.* Giannini appears to have taken Pls. XXXIII–XXXVIII directly from the building as he saw it.

5. *Sections through the oratory and library.* Once again it is helpful to distinguish between Giannini's conceptual model and his factual sources. In Giannini's conception, sections in Pls. XXXIX–XLVIII are indebted to the sections through the oratory by the draftsman Anonymous B of the *Opus* manuscript (Cat. 85a, c, e). However, he updated his models in detail, particularly by showing the new oratory altar of 1653 and the library expansion of 1665. A comparison between one of his sections (Pl. XLII, Fig. 27) and the section in the manuscript (Cat. 85a) gives a good idea of Giannini's debt to Anonymous B but also of his own independent contribution.

6. *First and second courtyards.* The conceptual model of Giannini's Pls. L and LIII is to be found either in a drawing in the *Opus* manuscript (Cat. 86m) or in one of Barrière's prints (Cat. 89c). However, as usual, the prints were updated in matters of detail to match the building as it stood in 1725. The same is true for his sections through the building, Pls. LIV, LV, LVI, and LVIII (Figs. 25, 26), which show the casa as Maruscelli would have done had he come back to life in 1725.

7. *Lavamani, refectory,* and *sala di ricreazione.* Pls. LIX–LXVI generally represent the eighteenth-century state of the casa, although some of them (Pls. LIX, LX, LXIV) show the influence of Cat. 86o and 86p, drawings in the *Opus* manuscript by draftsman Anonymous C.

At some point after 1725 Giannini began work on a third volume of his *Opera* series, which was dedicated to S. Carlo alle Quattro Fontane. It exists in a single proof copy in the Vallicella archives and consists of a dedication plate and five plates of the building but no text. Like the previous volumes, Giannini's edition of S. Carlo is based on a variety of sources, including identifiable Borromini drawings, prints in earlier books, and the actual building as it stood in the early eighteenth century. The volume is undated, but it would seem likely that it was undertaken before 1730, the approximate date when the collection of Borromini drawings that the architect had left to his nephew Bernardo Borromini (1643–1709) was acquired by Baron von Stosch, through whose *Atlas* the drawings passed on to Vienna. According to a notice in the *Giornale de' letterati d'Italia,* Venice, XXXIII, 1722, parte seconda, 509 ff. (quoted in De Bernardi Ferrero, xiv), Giannini was also preparing a fourth volume in the *Opera* series, but its content remains unknown. Although there is little external evidence about Giannini, the evidence of the plates themselves allows some conclusions about his working methods. Rather than being a mere literal copyist, he was an active editor who transformed his sources in characteristic ways; to understand these transformations it helps to distinguish between his conceptual models, which were often older drawings, and his factual sources, which included the buildings as they stood in the period 1720–30. Giannini was a direct competitor of Domenico de Rossi, and a sense of mutual rivalry and interaction can be detected between the volumes of the *Opera* and the later volumes of the *Studio*. Giannini's great strength was his access to the "entire studio" of Borromini at a time when Borromini drawings were in great demand; although he did not entirely understand the material in his hands, his edition of Borromini was quite authentically "cavata da suoi originali." This much can be deduced from the evidence of the books themselves. On the other hand, the questions of who Giannini was, why he undertook the publication of the *Opera,* why the volume on S. Carlo was abandoned, and when the engraver died, all remain unanswered.

Bibl.: *De Bernardi Ferrero, Pls. 124–279, which form a reduced format facsimile of all three volumes of the *Opera,* although Pl. 275 of S. Carlo is upside down and Pl. 279 of S. Carlo is reversed; Wittkower, "Francesco Borromini: Personalità e destino," *Studi sul Borromini,* I, Rome, 1967, 40–43; Incisa della Rocchetta, *Dialogo,* 165–67.

111.   Anonymous. Before 1743.
Plan of the Piazza della Chiesa Nuova.
ASR, Disegni e mappe, c. 80. Ink and wash.

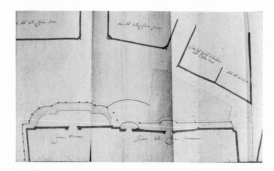

111

Inscriptions:
R. PP. della Chiesa Nova. R. R. PP. della Chiesa Nova. Eredi del quondam Giulio Strada habb.o a Strada Nova. RR. PP. del Popolo. Chiesa Nuova. Oratorio della Chiesa Nuova.

The plan is part of a survey of the urban spaces of the area conducted by the Mastri di Strade prior to the expansion of the

Piazza della Chiesa Nuova in 1743. The so-called "anima" of the piazza is indicated by the shaded area on the right. The curved lines in front of the Filippini portal apparently represent a slope that caused difficulty to approaching carriages until it was leveled and replaced by steps between 1745 and 1758 (Decr. 591–593; Cat. 113). The plan is awkward in proportions but accurate in its representation of minor urban features such as the colonettes in front of the Vallicella stairs and the fountain on the corner where the Strada Nuova and the piazza intersect. Unpublished.

112.   Anonymous. April 6, 1743.
Chirograph of Benedict XIV authorizing the enlargement of the Piazza della Chiesa Nuova.
ASR, Disegni e mappe, c. 80, n. 250; duplicate copy in AV, small cartella. 49.0 × 48.5 (excluding text). Ink and wash.
Text of the chirograph:
Monsignore Niccolo Casoli Chierico della Nostra Camera, e Presidente delle Strade.

Ci avete rappresentato che la Congregatione e Preti dell'Oratorio di S. Filippo Neri di Roma, avendo già ottenuto dalla Santa memoria di Urbano VIII nostro predecessore diverse grazie, indulti, e concessioni, affinche per ornamento di questa nostra città, e della loro chiesa, ed anche per commodo pubblico potessero aprire lo stradone, che dalla suddetta chiesa va il Pellegrino, ed anche fare una congrua piazza avanti la medesima chiesa, come appare da un chirografo di detto pontefice in data de 27 gennaro dell' anno 1627, al quale essendosi già da gran tempo data essecuzione, restarebbe ora da perfezzionarsi l'ornato di detta Piazza con ridurla più ampia, ed in simetria quasi uguale, anche dalla parte, ch'è situata in faccia all'Oratorio contiguo a detta chiesa, innalzando le fabbriche delle case con l'istesso ordine, ed architettura delle altre, e riducendo essa piazza in concertato, e convenevol prospetto: e però datasi l'occasione, che il convento, e Padri di Santa Maria del Popolo abbino cominciato a demolire una loro casa posta, e situata incontro all'Oratorio suddetto nel sito disegnato nella qui sopra delineata pianta alla Lettera A, si siano esibiti di comprare al giusto prezzo, senza pero l'augumento della Bolla Gregoriana, la suddetta casa, già smantellata, coll'altra contigua posseduta dalla Contessa Marscianni disegnata in detta pianta alla lettera B, rifabbricarle ambedue, facendo il prospetto di esse

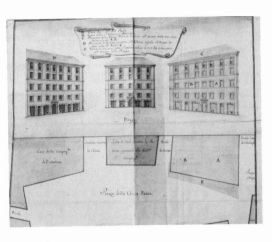

112

corrispondente sulla piazza, come sta delineato in detta pianta alla Lettera C, colla stessa simmetria, ed architettura delle altre case che fanno angolo dall'altro parte, dimostrate in pianta alla lettera D, ed inoltre di rilasciare a benfizio pubblico il sito, e suolo libero sulla Piazza incontro l'Oratorio in quantità di canne ventitre quadrata in circa, come vien dimostrato da essa pianta nella striscia di color piombino alla lettera E, con averne di ciò anco fatto obbligo in scritto, stante il quale obbligo prodotto negli atti del vostro Tribunale di vostro ordine, siano stati inibiti ad istanza del detto Tribunale li nominati Padri del Popolo, accioche non proseguissero la demolizione di dette case, ne innovassero altro. Per tanto essendoci a cuore il publico ornato, ed avendo considerato, che riducendosi ad effetto, quanto voi ci avete riferito, secondo l'esibizione fatta da suddetti preti, ciò sarà di grande ornamento alla detta nostra città, e di commodo al pubblico, ed all'Oratorio suddetto. . . . Vi ordiniamo e commandiamo . . . tanto il Convento, e Padri di Santa Maria del Popolo, quanto la Contessa Marsciani a vendere alli detti Preti della Congregatione le loro case situate incontro all'Oratorio suddetto, e delineate nella suddetta pianta col colore rossino alle lettere A, e B, con tutti li loro membri, ragioni, e pertinenze per il prezzo da stimarsi da due periti da eleggersi uno per parte . . . conche detti preti della Congregatione, oltre il dover fare a loro spese l'edificio suddetto, secondo la predetta delineazione, rilascino a favore del pubblico il sito di canne ventitre quadrate in circa lineato in detta pianta colore piombino alla Lettera A. . . . Perche poi li suddetti Padri del Popolo hanno già cominciato a fare la sudetta demolizione con animo di rifabricare. Perchio vi ordiniamo, e commandiamo, che prefiggiate alli

medesimi un congruo termine, dentro il quale obbligandosi li medesimi a fare la detta fabbrica coll'istesso ordine e simetria, colla quale intendono di farla i Preti dell'Oratorio, e a rilasciare a benefitizio pubblico le canne ventitre quadrate in circa, come abbiamo di sopra disposto, e facendo l'attuale deposito del prezzo della detta casa spettante alla Contessa Marsciani . . . affinche in tutto, e per tutto segua prontamente il suddetto ornato a forma della riferita pianta. . . .

Data dal nostro Palazzo Apostolico di Monte Cavallo questo di 6 Aprile 1743. Benedictus PP. XIV.

Other inscriptions:

A. Casa de i PP. del Popolo.

B. Casa della S.ra Contessa Marciani.

C. Prospetto della nuova fabrica da farsi coll'unione delle due case contra segnate A.B.

D. Prospetto delle Case incontro alla chiesa eguale al nuovo da farsi alla detta Lettera C.

E. Tutta la striscia color piombino indica il sito da rilasciarsi per ornato della piazza.

Piazza. Case della Congreg.ne dell'Oratorio. Stradone incontro la chiesa. Isola di case incontro la porteria spettante alla med.ma Congreg.ne. Vicolo de Cartari. Vicolo detto di Calabraghe. Piazza Sforza. Piazza della Chiesa Nuova. Vicolo. Case spettanti alla med. Cong.ne. Stradone in fianco la Chiesa. Scalinata. Chiesa. Muricciolo. Oratorio. Strada che tende alla Piazza dell'Orologio. Case de Particolari.

In addition, a chirograph of March 3, 1742 on the regularization of Piazza Sforza sheds further light on town-planning in the area of the Piazza della Chiesa Nuova (ASR, Disegni e mappe, c. 81, n. 312):

Monsignor Niccolo Casoni Ch.co della Nostra Camera Apostolica, e Presidente delle Strade.

Essendoci stato rappresentato, che avendo il Duca Sforza Cesarini Savelli fatto demolire alcune casette contigue al suo palazzo corrispondenti in Piazza Sforza, che risoltavano in fuori fino alla larghezza di palmi 17¼ ragguagliatamente, e longhezza di palmi 123 attesa la rovina, che minacciavano, potrebbesi con tale occasione toglier di mezzo la deformità da tanto tempo osservata, che dette casette rendevano a detta piazza, mentre tirandosi a diritto filo rimarrebbe quadrata la detta piazza, ed inoltre sarebbe libera l'entrata alla strada, che tende alla Piazza dell'Orologio della Chiesa Nuova, e finalmente resterebbe esente quel sito dall'immondizie, che si radunano ne i due lati di detto risalto, e che per la spesa del sito di dette casette se ne potrebbe fare una tassa alli possessori delle case, che godono la vista di essa piazza, nel modo, e forma si è pratticato in altri simili casi dal nostro Tribunale delle Strade; e desiderando Noi, che questa nostra città si renda ornato più che sia possibile, e che il pubblico goda il beneficio non meno della pulizia, che dell'ampiezza, e dirittura di detta piazza, abbiamo determinato doversi porre in esecuzione quanto, come sopra ci è stato rappresentato. Per tanto di nostro moto proprio, etc. . . . diamo a Voi . . . la facoltà di acquistare il sito di dette casette, che facevano risalto fino ai limiti del palazzo, ed altro adiacente, al qual effetto dovrete invigilare, che il nuovo muro da eriggersi in fianco il giardino di detto Duca Sforza sia fatto a diritto filo, nel modo, che si dimostra nella qui sopra delineata pianta con il colore di rossino. . . . Tassa: ed in quella tassare tutte le case in vicinanza di detta piazza a proportione del commodo, e vista, che conseguitanno, secondo il pratticato in simili casi . . .

Dato dal nostro Palazzo Apsotolico di Monte Cavallo questo di 3 Marzo 1742. Benedictus PP. XIV.

In 1743 the Augustinians of S. Maria del Popolo began to demolish one of their houses in the piazza (A); a legal battle ensued which resulted in the present license. The document gives the Oratorians the right to purchase both the Augustinians' house and its neighbor (B), and to rebuild it on a new property line and with a new elevation (C) matching the Casa Lancisi of 1702 at the other end of the piazza (D). Should the Congregation exercise this right, they were obligated to cede a swath of land (E) to the public, an act which gave the piazza its definitive outline. A clause in the chirograph allowed the Augustinians to retain ownership of the house if they agreed to rebuild it as the drawing proposes; the option was declined.

The construction of the new house was the occasion for raising the heights of the houses already standing around the piazza. The center house, dating from 1655, was raised from four to five stories in 1744–45; the large *appartamento* along the eastern flank of the church, called the Fabrica Brugiotti, was apparently given its uppermost story in 1748–57. Finally the new house of 1743 is shown in old photographs with an attic story that does not appear on the present drawing (Decr. 575–593, 595, 597, 602, 606, 607, 609, 610; Cat. 87, 98a, 103, 106).
Unpublished.

113. Francesco Ferruzzi. 1745.
Project for the steps and platform in front of the oratory.
AV, small cartella. Pen and wash. Scale: 50 p.
Inscriptions:
Porta dell'Oratorio. Entrata. Porta piccola della chiesa che risponde in faccia le navate. Porta grande della chiesa.

The drawing proposes a series of ledges and steps to make the transition between the low unpaved surface of the piazza and the higher level of the oratory and *portaria*. The need for such steps was neglected in Borromini's early projects (Cat. 39, 40) and first recognized in his revisions of the oratory facade of 1658–60 (Cat. 89b, 90). When Falda and Cruyl depicted the piazza in 1665, the approach to the oratory was over a steep rise of unpaved earth which caused trouble for carriages and turned to a swamp in heavy rains (Cat. 98a, 99). In 1745 the Congregation approved a plan by their architect to pave the piazza and to replace the sloping terrain in front of the casa portal with steps. The present drawing was apparently the one considered at that time; some of its more dramatic curves were simplified into a straight terrace when the design was put into execution (Fig. 9). Francesco Ferruzzi (1678–1745) became the Congregation's

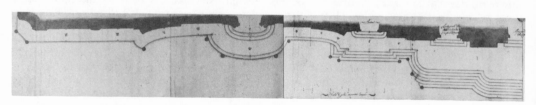

architect in 1725; he was still active in 1743 and was apparently called on to do the present plan in March 1745. By December 1745, however, he was near death and had to be replaced (Decr. 477, 580, 591–593, 599).
Unpublished.

114.   Giuseppe Vasi. 1756.
   View of the Piazza della Chiesa Nuova.
   Delle magnificenze di Roma antica e moderna, VII, Rome, 1756, Pl. 157. 21.5 × 37.2 (plate mark). Etching.
Inscription:
   Chiesa di S. Maria in Vallicella, e Casa dei Preti della Cong.ne dell'Oratorio. 1. Prospetto dell'Oratorio. 2. Piazza Sforza, e Palazzo Cesarini, gia Dataria Apostolica.

The view is not accurate in all respects. It shows the house opposite the oratory facade as seven bays wide instead of five (Fig. 9). The house at the extreme southwest corner of the piazza is misaligned in order to exaggerate the view into the neighboring Piazza Sforza. The low houses along the Via dei Filippini are shown as three stories high, as opposed to four stories in other sources (Fig. 9 and Cat. 99). However, the print offers the earliest view of the steps and platform installed in front of the oratory facade in 1745 (Cat. 113). Furthermore, it is a valuable source for the appearance of the corner where the Strada Nuova emerged into the piazza. It shows an icon not recorded by other sources and the fountain approved in 1641 and probably installed in about 1657. The fountain is shown on a plan of 1743 (Cat. 111), but is obscured by a passing horse on Fig. 9 (Decr. 163, 349, 591–593).
*Bibl.: *Ragguagli,* 254 ff., Pl. 7.*

115.   Anonymous. 1871–1922.
   Plans of the casa at four levels.
   Ministero di Grazia e Giustizia, Roma, Archivio Generale, Affari Civili, busta 1919, fasc. 5.

115a.   Ground floor plan.
Inscriptions:
   Palazzo dei Tribunali. Iconografia del piano terreno. I. Via del Governo Vecchio; Via dei Filippini; Via della Chiesa Nuova; Piazza della

Chiesa Nuova. Limite fra i locali occupati dai Tribunali e la parte rimasta ai monaci.

115b.   Second floor plan.
   . . .primo piano II . . .

115c.   Mezzanine floor plan.
   . . . piano mezzato fra il 1° e 2° piano.

115d.   Top floor plan.
   . . . secondo piano . . .

Pacini published two plans made in conjunction with the transformation of the casa into a Court of Assizes in 1871–72 (his Figs. 28–29, no source cited, originals untraceable in the Ministero di Grazia e Giustizia). Apparently a survey of the entire building was made upon completion of the work; the present drawings are mechanical copies of that survey. Their value lies in absolute fidelity to the building as it stood in 1872. Cat. 115a along with Pacini's Fig. 29 are the first plans to depart from the inaccuracies of the *Opus* MS drawings and Giannini's prints (Fig. 5). Cat. 115b–d are the only known plans of the upper stories, and as such they record important information about the design as built. Cat. 115b shows the stairs of 1633 between the church and casa, and proves that the alterations suggested by Borromini on Cat. 66^r were put into effect. Cat. 115b shows the two small corridors at the head and foot of the sacristy that provide access to the upper *nicchioni* of the first court (Fig. 49); although only one was projected on Maruscelli's initial plans (Cat. 20b, no. 16), both exist in the present building. The same plan also shows the space above the *lavamani* as a simple rectangular room without niches. Cat. 115c and 115d are useful in showing the system of corridors and suites worked out in Arcucci's plans of 1659 (Cat. 95). The connection between the third landing of the *scalone* and the mezzanine story is confirmed by Cat. 96 and by *Opus* Pls. LI and LVIII; at present this doorway, located under the *Attila* relief, is sealed (Fig. 59). The one detectable error occurs in the rendering of the library on Cat. 115d, where the partition walls of the lower stories have been carelessly transposed to the library *salone*.

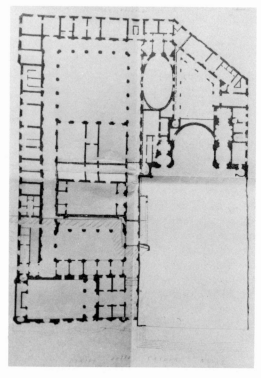

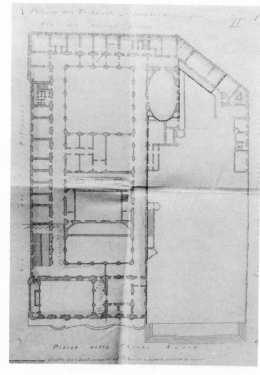

115a

115b

The plans also document the alterations of 1871–72. They show the lumbering courtroom structure which reduced the number of bays in the garden courtyard from eight to five. The transformations shown in the oratory agree with old photographs, particularly the sealing of the two upper loggie and the opening of doors in the north wall. Transformations in the first courtyard included partitioning the loggia into small cubicles and constructing a single-story room between the *nicchioni,* all of which are visible in a photograph published in 1928 (Fig. 48).

Documents kept with the drawings indicate projects for the further transformation of the building after 1872. By Law N. 755 of July 15, 1911, the oratory, Biblioteca Vallicelliana, and other rooms occupied by the "Corpo di Guardia dei Reali Carabinieri addetti agli Uffici Giudiziari" were transferred to the possession of the Comune di Roma. A report of 1911 examines the possibility of converting the rest of the building

into a center for the Preture Mandamentali; its tone is negative owing to lack of office space and the deplorable condition of the rooms. An undated report estimates the cost of repairs and new construction including a "passeggio coperto al 1º piano," curiously remedying the defect described by Borromini in *Opus,* XIII, 41^{r-v} (Cat. 57, 63). A report of May 2, 1923 notes that the building has been occupied by the Archivio Storico, Archivio Notarile, and all the administrative archives of the Comune that were formerly located in the Campidoglio (cf. also *GR,* Parione, II, 44 ff. on the restorations of 1922–24 and the archives presently located in the casa).

Unpublished. Related drawings in R. Pacini, "Alterazioni dei monumenti borrominiani," *Studi sul Borromini,* I, Rome, 1967, Figs. 28–29. G. Incisa della Rocchetta kindly offered the initial suggestion that Pacini's plans might be found in the Ministry of Grace and Justice.

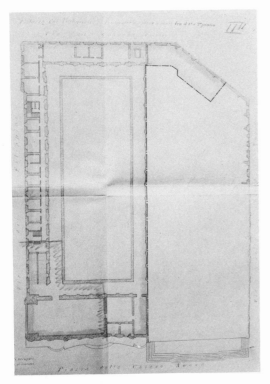

115c

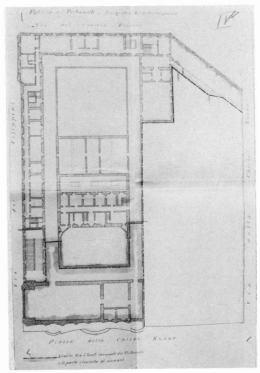

115d

The Plates

1. Vallicella area.

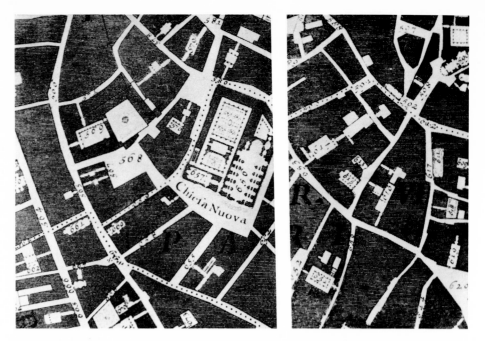

2. G. B. Nolli, plan of Rome, detail of the Vallicella area, 1748.

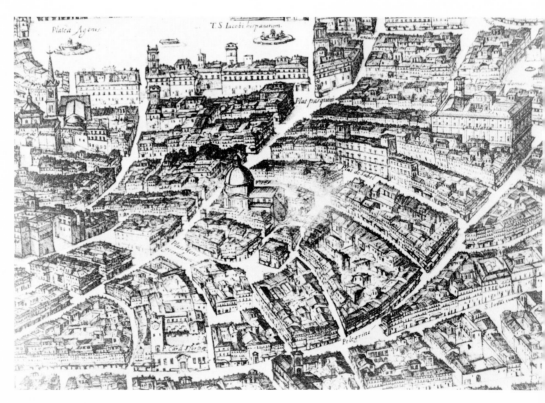

3. A. Tempesta, plan of Rome, detail of the Vallicella area, 1593.

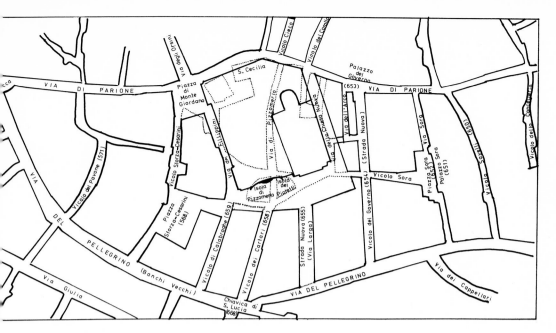

Plan of the Vallicella area.

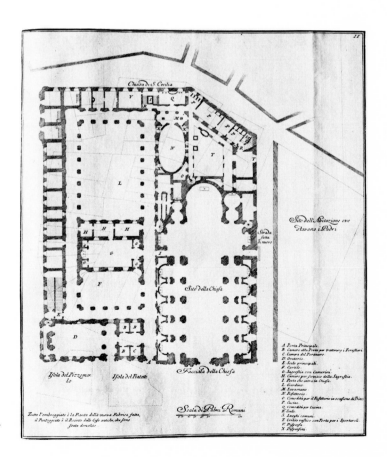

5. S. Giannini, plan of the
Casa dei Filippini, 1725.
(Cat. 110.II.)

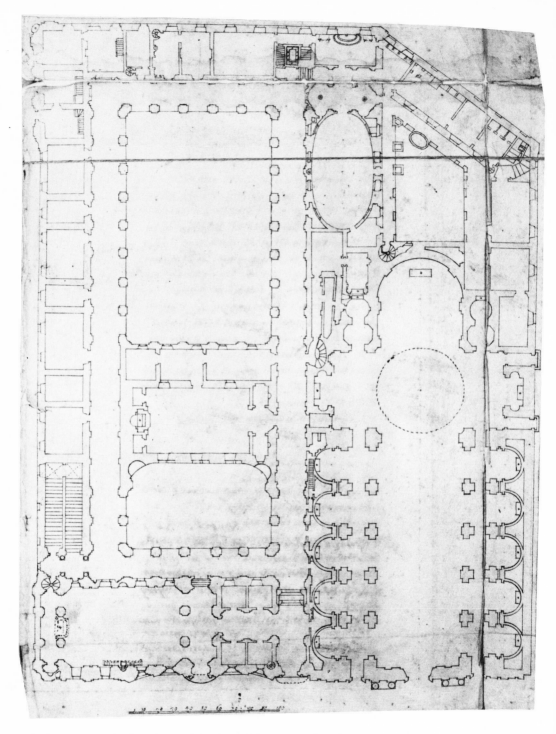

6. Anonymous A after Borromini, plan of the casa and project
   for its completion, 1650–53. (*Opus* MS, Pl. VIII; Cat. 84a.)

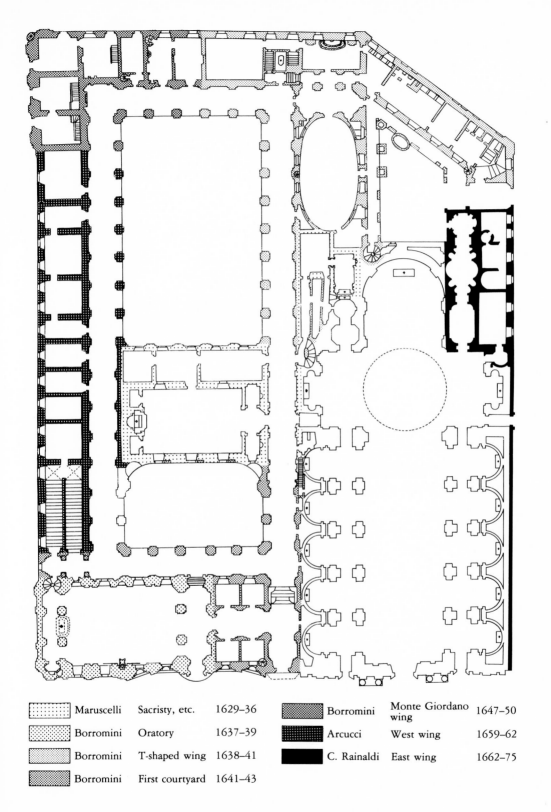

	Maruscelli	Sacristy, etc.	1629–36
	Borromini	Oratory	1637–39
	Borromini	T-shaped wing	1638–41
	Borromini	First courtyard	1641–43

	Borromini	Monte Giordano wing	1647–50
	Arcucci	West wing	1659–62
	C. Rainaldi	East wing	1662–75

7. Building phases of the casa.

8. Oratorio dei Filippini and S. Maria in Vallicella.

9. View of the Piazza della Chiesa Nuova, before 1885.

10. Piazza della Chiesa Nuova, view from the Piazza Sora
    facing west, 1885.

11. Casa Cerosi and Casa Lancisi, with the oratory facade
    visible down the Vicolo di Sora, 1885. (Discussed in Cat. 106.)

12. Oratory facade.

13. Casa dei Filippini, reconstruction of Paolo Maruscelli's project
for the south facade, 1627. (Photomontage based on Fig. 8 and Cat. 23c.)

Stage 1: five-bay facade, early 1637.

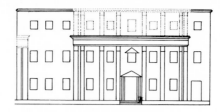

*Stage 2: five-bay facade with two flank-
ing bays of rougher brickwork,
May 1637.*

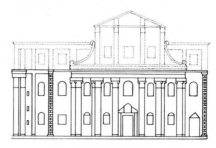

*Stage 3: Seven-bay facade, August
1638.*

14. Oratory facade,
three stages of development.

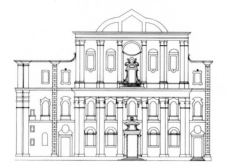

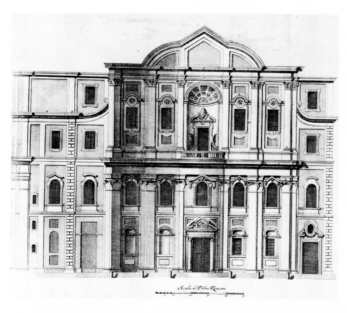

15. S. Giannini, view of the oratory facade, 1725. (Cat. 110.VI.)

16. S. Giannini, idealized view of the oratory facade, 1725,
based on a plate of ca. 1660 by Borromini and Barrière. (Cat. 110.V.)

17. Oratory facade, second story windows.

18. Oratory facade, niche windows of the lower story.

19. Oratory facade, central bays.

20. Oratory facade, southwest corner.

21. West side facade.

22. S. Giannini, west side facade of the casa, 1725. (Cat. 110.XXVII.)

23. Clocktower facade.

24. Northwest corner
of the casa, shrine.

25. S. Giannini, section through the casa including (from left to right): oratory and
library, first courtyard, sacristy, sacristy service rooms, garden courtyard, north
wing, 1725. (Cat. 110.LVI.)

26. S. Giannini, section through the west wing, including (from left to right):
oratory and library, *scalone,* residential rooms, clocktower, 1725. (Cat.
110.LVIII.)

27. S. Giannini, section through the south wing of the casa
    including: *portaria, forestaria,* oratory, and library, 1725.
    (Cat.110.XLII.)

28. S. Giannini, section through the oratory and library facing
    west, 1725. (Cat. 110.XXXIX.)

29. Oratory vault.

30. Underground oratory, northeast corner.

31. West end of oratory with Vaj altar.

32. Anonymous B, elevation of
Borromini's original wooden model
for the oratory altar, 1652?–53.
(*Opus* MS, Pl. XI; Cat. 85b.)

33. West end of oratory,
musicians' loggia.

34. East end of oratory, with entrance loggia below and cardinals' loggia above.

35. East end of oratory, detail.

36. West end of oratory after conversion to a tribunal, 1871–1924.

37. North and east sides of oratory after conversion to a tribunal, 1871–1924.

38. Preacher's seat in the south wall of the oratory.

39. Entrance loggia of oratory facing south.

40. Aperture over north door of oratory leading to the first courtyard.

41. Aperture over south door of oratory leading to the piazza.

42. *Portaria* and entrance to the casa, facing south.

44. Portal and entrance atrium to the oratory, facing west.

43. Steps between *portaria* and first courtyard, facing north.

45. S. Giannini, oratory
    entrance portal, 1725.
    (Cat. 110.XXXIII.)

46. Andrea Bolgi, marble bust
    of S. Filippo, 1650, formerly installed
    in the oratory entrance portal.

47. First courtyard facing southwest.

49. First courtyard, north side with *nicchioni* and sacristy windows.

48. First courtyard facing west, with alterations of 1871–1924 on the lower left and lower right. (A. Muñoz, *Roma barocca,* Milan and Rome, 1928, 236.)

50. Anonymous C, north side of first courtyard with original balcony window, after 1647. (*Opus* MS, Pl. XXX, detail; Cat. 86m.)

51. First courtyard, with original balcony window on the upper right, 1871–1924. (O. Pollak, "Die Decken des Palazzo Falconieri," *Jahrbuch des Kunsthistorischen Institutes der K.K. Zentralkommissio für Denkmalpflege,* V, 1911, 134, Fig. 92.)

52. S. Giannini, balcony window above sacristy,
elevation and molding profiles, 1725.
(Cat. 110.LII.)

53. S. Giannini, first courtyard,
perspectival section facing north, 1725.
(Cat. 110.L.)

54. S. Giannini, first courtyard
and *scalone,* section facing north, 1725.
(Cat. 110.LI.)

55. Main *scalone,* niche at entrance.

56. Entrance vestibule of the main *scalone,* view facing west, 1871–1924.

57. S. Giannini, entrance vestibule of the main *scalone,*
view facing west, 1725. (Cat. 110.XLIX.)

58. Main *scalone,* view facing north
up the third flight.

59. Main *scalone,* view facing north
down the fourth flight.

60. First courtyard, view facing southwest with library, library extension, and roof of *scalone.*

61. *Forestaria* on *piano nobile*,
    door to cardinals' apartment.

62. *Forestaria* on *piano nobile*,
    door to cardinals' loggia in the oratory.

63. *Forestaria, camerotto grande* with door formerly
    opening onto the cardinals' loggia of the oratory.

64. *Forestaria,* vault of *camerino* in the cardinals' apartment.

65. Library *salone,* view facing east.

66. Library ceiling.

67. Library *salone,* bust of Cardinal Baronius and door to balcony in the center of the oratory facade.

68. Library *salone,* spiral staircase in the northeast corner.

69. Corridor between church and sacristy with twin portals by Paolo Maruscelli, view facing south.

70. Pilaster by Borromini
in the garden courtyard.

71. Door to the sacristy from the
transept of S. Maria in Vallicella.

72. Sacristy, high altar with statue
of S. Filippo by Algardi.

1. Door from sacristy area.
2. Site of steep stairway between 1634–38, converted into a corridor in 1638.
3. Borromini door with oval window on top which was opened onto a corridor in 1638 (Cat. 54).
4. Door (Fig. 77) identical to no. 3. It was opened onto courtyard (20) in 1638, but mutilated by the low corridor from the saint's chapel (19) built in 1641.
5. Sala Rossa. Originally a *dispensa* (Cat. 21, no. 24), built in 1634; vault frescoes by Niccolo Tornioli in 1643–52, completed by the Cortona workshop (Decr. 191, 205, 206, 219, 220, 308); redecorated 1745 (Decr. 596, 598).
6. Original entrance to the Sala Rossa, with a simple black doorframe by Maruscelli. Door sealed and converted into a reliquary niche in 1638.
7. Door to the Capella Interna, with a frame identical to no. 6 (illustrated in Bruschi, "Stanze," 19).
8. Refectory, 1638 ff.
9. Refectory service room, used for storage of cardinals' dining service (*Opus,* XXI, 58˅).
10. Capella Interna. Originally a storage room for glasses and bottles (Cat. 21, no. 25).
11. Charred fragments of S. Filippo's room, installed in the original doorway of room no. 10 in December 1635 (Decr. 96).
12. Marble doorframe by Maruscelli, built ca. 1634–35, sealed with Borromini stucco niche when passageway no. 13 was closed in 1641 (Fig. 75).
13. Passageway on epistle side of the Capella Esterna (16), closed in 1641.
14. Donati Chapel, 1641–43.
15. Casket of S. Filippo, located underneath the altars in both chapel no. 14 and chapel no. 16 (cf. Cat. 65).
16. Chapel of S. Filippo (Cappella Esterna) by Honorio Longhi and Giovanni Guerra, 1600 ff.
17. Vestibule to the Cappella Esterna.
18. Door opened in 1605 from Chapel of S. Filippo onto the Via di Pizzomerlo (*Licenze,* 106, no. 43). Between 1638 and 1641, the door opened onto the *cortiletto* (20); after 1641, onto the corridor (19).
19. Low corridor built in 1641 to provide a covered passageway built the Cappella Esterna (16) and the Sala Rossa (5). It cut Borromini's door (4) in half and damaged the moldings.
20. *Cortiletto,* a vestige of the former Via di Pizzomerlo.

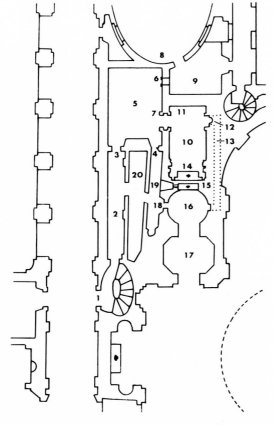

73. Rooms of S. Filippo, plan of ground floor (detail of Fig. 6, caption numbers added).

Piano nobile

21. Spiral stairs. Built by Borromini September 1638–February 1639. (*Opus,* XI, 39ʳ; Cat. 51.)

22. Doorway between spiral stairs (21) and corridor (23). The upper oval with the bust of Giovenal Ancina (1545–1604) lights another full turn of the spiral, as in the spiral ramp of the Palazzo Carpegna.

23. Corridor which replaced the straight stairs (Cat. 39) in 1638.

24. Former landing of the straight stairs, incorporated into the new corridor. The vault, visible on Cat. 39, was decorated by Borromini with Fillippini heraldry in 1638. The door with the bust of S. Filippo is by Maruscelli, ca. 1634–35 (Fig. 79).

25. Anticamera del Santo. Originally planned as a *dispensa* (Cat. 21 no. 30), converted to the Anticamera on Spada's drawing of 1634 (Cat. 27, no. 7). Vault frescoes by Cortona, April 1634.

26. Door (without frame) which leads to makeshift elevated walkway to the old casa. Complete route: 28–27–26–25–24–23–22–21–1.

27. Room off one corner of the Sala di Ricreazione, used as a chapel for convalescents (*Opus,* XXV, 69ʳ).

28. Outer door to makeshift walkway.

29. Sala di Ricreazione.

30. Borromini's green marble door to the Cappelletta di S. Filippo (Fig. 80, Cat. 55, 56).

31. Cappelletta di S. Filippo, transported intact from old casa in 1634–35.

32. Altar of Cappelletta. A proposal to move it was defeated in May 1639, even though the celebrant, who faced west, would continue to be disturbed by traffic along the route from the old casa to the sacristy (Decr. 134).

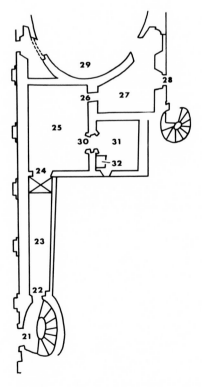

74. Rooms of S. Filippo, *piano nobile.*

75. Door in the Cappella Interna:
    frame by Maruscelli, ca. 1634–35;
    niche and stucco decorations by Borromini, 1641
    (no. 12 on Fig. 73).

76. Borromini and others, Donati Chapel, 1641–43
    (no. 14 on Fig. 73).

77. Door to the Sala Rossa, 1638
(no. 4 on Fig. 73), closed by corridor of 1641.

78. Door to the spiral staircase
(no. 22 on Fig. 74).

79. Door to the Anticamera del Santo
(no. 24 on Fig. 74).

80. Door to the Cappelletta di S. Filippo
(no. 30 on Fig. 74).

81. Area over sacristy service rooms: 1871 tribunal structure on left, east wing of casa and Vallicella transept at center, sacristy on right.

82. Garden courtyard.

83. Garden courtyard, view facing south.

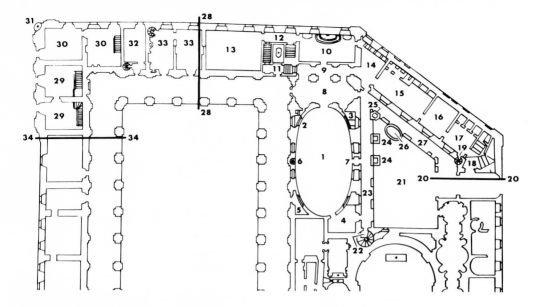

84. Plan of the north wing (detail of Fig. 6, caption numbers added).

Refectory and kitchen area

1. Refectory (*piano nobile:* Sala di Ricreazione).
2. Closet with bell rope and access to an underground well (*piano nobile:* firewood storage).
3. Closet for table linen (*piano nobile:* auditor's chamber).
4. Closet for special table service for distinguished guests (*piano nobile:* convalescents' chapel with access to the saint's rooms).
5. Closet for garden tools (*piano nobile:* passage to the adjacent loggia and spiral staircase to the upper floor).
6. Pulpit.
7. Passage to service courtyard.
8. *Lavamani.*
9. Transit corridor.
10. *Piazza d'arme* or food distribution room.
11. Square staircase.
12. Transit corridor.
13. *Dispensa* or larder.
14. *Lavapiatti.*
15. Kitchen.
16. Room for working pasta, with mezzanine overlooking the kitchen.
17. Storage room for dirty wash, meat and leftovers, with mezzanine for the cook.
18. Ramp for pack animals to descend to the cellars, with mezzanine for cook's assistant.

19. Spiral staircase to the mezzanine of rooms 16–18.
20. End of construction in the campaign of 1638–41 (Fig. 96).

Service Courtyard

21. Service courtyard.
22. Spiral staircase to preacher's apartment on the top floor.
23. *Portichetto* or covered passage, later removed.
24. Cisterns.
25. Well.
26. Basin for a fountain of Acqua Paola.
27. Loggia with three stories of corridors above.
28. End of construction in the campaign of 1638–41.

Monte Giordano Wing

29. Shops (Cat. 89).
30. Corner shop with two rooms (cf. Cat. 84).
31. Corner fountain (Cat. 82, 89).
32. Designation unknown.
33. *Spettiaria* or pharmacy.
34. End of construction in the campaign of 1647–50.

85. *Lavamani,* view looking west with refectory door on left
(Fig. 84, no. 8).

86. S. Giannini, *lavamani* and fountains, section looking south, 1725.
(Cat. 110.LX.)

87. Fountain in the *lavamani.*

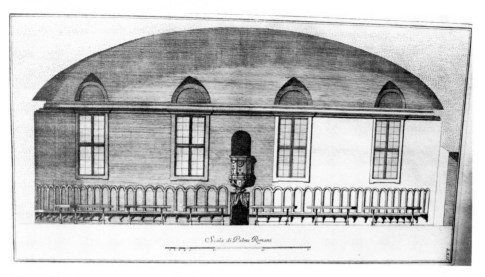

88. S. Giannini, refectory, section looking west, 1725 (Fig. 84, no. 1). (Cat. LXII.)

89. Refectory pulpit, transferred to S. Maria in Vallicella.

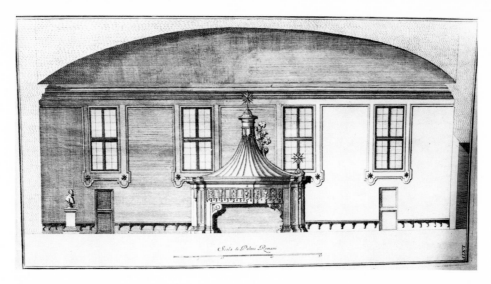

90. S. Giannini, *sala di ricreazione,* section looking west, 1725.
(Cat. 110.LXIV.)

91. Fireplace in the *sala di ricreazione.*

92. Square staircase (Fig. 84, no. 11).

93. Square staircase (Fig. 84, no. 11).

94. East wing, with the
Spada Chapel on left.

95. Service courtyard, view facing north.

96. Service courtyard, truncated end of the north wing (Fig. 84, no. 20).

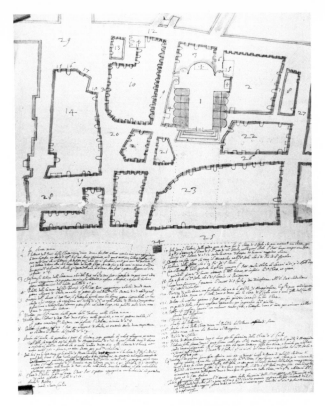

97. Anonymous, plan of the Vallicella area, with
captions relating to the Barnabite project for the
church of S. Carlo a Monte Giordano, 1611.
(AV, C.II.8, no. 107.)

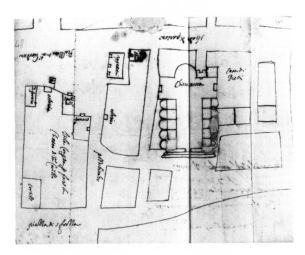

98. Anonymous, plan of the Vallicella area,
1611. (Bibl. Vallicelliana, 0 57², fol. 48.)

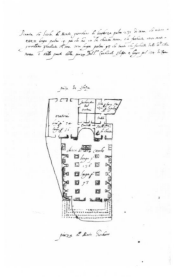

99. Anonymous, project for the church of
S. Carlo a Monte Giordano, 1611.
North at bottom of the sheet. (AV,
C.II.8, no. 108.)

100. G. B. Falda, view of the Piazza della Chiesa Nuova,
east side, 1665 (detail of Cat. 98a).

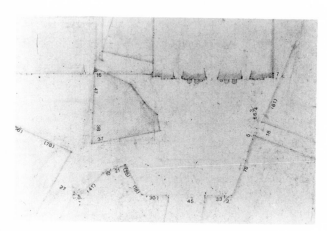

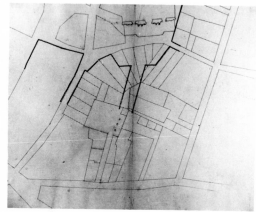

101. Borromini, measured plan of the Piazza
della Chiesa Nuova, 1637–41 (detail of
Cat. 38). Numbers without parentheses
correspond to the dimensions inscribed on
the drawing; numbers with parentheses
have been measured on the accompanying
scale.

102. Paolo Maruscelli, site plan, late
1626. Dark lines added to clarify
the disposition of houses shown in
Fig. 101. (AV, C.II.8, no. 99; Cat.
17a.)

103. Via della Chiesa Nuova, view facing south,
with the *appartamento* of 1673–75 on the left
and S. Maria in Vallicella on the right.

104. Anonymous, Cardinal Alessandro Farnese as patron of the Gesù and
     Cardinal Odoardo Farnese as patron of the Casa Professa, early
     seventeenth century. (Gesù sacristy.)

105. S. Giannini after Borromini, project of 1648 for the clocktower, 1725. (Cat. 110.XXX; cf. Cat. 89a.)

106. Casa Professa, courtyard clock, 1599 ff.

107. Girolamo Rainaldi (?), fountain in the sacristy of the Gesù, ca. 1600.

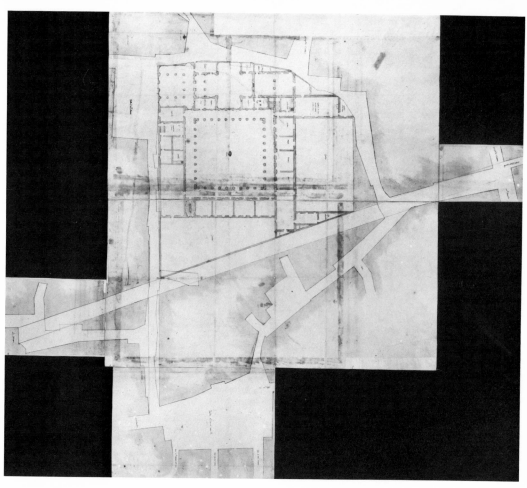

108. Anonymous, project for the Collegio Romano
and the church of the SS. Annunziata, ca. 1560.
(Uffizi A 4180.)

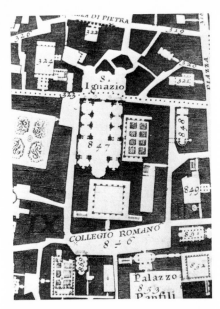

109. G. B. Nolli, plan
of the Collegio Romano area, 1748.

111. Oratio Grassi, S.J., northeast corner
of the Collegio Romano, ca. 1628–31.
Oratory of the Caravita on the left, 1631–33.

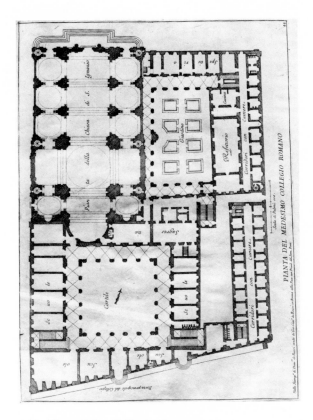

110. Plan of the Collegio Romano.
(Ferrerio-Falda, I, Pl. 44.)

112. Paolo Maruscelli, sacristy of S. Andrea della Valle, 1629.

113. Paolo Maruscelli, S. Maria in Vallicella, sacristy door, 1634.

114. Paolo Maruscelli, S. Andrea della Valle, sacristy door, 1629 ff.

115. A. Palladio, Convent of the Carità in Venice.
(*Quattro libri,* 1570, II, 30.)

116. A. Palladio, Palazzo Iseppo da Porto
in Vicenza. (*Quattro libri,* 1570, II, 10.)

117. Pellegrino Tibaldi, Archepiscopal Palace of Milan,
courtyard, designed 1564 and built 1571–1604.

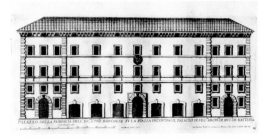

118. G. B. Soria and others,
Palazzo della Famiglia Borghese, 1624–27.
(Ferrerio-Falda, I, Pl. 25.)

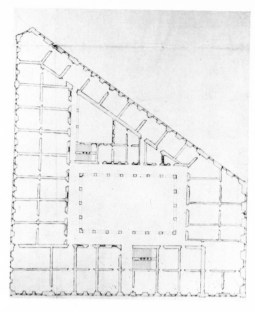

119. Attributed to G. B. Soria,
Palazzo della Famiglia Borghese,
ground floor plan. (AV, C.II.8, no. 162.)

120. Attributed to G. B. Soria,
Palazzo della Famiglia Borghese,
piano nobile plan. (AV, C.II.8, no. 161.)

121. Girolamo Rainaldi, S. Teresa in Caprarola, nave, 1621 ff.

122. Francesco da Volterra and
     Carlo Maderno, S. Giacomo degli
     Incurabili, facade, ca. 1600–1608.

123. Martino Longhi the Elder,
     S. Girolamo degli Schiavoni,
     facade, 1588.

124. Ercole Fichi,
     S. Paolo in Bologna,
     facade, 1634–36.

125. Carlo Maderno, S. Susanna, facade, 1603.

126. Oratorio dei Filippini, facade detail.

127. Antonio da Sangallo, Palazzo del Vescovo di Cervia, facade detail.

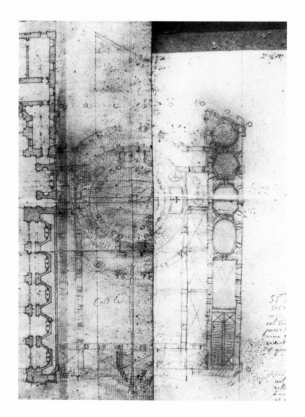

128. Borromini, project for
a Pamphilj chapel attached to
S. Maria in Vallicella, 1644
(detail of Cat. 39).

129. G. B. Montano, reconstruction
of an antique rotonda.
(*Scielta di varii tempietti antichi,* Rome,
1624, Pl. 46.)

130. Casa dei Filippini, first courtyard,
nicchioni.

131. Vignola and G. Rainaldi (?), Palazzo Farnese in Piacenza,
courtyard, *nicchioni,* 1558–93.

132. Antonio da Sangallo, Palazzo Baldassini, entrance atrium, 1516–19.

133. G. B. Soria, shelves for the library of the Palazzo Barberini, 1633, installed in the Vatican Library in 1902.

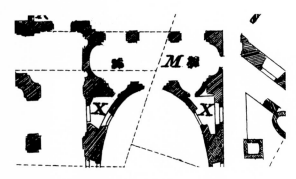

134. Casa dei Filippini,
plan of *lavamani* area
(detail of Fig. 5).

135. Donato Bramante, project for St. Peter's,
detail of entrance vestibule, 1506.
(Uffizi A 1.)

137. Borromini, S. Giovanni in Laterano,
detail of ornament, 1648–50.

136. Casa dei Filippini,
square staircase (Fig. 84, no. 11),
detail of moldings on the *piano nobile.*

138. Borromini, Propaganda Fide, Re Magi Chapel, 1660–62.

Works Cited

Accolti, Pietro. *Lo inganno de gl'occhi, prospettiva pratica.* Florence, 1625.

Ackerman, James S. *The Architecture of Michelangelo.* 2 vols. New York and London, 1964.

———. *Palladio.* Harmondsworth, 1966.

Alaleona, Domenico. *Studi sulla storia dell'oratorio musicale in Italia.* Turin, 1908. Reprinted as *Storia dell'oratorio musicale in Italia.* Milan, 1945.

Ammannati, Bartolomeo. *La città.* Ed. Mazzino Fossi. Rome, 1970.

Ancina, Giovenale. *Tempio armonico. . . .* Rome, 1599.

Anonymous. *Pianta del sito degli Ecc.mi SS.ri Barberini a piazza Grimana, overo quattro fontane.* BV, Barb. lat. 4360, n.d. [ca. 1626–28].

———. *Biografia di Monsignore Alessandro Sperelli patrizio di Assisi e vescovo di Gubbio.* Spoleto, 1872.

Antonazzi, Giovanni. "La sede della Sacra Congregazione e del Collegio Urbano." *Sacrae Congregationis de Propaganda Fide Memoria Rerum.* Ed. J. Metzler. Rome-Freiburg-Vienna, 1971, 306–34.

Aringhi, Paolo. *Memorie istoriche della vita del Padre Virgilio Spada. . . .* Venice, 1788.

Ashby, Thomas. "Sixteenth-Century Drawings of Roman Buildings Attributed to Andrea Coner." *Papers of the British School at Rome.* II, 1904; VI, 1913, 184 ff.

———. "Lieven Cruyl e le sue vedute di Roma (1664–1670)." *Memorie della Pontificia Accademia Romana di Archeologia.* Ser. III, I, 1, 1923, 221–29.

Bacci, Pietro Giacomo. *L'a Dio del p. Bacci all' amata Vallicella nel partirsi per Monte Giordano, alla nova abitazione.* Bibl. Vallicelliana, Cod. 0 57², fols. 530ʳ–531ᵛ, n.d. [1643].

Baglione, Giovanni. *Le vite de pittori, scultori, et architetti. . . .* Rome, 1642. Facsimile edition by V. Mariani. Rome, 1935.

Baillie, Hugh Murray. "Etiquette and the Planning of the State Apartments in Baroque Palaces." *Archaeologia.* CI, 1967, 167–99.

Baldelli, D. Pietro. *Brevi cenni di storia sulla chiesa e parrocchia della Madonna del Prato.* Gubbio (mimeographed), ca. 1970.

Bandini, Angelo Maria. *Commentariorum de vita et scriptis Ioannis Bapt. Doni . . . Libri quinque.* Florence, 1755.

Baroni, Costantino. *Documenti per la storia dell'architettura a Milano nel Rinascimento e nel Barocco.* I, Florence, 1940; II, Rome, 1968.

Bassi, Elena. *Il convento della Carità.* Corpus Palladianum, VI. Vicenza, 1971.

Beltrame Quattrocchi, Enrichetta. *Il Palazzo del Collegio Romano e il suo autore.* Rome, 1956.

Bentivoglio, Enzo. "Un palazzo 'barocco' nella Roma di Leone X. Il progetto per Palazzo Medici in piazza Navona di Giuliano da Sangallo." *Architettura.* XVIII, 1972, 196–204.

Bianchi, Arturo. "Le vicende e le realizzazioni del piano regolatore di Roma capitale." *Capitolium.* X, 1934, 33–43.

Bibliografia romana. I (no subsequent volumes). Rome, 1880.

Blondel, Jacques François. *Cours d'architecture.* 12 vols. Paris, 1771–77.

Blunt, Anthony. "The Palazzo Barberini: The Contributions of Maderno, Bernini and Pietro da Cortona." *Journal of the Warburg and Courtauld Institutes.* XXI, 1958, 256–87.

———. "Introduction." *Acts of the Twentieth International Congress of the History of Art.* III, Princeton, 1963, 3–12.

———. *Supplements to the Catalogues of Italian and French Drawings.* In Edmund Schilling, *The German Drawings in the Collection of Her Majesty the Queen at Windsor Castle.* London and New York, n.d.

———. *Borromini.* Cambridge, Mass., 1979.

Boëthius, Axel, and Ward-Perkins, J. B. *Etruscan and Roman Architecture.* The Pelican History of Art. Harmondsworth, 1970.

Borromini, Francesco. *Opera del Caval. Francesco Boromino Cavata da Suoi Originali cioè La Chiesa, e Fabrica della Sapienza di Roma. . . .* Ed. Sebastiano Giannini. Rome, 1720.

———. *Opera del Cav. Francesco Boromini Cavata da Suoi Originali cioè L'Oratorio, e Fabrica per l'Abitazione De PP. dell'Oratorio di S. Filippo Neri di Roma. . . .* Ed. Sebastiano Giannini. Rome, 1725.

Bottari, Giovanni. *Dialoghi sopra le tre arti del disegno.* Naples, 1772.

Brauer, Heinrich, and Wittkower, Rudolf. *Die Zeichnungen des Gianlorenzo Bernini.* Römische Forschungen der Bibliotheca Hertziana, IX. 2 vols. Berlin, 1931.

Brown, Howard M. "How Opera Began: An Introduction to Jacopo Peri's *Euridice* (1600)." In *The Late Italian Renaissance 1525–1630.* Ed. E. Cochrane. London, 1970, 401–43.

Bruschi, Arnaldo. "Il Borromini nelle stanze di S. Filippo alla Vallicella." *Palatino.* XII, 1968, 13–21.

Bukofzer, Manfred. *Music in the Baroque Era.* New York, 1947.

Cancellieri, Francesco. *Le due nuove campane di Campidoglio. . . .* Rome, 1806.

Castagnoli, Ferdinando, and others. *Topografia e urbanistica di Roma.* Istituto di Studi Romani, Storia di Roma, XXII. Bologna, 1958.

Cavalieri, Emilio dei. *Rappresentatione di anima, et di corpo.* Rome, 1600.

Cerasoli, F. "Notizie circa la sistemazione di molte strade di Roma nel sec. XVI." *Bollettino della Commissione Archeologica Comunale di Roma.* XXVIII, 1901, 342–62.

Ceschi, Carlo. "S. Urbano ai Pantani." *Capitolium.* IX, 1933, 380–91.

Ciacconio [Chacon], Alphonsus. *Vitae et res gestae pontificum romanorum et S. R. E. cardinalium ab initio nascentis Ecclesiae usque ad Clementem IX P. O. M.* 4 vols. Rome, 1677.

Cicinelli, Aldo. *The Church of S. Maria dell'Umiltà and the Chapel of the North American College.* Rome, 1970.

Cistellini, Antonio. "I primordi dell'Oratorio filippino in Firenze." *Archivio Storico Italiano.* CXXVI, 1968, 191–285.

Connors, Joseph. "Early Projects for the *Casa dei Filippini* in Rome." *Oratorium. Archivum Historicum Oratorii Sancti Philippi Neri.* VI, 1975, 107–17.

———. Review of H. Thelen, *Francesco Borromini. Die Handzeichnungen,* Graz, 1967, in *Journal of the Society of Architectural Historians.* XXXV, 1976, 144–46.

———. Review of M. Heimbürger Ravalli, *Architettura scultura e arti minori nel barocco italiano. Ricerche nell'Archivio Spada,* Florence, 1977, and of L. Neppi, *Palazzo Spada,* Rome, 1975, in *Journal of the Society of Architectural Historians,* XXXVIII, 1979, 193–96.

Corbo, Anna Maria. *L'Archivio della Congregazione dell'Oratorio di Roma e l'archivio della Abbazia di S. Giovanni in Venere: Inventario.* Quaderni della Rassegna degli Archivi di Stato, 27. Rome, 1964.

———. "Apertura di una strada alla Chiesa Nuova nel 1673: ritrovamenti archeologici e polemiche." *Commentarii.* XXIII, 1972, 181–85.

Crescimbeni, Giovanni Mario. *L'historia della chiesa di S. Giovanni avanti Porta Latina.* Rome, 1716.

Damilano, Piero. *Giovenale Ancina musicista filippino (1545–1604).* Florence, 1956.

Danti, Egnatio. *La prospettiva di Euclide. . . .* Florence, 1573.

de Bernardi Ferrero, Daria. *L'opera di Francesco Borromini nella lettera artistica e nelle incisioni dell'età barocca.* Turin, 1967.

del Piazzo, Marcello, ed. *Ragguagli borrominiani.* Ministero dell'Interno, Pubblicazioni degli Archivi di Stato, LXI. Rome, 1968.

Delumeau, Jean. *Vie économique et sociale de Rome dans la seconde moitié du XVIe siècle.* 2 vols. Paris, 1957.

de Rossi, Domenico. *Studio d'architettura civile.* 3 vols. Rome, I, 1702. II, 1711. III, 1721.

de Rossi, Giovanni Giacomo. *Insignium Romae Templorum Prospectus.* Rome, 1683. Enlarged ed. 1684.

de Rossi, Matteo Gregorio, and Cruyl, Lieven. *Prospectus Locorum Urbis Romae.* Rome, 1666.

D'Onofrio, Cesare. *Roma nel seicento.* Edition of F. Martinelli, *Roma ornata . . . ,* MS Casanatense 4984, 1660–62. Florence, 1969.

———. *Scalinate di Roma.* Rome, 1974.

Dorez, Léon. *La cour du Pape Paul III.* 2 vols. Paris, 1932.

Egger, Hermann. *Römische Veduten. Handzeichnungen aus dem XV.–XVIII. Jahrhundert.* 2 vols. Vienna and Leipzig, I, 1911. II, 1931.

Ehrle, Francesco. "Dalle carte e dai disegni di Virgilio Spada (d. 1662) (Codd. Vaticani lat. 11257 e 11258)." *Atti della Pontificia Accademia Romana di Archeologia.* Ser. III, Memorie, II, 1928, 1–98.

Eimer, Gerhard. *La fabbrica di S. Agnese in*

Navona. 2 vols. Stockholm, 1970.

Eubel, Conrad. *Hierarchia Catholica.* . . . 7 vols. Munich, 1913 ff.

Evelyn, John. *The Diary of John Evelyn.* Ed. E. S. de Beer. 6 vols. Oxford, 1955.

Falda, Giovanni Battista. *Il nuovo teatro delle fabriche.* . . . 4 vols. Rome, I, II, 1665. III, 1667–69. IV, with plates by A. Specchi, 1699.

Fasolo, Furio. *L'opera di Hieronimo e Carlo Rainaldi (1570–1655 e 1611–1691).* Rome, 1961.

Ferrerio, Pietro, and Falda, Giovanni Battista. *Palazzi di Roma.* Ed. Giovanni Giacomo de Rossi. 2 vols. Rome, I, n.d. [1655 ff.]. II, n.d. [1670–77].

Fontana, Domenico. *Della trasportazione dell' obelisco vaticano et delle fabbriche di Nostro Signore Papa Sisto V.* Rome, 1590.

Fossi, Mazzino. *Bartolomeo Ammannati architetto.* Florence, n.d.

Frey, Dagobert. "Beiträge zur Geschichte der römischen Barockarchitektur". *Wiener Jahrbuch für Kunstgeschichte.* III (XVII), 1924, 5–113.

Frommel, Christoph. "Bramantes 'Ninfeo' in Genazzano." *Römisches Jahrbuch für Kunstgeschichte.* XII, 1969, 137–60.

———. "Caravaggios Frühwerk und der Kardinal Francesco Maria del Monte." *Storia dell' Arte.* 9/10, 1971, 5–52.

———. *Der Römische Palastbau der Hochrenaissance.* Römische Forschungen der Bibliotheca Hertziana, XXI. 3 vols. Tübingen, 1973.

Gaizo, V. del, and others. *Il Palazzo Madama sede del senato.* Rome, 1969.

Gasbarri, Carlo. *L'Oratorio romano dal cinquecento al novecento.* Rome, 1962.

Girouard, Mark. *Life in the English Country House.* New Haven and London, 1978.

Giustiniani, Vincenzo. Discourse on architecture in the form of a letter to T. Ameyden, in G. Bottari and S. Ticozzi, *Raccolta di lettere sulla pittura, scultura ed architettura.* Rome, VI, 1822, 99–120.

Gnoli, Domenico. "Il Palazzo del Senato già Madama." *Nuova Antologia.* August 1, 1926, 249–64.

Gnoli, Umberto. *Alberghi ed osterie di Roma nella rinascenza.* Spoleto, 1935.

———. *Topografia e toponomastica di Roma medioevale e moderna.* Rome, 1939.

Gonzales-Palacios, Alvar. "Giovanni Battista Calandra, un mosaicista alla corte dei Barberini." *Ricerche di Storia dell'Arte.* 1–2, 1976, 211–40.

Gosebruch, Martin. "Vom Pantheon Vergleichlich-Unvergleichliches. Römische Thermenarchitektur und ihre Auswirkungen auf die Baukunst des Cinquecento." *Römische Quartalschrift.* 30. Supplementheft. 1966, 147–68.

Güthlein, Klaus. "Die Fassade der Barnabiterkirche San Paolo in Bologna." *Römisches Jahrbuch für Kunstgeschichte.* XVII, 1978, 125–55.

———. Review of M. Heimbürger Ravalli, *Architettura scultura e arti minori nel barocco italiano. Ricerche nell'Archivio Spada,* Florence, 1977, in *Zeitschrift für Kunstgeschichte.* XLI, 1978, 336–42.

Guide rionali di Roma. Prepared by Carlo Pietrangeli and others. Rome, 1968 ff.

Hager, Hellmut. "Carlo Fontana's Project for a Church in Honour of the 'Ecclesia Triumphans' in the Colosseum, Rome." *Journal of the Warburg and Courtauld Institutes.* XXXVI, 1973, 319–37.

———. "Puntualizzazioni su disegni scenici teatrali e l'architettura scenografica del periodo barocco a Roma." *Bollettino del Centro Internazionale di Studi di Architettura Andrea Palladio.* XVII, 1975, 119–29.

Harris, Ann Sutherland. "Andrea Sacchi and Emilio Savonanzi at the Collegio Romano." *Burlington Magazine.* CX, 782, 1968, 249–57.

———. *Andrea Sacchi.* Princeton, 1977.

Haskell, Francis. *Patrons and Painters.* New York, 1963.

Heimbürger Ravalli, Minna. "Disegni sconosciuti del Borromini per il Banco di Santo Spirito e per Palazzo Spada." *Paragone* (Arte). 275, 1973, 57–63.

———. *Architettura scultura e arti minori nel barocco italiano. Ricerche nell'Archivio Spada.* Florence, 1977.

Hempel, Eberhard. *Francesco Borromini.* Römische Forschungen des Kunsthistorischen Institutes Graz. Vienna, 1924.

Henneberg, Josephine von. "An Early Work by Giacomo della Porta: The Oratorio del Santissimo Crocefisso di San Marcello in Rome." *Art Bulletin.* LII, 1970, 157–71.

Hess, Jacob. *Die Künstlerbiographien von Giovanni Battista Passeri.* Römische Forschungen der Bibliotheca Hertziana, XI. Leipzig and Vienna, 1934.

———. "Contributi alla storia della Chiesa Nuova (S. Maria in Vallicella)." *Scritti di storia dell'arte in onore di Mario Salmi.* III, Rome, 1963, 215–38 and 431–33. Reprinted in J. Hess, *Kunstgeschichtliche Studien zu Renaissance und Barock.* Rome, 1967, 353–67.

———. "Some Notes on Paintings in the Vatican Library." In J. Hess, *Kunstgeschichtliche Studien zu Renaissance und Barock.* Rome, 1967, 163–79.

Heydenreich, Ludwig. "Spätwerke Brunelleschis." *Jahrbuch der Preusschischen Kunstsammlungen.* LII, 1931, 1–28.

———, and Lotz, Wolfgang. *Architecture in Italy 1400 to 1600.* The Pelican History of Art. Harmondsworth, 1974.

Hibbard, Howard. *The Architecture of the Palazzo Borghese.* Memoirs of the American Academy in Rome, XXVII. Rome, 1962.

———. "Di alcune licenze rilasciate dai Mastri di Strade per opere di edificazione a Roma (1586–'89, 1602–'34)." *Bollettino d'arte.* LII, 1967 [published 1970], 99–117.

———. *Carlo Maderno and Roman Architecture 1580–1630.* London, 1971.

Hiersche, Waldemar. *Pellegrino de' Pellegrini als Architekt.* Parchim i. M., 1913.

Huelsen, Christian, and Egger, Hermann, *Die römischen Skizzenbücher von Marten van Heemskerck.* 2 vols. Berlin, I, 1913. II, 1916.

Huelsen, Christian. *Le chiese di Roma nel medio evo.* Florence, 1927.

Incisa della Rocchetta, Giovanni. Review of O. Pollak, *Die Kunsttätigkeit,* Vienna-Augsburg-Cologne, I, 1928, in *Roma.* VI, 1928, 347–55.

———. "La chiesa di San Carlo sulla piazza di Monte Giordano". *Strenna dei Romanisti.* XXII, 1961, 43–48.

———. "Un dialogo del p. Virgilio Spada sulla fabbrica dei Filippini." *Archivio della Società Romana di Storia Patria.* XC, 1967, 165–211.

———. "La Chiesa Nuova nel marzo 1622." *Oratorium. Archivum Historicum Oratorii Sancti Philippi Neri.* III, 1972, 33–40.

———. "La Cappella di San Filippo alla Chiesa Nuova; II–L'anticamera privata di s. Filippo; III–La 'sala rossa' e la cappella interna di s. Filippo." *Oratorium. Archivum Historicum Oratorii Sancti Philippi Neri.* III, 1972, 46–52, and 74–101.

———. "Il salone della Biblioteca Vallicellana". *Palladio.* XXIII, 1973, 121–28.

———. "Il santuario filippino della Vallicella." *Quaderni dell' Oratorio.* II, n.d., 1–20.

———. *Studi offerti a Giovanni Incisa della Rocchetta.* Miscellanea della Società Romana di Storia Patria, 23. Rome, 1973.

Iversen, Erik. *Obelisks in Exile.* Copenhagen, I, 1968. II, 1972.

Jedin, Hubert. *A History of the Council of Trent.* Vol. I. St. Louis, 1957.

Koschatzky, Walter, and others. *I grandi disegni italiani dell'Albertina di Vienna.* Milan, 1972.

Kostof, Spiro. *The Third Rome 1870–1950* (exhibition catalogue). Berkeley, University Art Museum, 1973.

Krautheimer, Richard; Corbett, Spencer; and Frazer, Alfred. *Corpus Basilicarum Christianarum Romae.* Vol. V. Vatican City and New York, 1977.

Krautheimer, Richard, and Jones, R. S. B. "The Diary of Alexander VII: Notes on Art, Artists and Buildings." *Römisches Jahrbuch für Kunstgeschichte.* XV, 1975, 199–233.

Labacco, Antonio. *Libro . . . appartenente à l'architettura nel qual si figurano alcune notabili antiquità di Roma.* Rome, 1559.

Lanciani, Rodolfo. *Storia degli scavi di Roma e notizie intorno le collezioni romane di antichità.* 4 vols. Rome, 1902–12.

Letarouilly, P. *Édifices de Rome moderne. . . .* 3 text vols. and 3 plate vols. Liège, 1849 ff. Enlarged ed., Paris, 1868 ff.

Lewine, Milton. *The Roman Church Interior 1527–1580.* Unpublished Ph.D. dissertation. Columbia University, New York, 1960.

Lohninger, J. S. *Maria dell'Anima, Die deutsche Nationalkirche in Rom.* Rome, 1909.

Longhi, Martino, the Younger. *Discorso . . . delle cagioni delle ruine della facciata e campanile del famoso tempio di S. Pietro in Vaticano. . . .* Rome, 1645. Facsimile in M. Fagiolo dell' Arco, ed., *Architettura barocca a Roma.* Rome, 1972, 115–28.

Lumbroso, Giacomo. *Notizie sulla vita di Cassiano dal Pozzo.* Miscellanea di Storia Italiana, XV. Turin, 1874.

Lunadoro, Girolamo [Leti, G.]. *Relatione della corte di Roma.* Venice, 1664.

Magnuson, Torgil. *Studies in Roman Quattrocento Architecture.* Figura, IX. Stockholm, 1958.

Magrini, Antonio. *Memorie intorno la vita e le opere di Andrea Palladio.* Padua, 1845.

Mancini, C. *S. Apollinare.* Le Chiese di Roma Illustrate, 93. Rome, n.d.

Martinelli, Domenico. *Horologi elementari divisi in quattro parti.* Venice, 1669.

Martinelli, Fioravante. *Primo trofeo della S.ma croce eretto in Roma nella via Lata da S. Pietro apostolo.* Rome, 1655.

———. *Roma ricercata nel suo sito, et nella scuola di tutti gli antiquarij.* Rome, 1st ed. 1644. 2nd. ed. 1650. 3rd ed. with plates by Domenico Barrière, 1658.

———. *Roma ornata dall'architettura, pittura e scoltura.* MS Casanatense 4984, 1660–62. Ed.

by C. D'Onofrio as *Roma nel seicento.* Florence, 1969.

——. *Carbognano illustrato.* Rome, 1695.

Martinori, Edoardo. *Annali della zecca di Roma.* 24 fasc. Rome, 1917–22.

——. *I Cesi.* Rome, 1931.

Mellini, Benedetto. *Dell'antichità di Roma.* BV, Vat. lat. 11905, n.d. [ca. 1656 ff.].

Million, Henry. "An Early Seventeenth Century Drawing of the Piazza San Pietro." *Art Quarterly.* XXV, 1962, 229–41.

Mola, Giovanni Battista. *Breve racconto delle miglior opere d'architettura, scultura et pittura fatte in Roma et alcuni fuor di Roma.* 1663. Ed. K. Noehles. Quellen und Schriften zur bildenden Kunst, 1. Berlin, 1966.

Montagu, Jennifer. "Alessandro Algardi and the Statue of St. Philip Neri." *Jahrbuch der Hamburger Kunstsammlungen.* XXII, 1977, 75–100.

Montalto, Lina. "Il problema della cupola di Sant'Ignazio di padre Orazio Grassi e fratel Pozzo a oggi." *Bollettino del Centro di Studi per la Storia dell'Architettura.* XI, 1957, 33–62.

Montano, Giovanni Battista. *Scielta di varii tempietti antichi.* Ed. G. B. Soria. Rome, 1624.

Morelli, Gonippo. *Le corporazioni romane di arti e mestieri dal XIII al XIX secolo.* Rome, 1937.

Morello, Giovanni, and Dante, Francesco. "L'Archivio della Congregazione dell'Oratorio di Roma alla Chiesa Nuova." *Ricerche per la Storia Religiosa di Roma.* 2, 1978, 275–362.

Moroni, Gaetano. *Dizionario di erudizione storico-ecclesiastica da S. Pietro sino ai nostri giorni.* 103 vols. and 6 index vols. Rome and Venice, 1840–79.

Mortoft, Francis. *Francis Mortoft: His Book. Being His Travels Through France and Italy 1658–1659.* The Hakluyt Society, 2nd ser., LVII. London, 1925.

Muñoz, Antonio. *Roma barocca.* Milan and Rome, 1928.

Nash, Ernest. *Pictorial Dictionary of Ancient Rome.* Revised ed. 2 vols. London, 1968.

Nava Cellini, Antonia. "Per il Borromini e il Duquesnoy ai S.S. Apostoli di Napoli." *Paragone* (Arte). 329, 1977, 26–38.

Neppi, Lionello. *Palazzo Spada.* Rome, 1975.

Nicolai, Niccola Maria. *Sulla presidenza delle strade ed acque e sua giurisdizione economica.* 2 vols. Rome, 1829.

Noehles, Karl. *La chiesa dei SS. Luca e Martina nell'opera di Pietro da Cortona.* With contributions by G. Incisa della Rocchetta and C.

Pietrangeli. Rome, 1970.

Ortolani, Sergio. *S. Andrea della Valle.* Le Chiese di Roma Illustrate, 4. Rome, n.d.

——. *San Carlo a' Catinari.* Le Chiese di Roma Illustrate, 18. Rome, n.d.

Ost, Hans. "Studien zu Pietro da Cortonas Umbau von S. Maria della Pace." *Römisches Jahrbuch für Kunstgeschichte.* XIII, 1971, 231–85.

Pacini, Riccardo. "Alterazioni dei monumenti borrominiani e prospettive di restauro." *Studi sul Borromini. Atti del Convegno promosso dall'Accademia Nazionale di San Luca.* Vol. I. Rome, 1967, 317–41.

Palisca, Claude. "Musical Asides in the Diplomatic Correspondence of Emilio de' Cavalieri." *The Musical Quarterly.* XLIX, 1963, 339–55.

——. *Baroque Music.* Englewood Cliffs, 1968.

Palladio, Andrea. *Li quattro libri dell'architettura.* Venice, 1570.

Partner, Peter. *Renaissance Rome 1500–1559.* Berkeley, 1976.

Passeri, Giovanni Battista. *Vite de pittori scultori et architetti Dall'anno 1641 sino all'anno 1673.* Ed. by J. Hess as *Die Künstlerbiographien von Giovanni Battista Passeri.* Römische Forschungen der Bibliotheca Hertziana, XI. Leipzig and Vienna, 1934.

Pastor, Ludwig von. *The History of the Popes.* 40 vols. London, 1891–1953.

Pecchiai, Pio. *Il Gesù di Roma.* Rome, 1952.

Pernier, A. "Documenti inediti sopra un'opera del Borromini. La fabbrica dei Filippini a Monte Giordano". *Archivi d'Italia.* 2nd ser., II, 1935, 204 ff.

Piacentini, Michelangiolo. "Architetti romani minori nel 600: Andrea Sacchi architetto, Pietro Ferrerio pittore incisore e architetto". *Palladio.* IV, 1940, 29–33.

Pinkney, David. *Napoleon III and the Rebuilding of Paris.* Princeton, 1958.

Pinto, Elena. *La Biblioteca Vallicelliana in Roma.* Miscellanea della R. Società Romana di Storia Patria. Rome, 1932.

Pirri, Pietro, S.J. "La topografia del Gesù di Roma e le vertenze tra Muzio Muti e S. Ignazio secondo nuovi documenti." *Archivium Historicum Societatis Iesu.* X, 1941, 177–217.

——. *Giovanni Tristano e i primordi della architettura gesuitica.* Bibliotheca Instituti Historici S. I., VI. Rome, 1955.

——. *Giuseppe Valeriano S. I. architetto e pittore 1542–1596.* Bibliotheca Instituti Historici S. I., XXXI. Rome, 1970.

Platner, Samuel Ball, and Ashby, Thomas. *A*

Topographical Dictionary of Ancient Rome. Oxford and London, 1929.

Pollak, Oskar. "Antonio del Grande, ein unbekannter römischer Architekt des XVII. Jahrhunderts." *Kunstgeschichtliches Jahrbuch der K. K. Zentral-Kommission*. III, 1909, 133–61.

———. "Architektenmärchen." *Kunstgeschichtliches Jahrbuch der K. K. Zentral-Kommission für Erforschung und Erhaltung der Kunst- und historischen Denkmale*. IV, 1910, Beiblatt, 163–74.

———. "Die Decken des Palazzo Falconieri in Rom und Zeichnungen von Borromini in der Wiener Hofbibliothek." *Jahrbuch des Kunsthistorischen Institutes der K. K. Zentralkommission für Denkmalpflege*. V, 1911, 111–41.

———. *Die Kunsttätigkeit unter Urban VIII*. 2 vols. Vienna, 1928–31.

Pommer, Richard. *Eighteenth-Century Architecture in Piedmont. The Open Structures of Juvarra, Alfieri, and Vittone*. New York and London, 1967.

Ponnelle, Louis, and Bordet, Louis. *Saint Philippe Néri et la société romaine de son temps (1515–1595)*. Paris, 1929. Translated into English by R. F. Kerr as *St. Philip Neri and the Roman Society of his Times*. London, 1932.

Ponti, Ermanno. *Il Banco di Santo Spirito*. Rome, 1941.

Portoghesi, Paolo. "Intorno a una irrealizzata immagine borrominiana". *Quaderni dell'Istituto di Storia dell'Architettura dell'Università di Roma*. 6, 1954, 12–28.

———. *Borromini nella cultura europea*. Rome, 1964.

———. *Roma barocca. Storia di una civiltà architettonica*. Rome, 1966; rev. ed. Bari, 1978.

———. *Borromini. Architettura come linguaggio*. Rome and Milan, 1967.

———. *Disegni di Francesco Borromini*. Rome, 1967.

Poultney, David. "Alessandro Scarlatti and the Transformation of Oratorio." *The Musical Quarterly*. LIX, 1973, 584–601.

Pugliese, Antonia, and Rigano, Salvatore. "Martino Lunghi il giovane architetto," in M. Fagiolo dell'Arco, ed., *Architettura barocca a Roma*. Rome, 1972, 7–191.

Rasponi, Cesare. *De Basilica et Patriarchio Lateranensi Libri Quattuor*. Rome, 1656. Colophon 1657.

Re, Emilio. "L'edificio dei Filippini dal 1870 ai giorni nostri." *Studi Romani*. VI, 1958, 680–84.

Ricci, Ettore, d. O. *La Chiesa dell'Immacolata Concezione e di San Filippo Neri (Chiesa Nuova) in Perugia*. Deputazione di Storia Patria per l'Umbria. Appendici al Bollettino. No. 10. Perugia, 1969.

Rinaldi, Ernesto, S. J. *La fondazione del Collegio Romano*. Arezzo, 1914.

Rome. *Piano regolatore di Roma 1931*. Rome and Milan, n.d.

Rosci, Marco. *Il trattato di architettura di Sebastiano Serlio*. 2 vols. Milan, 1966.

Rotili, Mario. *Filippo Raguzzini e il rococò romano*. Rome, 1952.

Russo, Maria T. "Il contributo della Congregazione dell'Oratorio alla topografia romana: Piazza della Chiesa Nuova." *Studi Romani*. XIII, 1965, 21–43.

———. "I Cesi e la Congregazione dell'Oratorio." *Archivio della Società Romana di Storia Patria*. XC, 1967, 101–63. XCI, 1968, 101–55.

———. "Appunti sull'antica parrocchia vallicelliana." *Studi offerti a Giovanni Incisa della Rocchetta*. Miscellanea della Società Romana di Storia Patria, 23. Rome, 1973, 89–115.

———. "Origini e vicende della Biblioteca Vallicellana." *Studi Romani*. XXVI, 1978, 14–34.

Sabatini, Francesco. *La chiesa di S. Salvatore in Thermis*. Rome, 1907.

Salerno, Luigi; Spezzaferro, Luigi; and Tafuri, Manfredo. *Via Giulia. Una utopia urbanistica del 500*. Rome, 1973.

San Bonaventura, Fra Giovanni di. *Relazione del Convento di S. Carlo alle 4° fontane. . . .* Archivio del Convento di S. Carlo alle Quattro Fontane, MS vol. 77, n.d. [1650–52]. Partly transcribed in O. Pollak, *Die Kunsttätigkeit unter Urban VIII*. Vol. I. Vienna, 1928, 36–51, reg. 225.

Sanjust di Teulada, Edmondo. *Relazione presentata al Consiglio Comunale di Roma*. Rome, 1908.

Sarti, Mauro. *De Episcopis Eugubinis*. Pesaro, 1755.

Scarafone, Giuseppe. "L'edicola mariana di Piazza dell'Orologio e i suoi autori." *L'Urbe*. XL, 1977, 17–21.

Scavizzi, C. Paola. "Le condizioni per lo sviluppo dell'attività edilizia a Roma nel sec. XVII: la legislazione." *Studi Romani*. XVII, 1969, 160–71.

Schmidlin, J. *Geschichte der deutschen Nationalkirche in Rom S. Maria dell'Anima*. Freiburg im Breisgau, 1906.

Schudt, Ludwig. *Le guide di Roma*. Vienna and Augsburg, 1930.

Schulze, Robert. *Gubbio und seine mittelalterlichen*

Bauten. Berlin, 1915.

Schwager, Klaus. "Giacomo della Portas Herkunft und Anfänge in Rom—Tatsachen, Indizien, Mutmassungen." *Römisches Jahrbuch für Kunstgeschichte.* XV, 1975, 109–42.

Sebastiani, Leopoldo. *Descrizione e relazione istorica del Nobilissimo e Real Palazzo di Caprarola.* Rome, 1741.

Serlio, Sebastiano. *Tutte l'opere d'architettura et prospettiva.* Venice, 1619.

———. *On Domestic Architecture.* Intro. by Myra Nan Rosenfeld. New York, 1978.

Sestini, Francesco. *Il maestro di camera.* Venice, 1664.

Shearman, John. "Raphael as Architect." *Journal of the Royal Society of Arts.* CXVI, 1968, 388–409.

Smither, Howard E. "The Baroque Oratorio. A Report on Research Since 1945." *Acta Musicologica.* XLVIII, 1976, 50–76.

———. *A History of the Oratorio, Volume I: The Baroque Era: Italy, Vienna, Paris.* Chapel Hill, 1977.

Solerti, Angelo. *Le origini del melodramma. Testimonianze dei contemporanei.* Turin, 1903.

———. "Lettere inedite sulla musica di Pietro della Valle a G. B. Doni." *Rivista Musicale Italiana.* XII, 1905, 221–338.

Spada, Virgilio. *Discorso . . . sopra i disordini della facciata della chiesa, e portico di S. Pietro.* BV, Vat. lat. 11899, May 1645.

———. *Descrittione della nostra fabrica. . . .* AV. C.II.7, n.d. [ca. 1648–49]. Transcription in G. Incisa della Rocchetta, "Un dialogo del p. Virgilio Spada sulla fabbrica dei Filippini." *Archivio della Società Romana di Storia Patria.* XC, 1967, 165–211.

———. *Trattato di monete.* BV, Cod. Ferrajolus 369. Also BV, Chigi C.III.64. Also Bibl. Casanatense, n.d.

Spezzaferro, Luigi. "La cultura del cardinal Del Monte e il primo tempo del Caravaggio." *Storia dell'Arte.* 9/10, 1971, 57–92.

Steinberg, Leo. *Borromini's San Carlo alle Quattro Fontane. A Study in Multiple Form and Architectural Symbolism.* Rev. Garland ed. of a dissertation of 1960. New York, 1977.

Steinhuber, Andrea, S.J. *Geschichte des Collegium Germanicum Hungaricum in Rom.* Freiburg im Breisgau, 1895.

Strazzullo, Franco. *La chiesa dei SS. Apostoli.* Naples, 1959.

Strong, Eugénie. *La Chiesa Nuova (Santa Maria in Vallicella).* Rome, 1923.

Tacchi Venturi, Pietro, S.J. *La prima casa di S. Ignazio di Loyola in Roma e le sue cappellette al Gesù.* 2nd. rev. ed. Rome, 1951.

Tafuri, Manfredo. "Borromini in Palazzo Carpegna. Documenti inediti e ipotesi critiche." *Quaderni dell'Istituto di Storia dell' Architettura dell'Università di Roma.* 79/84, 1967, 85–107.

Tetius [Teti], Hieronymus. *Aedes Barberinae ad Quirinalem.* Rome, 1642. 2nd. ed. 1647.

Thelen, Heinrich. *70 disegni di Francesco Borromini dalle collezioni dell'Albertina di Vienna.* Istituto Austriaco di Cultura in Roma. Gabinetto Nazionale delle Stampe Farnesina. Rome, 1958.

———. *Francesco Borromini. Die Handzeichnungen.* I. Abteilung. Zeitraum von 1620/32. Text volume and plate volume. Graz, 1967.

———. *Francesco Borromini. Mostra di disegni e documenti vaticani.* Vatican City, 1967.

Thieme, Ulrich; Becker, Felix. *Allgemeines Lexikon der bildenden Künstler von der Antike bis zur Gegenwart.* Leipzig, W. Engelmann, 1907–50 (Zwichan F. Ullmann, 1934–64). 37 vols.

Tomei, Piero. "Un elenco dei palazzi di Roma del tempo di Clemente VIII." *Palladio.* III, 1939, 163–74 and 219–30.

———. *L'architettura a Roma nel Quattrocento.* Rome, 1942.

Totti, Pompilio. *Ritratto di Roma moderna.* Rome, 1638.

Valle, Pietro della. *Della musica dell'età nostra.* January 1640. Reprinted in A. Solerti, *Le origini del melodramma.* Turin, 1903, 148–79.

Vallery-Radot, Jean. *Le recueil de plans d'édifices de la Compagnie de Jésus conservé à la Bibliothèque Nationale de Paris.* Paris, 1960.

Vasari, Giorgio, the Younger. *La città ideale.* Ed. Virginia Stefanelli. Rome, 1970.

Vasi, Giuseppe. *Delle magnificenze di Roma antica e moderna.* 10 vols. Rome, 1747–61.

Villoslada, Riccardo, S.J. *Storia del Collegio Romano dal suo inizio (1551) alla soppressione della Compagnia di Gesù (1773).* Rome, 1954.

Viollet-le-Duc, Eugène-Emmanuel. *Entretiens sur l'architecture.* 2 vols. Paris, 1863–70.

Waddy, Patricia. *Palazzo Barberini: Early Proposals.* Unpublished Ph.D. dissertation. Institute of Fine Arts, New York, 1973.

———. "The Design and Designers of Palazzo Barberini." *Journal of the Society of Architectural Historians.* XXXV, 1976, 151–85.

Walker, Obadiah. *Of Education.* Oxford, 1673. Scolar Press facsimile 1970.

Wasserman, Jack. *Ottaviano Mascarino and His Drawings in the Accademia Nazionale di San Luca.* Rome, 1966.

Wittkower, Rudolf. "S. Maria della Salute: Scenographic Architecture and the Venetian Baroque." *Journal of the Society of Architectural Historians.* XVI, 1957, 3–10.

———. *Art and Architecture in Italy 1600–1750.* The Pelican History of Art. Harmondsworth. 1st ed. 1958. 2nd ed. 1965. 3rd ed. 1973. Citations are from the 3rd paperback edition.

———. "Francesco Borromini: Personalità e destino." *Studi sul Borromini. Atti del Convegno promosso dall'Accademia Nazionale di San Luca.* I, Rome, 1967, 19–48.

———. *Gothic vs. Classic. Architectural Projects in Seventeenth-Century Italy.* New York, 1974.

Ziino, Agostino. "Pietro Della Valle e la 'musica erudita.' Nuovi documenti." *Analecta Musicologica. Studien zur italienisch-deutschen Musikgeschichte.* IV, 1967, 97–111.

Zorzi, Giangiorgio. *Le opere pubbliche e i palazzi privati di Andrea Palladio.* Venice, 1965.

Index

Numbers in italics refer to the plates

Accolti, Pietro, 36, 122 n.59
Acqua Felice, 60
Acqua Paola, 60, 65–66
Acqua Vergine, 66, 253
Alberti, Gasparo, 152
Albertini, Matteo, 163
Alexander VII, Pope, 54, 63, 67, 273
Algardi, Alessandro: *Attila* relief, 54; statue of
     San Filippo, 2, 203–05, *72*
Altars, 223; oratory, 29, 31, 53, 55, 226–28,
     256, *31, 32;* sacristy, 203–06, *72*
Ammannati, Bartolomeo, 113 n.2, 131
     n.4
Ancina, Blessed Giovenale, bust of, 229, *78*
Anerio, Giovanni Francesco, 70
Angeletti, Pietro, 55, 116 n.28
Animuccia, Giovanni, 72
Antiquity, as source of design, 31, 34, 75–76,
     121–22 n.48
Appartamento, on west side of Piazza della Chiesa
     Nuova, 280–81
Apse-ended spaces, 129–30 n.105
Aqueducts, 60, 65–66
Arconio, Mario, 13–14, 17, 32, 85, 115 n.1
     documents and drawings
          1618–21: site plan, 172
          1620: valuation of Casa dei Rusconi,
          142–43
          1621–3: project for casa, 172–75
          date uncertain: site plan, 182
Arcucci, Camillo, 42, 53–56, 63, 76, 125 n.74,
     226–27, 285; outline of dates, 104
     documents and drawings
          1652: license to build *mucciolo,* 251–52
          1659: projects for west wing, 270–71
          1661: design of garden and model for foun-
          tain, 157
Arcucci, Giuseppe Brusati, 104, 125 n.74, 279,
     280
Attaccanti, Domenico, 162

Bacci, Giacomo, 114 n.26, 117 n.40
Baldinucci, Filippo: revised biographical sketch
     of Borromini, 157–60
Balducci, Francesco, 71–72
Banco di Santo Spirito, 273–74, 276
Barberini, Cardinal Antonio, 144
Barnabites, 11–12; project for church on Piazza
     di Monte Giordano, 85, 142, *97*
Baronius, Cardinal Caesare, 7; bust of, 50, *67*
Barrière, Domenico, 268; de Rossi's engraving
     after, 281–82; views of casa (after Bor-
     romini), 263–66
Belli, Angello, 169
Belluzzi, Ascanio, 279, 280
Benedict XIV, Pope: chirographs of 1742–3
     regulating enlargement and construction
     in area of Piazza della Chiesa Nuova, 288–
     90
Bernini, G.L., 118 n.14, 122 n.59, 134 n.41
Berrettini, Luca, 162–63, 227
Berti, Gasparo, 130 n.112
Bini, Pietro, 117 n.40
Bogi, Andrea: bust of San Filippo, *46*
Bologna, San Paolo, 33, 36, 120 n.39, 124
Boncompagni-Corcos family, 203–05, 252
Borromeo, Carlo, 19, 20, 116 n.31
Borromini, Bernardo, 268–69, 287; biographi-
     cal sketch of Francesco Borromini, 157–60
Borromini, Francesco, 1, 13, 18, 20–39, 48, 51–
     54, 73–79, 96, 97–103, 124–25 n.66, 140
     n.44, 157–60, 236–37; *see also* individual
     buildings and Casa dei Filippini
     drawings
          1634–8: Sala Rossa door and window,
          229–30
          1634–9: Cappella di San Filippo, door to,
          230–31
          1636: sacristy altar, 203–06
          1636–7: copies of Maruscelli's plans and
          sections, 211–12, 214

1636–7, 1644: plan of casa in three stages, 214–18

1637: oratory, ground floor plan, 206–07

1637–8: oratory, altar loggia, 226–28

1637–41: Piazza della Chiesa Nuova, plan of, 213–14, *101*

1638: casa, ground floor plan, 218–20

1638: oratory facade, 220–23

1638: molding profiles and columns framing doorway, 223

1638: altar, 223

1638: iron window grilles, 223–24

1638–9: contributions to Phase II of building activities, 202–03

1638–9: windows of oratory facade, 225

1638–9: spiral staircase, 228–29

1638–9: oval refectory, 232

1639: pilaster elevation of garden court, 231–32

1639: *lavamani* area, 233

1639–41: doorframe, 224–25

date uncertain: decorative grille, 228

1639–41: garden courtyard, 234–36

1640: casa plan, 232–33

1640–1: courtyards, plans for, 233–34

ca. 1641: Donati Chapel project, 236–37

1641: *portaria* and first courtyard, 237–41

1641: casa, entrance portal of, 241

date uncertain: Santa Maria in Vallicella, facade of, 241–43

1641–3: contributions to Phase III of building activities, 203

1641–3: door to oratory, 243

1642: library, 245–46

1642–3: window of room over sacristy, 243–44

1643: entrance vestibule to main stairway, 244–45

date uncertain: fountain, projects for, 245

1643: library shelves, 246–47

1643: doors of library *salone,* 247

1647: north and west wings, 249–50

1647: north wing and Monte Giordano projection, 247–49

1650: northwest corner and fountain, 250–51

1659–60: oratory facade, ornament of, 269–70

ca. 1660: oratory facade, 266–69

Bramante, Donato, 76; project for Saint Peter's, *135*

Breccioli, F., 142–43

Brickwork, 33–34, 75, 88, 120–21 n.45, 121 n.46, 121–22 n.48, 161, 162

Brugiotti, Andrea, 63–64

Brusati, Giuseppe, *see* Arcucci, Giuseppe Brusati

Bugnato, 37

Buzio, Carlo, 197, 200

Calcagni, Giuseppe, 108

Campidoglio, brickwork, 120

Carissimi, Giacomo, 72

Carpegna, Cardinal Ulderico, 119 n.18

Cartari, Carlo, 280; descriptions of Roman libraries, 155–57

Casa Cerosi, 284, *11*

Casa degli Arditi, 10

Casa dei Filippini, *6, 7;* andito, 47; cisterns, 66; clocktower *(torre dell'orologio),* 2, 52, 88–89, 152, 248–49, 263–65, 287, *23, 105;* corridors, 15–18, 47, 68, 200, 207, *69;* courtyards, 1, 18, 54, 68, 192, 196, 216; courtyard (first), 1, 15, 41, 46–50, 54, 56, 76, *43, 47–51, 53, 54, 60, 130;* courtyard (second or garden), 2, 15, 16, 45, 54, 56, 91, 292, *70, 82, 83;* courtyard (third or service), 2, 15, 42, 45, 55, *95, 96; dispensa* (larder), 43–44, 57, 65; distribution room *(piazza d'arme),* 43, 57, 65, 232–33; east wing, 42, *81, 94;* "elbow" wing, 42–44, 55, 57; enfilades, 15, 18, 85, 192; entrance portal, 133 n.13, *42;* fireplaces, 2, 43, 57, 69, 75, 78, 233–34, 260, *91; forestaria* (guest rooms), 2, 41, 47, 48, *61–64;* fountains, 52, 65, 245, 250–51, *87;* hydraulic system, 66; kitchen, 42–44, 218; *lavamani,* 2, 43, 57, 65, 123 n.11, 233, 260, 287, *85–87, 134; lavapiatti,* 44, 65; library, 49–50, 56, 122 n.50, 150–51, 245–47, 276–78, *2, 65–68;* loggie, 2, 15–16, 29–30, 45–47, 56, 68, 73, 98, 192, 195–96, 216, 231–32, 235–36, 250, *39;* Monte Giordano wing, 42, 51–53, 62, 89, 120, 162, 265–66; north wing, 42, 251–52, 255–58, *84;* oratory, 1, 16, 28–31, 52–53, 55–56, 70–71, 73, 98, 214–15, 226–28, 258, 284, *8, 29–31, 33–41, 62, 63;* oratory facade, 19, 88, 89, *12, 14, 17–20, 126;* pharmacy *(spettiaria),* 51, 57, 124 n.50, 249; *portaria,* 1–2, 41, 42, 47, 237–41, 253–54, 256, 282, *42;* privies, 44, 65, 67; recreation room *(sala di ricreazione),* 2, 42–43, 57, 68–69, 192, 233, 260, 284, 287, *90, 91;* refectory, 2, 41–43, 57, 68–69, 75, 78, 162, 196, 202, 216, 218, 232, 287, *88, 89;* residential quarters, 43, 45, 51, 66, 68; rooms of San Filippo Neri, 17–18, 117–18 n.1, 201–03, 229–30, *73–79; seditori,* 47, 77, 240; staircases, main *scalone,* 2, 16–17, 47, 54–55, 75–77, 196, 207, 215–16, 244–45, 271–72, *55–60;* staircase, northwest, 57; staircase, spiral, 2, 29, 98, 162, 202, 228–29, *24, 68, 78;* staircase, square, 43,

44–45, 218, *92, 93, 136;* west wing, 42, 52, 54–55, 63, 249–50, 270–71, *21, 22, 26*
Casa dei Rusconi, valuation of, 142–43
Casa Lancisi, 283–84, *11*
Casa Professa del Gesù, 3, 15, 60, 88, 90, 113 n.3, 121 n.46, 134 n.39; brickwork, 120; courtyard clock, *106*
Casa Vecchia dei Filippini, 11, 114 n.26, 127 n.23
Castellani bequest, 62
Castello, Matteo da, 9
Cavalieri, Emilio de', 11, 70, 72, 128 n.88
Cerri, Antonio, 87, 185
Cesi family, 64; Angelo, 10, 162; Ludovico, 64; Pierdonato, 9–10, 64, 74, 113 n.5
Chaining of vaults, 29, 54, 55, 119 n.22
Chenna, Domenico, 147
Cherub over oratory window, 36–37
Churches in Rome
    Sant'Agostino, 123 n.35
    Sant'Andrea delle Fratte, 98
    Sant'Andrea della Valle, 18, 85, 108, 116 n.29, *112, 114*
    San Carlo ai Catinari, 12
    San Carlo alle Quattro Fontane, 35, 43, 88, 98, 118 n.1, 122 n.49, 227–28; anonymous project for, *97, 99;* construction costs, 59–60; Giannini's prints, 287–88
    Santa Cecilia a Monte Giordano, 8, 12, 17
    Sant'Elisabetta, 10–11, 120 n.34
    San Giacomo degli Incurabili, 35, 222, *122*
    San Giovanni dei Fiorentini, 6, 9
    San Giovanni in Laterano, *see* Lateran basilica and palace
    San Giovanni a Porta Latina, 121 n.48
    San Girolamo della Carità, 5–6, 163
    San Girolamo degli Schiavoni, 35, *123*
    Sant'Ignazio, 82
    Sant'Ivo alla Sapienza, 53, 98, 136–37 n.24, 286; brickwork, 120; mason's contract, 163
    Santa Maria dell'Anima, 108–09; brickwork, 120
    Santa Maria di Loreto: brickwork, 120
    Santa Maria sopra Minerva, 15, 109
    Santa Maria ai Monti, 115 n.9
    Santa Maria del Popolo, 162
    Santa Maria delle Sette Dolori, 98
    Santa Maria in Vallicella, 1, 7–10, 55, 64, 84–85, 142, 200, *8–10, 101, 103;* Capella di San Filippo Neri, 17–18, 200–02, 230–31, *80;* chapel of Vincenzo Lavaiana, 162; chapels, 55; cupola, 30–31, 163; curtain wall, 278–79; facade, 162, 241–43; old basilica, 181–82; parish, 90; projects, 167–69, 181–82; pulpit, *89;* sacristy, 2, 14, 17–18, 23, 41–42, 44–45, 146–47, 169, 192–94, 195,

215, *72;* sacristy *credenzoni,* 17, 197–200, 203–06; Spada chapel, 42, 54, 285, *94;* transept, *71*
    Sant'Orsola della Pietà, 6
    San Paolo fuori le mura, 51, 124 n.47
    Saint Peter's Basilica, 60, 76; Bramante's project for, *135*
    San Salvatore in Lauro, 15
    Santo Spirito dei Napoletani, 15
    Santa Susanna, 33, 35, *125;* brickwork, 120
    Santa Teresa in Caprarola, 30, *121*
Clement VIII, Pope, 20
Clement XI, Pope, 72
Cocciani, Laetitia, 143
Codex Coner, 75, 130 n.106
Collegio Romano, 3, 51–52, 60, 82–83, 88, 90, 125 n.46, 130–31 n.4, *108–111;* brickwork, 120
Colloredo, Leandro, 285
Colutio, Pietro, 143
Consulta, 16, 27
Contini, Francesco, 48
Corso Vittorio Emanuele, 92–93
Cortona, Pietro da, 17, 52; personal library, 140 n.44
Counter Reformation, influence on architecture, 2–3, 19, 95
Cruyl, Lieven, 276

Del Bufalo, Marchese, 121 n.48
Del Monte, Cardinal Francesco, 113 n.5
Donati, Giulio, 203

Eritreo, J. N., 71
Evelyn, John, 71
Expropriation laws, 41, 81, 91

Fabrica Brugiotti, 290
Facades (curved), 36, 98, 122 n.57, 133 n.24
Falconieri, Orazio, 228
Falda, G. B.: view of Piazza della Chiesa Nuova, 274–76, *100;* view of Piazza di Monte Giordano, 275–76
Famiglia palace design, 18–20, 45, 67, 95, 116–17 n.35
Farnese, Cardinal Alessandro, *104*
Farnese, Cardinal Odoardo, 3, 9, *104*
Ferrata, Ercole, 280
Ferruzzi, Antonio, 104
Ferruzzi, Francesco, 104, 228
Fichi, Ercole: San Paolo, Bologna, *124*
Filomarino altar, 98, 228
Finance, 9, 53, 59–64
    documents: 142–44, 147, 151–55, 162–63
Finelli, G., 118 n.14
Fiori, Giovanni, 104

Fiori, Raffaele, 104
Florence, Uffizi, 60
Fontana, Antonio, 163
Fontana, Carlo: plan of *isola,* 272–74
Fontana, Domenico, 9, 162

Gesù, Il, 15, 60, 85; brickwork, 120; fountain in sacristy, *107*
Giannini, Sebastiano, 252, 268; prints of the casa, 285–88, *5, 15, 16, 22, 25, 26, 27, 28, 45, 52, 53, 54, 57, 86, 88, 90, 105*
Giusti, Horatio, 162
Grassi, Oratio: plans of Collegio Romano and Oratory of the Caravita, *111*
Greca, Felice della, 53
Gregory XIII, Pope, 3, 7, 20, 72, 82
Griffi, Orazio, 70
Guardarobba, 192, 196
Gubbio, Santa Maria del Prato, 119 n.18
Guercino, 203
Guidici, Domenico de, 162

Honorati, Marsilio, 162
Houses on casa site
   documents: 142–43, 147, 162
   drawings: 181–82, 261–62, 282–83

Iannarelli, G. A., 247
Ignatius of Loyola, Saint, 7, 90
Innocent X, Pope, 51–53, 97, 163, 216
Institutional buildings, effect of 16th-century urbanism on, 81–82
Isola dei Piatetti, 213
Isola di Pizzomerlo, 213
Isorello, Dorisio, 128 n.89

Jacomelli, G. A., 247
Jesuits, 6–7, 34, 82–83, 90

Labacco, Antonio, 75
Lancisi, Giovanni Maria, 283–84
Landi, Taddeo, 28, 199–200, 205
Latera, Duchessa di; building of, 163
Lateran basilica and palace, 51, 53, 98–99; bronze doors, 124 n.61; costs of reconstruction, 59–60; excavations under, 34, 121–22 n.48; ornament, detail of, *137*
Lauda, 70
Leo XI, Pope, 129 n.90
Licenses: for arch over *vicoletto,* 279–81; for rebuilding house in piazza, 261–62; for sidewalks, 251–52, 279–81
Lombard tiburio, 30
Longhi, Martino, the Elder, 9–10, 35; project for church and casa, 167–68; San Girolamo degli Schiavoni, *123*

Maderno, Carlo, 33, 35, 60, 205; personal library, 112; San Giacomo degli Incurabili, *122;* Santa Susanna, *125;* valuation of Casa dei Rusconi, 142–43
Maderno, Domenico: valuation of house of P. Colutio and L. Cocciani, 143
Madonna, street icons, 92, 135 n.74
Magni, G. B., 111
Marchesi, Domenico de, 162
Martinelli, Fioravante, 75, 222, 263–64
Maruscelli, Paolo, 14–21, 51–52, 66, 73, 95; background and career, 107–12; Cappella Interna, doorframe, *75;* Chapel of San Filippo, 17, 201–02; construction of casa (1629–34), 17–18; corridor system, 68; cost of doorframe under, 60; courtyards, 45–46; drawing style, 111; *lavamani,* 43; library, 42; oratory, 29, 32; outline of dates, 101–104; personal library, 112; residential quarters, 45; resignation and replacement, 23–28; sacristy, 17–18, 47, *113;* Sant'Andrea della Valle, *112, 114;* service rooms, 17, 42; sewer, 65; sources of imagery, 18–21, 74, 77; twin portals in corridor, *69;* as urbanist, 85–87
documents
   1622: valuation of house of P. Colutio and L. Cocciani, 143
   1625: valuation of Casa dei Rusconi, 143
   1630: *misura e stima* of Strada Nuova, 143
   1634: *misura e stima* for work done by *scarpellini,* 147
   1636: *misura e stima* for work on houses along Strada Nuova, 147
   1637: estimate of value of a house, 162
   1649: inventory of possessions, 152
drawings
   1624: preliminary casa project, 176–78
   ca. 1624: casa project, 178
   1624–7: casa project, 178–81
   date uncertain: site plan, 182
   1626: projects for Piazza della Chiesa Nuova and Strada Nuova, 182–84, *102*
   1626–7: project for old Santa Maria in Vallicella with adjacent streets and houses, 181–82
   1627: casa projects, 185–97, *13*
   1636–7: Borromini's copies of plans and sections, 211–12, 214
   1637: oratory project, 210–11
Masi, Girolamo, 104
Mattei, Tommaso, 104
Mazzei, Cesare, 72
Messengers' seats, *see* Casa dei Filippini: *seditori*
Michelangelo, 75–76

Milan, Archepiscopal Palace of, 19, 116 n.31, *117*
Milan, Collegio Elvetico, 122 n.57
Mola, Giovanni Battista: oratory plan, 26, 207–08
Montano, G. B., 38, 217; reconstruction of antique rotonda, 75, *129*
Montoliveto, Ludovico, 62, 64
Morelli, Carlo, 280
Mortoft, Francis, 71–72
Muricciolo (pedestrian sidewalk), licenses to build, 251–52, 279–81
Music, 6, 11, 20, 69–73, 78–79
Musicians' choir, oratory, 29, 70–71, *33*

Naples, SS. Apostoli: Filomarino altar, 136 n.21
Nebbia, Cesare, 162
Neri, San Filippo, 1, 4–7, 9–10, 13, 19; Algardi's statue of, 2, 203–05, *72;* apartment in *casa vecchia,* 11, *73, 74, 79;* Bolgi's bust of, *46;* books, 247; deposition, translation, and systemization of body, 237; heraldry, 5
Nicchioni (niches), 47, 76, 240, 129–30 n.105, *49, 130;* Palazzo Farnese in Piacenza, *131*
Nolli, G. B.: plan of Collegio Romano, *109;* plan of Rome, detail of Vallicella area, *2*

Oppenort, Gilles Marie, 236
Optical theories, 36, 122 n.59
Opus Architectonicum, 23, 27, 32–34, 36, 46, 48–51, 54, 75–76, 105–08, 252–61, 286
Oratoria della Caravita, 32, 83, 120 n.35, 131–32 n.6, *111*
Oratorio del Gonfalone, 120 n.35
Oratorio del SS. Crocefisso a San Marcello, 120 n.35
Oratorio di San Giovanni Decollato, 32
Oratorio (musical genre), 69–73
Oratory (devotion), 6, 69–71
Oratory, Congregation of the, 1, 3, 5–7, 10, 12, 19–21 59–74, 127 n.48, 141
Ornamentation, 3–4; Borromini's use of, 36–37, 60, 78, 96; Maruscelli's courtyards, 19
Ossatura of capital, 33, 120–21 n.41
Osteria della Spada, 273

Palace ceremonial, 73, 129 n.93
Palace design, 75–77, 83, 96; *see also Famiglia* palace design
Palazzetto Turci, 84
Palazzi in Rome
    Alberini-Cicciaporci, 76
    Alessandrino-Bonelli, 119 n.20
    Baldassini, 76, *132;* brickwork, 120
    Barberini, 77, 86, 96, 122 n.62, 133 n.24; brickwork, 120; library, 49, 155–57; library

shelves, 49, *133;* mason's contract for work on, 163
    Bufalo, 117 n.35, 123 n.17
    Carpegna, 98, 163
    Cerri, 87, 133 n.21, 163
    Falconieri, 125 n.74, 163, 269
    Famiglia Borghese, 19, 60, *118–120*
    Famiglia Ludovisi, 117 n.35
    Fieschi-Sora, 84; brickwork, 120
    Laterno, *see* Lateran basilica and palace
    Medici-Madama, 109–10
    Pamphilj, 51, 97–98
    Sforza-Cesarini, 89
    Spada-Capodiferro, 110–11
    Spagna, 130 n.74
    Vescovo di Cervia, *127;* brickwork, 120
Palladio, Andrea, 76–77, 99, 119 n.25; Convent of the Carità, Venice, 18, *115;* Palazzo Iseppo da Porto, Vicenza, *116*
Pamphilj Chapel project, 31, 38, 51, 75, 87, 216–18, *128*
Pamphilj, Giovanni Battista, *see* Innocent X, Pope
Papal court, relations with Oratorians, 20
Patronage system, in architecture, 3, 64
Paul V, Pope, 12, 65
Pediment, oratory facade, 37
Peparelli, Francesco, 87
Peschal, Defendino, 52, 62, 162–63
Piacenza, Palazzo Farnese, 34, 67, 76–77, 121 n.46, 129 n.104, 129–30 n.105, *131*
Piazza dell'Arco di Camillo, 83
Piazza di Monte Giordano, 8, 12, 14, 57, 85, 87, 114 n.12
    drawings: 273–76
Piazza di San Macuto, 82–83
Piazza Farnese, 86
Piazza Sant'Ignazio, 83
Piazza Sforza, 273, 289–90, *291*
Pinselli, Marco Antonio, 104
Pomis, G. A. de, 143
Porta, Giacomo della, 9
Propaganda Fide, Collegio di, 60, 99–100, 133 n.24, 137 n.30; Re Magi Chapel, 99, 137 n.32, *138*
Pumpkin vault, 33

Raguzzini, Filippo, 83
Rainaldi, Carlo, 42, 280–81; Chapel of San Carlo Borromeo, 55; curtain wall along east flank of church, 278–79; outline of dates, 104
Rainaldi, Girolamo, 16; oratory plans, 26–29, 75–76, 208–09; Palazzo Farnese, *131;* sacristy fountain, Gesù, *107;* Santa Teresa in Caprarola, 30, *121*
Raphael, 76, 99

Regilla, Annia, tomb of, 34
Resta, Sebastiano, 278
Ricchino, F. M., 122 n.57
Righi, Francesco, 52, 111; Bernardino Spada's letter to, 124–25 n.66
Roberti, Isodoro, 48
Rodriquez, Felippo, 162
Roman architecture, ancient, 31, 34, 75–77, 121–22 n.48
Romanelli, Giovanni Francesco, 29, 30, 50, 55, 119 n.28, 246
Romani, Girolamo: report on structural problems, 161
Roncalli, Simone, 162
Rosa, Persiano, 5
Rosciani, Simone, 247; contract for carpentry work on library, 149–50; payment for work, 152
Rosini, Girolamo, 70–71
Rossi, Domenico de: *Studio d'architettura civile*, 284–85
Rossi, Giovanni Jacomo de, 269, 281–82
Rubble masonry, 33–34
Rughesi, Fausto, 10, 27, 162

Sacchi, Andrea, 109
Saluzzi, Angelo, 24–25, 64
San Carlo Borromeo, Chapel of, 55, 278
Sangallo, Antonio da, 75; Palazzo Baldassini, *132;* Palazzo del Vescovo di Cervia, *127*
Sanjust Plan of 1908, 93
Scarlatti, Alessandro, 72
Serlio, Sebastiano, 77, 113 n.2
Shops on casa site, 51, 57, 91, 127 n.23, 265
Somazzi, Giovanni, 162
Sora, Duca di, 184–85
Soria, G. B., 16, 19, 48; library shelves in Palazzo Barberini, 49, 123 n.36, *133;* Palazzo della Famiglia Borghese, 116–17 n.35, *118–120*
Sorrisi, Giovanni Maria, 118 n.18, 119 n.22; Borromini's critique of stucco work, 148–49
Spada, Bernardino, 53, 97, 112, 124–25 n.66
Spada, Orazio, 55, 274, 278
Spada, Paolo, 96
Spada, Virgilio, 13, 15, 19, 33, 43, 49, 77, 96–100, 124–25 n.66, 135–36 n.8; apartment, description of, 67; and Borromini, 28, 48, 52–54; coin and curiosity collection, 127 n.55; criticism of alterations to oratory altar, 226–27; *Dialogo,* 24; financing of demolition and construction, 59–64; Innocent X, service to, 51; invention of features in the casa, 115 n.13; *Opus Architectonicum,* 23–24, 50; Pamphilj Chapel, 216–18; on problem

of shops, 91; on visitors to singers' choir, 73; unpublished monetary treatise, 126–27 n.20
documents
    1644: first testament, 152
    1644: draft of ways that Innocent X might show his affection for the Vallicella, 163–64
    1662: second testament, 157
drawings
    1629–30: pavement levels for Strada Nuova, 184–85
    1634: project for sanctuary behind chapel and *piano nobile* plan, 200–03
    1644: critique of chapel project, 247
Specchi, Alessandro: details of oratory facade and *sala di ricreazione,* 284
Sperelli, Alessandro, 118–19 n.18
Statera, Flaminio, 147
Stonecutters *(scarpellini),* 161–62; documents pertaining to work of, 146–47, 161–63
Strada del Paradiso, 133 n.9
Strada Nuova, 84, 86–87
    documents: 143, 162
    drawings: 182–84, 211
Streets of Rome, 81, 84, 93, 132–33 n.9

Tarugi, Francesco Maria, 72
Tempesta, A.: plan of Rome, detail of Vallicella area, *3*
Tempio armonico, 32
Theft, precautions against, 50, 91
Tibaldi, Pellegrino, 19; Archepiscopal Palace, Milan, *117*
Tornioli, Niccolo, 203
Torriani, Orazio, 108, 143
Totti, Pompilio: view of Vallicella area and Strada Nuova, 211
Trinità dei Pellegrini, 5, 122 n.8
Tristano, Giovanni, S. J., 131 n.4

Underground oratory, 56, 71, 256, *30*
Urban VIII, Pope, 86, 89, 91
documents
    1627: decree authorizing opening of Strada Nuova, 143
    1633: report made to Sacra Visita of, in favor of continuing building program, 144–46

Vaj bequest, 30, 53, 55, 226–27
Valeriano, Giuseppe, 82, 131 n.4
Valle, Pietro della, 71–72, 128 n.89
Vallicella area, 7–8, 90–93, *1–4, 97, 98;* Totti's view of, 211; water supply, 65
Vanni, Raffaello, 220, 227
Vanvitelli, Luigi, 104

Vasari, Giorgio, the Younger, 113 n.2
Vasi, Giuseppe: view of Piazza della Chiesa Nuova, 291
Vatican Library, 49; library shelves, *133*
Vecchi, Gaspare de, 16
Venice, Convent of the Carità, 18, *115*
Venturi, Sergio, 162
Vescovo di Cervia, 34
Via dei Baullari, 86, 133 n.9
Via dei Filippini-Calabraghe-Cellini, 132 n.9
Via del Pellegrino, 8, 84–86, 92, 114 n.12
Via della Chiesa Nuova, 55, 86, *103*
Via dell'Arco della Chiesa Nuova, 132 n.9
Via di Parione, 8, 11, 65, 83–87, 92
Via di Pizzomerlo, 12, 132 n.9
Via Sora, 84, 132–33 n.9
Vicenza, Palazzo Chiericati, 76
Vicenza, Palazzo Iseppo da Porto, 197
Vicoli, 84
Vicolo dei Cartari, 84

Vicolo dei Leutari, 133 n.9
Vicolo del Corallo, 132 n.9
Vicolo del Governo, 10, 84–85, 132 n.9
Vicolo del Pavone, 132 n.9
Vicolo della Cancelleria, 84, 133 n.9
Vicolo di Pizzomerlo, 13, 84
Vicolo Savelli, 84, 133 n.9
Vicolo Sforza-Cesarini, 132 n.9
Vicolo Sora, 132–33 n.9
Vignola, Giacomo da, 76, 130 n.105; Palazzo Farnese, in Piacenza, *131*
Villa Giulia: brickwork, 120
Visitors, provisions for, 72–73
Vittori, Loreto, 71
Viviani Plan of 1873, 92
Volterra, Francesco da, 35, 75; San Giacomo degli Incurabili, *122*

Water supply, 65–66
Wells, 66